# Communication Yearbook 33

# Communication Yearbook 33

**Edited by**
**Christina S. Beck**

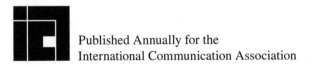

Published Annually for the
International Communication Association

Routledge
Taylor & Francis Group

NEW YORK AND LONDON

First published 2009
by Routledge
270 Madison Ave, New York, NY 10016

Simultaneously published in the UK
by Routledge
2 Park Square, Milton Park, Abingdon, Oxon OX14 4RN

*Routledge is an imprint of the Taylor & Francis Group, an informa business*

Typeset in Times by EvS Communication Networx, Inc.
Printed and bound in the United States of America on acid-free paper by Edwards Brothers, Inc.

ISSN: 0147-4642

ISBN10: 0-415-99961-8 (hbk)
ISBN10: 0-203-87156-1 (ebk)

ISBN13: 978-0-415-99961-8 (hbk)
ISBN13: 978-0-203-87156-0 (ebk)

# Contents

# The International Communication Association

The International Communication Association (ICA) was formed in 1950, bringing together academics and other professionals whose interests focus on human communication. The Association maintains an active membership of more than 4,000 individuals, of whom some two-thirds teach and conduct research in colleges, universities, and schools around the world. Other members are in government, law, medicine, and other professions. The wide professional and geographic distribution of the membership provides the basic strength of the ICA. The Association serves as a meeting ground for sharing research and useful dialogue about communication interests.

Through its divisions and interest groups, publications, annual conferences, and relations with other associations around the world, ICA promotes the systemic study of communication theories, processes, and skills. In addition to *Communication Yearbook*, ICA publishes the *Journal of Communication, Human Communication Research, Communication Theory, Journal of Computer-Mediated Communication, Communication, Culture & Critique, A Guide to Publishing in Scholarly Communication Journals*, and the *ICA Newsletter*.

For additional information about the ICA and its activities, visit online at www.icahdq.org or contact Michael L. Haley, Executive Director, International Communication Association, 1500 21st Ave. NW, Washington, DC 20036 USA; phone (202) 202-955-1444; fax 202-955-1448; email ica@icahdq.org.

Editors of the *Communication Yearbook* series:

Volumes 1 and 2, Brent D. Ruben
Volumes 3 and 4, Dan Nimmo
Volumes 5 and 6, Michael Burgoon
Volumes 7 and 8, Robert N. Bostrom
Volumes 9 and 10, Margaret L. McLaughlin
Volumes 11, 12, 13, and 14, James A. Anderson
Volumes 15, 16, and 17, Stanley A. Deetz
Volumes 18, 19, and 20, Brant R. Burleson
Volumes 21, 22, and 23, Michael E. Roloff
Volumes 24, 25, and 26, William B. Gudykunst
Volumes 27, 28, and 29, Pamela J. Kalbfleisch
Volumes 30, 31, 32, and 33, Christina S. Beck

# INTERNATIONAL COMMUNICATION ASSOCIATION
## EXECUTIVE COMMITTEE

**President and Chair**
Patrice M. Buzzanell
*Purdue University*

**President-Elect**
Barbie Zelizer
*University of Pennsylvania*

**Immediate Past President**
Sonia Livingstone
*London School of Economics*

**Executive Director**
Michael L. Haley (ex-officio)
*ICA Headquarters*

**Past President**
Ronald E. Rice
*University of California, Santa Barbara*

**Finance Chair**
Jon F. Nussbaum
*Pennsylvania State University*

## BOARD OF DIRECTORS

**Members-at-Large**

Yu-li- Liu, *National Chengchi University*

Gianpietro Mazzoleni, *University of Milan*

Elena E. Pernia, *University of the Philippines, Diliman*

Juliet Roper, *University of Waikato*

Aldo Vasquez Rios, *University De San Mart*

**Student Members**

Michele Cheng Hoon Khoo, *Nanyang Technology University*

Michaela L. Marlow, *University of Idaho*

## DIVISION CHAIRS

Mass Communication
Robin Nabi, *University of California, Santa Barbara*

Organizational Communication
Dennis K. Mumby, *University of North Carolina, Chapel Hill*

Intercultural Communication
James W. Neuliep, *St. Norbert College*

Political Communication
Kevin G. Barnhurst, *University of Illinois, Chicago*

Information Systems
Paul David Bolls, *University of Missouri, Columbia*

Interpersonal Communication
Pamela Kalbfleisch, *University of North Dakota*

Health Communication
David B. Buller, *Klein Buendel, Inc.*

Philosophy of Communication
Ingrid Volkmer, *University of Melbourne*

Communication & Technology
S. Shyam Sundar, *Pennsylvania State University*

Popular Communication
Cornel Sandvoss, *University of Surrey*

Public Relations
Craig E. Carroll, *University of North Carolina, Chapel Hill*

Feminist Scholarship
Vicki Mayer, *Tulane University*

Communication Law & Policy
Stephen D. McDowell, *Florida State University*

Instructional/Development Chair
Kristen Harrison, *University of Illinois*

Language & Social Interaction
Mark Aakhus, *Rutgers University*

Visual Communication Studies
Marion G. Mueller, *Jacobs University, Bremen*

Global Communication/Social Change
Oliver Boyd-Barrett, *Bowling Green State University*

Journalism Studies
Maria Elizabeth Grabe, *Indiana University*

Ethnicity and Race in Communication
Kumarini Silva, *Northeastern University*

## SPECIAL INTEREST GROUP CHAIRS

Gay, Lesbian, Bisexual, and Transgender Studies
David Phillips, *University of Toronto*
Lynn A. Comella, *University of Nevada – Las Vegas*

Communication History
David W. Park, *Lake Forest College*

Intergroup Communication
Bernadette Maria Watson, *University of Queensland*

Game Studies
John L. Sherry, *Michigan State University*

Children, Adolescents, and the Media
Patti, M. Valkenburg, *University of Amsterdam*

# Editorial Board

| Christina Holtz-Bacha | *Universität Erlangen-Nürnberg* |
| Philip N. Howard | *University of Washington* |
| Elly Konijn | *VU University Amsterdam* |
| Michael L. Kent | *University of Oklahoma* |
| Kimberly N. Kline | *University of Texas at San Antonio* |
| Eric Mark Kramer | *University of Oklahoma* |
| Wendy Leeds-Hurwitz | *University of Wisconsin-Parkside* |
| Dafna Lemish | *Tel-Aviv University* |
| Leah A. Lievrouw | *University of California, Los Angeles* |
| John Lucaites | *Indiana University* |
| Gianpietro Mazzoleni | *University of Milan* |
| Raymie E. McKerrow | *Ohio University* |
| Caryn Medved | *Baruch College – City University of New York* |
| Michaela D. E. Meyer | *Christopher Newport University* |
| Renee Meyers | *University of Wisconsin-Milwaukee* |
| Claude Miller | *University of Oklahoma* |
| Eric Morgan | *New Mexico State University* |
| Judy Motion | *University of Wollongong* |
| Dennis Mumby | *University of North Carolina-Chapel Hill* |
| Anne M. Nicotera | *George Mason University* |
| Susan Ohmer | *University of Notre Dame* |
| Daniel J. O'Keefe | *Northwestern University* |
| Kellie Carlyle Palazzolo | *Arizona State University* |
| Michael J. Papa | *Central Michigan University* |
| Ronald J. Pelias | *Southern Illinois University* |
| Elizabeth Perse | *University of Delaware* |
| Brian Quick | *University of Illinois at Urbana-Champaign* |
| Sandra Ragan | *University of Oklahoma* |
| Daniel Riffe | *University of North Carolina – Chapel Hill* |
| Anthony J. Roberto | *Arizona State University* |
| Jeffery D. Robinson | *Rutgers University* |
| Matthew W. Seeger | *Wayne State University* |
| Barbara Sharf | *Texas A&M University* |
| Christina Slade | *Macquarie University* |
| Brian H. Spitzberg | *San Diego State University* |
| J. Michael Sproule | *Saint Louis University* |
| Jeffrey St. John | *University of Maine* |
| Suzanne Suggs | *University of Lugano* |
| Bryan C. Taylor | *University of Colorado at Boulder* |
| Maureen Taylor | *University of Oklahoma* |
| Candice Thomas-Maddox | *Ohio University - Lancaster* |
| Teresa Thompson | *University of Dayton* |
| Scott Titsworth | *Ohio University* |
| Nick Trujillo | *California State University, Sacramento* |
| Robert Ulmer | *University of Arkansas at Little Rock* |
| Patti M. Valkenburg | *University of Amsterdam* |
| Robert Westerfelhaus | *College of Charleston* |
| Andrew Wood | *San José State University* |
| Jason Wrench | *State University of New York – New Paltz* |
| Gust A. Yep | *San Francisco State University* |

# Guest Reviewers

| | |
|---|---|
| Yoshitaka Miike | *University of Hawaii at Hilo* |
| Rohan Miller | *University of Sydney* |
| Dan Modaff | *Ohio University* |
| Emily Moyer-Gusé | *Ohio State University* |
| Michelle Nelson | *University of Illinois – Urbana Champaign* |
| Natalie Nelson-Marsh | *Boise State University* |
| Simon Niemeyer | *Australian National University* |
| Hye-Jin Paek | *Michigan State University* |
| Carol J. Pardun | *University of South Carolina* |
| Alice Pawley | *Purdue University* |
| Jorge Peña | *University of Texas at Austin* |
| Roxanne Parrott | *Pennsylvania State University* |
| Sandra Petronio | *Indiana University Purdue University, Indianapolis* |
| Penny Powers | *Thompson Rivers University* |
| Mark Ivan Rieker | *University of KwaZulu-Natal* |
| Peter Sandman | *Private Sector* |
| Steven Schnell | *Kutztown University* |
| Mike Schmierbach | *The Pensylvania State University* |
| Tamir Sheafer | *Hebrew University of Jerusalem* |
| Corinne Shefner-Rogers | *University of New Mexico* |
| Sherianne Shuler | *Creighton University* |
| Mary Simpson | *University of Waikato* |
| Suruchi Sood | *Johns Hopkins Bloomberg School of Public Health* |
| Sandy Staples | *Queen's University* |
| John Street | *University of East Anglia* |
| Hwee Hoon Tan | *Lee Kong Chian School of Business, Singapore Management University* |
| Jennifer Theiss | *Rutgers University* |
| Bart van den Hooff | *VU University Amsterdam* |
| Judy VanSlyke Turk | *Virginia Commonwealth University* |
| C. Arthur VanLear | *University of Connecticut* |
| Steven Venette | *University of Southern Mississippi* |
| Erika A. Waters | *National Cancer Institute* |
| Neil Weinstein | *University of Arizona* |
| Kevin Wright | *University of Oklahoma* |
| Itzhak Yanovitzky | *Rutgers University* |
| Yan Bing Zhang | *University of Kansas* |
| Joanna Zylinska | *Goldsmiths, University of London* |

# Editor's Introduction

## Christina S. Beck

> *I lingered in the movie theater, staring at the scrolling credits. "Mommy, are you ready to go?" Emmy asked. "Yeah, just a sec," I replied. She nervously glanced around at the now empty auditorium, imploring "Come on, Mom, everyone else is gone." I stood, slowly collected my coat, and stepped toward the entrance, glancing back to glimpse the screen as it faded to black...*

I am truly grateful for the privilege of serving as editor of *Communication Yearbook*. Without a doubt, this experience constitutes one of the most inspiring and influential moments in my professional life. I will never be the same, and I hope that I have impacted others and contributed to our discipline in a positive manner. Through many interactions with potential contributors, reviewers, selected authors, and readers of the published volumes, I have come to understand just how much that various stakeholders collectively shape emergent scholarly dialogues about issues, concepts, theories, methodological approaches, etc.; indeed, I have been awed and humbled by my own part in the process as editor.

For example, throughout my editorship, I challenged selected authors to discuss the relevancies of more narrow topics for others in the discipline. I stressed my perspective that we, as communication scholars, could benefit from interacting with others more and dismissing unfamiliar ideas as "irrelevant" much less (see related argument by Gumpert, 2007). Although I cast a "broad net" in terms of potential literatures that could be reviewed in each volume, chapters in the previous three volumes (as well as in this one) suggest ways in which particular bodies of work could inform other areas in communication. Each volume challenges us to reflect on underlying concerns that span communication contexts.

> *I settled into the car, adjusting my seatbelt and then shifting gears as images from* High School Musical 3 *streamed through my mind. I'm far beyond high school, but I felt intensely drawn to the movie, in more ways than one. Yeah, I'm a huge Disney fan so it "had me at 'hello.'" Yet, core issues in the film mirror ones from everyday life that transcend mere teen angst... dilemmas, decisions, and relationships that constrain and enable us throughout our life spans...*

> *I recognized the characters' respective struggles with legitimacy—How does one "pull off" a role? What counts as "acceptable"? What do others*

*critique and dismiss as "unacceptable"? I admired the drama teacher's efforts to persuade Troy, the male lead, to redefine himself. By pushing his boundaries and resisting stereotypes and parental/peer pressure, Troy could be a star on the basketball court as well as the stage.*

*We pulled into our neighborhood, and, silently, I applauded the collective realization by the diverse young people that they really "are in this together" (the refrain of the movie's main song)... that they could accomplish much more by appreciating their differences, embracing unique attributes, and balancing community and individualism.*

In *Communication Yearbook 30, 31, 32*, and, now, *33*, authors have offered a wide range of reviews of literature on important communication topics. Moreover, they have contributed to larger conversations about labeling and legitimacy (see, especially, CY30), the dialectic of fluidity and stability (see, especially, CY31), the positioning of communication as co-constructed, co-negotiated, and consequential (see, especially, CY32), and communication as implicitly persuasive and power-laden (see, especially, CY33). By noting potential connections and discussing broader implications, each volume emphasizes that, in spite of our many differences, communication scholars can gain insights from intra-disciplinary interactions and sharing of resources. As a discipline (and as global citizens), we are "all in this together."

My editorial emphasis on intersections underscores and exemplifies that, as co-participants in the publication process, we implicitly bring our unique "baggage" (i.e., assumptions, agendas, theoretical frameworks, political commitments, methodological beliefs, awareness of literature, even convictions about "appropriate" grammar and punctuation, etc.) with us during submission, review, selection, and revision of manuscripts. I like to believe that my personal editorial preconceptions, convictions, and priorities facilitated the publication of "quality" and "valuable" chapters in *Communication Yearbook*. Yet, as I have pondered many times during my term, decisions about what to publish (or not) and in what form depend not on clear cut absolutes ("right," "wrong," "good," or "bad") but on the ability of an author to articulate a persuasive "case" to a certain team of reviewers and a particular editor (see related arguments by Jackson, 1989).

The primary burden obviously rests squarely on the shoulders of potential contributors in terms of sending work that meets the criteria outlined in a given call. However, as a discipline, I urge us to engage in more of the reflexivity advocated by Blair, Brown, and Baxter (1994) regarding the publication process. If we are, indeed, "all in this together," how should/could we collectively determine what constitutes, for instance, "cutting edge" as opposed to "obscure," "unimportant," or "insignificant"? An editor may receive input from two scholars with sound expertise, but the very process of choosing reviewers and determining and communicating review criteria constitutes a subjective endeavor; those actions implicitly impact reactions to submissions.

The editor must decide which people possess the "right" viewpoints and experiences to assess a submission, and, necessarily, the selection of reviewers affects the frame through which that manuscript will be evaluated. Further, by virtue of outlining criteria, the editor specifies what attributes should be treated as more or less salient. How can prospective contributors "get in the loop" regarding what "counts as" "strong" or "valuable" for a publication at any given moment in time? Further, how should we discuss priorities in terms of types of research to be published? Most importantly, how can we give voice to diverse perspectives, orientations, and approaches while ensuring "quality" in our publications?

Space constraints implicitly limit what can appear in print, and, thus, editors and review boards confront tough choices. Indeed, most communication publications reject far more submissions than they accept. *Communication Yearbook 33* boasts a mere 15% acceptance rate. Clearly, journals cannot (and should not) err on the flip side by accepting everything, but I offer these reflections as an outgoing editor to prompt discussion about often unspoken "taken-for-granteds" in the publication process that receive far too little attention and transparency.

> *"Mommy, can I have a snack when we get inside?" Emmy asked. "Hmm? Yeah, sure," I replied. I eased the car into the driveway as I recalled the bittersweet end of the movie. The seniors turn their tassels, take a final bow, and begin a new phase in their respective life journeys as a new group of underclassmen prepare to take the stage at East High. The next trilogy will tell their similar yet unique story ...*

As students will attest, four years can seem like an eternity and yet pass in a flash. I feel the same way about the past four years with *Communication Yearbook*. Although I will always treasure this amazing experience, I am ready to encounter new professional and personal adventures and to "pass the torch" to the very qualified Charles Salmon. I wish him the very best with his own enactment of this most special publication.

## Overview of *Communication Yearbook 33*

I received 70 submissions for *Communication Yearbook 33*, the highest number under my four-year editorship. I received proposals from across our discipline and around the world. With the exception of manuscripts that did not fit the call or overlapped with chapters in recent volumes of CY, I obtained feedback from at least two reviewers for each submission in a blind, peer-review process. Based on that valuable input, I selected 11 proposals for development into chapters for CY33. The selected authors received reviewer input during at least two rounds of full review as well as editorial feedback on multiple versions of their manuscripts.

I encouraged international submissions, and the selected chapters include authors from Germany, the Netherlands, New Zealand, and the United States. I invited potential contributions from any area of communication research, and the 11 chapters in this volume exemplify the rich diversity of our field.

Although unintentional in terms of the call, these chapters reveal the importance of persuasion in our discipline (see, especially, Byrne & Hart, chapter 1, this volume; Hornikx & O'Keefe, chapter 2, this volume; Noar, Harrington, & Aldrich, chapter 3, this volume; Skubisz, Reimer, & Hoffrage, chapter 5, this volume), with a secondary emphasis on technology (Heinz & Rice, chapter 4, this volume) and science (see, especially, Galvin & Grill, chapter 6, this volume; Kisselburgh, Berkelaar, & Buzzanell, chapter 7, this volume). Even chapters that do not directly and explicitly fit those categories relate to the general themes of interpersonal and public persuasion. Negotiating gendered divisions of labor (Medved, chapter 8, this volume), volunteerism (Ganesh & McAllum, chapter 9, this volume), public interest media activism (Napoli, chapter 10, this volume), and apologia (Towner, chapter 11, this volume) all underscore the importance of interaction as individuals and organizations present themselves in preferred ways and position themselves in relation to others.

*Communication Yearbook 33* addresses issues that truly pervade our discipline, span communication contexts, and affect our daily lives as individuals, family members, organizational participants, media consumers, and citizens. I believe that each of these chapters provides a useful review of a particular body of literature as well as contributes to broader scholarly conversations.

## Grateful Acknowledgments

I will always cherish this editorial experience, and I am grateful to the ICA Publications Committee for permitting me to serve as editor of *Communication Yearbook*. I have had the opportunity to interact with people from around the world, and I value the many relationships that I have developed because of this journey.

I am grateful to the members of my editorial board and our guest reviewers for each of the four volumes under my editorship. I have received thank you notes from potential contributors, praising the valuable and insightful feedback that they have received. I applaud and appreciate each of these scholars for taking the time and energy to share important words of encouragement, support, and guidance to people that they may well never know. On behalf of the potential contributors and selected authors from CY30–33, thank you for agreeing to review and for sending pages upon pages of excellent expert input.

I appreciate the support of the School of Communication Studies at Ohio University for providing me with time to edit and with support staff. I would especially like to thank Michael Pfahl and Tennley Vik for their assistance with *Communication Yearbook 33*.

I am profoundly grateful to Jennifer Scott, my senior editorial associate. Jennifer has been with me since the beginning of my editorship, and, as many of the contributors to these four volumes will attest, Jennifer has offered ideas for titles, searched for pesky pieces of information, shared thoughts on organization, and communicated with authors about important details. She has truly been my "Nancy Drew" and "right hand" throughout this process, and I appreciate her willingness to serve as my sounding board over the years and to exchange e-mails with me at all hours of the day and night. Thank you for everything, Jenn!!

Finally, I would like to thank my family. As I was writing this introduction, I realized that I have been editor of *Communication Yearbook* for over half of my youngest daughter, Emmy's, life. She'll possibly enjoy going to the movies with me much more after I send this book to press. I dedicate this volume of *Communication Yearbook* to my daughters, Brittany, Chelsea Meagan, and Emmy, and to my husband, Roger Aden. Thank you for permitting me to enjoy the opportunity and experience of a lifetime and for sharing me with this wonderful and important publication.

## References

Blair, C., Brown, J., & Baxter, L. (1994). Disciplining the feminine. *Quarterly Journal of Speech, 80*, 383–409.

Gumpert, G. (2007). Looking past disciplines. *Critical Studies in Media Communication, 24*, 170–171.

Jackson, S. (1989). Method as argument. In B. Gronbeck (Ed.), *Spheres of argument: Proceedings of the sixth SCA/AFA conference on argumentation* (pp. 1–8). Annandale, VA: SCA.

# Communication Yearbook 33

# CHAPTER CONTENTS

# 1 The Boomerang Effect

## A Synthesis of Findings and a Preliminary Theoretical Framework

*Sahara Byrne*
*Philip Solomon Hart*
Cornell University

Communicative messages are often constructed strategically. In many cases, the creators of such messages strive to curtail specific anti-social or unhealthy attitudes and behaviors held by the target audience. However, these messages are not always successful in achieving the intended effect. Messages with a specific intent can backfire and cause an increase in the unhealthy or anti-social attitude or behavior targeted for change. We present a review of findings that have resulted in *boomerang* effects, broadly defined. An analysis of theoretical mechanisms for the effect eventuates in the proposal of two distinct paths to the boomerang. One path predicts that message receivers will process harmful elements in a message at the expense of those that were intended. The other path predicts that receivers will process the message as intended, but then resist complying with it. Finally, we offer a preliminary theoretical framework of boomerang effects.

S trategic communication encompasses any communication with a well-defined intent on the part of the sender or message creator (Piotrow & Kincaid, 2001). Examples of this type of communication include commercial advertising that aims to persuade individuals to purchase a specific product, social marketing campaigns that attempt to change unhealthy attitudes and behaviors, and media literacy interventions given to children with the intent of preventing negative effects of the media. Many strategic messages intend to have a pro-social effect on individuals, namely to curtail the manifestation of anti-social or unhealthy attitudes or behaviors. However, strategic messages do not always succeed in achieving this intended effect. Often, they result in the opposite effect, causing an increase in the unhealthy or anti-social attitude or behavior targeted for change (Pechmann & Slater, 2005). This outcome is of broad concern to scholars of communication who are interested in understanding how messages can be misinterpreted or fail.

This chapter examines the literature for evidence of *boomerang effects* in response to strategic messages. We pay particular attention to the unintended effects of messages that attempt to change anti-social or unhealthy attitudes and behaviors. We synthesize theories of communication, persuasion, psychology,

---

Correspondence: e-mail: seb272@cornell.edu

and education, and we discuss two distinct paths to the boomerang effect. Finally, we present a preliminary framework of boomerang effects.

## Concepts and Terminology

The term *strategic message* has emerged from the broader field of persuasion to describe messages that are specifically conceived, constructed, and delivered with the clear intention to result in a specific effect (Piotrow & Kincaid, 2001; E. M. Rogers, 1995). Sometimes, the intended effect encompasses a change in attitude or behavior. For example, stakeholders design strategic messages with the specific intention of reducing smoking in adolescents, increasing voter turnout, selling a product, or lowering aggression.

In addition to intended effects, messages can result in many types of effects that are not intended (for a review, see Cho & Salomon, 2007). *Intention* guides message creators as they design and construct a message as well as scholars when they investigate message effects (Berger, 1995; Dillard, Anderson, & Knobloch, 2002). In this chapter, we synthesize evidence of, and explanatory mechanisms for, one type of unintended effect—a *boomerang effect*, which occurs when a strategic message generates the opposite attitude or behavior than was originally intended (Cho & Salomon, 2007; Hovland, Janis, & Kelly, 1953).

The boomerang effect can be documented by change within an individual due to message exposure, or in comparison to other individuals who were exposed to an alternative message, or no message at all. For example, if a media literacy intervention seeks to *reduce* a child's desire for products that are advertised in television commercials, a boomerang effect would entail an *increase* in the child's desire for the product beyond that which would have occurred without the intervention. We believe that one of the most serious implications of boomerang effects is that messages created with a pro-social intent can result in the targeted attitude or behavior becoming worse. While communicators create many messages with a pro-social intent, we also discuss messages without such positive intentions.

We should note that message creators may actually intend to elicit resistance to messages, what might be considered an intentional boomerang effect (S. S. Brehm & J. W. Brehm, 1981; Farrelly et al., 2002; Papageorgis & McGuire, 1961). Because we focus on understanding why messages sometimes result in the opposite effect than intended, resistance effects that are intended do not constitute the types of boomerang effects of primary concern to this review.

Finally, while messages may have intended effects and unintended effects, they can also result in null effects. However, in this chapter, we primarily investigate why strategic messages sometimes result in unintended effects, with a particular interest in explaining boomerang effects.

## Evidence of the Boomerang Effect

This review of literature mainly centers on strategic messages created with intention of changing anti-social or unhealthy attitudes and behaviors. As stated in the introduction, strategic messages often function as a vehicle to persuade individuals to change certain attitudes or behaviors. However, people do not always comply, and they often do the opposite. We now review the evidence for the boomerang effect across multiple contexts.

### *Health Behavior Modification Campaigns*

Media campaigns often strive to promote health promotion messages, usually with the aim of curtailing negative or dangerous health behaviors such as the abuse of drugs and alcohol or engaging in unprotected sex. Some of these messages have resulted in boomerang effects (Pechmann & Slater, 2005; Ringhold, 2002). For example, boomerang effects have been reported in response to campaigns attempting to reduce smoking, alcohol consumption, and drug use (Crano & Burgoon, 2002).

Messages that intend to lower smoking behavior can actually increase smoking rates (Wolburg, 2006). Grandpre, Alvaro, Burgoon, Miller, and Hall (2003) found that 10th grade adolescents who viewed anti-smoking messages were more likely say that they would try a cigarette soon if they heard an explicit message telling them not to smoke than they would have been if they did not hear this type of message.

Several communication efforts aiming to lower both alcohol consumption and positive attitudes toward drinking have resulted in boomerang effects (Campo & Cameron, 2006; Foxcroft, Lister-Sharp, & Lowe, 1977; Gordon & Minor, 1992; Perkins, Haines, & Rice, 2005; Ringhold, 2002; Wechsler et al., 2003). For example, Wechsler et al.'s nationwide study of 118 colleges revealed that many formal attempts to reduce alcohol consumption through social norms campaigns resulted in an increase of alcohol consumption. Social norms campaigns attempt to reduce anti-social behavior by changing misconceptions about the prevalence of such behaviors (Cialdini, Kallgren, & Reno, 1991).

The social norms approach is not the only type of strategic message that has resulted in reports of increased drinking. A boomerang effect has been found in other types of strategic efforts, particularly those that advocate restrictions on individuals' behaviors. For example, one study demonstrated that some college students, especially males who drink often, drank more alcohol directly after observing a message telling them to abstain from drinking, while similar students who heard a less restrictive message to drink "in moderation" did not exhibit this boomerang effect (Bensley & Wu, 1991).

Similarly, messages aiming to reduce drug use have, at times, had the opposite effect on viewers (Atkin, 2002). Fishbein, Hall-Jamison, Zimmer, von Haeften, and Nabi (2002) examined the effectiveness of 30 anti-drug public service announcements, and they concluded that humorous messages and messages that specifically target marijuana use hold the potential to result in a boomerang effect. This effect is not atypical. For example, Rosenbaum and Hanson (1998) concluded that suburban children who participated in project Drug Abuse Resistance Education (D.A.R.E.) use drugs significantly more through high school than both all urban participants and the suburban control group.

Health campaigns with the goal of promoting healthy behaviors also sometimes produce the opposite effect, where individuals are less likely perform the preventative behavior. This pattern has been found in reaction to some messages utilizing fear appeals (see Leventhal, 1971; Witte, 1992), such as the threat of death if a woman does not perform self-administered routine breast cancer exams (Kline, 1995; Kline & Mattson, 2000), interventions to promote healthy nutrition (Schwartz, Thomas, Bohan, & Vartanian, 2007), and safe sex campaigns (Priester, 2002).

The possibility of boomerang effects has also been a concern of suicide prevention efforts. In this area of research, the emergence of a boomerang effect is extremely risky because, if messages of suicide prevention glorify the act in the recipient's mind or present it as normative, individuals might be more inclined to attempt suicide (Chambers et al., 2005). The line of research linking media coverage of suicide to an increase in the number of suicides led the Surgeon General of the United States (1999) to officially warn that suicide "can be facilitated in vulnerable teens by exposure to real or fictional accounts of suicide" (para 30). While it is obviously difficult to test for a boomerang effect directly, Chambers et al. argued that any suicide prevention campaign must first undergo careful evaluation because the message may unintentionally generate suicidal thoughts and behaviors.

### Advertising

Messages intending to sell products can also backfire. In some cases, advertising has resulted in a dislike for the product or service being advertised (Petrova & Cialdini, 2005). For example, as Petrova and Cialdina asserted, ads with imagery appeal, or that ask people to imagine using a product, have been found to cause some people to be less persuaded than they would have been without the imagery request. Petrova and Cialdina determined a similar reaction if the vividness of a product, or photographic image, is "fuzzy" or dulled.

Boomerang effects also emerge at times in response to advertisements that attempt to play on the emotions of viewers (Campbell, 1995; Cotte, Coulter, & Moore, 2005). According to Cotte et al., viewers more likely hold a negative attitude toward an advertisement, as well as the sponsor, if they perceive the intent to manipulate their emotions.

Advertisements that are intended to promote political candidates and agendas have also sometimes resulted in boomerang effects, particularly in the case of negative advertising about an opposing candidate's image or stance on an issue (Garramone, 1984; King & McConnell, 2003; Lau, Sigelman, & Rovner, 2007; Shapiro & Rieger, 1992). Additionally, when news reports called "ad-watches" have critiqued negative political advertisements, individuals have tended to be more persuaded by the ad than they would have been if they had not been exposed to the critique (Ansolabehere & Iyengar, 1996; Pfau & Louden, 1994).

### Entertainment-Education Efforts

Entertainment programs intentionally designed to enhance pro-social attitudes and behaviors can also lead to boomerang effects. Critics widely expected the popular CBS show, *All in the Family*, to reduce bigotry. Instead, bigots perceived the show to be "telling it like it is," while liberals praised the show for its message of tolerance and the potential to spread pro-social effects. For both groups, watching the show reinforced their original beliefs (Vidmar & Rokeach, 1974), which sparked a boomerang effect with respect to an increase in bigoted beliefs.

Media messages that intend to sensitize viewers to rape myths have also resulted in boomerang effects under certain conditions (B. J. Wilson, Linz, Donnerstein, & Stipp, 1992; Winkel & De Kleuver, 1997). B. J. Wilson et al. argued that some viewers selectively interpreted a movie to reinforce their attitudes. This study examined the effects of a made-for-TV movie designed to make viewers sympathetic to victims of acquaintance rape. They only found a boomerang effect among older men who viewed the movie. Older men reported an increase in blame for victims of rape, but women and younger men did not. Further analysis revealed that these men tended to embrace rape myths before viewing the film. Viewing this movie may have reinforced these myths, compared to similar men who did not see the movie.

Adolescent males also remain susceptible to similar boomerang effects in this context (Moyer-Gusé & Nabi, 2008; Winkel & De Kleuver, 1997). In an experiment testing the effectiveness of techniques to reduce violence against women, participants saw a video depicting either the consequences to a victim of sexual assault (distress) or perpetrator consequences (going to jail). Winkel and De Kleuver determined that young males who viewed the video portraying consequences for the perpetrator reported an increase (instead of a decrease) in acceptance of coerced sex, rape myths, and macho behavior; however, boys that saw a video depicting the consequences to the victim reported a change in the intended direction.

### Strategies to Reduce Negative Effects of the Media

Research on specific strategies to reduce or prevent negative effects of the media has evidenced a pattern of boomerang effects. These strategies include media literacy interventions or mediations, enforcing rules to prevent exposure, and the implementation of ratings, advisories, and warning labels.

*Interventions*

Many media literacy interventions seek to provide people with cognitive defenses against negative media effects (Potter, 2004). Most of the research in this area has examined the potential of media literacy interventions to prevent children from enacting media-induced aggression, one of the most consistently documented media effects in media effects research (Bandura, Ross, & Ross, 1963; Josephson, 1987).

Research on these strategies has uncovered many instances of boomerang effects (see Cantor & Wilson, 2003). For example, Doolittle's (1980) intervention attempted to reduce the effect of media violence on children by having children create their own violent film, thereby trying to teach them that the content is unrealistic. This treatment resulted in a boomerang effect in boys—those who participated in this treatment group were more aggressive after viewing violent video clips than those in the control group.

Certain types of intervention efforts more likely result in a boomerang effect compared to others. Nathanson (2004) argued that teaching facts about media production, such as "those people are just actors," can cause some children (especially older, lighter viewers) to be more vulnerable to violent content after receiving the mediation compared to others who were taught to evaluate the characters negatively. Similarly, Byrne (2009) reported that children who participated in an intervention that did not contain an activity to encourage deeper processing of the elements in the intervention were more willing to use aggression after viewing a violent clip, but children who did complete the learning activity were less willing to use aggression after viewing the same clip. Nathanson and Yang (2003) concluded that, for some age groups, mediation efforts that pose questions to children about the inappropriateness of aggressive behavior can cause younger children to develop more positive attitudes toward a violent program, while lessons in statement form cause older children to boomerang. According to Nathanson and Yang, some children also exhibit a boomerang response to a social reality lesson (people in real life do not act like people on TV) by having more positive attitudes toward a violent program after the lesson.

Boomerang effects also emerge in media literacy interventions outside the context of preventing aggression. In the health context, interventions aiming to generate critical analysis of the media's role in promoting poor body image and eating disorders have sometimes backfired (Choma, Foster, & Radford, 2007), and some evidence indicates that efforts to mitigate the media's role in the desire to smoke cigarettes may increase the appeal of engaging in those behaviors (Austin, Pinkleton, Hust, & Cohen, 2005). Recent evidence also suggests that media literacy interventions that are intended to reduce stereotypical attitudes generated from viewing media messages may sometimes increase prejudicial responses when compared to a control group (Ramasubramanian & Oliver, 2007).

## Rules and Restrictions

Another way to protect individuals from the potential negative effects of the media involves preventing them from being exposed to it in the first place. These efforts include household rules, preventative warnings, restrictions, and advisories. These attempts have also resulted in the unintended effect of creating more interest in the restricted message (McLeod, Atkin, & Chaffee, 1972; Nathanson, 1999).

Nathanson (1999) demonstrated a curvilinear relationship between aggression and media restrictions in the home. Findings linked moderate levels of restriction with the least aggression, while both very high and very low restriction of media corresponded to higher aggressive tendencies in children. Parental restrictions on adolescent media use were also related to more positive feelings about the restricted content and more negative attitudes toward their relationship with their parents (Nathanson, 2002).

Parental restrictiveness tends to be associated with higher levels of both violence viewing and aggression (Krcmar & Cantor, 1997; McLeod et al., 1972). Some children place value on restricted material; in fact, Krcmar and Cantor found that 23% of the children in their study chose to view the parentally restricted movie after the parent left the room. While this data does not indicate a boomerang per se, it does demonstrate that restriction can cause some children to have a greater preference for the restricted material.

Additionally, barring children from viewing news may have differentially negative effects compared to talking with them about their fears. Buijzen, Walma van der Molen, and Sondij (2007) surveyed 451 elementary school children in The Netherlands, and they discovered that actively helping children understand what they see on the news moderates resulting fear and worry, but restricting exposure can increase these negative emotions among the youngest children in their sample (8- to 10-year-olds) (for related review of media literacy literature, see Rosenbaum, Beentjes, & Konig, 2008).

## Ratings, Warnings, and Advisories

Movie and television ratings exist primarily to help parents identify potentially harmful or offensive media content. Movie ratings are intended to identify how appropriate a parent would find the content in a given movie for a child of a certain age (J. B. Wilson, Linz, & Randall, 1990). Television ratings are based on the potential harm of a certain type of content to children of a certain age range. The ratings are applied to shows based on a voluntary system designed by the media industry to serve as a companion to v-chip technology. Parents can identify violent or sexual content, as well as objectionable language or suggestive dialogue (Cantor, 1998). General advisories, such as "parental discretion advised," have also been used to help parents navigate media choices. While ratings, warning labels, advisories, and descriptive identifiers were designed to help parents with filtering media exposures and preventing negative effects, research on these efforts has evidenced some unintended effects.

An increase in the desire to watch a program with a certain rating is not always a boomerang effect, as we have defined it. Strictly speaking, industry officials do not share ratings and advisories with the goal of dissuading potential viewers but instead to inform them (or their caregivers). To the extent that a warning label actually carries the intention of reducing the desirability of that product, this effect would be considered a boomerang. However, the messages are primarily created to protect individuals, especially children, from experiencing a negative effect. We describe the findings because these types of messages may cause children to be more interested in the programs and, in turn, more likely to view it and exhibit the effect in question.

In a meta-analysis, Bushman and Cantor (2003) found that, across 18 reports (70 independent samples) that examined the effects of ratings on attraction to content, restrictive ratings tended to make programs more attractive to viewers overall. Krcmar and Cantor (1997) examined communication patterns between children and parents as they made program choices. The researchers randomly assigned ratings and advisories to different programs. Results revealed that some children responded positively to programs that were both disapproved by parents and prohibited by rating or advisory.

Earlier studies noted that older boys tend to be most attracted to advisory labels, such as "parental discretion advised" (Cantor & Harrison, 1996; Cantor, Harrison, & Nathanson, 1997). Similarly, Sneegas and Plank (1998) discovered that boys prefer content labeled as violent over other types of questionable content, but girls did not exhibit such a preference.

Considerable evidence attests that children, particularly boys, are drawn to restrictive ratings and advisories, adults are not immune to the attractiveness of ratings. College age participants reported greater interest in seeing films labeled as containing harmful violent content, compared to when they were not labeled, or simply described as violent (Bushman & Stack, 1996).

### Environmental Messages

The boomerang effect has also emerged in environmental messages. One of the most famous research examples of the boomerang effect occurred in the context of environmental communication. People who were explicitly told not to litter were more likely to litter than those who did not receive an anti-littering appeal (Reich & Robertson, 1979). Similarly, Schultz et al. (2007) asserted that an appeal to reduce energy consumption backfired among households that were already comparatively low energy consumers prior to hearing the message. Households in the experimental conditions were exposed to two waves of pamphlets containing information about their current household energy consumption and an appeal to conserve. In response, households that were low energy consumers tended to increase their short and long-term energy usage.

Environmental communication researchers have also examined whether we should highlight the gains or losses associated with a certain issue (for the theoretical foundation of gain and loss frames, see Kahneman & Tversky, 1979; Tversky & Kahneman, 1981, as well as related review by O'Keefe & Jensen, 2006). For example, Obermiller (1995) examined the difference between framing a message around the severity of an environmental problem or the positive impact that would be created by individual action. Obermiller argued that, when individuals already possess a high degree of concern for an issue, stressing the gravity of an environmental problem can actually lower their willingness to take action on the issue.

### Interpersonal Communication

Researchers examining interpersonal influence have largely focused on how best to gain compliance in sales and donation contexts (Dillard et al., 2002). Of the myriad strategies born out of this research area, very few have resulted in boomerang effects (Cody, Canary, & Smith, 1994). As a notable exception, Abrahams and Bell (1994) tested three different types of *door-in-the-face* strategies (asking for a large donation first and then lowering the amount) and discovered that the strategy may backfire only when the solicitation attempt was not expected by a potential donor. Similarly, a strategy called *that's-not-all* (offering more before purchaser declines) appears to boomerang only when individuals are explicitly mindful of the decision to purchase a product, such as when the product is relatively expensive (Pollack, Smith, Knowles, & Bruce, 1998). In a closely related research area, telephone survey refusals tend to be even greater when interviewers attempt to persuade respondents to participate by strategically revealing information about the legitimacy of the study (Fuse & Xie, 2007).

### Social Accounts

Individuals often construct polite messages, like *please* and *thank you*, and apologies with the intent of increasing receiver's perceptions of fairness—with the ultimate goal of reducing the likelihood of receiver retaliation (Bies, 1989). Unfortunately, these efforts don't always go as planned (Skarlicki & Folger, 1997; Skarlicki, Folger, & Gee, 2004). For example, according to Skarlicki et al., when offered low compensation with an apology or polite message, participants become less likely to perceive fairness and more likely to retaliate than if the offer had been made without such niceties. (For a related review on apologies, see Towner, this volume.)

### Other Communication Contexts

#### Organizational

In an organizational setting, individuals often rely on excuses for poor performance in an attempt to reduce expectations and manage impressions.

Unfortunately, these excuses can lead to the opposite effect. For example, Greenberg (1996) discovered across three experiments that, when workers blame their poor performance on being new at a job, individuals who are adversely affected by the performance rated the workers lower than individuals who did not hear an excuse.

*Legal*

One of the most difficult communication problems in courtroom settings involves how judges should best handle instructing juries to disregard inadmissible evidence (Cook, Arndt, & Lieberman, 2004). Across studies, evidence suggests a strong relationship between such admonitions and the tendency for jury members to give even more weight to the evidence than they would have if no such instruction were given (for a review, see Lieberman & Arndt, 2000).

*Donation Appeals*

Research on donation appeals affirms that individuals are more willing to give a donation to an identifiable victim (e.g., one child in need) than a group of statistical victims (e.g., 20,000 children in need) (Kogut & Ritov, 2005; Small & Loewenstein, 2003). Small, Loewenstein, and Slovic (2007) investigated whether it was possible to lower the discrepancy between contributions to identifiable and statistical victims, and raise the contributions to statistical victims, by educating individuals about the identifiable victim effect. The education effort resulted in a boomerang effect. Although it removed the discrepancy of donations, it did so by reducing contributions to identified victims, while not changing contributions to statistical victims, which resulted in a lowering of overall contributions.

*Instructional*

Various strategic instructional messages have been given to students in an effort to raise academic performance. Research indicates that messages intending to boost self-esteem tend to fail (Valentine, DuBois, & Copper, 2004). For example, Forsyth, Lawrence, Burnette, and Baumeister (2007) concluded that providing low-performing students in an introductory psychology course with academically focused self-esteem messages resulted in lower test scores, both within-subjects and compared to similar students given no such messages.

**Patterns of Individual Differences**

Human beings possess many attributes which moderate the effects of a communicative interaction. Developmental abilities of individuals are usually marked by average differences between people at various ages. Boomerang effects have been found to depend on the age of participants when examining the ability of media to change attitudes (B. J. Wilson et al., 1992), reactions to ratings and labels (Bushman & Cantor, 2003; Cantor, 1998; Cantor & Harrison, 1996), and media literacy interventions (Nathanson & Yang, 2003).

Gender of message receivers also plays a role in the emergence of a boomerang effect. Males appear to be more likely to exhibit boomerang effects in studies that have investigated messages that target issues that may be more salient to men, such as messages regarding alcohol consumption (Bensley & Wu, 1991) and restrictive labels or warnings on aggressive material (Bushman & Cantor, 2003; Bushman & Stack, 1996). The gender discrepancy of the boomerang effect can work in both directions, however, as evidenced by women's, but not men's, responses to negative political advertising in some studies (King & McConnell, 2003; Pfau & Louden, 1994).

Personality differences also influence the boomerang effect. For example, Cantor et al. (1997) argued that individuals high in trait aggression tend to be most interested in movies with restrictive ratings. Other factors that moderate boomerang effects include processing ability (Petrova & Cialdini, 2005), trait reactance (Bushman & Stack, 1996), and previous tendencies toward the targeted behaviors such as TV viewing (Nathanson & Yang, 2003) and energy consumption (Schulz et al., 2007).

### Patterns of Message Differences

In addition to differences between individuals, the actual messages may influence the likelihood of a boomerang effect. Messages can be framed, presented, or constructed in many ways. One of the most long-standing debates, for example, pertains to the use of fear appeals in persuasive messages. When individuals receive a high fear-inducing message aimed to promote behavior change, a boomerang effect will result if they do not feel that they have high personal efficacy regarding the behavior (Gore & Bracken, 2005; Leventhal, 1970; Witte, 1992, 1994).

Similar patterns have emerged in messages using a social norms approach (Wechsler et al., 2003), overly explicit messages (Grandpre et al., 2003), messages with an authoritative or demanding source (S. S. Brehm & J. W. Brehm, 1981; Bushman & Stack, 1996; Pennebaker & Sanders, 1976), and messages that demonstrate consequences to perpetrators rather than victims (Winkel & De Kleuver, 1997). Additionally, warnings against violent material more likely boomerang than warnings against sexual material (Bushman & Cantor, 2003). Finally, across contexts, scholars have argued that messages with weak arguments (those that are circular, without support, or vacuous) more likely result in unintended or boomerang effects than messages with strong arguments (based in logic with valid and clear presentation of data) (Park, Levine, Westerman, Orfgen, & Foregger, 2007).

## Two Paths to the Boomerang Effect

Various explanations for the boomerang effect are proposed within theories of communication, persuasion, psychology, and education. This section reviews possible explanations for this effect and provides examples of how the effect would manifest under the predictions of each explanation. Many of the theoretical explanations in this section do not address boomerang effects specifically. However, the theoreticians provide insight on several key constructs and explanatory mechanisms that enhance our understanding of the process.

These explanations for the boomerang effect can be grouped into two broad categories. One set of mechanisms operates from the assumption that receivers process the strategic message as intended, but do not properly comply. This family of mechanisms includes psychological reactance (J. Brehm, 1966; S. S. Brehm & J. W. Brehm, 1981), increased interest in a scare resource (Brock, 1968; Fromkin & Brock, 1973), implications of lack of self-efficacy (Leventhal, 1971; R. W. Rogers, 1983; Witte, 1992), and the inability to resist thinking about the attitude or behavior in question (Wegner, 1994).

However, what if the receiver does not interpret the message as intended? McGuire (2001) argued that two of the major steps to being persuaded occur at the time of message exposure. These steps encompass perceiving and comprehending the message *as intended*. While McGuire's steps help us to understand how difficult it is to be persuaded, he does not detail the implications for those individuals who are not persuaded—those who do *not* perceive and understand the message as intended—or even move in the opposite direction, at any of these stages.

A second set of theories addresses this issue, holding that some recipients are susceptible to greater risks than simply not being persuaded. These theories postulate that some aspects of a message may be processed by the receiver at the expense of other aspects. Explanations in this category include observational learning (Bandura, 1986), activation of social norms (Cialdini, 2003; Gascoinge, 2001), the priming of cognitions related to an opposing set of ideas (Berkowitz & Rogers, 1986), and ambiguity reduction (Bushman & Stack, 1996).

In the next section, we review the theoretical mechanisms under these two broad, but conceptually distinct pathways to the boomerang effect (see Table 1.1). One path, *intended construct activation*, involves processing the content of the message as intended, but not complying with it. The other path involves message receivers processing harmful elements in a message at the expense of those that were intended, a mechanism we label *unintended construct activation*.

### *Intended Construct Activation*

Stakeholders deliberately insert content into strategic messages to achieve the intended effect of changing beliefs, attitudes, or behaviors (Piotrow & Kin-

*Table 1.1* Categorizing Some Theoretical Mechanisms for the Boomerang Effect

| Path A | Path B |
| --- | --- |
| *Intended Construct Activation* | *Unintended Construct Activation* |
| Valuing a commodity or freedom | Observational learning |
| Reactance | Internalizing attributions |
| Ironic processing | Ambiguity reduction |
| Engaging in fear control | Accessibility/priming |
| | Peripheral processing |
| | Selective exposure and attention |
| | Selective perception |
| | Activation of social norms |

caid, 2001). Ideally, these elements have been constructed by drawing on theory and research. For example, a message may be created with the intention of persuading teenagers to adopt the belief that taking drugs is unhealthy. This belief may be targeted with the intention of ultimately creating a behavior change—making teens less likely to use drugs. To achieve this desired effect, the message must contain elements specifically designed to achieve this goal, such as testimonials from teenagers who have suffered from drug abuse. The information in these testimonials—that using drugs leads to health complications—exemplifies an *intended element*, or a specific component in a message, expected to lead to receivers to exhibit certain predicted effects. We will now review some theories postulate that the message receiver processes but then rejects or resists those elements.

*Valuing a Commodity*

Commodity theory (Brock, 1968; Fromkin & Brock, 1973) focuses on how people psychologically respond to scarce resources. According to Fromkin and Brock, a commodity comprises anything that has "usefulness or relevance to the person who possesses it" (p. 222). This theory affirms that the more receivers perceive a commodity to be unavailable, the more that they value, desire, or accept it. Brock argued that media messages and human behaviors constitute commodities. It follows that messages or behaviors that cannot be obtained, or can only be obtained through great effort, are judged to be more valuable by individuals. For example, if a message attempts to persuade individuals to quit smoking, those individuals who do smoke may more highly value the ability to do so. Similarly, a rule preventing exposure to sexual media messages may instead function to add value to that particular kind of message. If such a rule intends to ultimately prevent exposure to audiences at risk, a boomerang effect may occur as those messages become more highly sought-after.

*Reactance*

The theory of psychological reactance (J. Brehm, 1966; S. S. Brehm & J. W. Brehm, 1981) also predicts the conditions under which a strategic message will fail. The theory holds that individuals perceive themselves as having specific behavioral freedoms. As S. S. Brehm and J. W. Brehm noted, if these freedoms are threatened or eliminated, individuals will be motivated to reestablish them.

The level of reactance arousal in an individual depends on both how much he or she values a specific freedom and the degree of threat the person perceives toward that freedom. Recent work on the theory has attributed reactance to "an intermingling of negative cognition and anger" (Dillard & Shen, 2005, p. 160). In other words, the threat makes individuals angry and motivates them to take action. For example, if a man highly values the freedom to smoke and his wife tells him that he should not smoke, he may experience reactance arousal. This arousal may, in turn, motivate him to smoke even more when he is not in his wife's presence, in an effort to re-establish his freedom to smoke.

When an individual freedom is taken away, individuals can re-establish the freedoms through restoration, which can be accomplished either by engaging in the behavior that is threatened or, if the threat is directed toward an idea, embracing that idea even more (S. S. Brehm & J. W. Brehm, 1981). This process provides a sense of control for the individual experiencing reactance.

Several outcomes of reactance have been proposed in addition to direct restoration of the threatened freedom, including an increase in perceived value of the threatened freedom, hostility toward the source of the threat, denial that a threat exists, and protection of future freedoms (S. S. Brehm & J. W. Brehm, 1981). Of these effects, two are most important to the boomerang effect—the freedom increases in value and source derogation.

The first factor, additional value being attached to the freedom in question, entails a minor point in the reactance theory and borrows heavily from commodity theory (S. S. Brehm & J. W. Brehm, 1981; Brock, 1968; Worchel, 1972). However, it is important in understanding why boomerang effects, as predicted by psychological reactance theory, may occur. If a person perceives a freedom as more valuable than it was perceived to be before exposure to the threat, it follows that he or she may become more likely to engage in restoration of the freedom.

The second effect, source derogation, may be particularly damaging because individuals may not only reject the message at hand but also become more likely to reject any future messages from that particular source (S. S. Brehm & J. W. Brehm, 1981). In addition, elimination of source derogation effects can be intentionally constructed by designing a message with a more likeable source, or a source more similar to the receiver. Such strategies may help reduce the sense of threat and, in turn, reduce potential boomerang effects (C. H. Miller, Lane, Deatrick, Young, & Potts, 2007; Silvia, 2005).

*Ironic Processing*

Another explanation for boomerang effects may be that humans simply experience difficulty with *not* thinking about something that they are told not to think about. The theory of ironic processes (Wegner, 1994) identifies the mechanisms underlying this phenomenon. The theory explains the findings of the famous "white bear" studies (Wegner, Schneider, Carter, & White, 1987). In these experiments, participants who were told not to think of a white bear had more white bear-related thoughts than those who were encouraged to think of the bear.

Wegner (1994) proposed a dual process model to explain why individuals can access suppressed thoughts more easily than free thoughts. In the model, when individuals attempt to suppress thoughts, they activate two cognitive mechanisms—an *operating process* and a *monitoring process*. If an individual tries not to think of a white bear, for example, the operating process searches for distracting thoughts while the monitoring process waits for evidence that the individual has failed (Wenzlaff & Wegner, 2000). Both of these processes increase accessibility of the target construct. Because maintaining this state requires a great deal of effort, the more active and demanding operating process eventually becomes taxed. When this fatigue happens, the more automatic monitoring process continues to linger, as its function is to draw an individual's attention to the unwanted accessible constructs. As the operating process becomes more and more taxed, the monitoring process continues to observe occurrences of the target thought, increasing the accessibility of the thought.

The boomerang effect occurs when the operating system slows due to a lack of cognitive resources, and the monitoring system takes over. This condition holds important implications for health campaigns that attempt to curtail substance cravings. If an individual's operating process successfully focuses on anti-smoking messages based on a "don't smoke" message, that element of the message may eventually subside as the individual becomes taxed. The theory holds that positive thoughts related to smoking suddenly become "hyperaccessible" in ones' mind (Wegner & Erber, 1992). This state of hyperaccessiblity allows the unwanted constructs more influence on behavior than they would have had if the message had not been heard in the first place (Monteith, Sherman, & Devine, 1998).

*Engaging in Fear Control*

There have been several efforts to explain the failure of strategic messages that employ the use of fear appeals, in particular (Leventhal, 1971; R. W. Rogers, 1983; Witte, 1992). Witte's (1992) extended parallel process model proposed that messages should possess content intended to increase both the perceived threat and efficacy. She argued that maladaptive effects may occur if one set of cognitions, those related to efficacy, are not as accessible as another set of cognitions, those related to the perceived threat. When the cognitions related to the threat (perceived susceptibility and perceived severity) override those related to efficacy (self and response) an individual may attempt to reduce the emerging fear by rejecting the message. While the model mainly addresses message rejection, boomerang effects may result from an individual engaging in extreme "fear control" mechanisms that include defensive avoidance, selective exposure and even reactance (Witte, 1994).

### Unintended Construct Activation

Ideally, strategic messages encompass only elements that were universally interpreted by receivers as intended. However, as in any communicative message, most elements remain open to interpretation (Lang et al., 1997). As a result, receivers may process a message in a way that leads to an effect that was not intended.

In order to identify elements that would predict a boomerang effect, we suggest first clearly specifying the intended effect. Next, we should examine the message for elements that based on existing research, and face value, hold the potential to send unintended signals that can lead the receiver to adopt the opposite attitude (or exhibit the opposite behavior). For example, if potential persuaders want to reduce the likelihood of drug use in teenagers, they should examine the message for elements with the potential to *increase* the likelihood that teens will use drugs. As with the intended elements, researchers are able to identify parts of messages that are likely to result in an increase in likelihood to use drugs by applying existing theory and drawing on research. Receivers might, for example, experience ambiguity reduction (Bushman & Stack, 1996), identify a social norm (Cialdini, 2003; Gascoinge, 2001), engage in observational learning (Bandura, 1986), or receive priming of unintended constructs (Berkowitz & Rogers, 1986).

These processes occur because a receiver selects (consciously or unconsciously) specific elements, or responds to a lack of necessary elements, in the message. We should clarify that messages often contain both unintended and intended elements with the potential to lead to unintended effects. To follow through on the teen drug use example: The use of teens as spokespersons may have the intended element of signaling to a teen audience that the message is credible, but it might also unintentionally signal that drug use comprises a normative behavior. By specifically examining the message for elements that may signal the desirability of drug use to teens, researchers can pinpoint *unintended elements* that can lead to a boomerang effect. The following theories adopt this perspective.

### Observational Learning

To the extent that a message does not explicitly identify harmful consequences of a target behavior, social cognitive theory postulates that receivers may encode a message for later use, just as if the behavior had been rewarded (Bandura, 1986, 2002). Viewers may perceive rewards (or no consequences) in social influence messages, such as anti-drug ads. If a public service announcement portrays a drug user as thin and beautiful, it may concurrently communicate certain rewards associated with using drugs. If the viewer wants to become thin, those behaviors (i.e., drug use) may be easily accessible and may later be retrieved as a potentially rewarding solution.

### Internalizing Attributions

Self-perception theory explains why people might reject the persuasive appeal of authority, or any other extrinsic motivating force, such as expectations of punishment or rewards (Bem, 1972; Conway & Schaller, 2005). This theory helps us understand what happens when individuals are offered an extrinsic reward to engage in activity that they were already doing, or were about to do, without any reward. In this situation, people may discount their intrinsic motivations for engaging in the behavior and instead attribute compliance solely to the possibility of gaining the extrinsic reward (Festinger & Carlsmith, 1959; T. D. Wilson & Lassiter, 1982). For example, if people who desire to quit smoking receive a financial incentive to quit, they could perceive earning money (not a healthier life) as their reason for stopping.

According to Aronson and Carlsmith (1963), if people receive extrinsic rewards *not* to perform an undesirable behavior, they may actually increase their intrinsic interest in that behavior. If a smoker listens to a message that he should discontinue smoking because it harms others around him, he may attribute his reasons for not smoking to potential consequences on other people, not himself. This condition may cause him to become more intrinsically interested in smoking. Essentially, the smoker might say to himself, "I shouldn't smoke around other people, so I'll just smoke more often in private." Aronson and Carlsmith argued that individuals are not likely to be persuaded on the basis of extrinsic rewards or punishments because the experience does not afford them the opportunity to self-persuade.

### Ambiguity Reduction

Undesirable constructs may become accessible simply by introducing new concepts into a network of ideas (Bushman & Stack, 1996). This newly acquired knowledge may influence the attitudes and behaviors of the individual. For example, when a person sees a movie rating, she or he attains knowledge about the movie that did not exist before exposure to the rating. As Bushman and Stack asserted, armed with this new knowledge, the individual may experience an increase in desire to view the movie based on past positive experiences with movies with the same rating.

## Accessibility and Priming

Boomerang effects may be caused by an undesirable set of mental constructs becoming more accessible than a desired set. Berkowitz and Rogers (1986) labeled the mechanism behind this effect as priming. Based on associative models of memory, this framework suggests that the human mind consists of links and nodes that, when activated in response to a stimulus, become more easily accessed (Anderson & Bower, 1974; Collins & Loftus, 1975). Additionally, because individuals have limited mental capacity (Mayer, 2003), they likely devote cognitive resources to processing certain pieces of information at the expense of others (Lang, 2000). These pieces of information may be linked to cognitions that may ultimately cause an individual to respond in a way that was not intended by the strategic message.

Concepts can become more accessible by reaction to message frames. Frames constitute "schemata of interpretation" that allow individuals "to locate, perceive, identify, and label" issues and topics within their own personal context (Goffman, 1974, p. 21). Gamson and Modigliani (1989) described frames as interpretative packages that give meaning to an issue by presenting "a central organizing idea...for making sense of relevant events, suggesting what is an issue" (p. 3). A primary area of framing research examines *frame-setting* (Scheufele, 2000), which examines how frames resonate with individuals and affect their interpretation of events and situations. The related *emphasis framing effect* (Druckman, 2001) holds that, if a message emphasizes specific attributes of an object or issue, message receivers (audiences) will tend to focus on the emphasized components when making evaluations and decisions on the object or issue. In other words, frames select and present a subset of issue considerations or attributes over others to an audience or target—altering accessibility of related concepts. For some audiences, framing a message in a certain way may unintentionally activate cognitions at odds with the original goal of the message.

## Peripheral Processing

According to the elaboration likelihood model (Petty & Cacioppo, 1986), if an individual lacks motivation or the ability to process deeply, he more likely processes peripherally and fails to seriously consider arguments presented in the message. If the unintended (or harmful) elements of a message happen to be the easiest to process and the intended (or helpful) elements of a message are the hardest to process, boomerang effects may occur in individuals low in motivation and ability. According to Petty and Cacioppo, these individuals tend to prioritize the easier, unintended elements over the more difficult intended elements. For example, a television viewer may not be motivated or able to process a campaign advertisement that intends to portray an opposing candidate in a negative light. Instead, the viewer may pick up on peripheral cues, such as the candidate's appearance. In fact, simply being repeatedly exposed to these ads may be boomerang on individuals who process peripherally (Ansolabehere & Iyengar, 1996).

Similarly, if a viewer watches a message intended to curtail anti-social behaviors but does so without processing the main argument against the behavior, the message could prompt positive thoughts about the behavior. For example, if a public service announcement (PSA) that discourages drug use depicts good-looking teens using drugs, the viewer may not focus on the arguments in the message. Instead, she or he may develop positive attitudes about drug use while processing the message peripherally.

### Selective Exposure and Attention

Individuals also possess the ability to attend to certain messages, or parts of messages, and ignore others (Freedman & Sears, 1965). If children are more intrinsically interested in, for example, the violent clips used as examples in a media literacy intervention than in the concepts being taught, attention to these concepts may activate unintended aggressive constructs (Byrne, 2009).

Individuals also might interpret a message that they are forced to view in a very different way than viewers who elect to view the message. Under forced viewing conditions, a viewer may be susceptible to anti-social thoughts that emerge as a result of limited previous exposure. This argument may explain the results of experimental situations that ask viewers to watch a program that they would not otherwise watch (B. J. Wilson et al., 1992) or in media literacy interventions, when children who watch little television are asked to pay close attention to a type of content that they would not normally view in their daily lives (Nathanson & Yang, 2003). Without the pre-established knowledge structures needed to processes and store the intended information, the viewer might instead be more influenced by the anti-social message, given his or her unusually close attention to it (Nathanson, 2004).

### Selective Perception

What if viewers receive the exact same message but perceive different meanings in it? According to theories and research on selective perception, interpretations depend on individual differences (DeFleur & Ball-Rokeach, 1989; Mullin, Imrich, & Linz, 1996; Oliver, 2002). If producers of a movie intend to increase rape awareness, but instead the film is sexually arousing to certain individuals, this finding clearly constitutes a boomerang effect (B. J. Wilson et al., 1992). Additionally, if receivers perceive a pro-social message or an advertisement as being manipulative in intent, the likelihood of rejection, and boomerang effects, may be increased (Skarlicki et al., 2004).

Social judgment theory (Sherif & Hovland, 1961) postulates that individuals sometimes distort messages depending on their current attitudes. This process could lead to a boomerang effect. For example, a 40-year-old man could believe that prostate exams are important, but he doesn't feel that he is old enough to begin routine prostate examinations. If he were exposed to a campaign that attempted to encourage prostate examinations, and the source of the ad appeared older than the viewer, the younger viewer might assimilate the message toward his own attitude and perceive that the message agrees with him—that he doesn't need exams yet and that routine exams are for older men. This perception might make him even less likely to seek an exam than before watching the advertisement.

### Activation of Social Norms

A boomerang effect may occur when, as a result of exposure to a strategic message, the receiver deduces that the undesirable behavior being targeted is a social norm (Cialdini, 2003; Gascoinge, 2001; Schultz et al., 2007). For example, an adolescent female may observe a campaign intending to promote sexual abstinence and deduce that most of her peers must be having sex. Otherwise, no need would exist for such a campaign. Armed with this set of beliefs, the girl may be more likely to engage in sexual behavior than she would have been in the absence of exposure to the message.

## Integrated Theoretical Framework

Proceeding with two paths to the boomerang effect as argued above, the presence of various elements within a single strategic message sets up a competition of sorts in the mind of the receiver of a strategic message. The boomerang effect may be, in part, the result of how this competition plays out. Based on our review of the literature, we advance the following integrated theoretical framework for the boomerang process.

### Competitive Processing

Through a process that we call *competitive processing*, certain aspects of the message become more salient than others in the mind of the receiver. This process can be conscious or automatic. The end result of this competitive processing is the primary activation of cognitive associations, or constructs, linked to the message elements that essentially win this competition by the receiver (R. R. Miller & Grace, 2003) (see Figure 1.1 for a detail of competitive processing). If intended elements in the message win out, the receiver enters *intended construct activation*. If unintended elements win out, the receiver enters *unintended construct activation*.

> Proposition 1: If a receiver processes intended elements, then cognitions related to these elements become more accessible in the mind of the receiver than those related to unintended elements.

> Proposition 2: If a receiver processes *un*intended elements, then related unintended cognitions become more accessible in the mind of the receiver than those related to the intended elements.

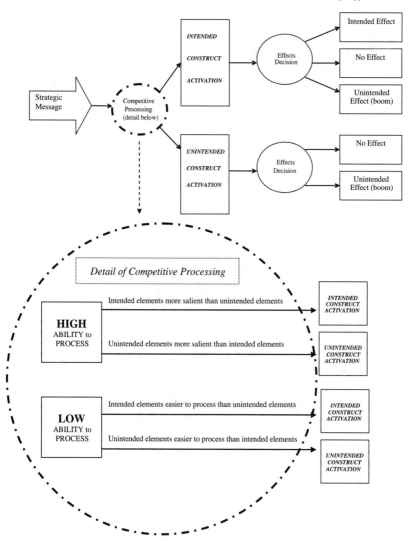

*Figure 1.1* A preliminary theoretical framework of the boomerang effect.

The selection and processing of one set of elements over the other is central to explaining the mechanisms driving the boomerang effect. An individual may process both kinds of elements, but one set ultimately "wins," overriding the other. According to R. R. Miller and Grace (2003), the likelihood that one stimulus will overshadow or block associations previously linked with the other depends on the "relative salience" of two stimuli, which we respectively label X and Y. If we apply this concept to boomerang effects, the associative network within the mind of an individual upon exposure to a message will either be related to the intended elements (functioning as stimulus Y) or the unintended elements (functioning as stimulus X). Therefore, in order for the intervention to be considered effective, the mental constructs related to the intended elements will be more accessible to the receiver than those associated with the undesirable, unintended elements. If not, the undesirable constructs may instead be activated in the mind of the receiver, increasing the likelihood of boomerang effects. These ideas lead to the third proposition:

> Proposition 3: For the strategic message to result in the intended effect, constructs related to the intended elements should be more accessible in the mind of the receiver than those related to unintended elements.

An individual will cognitively process one or the other set of elements of the message depending on (a) how able he or she is to process one set of message elements versus the other and (b) how salient one set of elements is perceived compared to the other set.

These theoretical ideas resemble to the motivation and ability constructs of the elaboration likelihood model of persuasion (Petty & Cacioppo, 1986), but the framework proposed here applies these ideas in a different way. Whereas ELM applies these ideas to the cognitive processing of the strategic message as a whole to predict likelihood of persuasion, the present framework emphasizes that several possible messages exist within what appears to be a unified message. Persuasion (or the opposite) results from which set of elements within the same message earns priority in a receiver's mind.

This framework envisions "ability" as a receiver trait that increases or decreases the likelihood of selecting the easiest elements to process, relative to each other (Petty & Cacioppo, 1986). If the receiver can successfully process both elements in a message, then this framework expects that motivation will be the central predictor of the selection of the intended or unintended elements of the message.

### The Role of Ability

If receivers' ability to process a strategic message remains low, they will process the easiest elements of the message (Lang, 2000). Cognitive ability has been previously operationalized as the degree to which an individual has mastered problem solving skills, scholastic ability, musical ability, and social skills (Dewey, Crawford, Creighton, & Suave, 2000; Williams, Ochs, Williams, & Mulhern, 1991). For viewers with less developed cognitive skills, such as children, the easiest part of the message will likely be elements such as the visuals (Lang, 1995), the least abstract (Nathanson, 2004) or familiar concepts (Lang, 2000).

The question then becomes, how does variance in cognitive ability predict the likelihood of the intended elements in a strategic message being successfully selected and processed instead of the unintended elements? Due to limited capacity, if the unintended elements of a message are easier to process than the intended elements, receivers low in ability will be more likely to experience an unintended effect. These ideas lead to the following proposition:

Proposition 4: Receivers low in ability will process the easiest elements of a message such that:

(a) If unintended elements of a message are easier to process than the intended elements, then constructs related to unintended elements will be activated in the mind of the receiver.

(b) If intended elements of a message are easier to process than the intended elements, then constructs related to intended elements will be activated.

## The Role of Relative Motivation

If receivers possess high ability overall, we can predict competitive processing by the relative motivation to process one set of elements over the other. One such motivator involves the degree to which the elements in the message remain personally salient. Specific message characteristics that may be indices of personal salience encompass the relative degree to which the individual enjoys, finds importance in, values, likes, identifies with, and has previous experience with one set of elements versus the other (Pfau et al., 1997). Participants will ultimately prioritize elements of the message that are more personally salient.

If the "relative personal salience" of the intended elements is given more weight than the unintended elements, the receivers will be motivated to process the intended elements and, therefore, engage in intended construct activation. If however, they emphasize the unintended elements, receivers will, instead, be motivated to process the unintended elements and engage in *unintended construct activation*. The following propositions state these ideas more formally:

Proposition 5: Receivers high in ability will process the most salient elements of a message such that:

(a) If the unintended elements of a message are more personally salient than the intended elements then constructs related to unintended elements will be activated in the mind of the receiver.

(b) If the intended elements of a message are more personally salient than the intended elements then constructs related to intended elements will be activated.

When receivers activate one set of constructs, they prime related ideas and become ready for the next stage of the framework—the effects decision.

## The Effects Decision

Once the outcome of competitive processing has been determined, the receiver proceeds to make an effects decision (see Figure 1.1), which constitutes the process whereby more specific mechanisms determine the likelihood of an effect. Like competitive processing, this phase of the framework is not necessarily a conscious decision, but can often occur automatically, without awareness.

### Effects via Intended Construct Activation

Logically, if the receiver processes the intended elements of the message then he or she should exhibit the intended effect. However, even if the receiver engages in intended construct activation, the intended effect, observable, may not actually manifest. Many theories of persuasion and media effects begin with this step, assuming that the receiver enters intended construct activation (J. Brehm, 1966; S. S. Brehm & J. W. Brehm, 1981; Brock, 1968; Fromkin & Brock, 1973; Leventhal, 1971; R. W. Rogers, 1983; Wegner, 1994; Witte, 1992). This perspective assumes that the receiver can and does process the message as intended but not exhibit the intended effect for theoretically proposed reasons. The present framework adheres to this line of thinking. We argue that, if a receiver experiences intended construct activation, three possible final outcomes could ensue—the intended effect is manifested; no effect is manifested, or an unintended effect is manifested (one of which may be a boomerang effect).

The intended effect occurs when the receiver selects, processes, and is persuaded by the intended elements as the creators of that message hoped (Piotrow & Kincaid, 2001). For example, an intended effect occurs when an ad campaign to promote use of birth control results in a significant increase in the use of condoms. While we do believe that the intended effect might possibly come about accidentally after exposure to the message, these instances are rare and not necessarily indicative of a successful strategic message.

An unintended effect, such as a boomerang effect, occurs when the receiver cognitively processes the message as intended, but then resists it. The effects can occur through several mechanisms (see Table 1.1, path A). For example, an unintended effect may occur via psychological reactance. An individual who comprehends a message that is intended to curtail drug use may become angry (when he or she feels that his freedom to use drugs is threatened), experience reactance, and, after reactance arousal, might exhibit an unintended or boomerang effect in an effort to restore the freedom to use drugs.

> Proposition 6: If the intended constructs produce resistance and/or negative affect toward the intended outcome, the receiver will exhibit an unintended effect.

Additionally, no (or null) effect(s) will result when the intended constructs have been activated in the mind of the receiver, but those constructs simply fail to persuade the individual. For example, scholars of the extended parallel process model (Witte, 1992) might argue that the receiver may lack sufficient efficacy.

### Effects via Unintended Construct Activation

This framework allows for boomerang effects to occur via two very different general mechanisms. While the pathway presented above posits that boomerang effects can occur when a receiver has comprehended the message as intended but then proceed to resist it, the framework holds that boomerang effects can also happen due to the selection and processing of elements in the message that were not intended (Table 1.1, Path B). The receiver processes the *unintended* elements instead of the intended elements, and two outcomes can emerge—an unintended effect (such as a boomerang effect) or no effect. If a null effect occurs, the reasons are probably not message-based. For example, the individual may be subjected to external social pressure, such as not to smoke, not to act aggressively, not to drink and drive. An unintended effect, like a boomerang effect, develops if the rewards associated with expressing an attitude or behavior linked to the unintended constructs outweigh factors external to the message that might suppress it (Bandura, 2002). If, for example, unintended elements in an anti-smoking message activate social norms cognitions that encourage smoking, the individual may still experience sufficient social pressure, external to the message, not to engage in smoking.

However, in the absence of these external factors, an unintended effect will result if the receiver finds sufficient value in the unintended elements in the message. Mechanisms that might contribute to this effect include perceiving rewards associated with the attitude or behavior in question, as proposed by social cognitive theory (Bandura 1986, 2002); perceiving the attitude or behavior to be normative (Cialdini, 2003; Gasciogne, 2001); being introduced to new ideas, as suggested by ambiguity reduction theory (Bushman & Stack, 1996), or being cognitively primed by the unintended elements of the message (Berkowitz & Rogers, 1986).

> Proposition 7: If unintended constructs have been activated in the mind of the receiver, then an unintended effect will result. In an open system, this effect may be suppressed by factors external to the message.

### Manifestation of Effects

In the proposed framework, five boxes on the far right of Figure 1.1 represent the effects. As noted, a boomerang effect can occur due to either intended or unintended construct activation. Notably, this framework asserts that these two types of effects may look identical, but the process through which each effect manifests itself is very different. This idea pertains to scholars and practitioners of strategic messages because, when a message boomerangs, this framework provides two possible explanations for the failure. Within those two explanations, a message can fail at two different points; during competitive processing or during the effects decision.

## Discussion

After a review of the research findings and existing theories that contribute to our understanding of the boomerang effect, we proposed two paths to the boomerang. First, message receivers may process and encode the message as intended but proceed to resist it. Second, instead of processing the message as intended, receivers of the message may essentially "miss the point" and instead be persuaded and affected by elements of the message that induce a boomerang effect. These two paths to the boomerang, manifesting through intended and unintended construct activation are the main components of a preliminary theoretical framework.

### Future Research

Several aspects of the framework require future refinement before it rises to the level of a formal model. First, the framework does not allow for a mechanism that we call *directed attention*. We can imagine a scenario where the intended elements (e.g., teacher's instructions) actually serve to direct the receiver's attention and processing resources toward unintended elements (anti-social message) and that, without such direction, the receiver might not have noticed or paid much attention to the unintended elements. In an experiment, this effect would emerge as an interaction, where the presence of both unintended *and* intended elements were necessary for a boomerang effect to emerge, rather than observing a main effect for one or the other.

Additionally, because we believe that both unintended and intended elements can be processed (and then one "overrides" the other), the degree of the override can affect the magnitude of the effect. For example, if the unintended constructs are extremely powerful, and the intended are weak, a boomerang effect would be stronger than it would have been if the unintended constructs are only slightly powerful. The framework can be refined to clarify this possibility.

However, the framework presented here can serve to assist researchers and practitioners in identifying the points in information processing where receivers may boomerang—either at the time of competitive processing or at the effects decision. The framework will be also be useful for researchers of strategic messages as they strive to further understand how to maximize the positive effects of these messages and minimize unintended effects. For example, a few studies that managed to override the boomerang effect by strategically directing receiver's attention away from unintended elements and toward those that were intended (Byrne, 2009; Cook et al., 2004) or by removing unintended elements altogether (Schwartz et al., 2007). Essentially, we hope that this chapter will activate research specifically examining why some individuals respond to strategic messages in ways that were not intended by the creators of the message and to generate specific solutions to prevent this outcome from occurring.

Finally, we believe that the ideas put forth in this chapter are relevant to scholars across the field of communication. The earliest models of communication were concerned with explaining why the communicative interaction sometimes fails (Shannon & Weaver, 1949). Because any message created with the intent to change attitudes, beliefs or behaviors is at risk of leading to the opposite response, we hope that this chapter contributes to what we know about message disruption processes in subfields such as organizational, group, interpersonal, intercultural, and mediated communication.

## References

Abrahams, M. F., & Bell, R. A. (1994). Encouraging charitable contributions—An examination of 3 models of door-in-the-face compliance. *Communication Research, 21*, 131–153.

Anderson, J. R., & Bower, G. H. (1974). *Human associative memory*. Washington, DC: Hemisphere.

Ansolabehere, S., & Iyengar, S. (1996). Can the press monitor campaign advertising? An experimental study. *Press/politics, 1*, 72–86.

Aronson, E., & Carlsmith, J. M. (1963). Effects of severity of threat in the devaluation of forbidden behavior. *Journal of Abnormal & Social Psychology, 66*, 584–588.

Atkin, C. (2002). Promising strategies for media health campaigns. In W. D. Crano & M. Burgoon (Eds.), *Mass media and drug prevention* (pp. 35–64). Mahwah, NJ: Erlbaum.

Austin, E. W., Pinkleton, B. E., Hust, S. J. T., & Cohen, M. (2005). Evaluation of an American Legacy Foundation Washington State Department of Health Media literacy pilot study. *Health Communication, 18*, 75–95.

Bandura, A. (1986). *Social foundations of thought and action: A social cognitive theory*. Englewood Cliffs, NJ: Prentice Hall.

Bandura, A. (2002). Social cognitive theory of mass communication. In J. Bryant & D. Zillmann (Eds.), *Media effects: Advances in theory and research* (pp. 121–154). Mahwah, NJ: Erlbaum.

Bandura, A., Ross, D., & Ross, S. A. (1963). Imitation of film-mediated aggressive models. *Journal of Abnormal and Social Psychology, 66*, 3–11.

Bem, D. J. (1972). Self-perception theory. In L. Berkowitz (Ed), *Advances in experimental social psychology* (Vol. 6, pp. 1–63). New York: Academic Press.

Bensley, L. S., & Wu, R. (1991). The role of psychological reactance in drinking following alcohol prevention messages. *Journal of Applied Social Psychology, 21*, 1111–1124.

Berger, C. R. (1995). A plan-based approach to strategic communication. In D. E. Hewes (Ed.), *The cognitive bases of interpersonal communication* (pp. 141–179). Hillsdale, NJ: Erlbaum.

Berkowitz, L., & Rogers, K. H. (1986). A priming effect analysis of media influences. In J. Bryant & D. Zillman (Eds.), *Perspectives on media effects* (pp. 57–81). Mahwah, NJ: Erlbaum.

Bies, R. J. (1989). Managing conflict before it happens: The role of accounts. In M. A. Rahim (Ed.), *Managing conflict: An interdisciplinary approach* (pp. 83–91). New York: Praeger.

Brehm. J. (1966). *A theory of psychological reactance.* New York: Academic Press.

Brehm, S. S., & Brehm, J. W. (1981). *Psychological reactance: A theory of freedom and control.* San Diego, CA: Academic Press.

Brock, T. C. (1968). Implications of commodity theory for value change. In A. G. Greenwald, T. C. Brock, & T. M. Ostrom (Eds.), *Psychological foundations of attitudes* (pp. 243–275). New York: Academic Press.

Buijzen, M., Walma van der Molen, J. H., & Sondij, P. (2007). Parental mediation of children's emotional responses to a violent news event. *Communication Research, 34,* 212–230.

Bushman, B. J., & Cantor, J. (2003). Media ratings for violence and sex: Implications for policymakers and parents. *American Psychologist, 58,* 130–141.

Bushman, B. J., & Stack, A. D. (1996). Forbidden fruit versus tainted fruit: Effects of warnings labels on attraction to television violence. *Journal of Experimental Psychology: Applied, 2,* 207–226.

Byrne, S. (2009). Media literacy interventions: What makes them boom or boomerang? *Communication Education, 58,* 1–14.

Campbell, M. C. (1995). When attention-getting advertising tactics elicit consumer inference of manipulative intent: The importance of balancing benefits and investments. *Journal of Consumer Psychology, 4,* 225–254.

Campo, S., & Cameron, K. A. (2006). Differential effects of exposure to social norms campaigns: A cause for concern. *Health Communication, 19,* 209–219.

Cantor, J. (1998). Ratings for program content: the role of research findings. *Annals of the American Academy of Political and Social Science, 557,* 54–69.

Cantor, J., & Harrison, K. (1996). Ratings and advisories for television programming. In Center for Communication and Social Policy (Ed.), *National television violence study* (Vol. 1, pp. 361–410). Thousand Oaks, CA: Sage.

Cantor, J., Harrison, K. S., & Nathanson, A. I. (1997). Ratings and advisories for television programming. In Center for Communication and Social Policy (Ed.), *National television violence study* (Vol. 2, pp. 267–322). Thousand Oaks, CA: Sage.

Cantor, J., & Wilson, B. J. (2003). Media and violence: Intervention strategies for reducing aggression. *Media Psychology, 5,* 363–403.

Chambers, D. A., Pearson, J. L., Lubell, K., Brandon, S., O'Brien, K., & Zinn J. (2005). The science of public messages for suicide prevention: A workshop summary. *Suicide and Life-Threatening Behavior, 35,* 134–145.

Cho, H., & Salomon, C. T. (2007). Unintended effects of health communication campaigns. *Journal of Communication, 57,* 293–317.

Choma, B. L., Foster, M. D., & Radford, E. (2007). Use of objectification theory to examine the effects of a media literacy intervention on women. *Sex Roles, 56,* 581–590.

Cialdini, R. B. (2003). Crafting normative messages to protect the environment. *Current Directions in Psychological Research, 12,* 105–109.

Cialdini, R. B., Kallgren, C. A., & Reno, R. R. (1991). A focus theory of normative conduct. *Advances in Experimental Social Psychology, 24,* 201–234.

Cody, M. J., Canary, D. J., & Smith, S. W. (1994). Compliance gaining goals: An indictive analysis of actors' and goal types, strategies, and successes. In J. A. Daly &

J. M. Wiemann (Eds.), *Strategic interpersonal communication* (pp. 33–90). Hillsdale, NJ: Erlbaum.

Collins, A. M., & Loftus, E. F. (1975). A spreading-activation theory of semantic processing. *Psychological Review, 82*, 407–428.

Conway, L. G., & Schaller, M. (2005). When authorities' commands backfire: Attributions about consensus and effects on deviant decision making. *Journal of Personality & Social Psychology, 89*, 311–326.

Cook, A., Arndt, J., & Lieberman, J. D. (2004). Firing back at the backfire effect: The influence of mortality salience and nullification beliefs on reactions to inadmissible evidence. *Law and Human Behavior, 28*, 389–408.

Cotte, J., Coulter, R. A., & Moore, M. (2005). Enhancing or disrupting guilt: The role of ad credibility and perceived manipulative intent. *Journal of Business Research, 58*, 361–368.

Crano W. D., & Burgoon M. (Eds.). (2002). *Mass media and drug prevention: Classic and contemporary theories and research*. Mahwah, NJ: Erlbaum

DeFleur M., & Ball–Rokeach, S. (1989). *Theories of mass communication* (5th ed.). White Plains, NY: Longman.

Dewey, D., Crawford, S. G., Creighton, D. E., & Suave, R. S. (2000). Parent's ratings of everyday cognitive abilities in very low birth weight children. *Journal of Developmental & Behavioral Pediatrics, 21*, 37–43.

Dillard, J. P., Anderson, J. W., & Knobloch, L. K. (2002). Interpersonal influence. In M. L. Knapp & J. A. Daly (Eds.), *Handbook of interpersonal communication* (pp. 425–474). Thousand Oaks, CA: Sage.

Dillard, J. P., & Shen, L. (2005). On the nature of reactance and its role in persuasive health communication. *Communication Monographs, 72*, 144–168.

Doolittle, J. C. (1980). Immunizing children against possible antisocial effects of viewing television violence: A curricular intervention. *Perceptual & Motor Skills, 51*, 498.

Druckman, J. (2001). On the limits of framing effects: who can frame? *The Journal of Politics, 63*, 1041–1066.

Farrelly, M. C., Healton, C. G., Davis, K. C., Messeri, P., Hersey, J. C., & Haviland, M. L. (2002). Getting to the truth: Evaluating national tobacco countermarketing campaigns. *American Journal of Public Health, 92*, 901–907.

Festinger, L., & Carlsmith, J. M. (1959). Cognitive consequences of forced compliance. *Journal of Abnormal and Social Psychology 58*, 203–210.

Fishbein, M., Hall-Jamison, K., Zimmer, E., von Haeften, I., & Nabi, R. (2002). Avoiding the boomerang: Tesing the relative effectiveness of antidrug public service announcements before a national campaign. *American Journal of Public Health, 92*, 238–245.

Forsyth, D. R., Lawrence, N. K., Burnette, J. L., & Baumeister, R. F. (2007). Attempting to improve the academic performance of struggling college students by bolstering their self-esteem: An intervention that backfired. *Journal of Social and Clinical Psychology, 26*, 447–459.

Foxcroft, D. R., Lister-Sharp, D., & Lowe, G. (1997). Alcohol misuse prevention for young people: A systematic review reveals methodological concerns and lack of reliable evidence of effectiveness. *Addiction, 92*, 531–537.

Freedman, J. L., & Sears, D. O. (1965). Selective exposure. In L. Berkowitz (Ed.), *Advances in experimental social psychology* (Vol. 2, pp. 57–97). New York: Academic Press.

Fromkin, H. L., & Brock, T. C. (1973). Erotic materials: A commodity theory analysis of the enhanced desirability that may accompany their unavailability. *Journal of Applied Social Psychology, 3,* 219–231.

Fuse, K., & Xie, D. (2007). A successful conversion or a double refusal: A study of the process of refusal conversion in telephone survey research. *Social Science Journal, 44,* 434–446.

Gamson, W., & Modigliani, A. (1989). Media discourse and public opinion on nuclear power: A constructionist approach. *American Journal of Sociology, 95,* 1–37.

Garramone, G. M. (1984). Voter responses to negative political ads. *Journalism Quarterly, 61,* 250–259.

Gascoinge, J. (2001). The power of positive peer pressure: Using social norm theory to address youth health issues. *The RMC Health Educator, 2,* 1–4.

Goffman, E. (1974). *Frame analysis.* Cambridge, MA: Harvard University Press.

Gordon, R. A., & Minor, S. W. (1992). Attitudes toward change in the legal drinking age: Reactance versus compliance, *Journal of College Student Development, 33,* 171–176.

Gore, T. D., & Bracken, C. C. (2005). Testing the theoretical design of a health risk message: Reexamining the major tenets of the extended parallel process model. *Health Education and Behavior, 32,* 27–41.

Grandpre, J., Alvaro, E. M., Burgoon, M., Miller, C. H., & Hall, J. R. (2003). Adolescent reactance and anti-smoking campaigns: A theoretical approach. *Health Communication, 15,* 349–366.

Greenberg, J. (1996). Forgive me, I'm new: Three experimental demonstrations of the effects of attempts to excuse poor performance. *Organizational Behavior and Human Decision Processes, 66,* 165–178.

Hovland, C. I., Janis, I. L., & Kelly, H. H. (1953). *Communication and persuasion: Psychological studies of opinion change.* New Haven, CT: Yale University Press.

Josephson, W. L. (1987). Television violence and children's aggression: Testing the priming, social script, and disinhibition predictions. *Journal of Personality and Social Psychology, 53,* 882–890.

Kahneman, D., & Tversky, A. (1979). Prospect theory: An analysis of decision under risk. *Econometrica, 47,* 263–291.

King, J. D., & McConnell, J. B. (2003). The effect of negative campaign advertising on vote choice: The mediating influence of gender. *Social Science Quarterly, 84,* 843–857.

Kline, K. N. (1995, November). *Applying Witte's extended parallel process model to pamphlets urging women to engage in BSE. Where are the efficacy messages?* Paper presented at the annual meeting of the Speech Communication Association, San Antonio, TX.

Kline, K. N., & Mattson, M. (2000). Breast self-examination pamphlets: A content analysis grounded in fear appeal research. *Health Communication, 12,* 1–21.

Kogut, T., & Ritov, I. (2005). The "identified victim" effect: An identified group, or just a single individual? *Journal of Behavioral Decision Making, 18,* 157–167.

Krcmar, M., & Cantor, J. (1997). The role of television advisories and ratings in parent-child discussion of television viewing choices. *Journal of Broadcasting & Electronic Media, 41,* 393–411.

Lang, A. (1995). Defining audio/video redundancy from a limited-capacity information processing perspective. *Communication Research, 22,* 86–115.

Lang, A. (2000). The limited capacity model of mediated message processing. *Journal of Communication, 50,* 46–70.

Lang, P. J., Bradley, M. M., & Cuthbert, B. N. (1997). Motivated attention: Affect, activation and action. In P. J. Lang, R. F. Simons, & M. T. Balaban (Eds.), *Attention and orienting: Sensory and motivational processes* (pp. 97–136). Hillsdale, NJ: Erlbaum.

Lau, R. R., Sigelman, L, & Rovner, I. B. (2007). The effects of negative political campaigns: A meta-analytic reassessment. *The Journal of Politics, 69,* 1176–1209.

Leventhal, H. (1970). Findings and theory in the study of fear communication. In L. Berkowitz (Ed.), *Advances in experimental social psychology* (Vol. 5, pp. 119–186). New York: Academic Press.

Leventhal, H. (1971). Fear appeals in persuasion: The differentiation of a motivational construct. *American Journal of Public Health, 61,* 1208–1224.

Lieberman, J. D., & Arndt, J. (2000). Understanding the limits of limiting instruction: Social psychology explanations for the failure of instructions to disregard pretrial publicity and other inadmissible evidence. *Psychology, Public Policy, and Law, 6,* 677–711.

Mayer, R. E. (2003). *Learning and instruction.* Upper Saddle Creek, NJ: Merrill-Prentice Hall.

McGuire, W. J. (2001). Input and output variables currently promising for constructing persuasive communications. In R. E. Rice & C. K. Atkin (Eds.), *Public communication campaigns* (pp. 22–48). Thousand Oaks, CA: Sage.

McLeod, J. M., Atkin, C. K., & Chaffee, S. H. (1972). Adolescents, parents, and television use: Adolescent self-report measures from Maryland and Wisconsin samples. In G. A. Comstock & E. A. Rubinstein (Eds.), *Television and social behavior: Vol. 3. Television and adolescent aggressiveness* (pp. 173–238). Washington, DC: U.S. Government Printing Office.

Miller, C. H., Lane, L.T., Deatrick, L. M., Young, A. M., & Potts, K. A. (2007). Psychological reactance and promotional health messages: The effects of controlling language, lexical concreteness, and the restoration of freedom. *Human Communication Research, 33,* 219–240.

Miller, R. R., & Grace, R. C. (2003). Conditioning and learning. In I. B. Weiner (Series Ed.) & A. F. Healy & R. W. Proctor (Vol. Eds.), *Handbook of psychology: Vol. 4. Experimental psychology* (pp. 357–363). New York: Wiley.

Monteith, M. J., Sherman, J. W., & Devine, P. G. (1998). Suppression as a stereotype control strategy. *Personality & Social Psychology Review, 2,* 63–82.

Moyer-Gusé, E., & Nabi, R. (2008, May). *Comparing the persuasive effects of entertainment-education and educational programming on risky sexual behavior.* Paper presented at the annual conference of the International Communication Association, Montreal, Canada.

Mullin, C., Imrich, D. J., & Linz, D. (1996). The impact of acquaintance rape stories and case-specific pretrial publicity on juror decision making. *Communication Research, 23,* 100–135.

Nathanson, A. I. (1999). Identifying and explaining the relationship between parental mediation and children's aggression. *Communication Research, 26,* 124–143.

Nathanson, A. I. (2002). The unintended effects of parental mediation of television on adolescents. *Media Psychology, 4,* 207–230.

Nathanson, A. I. (2004). Factual and evaluative approaches to modifying children's responses to television. *Journal of Communication, 54,* 321–336.

Nathanson, A. I., & Yang, M. (2003). The effects of mediation content and form on children's responses to violent television. *Human Communication Research, 29,* 111–143.

Obermiller, C. (1995). The baby is sick/The baby is well: A test of environmental communication appeals. *Journal of Advertising, 24,* 55–70.

O'Keefe, D., & Jensen, J. (2006). The advantages of compliance or the disadvantages of noncompliance? A meta-analytic review of the relative persuasive effectiveness of gain-framed and loss-framed messages. In C. S. Beck (Ed.), *Communication yearbook 30* (pp. 1–44). Mahwah, NJ: Erlbaum.

Oliver, M. B. (2002). Individual differences in media effects. In J. Bryant & D. Zillmann (Eds.), *Media effects: Advances in theory and research* (pp. 507–524). Mahwah, NJ: Erlbaum.

Papageorgis, D., & McGuire, W. J. (1961). The generality of immunity to persuasion produced by pre-exposure to weakened counterarguments. *Journal of Abnormal and Social Psychology, 62,* 475–481.

Park, H. S., Levine, T. R., Westerman, C. Y. K., Orfgen, T., & Foregger, S. (2007). The effects of argument quality and involvement type on attitude formation and attitude change: A test of dual-process and social judgment predictions. *Human Communication Research, 33,* 81–102.

Pechmann, C., & Slater, M. D. (2005). Social marketing messages that may motivate irresponsible consumption behavior. In S. Ratneshwar & D. G. Mick (Eds.), *Inside consumption: Consumer motives, goals, and desires* (pp. 185–207). New York: Routledge.

Pennebaker, J. W., & Sanders, D. Y. (1976). American graffiti: Effects of authority and reactance arousal. *Personality and Social Psychology Bulletin, 2,* 264–267.

Perkins, H. W., Haines, M. P., & Rice, R. (2005). Misperceiving the college drinking norm and related problems: A nationwide study of exposure to prevention information, perceived norms and student alcohol misuse. *Journal of Studies on Alcohol, 55,* 470–478.

Petrova, P. K., & Cialdini, R. B. (2005). Fluency of consumption imagery and the backfire effects of imagery appeals. *Journal of Consumer Research, 32,* 442–452.

Petty, R. E., & Cacioppo, J. T. (1986). *Communication and persuasion: Central and peripheral routes to attitude change.* New York: Springer-Verlag.

Pfau, M., & Louden, A. (1994). Effectiveness of adwatch formats in deflecting political attack ads. *Communication Research, 21,* 325–341.

Pfau, M., Tusing, K. J., Koerner, A. F., Lee, W., Godbold, L. C., Penaloza, L. J., et al. (1997). Enriching the inoculation construct: The role of critical components in the process of resistance. *Human Communication Research, 24,* 187–215.

Piotrow, P. T., & Kincaid, D. L. (2001). Strategic communication for international health programs. In R. E. Rice & C. K. Atkin (Eds.), *Public communication campaigns* (3rd ed., pp. 249–265). Thousand Oaks, CA: Sage.

Pollack, C., Smith, S., Knowles, E., & Bruce, H. (1998). Mindfulness limits compliance with the that's-not-all technique. *Personality and Social Psychology Bulletin, 24,* 1153–1157.

Potter, W. J. (2004). *Theory of media literacy: A cognitive approach.* Thousand Oaks, CA: Sage.

Preister, J. R. (2002). Sex, drugs and attitudinal ambivalence: How feelings of evaluative tension influence alcohol use and safe sex behaviors. In W. D. Crano & M.

Burgoon (Eds.), *Mass media and drug prevention* (pp. 145–162). Mahwah, NJ: Erlbaum.

Ramasubramanian, S., & Oliver, M. B. (2007). Activating and suppressing hostile and benevolent racism: Evidence for comparative media stereotyping. *Media Psychology, 9,* 623–646.

Reich, J. W., & Robertson, J. L. (1979). Reactance and norm appeal in antilittering messages. *Journal of Applied Social Psychology, 9,* 91–101.

Ringhold, D. J. (2002). Boomerang effects in response to public health interventions: Some unintended consequences in the alcoholic beverage market. *Journal of Consumer Policy, 25,* 27–63.

Rogers, E. M. (1995). *Diffusion of innovations* (4rd ed.). New York: Free Press.

Rogers, R. W. (1983). Cognitive and physiological processes in fear appeals and attitude change: A revised theory of protection motivation. In J. T. Cacioppo & R. E. Petty (Eds.), *Social psychophysiology: A sourcebook* (pp. 153–176). New York: Guilford Press.

Rosenbaum, D. P., & Hanson, P. S. (1998). *Assessing the effects of school-based drug education: A six-year multi-level analysis of project D.A.R.E.* Retrieved March 9, 2006, from http://www.drugsense.org/tfy/uic.htm

Rosenbaum, J., Beentjes, J., & Konig, R. (2008). Mapping media literacy: Key concepts and future directions. In C. S. Beck (Ed.), *Communication yearbook 32* (pp. 313–354). New York: Routledge.

Scheufele, D. A. (2000). Agenda-setting, priming, and framing revisited: Another look at cognitive effects of political communication. *Mass Communication and Society, 3,* 297–316.

Schultz, P. W., Nolan, J. M., Cialdini, R. B., Goldstein, N. J., & Griskevicius, V. (2007). The constructive, destructive, and reconstructive power of social norms. *Psychological Science, 18,* 429–434.

Schwartz, M. B., Thomas, J. J., Bohan, K. M., & Vartanian, L. R. (2007). Intended and unintended effects of an eating disorder education program: Impact of presenter identity. *International Journal of Eating Disorders, 40,* 187–192.

Shannon, C. E., & Weaver, W. (1949). *The mathematical theory of communication.* Urbana: University of Illinois Press.

Shapiro, M. A., & Rieger, R. H. (1992). Comparing positive and negative political advertising on radio. *Journalism Quarterly, 69,* 135–145.

Sherif, M., & Hovland, C. I. (1961). *Social judgment: Assimilation and contrast effects in communication and attitude change.* New Haven, CT: Yale University Press.

Silvia, P. J. (2005). Deflection reactance: The role of similarity in increasing compliance and reducing resistance. *Basic and Applied Social Psychology, 27,* 227–284.

Skarlicki, D. P., & Folger, R. (1997). Retaliation in the workplace: The roles of distributive, procedural, and interactional justice. *Journal of Applied Psychology, 82,* 434–443.

Skarlicki, D. P., Folger, R., & Gee, J. (2004). When social accounts backfire: The exacerbating effects of a polite message or an apology on reactions to an unfair outcome. *Journal of Applied Social Psychology, 34,* 322–341.

Small, D. A., & Loewenstein, G. (2003). Helping the victim or helping a victim: Altruism and identifiablity. *Journal of Risk and Uncertainty, 16,* 5–16.

Small, D. A., Loewenstein, G., & Slovic, P. (2007). Sympathy and callousness: The impact of deliberative thought on donations to identifiable and statistical victims. *Organizational Behavior and Human Decision Processes, 102,* 143–153.

Sneegas, J. E., & Plank, T. A. (1998). Gender differences in pre-adolescent reactance to age-categorized television advisory labels. *Journal of Broadcasting & Electronic Media, 42,* 423–434.

Surgeon General of the United States. (1999). *Mental health: A report by the Surgeon General* (Chap. 3). Retrieved November 26, 2008, from http://www.surgeongeneral. gov/library/ mentalhealth/chapter3/sec5.html

Towner, E. B. (this volume). Apologia, image repair, and reconciliation: The application, limitations, and future directions of apologetic rhetoric. In C. S. Beck (Ed.), *Communication yearbook 33* (pp. 431–468). New York: Routledge.

Tversky, A., & Kahneman, D. (1981). The framing decisions and the psychology of choice. *Science, 211,* 453–458.

Valentine, J. C., DuBois, D. L., & Cooper, H. (2004). The relation between self-beliefs and academic achievement. *Educational Psychologist, 39,* 111–113.

Vidmar, N., & Rokeach, M. (1974). Archie Bunker's bigotry: A study in selective perception and exposure. *Journal of Communication, 24,* 36–47.

Wechsler, H., Nelson, T. F., Lee, J. E., Seibring, M., Lewis, C., & Keeling, R. P. (2003). Perception and reality: A national evaluation of social norms marketing interventions to reduce college students' heavy alcohol use. *Quarterly Journal of Studies on Alcohol, 64,* 484–494.

Wegner, D. M. (1994). Ironic processes of mental control. *Psychological Review, 101,* 34–52.

Wegner, D. M., & Erber, R. (1992). The hyperaccessibilty of suppressed thoughts. *Journal of Personality & Social Psychology, 63,* 903–912.

Wegner, D. M., Schneider, D. J., Carter, S. R., & White, T. L. (1987). Paradoxical effects of thought suppression. *Journal of Personality & Social Psychology, 53,* 5–13.

Wenzlaff, R. M., & Wegner, D. M. (2000). Thought suppression. *Annual Review of Psychology, 51,* 59–91.

Williams, K. S., Ochs, J., Williams, J. M., & Mulhern, R. K. (1991). Parent report of everyday cognitive abilities among children treated for acute lymphoblastic leukemia. *Journal of Pediatric Psychology, 16,* 13–26.

Wilson, B. J., Linz, D., Donnerstein, E., & Stipp, H. (1992). The impact of social issue television programming on attitudes toward rape. *Human Communication Research, 19,* 179–208.

Wilson, J. B., Linz, D. & Randall, B. (1990). Applying social science research to film ratings: A shift from offensiveness to harmful effects. *Journal of Broadcasting and Electronic Media, 34,* 443–468.

Wilson, T. D., & Lassiter, G. D. (1982). Increasing intrinsic interest with superfluous extrinsic constraints. *Journal of Personality & Social Psychology, 42,* 811–819.

Winkel, F. W., & De Kleuver, E. (1997). Communication aimed at changing cognitions about sexual intimidation: Comparing the impact of perpetrator-focused versus a victim-focused persuasive strategy. *Journal of Interpersonal Violence, 12,* 513–529.

Witte, K. (1992). Putting the fear back in fear appeals: Reconciling the literature. *Communication Monographs, 59,* 329–349.

Witte, K. (1994). Fear control and danger control: An empirical test of the extended parallel process model. *Communication Monographs, 61*, 113–134.

Wolburg, J. M. (2006). College student's responses to antismoking messages: Denial, defiance and other boomerang effects. *Journal of Consumer Affairs, 40*, 294–323.

Worchel, S. (1972). The effects of films on the importance of behavioral freedom. *Journal of Personality, 40*, 417–435.

# CHAPTER CONTENTS

# 2 Adapting Consumer Advertising Appeals to Cultural Values

## A Meta-Analytic Review of Effects on Persuasiveness and Ad Liking

*Jos Hornikx*

Radboud University Nijmegen

*Daniel J. O'Keefe*

Northwestern University

It is a truism that successful persuasive messages should be adapted to audience values. A substantial research literature—not previously systematically reviewed—has examined whether advertisements with appeals adapted to the audience's important cultural values (e.g., individualism for North Americans) are more persuasive and better liked than appeals that are unadapted to such values. A meta-analytic review of that research finds that adapted ads are only slightly more persuasive (mean $r = .073$, 67 cases) and slightly better liked (mean $r = .082$, 66 cases) than unadapted ads. Moreover, these effects were mainly limited to North Americans and Asians and to values related to individualism-collectivism. In this chapter, we discuss explanations for these results and identify directions for future research.

Persuasion is a pervasive communicative function, occurring in personal relationships, the workplace, political settings, and in a variety of mediated contexts. Not surprisingly, persuasion has historically attracted considerable attention from scholars in many academic fields. For centuries, students of persuasion have taken it to be a commonplace that, in order to be effective, persuasive messages should be adapted to the audience. Indeed, this belief seems very nearly to be taken for granted, to the point that standard treatments of persuasion research do not give the matter much elaboration (e.g., Dillard & Pfau, 2002; O'Keefe, 2002; Perloff, 2003; Stiff & Mongeau, 2003). Of course, offering a systematic treatment of this question is complicated by the very large number of different possible specific bases of audience adaptation. A persuader might try to adapt to the audience's demographic characteristics such as sex and age (e.g., Martin, 2003; Yoon, Lee, & Danziger, 2007), psychographic characteristics such as values, attitudes, and lifestyles (e.g., Kahle, 1996;

Correspondence: e-mail: j.hornikx@let.ru.nl

Novak & MacEvoy, 1990), information-processing style (e.g., level of sensation-seeking; Stephenson & Southwell, 2006), regulatory focus (e.g., Keller, 2006), attitudinal ambivalence (e.g., Broemer, 2002), and so forth.

Of all the possible bases of persuasive message adaptation, however, adaptation to the audience's *values* might plausibly be supposed to be the most important. Values are people's guiding principles in life (Rokeach, 1973; Schwartz, 1992), affecting their attitudes, intentions, and behavior. To the extent that a persuader's arguments speak to the audience's values, surely to that same extent the persuader is likely to be successful. Conversely, an advocated action (whether buying a product, voting for a candidate, adopting a policy, and so on) that is justified in terms of attributes or outcomes not valued by the audience is not likely to find much support. In short, adapting persuasive appeals to the audience's values would seem to be an obviously important element of successful persuasion. Although it seems reasonable to suppose that value adaptation will be important—or indeed crucial—to persuasive success, until rather recently relatively little direct research attention had been given to this supposition. A substantial body of relevant research has quietly accumulated in the form of studies that compare the persuasiveness of consumer advertising appeals that vary in the degree to which the appeals invoke the audience's important cultural values.

## Cultural Values and Advertising Adaptation

People differ in the extent to which they prefer one specific value over another. One individual may prefer adventure over harmony, whereas another may prefer harmony over adventure. Not only do individuals vary in their value priorities, but cultures also differ in their value hierarchies, that is, their rankings of which values are relatively important and unimportant (Hofstede, 1980, 2001). In the United States, for instance, individualist values (e.g., independence) are relatively important; however, in the Korean culture, members prioritize collectivist values (e.g., interdependence) (Hofstede, 1980, 2001).

Values are the core element of culture, which can be defined as "collective programming of the mind that distinguishes the members of one group or category of people from another" (Hofstede, 2001, p. 9). Although various definitions of and approaches to the fuzzy concept of culture exist, researchers concur that values play a central role in distinguishing and characterizing different cultures (Fiske, Kitayama, Markus, & Nisbett, 1998; Hofstede, 1980, 2001; Smith & Schwartz, 1997). Hofstede (1980, 2001) identified five value dimensions on which cultures can be classified and compared: individualism-collectivism (the relationship between the self and groups), high-low uncertainty avoidance (the tolerance for uncertainty), large-small power distance (the acceptance of power inequality), masculinity-femininity (the distribution of gender roles), and long-term versus short-term orientation. This dimensional approach taken by Hofstede and by other scholars has been the most popular means of characterizing and studying cultural value variation (e.g., Fiske et al.,

1998). Within this approach, the Hofstede dimensions have been most widely adopted in cross-cultural marketing research in general (e.g., Soares, Farhangmehr, & Shoham, 2007), and—as will become apparent—in studies on adapting advertising appeals to cultural values in particular.

Given that cultures vary in what values are emphasized, advertising in different cultures naturally displays corresponding variation. Corpus analyses of advertising appeals in magazines (e.g., Han & Shavitt, 1994), on television (e.g., Lin, 2001), or on websites (e.g., Singh & Matsuo, 2004) indicate that advertisements in a given culture often reflect that culture's values (cf. Cutler, Erdem, & Javalgi, 1997). Han and Shavitt (1994), for instance, found that appeals in Korean ads were more frequently related to interdependence and harmony, whereas those in U.S. ads tend to feature independence and individuality.

It is plausible to hypothesize that adaptation to important cultural values enhances the persuasiveness of advertising. To be sure, it is possible to adapt advertising to a culture in other ways. For example, some studies comparing the effectiveness of culturally adapted ads with culturally unadapted ads have based adaptation on such message elements as (non)comparative advertising (Choi & Miracle, 2004), attribute-focused or context-focused pictures (Meng, 2004), and associational or claimless information (Wells & Van Auken, 2006). However, just as adaptation to an audience's basic values is likely to be more important (generally speaking) than adaptation to (say) age or information-processing style, so adapting advertising appeals to cultural values is likely to be an especially important contributor to persuasive success. In fact, the most prominently studied message element in cultural advertising adaptation has been the value appeal (see overviews of Gelbrich & Roschk, 2008; Shavitt & Zhang, 2004).

This research on adapting advertising appeals to culture can be seen to be spurred by the increasing globalization of brands and products and by the consequent need to address the question of the degree to which advertising can be standardized across cultures as opposed to culturally adapted (e.g., M. Agrawal, 1995; Taylor, 2005; Taylor & Johnson, 2002). For companies the benefits of standardization include not only economies of scale and the creation of a corporate brand image, but also the possibility to more fully exploit good creative ideas (see, for an overview, White, 2000). Adaptation, on the other hand, allows companies to tailor their ads to the needs and tastes of each local culture; the supposition is that the existence of different cultural values makes for corresponding differences in product use and purchase motives (e.g., De Mooij, 2005).

The paradigmatic research design in this area has compared the persuasiveness of two advertisements (appealing to different values) in each of two cultures, with one ad well-adapted to one culture and the other ad well-adapted to the other culture. For example, several studies have compared the persuasiveness of an ad appealing to individualist values and an ad appealing to collectivist values for both American and Chinese audiences (e.g., Aaker & Schmitt, 2001; J. Zhang, 2004). Researchers have generally expected that Americans will be more persuaded by (and will like better) an ad with an individualist appeal compared to one with a collectivist appeal, with the reverse expected for the Chinese. However, despite the apparent importance of illuminating the effects of advertising standardization or adaptation, the existing experimental research has not attracted much careful review. For example, Le Pair, Crijns, and Hoeken's (2000) narrative review identified six relevant experiments, but it did not address questions of the size of the observed effects.

Thus, we undertook a meta-analytic review of the effects of cultural value appeal adaptation on the persuasiveness of, and liking for, consumer advertisements. We sought not only to provide information about the practical issues concerning the question of the use of standardization or adaptation in international advertising—information called for by various scholars (e.g., Luna & Gupta, 2001; Zou, 2005)—but also to speak to broader theoretical questions about the effects of adapting persuasive appeals to audience values. Our analysis addressed two broad research questions, corresponding to the two outcome variables most commonly assessed in this research literature.

RQ1: Are ads with culturally adapted value appeals more persuasive than ads with culturally unadapted value appeals?

RQ2: Are ads with culturally adapted value appeals better liked than ads with culturally unadapted value appeals?

These two outcomes—persuasion and ad liking—are conceptually distinct; it is possible, for example, that a consumer positively evaluates an advertisement even if she or he is not persuaded by it. Indices of persuasiveness and ad liking are sometimes empirically positively associated. For example, with unfamiliar products, a positive evaluation of the advertisement can provide a basis for a similarly positive evaluation of the product (e.g., M. P. Gardner, 1985; Mitchell, 1986). However, ad liking and persuasion can also diverge, especially with more familiar products (e.g., Cox & Locander, 1987; Machleit, Allen, & Madden, 1993; Machleit & Wilson, 1988; for a relevant review, see Brown & Stayman, 1992). Hence, ad persuasiveness and ad liking are best treated as different outcomes, even if sometimes closely related empirically.

To help assess the generality of any obtained effects on these outcomes, we also examined the effects of two potential moderating factors. First, to examine the possibility that adaptation effects might vary from one culture to another, we distinguished cases on the basis of the audience's culture (specifically, on the basis of geographic region). Second, to explore the possibility that effects might vary from one value to another, we distinguished cases on the basis of the particular values invoked by the appeals.[1]

## Method

### Literature Search

We identified relevant research reports through personal knowledge of the literature and through examination of reviews, reference lists of located reports, and relevant conference proceedings such as from the American Academy of Advertising, the Association for Business Communication, the Association for Consumer Research, and the Society for Consumer Psychology. In addition, we located reports through the computerized database retrieval systems ABI-INFORM, Communication Abstracts, Dissertations Abstracts, and PsycINFO through at least March 2008. We used a number of terms (in appropriate combinations), including *adapt, adaptation, congruent, congruency, culture, cultural, match, matched, matching, tailor, tailored, tailoring, target, targeted, targeting, sensitive, sensitivity, standardize, standardized,* and *standardization*. Mindful of the possibility of publication bias and the attendant possibility that research appearing in the published research literature might yield an inflated estimate of the average effect size (Rothstein, Sutton, & Borenstein, 2005), we sought both published and unpublished research reports.

### *Inclusion Criteria*

We selected studies for the review if they met two criteria. First, the study had to compare at least two consumer ads that differed only in whether their value appeals were culturally adapted or culturally unadapted to an audience. By this criterion, we excluded studies in which it was not made clear which appeals were adapted or not adapted for a given cultural audience (e.g., Tai, 1999; Williams & Aaker, 2002). We also eliminated studies that presented only one ad appeal to two cultural audiences (e.g., Grier & Brumbaugh, 1999; Pitts, Whalen, O'Keefe, & Murray, 1989) or that confounded the adapted-versus-unadapted manipulation with other manipulations such as brand (e.g., Chiou, 2002; Donthu, 1998; Garcia, 2004) or product (e.g., Paik, 1995). We included any study whose design provided evidence relevant to our research questions, even if the study's rationale was not explicitly formulated in such terms (e.g., Lau-Gesk, 2003; Van Hartingsveldt, 2004).[2]

Second, appropriate quantitative information had to be available in order to compute effect sizes for a dependent variable of interest, namely, persuasion or ad liking. By this criterion, we excluded studies with other dependent variables, such as perceived persuasiveness (Cooperman, 2003), ad interpretation (Callow, 2000), and so on (e.g., Hornik, 1980; J. Zhang, 2004, study 2). Whenever reports did not provide sufficient quantitative information, we sought to obtain it from the authors. Studies for which we could not obtain enough information (either because the information was no longer available or because multiple e-mail requests went unanswered) included: Aaker (2000) study 1, and study 2; Aaker (2000) study 3, ad liking; Aaker and Williams (1998) pilot study and study 2; Callow (2000); Chang (2005, 2006b); Chiou (1996); Han and Shavitt (1994) study 2, Koreans, intention measure for chewing gum ad and running shoes ad; Lepkowska-White, Brashear, and Weinberger (2003), all dependent variables for Polish participants; Sara (2004); Shavitt, Nelson, and Yuan (1997); Shavitt, Zhang, and Johnson (2002); Shim (2002); Teng (2003); Wang and Mowen (1997) study 2; Wilcox, Ko, Gentry, Stricklin, and Jun (1996).

### Dependent Variables

Two dependent variables were relevant. We assessed the first one, persuasion, through measures such as attitude toward the product, attitude toward the brand, purchase intention, and product choice. Whenever a study reported multiple measures for persuasion, we computed an effect size estimate for each measure and then averaged these estimates into an overall persuasion measure.[3] The other dependent variable was liking for the ad (sometimes referred to as attitude toward the ad).[4] Most, but not all, studies collected both dependent variables of interest.

### Effect Size Measure

We computed an effect size $r$ for each comparison between the adapted version of an ad and the unadapted version of the ad. We chose $r$ as the effect size index because of its familiarity and easy interpretability. Effect sizes with a positive sign indicate an advantage of the adapted version over the unadapted version. We converted results not reported as correlations to $r$ using formulas provided by Rosenthal (1991). When effect sizes had to be averaged (such as with several measures of the persuasion dependent variable), we calculated an average $r$ using the $r$-to-$z$-to-$r$ transformation procedure, weighted by $n$.

### Moderators

We coded studies for two potential moderating factors, geographic region (as a proxy for culture) and the value dimension that was investigated.

#### Geographic Region

Adaptation effects might vary from one culture to another, so examining mean effects in different cultures could be informative. The studies reviewed included participants from a large number of different cultures (countries), but we often found too few cases for any given culture to permit useful analysis on a culture-by-culture basis. Hence, as a proxy for variation in the audience's cultural identity, we recorded each audience's geographic region: Asia-Pacific (e.g., China, New Zealand), Central and South America (e.g., Puerto Rico), Europe (e.g., France, The Netherlands), or North America (U.S.).

#### Value Dimension

In the majority of the cases, adaptation effects were hypothesized on the basis of cultural differences on Hofstede's (1980, 2001) value dimensions. For these cases, three such dimensions were distinguished: individualism-collectivism, masculinity-femininity, and high-low uncertainty avoidance. Hofstede's other value dimensions were not investigated in the studies under review.

## Unit of Analysis

The central comparison of interest was that between an adapted message and an unadapted message for a given cultural audience, and, hence, our fundamental unit of analysis was the conjunction of a given message pair and a given audience. For each message-pair-by-audience combination, we recorded an effect size. For instance, one common design in this research area has two audiences and two advertisements for a given product, with each advertisement's appeals designed to be adapted to one audience and unadapted to the other. As an example, Aaker and Schmitt (2001, study 1) compared differentiation and assimilation appeals for American and Chinese participants, using advertisements for a watch. They expected the differentiation appeal to be adapted for the American audience and unadapted for the Chinese audience and vice versa for the assimilation appeal. This kind of design provided two effect sizes indicating the relative effects of the adapted and the unadapted versions, one for each of the two audiences.

Usually, researchers used a given message pair only in a single investigation. Some message pairs, however, were used in more than one study. In such circumstances, we averaged the effect sizes for the message pair before inclusion in the analysis. We combined and recorded data from Hoeken et al. (2003) and Noordhoek (2003) as Hoeken et al. (2003) combined, and data from Y. Zhang and Gelb (1996) and Y. Zhang and Neelankavil (1997) as Y. Zhang and Gelb (1996).

For studies with more than one message pair, we recorded effect sizes for each pair if appropriate information was available (e.g., Gregory, Munch, & Peterson, 2002). When separate effect sizes could not be obtained, we computed composite effect sizes across the different message pairs (Gunaratne, 2000; Lepkowska-White et al., 2003, ad liking, and purchase intention for the American participants; Y. Zhang & Neelankavil, 1997, ad liking, attitude toward the brand).

When primary research data appeared in more than one publication, we treated the data as belonging to a single study. The same data were reported, in whole or in part, in: Briley and Aaker (2006, 2007), reported as Briley and Aaker (2006); Diehl, Terlutter, and Weinberg (2003) and Diehl and Terlutter (2004), recorded as Diehl and Terlutter (2004); Gregory (1997) and Gregory, Munch, and Peterson (1997, 2002), recorded as Gregory et al. (2002); Han (1990) and Han and Shavitt (1994) study 2, recorded as Han and Shavitt (1994); Hoeken et al. (2003), Hornikx and Starren (2004), and Van den Brandt, Domínguez, and Hoeken (2001), recorded as Hoeken et al. (2003) combined; Lau (2002) and Lau-Gesk (2003) study 1, recorded as Lau-Gesk (2003) study 1; Lepkowska-White (1999) and Lepkowska-White et al. (2003), recorded as Lepkowska-White et al. (2003), and Brunel and Nelson (1999) and Nelson (1997), recorded as Nelson (1997).

### Meta-Analytic Procedure

We initially transformed the effect sizes (correlations) to Fisher's $z$s. We analyzed these $z$s using Borenstein and Rothstein's (2005) random-effects procedures (Hedges & Vevea, 1998; Shadish & Haddock, 1994), with results transformed back to $r$. We employed a random-effects analysis in preference to a fixed-effects analysis because of an interest in generalizing across the different ads (Jackson, 1992).

## Results

### Overall Effect

We found effect sizes for 67 cases for persuasion outcomes (see Table 2.1) and for 66 cases for ad liking outcomes (see Table 2.2). Overall, as Tables 2.3 and 2.4 indicate, ads with culturally adapted value appeals were, compared to ads with culturally unadapted value appeals, more persuasive (RQ1; mean $r = .073$, $p = .001$), and better liked (RQ2; mean $r = .082$, $p = .002$).

### Alternative Analyses

As mentioned above, the usual design in this research area has two audiences and two advertisements for a given product, with each advertisement's appeals designed to be adapted to one audience and unadapted to the other. However, three variations on this design recommended some alternative analyses.

### Within-Subject Designs

In one design variation, participants saw both the adapted and unadapted advertisements (e.g., Nelson, 1997). Such a within-subjects design has the potential to artificially inflate effect sizes, so we conducted an alternative analysis excluding such cases. The results excluding within-subjects designs were virtually identical to those of the main analysis with all cases—persuasion: $k = 65$, mean $r = .071$ ($N = 6,579$), 95% CI limits of .026 and .115, $p = .002$, $Q(64) = 200.1$, $p < .001$; ad liking: $k = 55$, mean $r = .087$ ($N = 5,133$), 95% CI limits of .028 and .146, $p = .004$, $Q(54) = 233.3$, $p < .001$.

### Multiple Ads for Each Participant

In another design variation, participants were exposed to multiple advertisements for different products. In some such studies, a given participant saw either all adapted ads or all unadapted ads (e.g., J. Zhang, 2004, study 3); in other studies, a given participant saw some adapted ads and some unadapted ads (e.g., Han & Shavitt, 1994). These designs pose a methodological dilemma. If one records a separate effect size for each different pair of messages (each different product), the resulting effect sizes are not statistically independent,

*Table 2.1*  Cases Analyzed (Persuasion Outcomes)

| Study | r | N | Codings[a] |
|---|---|---|---|
| Aaker (2000) study 3, Japan, ruggedness | .221 | 48 | 4/1 |
| Aaker (2000) study 3, Japan, sophistication | .044 | 52 | 4/1 |
| Aaker (2000) study 3, US, peacefulness | −.025 | 66 | 4/4 |
| Aaker (2000) study 3, US, sophistication | −.002 | 52 | 4/4 |
| Aaker & Schmitt (2001) study 1, China | .272 | 50 | 1/1 |
| Aaker & Schmitt (2001) study 1, US | .235 | 71 | 1/4 |
| Aaker & Williams (1998) study 1, China | −.137 | 90 | 1/1 |
| Aaker & Williams (1998) study 1, US | −.274 | 60 | 1/4 |
| N. Agrawal & Maheswaran (2005) study 1 | .140 | 167 | 1/1 |
| N. Agrawal & Maheswaran (2005) study 2 | .219 | 198 | 1/4 |
| Gregory & Munch (1997) automobile | .043 | 316 | 1/2 |
| Gregory & Munch (1997) gelatin | .025 | 316 | 1/2 |
| Gregory et al. (2002) Colombia, toothbrush | −.052 | 135 | 1/2 |
| Gregory et al. (2002) Colombia, t–shirt | .023 | 135 | 1/2 |
| Gregory et al. (2002) Colombia, watch | −.092 | 135 | 1/2 |
| Gregory et al. (2002) US, toothbrush | −.053 | 141 | 1/4 |
| Gregory et al. (2002) US, t–shirt | .041 | 141 | 1/4 |
| Gregory et al. (2002) US, watch | .243 | 141 | 1/4 |
| Gunaratne (2000) New Zealand | .287 | 140 | 1/1 |
| Gunaratne (2000) Sri Lanka | .298 | 140 | 1/1 |
| Han & Shavitt (1994) Korea, chewing gum | −.063 | 64 | 1/1 |
| Han & Shavitt (1994) Korea, clothes iron | .324 | 64 | 1/1 |
| Han & Shavitt (1994) Korea, detergent | .330 | 64 | 1/1 |
| Han & Shavitt (1994) Korea, running shoes | −.268 | 64 | 1/1 |
| Han & Shavitt (1994) US, chewing gum | .352 | 64 | 1/4 |
| Han & Shavitt (1994) US, clothes iron | .294 | 64 | 1/4 |
| Han & Shavitt (1994) US, detergent | .284 | 64 | 1/4 |
| Han & Shavitt (1994) US, running shoes | .348 | 64 | 1/4 |
| Hoeken et al. (2003) combined, The Netherlands | .135 | 177 | 3/3 |
| Hoeken et al. (2003) combined, Spain | −.140 | 183 | 3/3 |
| Hoeken et al. (2003) Belgium | .137 | 142 | 3/3 |
| Hoeken et al. (2003) France | −.040 | 125 | 3/3 |
| Hoeken, Starren, Nickerson, Crijns, & Van den Brandt (2007) study 1, Belgium | .016 | 72 | 3/3 |
| Hoeken et al. (2007) study 1, The Netherlands | .271 | 57 | 3/3 |
| Hoeken et al. (2007) study 1, Spain | .121 | 123 | 3/3 |
| Hoeken et al. (2007) study 2, Germany | .204 | 98 | 2/3 |
| Hoeken et al. (2007) study 2, The Netherlands | −.076 | 79 | 2/3 |
| Hoeken et al. (2007) study 2, UK | .114 | 74 | 2/3 |
| Kirk (2003) | −.090 | 24 | 3/2 |
| Lau-Gesk (2003) study 1, easterners | .437 | 29 | 1/1 |
| Lau-Gesk (2003) study 1, westerners | .534 | 25 | 1/4 |
| Lepkowska-White et al. (2003) US, collectivistic | .005 | 275 | 1/4 |
| Lepkowska-White et al. (2003) US, functional | −.194 | 278 | 4/4 |
| Reesink (1994) The Netherlands | −.054 | 106 | 2/3 |
| Reesink (1994) UK | .383 | 70 | 2/3 |

(*continued*)

*Table 2.1* Continued

| Study | r | N | Codings[a] |
|---|---|---|---|
| Sanderse (2004) UK, camera | .115 | 78 | 2/3 |
| Sanderse (2004) UK, mp3 player | −.142 | 73 | 2/3 |
| Sanderse (2004) The Netherlands, camera | −.112 | 80 | 2/3 |
| Sanderse (2004) The Netherlands, mp3 player | −.123 | 92 | 2/3 |
| Van Hartingsveldt (2004) Belgium, added attributes | .009 | 50 | 2/3 |
| Van Hartingsveldt (2004) Belgium, product attributes | −.093 | 50 | 2/3 |
| Van Hartingsveldt (2004) The Netherlands, added attributes | −.142 | 50 | 2/3 |
| Van Hartingsveldt (2004) The Netherlands, product attributes | .064 | 50 | 2/3 |
| Wang, Bristol, Mowen, & Chakraborty (2000) China | .134 | 105 | 1/1 |
| Wang et al. (2000) US | .182 | 96 | 1/4 |
| J. Zhang (2004) study 3, China, body wash | −.320 | 93 | 1/1 |
| J. Zhang (2004) study 3, China, car | −.080 | 93 | 1/1 |
| J. Zhang (2004) study 3, China, chocolate | .273 | 93 | 1/1 |
| J. Zhang (2004) study 3, China, frozen food | .108 | 93 | 1/1 |
| J. Zhang (2004) study 3, US, body wash | −.180 | 74 | 1/4 |
| J. Zhang (2004) study 3, US, car | −.195 | 74 | 1/4 |
| J. Zhang (2004) study 3, US, chocolate | .075 | 74 | 1/4 |
| J. Zhang (2004) study 3, US, frozen food | .006 | 74 | 1/4 |
| Y. Zhang & Gelb (1996) China, camera | .459 | 80 | 1/1 |
| Y. Zhang & Gelb (1996) China, toothbrush | −.092 | 80 | 1/1 |
| Y. Zhang & Gelb (1996) US, camera | .046 | 80 | 1/4 |
| Y. Zhang & Gelb (1996) US, toothbrush | .355 | 80 | 1/4 |

*Note*: In labeling cases, we simply listed the authors and the date when that was sufficient to identify the study; we provided additional information only where disambiguation was needed, as when a given publication had several studies (thus "study 1"), audiences ("China"), products ("t-shirt"), comparisons of different appeals ("ruggedness"), or conditions ("added attributes").
[a]The coding judgments are, in order: value dimension (1 = individualism-collectivism, 2 = masculinity-femininity, 3 = uncertainty avoidance, 4 = other), and geographic region (1 = Asia-Pacific, 2 = Central/South America; 3 = Europe, 4 = North America).

because they are based on the same human sample. On the other hand, if one records a composite effect size for the human sample in question (by averaging effect sizes across the different message pairs), the resulting effect size conceals any differences in effects from one product (message pair) to another, that is, artificially reduces the apparent heterogeneity of effects. We approached this problem by recording separate effect sizes for each message pair by audience combination (this is the main analysis reported above) and then conducting a subsequent alternative analysis using effect sizes collapsed across message pairs for a given human sample. The mean effect sizes of the latter analysis were virtually identical to those of the main analysis—persuasion: $k = 45$, mean $r = .078$ ($N = 4,665$), 95% CI limits of .031 and .125, $p = .001$, $Q(44) =$

*Table 2.2* Cases Analyzed (Ad Liking Outcomes)

| Study | r | N | Codings[a] |
|---|---|---|---|
| Aaker & Williams (1998) study 1, China | −.164 | 90 | 1/1 |
| Aaker & Williams (1998) study 1, US | −.320 | 60 | 1/4 |
| Briley & Aaker (2006) study 1, China | .222 | 80 | 4/1 |
| Chang (2006a), US | .304 | 112 | 2/4 |
| Diehl & Terlutter (2004) China | .121 | 36 | 1/1 |
| Diehl & Terlutter (2004) Germany | .247 | 39 | 1/3 |
| Gregory & Munch (1997) automobile | .067 | 316 | 1/2 |
| Gregory & Munch (1997) gelatin | .084 | 316 | 1/2 |
| Gregory et al. (2002) Colombia, toothbrush | −.081 | 135 | 1/2 |
| Gregory et al. (2002) Colombia, t-shirt | .015 | 135 | 1/2 |
| Gregory et al. (2002) Colombia, watch | −.095 | 135 | 1/2 |
| Gregory et al. (2002) US, toothbrush | .203 | 141 | 1/4 |
| Gregory et al. (2002) US, t-shirt | .047 | 141 | 1/4 |
| Gregory et al. (2002) US, watch | .238 | 141 | 1/4 |
| Gunaratne (2000) New Zealand | .303 | 140 | 1/1 |
| Gunaratne (2000) Sri Lanka | .308 | 140 | 1/1 |
| Han & Shavitt (1994) Korea, chewing gum | −.130 | 64 | 1/1 |
| Han & Shavitt (1994) Korea, clothes iron | .311 | 64 | 1/1 |
| Han & Shavitt (1994) Korea, detergent | .274 | 64 | 1/1 |
| Han & Shavitt (1994) Korea, running shoes | −.260 | 64 | 1/1 |
| Han & Shavitt (1994) US, chewing gum | .411 | 64 | 1/4 |
| Han & Shavitt (1994) US, clothes iron | .296 | 64 | 1/4 |
| Han & Shavitt (1994) US, detergent | .278 | 64 | 1/4 |
| Han & Shavitt (1994) US, running shoes | .306 | 64 | 1/4 |
| Hoeken et al. (2003) combined, The Netherlands | .036 | 178 | 3/3 |
| Hoeken et al. (2003) combined, Spain | −.085 | 183 | 3/3 |
| Hoeken et al. (2003) Belgium | −.039 | 142 | 3/3 |
| Hoeken et al. (2003) France | .122 | 124 | 3/3 |
| Hoeken et al. (2007) study 1, Belgium | −.313 | 72 | 3/3 |
| Hoeken et al. (2007) study 1, The Netherlands | .324 | 57 | 3/3 |
| Hoeken et al. (2007) study 1, Spain | −.171 | 123 | 3/3 |
| Hoeken et al. (2007) study 2, Germany | −.071 | 98 | 2/3 |
| Hoeken et al. (2007) study 2, The Netherlands | .258 | 79 | 2/3 |
| Hoeken et al. (2007) study 2, UK | −.114 | 74 | 2/3 |
| Kirk (2003) | .003 | 24 | 3/2 |
| Lau-Gesk (2003) study 1, easterners | .528 | 29 | 1/1 |
| Lau-Gesk (2003) study 1, westerners | .643 | 25 | 1/4 |
| Lau-Gesk (2003) follow up, westerners | .247 | 43 | 1/4 |
| Lepkowska-White et al. (2003) US, cleanser, collectivist | −.187 | 68 | 1/4 |
| Lepkowska-White et al. (2003) US, cleanser, functional | −.267 | 70 | 4/4 |
| Lepkowska-White et al. (2003) US, chocolate, collectivist | .242 | 71 | 1/4 |
| Lepkowska-White et al. (2003) US, chocolate, functional | −.214 | 70 | 4/4 |

*(continued)*

*Table 2.2* Continued

| Study | r | N | Codings[a] |
|---|---|---|---|
| Lepkowska-White et al. (2003) US, fridge, collectivist | −.311 | 69 | 1/4 |
| Lepkowska-White et al. (2003) US, fridge, functional | −.310 | 70 | 4/4 |
| Lepkowska-White et al. (2003) US, jeans, collectivist | .312 | 67 | 1/4 |
| Lepkowska-White et al. (2003) US, jeans, functional | −.220 | 68 | 4/4 |
| Nelson (1997) Denmark | .209 | 37 | 1/3 |
| Nelson (1997) US | −.217 | 71 | 1/4 |
| Reesink (1994) The Netherlands | −.054 | 106 | 2/3 |
| Reesink (1994) UK | .383 | 70 | 2/3 |
| Sanderse (2004) UK, camera | −.040 | 79 | 2/3 |
| Sanderse (2004) UK, mp3 player | .147 | 76 | 2/3 |
| Sanderse (2004) The Netherlands, camera | .246 | 79 | 2/3 |
| Sanderse (2004) The Netherlands, mp3 player | .086 | 93 | 2/3 |
| Terlutter, Mueller, & Diehl (2005) France | −.153 | 84 | 4/3 |
| Terlutter et al. (2005) Germany | −.046 | 182 | 4/3 |
| Terlutter et al. (2005) UK | −.057 | 89 | 4/3 |
| Terlutter et al. (2005) US | .000 | 132 | 4/4 |
| Van Hartingsveldt (2004) Belgium, added attributes | .235 | 50 | 2/3 |
| Van Hartingsveldt (2004) Belgium, product attributes | .238 | 50 | 2/3 |
| Van Hartingsveldt (2004) The Netherlands, added attributes | .112 | 50 | 2/3 |
| Van Hartingsveldt (2004) The Netherlands, product attributes | .163 | 50 | 2/3 |
| Y. Zhang & Gelb (1996) China, camera | .610 | 80 | 1/1 |
| Y. Zhang & Gelb (1996) China, toothbrush | −.029 | 80 | 1/1 |
| Y. Zhang & Gelb (1996) US, camera | .045 | 80 | 1/4 |
| Y. Zhang & Gelb (1996) US, toothbrush | .399 | 80 | 1/4 |

*Note*: In labeling cases, we simply listed the authors and the date when that was sufficient to identify the study; we provided additional information only where disambiguation was needed, as when a given publication had several studies (thus "study 1"), audiences ("China"), products ("t-shirt"), comparisons of different appeals ("ruggedness"), or conditions ("added attributes").
[a]The coding judgments are, in order: value dimension (1 = individualism-collectivism, 2 = masculinity-femininity, 3 = uncertainty avoidance, 4 = other), and geographic region (1 = Asia-Pacific, 2 = Central/South America; 3 = Europe, 4 = North America).

107.7, $p < .001$; ad liking: $k = 49$, mean $r = .080$ ($N = 4,564$), 95% CI limits of .023 and .136, $p = .006$, $Q(48) = 167.3$, $p < .001$.

## Hypothesized Within-Study Moderating Factors

In some studies, researchers hypothesized that a moderating factor, such as participants' age (J. Zhang, 2004) or the type of product (e.g., Han & Shavitt,

Table 2.3 Summary of Results: Effects on Persuasion

| | k | N | mean r | 95% CI | power[a] | Q (df) |
|---|---|---|---|---|---|---|
| All cases | 67 | 6,755 | .073 | .029, .118 | — | 209.3 (66)*** |
| Geographic region | | | | | | |
| North America | 22 | 2,256 | .096 | .010, .181 | — | 82.7 (21)*** |
| Europe | 20 | 1,829 | .034 | −.032, .100 | .84 | 36.7 (19)** |
| Asia-Pacific | 19 | 1,609 | .124 | .020, .225 | — | 76.0 (18)*** |
| Central/South America | 6 | 1,061 | .003 | −.057, .064 | .63 | 2.5 (5) |
| Specific values appealed to | | | | | | |
| Individualism-collectivism | 41 | 4,406 | .105 | .046, .163 | — | 146.9 (40)*** |
| Masculinity-femininity | 13 | 950 | .015 | −.075, .105 | .57 | 22.7 (12)* |
| Uncertainty avoidance | 8 | 903 | .053 | −.044, .149 | .55 | 13.8 (7) |
| Other | 5 | 496 | −.022 | −.176, .133 | .34 | 9.1 (4) |

*p < .05; **p < .01; ***p < .001
[a]These are power figures for detecting a population effect size of $r = .10$, assuming large heterogeneity, with a random-effects analysis, .05 alpha, and a two-tailed test (Hedges & Pigott, 2001).

1994), would influence the size of the persuasive advantage expected for adapted appeals. For example, J. Zhang hypothesized that, for younger participants, the usual persuasive advantage of adapted appeals would diminish or vanish. In a subsidiary analysis, we recomputed effect sizes so as to remove such conditions and, hence, analyzed only circumstances in which researchers expected the persuasive advantage of adapted appeals to be maximized. This analysis produced a pattern of significant effects identical to those of the main analysis, although, unsurprisingly, the means commonly showed a slightly greater advantage for adapted appeals than in the main analysis—persuasion: $k = 62$, mean $r = .095$ ($N = 5,638$), 95% CI limits of .046 and .143, $p < .001$, $Q(61) = 193.2$, $p < .001$; ad liking: $k = 61$, mean $r = .112$ ($N = 5,299$), 95% CI limits of .055 and .168, $p < .001$, $Q(60) = 245.6$, $p < .001$.

### Moderators

Two potential moderators were examined, geographic region and value dimension.

*Table 2.4* Summary of Results: Effects on Ad Liking

| | $k$ | $N$ | mean $r$ | 95% CI | power[a] | $Q$ (df) |
|---|---|---|---|---|---|---|
| All cases | 66 | 6091 | .082 | .029, .135 | — | 265.2 (65)*** |
| Geographic region | | | | | | |
| North America | 23 | 1835 | .084 | −.026, .191 | .84 | 118.0 (22)*** |
| Europe | 25 | 2264 | .050 | −.017, .116 | .91 | 57.5 (24)*** |
| Asia-Pacific | 12 | 931 | .184 | .024, .335 | — | 64.6 (11)*** |
| Central/South America | 6 | 1,061 | .025 | −.037, .086 | .63 | 5.1 (5) |
| Specific values appealed to | | | | | | |
| Individualism-collectivism | 35 | 3277 | .139 | .062, .215 | — | 159.4 (34)*** |
| Masculinity-femininity | 14 | 1066 | .132 | .045, .218 | — | 26.4 (13)* |
| Uncertainty avoidance | 8 | 903 | −.023 | −.139, .094 | .55 | 19.8 (7)** |
| Other | 9 | 845 | −.108 | −.209, −.004 | — | 17.5 (8)* |

*$p < .05$; **$p < .01$; ***$p < .001$
[a]These are power figures for detecting a population effect size of $r = .10$, assuming large heterogeneity, with a random-effects analysis, .05 alpha, and a two-tailed test (Hedges & Pigott, 2001).

## Geographic Region

Adaptation effects varied depending on the audience's geographic region (that is, cultural identity). Adapted appeals were significantly more persuasive than unadapted appeals for Asian-Pacific audiences ($r = .124$, $p = .019$) and for North American audiences ($r = .096$, $p = .029$); there was no such adaptation effect for European ($r = .034$, $p = .315$) or for Central/South American ($r = .003$, $p = .916$) audiences, despite reasonable statistical power (as indicated in Table 2.3). The difference between the effect for Asian-Pacific audiences and the effect for Central/South American audiences was significant; $Q(1) = 3.9$, $p = .049$; differences between other pairs of effects were not significant.

Ads with adapted appeals generated significantly greater ad liking than did ads with unadapted appeals only for Asian-Pacific audiences ($r = .184$, $p = .024$). Despite generally good statistical power (see Table 2.4), we found no significant difference in ad liking between adapted and unadapted appeals by audiences in North America ($r = .084$, $p = .134$), Europe ($r = .050$, $p = .142$), or Central/South America ($r = .025$, $p = .433$). These four effects were not significantly different from each other.

*Value Dimension*

Ads with adapted appeals were significantly more persuasive than ads with unadapted appeals when the appeals were based on individualism-collectivism values ($r = .105$, $p = .001$), but not when the appeals involved high-low uncertainty avoidance ($r = .053$, $p = .281$) or masculinity-femininity ($r = .015$, $p = .741$) values. These three effects were not significantly different from each other.

Ad liking for ads with adapted appeals was significantly higher than that for ads with unadapted appeals when the appeals were based on individualism-collectivism values ($r = .139$, $p < .001$) or on masculinity-femininity values ($r = .132$, $p = .003$), but not when the appeals concerned high-low uncertainty avoidance values ($r = -.023$, $p = .700$). The effect for high-low uncertainty avoidance appeals was significantly smaller than both the effect for individualism-collectivism-based appeals—$Q(1) = 5.2$, $p = .023$—and the effect for masculinity-femininity-based appeals—$Q(1) = 4.4$, $p = .037$; the latter two effects did not significantly differ.

## Discussion

These meta-analytic results, perhaps unsurprisingly, confirm that ads with culturally adapted value appeals are significantly more persuasive and better liked than ads with culturally unadapted value appeals. The signal advantage of meta-analytic reviews, of course, is the diversity of evidence on which such conclusions are based. The studies reviewed here used appeals with a variety of different values (e.g., adventure, modesty, peacefulness) and value dimensions (e.g., individualism-collectivism, masculinity-femininity), advertisements for various kinds of products (e.g., detergent, jeans, watches), and participants from a large number of different countries (e.g., Belgium, Sri Lanka, Mexico). Thus, taken at face value, these results favor cultural value adaptation rather than standardization in advertising appeals. However, two caveats need to be addressed—one about the size of the effects and one about moderating variables.

### Size of the Effects

The mean effect size for persuasion in this meta-analysis was $r = .073$, which is a rather small effect. This effect magnitude is, however, typical of those found in persuasive effects research. O'Keefe's (2005) review of 12 meta-analyses of persuasion variables reported an average effect size (expressed as a correlation) of .07. However, those meta-analyses concerned studies of what would seem to be relatively superficial variations in persuasive messages, such as including rhetorical questions or explicit conclusions. By contrast, in the studies reviewed here, researchers varied the values invoked in the persuasive appeals. One would naturally suppose that this more fundamental aspect of persuasive messages would correspondingly have much greater impact, but it does not.

The observed mean effect size is, if anything, surprisingly small, even though statistically significant. So why is the effect characteristically so small? We consider five possible explanations: poor choice of values to be invoked in the advertisements, poor realization of values in the advertisements, divergence between the sex of the study participants and the sex of the participants in Hofstede's (1980, 2001) research, divergence between the individual values of the study participants and the values of their cultures, and processes of globalization.

One explanation might be that the values researchers selected were not culturally important ones, and so appeals invoking those values did not make the ads that much more persuasive. Conveniently, assessing this explanation is made possible by the large number of studies that used values drawn from Hofstede's (1980, 2001) work. Hofstede's value dimension indices provide assessments of the importance of specified values in different cultures. The maximum score 100 stands for the culture in which the set of values is the most important relative to the other 52 cultures (nations or groups of nations) Hofstede investigated. Examination of these scores yielded two indications that the explanation of a selection of culturally unimportant values is unsound. First, in the studies reviewed here that used values examined by Hofstede, the values had mean importance scores of 83.9 ($SD$ = 11.24) in the persuasion subset ($k$ = 50) and 81.1 ($SD$ = 12.76) in the ad liking subset ($k$ = 51). That is, these values were plainly important ones. Second, although this explanation implies that the size of the adaptation effect should increase as value importance increases, the correlations between the effect size and its related value importance were not significant—persuasion: $r$ (48) = −.13, $p$ = .38; ad liking: $r$ (49) = −.15, $p$ = .31.[5]

A second possible explanation for the small effect size is that the experimental advertisements were in some way uncharacteristic of actual consumer advertising and, specifically, were poorly designed with respect to engaging the relevant cultural values. However, the advertisements used in the included studies appeared to employ appeals quite typical of consumer advertising. Indeed, in some studies, experiments were preceded by corpus analyses— analyses of extant consumer advertisements—to ensure the realism of the experimental materials (e.g., Han & Shavitt, 1994; J. Zhang, 2004); other studies referred to these or other corpus analyses (such as Albers-Miller & Gelb, 1996) as a basis for their experimental variations (e.g., Hoeken, Starren, Nickerson, Crijns, & Van den Brandt, 2007; Y. Zhang & Gelb, 1996). That is, generally speaking, the value-appeal variations in the studies reviewed here were based on research on cultural dimensions and advertising characteristics. Although it is possible that some ads activated the relevant values better than did others, examination of the ads did not suggest any manifestly implausible invocations of cultural values.

A third potential explanation for the small effect size might arise from the sex of the participants. Hofstede's (1980, 2001) research was based on a predominantly male sample, and some evidence suggests that males and females differ in their reactions to Hofstede's cultural value dimensions (e.g., Hofstede, 2001, p. 91, p. 286). The mean percentage of female participants in the studies reviewed here (for which relevant information was available) is much higher than in Hofstede's original work: 52.93 ($SD$ = 20.55, $k$ = 53) for the persuasion subset, and 56.36 ($SD$ = 14.08, $k$ = 54) for the ad liking subset. However, the correlations between the percentage of female participants in a study and the study's effect size are neither large nor significant—persuasion: $r$ (51) = –.10, $p$ = .47; ad liking: $r$ (52) = –.12, $p$ = .40). Therefore, the higher proportion of female participants in these studies (compared to that in Hofstede's research) is apparently not the cause of the small observed effect.

A fourth possible explanation is that the participants in these studies might not themselves have endorsed the relevant cultural values; that is, the participants' individual value preferences might have diverged in some way from those of their larger culture. Unfortunately, in most cases, we could not confirm or disconfirm whether the relative value rankings of participants matched the relative rankings in the participants' culture. Even where researchers collected individual-level value assessments (such as Singelis's, 1994, scale related to individualism-collectivism and Schwartz's, 1992, values that have been related to several Hofstede dimensions), the reported information was not always sufficient to compare the relevant rankings. Moreover, some significant methodological questions have been raised about individual- and cultural-level value measurement (e.g., Fischer, 2006; Levine et al., 2003; Smith & Schwartz, 1997). In short, the individual-level value assessments in hand are limited and of uncertain value. Still, in the relatively few cases in which such information was available, participants' relative value rankings were usually, though not always, congruent with their culture's value rankings. We observed such congruency in 15 of 22 persuasion effect sizes and 14 of 21 ad liking effect sizes. Thus, the relatively small effect sizes cannot be ascribed to some general divergence between the participants' value rankings and the value rankings in the participants' culture; the individual-level value assessments available in these studies suggest that the cultural value variations relevant to a given experiment were for the most part mirrored in the judgments of the individual participants.

Even though participants' value preferences and those of their culture did not generally diverge, one would naturally expect that, if the value rankings of a particular set of participants differed from those of the participants' culture, to that same extent the advantage of culturally adapted advertising value appeals would be diminished. In the current set of studies, for each of the two outcome measures, the advantage of culturally adapted appeals was not significantly larger when participants' rankings matched their culture's rankings than when the rankings were noncongruent. For persuasion, congruent value rankings ($k$ = 15) mean $r$ = .120, noncongruent value rankings ($k$ = 7) mean $r$ = .009; $Q(1)$ = 3.0, $p$ = .09. For ad liking, congruent value rankings ($k$ = 14) mean $r$ = .142, noncongruent value rankings ($k$ = 7) mean $r$ = .042; $Q(1)$ = 0.9, $p$ = .35. One might thus suspect that a factor moderating the size of the advantage of culturally adapted value appeals is the degree to which the audience's value preferences match those of its culture. Such moderation would be unsurprising, but also likely of little practical utility to advertisers, who commonly will not have individual-level value assessments available. In the absence of such individual-level assessments and corresponding appeal-adaptation possibilities, adapting advertising appeals to broad cultural values will likely on average yield only relatively small effects, as observed here.

One final possible explanation for the small observed effects is that processes of globalization may have eroded the salience of cultural values—or even cultural value differences themselves (Featherstone, 1990). Although cultural value hierarchies have been claimed to be stable over time because of the reinforcement of cultural patterns within cultures (Hofstede, 1980, 2001), globalization in advertising may affect the salience of important values in a given culture (Craig & Douglas, 2006; Shavitt, Lee, & Johnson, 2008). A number of corpus-analytic studies have suggested changes in the value appeals used in ads in Eastern cultures (e.g., Lin, 2001; J. Zhang & Shavitt, 2003). For instance, J. Zhang and Shavitt determined that appeals to youth and modernity, which are characteristically individualistic appeals, appeared frequently in Chinese ads. In Europe, where geographically close cultures differ sharply in femininity-masculinity, uncertainty avoidance, and power distance, individuals are exposed to a variety of advertising appeals related to different value dimensions, which might diminish the salience of one's own cultural values. Ideally, the plausibility of this account might be assessed by seeing whether the advantage of culturally adapted value appeals has diminished over time, but the time span of this research is quite short—we discovered no studies appearing before 1994, for example. This time span naturally corresponds precisely to the period of time in which globalization has been prominent. (Without globalization, advertisers may have little need to consider whether to standardize or adapt their advertising.) Still, to the extent that such erosion of cultural differences underlies the small effects, the plain implication is that even the currently observed small persuasive advantage of culturally adapted value appeals may well diminish in the future.

### Moderators: When Does the Adaptation Effect Disappear?

The moderator variables that were explored—geographic region and specific values—do, indeed, affect the effect sizes for adaptation, but, even under optimum conditions, the maximum mean correlation hardly exceeds .18. That is, rather than identifying conditions under which notably large effects occur, these results indicate particular geographic regions and specific values for which adaptation effects disappear. An adaptation effect on persuasion was not found for Europe or Central/South America; an effect on ad liking was absent for both these two areas and for North America. For the value dimension of high-low uncertainty avoidance, adaptation effects on persuasion and ad liking did not occur; for masculinity-femininity, an effect on persuasion did not occur.

Broadly speaking, cultural value adaptation of ads seems dependably effective for only some cultural audiences (Asia-Pacific and North America) and for only one value dimension (individualism-collectivism). However, these two apparent limitations are related; in the studies reviewed in this chapter, value dimensions were confounded with the audiences' geographic regions. For example, of the 41 persuasion effect sizes based on individualism-collectivism-based appeals, 36 involved a North American or an Asian-Pacific audience; of the 35 ad liking effect sizes based on individualism-collectivism-based appeals, 28 involved a North American or an Asian-Pacific audience. This confounding, of course, is entirely natural given that these cultures vary with respect to individualism-collectivism, but the question that arises is whether the observed adaptation effects result from the particular value dimension (individualism-collectivism), the particular audiences (Asia-Pacific and North America), or the combination of the two.

As another example, all of the 13 studies concerned with the persuasive effectiveness of appeals based on the masculinity-femininity value dimension used European audiences, a natural confounding given that European cultures are thought to vary with respect to masculinity-femininity (Hofstede, 1980, 2001). Across these cases, the overall effect on persuasion was nonsignificant ($r = .015, p = .741$). The question is whether this finding is a consequence of the particular value dimension (masculinity-femininity), the particular audience (Europeans), or the combination.

Consider first the hypothesis that the observed variation in effects is a consequence of the particular values involved. This hypothesis implies that something about individualism-collectivism makes it an especially receptive basis for developing ad appeals (compared to other value dimensions). This suggestion gains some plausibility from the extensive research indicating the importance of this value dimension (see, for a review, Oyserman, Coon, & Kemmelmeier, 2002). Individualism-collectivism may be more closely related to important personality characteristics (e.g., self-schema; Markus & Kitayama, 1991; cf. Levine et al., 2003) than are other value dimensions such as high-low uncertainty avoidance and masculinity-femininity, perhaps reflecting greater individual internalization of individualism-collectivism values compared to others. Fischer (2006, study 1) reported congruence between important values at a cultural level and important values at an individual level for values related to individualism-collectivism in particular. For values related to, for instance, masculinity-femininity, such internalization may be less apparent (for a further discussion of the two levels of values, see Smith & Schwartz, 1997; Van de Vijver & Leung, 1997).

If the observed adaptation effects for Asian-Pacific and North American audiences are, indeed, explained by researchers' use of the individualism-collectivism value dimension, then similar effects should be found for individualist and collectivist appeals in Europe (with predominantly individualist cultures, like North America). Thus, future research might usefully compare the effects on European participants of individualist (adapted) and collectivist (unadapted) appeals. Similarly, more studies should be conducted in which individuals from Asia-Pacific and North America receive appeals based on other value dimensions such as masculinity-femininity. As an example for North America, masculine or low-uncertainty-avoidant value appeals could be selected as culturally adapted appeals for Americans and Canadians (Hofstede, 2001). Such work would illuminate the possibility that individualism-collectivism is a value dimension that provides a distinctively good basis for developing culturally adapted ad appeals.

Alternatively, the observed variation in effects could stem from the particular cultural audiences involved, reasoning that some cultural audiences are more sensitive to cultural value appeal variations than other audiences. This explanation would have it that Europeans and Central and South Americans are not sensitive to differences in value appeals as are people from North America and Asia-Pacific. The suggestions for future research mentioned above are also well-suited to examining this explanation. The current data do, however, contain one bit of evidence against this hypothesis. Adapted appeals based on the masculinity-femininity dimension produced significantly greater ad liking than did unadapted appeals for European audiences ($k = 13$, $r = .115$, $p = .011$). This finding suggests that European audiences are not entirely insensitive to these appeal variations. Still, more direct research evidence will certainly be welcomed.

### Submerged Complexities in Value Variation and Functioning

Our discussion thus far has offered a relatively simple picture of value variations and of value functioning. In this brief section, we note some submerged complexities concerning each of these matters.

#### Value Variation

In research on cultural value adaptation of advertising, the conceptualization of value variation has been dominated by Hofstede's (1980, 2001) analysis. Indeed, the design of experimental appeal variations in this research literature is commonly aimed at producing appeals that vary in their invocation of one or another of Hofstede's value dimensions, especially (as we have seen) individualism-collectivism. However, this approach may be too simple in two ways.

First, although individualism-collectivism is the most broadly used of Hofstede's value dimensions, it is arguably insufficient as a basis for capturing cultural variations. Shavitt, Lalwani, Zhang, and Torelli (2006) underlined the importance of also distinguishing between horizontal (equality) and vertical (hierarchy) individualism-collectivism (e.g., Triandis, 1995). Regardless of whether this distinction, which resembles power distance, is integrated into individualism-collectivism or is disentangled from it (e.g., Oyserman, 2006), various scholars have urged an expansion of the set of cultural value dimensions beyond individualism-collectivism (e.g., Shavitt et al., 2008).

Second, it may be useful to consider ways of capturing cultural value dimensions that are wholly different from Hofstede's. For example, the Global Leadership and Organizational Behavior Effectiveness (GLOBE) research program provided a large-scale study of cross-cultural values (House, Hanges, Javidan, Dorfman, & Gupta, 2004). GLOBE distinguished nine dimensions of variation, dimensions conceptually dissimilar to the five identified by Hofstede (1980, 2001). Okazaki and Mueller (2007) argued that the GLOBE project offers a potentially useful typology for research on cultural value adaptation. The GLOBE project may be imperfect (see, in particular, Hofstede, 2006), but it underlines the desirability of continuing attention to the task of developing a reliable and valid set of dimensions that are useful for the study of human values generally and cultural value variation in particular.

*Value Functioning*

Cultural values do not always function straightforwardly in human behavior. Two specific complexities are worth noting. First, the salience of cultural values can be situationally primed (e.g., Hong, Morris, Chiu, & Benet-Martínez, 2000). Activating a value makes it salient, even if the value is relatively unimportant for the individual, and such activation can affect subsequent judgments (e.g., W. L. Gardner, Gabriel, & Lee, 1999; Monga & John, 2007). In W. L. Gardner et al., for instance, American participants endorsed more collectivist values when primed with interdependence than when not exposed to such a prime. In a similar vein, Asian participants who were primed with independence endorsed more individualistic values than those not exposed to such a prime. It might be that advertising appeals adapted to cultural values might gain effectiveness if the relevant values are situationally primed (as might occur, for instance, when television program content primes the values invoked by a subsequent commercial).

Second, a given culture can appear to embrace contradictory values simultaneously—a phenomenon that De Mooij (2005) referred to as the "value paradox," which arises from a conflict between the desired (what people desire) and the desirable (what people think ought to be desired). For example, in cultures with low uncertainty avoidance, innovation may be an especially appropriate basis for an appeal. However, as De Mooij explained, appealing to innovation can also be important in a high uncertainty avoidance culture, such as France, in which citizens desire innovation yet also traditional, conservative behavior. Taken together, the value paradox and the situational priming of values underscore the potentially complex relationships among culture, values, persuasion, and behavior, and affirm the usefulness of future research that recognizes these complexities.

**Broader Implications**

The research reviewed in this chapter addresses both narrower practical questions and broader theoretical ones. In practical terms, this meta-analysis obviously speaks to the adaptation-standardization debate in international advertising, where each approach has received some critical attention (e.g., Luna & Gupta, 2001; Okazaki, Taylor, & Zou, 2006; Taylor, 2005; Zou, 2005). The results show that adapting ads to the audience's cultural values makes ads more persuasive and better-liked—but they also demonstrate that these effects are not especially large. By implication, advertisers should carefully consider the costs of adapting ads to ensure appropriate return on investment.

More generally, these results appear to cast doubt on a common assumption about the role of audience values in reactions to persuasive messages. Values are widely presumed to exert substantial influence on conduct (e.g., Rokeach, 1973). Naturally, then, advertising appeals invoking a consumer's important values should be considerably more persuasive than appeals based on other values. However, as the current review indicates, value-adapted appeals are only slightly more persuasive than unadapted appeals, and, in some circumstances, value adaptation confers no dependable advantage.

This observed weak effect coincides with a good deal of previous work on the effects of value on behavior. As Shrum and McCarty (1997, p. 140) observed, "When relationships between values and behavior have been observed, they have tended to be relatively weak." However, Shrum and McCarty also noted that "the lack of robust relationships in past research does not necessarily suggest a true weak effect" (p. 141). For instance, results that underestimate the true effect might arise from various methodological shortcomings, individual differences, or situational variations (e.g., Maio, Olson, Allen, & Bernard, 2001).

In the present case, one might wonder whether the use of broad cultural values (as opposed to the specific values of individuals) has contributed to the observed weak effects. Members of a culture do vary in their endorsement of that culture's values, and individual-level value assessments might therefore produce larger effects (see Chang, 2006b; Wang & Mowen, 1997; more generally, see Hullett, 2002, 2006). As discussed earlier in this chapter, the present data hint that variation in individual subscription to cultural values might moderate the size of these effects. However, even where participants' value preferences could be confirmed to match those of their culture, the mean persuasive advantage was only $r = .12$—still not a remarkably large effect if one imagines values to be powerfully influential.

So it may simply be that values are only weakly related to behavior—and so only weakly related to audience reactions to persuasive appeals. It remains to be seen whether other kinds of persuasive message adaptation might yield larger effects, but, if similar conclusions were to be confirmed in other areas of message-adaptation research, it would obviously warrant far-reaching reexamination of widespread fundamental assumptions about what makes for successful persuasive messages.

In a similar vein, these results may have implications beyond the narrow context of consumer advertising. In particular, these results are suggestive with respect to the practice of devising "culturally tailored" health interventions (see related review by Noar, Harrington, and Aldrich, this volume). An intervention might be culturally or ethnically tailored in any number of ways. For example, the communicator's ethnicity might match that of the audience (e.g., Anderson & McMillion, 1995; Ramirez, 1977), or an intervention designer might choose what is taken to be a culturally-appropriate communicative vehicle. For example, Larkey and Gonzalez (2007, p. 272) compared a "culturally aligned, brief storytelling intervention" against a "numeric risk tool intervention" for promoting colorectal cancer screening among Latinos.

However, these other kinds of cultural adaptation commonly involve tailoring through relatively peripheral considerations (e.g., message format) as opposed to tailoring by adapting appeals to the audience's basic values. It seems unlikely that, as a general matter, such peripheral adaptations will produce greater persuasive advantages than are obtained by value adaptation. This is not to say that other varieties of cultural tailoring will be without benefit, but such tailoring will not likely yield persuasive advantages any larger than those observed in this review. In the end, these are empirical questions for future research; our results can be no more than suggestive concerning the effects of other kinds of cultural tailoring, but little in the present results gives much hope that other sorts of cultural tailoring will yield dramatic persuasive benefits (tailoring based on considerations other than culture might yield larger benefits; see Noar et al., this volume).

This meta-analysis may point to the limits of general cultural stereotypes as a basis for understanding or influence. The sorts of broad value characterizations employed in the research reviewed in this chapter ("Americans are individualistic") amount to a form of cultural stereotyping, in the sense that a general description ("individualistic") is deployed to cover a large cultural category that contains substantial intra-category variation ("Americans"). Simply put, such characterizations may contain a grain of truth (as indicated by the persuasive advantage of appeals adapted on such bases)—but it is a very small grain indeed.

## Acknowledgments

This research was funded by a grant from the Niels Stensen Foundation (The Netherlands) awarded to the first author. The authors thank Gary Gregory, Helen van Hartingsveldt, Hans Hoeken, Mathilde Kirk, Loraine Lau-Gesk, Michelle Nelson, Femke Noordhoek, Wouter Sanderse, Ralf Terlutter, Jing Zhang, and Yong Zhang for supplying primary-research information.

## Notes

1. As with any literature review, exploration of potential moderating factors is to some degree constrained by the character of the research under review. In this research area, a number of different possible moderating factors have been suggested, such as the level of brand commitment (Agrawal & Maheswaran, 2005) and the decision risk associated with product purchase (Gregory & Munch,

1997). However, primary research on any given moderator is sparse, making meta-analytic treatment of such factors problematic. As another example, a reader suggested that the medium of communication (video, audio, print) might be explored as a potential moderator, but, unfortunately, the research to date has relied exclusively on print materials.

2. We accepted at face value researchers' assertions about what constituted value adaptation of appeals. We realize that researchers might, upon seeing experimental results, construct post hoc some hypothesis that matches the obtained pattern of significant and nonsignificant effects—such that in a condition where no significant effect of value adaptation occurred, the reasoning is presented as being that in that condition neither appeal was adapted and hence no difference was hypothesized. In such a circumstance, our procedure would exclude the condition in which the researchers indicated neither appeal was adapted (i.e., the condition in which the nonsignificant effect occurred). The plain implication is that our procedure is, if anything, likely to have overestimated the size of the effects of adaptation.

3. These various persuasion outcomes are of course distinct variables but nevertheless appropriately combined as indicators of *relative* persuasiveness (comparing the adapted and unadapted appeal conditions). It might be the case that, for example, attitudes are more easily changed than behaviors, but this tendency does not mean that the difference in persuasiveness between one message form and another will vary between these outcomes. As a relevant bit of empirical evidence, consider that Witte and Allen's (2000) meta-analytic review reported that the mean effects of variations in depicted threat severity (high versus low depicted severity) were statistically indistinguishable for attitudinal (mean $r$ = .15), intention (mean $r$ = .14) and behavioral (mean $r$ = .13) outcomes. That is, conclusions about the relative persuasiveness of high- versus low-depicted-severity messages were identical regardless of whether attitude, intention, or behavior was the outcome variable. Witte and Allen reported a similar pattern of effects for variations in depicted threat susceptibility (mean $rs$ of .12, .17, and .14, respectively), variations in depicted response efficacy (mean $rs$ of .14, .17, and .13), and variations in depicted self-efficacy (mean $rs$ of .12, .17, and .13). We do not argue that, for example, product attitude and purchase behavior are the same thing. But these results do suggest that, where one's research question concerns the relative persuasiveness of two message forms (as in the present enterprise), one's conclusions are not likely to be much affected by whether the persuasive outcome assessed is attitude, intention, or behavior. That is, as indicators of the *relative* persuasiveness of two messages, these outcome variables appear to function similarly and hence are appropriately combined.

4. As Smit, Van Meurs, and Neijens (2006) observed, researchers have commonly assessed ad liking in one of two ways, either through assessment of multiple specific dimensions (e.g., the degree to which the ad is entertaining, irritating, etc.—though these items are commonly highly correlated; see, e.g., Mitchell & Olson, 1981) or through a global evaluative judgment (though this assessment is commonly based on multiple general-evaluation scale items; see, e.g., Biehal, Stephens, & Curlo, 1992). Following Brown and Stayman (1992) and Smit et al., we treated these as alternative assessments of a single underlying construct.

5. These results excluded cases involving China, for which Hofstede (2001, p. 502) provided only an estimated score for collectivism (80). However, means and correlations based on a larger dataset including these estimated scores hardly differ from those reported in the text. The mean importance scores were 83.3 (*SD* = 10.35) in the persuasion subset (*k* = 60) and 81.0 (*SD* = 12.07) in the ad liking subset (*k* = 57). The correlations between the effect size and its related value importance were not significant—persuasion: *r* (58) = –.12, *p* = .38; ad liking: *r* (55) = –.14, *p* = .31.

# References

References marked with an asterisk indicate studies included in the meta-analysis.

*Aaker, J. L. (2000). Accessibility or diagnosticity? Disentangling the influence of culture on persuasion processes and attitudes. *Journal of Consumer Research, 26*, 340–357.

*Aaker, J. L., & Schmitt, B. (2001). Culture-dependent assimilation and differentiation of the self: Preferences for consumption symbols in the United States and China. *Journal of Cross-Cultural Psychology, 32*, 561–576.

*Aaker, J. L., & Williams, P. (1998). Empathy versus pride: The influence of emotional appeals across cultures. *Journal of Consumer Research, 25*, 241–261.

Agrawal, M. (1995). Review of a 40-year debate in international advertising: Practitioner and academician perspectives to the standardization/adaptation issue. *International Marketing Review, 12*, 26–48.

*Agrawal, N., & Maheswaran, D. (2005). The effects of self-construal and commitment on persuasion. *Journal of Consumer Research, 31*, 841–849.

Albers-Miller, N. D., & Gelb, B. D. (1996). Business advertising as a mirror of cultural dimensions: A study of eleven countries. *Journal of Advertising, 25*(4), 57–70.

Anderson, R. B., & McMillion, P. Y. (1995). Effects of similar and diversified modeling on African American women's efficacy expectations and intentions to perform breast self-examination. *Health Communication, 7*, 327–343.

Biehal, G., Stephens, D., & Curlo, E. (1992). Attitude toward the ad and brand choice. *Journal of Advertising, 21*(3), 19–36.

Borenstein, M., & Rothstein, H. (2005). Comprehensive meta-analysis (Version 2.2.023) [Computer software]. Englewood, NJ: Biostat.

*Briley, D. A., & Aaker, J. L. (2006). When does culture matter? Effects of personal knowledge on the correction of culture-based judgments. *Journal of Marketing Research, 43*, 395–408.

*Briley, D. A., & Aaker, J. L. (2007). When does culture matter? Effects of personal knowledge on the correction of culture-based judgments. In G. J. Fitzsimons & V. G. Morwitz (Eds.), *Advances in consumer research* (Vol. 34, p. 148). Duluth, MN: Association for Consumer Research.

Broemer, P. (2002). Relative effectiveness of differently framed health messages: The influence of ambivalence. *European Journal of Social Psychology, 32*, 685–703.

Brown, S. P., & Stayman, D. M. (1992). Antecedents and consequences of attitude toward the ad: A meta-analysis. *Journal of Consumer Research, 19*, 34–51.

*Brunel, F. F., & Nelson, M. R. (1999). Toward an understanding of gender, personality and cultural differences in responses to charity ad appeals. In E. J. Arnould & L. M. Scott (Eds.), *Advances in consumer research* (Vol. 26, p. 267). Provo, UT: Association for Consumer Research.

Callow, M. A. (2000). Do you see what I see? A cross-cultural analysis of the social identity metaphor in visual print advertisements (Doctoral dissertation, City University of New York, 2000). *Dissertation Abstracts International, 61*(04), 1512A. (UMI No. 9969681)

Chang, C. (2005). The moderating influence of ad framing for ad-self-congruency effects. *Psychology and Marketing, 22,* 955–968.

*Chang, C. (2006a). Cultural masculinity/femininity influences on advertising appeals. *Journal of Advertising Research, 46,* 315–323.

Chang, C. (2006b). Seeing the small picture: Ad-self versus ad-culture congruency in international advertising. *Journal of Business and Psychology, 20,* 445–465.

Chiou, J.-S. (1996). International marketing standardization versus adaptation from the consumer's perspective (Doctoral dissertation, Michigan State University, 1996). *Dissertation Abstracts International, 57*(09), 4034A. (UMI No. 9706461)

Chiou, J.-S. (2002). The effectiveness of different advertising message appeals in the Eastern emerging society: Using Taiwan TV commercials as an example. *International Journal of Advertising, 21,* 217–236.

Choi, Y. K., & Miracle, G. E. (2004). The effectiveness of comparative advertising in Korea and the United States: A cross-cultural and individual-level analysis. *Journal of Advertising, 33*(4), 75–87.

Cooperman, R. A. (2003). The effectiveness of localized versus standardized international industrial advertising in the European Union (Doctoral dissertation, Nova Southeastern University, 2003). *Dissertation Abstracts International, 65*(05), 1856A. (UMI No. 3132804)

Cox, D. S., & Locander, W. B. (1987). Product novelty: Does it moderate the relationship between ad attitudes and brand attitudes? *Journal of Advertising, 16*(3), 39–44.

Craig, C. S., & Douglas, S. P. (2006). Beyond national culture: Implications of cultural dynamics for consumer research. *International Marketing Review, 23,* 322–342.

Cutler, B. D., Erdem, S. A., & Javalgi, R. G. (1997). Advertisers' relative reliance on collectivism-individualism appeals: A cross-cultural study. *Journal of International Consumer Marketing, 9*(3), 43–55.

De Mooij, M. (2005). *Global marketing and advertising: Understanding cultural paradoxes* (2nd ed.). Thousand Oaks, CA: Sage.

*Diehl, S., & Terlutter, R. (2004). Comparing the effects of individualistic versus collectivistic advertising on Germans and Chinese. In P. Neijens, C. Hess, B. van den Putte, & E. Smit (Eds.), *Content and media factors in advertising* (pp. 62–47). Amsterdam: Het Spinhuis.

*Diehl, S., Terlutter, R., & Weinberg, P. (2003). Advertising effectiveness in different cultures: Results of an experiment analyzing the effects of individualistic and collectivistic advertising on Germans and Chinese. In D. Turley & S. Brown (Eds.), *European advances in consumer research* (Vol. 6, pp. 128–136). Provo, UT: Association for Consumer Research.

Dillard, J. P., & Pfau, M. (Eds.). (2002). *The persuasion handbook: Developments in theory and practice.* Thousand Oaks, CA: Sage.

Donthu, N. (1998). A cross-country investigation of recall of and attitude toward comparative advertising. *Journal of Advertising, 27*(2), 111–122.

Featherstone, M. (Ed.). (1990). *Global culture: Nationalism, globalization and modernity.* London: Sage.

Fischer, R. (2006). Congruence and functions of personal and cultural values: Do my values reflect my culture's values? *Personality and Social Psychology Bulletin, 32,* 1419–1431.

Fiske, A. P., Kitayama, S., Markus, H. R., & Nisbett, R. E. (1998). The cultural matrix of social psychology. In D. T. Gilbert, S. T. Fiske, & G. Lindzey (Eds.), *The handbook of social psychology* (4th ed., Vol. 2, pp. 915–981). Boston: McGraw-Hill.

Garcia, E. (2004). The effects of cultural values on international advertising effectiveness: A study of sex appeals in fashion advertising. (Master's thesis, University of Texas at El Paso). *Masters Abstracts International, 43*(03), 646. (UMI No. 10783)

Gardner, M. P. (1985). Does attitude toward the ad affect brand attitude under a brand evaluation set? *Journal of Marketing Research, 22,* 192–198.

Gardner, W. L., Gabriel, S., & Lee, A. Y. (1999). "I" value freedom, but "we" value relationships: Self-construal priming mirrors cultural differences in judgment. *Psychological Science, 10,* 321–326.

Gelbrich, K., & Roschk, H. (2008). Cross-cultural advertising. In W. Donsbach (Ed.), *International encyclopedia of communication* (pp. 50–56). Malden, MA: Wiley-Blackwell.

*Gregory, G. D. (1997). An examination of the moderating role of attitude functions in the value-attitude relationship: Implications for the development of cross-cultural advertisements (Doctoral dissertation, University of Texas at Arlington, 1997). *Dissertation Abstracts International, 58*(08), 3218A. (UMI No. 9804666)

*Gregory, G. D., & Munch, J. M. (1997). Cultural values in international advertising: An examination of familial norms and roles in Mexico. *Psychology and Marketing, 14,* 99–119.

*Gregory, G. D., Munch, J. M., & Peterson, M. (1997, December). *Extending attitude function theory to cross-cultural consumer research: A comparison of value-attitude relations in the U.S. and Columbia.* Paper presented at the Sixth Symposium on Cross-Cultural Consumer and Business Studies, Honolulu, HI.

*Gregory, G. D., Munch, J. M., & Peterson, M. (2002). Attitude functions in consumer research: Comparing value-attitude relations in individualist and collectivist cultures. *Journal of Business Research, 55,* 933–942.

Grier, S. A., & Brumbaugh, A. M. (1999). Noticing cultural differences: Ad meanings created by target and non-target markets. *Journal of Advertising, 28*(1), 79–93.

*Gunaratne, K. A. (2000). The influence of culture and product consumption purpose on advertising effectiveness. In A. O'Cass (Ed.), *Visionary marketing for the 21st century: Facing the challenge* (pp. 443–447). Brisbane, Australia: Griffith University.

*Han, S.-P. (1990). Individualism and collectivism: Its implications for cross-cultural advertising (Doctoral dissertation, University of Illinois at Urbana-Champaign, 1990). *Dissertation Abstracts International, 51*(12), 3942A. (UMI No. 9114257)

*Han, S.-P., & Shavitt, S. (1994). Persuasion and culture: Advertising appeals in individualistic and collectivistic societies. *Journal of Experimental Social Psychology, 30,* 326–350.

Hedges, L. V., & Pigott, T. D. (2001). The power of statistical tests in meta-analysis. *Psychological Methods, 6,* 203–217.

Hedges, L. V., & Vevea, J. L. (1998). Fixed- and random-effects models in meta-analysis. *Psychological Methods, 3,* 486–504.

*Hoeken, H., van den Brandt, C., Crijns, R., Dominguez, N., Hendriks, B., Planken, B. et al. (2003). International advertising in Western Europe: Should differences in uncertainty avoidance be considered when advertising in Belgium, France, The Netherlands and Spain? *Journal of Business Communication, 40*, 195–218.

*Hoeken, H., Starren, M., Nickerson, C., Crijns, R., & van den Brandt, C. (2007). Is it necessary to adapt advertising appeals for national audiences in Western Europe? *Journal of Marketing Communications, 13*, 19–38.

Hofstede, G. (1980). *Culture's consequences: International differences in work-related values.* Beverly Hills, CA: Sage.

Hofstede, G. (2001). *Culture's consequences: Comparing values, behaviors, institutions, and organizations across nations* (2nd ed.). Thousand Oaks, CA: Sage.

Hofstede, G. (2006). What did GLOBE really measure? Researchers' minds versus respondents' minds. *Journal of International Business Studies, 37*, 882–896.

Hong, Y., Morris, M. W., Chiu, C., & Benet-Martínez, V. (2000). Multiple minds: A dynamic constructivist approach to culture and cognition. *American Psychologist, 55*, 709–720.

Hornik, J. (1980). Comparative evaluation of international vs. national advertising strategies. *Columbia Journal of World Business, 15*(1), 36–48.

*Hornikx, J., & Starren, M. (2004). Publicités en France et aux Pays-Bas: Peut-on standardiser ou faut-il adapter? [Advertising in France and in The Netherlands: Should we standardize or adapt?]. *Studies in Communication Sciences, 4*(1), 219–233.

House, R. J., Hanges, P. J., Javidan, M., Dorfman, P. W., & Gupta, V. (Eds.). (2004). *Culture, leadership, and organizations: The GLOBE study of 62 societies.* Thousand Oaks, CA: Sage.

Hullett, C. R. (2002). Charting the process underlying the change of value-expressive attitudes: The importance of value-relevance in predicting the matching effect. *Communication Monographs, 69*, 158–178.

Hullett, C. R. (2006). Using functional theory to promote HIV testing: The impact of value-expressive messages, uncertainty, and fear. *Health Communication, 20*, 57–67.

Jackson, S. (1992). *Message effects research: Principles of design and analysis.* New York: Guilford Press.

Kahle, L. R. (1996). Social values and consumer behavior: Research from the List of Values. In C. Seligman, J. M. Olson, & M. P. Zanna (Eds.), *The psychology of values: The Ontario symposium* (Vol. 8, pp. 135–151). Mahwah, NJ: Erlbaum.

Keller, P. A. (2006). Regulatory focus and efficacy of health messages. *Journal of Consumer Research, 33*, 109–114.

*Kirk, M. D. (2003). *How to make a "splash" for Puerto Rican women? An exploratory investigation into the effectiveness of appealing to "security" and "stimulation" values in written advertisements for "Splash Lotions," targeted at female Puerto Rican migrants in New York state.* Unpublished master's thesis, Radboud University Nijmegen, Nijmegen, The Netherlands.

Larkey, L. K., & Gonzalez, J. (2007). Storytelling for promoting colorectal cancer prevention and early detection among Latinos. *Patient Education and Counseling, 67*, 272–278.

*Lau, L. G. (2002). Activating culture-related selves through persuasion appeals. In S. M. Broniarczyk & K. Nakamoto (Eds.), *Advances in consumer research* (Vol. 29, p. 454). Valdosta, GA: Association for Consumer Research.

*Lau-Gesk, L. G. (2003). Activating culture through persuasion appeals: An examination of the bicultural consumer. *Journal of Consumer Psychology, 13*, 301–315.

Le Pair, R., Crijns, R., & Hoeken, H. (2000). Het belang van cultuurverschillen voor het ontwerp van persuasieve teksten [The importance of cultural differences for the design of persuasive texts]. *Tijdschrift voor Taalbeheersing, 22*, 358–372.

*Lepkowska-White, E. (1999). The influence of cultural and socioeconomic variables on reactions to ad appeals (Doctoral dissertation, University of Massachusetts Amherst, 1999). *Dissertation Abstracts International, 60*(11), 4096A. (UMI No. 9950182)

*Lepkowska-White, E., Brashear, T. G., & Weinberger, M. G. (2003). A test of ad appeal effectiveness in Poland and the United States: The interplay of appeal, product, and culture. *Journal of Advertising, 32*(3), 57–67.

Levine, T. R., Bresnahan, M. J., Park, H. S., Lapinski, M. K., Wittenbaum, G. M., Shearman, S. M., et al. (2003). Self-construal scales lack validity. *Human Communication Research, 29*, 210–252.

Lin, C. A. (2001). Cultural values reflected in Chinese and American television advertising. *Journal of Advertising, 30*(4), 83–94.

Luna, D., & Gupta, S. F. (2001). An integrative framework for cross-cultural consumer behavior. *International Marketing Review, 18*, 45–69.

Machleit, K. A., Allen, C. T., & Madden, T. J. (1993). The mature brand and brand interest: An alternative consequence of ad-evoked affect. *Journal of Marketing, 57*(4), 72–82.

Machleit, K. A., & Wilson, R. D. (1988). Emotional feelings and attitude toward the advertisement: The roles of brand familiarity and repetition. *Journal of Advertising, 17*(3), 27–35.

Maio, G. R., Olson, J. M., Allen, L., & Bernard, M. M. (2001). Addressing discrepancies between values and behavior: The motivating effects of reasons. *Journal of Experimental Social Psychology, 37*, 104–117.

Markus, H. R., & Kitayama, S. (1991). Culture and the self: Implications for cognition, emotion, and motivation. *Psychological Review, 98*, 224–253.

Martin, B. A. S. (2003). The influence of gender on mood effects in advertising. *Psychology and Marketing, 20*, 249–273.

Meng, L. (2004). The role of culture and gender in consumer information processing styles: Exploring the effects on ad memory and attitude. In B. E. Kahn & M. F. Luce (Eds.), *Advances in consumer research* (Vol. 31, pp. 694–695). Valdosta, GA: Association for Consumer Research.

Mitchell, A. A. (1986). The effects of verbal and visual components of advertisements on brand attitudes and attitude toward the advertisement. *Journal of Consumer Research, 13*, 12–24.

Mitchell, A. A., & Olson, J. C. (1981). Are product attribute beliefs the only mediator of advertising effects on brand attitude? *Journal of Marketing Research, 18*, 318–332.

Monga, A. B., & John, D. R. (2007). Cultural differences in brand extension evaluation: The influence of analytic versus holistic thinking. *Journal of Consumer Research, 33*, 529–536.

*Nelson, M. R. (1997). Examining the horizontal and vertical dimensions of individualism within the United States and Denmark: How culture affects values, moral orientations and advertising persuasion (Doctoral dissertation, University of Illinois at Urbana-Champaign, 1997). *Dissertation Abstracts International, 58* (10), 3768A. (UMI No. 9812720)

Noar, S. M., Harrington, N. G., & Aldrich, R. S. (this volume). The role of message tailoring in the development of persuasive health communication messages. In C. S. Beck (Ed.), *Communication Yearbook 33* (pp. 73–133). New York: Routledge.

*Noordhoek, F. (2003). *Waarde-appels in Nederlandse en Spaanse advertenties [Value appeals in Dutch and Spanish ads].* Unpublished master's thesis, Radboud University Nijmegen, Nijmegen, The Netherlands.

Novak, T. P., & MacEvoy, B. (1990). On comparing alternative segmentation schemes: The List of Values (LOV) and Values and Life Styles (VALS). *Journal of Consumer Research, 17,* 105–109.

Okazaki, S., & Mueller, B. (2007). Cross-cultural advertising research: Where we have been and where we need to go. *International Marketing Review, 24,* 499–518.

Okazaki, S., Taylor, C. R., & Zou, S. (2006). Advertising standardization's positive impact on the bottom line: A model of when and how standardization improves financial and strategic performance. *Journal of Advertising, 35*(3), 17–33.

O'Keefe, D. J. (2002). *Persuasion: Theory and research* (2nd ed.). Thousand Oaks, CA: Sage.

O'Keefe, D. J. (2005). News for argumentation from persuasion effects research: Two cheers for reasoned discourse. In C. A. Willard (Ed.), *Selected papers from the thirteenth NCA/AFA conference on argumentation* (pp. 215–221). Washington, DC: National Communication Association.

Oyserman, D. (2006). High power, low power, and equality: Culture beyond individualism and collectivism. *Journal of Consumer Psychology, 16,* 352–356.

Oyserman, D., Coon, H. M., & Kemmelmeier, M. (2002). Rethinking individualism and collectivism: Evaluation of theoretical assumptions and meta-analyses. *Psychological Bulletin, 128,* 3–72.

Paik, K. H. (1995). The development of individualist and collectivist self-concept across cultures and its effects on the response to television commercials (Doctoral dissertation, Cornell University, 1995). *Dissertation Abstracts International, 55* (11), 5098B. (UMI No. 9509468)

Perloff, R. M. (2003). *The dynamics of persuasion: Communication and attitudes in the 21st century* (2nd ed.). Mahwah, NJ: Erlbaum.

Pitts, R. E., Whalen, D. J., O'Keefe, R., & Murray, V. (1989). Black and white response to culturally targeted television commercials: A values-based approach. *Psychology and Marketing, 6,* 311–328.

Ramirez, A. (1977). Social influence and ethnicity of the communicator. *Journal of Social Psychology, 102,* 209–213.

*Reesink, R. (1994). *Waarden in internationale reclame [Values in international advertising].* Unpublished master's thesis, Radboud University Nijmegen, Nijmegen, The Netherlands.

Rokeach, M. (1973). *The nature of human values.* New York: Free Press.

Rosenthal, R. (1991). *Meta-analytic procedures for social research* (2nd ed.). Beverly Hills, CA: Sage.

Rothstein, H. R., Sutton, A. J., & Borenstein, M. (Eds.). (2005). *Publication bias in meta-analysis: Prevention, assessment and adjustments.* Chichester, England: Wiley.

*Sanderse, W. (2004). *De overtuigingskracht van culturele waardeappèls in internationale reclame: Een vergelijking tussen Groot-Brittannië en Nederland [The persuasiveness of cultural value appeals in international advertising: A comparison* *between the United Kingdom and The Netherlands].* Unpublished master's thesis, Radboud University Nijmegen, Nijmegen, The Netherlands.

Sara, H. K. (2004). *Effects of cultural differences and product types on advertising effectiveness in Costa Rica and the U.S.* Unpublished master's thesis, University of Florida, Gainesville, FL.

Schwartz, S. (1992). Universals in the content and structure of values: Theoretical advances and empirical tests in 20 countries. In M. P. Zanna (Ed.), *Advances in experimental social psychology* (Vol. 25, pp. 1–65). Orlando, FL: Academic.

Shadish, W. R., & Haddock, C. K. (1994). Combining estimates of effect size. In H. Cooper & L. V. Hedges (Eds.), *Handbook of research synthesis* (pp. 261–281). New York: Russell Sage Foundation.

Shavitt, S., Lalwani, A. K., Zhang, J., & Torelli, C. J. (2006). The horizontal/vertical dimension in cross-cultural consumer research. *Journal of Consumer Psychology, 16,* 325–342.

Shavitt, S., Lee, A. Y., & Johnson, T. P. (2008). Cross-cultural consumer psychology. In C. P. Haugtvedt, P. M. Herr, & F. R. Kardes (Eds.), *Handbook of consumer psychology* (pp. 1103–1131). New York: Erlbaum.

Shavitt, S., Nelson, M. R., & Yuan, R. M. L. (1997). Exploring cross-cultural differences in cognitive responding to ads. In M. Brucks & D. J. MacInnis (Eds.), *Advances in consumer research* (Vol. 24, pp. 245–250). Provo, UT: Association for Consumer Research.

Shavitt, S., & Zhang, J. (2004). Advertising and culture. In C. Spielberger (Ed.), *Encyclopedia of applied psychology* (pp. 47–51). San Diego, CA: Academic Press.

Shavitt, S., Zhang, J., & Johnson, T. P. (2002). Horizontal and vertical orientations in cross-cultural consumer persuasion. In S. M. Broniarczyk & K. Nakamoto (Eds.), *Advances in consumer research* (Vol. 29, p. 47). Valdosta, GA: Association for Consumer Research.

Shim, S. W. (2002). Advertising appeals and culture: The difference between culturally congruent and culturally deviant individuals in Korea (Doctoral dissertation, University of Florida, 2002). *Dissertation Abstracts International, 63* (10), 3409A. (UMI No. 3065986)

Shrum, L. J., & McCarty, J. A. (1997). Issues involving the relationship between personal values and consumer behavior: Theory, methodology, and application. In L. R. Kahle & L. Chiagouris (Eds.), *Values, lifestyles, and psychographics* (pp. 139–159). Mahwah, NJ: Erlbaum.

Singelis, T. M. (1994). The measurement of independent and interdependent self-construals. *Personality and Social Psychology Bulletin, 20,* 580–591.

Singh, N., & Matsuo, H. (2004). Measuring cultural adaptation on the Web: A content analytic study of U.S. and Japanese Web sites. *Journal of Business Research, 57,* 864–872.

Smit, E. G., van Meurs, L., & Neijens, P. C. (2006). Effects of advertising likeability: A 10-year perspective. *Journal of Advertising Research, 46,* 73–83.

Smith, P. B., & Schwartz, S. H. (1997). Values. In J. W. Berry, M. H. Segall, & C. Kagitçibasi (Eds.), *Handbook of cross-cultural psychology: Vol. 3. Social behavior and applications* (2nd ed., pp. 77–118). Boston: Allyn & Bacon.

Soares, A. M., Farhangmehr, M., & Shoham, A. (2007). Hofstede's dimensions of culture in international marketing studies. *Journal of Business Research, 60,* 277–284.

Stephenson, M. T., & Southwell, B. G. (2006). Sensation seeking, the activation model, and mass media health campaigns: Current findings and future directions for cancer communication. *Journal of Communication, 56,* S38–S56.

Stiff, J. B., & Mongeau, P. A. (2003). *Persuasive communication* (2nd ed.). New York: Guilford.

Tai, H. C. S. (1999). Advertising ethics: The use of sexual appeal in Chinese advertising. *Teaching Business Ethics, 3,* 87–100.

Taylor, C. R. (2005). Moving international advertising research forward: A new research agenda. *Journal of Advertising, 34*(1), 7–16.

Taylor, C. R., & Johnson, C. (2002). Standardized vs. specialized international advertising campaigns: What we have learned from academic research in the 1990s. *New Directions in International Advertising Research, 12,* 45–66.

Teng, L. (2003). Effects of competition on consumer decision-making: Matching advertising to culture (Doctoral dissertation, Concordia University, 2003). *Dissertation Abstracts International, 64*(04), 1336A. (UMI No. NQ78630)

*Terlutter, R., Mueller, B., & Diehl, S. (2005). The influence of culture on responses to assertiveness in advertising messages: Preliminary results from Germany, the U.S., the U.K., and France. In S. Diehl, R. Terlutter, & P. Weinberg (Eds.), *Advertising and communication: Proceedings of the 4th international conference on research in advertising* (pp. 183–190). Wiesbaden, Germany: Gabler.

Triandis, H. C. (1995). *Individualism and collectivism.* Boulder, CO: Westview Press.

*Van den Brandt, C., Domínguez, N., & Hoeken, H. (2001). De relatieve overtuigingskracht van waarde-appèls in Nederlandse en Spaanse advertenties: Spelen cultuurverschillen een rol? [The relative persuasiveness of value appeals in Dutch and Spanish ads: Do cultural differences play a role?] *Toegepaste Taalwetenschap in Artikelen, 66,* 101–112.

Van de Vijver, F. J. R., & Leung, K. (1997). *Methods and data analysis for cross-cultural research.* Thousand Oaks, CA: Sage.

*Van Hartingsveldt, H. (2004). *Internationaal adverteren: Standaardisatie of adaptatie? [Advertise internationally: Standardization or adaptation?].* Unpublished master's thesis, Radboud University Nijmegen, Nijmegen, The Netherlands.

*Wang, C. L., Bristol, T., Mowen, J. C., & Chakraborty, G. (2000). Alternative modes of self-construal: Dimensions of connectedness-separateness and advertising appeals to the cultural and gender-specific self. *Journal of Consumer Psychology, 9,* 107–115.

Wang, C. L., & Mowen, J. C. (1997). The separateness-connectedness self-schema: Scale development and application to message construction. *Psychology and Marketing, 14,* 185–207.

Wells, L. G., & van Auken, S. (2006). A comparison of associational and claimless-informational advertising in Russia. *Journal of East-West Business, 12,* 29–48.

White, R. (2000). International advertising: How far can it fly? In J. P. Jones (Ed.), *International advertising: Realities and myths* (pp. 29–40). Thousand Oaks, CA: Sage.

Wilcox, J. S., Ko, G., Gentry, J. W., Stricklin, M., & Jun, S. (1996). Advertising presentations of the independent versus interdependent self to Korean and U.S. college students. *Advances in International Marketing, 7,* 159–174.

Williams, P., & Aaker, J. L. (2002). Can mixed emotions peacefully coexist? *Journal of Consumer Research, 28,* 636–649.

Witte, K., & Allen, M. (2000). A meta-analysis of fear appeals: Implications for effective public health programs. *Health Education and Behavior, 27*, 591–615.

Yoon, C., Lee, M. P., & Danziger, S. (2007). The effects of optimal time of day on persuasion processes in older adults. *Psychology and Marketing, 24*, 475–495.

*Zhang, J. (2004). Cultural values reflected in Chinese advertisements: Self-construal and persuasion implications (Doctoral dissertation, University of Illinois at Urbana-Champaign, 2004). *Dissertation Abstracts International, 65*(11), 4037A. (UMI No. 3153479)

Zhang, J., & Shavitt, S. (2003). Cultural values in advertisements to the Chinese X-generation: Promoting modernity and individualism. *Journal of Advertising, 32*(1), 23–33.

*Zhang, Y., & Gelb, B. D. (1996). Matching advertising appeals to culture: The influence of products' use conditions. *Journal of Advertising, 25*(3), 29–46.

*Zhang, Y., & Neelankavil, J. P. (1997). The influence of culture on advertising effectiveness in China and the USA: A cross-cultural study. *European Journal of Marketing, 31*, 134–149.

Zou, S. (2005). Contributions to international advertising research: An assessment of the literature between 1990 and 2002. *Journal of Advertising, 34*(1), 99–110.

# CHAPTER CONTENTS

# 3 The Role of Message Tailoring in the Development of Persuasive Health Communication Messages

*Seth M. Noar*
*Nancy Grant Harrington*
*Rosalie Shemanski Aldrich*
University of Kentucky

This chapter provides an overview of the literature on tailored health communication messages, an innovative area of health communication research that has broad applicability to other areas of communication. Unlike traditional message targeting practices, which operate at the group level, tailored interventions involve the development of persuasive health communications designed for (and based upon an assessment of) the individual. We introduce tailoring and discuss the historical context of message tailoring research. We then provide a broad review of seminal and more recent message tailoring studies. Next, we discuss the mechanisms through which tailored messages may exert their effects, reviewing theoretical perspectives as well as empirical data. Finally, we consider future directions for research on tailored health communication.

## Introduction

For decades, persuasion research has focused on answers to what seems like a relatively simple question: What elements of a message make it persuasive? A glance at any persuasion volume reveals that the persuasiveness of a message involves factors including its source, receiver, channel, content, and contextual characteristics. Because the receiver in this equation can have markedly different responses to the other elements (e.g., source evaluation, channel preference), a major implication for persuasion thus encompasses "knowing your audience" (see also related review by Hornikx & O'Keefe, this volume). In the area of mass communication campaigns, scholars discussed this critical mantra years ago (although it took several decades to be consistently put into action; see Rogers & Storey, 1987). For example, in 1947, Hyman and Sheatsley argued that simply providing individuals with *more* information would *not* necessarily lead to a more enlightened American public. Instead, individuals must be exposed to and absorb the information that is presented. Given that Hyman and Sheatsley's (1947) data suggested

---
Correspondence: e-mail:snoar2@uky.edu

that many Americans were apathetic and uninterested in acquiring new infor-mation, the possibility of public information campaigns reaching their goals seemed unlikely. They concluded that "the psychological characteristics of human beings must be taken into account" (p. 413) with regard to successfully carrying out campaigns that effectively impacted populations.

Rejecting one interpretation of Hyman and Sheatsley's (1947) work, namely that an apathetic public was to blame for failed mass communication cam-paigns, Mendelsohn (1973) suggested another probable cause:

> An impressive fund of data gathered over the past thirty years indicates that the publics who are most apt to respond to mass-mediated informa-tion messages have a prior interest in the subject areas presented. As a consequence, information directed to this *segment of a potential audi-ence* requires *totally different communications strategies* and tactics from information that is to be disseminated to an audience that is initially indif-ferent. (p. 50, emphasis added)

Mendelsohn added that "communicators who intend to use the mass media to produce information gains or attitudes and behavior modification must real-ize that their targets do not represent a monolithic mass" (pp. 50–51).

As we discuss next, this insight led to practices that have become wide-spread in communication and health communication—audience segmen-tation and message targeting. These practices, however, focus entirely on identifying group-level similarities and designing messages that may reso-nate with particular groups and subgroups. This chapter introduces a newer practice that focuses on *individual*-level characteristics and designing mes-sages to resonate with individuals. This practice is termed message tailoring (see Kreuter, Farrell, Olevitch, & Brennan, 2000; Kreuter & Skinner, 2000; Kreuter & Wray, 2003).

In this chapter, we broadly overview message tailoring research, a health communication research area that has broad applicability to other areas of com-munication. We accomplish this goal by introducing message tailoring and dis-cussing the historical context of message tailoring research. We then provide a broad review of seminal and more recent message tailoring studies. Next, we discuss the mechanisms through which tailored messages may exert their effects, reviewing theoretical perspectives as well as empirical data. Finally, we consider future directions for research on tailored health communication.

## Audience Segmentation and Message Targeting

Research indicates that, in order to develop effective communications, schol-ars/practitioners must carefully define their audience—that is, they must engage in audience segmentation (Grunig, 1989; Rogers & Storey, 1987). According to Grunig, as well as Rogers and Storey, *audience segmentation* refers to the practice of dividing one's audience into homogenous subgroups that are internally similar yet differ from one another. Why might this practice be effective? When audiences are divided into groups with more similar than different members, research suggests that they react similarly (and positively) to campaign messages designed for the segment. This practice of designing campaign messages for particular audience segments can be referred to as *message targeting* (Kreuter, Strecher, & Glassman, 1999; Palmgreen & Donohew, 2003).

Given that audiences can be segmented on an almost infinite number of variables, a large literature has been devoted to approaches to segmentation and targeting. Indeed, modern applications encompass segmenting audiences on demographic, geographic, psychographic, attitudinal, cultural (see Hornikx & O'Keefe, this volume), and behavioral variables (Albrecht & Bryant, 1996; Goldberg, Fishbein, & Middlestadt, 1997; Slater, 1996). Albrecht and Bryant noted that many writings center on criteria to be used in making segmentation decisions (see also Hornik & Ramirez, 2006; Slater, 1995, 1996). According to Hornik and Ramirez, considerations in such decisions include potential differences in audience segments according to the behavior under study, message preferences, channel preferences, and issues related to campaign execution. Although simple segmentation on demographic variables comprises the most widely used method (Slater, 1995), a number of more sophisticated approaches to segmentation exist (Albrecht & Bryant, 1996; Palmgreen et al., 1995; Slater, 1996).

## Tailoring at the Individual Level

The above approach relies entirely on identifying group similarities and subsequently targeting messages at the group level. For example, in a discussion of using race/ethnicity as a potential segmentation and targeting variable in the National Youth Anti-Drug Media Campaign, Hornik and Ramirez (2006) presented data on beliefs about drug use across different racial/ethnic groups, finding many similarities across these groups but some differences. However, a key question remains: Are the differences large enough to warrant segmenting the audience by racial/ethnic groups to target different messages to the different groups? An equally important question may be whether these beliefs about drug use differ as much within the groups as they do between them. That is, despite significant differences between the groups, much within-group variability likely still exists, such that at least some of the messages ultimately designed for African Americans may be more relevant for Whites, and vice versa. Such diversity of beliefs and attitudes *within* audience segments poses problems for message targeting; however, message tailoring can uniquely address such a challenge (Kreuter & Wray, 2003; Rimal & Adkins, 2003).

### Introduction and Definitions

*Message tailoring* refers to the practice of designing messages at the *individual level* (Kreuter et al., 2000). Consider these everyday examples of tailoring:

Devices on the highway assess driving speed and provide instant, tailored feedback on one's speed; computer programming in search engines, such as Google, process search terms and produce tailored advertisements for the user; supermarket scanners examine scanned grocery items and, using computer-driven algorithms, produce coupons tailored to one's food preferences, and Web sites, such as Amazon.com and Netflix.com, present tailored suggestions for items of interest when users log on to these sites based upon a large empirical database that has been created for this purpose.

Thus, unlike targeted messages that researchers develop to be effective with an entire segment of the population, tailored communication is customized to each individual person. This practice has been formally defined as "any combination of strategies and information intended to reach one specific person, based on characteristics that are unique to that person, related to the outcome of interest, and derived from an individual assessment" (Kreuter, Strecher, & Glassman, 1999, p. 277). Scholars have typically assessed those attributes through quantitative surveys. Additionally, computer technologies can efficiently and effectively match responses to survey items and scales with particular customized messages (Kreuter et al., 2000). Indeed, after advances in computer technology made individual tailoring on a large-scale basis possible, the literature on individualized tailoring "took off" (Velicer, Prochaska, & Redding, 2006).

### Relevance to the Communication Discipline

Message tailoring clearly pertains to a variety of areas in the communication discipline (see Table 3.1). While tailoring research has to date been conducted almost exclusively in the health communication domain—our review found only one study outside the health domain (Abrahamse, Steg, Vlek, & Rothengatter, 2007)—a variety of applications to other areas of communication should be considered. For example, those researchers studying interpersonal and computer-mediated communication may be interested in the similarities and differences of computer-tailored versus face-to-face communication. Those studying mass communication may be interested in the potential of tailored news and tailored polls on news Web sites. Those studying political communication may be interested in how tailoring could be used in political campaigns to narrowcast messages to various kinds of supporters. Finally, those studying persuasion may be interested in what comparisons of tailored and targeted messages reveal about message relevance, message processing, and persuasiveness. Thus, given the broad applicability of message tailoring to a variety of areas of communication, researchers in these areas should consider testing tailoring hypotheses in these domains.

While this chapter will reveal the many varied and diverse tailoring applications that have been developed in the health communication domain, there are also basic elements that all tailored interventions share (see Dijkstra & De Vries, 1999; Halder et al., 2008; Kreuter et al., 2000; Rimer & Glassman,

*Table 3.1* Relevance of Tailored Messages to a Variety of Domains across the Communication Discipline

| Area of Communication | Application of Computer-Tailoring |
| --- | --- |
| Interpersonal Communication /Computer-mediated Communication | Tailoring messages as adjunct to face-to-face counseling; similarities and differences of face-to-face versus computer-tailored messages |
| Mass Communication | Tailoring content on news websites; tailored polls; tailored communication campaigns (e.g., narrowcasting) |
| Political Communication | Tailoring campaign messages to supporters and interest groups |
| Persuasion | How to conduct effective tailoring; tailoring messages to understand message relevance; tailored versus targeted messages |
| Risk and Crisis Communication | Tailoring messages for differing risk groups and audiences; tailoring according to levels of risk |
| New Media | Tailoring messages on websites, email, and cell phones |
| Organizational Communication | Tailoring messages to differing audiences within an organization |
| Advertising/Public Relations | Simple tailored Internet advertising within search engines (e.g., Google); Complex tailored Internet advertising (e.g., Amazon, Netflix); Internet tailoring on data captured by "cookies" |

1998; Velicer & Prochaska, 1999). Briefly, tailored interventions begin by assessing an individual on a variety of characteristics that are relevant to the behavior under study (e.g., demographic, behavioral, psychosocial characteristics). Assessments can be made in a variety of ways—for example, through telephone, mail, or computer surveys. Computer algorithms are then used to drive decision rules that have been developed and programmed to select particular messages that are most appropriate for an individual. Messages are derived from a *message library*, which consists of hundreds or even thousands of messages that have been created by the researchers. A feedback report is then compiled (again by the computer program), printed out, and presented to the participant in person or through the mail. Tailored computer programs that operate in clinical/community settings or programs on the Internet occur similarly. In the case of tailored counseling interventions, the process is again similar, but the message source differs. In this case, a counselor delivers the tailored content, either in person or over the phone.

## Historical Examination of Tailoring

Before we present a review of seminal and more recent tailoring studies, we discuss the context in which this literature began. The first studies of tailoring largely involved computer-generated print materials, but subsequent studies quickly expanded to include other forms of tailored messages (e.g., tailored telephone counseling, tailored on-screen computer programs). Among early studies of tailored messaging, researchers described the vast potential of tailoring in the context of a health communication strategy that could be delivered at the population level while being tailored at the individual level (Velicer et al., 2006), and this dissemination largely occurred through the use of telephone and mail. For example, researchers made assessments by telephone or through the mail, and they then mailed tailored print materials to participants or engaged in tailored counseling over the telephone. This strategy achieved the kind of broad reach typically only attained with mass media while accomplishing a level of persuasion usually only gained with interpersonal communication (Rimal & Adkins, 2003).

More recently, tailoring has been applied to Internet-based health promotion programs (Lustria, Cortese, Noar, & Glueckauf, 2009). We discuss these types of interventions in the context of an updated review of the tailored message literature in this chapter. The Internet itself is a medium with great potential, and it has been described by many as holding great promise in delivering health communication messages (Cassell, Jackson, & Cheuvront, 1998; Neuhauser & Kreps, 2003; Noar, Clark, Cole, & Lustria, 2006). In fact, according to Cassell et al., the Internet constitutes a "hybrid" channel with the reach of mass communication and the persuasive properties of interpersonal communication. The Internet, thus, lends itself very well to tailored messaging, and, not surprisingly, researchers are increasingly developing and testing tailored interventions on the Internet and with other new media technologies (e.g., cellular phones).

## Approach to Review of Message Tailoring Studies

Throughout the years, a large number of reviews of message tailoring studies have been published. Previous reviews have catalogued a number of tailored intervention studies in a number of health domains. While most reviews have focused on particular behavioral areas, such as smoking cessation (Strecher, 1999; Velicer et al., 2006), diet and exercise (Brug, Campbell, & van Assema, 1999; Kroeze, Werkman, & Brug, 2006), and mammography screening (Sohl & Moyer, 2007), a few embraced a more integrative approach of reviewing the application of tailoring across many health behaviors (Noar, Benac, & Harris, 2007; Richards et al., 2007; Rimer & Glassman, 1999; Skinner, Campbell, Rimer, Curry, & Prochaska, 1999). In addition, general reviews of computer and Internet-based interventions also typically include a number of tailoring studies (S. Bull, 2008; Portnoy, Scott-Sheldon, Johnson, & Carey, 2008; Revere & Dunbar, 2001; Suggs, 2006; Walters, Wright, & Shegog, 2006). To date, the majority of reviews have concluded that participants perceive tailored messages as more relevant, and that they are also more likely read and recall such messages. Most reviews also have concluded that tailored messages are, indeed, more effective at impacting health behavior change as compared with targeted interventions or no-treatment control conditions (e.g., Kreuter et al., 2000; Kroeze et al., 2006; Richards et al., 2007; Rimer & Glassman, 1999; Skinner et al., 1999; Strecher, 1999). This has also been the conclusion of two recent meta-analyses on the topic of tailored interventions (Noar et al., 2007; Sohl & Moyer, 2007).

To provide a review of both seminal as well as more recent tailoring literatures across health behaviors, we supplemented the significant search effort from our previous meta-analysis (Noar et al., 2007) with a major new review to identify tailoring studies. We sought to conduct a large and representative review of the literature on individualized tailoring in the health domain. Although we could not possibly include every study that we located in our review, we chose instead to represent the literature as accurately as possible in terms of health behaviors studied and channels used for intervention delivery (e.g., traditional versus new media). Studies in our review included those in which the ultimate product of interventions consisted of print materials or on-screen feedback, including tailored Internet and cell phone/personal desktop assistant (PDA) interventions. Our review consisted of major searches of the PsycINFO and Medline databases, examination of studies identified from published review articles, and reliance on our personal knowledge of the literature. While these search efforts primarily took place through March 2008, we continued to add tailoring studies to this review throughout the summer of 2008.

The result of these efforts indicates that the tailoring literature has continued to burgeon over the past decade. As we report later in this chapter, the largest literature entails interventions with a primary focus on tailored print materials, or what have been termed the "first generation" of tailored interventions (Skinner et al., 1999). These studies examined the ability of computer-generated print materials to impact health behavior change, whether individually or in combination with other intervention components (e.g., print materials plus tailored telephone counseling). Within this "first generation" literature, researchers have most frequently studied smoking cessation, diet, and mammography screening. A fourth "area" also emerged as widely studied—that of multiple behavior change. Such studies use tailoring to attempt to impact multiple health behaviors in the context of a single intervention. While a number of multiple behavior interventions have concentrated on the two behaviors of diet and exercise together, a number considered diverse behaviors within the context of a single intervention (e.g., skin self-exam, physician screening, sun screen use).

In our reporting of the results of this review, we first discuss seminal studies of message tailoring (Table 3.2). Next we describe "first generation" tailored print-based studies within the behavioral areas that have been most commonly studied—smoking, diet, mammography, and multiple behavior changes (Table

Table 3.2 Seminal Studies of Message Tailoring

| Behavior | Population | Study Conditions | Intervention Intensity | Assessment | Materials/Delivery | Theory | Tailoring Variables | Type of Feedback |
|---|---|---|---|---|---|---|---|---|
| *Diet* | | | | | | | | |
| Brug et al. (1996) | Oil company employees (Netherlands) | Tailored intervention, comparison intervention | 1 contact | In person paper/pencil (at work) | Tailored letter | TPB, SCT | Attitudes, social influences, self-efficacy, dietary behavior, awareness levels | Normative |
| Campbell et al. (1994) | Adult family practice patients (central North Carolina) | Tailored intervention, comparison intervention, control | 1 contact | In person paper/pencil (physician's office) | Tailored one-page handouts | TTM, HBM | Stage of change, dietary intake, motives, barriers, beliefs, self-efficacy | Normative |
| *Mammography* | | | | | | | | |
| Skinner et al. (1994) | Women age 40–65 (North Carolina) | Tailored intervention, comparison intervention | 1 contact | Telephone (CATI) | Tailored letter | HBM, TTM | Stage of change, benefits, barriers, risk factors, screening status | Normative |
| *Smoking Cessation* | | | | | | | | |
| Curry et al. (1991) | Adult HMO members (western Washington state) | Intrinsic tailored, extrinsic tailored, both, control | Up to 3 contacts over 12 weeks | Mail | Written personalized feedback (intrinsic); prize drawing information, gift (extrinsic) | Intrinsic/Extrinsic Motivation Framework | Smoking and quitting history, health concerns, desire for self-control | Normative, Ipsative |

| Prochaska et al. (1993) | Adult smokers (Rhode Island) | 3 tailored conditions, 1 standardized comparison | Up to 4 contacts over 6 months | Mail | Stage-matched manuals, interactive feedback, counselor telephone calls | TTM | Stage of change, pros and cons, processes of change, temptations, confidence, techniques for coping | Normative, Ipsative |
|---|---|---|---|---|---|---|---|---|
| Strecher et al. (1994) | Adult family practice patients age 40-65 (North Carolina) | Tailored, generic, control | 1 contact | Telephone (CATI) or in person paper/pencil (physician's office) | Tailored letter | HBM, TTM, Attribution theory | Stage of change, benefits, barriers, perceived risks, attribution for past failure | Normative |

*Note:* HBM = Health Belief Model; SCT = Social Cognitive Theory; TPB = Theory of Planned Behavior; TTM = Transtheoretical Model

3.3). We then specify "first generation" studies in a number of other behavioral areas that have been examined (Table 3.4). In Tables 3.3 and 3.4, we aim to represent the literature as accurately as possible in terms of scope, but we focus on more recent studies (i.e., those published since the year 2000) because many previous publications (noted above) have reviewed studies throughout the 1990s. Finally, we detail what might be termed "second generation" studies, that is, studies that have delivered tailored interventions using more recent technological advances, such as the Internet and wireless handheld computers (Table 3.5). In all of these areas, we sought to overview the diversity of approaches that have been taken in this literature, in both the more established "first generation" studies as well as the newer "second generation" studies. However, given the size of the literature and the fact that our searches likely did not uncover every study, the studies listed in the tables constitute exemplars, rather than a comprehensive listing of all studies conducted in these areas to date. In choosing which studies to put into the tables, we prioritized studies that were newer, more innovative, and contributed to our goal of representing the diversity of applications of tailoring in terms of both behaviors and channels.

Across all of the tables, we listed the authors of the study and the publication date; for multiple behavior studies, we included the behaviors addressed by the intervention. We identified the study sample, including information on age, gender, and race/ethnicity if sampling was purposive, and as much detail on the sample's geographic location as possible. We detailed study conditions and described intervention intensity, indicating how many times the intervention group(s) was (were) provided with materials over what period of time. We indicated whether subjects were assessed (for message tailoring purposes) in person (paper and pencil questionnaire or interview), by computer, by telephone, or by mail. Next, we specified the intervention materials and how they were delivered, and we listed, where possible, the theory(ies) that guided the intervention design. We also listed the variables on which the intervention was tailored. Finally, we noted the type of feedback that participants received.

### Seminal Studies of Tailored Messages

The first studies in the area of individually tailored health messages were published in the early 1990s (for reviews, see Brug et al., 1999; Skinner et al., 1999; Strecher, 1999). Given the importance of this seminal work, a number of these early applications of tailoring are presented in Table 3.2 and summarized here.

These early studies sought to test the concept that print materials tailored on individual characteristics would outperform "one size fits all" generic materials or materials targeted on group-level characteristics. The outcomes of interest were behavioral, including smoking cessation and dietary change. Researchers derived characteristics to tailor on from theories of behavior and behavior change, such as stage of change (i.e., readiness to change behavior), self-efficacy, attitudes/beliefs, perceived susceptibility/risk, and social norms. In these studies, individuals were randomized to receive either tailored materials or generic/targeted materials. Studies were longitudinal and followed individuals up for many months after the interventions took place. In some cases, individuals participated for as long as 12 or 18 months.

These studies made an impact both because they tested an innovative health communication practice and because they achieved impressive results. While results varied considerably both within and across these studies, all of the studies demonstrated that tailored materials outperformed the more generic materials on the behavioral outcomes under study. These findings thus represented the first evidence that computer-generated print materials tailored on individual characteristics were more efficacious in changing behavior than generic or targeted print materials. This conclusion can hardly be overstated given the widespread use of both generic (e.g., brochures) and targeted print materials (e.g., self-help manuals).

Although these early studies revealed similar overall findings (that tailored materials were more efficacious than nontailored materials), the studies varied in important ways. Indeed, just as scholars use the term *campaign* to denote health communication efforts that vary on a multitude of dimensions (Salmon & Atkin, 2003), the term *tailored intervention* refers to a broad range of materials that have been tailored and tested in a variety of ways. Thus, although these early studies provided the basis for a literature, they did little to quell an ensuing debate regarding what makes an effective tailored message.

One factor that might be implicated in tailored message effectiveness entails behavioral theory or theories used to drive the tailoring in these studies. While some studies employed a single theory (e.g., Prochaska, DiClemente, Velicer, & Rossi, 1993), others employed multiple theories to inform the tailored messages (e.g., Skinner, Strecher, & Hospers, 1994; Strecher et al., 1994). Choice of theory impacted variable selection in tailoring, resulting in studies tailoring on many different (although largely psychosocial) characteristics. As a result, these seminal studies do not provide clear findings on what factors may be best utilized in tailoring. The dialogue on this issue has only grown since these early studies.

Another factor that varied among these studies involves choice of comparison conditions. For example, some studies aimed to make the tailored and generic letters as similar as possible (Strecher et al., 1994), increasing the possibility that any effects observed could be attributed to the tailoring itself. Other studies compared tailored materials to existing self-help materials (Curry, Wagner, & Grothaus, 1991; Prochaska et al., 1993). In these cases, it is less clear that the tailoring per se was responsible for the observed effects because the intervention and comparison conditions varied on many factors beyond tailoring. For instance, study conditions differed in terms of content and length of messages, which could potentially play a part in the efficacy of interventions. We will discuss this issue further throughout the chapter.

*Table 3.3* Exemplar Studies of Message Tailoring Applied to Health Behaviors Most Often Addressed in Tailoring Studies

| Behavior | Population | Study Conditions | Intervention Intensity | Assessment | Materials/ Delivery | Theory | Tailoring Variables | Type of Feedback |
|---|---|---|---|---|---|---|---|---|
| *Diet* | | | | | | | | |
| Brug et al. (1998) | Adults (Netherlands) | Tailored intervention (with or without ipsative follow up), generic intervention | 1 contact or 2 contacts over 4 weeks | Mail | Tailored letter(s) | TTM, PAPM | Dietary behavior, attitudes/beliefs, self-efficacy, intentions | Normative, Ipsative |
| de Bourdeaudhuij et al. (2007) | Adult employees (Belgium) | Tailored intervention, generic intervention, control | 1 contact | Computer | Computer presentation of information | TPB, TTM | Intentions, attitudes, self-efficacy, social support, benefits, barriers, knowledge, stage of change | Normative |
| Elder et al. (2005) | Spanish language-dominant Latinas (San Diego, California) | Lay health advisor plus tailored print materials, tailored print materials only, targeted print materials | 12 contacts over 12 weeks | In person interview (home visit) | Mailed newsletters and activity inserts | NR | Body Mass Index (BMI), goal setting, barriers, stage of change, behavioral strategies, points of influence for change | Normative |

| Study | Population | Design | Contacts | Delivery | Format | Theory | Variables | Type |
|---|---|---|---|---|---|---|---|---|
| Haerens, Deforche, Maes, et al. (2007) | Adolescents in the 7th grade (Belgium) | Tailored intervention, control | 1 contact | In person paper/ pencil (at school) | Computer presentation of information | TTM; TPB; SCT; Attitude, Social Influence and Self-efficacy Model | Stage of change, attitudes, self-efficacy, social support, perceived benefits and barriers | Normative |
| Heimendinger et al. (2005) | Adult callers to the Cancer Information Service (United States) | Single untailored, single tailored, multiple tailored, multiple retailored | Up to 4 contacts over 12 months | Telephone | Mailed booklet followed by 2 pamphlets and 1 letter | TTM, HBM, SCT | Stage of change, outcome expectations, beliefs, diet, cost comparison with snack foods, benefits, barriers, environmental issues | Normative, Ipsative |
| Irvine et al. (2004) | Hospital and corporation employees (Colorado; Illinois) | Tailored intervention, waitlist control | 1 contact plus unlimited use over 4 weeks | Mail | Interactive multimedia computer-based program plus printout | TTM, TRA, SCT | Gender, race, age, dietary behavior, perceived barriers, content interest | Normative |

(continued)

Table 3.3 Continued

| Behavior | Population | Study Conditions | Intervention Intensity | Assessment | Materials/ Delivery | Theory | Tailoring Variables | Type of Feedback |
|---|---|---|---|---|---|---|---|---|
| Kristal et al. (2000) | Health plan enrollees (western Washington state) | Tailored intervention, control | At least 6 contacts over 1 year | Telephone | Self-help materials package, dietary analysis feedback, motivational phone call, semi-monthly newsletters | SLT, TTM, Diet individuation model | Stage of change, motives for and interest in change, dietary habits | Normative, Ipsative |
| *Mammography* | | | | | | | | |
| Bastani et al. (1999) | Female relatives of breast cancer patients (United States; Canada) | Tailored intervention, control | 1 contact | Telephone (CATI) | Tailored letter plus targeted booklet, notepad, bookmark | Adherence Model | Personal risk factors for breast cancer | Normative |

| Study | Population | Intervention | Contacts | Delivery mode | Comparison materials | Theory | Constructs | Type |
| --- | --- | --- | --- | --- | --- | --- | --- | --- |
| Champion et al. (2007) | Low income women from a general medicine clinic and HMO enrollees non-adherent to mammography guidelines (St. Louis, Missouri; Indianapolis, Indiana | Tailored print, tailored telephone, tailored print and telephone, usual care control | 1 or 2 contacts over 1 week | Telephone (CATI) | Newsletter plus physician's letter, telephone call with same information plus responses to any questions | TTM, HBM | Perceived risk, benefits, barriers, self-efficacy, knowledge of mammography, age, family history, stage of change | Normative |
| Kreuter et al. (2005) | Lower income African-American women 40-65 years old (Saint Louis, Missouri) | Interventions tailored on behavioral constructs, cultural beliefs, or both, usual care control | 6 contacts over ~18 months | In person paper/pencil (health center) | Mailed magazines | Theories of health behavior change | Knowledge, barriers, stage of change, perceived risk, breast cancer family history, exposure/interest in fruits and vegetables, doctor or nurse advice, behaviors, religiosity, collectivism, racial pride, time orientation | Normative |

(continued)

Table 3.3 Continued

| Behavior | Population | Study Conditions | Intervention Intensity | Assessment | Materials/ Delivery | Theory | Tailoring Variables | Type of Feedback |
|---|---|---|---|---|---|---|---|---|
| Lipkus et al. (2000) | Women 50 years and older enrolled in a health plan (Raleigh, Durham, and Chapel Hill, North Carolina) | Tailored print, tailored telephone, usual care control | 2 contacts over 1 or 2 years | Telephone | Booklet, telephone counseling | TTM | Name, barriers, facilitators, pros/ cons, reasons for mammography, stage of change | Normative, Ipsative |
| Vernon et al. (2008) | Women veterans 52 years and older (United States) | Tailored and targeted intervention, targeted intervention, control | 2 contacts over ~12 months | Mail | Tailored letter and bookmarks, targeted materials (booklets, letter, pamphlets) | TTM, HBM, SCT, TPB | Mammography behavior and intention, mammography reminder, stage of change, pros/ cons, processes of change, objective and perceived risk, perceived barriers, self-efficacy, processes of change | Normative, Ipsative |

*Smoking Cessation*

| Study | Population | Conditions | Contacts | Channel | Materials | Theory | Constructs | Norm type |
|---|---|---|---|---|---|---|---|---|
| Dijkstra et al. (2006) | Adult smokers and ex-smokers (Netherlands) | Matched tailored, mis-matched tailored | 1 contact | Mail | Tailored letter | Social Cognitive Stage Model | Stage of change, pros/cons, self-efficacy | Normative |
| Hoffman et al. (2006) | Low income African American smokers (Chicago, Illinois) | Tailored intervention w/ information audiotape, Tailored intervention w/ information and instruction audiotape | 2 contacts over 3 months | Computer | Computer expert system, stage-based manual, stress reduction audiotape | TTM | Stage of change, pros/cons, temptations, processes of change | Normative, Ipsative |
| Meyer et al. (2007) | Adult patients age 18–70 years who smoke (northeast Germany) | Tailored print, physician advice, control | 3 contacts over 6 months | In person (physician's office) and telephone (CATI) or mail | Tailored letters, self-help manual | TTM | Stage of change, pros/cons, self-efficacy, processes of change | Normative, Ipsative |

(*continued*)

Table 3.3 Continued

| Behavior | Population | Study Conditions | Intervention Intensity | Assessment | Materials/ Delivery | Theory | Tailoring Variables | Type of Feedback |
|---|---|---|---|---|---|---|---|---|
| Prochaska et al. (2001) | Adult smokers in an HMO (United States) | Tailored only, tailored plus counselor, tailored plus stimulus control enhancement, assessment only | 3 contacts over 6 months | Mail or telephone | Mailed tailored feedback reports, stage-matched manuals, telephone calls based on tailored feedback, hand-held computer to provide stimulus control | TTM | Stage of change, pros/cons, self-efficacy, processes of change, small steps to change | Normative, |

*Ipsative*

| | | | | | | | | Normative |
|---|---|---|---|---|---|---|---|---|
| Sutton & Gilbert (2007) | Callers to a "Quitline" (United Kingdom) | Tailored intervention, usual care control | 1 contact | Telephone | Tailored letter plus standard information packet | Theories of smoking cessation and behavior change, including SCT and Perspectives on Change Model | Gender, age, cigarette consumption, length of longest previous abstinence, motivation and determination to quit, dependence, reasons for quitting, self-image, advantages and disadvantages of quitting, difficult situations, children, living with other smokers, social support, current health problems | |

*(continued)*

Table 3.3 Continued

| Behavior | Population | Study Conditions | Intervention Intensity | Assessment | Materials/ Delivery | Theory | Tailoring Variables | Type of Feedback |
|---|---|---|---|---|---|---|---|---|
| **Multiple Behaviors** | | | | | | | | |
| Blalock et al. (2002) – calcium intake, exercise | Adult females age 40-56 (western North Carolina) | Tailored, non-tailored intervention | 3 contacts over 3-4 weeks | Telephone (CATI) | Two mailed packets of tailored materials, a telephone counseling session | PAPM | Current calcium intake and exercise, perceived adequacy of current calcium intake and exercise, stage of change, behavioral goals, barriers | Normative, Ipsative |
| Campbell et al. (2002) – nutrition, exercise, smoking, cancer screening | Women employed in rural, blue collar worksites (eastern North Carolina) | Intervention, delayed intervention | 2 contacts over 6 months | In person (at workplace) and mail or telephone if necessary | Tailored magazines, "natural helpers" | Ecological framework, SCT, TTM, social support models | Name, workplace, age, shift, health concerns, diet, physical activity, smoking, cancer screening, choice of behavioral priority for change | Normative, Ipsative |

| Study | Population | Groups | Contacts/timing | Delivery mode | Intervention materials | Theory | Constructs | Tailoring type |
|---|---|---|---|---|---|---|---|---|
| Geller et al. (2006) – skin self-exam, physician screening, sunscreen use | Siblings of melanoma patients (United States) | Tailored, usual care | 3 mailings and 4 phone calls over 5 months | Mail | Tailored materials plus motivational telephone counseling | SCT, HBM, TPB, PAPM | Skin self-exam, physician screening, sunscreen use, self-efficacy, beliefs | Normative |
| Glasgow et al. (2006) – nutrition, physical activity | Adults with Type 2 diabetes at least 25 years of age (Denver, Colorado) | Tailored intervention, enhanced usual care | 4 contacts over 6 weeks | Computer | CD-ROM, telephone calls from health coach, tailored newsletter | SCT | Health behavior, benefits, barriers, goals and strategies for change, self-efficacy | Normative |
| Prochaska et al. (2005) – diet, smoking, sun exposure, mammography | Primary care patients from health insurance organization (northeastern United States) | Tailored intervention, control | 3 contacts over 12 months | Telephone and mail survey | Tailored reports | TTM | Stage of change, readiness to change, pros/cons, processes of change, self-efficacy, small steps to change | Normative, Ipsative |
| Rimer et al. (1999) – Pap test, mammography, overall cancer screening | Low income African American women (Durham, North Carolina) | Provider prompt plus tailored print plus telephone counseling, provider prompt plus tailored print, provider prompt only | Up to 4 contacts over 16 months | Telephone | Tailored birthday card, newsletter, telephone counseling | TTM | Previous screening, stage of change, barriers, pros/cons, race, age, hysterectomy | Normative |

*Note:* HBM = Health Belief Model; NR = Not reported; PAPM = Precaution Adoption Process Model; SCT = Social Cognitive Theory; SLT = Social Learning Theory; TPB = Theory of Planned Behavior; TRA = Theory of Reasoned Action; TTM = Transtheoretical Model

### Updated Review of Tailoring Studies

Our updated review of tailoring studies provides a "snapshot" of the more recent literature on tailored health messages and interventions (see Tables 3.3–3.5). These tables demonstrate that the literature has continued to grow, and, with that growth, scholars have now tested a wealth of diverse tailoring applications. While most studies have been conducted within the United States, explorations of tailoring have occurred in other countries, spanning the Netherlands, Belgium, Germany, Australia, Norway, Canada, Iran, Sweden, and the United Kingdom (Tables 3.3–3.5). Studies have been conducted with a large diversity of populations, from adolescents to adults and from U.S Marines to chemotherapy patients. In addition, virtually all of the randomized trials conducted to date have some form of comparison group, such as a "usual/ standard care," control group, or several different levels of treatment. Many studies compare tailored interventions to control conditions or generic or personalized conditions, while others contrast tailoring across different channels (e.g., print versus telephone) or examine additive effects of different channels (e.g., print plus telephone; see Tables 3.3–3.5).

Intervention intensity comprises a factor that varies across many types of health communication interventions, and, in this literature, it also ranges greatly. While some studies used one contact with participants and followed up shortly after that contact, others had 6 or 12 contacts and followed individuals for 12, 18, or 24 months (Tables 3.3–3.5). Studies that followed people over time had an opportunity to provide not only normative feedback (i.e., a person compared to his or her peers) but also ipsative feedback (i.e., a person compared to him- or herself at a previous time point) (Velicer et al., 1993). Notably, several studies in this literature had only one contact and, thus, did not take advantage of the full potential that tailoring has to offer. For example, in the table that presents studies of tailoring across a large number of health behaviors (Table 3.4), 15 of 30 studies (50%) had only one intervention contact and could provide only normative feedback to participants. In many ways, such studies differ from those that followed individuals over time and also delivered ipsative feedback. In fact, the potential for ipsative feedback is arguably one of the most compelling and potentially effective aspects of message tailoring, yet it was *not* used in the majority of studies. Indeed, across all of the studies in Tables 3.2 to 3.5, only 28 of 72 interventions (39%) provided ipsative feedback to participants.

Tables 3.3 to 3.5 also reveal the differing assessment and delivery approaches that have been used in message tailoring interventions. Assessments have been conducted through paper/pencil surveys in person or through the mail, telephone conversations, face-to-face interactions with data collected on a laptop/ desktop computer or computer kiosk (in a variety of settings), Internet-based surveys, wireless handheld computers, and investigation of medical records and billing databases. Delivery options also ranged widely, including print materials (such as letters, newsletters, magazines, booklets, and birthday cards sent

Table 3.4 Exemplar Studies of Message Tailoring Applied to a Variety of Health-related Behaviors

| Behavior | Population | Study Conditions | Intervention Intensity | Assessment | Materials/ Delivery | Theory | Tailoring Variables | Type of Feedback |
|---|---|---|---|---|---|---|---|---|
| *Alcohol Use* | | | | | | | | |
| Neumann et al. (2005) | Emergency department adult patients with acute injury (Berlin, Germany) | Tailored intervention, control | 1 contact | In person paper/pencil (at hospital) and computer | Computer program, tailored letter | TTM | Alcohol use, readiness to change | Normative |
| Werch et al. (2005) | Suburban high school students (northeast Florida) | Counselor plus tailored print materials, minimal intervention control | 2 contacts over 1 week | In person paper/pencil (school) | One-on-one counseling session, mailed tailored tip sheet | SCT, HBM, TPB | Type of alcoholic beverage consumed | Normative |
| *Cervical Cancer* | | | | | | | | |
| Campbell et al. (1997) | Adult women (Australia) | Tailored materials, control | 1 contact | Computer | Tailored printout | NR | Risk factors | Normative |
| *Colorectal Cancer Screening* | | | | | | | | |
| Jerant et al. (2007) | Adults 50 years or older (California) | Tailored computer program, non-tailored control | 1 contact | Computer | Interactive multimedia computer program | TTM | Patient preference for testing, self-efficacy, barriers, stage of change, prior screening | Normative |

*(continued)*

*Table 3.4* Continued

| Behavior | Population | Study Conditions | Intervention Intensity | Assessment | Materials/ Delivery | Theory | Tailoring Variables | Type of Feedback |
|---|---|---|---|---|---|---|---|---|
| Marcus et al. (2005) | Callers to the Cancer Information Service 50 years or older (United States) | Single untailored, single tailored, multiple tailored, multiple retailored | Up to 4 contacts over 12 months | Telephone | Mailed booklet followed by 2 newsletters (for multiple conditions) | HBM, TTM | Name, stage of change, cancer risk, barriers | Normative, Ipsative |
| *Drug Use* | | | | | | | | |
| Wolde et al. (2008) | Chronic benzo- diazepine users (Netherlands) | Single untailored, single tailored, multiple tailored | Up to 3 contacts over 3 months | Mail and telephone | Mailed tailored letter(s) | SCT | Name, type of benzodiazepine used, outcome expectations, self-efficacy | Normative, Ipsative |
| *Early Cancer Detection* | | | | | | | | |
| de Nooijer et al. (2004) | Adults (Netherlands) | Tailored materials, standard information, control | 1 contact | Mail | Mailed tailored letter | Attitude- Social Influence- Self Efficacy Model | Knowledge of cancer symptoms, early detection intentions, reasons for early detection, risk perception, attitudes, social influence, self- efficacy, fear of cancer, fatalistic attitudes, gender | Normative |

*Health Care Provider Behavior*

| | | | | | | | | |
|---|---|---|---|---|---|---|---|---|
| Fretheim et al. (2006) | General practitioners (Norway) | Tailored program, control | 1 contact, multiple computer "pop-ups" | Patient records | Computer "pop-up" messages associated with patient visits | NR | Performance of patient risk estimation, choice of prescription drugs, achievement of treatment goals | Normative |
| Rose et al. (1997) | Anesthesiologists (Toronto, Canada) | Tailored program, control | 6-month education period plus 4 contacts over 22 months | Patient records | Feedback forms on pain management behavior | NR | Rate of use of promoted patient pain management strategies, rate of excessive pain in the post-anesthesia care unit, pain scores | Normative, Ipsative |
| *Hypertension* | | | | | | | | |
| Friedman et al. (1996) | Hypertension patients age 60 or older (Boston, Massachusetts) | Computer-controlled telephone system, usual care | 26 contacts over 6 months | In person (home) and telephone | Computer-controlled voice feedback to patients | NR | Blood pressure, understanding of prescribed medication, patient adherence, side effects | Normative |
| *Immunization* | | | | | | | | |
| Baker et al. (1998) | Adult high risk patients (southeast Michigan) | Tailored materials, generic or personal postcard, control | 1 contact | Billing database | Tailored letter | HBM | Name, risk factors | Normative |

*(continued)*

Table 3.4 Continued

| Behavior | Population | Study Conditions | Intervention Intensity | Assessment | Materials/ Delivery | Theory | Tailoring Variables | Type of Feedback |
|----------|-----------|------------------|------------------------|------------|---------------------|--------|--------------------|------------------|
| Kreuter et al. (2004) | Parents of infants 0-1 year (St. Louis, Missouri) | Tailored materials, control | Up to 6 contacts over 24 months | In person interview (physician's office) and patient records | Tailored calendar | Social marketing | Age, gender, height, weight, name, photograph, ethnicity, parents/ siblings, home environment, baby's health, appointment date and time | Normative |
| *Injury Prevention* | | | | | | | | |
| Gielen et al. (2007) – child safety seat use, smoke alarm use, poison storage | Parents of young children making emergency department visits (Baltimore, Maryland) | Tailored intervention, personalized but generic intervention | 1 contact | Computer | Tailored safety report | ELM, PAPM | Self-reported behavior related to child safety seats, smoke alarms, and poison storage; PAPM stage; child's name, age, weight, gender; ethnicity | Normative |

| Study | Population | Conditions | Contacts | Delivery | Intervention | Theory | Tailored variables | Feedback |
|---|---|---|---|---|---|---|---|---|
| Lusk et al. (2003) – hearing protection | Automotive factory workers (Michigan) | Tailored, non-tailored, control | 1 contact | Computer | Computer-based intervention, hard copy handout | Health Promotion Model, SCT | Perceived benefits, self-barriers, interpersonal support, situational factors, type of hearing protection device (HPD) used, perceived hearing ability, self-reported use of HPDs | Normative |
| Nansel et al. (2002) – home and car safety | Parents of children ages 6-20 months (Washington, DC) | Tailored materials, generic materials | 1 contact | Computer | Tailored handout based on interactive computer program | NR | Child's name and gender, injury risk scores, locus of control, self-efficacy, injury risk information and prevention, response efficacy, barriers | Normative |

*Medical Appointments*

| | | | | | | | | |
|---|---|---|---|---|---|---|---|---|
| Campbell et al. (1994) | Parents of newborns (Rochester, New York) | Tailored letter, generic postcard, control | 1 contact | In person interview (clinic) | Mailed tailored reminder letter | HBM | Appointment date and time, age-specific interventions | Normative |

(continued)

*Table 3.4* Continued

| Behavior | Population | Study Conditions | Intervention Intensity | Assessment | Materials/ Delivery | Theory | Tailoring Variables | Type of Feedback |
|---|---|---|---|---|---|---|---|---|
| **Pain Management** | | | | | | | | |
| Ahles et al. (2006) | Adult patients (New Hamphire, Rhode Island, Vermont) | Tailored, tailored plus telephone consultations, usual care | 1 contact via letter, up to 9 telephone calls from nurse | Mail | Mailed tailored letter plus health education booklet, telephone consultations from nurse-educator, supplemental mailed written and audio materials | Cognitive-behavioral approaches, problem-solving therapy | Presence and level of pain, "psychosocial problems" | Normative |
| **Patient Information/ Decision Making** | | | | | | | | |
| Hoffmann et al. (2007) | Adult stroke patients (Brisbane, Australia) | Tailored intervention, generic control | 1 contact | In person interview (hospital) | Tailored booklet | NR | Topics about which the patient desired information, desired amount of information, font size preference | Normative |
| McBride et al. (2002) – hormone replacement therapy | Women 45-55 years old (United States) | Tailored intervention, delayed intervention control | 1 contact | Telephone | Trifold brochure, worksheet, booklet, question checklist | NR | Perceived menopausal status, hysterectomy, prior HRT use, accuracy of perceived cancer risk | Normative |

| Study | Population | Conditions | Contacts | Delivery | Format | Theory/Model | Tailoring variables | Type |
|---|---|---|---|---|---|---|---|---|
| Skinner et al. (2002) – *BRCA* testing | At risk adult women (United States) | Tailored materials, non-tailored control | 1 contact | Mail | Booklet | Decision counseling model | Sociodemographic characteristics, medical history, pros/cons of testing, intrusive thoughts, preference for information (type and amount), knowledge, probability of genetic mutation | Normative |
| *Physical Activity* | | | | | | | | |
| Bull et al. (1999) | Adult patients (southeastern Missouri) | Tailored and personalized, general and personalized, general only, usual care control | 1 contact | In person paper/pencil (physician's office) | Two-page printed materials | TTM | Stage of change, exercise goal, motives for exercising, barriers, preferred physical activity | Normative |
| Haerens, Deforche, Vandelanotte, et al. (2007) | Adolescents (Belgium) | Tailored intervention, control | 1 contact | In person paper/pencil (in school) | Computer-based (CD) intervention | TPB; SCT; Attitude, Social Influence and Efficacy Model; TTM | Attitudes, self-efficacy, social support, knowledge, benefits, barriers, stage of change | Normative |
| Kerr & McKenna (2000) | White collar employees (United Kingdom) | Tailored campaign materials, control | 1 contact | In person paper/pencil | Black and white A4 pages mailed through inter-office mail | TTM | Stage of change | Normative |

(continued)

Table 3.4 Continued

| Behavior | Population | Study Conditions | Intervention Intensity | Assessment | Materials/Delivery | Theory | Tailoring Variables | Type of Feedback |
|---|---|---|---|---|---|---|---|---|
| Marcus, Napolitano, et al. (2007) | Sedentary adults 18-65 years (northeastern United States) | Tailored via print, tailored via telephone, control | 14 contacts over 12 months | In person paper/pencil and mail | Computer expert system report, stage-targeted booklets, tip sheets; telephone counseling guided by same materials in print condition | TTM, SCT | Physical activity, stage of change, processes of change, pros/cons, self-efficacy | Normative, Ipsative |
| Shirazi et al. (2007) | Women 40-65 years (Iran) | Tailored, control | 9 contacts over 10 weeks | In person paper/pencil (health center) and physical assessment | Group-based instructional sessions, home-visit exercise instruction, mailed reminder cards and pamphlets | TTM | Stage of change | Normative, Ipsative |
| *Prostate Cancer* | | | | | | | | |
| Myers et al. (1999) | African American males 40-70 years (Chicago, Illinois) | Enhanced or minimal intervention | 2 contacts over 3 years | Telephone | Tailored print materials and telephone contact | Preventive Health Model | Name, age, race, family history of prostate cancer, presence or absence of prostate cancer symptoms | Normative |

*Safer Sex*

| | | | | | | | | |
|---|---|---|---|---|---|---|---|---|
| Kiene & Barta (2006) | College students (Connecticut) | Tailored program, control | 2 contacts over 2 weeks | Computer | Computer-based tailored program | Information-Motivation-Behavioral Skills Model of Health Behavior, TTM | Condom use information, motivation, behavioral skills, goal setting, barriers, benefits, gender | Normative, Ipsative |
| Roberto et al. (2007) | Rural high school students (Kentucky) | Tailored program, control | 6 contacts over 6 weeks | Computer | Computer-based tailored program, interactive CD-ROM | EPPM | Sensation seeking, impulsive decision making, knowledge | Normative |
| Scholes et al. (2003) | Sexually active adult women 18-24 years (North Carolina, Washington) | Tailored program, control | 2 contacts over 3 months | Telephone (CATI) | Tailored magazine, tailored newsletter | TTM, TRA | Stage of change, beliefs, norms, intentions, efficacy, barriers/facilitators, perceived STD risk, partner type, ethnicity, binge drinking, STD history, number of partners, oral contraceptive use, children | Normative, Ipsative |

*Sun Safety*

| | | | | | | | | |
|---|---|---|---|---|---|---|---|---|
| Lewis et al. (2005) | Zoo education directors (United States) | Tailored materials, generic materials | 3 contacts | Mail and telephone | Tailored project-related materials, follow-up phone calls | Diffusion theory | State-specific UVR and skin cancer data, zoo characteristics and resources | Normative, Ipsative |

Note: ELM = Elaboration Likelihood Model; HBM = Health Belief Model; NR = Not reported; PAPM = Precaution Adoption Process Model; SCT = Social Cognitive Theory; TPB = Theory of Planned Behavior; TRA = Theory of Reasoned Action; TTM = Transtheoretical Model through the mail or given in person), on screen feedback on a computer, Internet Web site, or handheld computer, or feedback delivered over the telephone.

Moreover, consistent with other reviews, theories used to guide tailoring as well as variables actually tailored on have differed greatly across studies. As we detail later in this chapter, similar to other reviews (Kreuter et al., 2000; Noar et al., 2007; Skinner et al., 1999), we find that theories widely applied in this literature include the transtheoretical model (TTM; Prochaska & DiClemente, 1983; Prochaska, DiClemente, & Norcross, 1992), the health belief model (Janz & Becker, 1984), social cognitive theory (Bandura, 1986), and the theory of planned behavior (Fishbein & Ajzen, 1975). Also similar to findings in earlier reviews, many studies use more than one theory to guide message tailoring, and few studies show "fidelity" to any one particular theoretical perspective in their choice of variables on which to tailor (Noar et al., 2007; Sohl & Moyer, 2007). Indeed, just because a researcher described a theory as informing a tailored intervention does *not* mean that researcher used all (or even most) of the components of that theory in tailoring. In that manner, researchers have used theory quite liberally in many of the applications of tailoring to date. Also, many studies tailored on additional variables that were not part of a particular theory.

This updated review finds that tailoring has now been applied to more than 20 different health behaviors and is increasingly being delivered with the use of technologies such as the Internet and cell phones/PDAs. In addition, a recent Internet intervention study aimed at reducing household energy use demonstrates that tailoring is now beginning to move beyond the health domain (Abrahamse et al., 2007). What does this updated review tell us as a whole, however? While the diversity of tailoring approaches that have been developed and evaluated to date comprises a strength of this literature, some aspects of this diversity can be considered a weakness. That is, one overriding conclusion about this literature is the lack of consensus regarding "best practices" in tailoring research. This issue is inextricably tied to understanding mechanisms of effective tailoring, which we address next. The discussions of tailoring mechanisms as well as future directions for research will also expose other gaps in this literature, such as the need for many more basic message design studies (as opposed to larger field trials) as well as meta-analyses to synthesize this large literature and help us to parse out the "active ingredients" of effective tailoring.

## Mechanisms of Tailoring

The updated literature review reveals that studies of tailored health messages and interventions have blossomed over the past decade. The vast number of randomized trials of such interventions has helped to answer the question of *whether* tailored interventions work. As we have described, many reviews (e.g., Brug et al., 1999; Skinner et al., 1999; Strecher, 1999) find support for the efficacy of numerous tailored interventions. Moreover, two recent meta-analyses of portions of the tailoring literature have concluded that tailored messages are more efficacious in sparking behavioral change when compared to nontailored messages (Noar et al., 2007; Sohl & Moyer, 2007). While many tailored interventions have been effective, we lack an understanding of *why* they have been effective. A critical question that must be raised as we move toward building a science of tailoring is the following: What are the ingredients of effective tailoring?

Early on in the tailored health literature, researchers referred to this "black box" of tailoring that often resulted from a "kitchen sink" approach where highly tailored interventions were compared to no-treatment control conditions (Abrams, Mills, & Bulger, 1999). In such cases, if the tailored communication was effective, scholars could not identify the components that led to efficacy (including whether tailoring was a significant contributor to intervention efficacy). Thus, Abrams et al. recommended moving beyond "basic 'first generation' research designs to more rigorous tests of the active ingredients in tailored communications" (p. 302).

This review suggests that most studies in this body of literature continue to be trials that primarily focus on whether tailored intervention packages are efficacious, rather than trials focused on *under what circumstances* tailoring is most efficacious. Thus, for the most part, Abrams et al.'s (1999) advice has not been heeded. For example, many newer trials explored whether tailored components delivered through different communication channels (e.g., print, telephone, in person) affect behavior change differently (see Tables 3.3–3.5). While the issue of channel selection remains an important question to answer, these studies tell us little about the ingredients of effective tailoring within individual channels.

Some recent empirical work, however, has advanced our understanding of how tailoring may exerts its effects as well as what may make for more versus less effective tailoring. We begin by detailing how tailoring may exert its effects from a theoretical perspective. Next, we consider perceived message relevance and a message effects perspective on tailoring. We then discuss theories that have been used for tailoring and discuss how the domains used in tailoring could be usefully expanded. Finally, we consider future directions for research in tailored communication.

### How Does Tailoring Exert its Effects?

From a theoretical perspective, how does tailoring achieve its effects? The elaboration likelihood model (ELM; Petty & Cacioppo, 1981; also see Kreuter & Wray, 2003) provides the most common explanation. The ELM comprises a dual process model of persuasion that has been used to explain the mechanisms of tailoring, and in that manner can be described as a theory "of" tailoring. The theory suggests that individuals engage in two types of message

Table 3.5 Exemplar Studies of Message Tailoring Using the Internet/New Media for Intervention Delivery

| Behavior | Population | Study Conditions | Intervention Intensity | Assessment | Delivery Site | Theory | Tailoring Variables | Type of Feedback |
|---|---|---|---|---|---|---|---|---|
| **Alcohol Use** | | | | | | | | |
| Simon-Arndt et al. (2006) | Active duty U.S. Marines (southern California) | Tailored intervention only | 1 session | Computer | Internet via office computers | EPPM | Alcohol use, risk information, estimated BAC, alcohol-related problems, money spent on alcohol, location of military base | Normative |
| Weitzel et al. (2007) | Private university students (southeastern United States) | Tailored messages, control | Up to 12-14 messages over 2 weeks | In person paper/pencil (at school) and wireless handheld computer | Wireless handheld computers | NR | Alcohol use, self-efficacy, outcome expectancies | Normative |
| **Asthma** | | | | | | | | |
| Joseph et al. (2007) | Urban African-American high school students (Detroit, Michigan) | Tailored intervention (with or without pretest), generic websites control | 4 sessions over 6 months (self-paced) | Computer | Internet via school computers | TTM, HBM | Controller medication adherence, rescue inhaler availability, smoking, beliefs, attitudes, barriers to change | Normative, Ipsative |

| Category / Study | Population | Groups | Sessions | Computer | Delivery | Theory | Outcomes | Feedback |
|---|---|---|---|---|---|---|---|---|
| *Bullying* | | | | | | | | |
| Evers et al. (2007) | Middle and high school students (United States) | Tailored intervention, control | 3 sessions over the school year (self-paced) | Computer | Internet plus CD-ROM via school computers | TTM | Bullying behavior (bully, victim, passive bystander), intention to stop bullying behavior, pros/cons, processes of change, self-efficacy | Normative, Ipsative |
| *Chemotherapy* | | | | | | | | |
| Kearney et al. (2006) | Chemotherapy patients (United Kingdom) | Tailored intervention | Daily sessions during two treatment cycles | Handheld computer | Handheld computers | NR | Symptoms of chemotherapy | Normative |
| *Injury Prevention* | | | | | | | | |
| Yardley & Nyman (2007) – falls | Adults 65 years or older (United Kingdom) | Tailored intervention, control | 1 session | Computer | Internet | NR | Self-rated balance, health problems, activity preference | Normative |

(continued)

Table 3.5 Continued

| Behavior | Population | Study Conditions | Intervention Intensity | Assessment | Delivery Site | Theory | Tailoring Variables | Type of Feedback |
|---|---|---|---|---|---|---|---|---|
| *Multiple Behaviors* | | | | | | | | |
| Ezendam et al. (2007) – nutrition, exercise, sedentary behaviors | Adolescents (Netherlands) | Intervention, control | 8 sessions over 10 weeks | Computer | Internet via school computer | PAPM, TPB | Knowledge, behavior, Body Mass Index (BMI), attitude, subjective norm, perceived behavioral control, stage of change, social support, skills, planning | Normative |
| Prochaska et al. (2008) – exercise, stress, smoking, weight | Medical university employees (United States) | Health risk intervention (HRI) only, HRI + motivational interview, HRI + tailored intervention | Unlimited sessions per behavior over six months (recommended minimum = 3 sessions per behavior) | Computer | Internet | TTM | Stage of change, pros/cons, efficacy, processes of change | Normative, Ipsative |

| | | | | | | | | |
|---|---|---|---|---|---|---|---|---|
| Tate et al. (2006) – diet, physical activity, tobacco use, alcohol use | Overweight adults 20-65 years old (United States) | Computer-automated e-mail feedback, human e-mail counseling, no counseling control | 1 in person session plus weekly Internet e-mails over 6 months; unlimited access to study Web site | In person (at clinic) and computer | Internet (e-mail) | Cognitive-behavioral theory | Weight, calorie intake, physical activity | Normative, Ipsative |
| Woolf et al. (2006) – diet, physical activity, tobacco use, alcohol use | Adult primary care patients (northern Virginia) | Tailored intervention, control | 1 or more sessions | Computer | Internet | TTM | Diet, physical activity, tobacco use, alcohol use, stage of change | Normative |
| *Physical Activity* | | | | | | | | |
| Marcus, Lewis, et al. (2007) | Sedentary adults age 18-65 (Providence, Rhode Island; Pittsburgh, Pennsylvania) | Tailored Internet, tailored print, standard Internet | At least monthly visits over 12 months | In person paper/pencil, interview and physical assessment (at research site) and computer | Internet | TTM, SCT | Stage of change, self-efficacy, pros/cons, processes of change, physical activity | Normative, Ipsative |

(continued)

Table 3.5 Continued

| Behavior | Population | Study Conditions | Intervention Intensity | Assessment | Delivery Site | Theory | Tailoring Variables | Type of Feedback |
|---|---|---|---|---|---|---|---|---|
| Spittaels et al. (2007) | Adults 25-55 years old at worksites (northern Belgium) | Tailored intervention only, tailored intervention plus email feedback, non-tailored advice | 1 session; 5 email messages over 8 weeks | Computer | Internet | TTM, TPB | Stage of change, intentions, attitudes, self-efficacy, social support, knowledge, benefits, barriers | Normative, Ipsative |
| *Smoking Cessation* | | | | | | | | |
| Etter (2005) | Adults (via Swiss-based program available in five languages) | "Original" and "modified" versions of a tailored intervention | 1 session; follow-up email messages at 1- and 2- months post session | Computer | Internet | TTM, TPB, theories of relapse prevention and tobacco dependence | Demographics, smoking status, stage of change, tobacco dependence, attitudes, self-efficacy, self-change strategies, coping methods, intention to use nicotine replacement therapy | Normative, Ipsative |

Note: EPPM = Extended Parallel Process Model; HBM = Health Belief Model; NR = Not reported; PAPM = Precaution Adoption Process Model; SCT = Social Cognitive Theory; TPB = Theory of Planned Behavior; TRA = Theory of Reasoned Action; TTM = Transtheoretical Model processing—central route and peripheral route. Central route processing is characterized by a careful examination of the arguments contained within a message, while peripheral route processing is characterized by a reliance on heuristics or cues that may be persuasive but tend to be unrelated to the core arguments contained within a message. In addition, as Petty and Cacioppo argued, central route processing results in attitudes that more likely remain stable over time and relate to future behaviors as compared with peripheral route processing.

Given that central route processing is advantageous from a persuasion and health behavior change perspective, what factors increase the chances that central route processing will take place? The ELM suggests that the extent to which individuals will elaborate with regard to a message and engage in central processing is heavily influenced by personal involvement with a message (Petty & Cacioppo, 1981). Personal involvement most likely occurs when one perceives a message to be personally relevant. As discussed above, individuals tend to interpret tailored messages as personally relevant more often than generic ones, thus increasing the chances that central processing will take place and that the result will be attitude and/or behavior change.

Indeed, Kreuter, Strecher, and Glassman (1999) suggested that communication messages range from the most generic to most customized along this continuum: (1) generic communication, (2) personalized generic communication, (3) targeted communication, (4) tailored communication, and (5) interpersonal communication. Generic communication pertains to all audiences, while personalized generic communication is similar except that superficial characteristics (e.g., name) are used to give the illusion of customization. Message designers customize targeted communication at the group level but tailored communication at the individual level. Interpersonal communication, being synchronous in nature, has the greatest potential to be the most efficacious of all communication types. However, Kreuter, Strecher, and Glassman observed that the impact of counseling interventions is limited by issues of reach and cost, while computer-based tailored interventions have an advantage on these issues. In addition, although interpersonal communication holds the *potential* to be the most highly tailored, not all interpersonal communication is tailored. Indeed, level of tailoring within interpersonal communication likely correlates with the knowledge, skill, and motivation of the communicator (Spitzberg & Cupach, 1984).

Surprisingly, these message types have yet to be compared within the context of a single study. Many studies have compared some of these message types (see Tables 3.3–3.5), although as mentioned earlier, the comparability of study conditions on features such as message content and length has not always been taken into account. Thus, while we may draw conclusions from some of the studies that have been conducted, we struggle to advance major conclusions regarding the relative efficacy of generic, targeted, and tailored messages. In fact, our review suggests that most tailoring studies have taken place in the context of larger "in the field" randomized controlled trials rather than smaller lab-based studies. Smaller studies would be capable of achieving finer manipulations of messages and examining the impact of those manipulations on various outcome variables. In fact, literatures such as message framing have engaged in many more small scale lab-based studies where elements of messages (e.g., gain versus loss frame) have been carefully manipulated, leading to stronger conclusions regarding the relative efficacy of those message types (e.g., see O'Keefe & Jensen, 2006).

As Kreuter and Wray (2003) observed, "Importantly, it is not yet known whether tailored or targeted messages are more effective.... There are, however, situations in which each approach would seem to have an advantage over the other" (p. S228). Kreuter and Wray acknowledged contextual influences on whether one or another approach may be wiser. For example, if little variability exists on a factor within the target audience, than targeting may be just as effective as tailoring because a lack of variability would result in most individuals in the population receiving a similar message (i.e., targeted message). In addition, tailoring requires a mechanism to gather data and then deliver feedback to the audience of interest. If such a mechanism does not exist in a particular context, than targeting may be a more sensible option. Thus, although theoretically more customized messages may be capable of greater impact (Kreuter, Strecher, & Glassman, 1999; Petty & Cacioppo, 1981), this issue is more complex than it appears on the surface.

One recent study attempted to fill a gap in this literature by comparing the efficacy of generic, targeted, tailored, and attention control messages in the context of a single experiment (Roberto, Raup-Krieger, & Beam, 2008). This project randomized Hispanic participants to receive a print message about kidney disease that was developed according to one of the four message conditions. The attention control condition contained a very basic informational message about kidney function. The generic condition featured a message that attempted to convince the participants that they were at high risk for kidney disease. The targeted message was identical to the generic condition except that the researchers created it to be specific to Hispanics (in both language and images). Finally, the tailored condition mirrored the targeted condition except that it presented tailored (rather than targeted) feedback on perceived susceptibility to kidney disease. Results indicated that the tailored message outperformed the generic and targeted messages, which, in turn, outperformed the control message on perceived susceptibility. According to Roberto et al., the tailored, targeted and generic messages outperformed the control message on behavioral intentions, but they did not significantly differ from one another. No significant differences on attitudes toward talking to a doctor about kidney disease emerged among any of the message types. Thus, the hypothesis that more customization would lead to greater persuasion was only partially supported.

## Perceived Message Relevance

An additional tenet of the ELM perspective on the effects of tailoring also deserves attention. The ELM suggests that tailoring achieves its effects by enhancing perceived relevance to the message. This suggestion essentially posits a meditational model where individuals perceive a more customized message as more personally relevant, and this enhanced personal relevance promotes greater attention, elaboration, message processing, and, ultimately, persuasion. Reviews of the tailored message literature have found that, compared with similar nontailored messages, tailored messages are generally more likely to be read, understood, recalled, rated highly, and perceived as credible (Kreuter et al., 2000; Kreuter & Holt, 2001; Rimer & Glassman, 1999; Skinner et al., 1999). Many of these factors indicate perceived message relevance. In addition, Kreuter, Bull, Clark, and Oswald (1999) explicitly sought to better understand the role of message relevance in tailoring by making a number of assessments of potential indicators of this construct, such as the number of positive thoughts about and personal connections to the materials and positive self-assessment thoughts. Kreuter et al. found that those participants who received tailored materials evaluated them more positively on all of these dimensions as compared with a generic brochure formatted to look like the tailored materials.

Dijkstra (2005) also examined potential indicators of perceived message relevance in tailored communications. Results suggested that participants rated the tailored materials significantly higher than the standard materials on being "directed at you personally" and "takes into account your personal situation as a smoker." This study also revealed, however, that *personalization* of generic materials may also enhance the relevance (and, in this case, the efficacy) of those materials. The term *personalization* refers to the incorporation of recognizable aspects of a person into tailored content, such as a person's name or the type of cigarettes smoked (Dijkstra, 2008). Dijkstra (2005) compared a personalized condition that contained the same text as the standard nontailored materials but included the person's name and number and type of cigarettes smoked. This condition fared about as well as the tailored condition on measures of perceived relevance and also on number of smoking quit attempts, although participants rated the message as significantly less "interesting" than the tailored condition. This study demonstrated that enhancing standard smoking cessation materials with even a minimal amount of personalized information may improve the perceived relevance and, potentially, the efficacy of those materials. It also raised the question of how much of the efficacy of tailored materials stems from individuals' perceptions that materials have been tailored as opposed to how much materials actually were tailored.

Webb, Simmons, and Brandon (2005) varied the amount of personalization in smoking cessation materials to explore potential mechanisms of tailoring. The study compared standard smoking cessation materials to both minimally and extensively personalized materials. The minimally personalized material contained the individual's name and a statement about how the report was created especially for them. The extensively personalized materials were similar except that approximately 50 personalized features were integrated into the report, including several instances of the participant's name, gender, age range, rate of cigarette consumption, length of time smoking, and cigarette brand smoked. In all cases, the actual smoking cessation content was identical. On measures related to perceived message relevance (e.g., caught attention, credible, trustworthy, interesting, etc.), Webb et al. reported a statistically significant linear pattern, indicating that participants interpreted the extensively personalized materials as most relevant, followed by minimally personalized and then standard materials. Webb et al. found a similar pattern on readiness to quit smoking, but it was not statistically significant. The study also revealed that those participants who most valued tailored information were most likely to exhibit changes on readiness to quit smoking in the personalized conditions. Similar to Dijkstra (2005), Webb et al. argued that personalizing health communication materials on even very basic features enhances the perceived message relevance and possibly the efficacy of those materials.

In some ways, however, these studies can be viewed as inconsistent with findings from the tailoring literature, which has relied almost entirely on tailoring on constructs from behavioral theories. The use of such behavioral theories and the matching of content based upon variables central to those theories (e.g., attitudes, self-efficacy) have been offered as an explanation for the efficacy of tailored messages (e.g., Prochaska et al., 1993). This matching of appropriate content to individuals based upon assessment has been referred to in recent writings as *adaptation* or *content-matching* (Dijkstra, 2008; Hawkins, Kreuter, Resnicow, Fishbein, & Dijkstra, 2008), and it comprises the central strategy employed in the early studies of message tailoring (see Table 3.2). The Webb et al. (2005) and Dijkstra (2005) studies, however, suggest that personalization may account for some of the effects of tailored interventions. As noted above, from an ELM perspective, even simple personalization has the potential to make the material appear more personally relevant to the reader and, thus, increase the chances of persuasion.

Moreover, Webb, Hendricks, and Brandon (2007) replicated the Webb et al. (2005) results almost exactly and provided evidence that priming individuals on the value of personalized or standard information enhances both perceived message relevance and readiness to quit smoking. Webb et al. concluded that "selling" participants on the value of the materials (whether standard or tailored) may enhance their effectiveness. Given that many tailored interventions appear to already contain messages that tell participants that the materials have been "specifically designed for them," this study raises the question of whether a placebo effect is responsible for some of the effects of tailored interventions. That is, does telling participants that a message has been specifically designed for them (whether or not it is in fact true) cause them to pay greater attention to such a message and view it as more personally relevant? The Webb et al. studies suggest that the answer is "yes," and that this suggestion of tailoring, in and of itself, could be responsible for some of the effects of tailoring (see Webb, Simmons, et al., 2005; Webb, Hendricks, et al., 2007).

Finally, while further studies may help us disentangle issues of personalization versus content matching, currently, many scholars (Hawkins et al., 2008; Rimer & Kreuter, 2006) agree that perceived message relevance is very important to the ultimate impact of tailored interventions. Scholars have rarely tested, however, whether perceived message relevance actually statistically mediates the relationship between exposure to the message and behavior change (Kreuter & Wray, 2003; Rimer & Kreuter, 2006) as well as whether a more complex relationship exists between exposure to a message, perceived relevance, message processing, and ultimate persuasion. To answer this important question, we need longitudinal studies that empirically examine the relationship between a variety of message-based factors, perceived message relevance, and later behavioral change. Such research will also need to address what exactly makes a message personally relevant (e.g., see F. C. Bull, Holt, Kreuter, Clark, & Scharff, 2001; Ruiter, Kessels, Jansma, & Brug, 2006). Obtaining answers to this large and complex question may advance our understanding of tailored health communication and also inform the issue of the importance of personalization compared with tailoring.

## Using Theory for Tailoring

In the realm of tailoring mechanisms, another issue that must be discussed constitutes the use of theories "for" tailoring. Tailoring can be achieved on virtually any variable that is capable of assessment (Rakowski, 1999). Thus, what variables should be tailored on to achieve the greatest intervention effects? Reviews of the tailoring literature demonstrate that, to date, a relatively small set of behavioral theories has been widely used in tailored interventions (see Kreuter et al., 2000; Kroeze et al., 2006; Noar et al., 2007; Skinner et al., 1999; Sohl & Moyer, 2007). These "usual suspect" theories are the transtheoretical or stages of change model (TTM; Prochaska & DiClemente, 1983; Prochaska, DiClemente, & Norcross, 1992), the health belief model (Janz & Becker, 1984), theories of reasoned action (Fishbein & Ajzen, 1975) and planned behavior (Ajzen & Madden, 1986), and social cognitive theory (Bandura, 1986). Each of these theories posits a number of psychosocial factors that may influence behavior change, and analyses of concepts from the theories reveal many similar constructs across the theories, including attitudes and beliefs, self-efficacy, social norms, perceived threat, behavioral intentions, and stages of change (Noar, 2005–2006; Noar & Zimmerman, 2005). Tailored interventions typically customize content based upon these concepts in efforts to match the right messages to the right individuals and, ultimately, persuade individuals to change their health behavior. This principle exemplifies one of the elegant features of tailored interventions. For a particular individual, theoretical mediators that do not need to change (e.g., perceived threat) can be de-emphasized or ignored altogether, while those that do need to change can be emphasized in intervention feedback (e.g., self-efficacy).

Notably, although these theories have been widely applied in tailoring, "application of theory" varies by study. Some researchers have suggested or implied that a tailored intervention should choose a single theory and tailor messages on all components from that theory in order to "count" as a "theory-based project" (Velicer et al., 1993, 2006). This standpoint, however, appears to be the minority view. Alternatively, other researchers suggest a process through which scholars select theoretical determinants on the basis of the empirical literature and subsequently use them in tailoring messages, regardless of theoretical origin (Kreuter et al., 2000; Rimer & Kreuter, 2006). Indeed, some reviews of tailored interventions demonstrate that multiple theories are used in tailoring, and, at times, little correspondence emerges between theories applied and variables tailored upon (e.g., see Noar et al., 2007; Richards et al., 2007; Sohl & Moyer, 2007). This fact makes it difficult to test which theory provides the most fruitful basis for tailored interventions, although testing which theoretical concepts may be most effective can and has been examined (see Noar et al., 2007; Sohl & Moyer, 2007).

To date, tailoring has almost entirely been conceived of as a way to customize intervention content (based on these behavioral theories) to individuals. As a result, nearly all tailoring has focused on what scholars believe to be the behavioral determinants of tailoring, which come from the theories of behavior and behavior change listed above (Kreuter et al., 2000; Noar et al., 2007; Rimer & Kreuter, 2006). A broader perspective would be that variables related to intervention content represent just one domain of tailoring that is possible. Indeed, Rimer and Kreuter argued that at least four approaches to tailoring can be used to enhance health communication and these approaches can be adapted to represent tailoring message domains. These four domains are (1) matching content to information needs and interests; (2) placing information in a meaningful context; (3) using design, production, and channel elements to capture attention and enhance message processing, and (4) presenting the type and structure of information preferred by participants. Table 3.6 lists these four domains, and includes possible theories and theoretical constructs that have been (or could be) applied in tailoring.

As noted above, matching content to individuals has been the main emphasis of the tailoring literature to date. In this domain, however, little work has been done applying behaviorally oriented theories within the communication discipline such as the extended parallel process model (Witte, 1992) and risk perception attitude framework (Rimal & Real, 2003). These theories lend themselves nicely to tailoring as they suggest "profiles" of individuals based on the theoretical concepts of perceived threat and self- and response-efficacy, variables that easily can inform the content of a message (see Rimal & Adkins, 2003; Skubisz, Reimer, & Hoffrage, this volume). Beyond manipulating content, placing information in a context meaningful to participants may be as important as the selection of particular theoretical determinants, especially in terms of the perceived relevance of the material (see Dijkstra, 2008; Hawkins et al., 2008; Noar et al., 2007). For example, creating materials that are tailored on factors such as gender, age, race, and culture may make that information more meaningful and relevant to participants. In fact, in their meta-analysis of print tailored materials, Noar et al. found that tailoring on demographic factors such as gender, race, or age enhanced the efficacy of tailored materials. They also found an additive effect such that tailoring in more areas (e.g., demographic, theoretical, behavioral) led to greater effects of interventions. Similarly, Kreuter et al. (2005) demonstrated the ability of tailoring on cultural variables to enhance the efficacy of materials tailored on behavioral theory constructs alone (also see Hornikx & O'Keefe, this volume). These studies suggest that moving beyond the content domain to include demographic and cultural variables in tailoring may lead to more efficacious interventions.

The third and fourth domains have to do with the design, structure, and type of messages. The third domain concentrates on gaining (and keeping) the attention of the participant and facilitating message processing. Demographic and cultural variables may go some way in gaining participants' attention, but variables such as message sensation value might also be used in tailoring to optimize the "look and feel" of messages for participants. For example, delivering high sensation value messages to high sensation seekers and low sensation value messages to low sensation seekers may be a strategy to help garner and keep the attention of individuals, particularly for high sensation seekers (Palmgreen & Donohew, 2003). In addition, tailoring based upon individuals' need for cognition, by applying "message cognition value," could facilitate central processing (Harrington, Lane, Donohew, & Zimmerman, 2006). Although the message cognition value construct is new to the field, several studies have demonstrated that tailoring messages on message sensation value can have positive effects (e.g., Harrington, Lane, Donohew, Zimmerman, Norling, et al., 2003; Lorch et al., 1994; Palmgreen et al., 1991; Roberto et al., 2007).

Finally, message structure and type in the delivery of tailored messages may also be important, particularly with regard to message processing. For example, delivering tailored messages in forms other than didactic materials, such as through the use of narratives (Kreuter, 2008) or tailoring message type based on preference for narrative or statistical presentation of information, comprise compelling avenues for research. Tailoring could also be conducted on preference for particular type of appeal, such as presenting information in the form of a fear appeal versus a guilt appeal. Tailoring on message frame—such as gain or loss frame—based upon individual differences found through assessment in this area could also be valuable (see Latimer, Salovey, & Rothman, 2007; Latimer et al., 2008).

## The Future of Tailored Health Communication

What is the future of tailored health communication? To be able to answer this question, we must begin with a clear understanding of the past. Although the literature has greatly progressed since the first tailoring studies were published, many basic questions about tailoring that were posed a decade ago remain unanswered (Abrams et al., 1999; Rakowski, 1999; Skinner et al., 1999). Indeed, this review reveals that we know much more about *whether* tailored interventions work than we do *why* and *under what conditions* they work. This conclusion has been drawn by other recent reviewers of the literature on tailored health interventions (e.g., Dijkstra, 2008; Hawkins et al., 2008; Kroeze et al., 2006; Noar et al., 2007; Richards et al., 2007; Rimer & Kreuter, 2006). We next discuss directions for future research in terms of 4 areas that may help advance a cumulative science of tailoring. These include additional meta-analyses, new primary studies, message design research, and message effects perspectives in tailoring.

### *Importance of Meta-Analyses*

While new studies can lend critical answers to such questions in tailoring, meta-analytic projects also hold the potential to be fruitful as conduits for cumulative knowledge. Two recent meta-analytic projects in the tailoring area (Noar et al., 2007; Sohl & Moyer, 2007) have just begun to synthesize this rapidly growing literature. Although narrative reviewers of the literature can report on the kinds of studies that have been conducted, meta-analytic studies can offer valuable insights in terms of answering questions involving study findings and outcomes (Noar, 2006b). Such projects could take advantage of the large literature that already exists in tailoring and glean insights from the many randomized trials that have already been conducted (Snyder et al., 2008). In this manner, such projects could facilitate reflection on the first decade and a half of tailoring research and help set the agenda for the future of tailoring studies. Over time, a set of "best practices" in tailoring, informed by both theory and data, could perhaps be developed to provide guidance for effective tailored interventions. Advancing our understanding of how tailoring does (and does not) work across particular health behaviors, channels, and populations is critical in building a cumulative science of tailored health communication. We must also determine how the diversity of theoretical variables, constructs, and domains can be most fruitfully applied to tailored messages and interventions. In addition, as tailored message researchers work to build this cumulative science, we strongly urge the adoption of clear and consistent reporting guidelines for publications, including clearly specifying features such as assessment strategies, tailoring variables (what was tailored on and how it was achieved), and detail on intervention materials.

## New Primary Studies

While meta-analyses are capable of examining the large number of studies that have already been conducted, new studies can test novel ideas in tailoring. Additional randomized trials examining the ability of tailored interventions to outperform alternative interventions, while useful in informing the "efficacy" question, may *not* lead us toward a more sophisticated science of tailoring (Abrams et al., 1999; Hawkins et al., 2008). A number of studies could be undertaken, however, that would help improve the knowledge base regarding what makes effective tailoring. Such studies would encompass randomized trials that tease out various components of tailoring by comparing a variety of intervention conditions that incrementally add various tailoring components and examine their influence on outcomes (e.g., behavior change; Abrams et al., 1999; Hawkins et al., 2008; Kreuter et al., 2005; Kroeze, Oenema, Dagnelie, & Brug, 2008; Resnicow et al., 2008; Strecher et al., 2008). Although scholars have long called for such studies in the tailored health literature, as Abrams et al. observed, few exist. In addition, many of these studies could be driven by research questions aimed at testing tailoring variables beyond the content domain, as suggested in Table 3.6. Studies could also be driven by more recent distinctions that have been made in the tailoring literature, such as the differences between personalization, content-matching/ adaptation, and various types of feedback (Dijkstra, 2008; Hawkins et al., 2008). These distinctions have given tailoring researchers a language with which to describe a variety of tailoring components and mechanisms that previously had simply been a part of the "black box" of tailoring. Newer studies, thus, can examine the unique role that each of these strategies plays in the efficacy of tailored messages.

## Message Design

Notably, many of the domains listed in Table 3.6 focus on message design of tailored interventions, and this area constitutes one in which health communication researchers can likely make important contributions. Indeed, not surprisingly, tailored interventions have mostly been tailored on content (i.e., content-matching) in part because much of the tailoring literature has been driven by theories of health behavior (rather than communication or persuasion theories). While behavioral theories tell us what theoretical content interventions should stress, they do not tell us how to design the intervention messages in ways that make them personally relevant and persuasive (Cappella, 2006; Noar, 2006a; Slater, 2006). For guidance on this question, communication theories related to message design and persuasion can be applied (Cappella, 2006; Harrington et al., 2006; Noar, 2006a; Slater, 2006). Communication researchers, thus, could contribute to this literature by considering (and empirically testing) how "message design" of tailored interventions can

Table 3.6 Domains in Which Tailoring Can be Achieved and Associated Theories and Variables

| Purpose | Theories | Variable Types | Specific Constructs/Variables | Outcomes |
|---|---|---|---|---|
| Match content to individual's information needs & interests | Transtheoretical Model and Stages of Change Health Belief Model Social Cognitive Theory Theory of Reasoned Action Theory of Planned Behavior Extended Parallel Process Model | Psychosocial variables, past behavior | Attitudes, beliefs, self-efficacy, social norms, perceived susceptibility, perceived severity, behavioral intentions, stage of change, previous behavior | Argument strength (content was convincing) |
| Place information in a meaningful context | Audience segmentation Personalization Culturally-oriented theories | Demographic, cultural variables | Gender, age, race Gender norms, cultural norms, ethnic identity, racial pride, religiosity, collectivism | Perceived relevance (intervention was designed for me and reflects my beliefs and values) |
| Use design, production, and channel elements to capture and keep individual's attention | Activation Model Sensation-seeking Targeting Limited Capacity Model | Message design variables ("look and feel") | Message sensation value | Attention (intervention kept my attention) |
| Present information in type and structure preferred by individual | Exemplification Theory/ Narratives Entertainment Education Message Framing Emotional appeals | Message structure variables (type of appeal) | Narrative vs. statistical Gain vs. loss framing Fear, guilt, warmth, and other appeals | Message processing (thought about information, recalled information later on) |

be enhanced, perhaps by careful experiments or randomized trials that compare differing message design approaches (see Table 3.6). This research should include testing basic design questions such as whether tailoring on visual elements increases the efficacy of tailored interventions, as implied by the findings of a recent meta-analysis (Noar et al., 2007).

### Message Effects

We also need to disentangle the process by which tailored messages exert their effects. Figure 3.1 presents one such hypothesized pathway. Based upon both the ELM (Petty & Cacioppo, 1981) and McGuire's persuasion model (McGuire, 1989), this message effects model suggests that exposure to a message results in an immediate judgment of perceived relevance. If receivers rate relevance as low, then they pay little attention to that message and likely turn their attention to something else. If receivers judge perceived relevance as moderate or high, they may instead attend more closely to that message and devote more cognitive resources to it. An interrelationship likely exists among these factors, such that processing of the message may ultimately lead to a judgment that the message is not relevant after all or that the arguments are not persuasive. Conversely, the design of the message may not be stimulating enough to keep attention. In any of these cases, the individual may turn away to something else and, again, fail to be persuaded (also see Byrne & Hart, this volume).

If the message is sufficiently compelling, however, and convinces an individual of its personal relevance, keeps attention, and results in central processing, the message may ultimately lead to information seeking, persuasion (e.g., attitude, behavior change), or both. Indeed, when we consider tailoring from a message effects perspective, the role of tailoring variables beyond the content domain becomes clearer. For instance, the role of content domain variables primarily entails the development of convincing arguments for change. Other tailoring variables, however, may be more useful in garnering attention, fostering perceived relevance, or encouraging message processing (also see Hawkins et al., 2008). For example, both Table 3.6 and Figure 3.1 suggest that tailoring on demographic factors and contextual variables, and using personalization strategies may aid in raising the perceived relevance of the message; theoretical concepts such as message sensation value might be applied to garner and keep attention to the message, and approaches such as narratives and message appeals might be used to enhance message processing. These assertions constitute empirically testable hypotheses that might be the subject of further tailoring research. Such work holds the potential to greatly advance our understanding of how tailored messages exert their effects and could provide guidance for the next generation of tailored health communication.

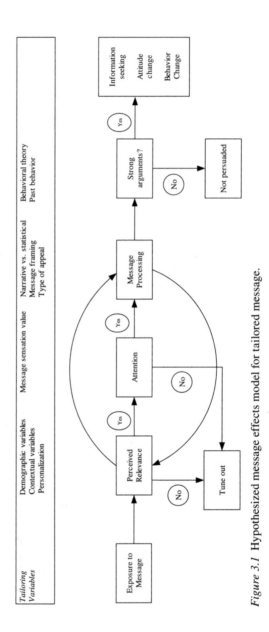

| Tailoring Variables | Demographic variables | Message sensation value | Narrative vs. statistical | Behavioral theory |
| --- | --- | --- | --- | --- |
| | Contextual variables | | Message framing | Past behavior |
| | Personalization | | Type of appeal | |

*Figure 3.1* Hypothesized message effects model for tailored message.

# Conclusion

This chapter has provided an overview of the area of individually tailored communication, an exciting area of persuasive messaging in health communication with strong possible implications for other areas of the communication discipline as well. Its focus on matching messages to the unique beliefs, attitudes, needs, and preferences of individuals makes it fundamentally different from the common mass communication practices of audience segmentation and message targeting, which operate at the group level. The possibility of reaching entire populations with individually tailored messages is upon us, and opportunities to bring such messages to populations will only grow with the further advancement of new technologies.

This chapter reveals the extraordinary breadth of the tailoring literature, yet it also reveals the limited depth with which we understand the effects of tailored communications. Future studies in this area could advance the science of tailored communication by studying the mechanisms and moderators of efficacious tailored interventions. While the roots of this literature lie in psychology and public health, communication researchers have a unique role to play by applying communication and persuasion theory to better inform this work from a theoretically-oriented, message-based perspective.

# References

Abrahamse, W., Steg, L., Vlek, C., & Rothengatter, T. (2007). The effect of tailored information, goal setting, and tailored feedback on household energy use, energy-related behaviors, and behavioral antecedents. *Journal of Environmental Psychology, 27*, 256–276.

Abrams, D. B., Mills, S., & Bulger, D. (1999). Challenges and future directions for tailored communication research. *Annals of Behavioral Medicine, 21*, 299–306.

Ahles, T. A., Wasson, J. H., Seville, J. L., Johnson, D. J., Cole, B. F., Hanscom, B., et al. (2006). A controlled trial of methods for managing pain in primary care patients with or without co-occurring psychosocial problems. *Annals of Family Medicine, 4*, 341–350.

Ajzen, I., & Madden, T. J. (1986). Prediction of goal-directed behavior: Attitudes, intentions, and perceived behavioral control. *Journal of Experimental Social Psychology, 22*, 453–474.

Albrecht, T. L., & Bryant, C. (1996). Advances in segmentation modeling for health communication and social marketing campaigns. *Journal of Health Communication, 1*, 65–83.

Baker, A. M., McCarthy, B., Gurley, V. F., & Ulcickas, M. (1998). Influenza immunization in a managed care organization. *Journal of General Internal Medicine, 13*, 469–475.

Bandura, A. (1986). *Social foundations of thought and action: A social cognitive theory.* Englewood Cliffs, NJ: Prentice-Hall.

Bastani, R., Maxwell, A. E., Bradford, C., Das, I. P., & Yan, K. X. (1999). Tailored risk notification for women with a family history of breast cancer. *Preventive Medicine, 29*, 355–364.

Blalock, S. J., DeVellis, M. M., Patterson, C. C., Campbell, M. K., Orenstein, D. R., & Dooley, M. A. (2002). Effects of an osteoporosis prevention program incorporating tailored educational materials. *American Journal of Health Promotion, 16*, 146–156.

Brug, J., Campbell, M., & van Assema, P. (1999). The application and impact of computer- generated personalized nutrition education: A review of the literature. *Patient Education and Counseling, 36*, 145–156.

Brug, J., Glanz, K., Assema, P. V., Kok, G., & Breukelen, G. J. P. V. (1998). The impact of computer-tailored feedback and iterative feedback on fat, fruit, and vegetable intake. *Health Education and Behavior, 25*, 517–531.

Brug, J., Steenhuis, I., van Assema, P., & de Vries, H. (1996). The impact of a computer-tailored nutrition intervention. *Preventive Medicine, 25*, 236–242.

Bull, F. C., Holt, C. L., Kreuter, M. W., Clark, E. M., & Scharff, D. (2001). Understanding the effects of printed health education materials: Which features lead to which outcomes? *Journal of Health Communication, 6*, 265–279.

Bull, F. C., Jamrozik, K., & Blansky, B. A. (1999). Tailored advice on exercise: Does it make a difference? *American Journal of Preventive Medicine, 16*, 230–239.

Bull, S. (2008). Internet and other computer technology-based interventions for STD/HIV prevention. In T. Edgar, S. M. Noar, & V. Freimuth (Eds.), *Communication perspectives on HIV/AIDS for the 21st century* (pp. 351–376). New York: Erlbaum.

Byrne, S., & Hart, P. S. (this volume). The boomerang effect: A synthesis of findings and a preliminary theoretical framework. In C. S. Beck (Ed.), *Communication Yearbook 33* (pp. 3–37). New York: Routledge.

Campbell, E., Peterkin, D., Abbott, R., & Rogers, J. (1997). Encouraging underscreened women to have cervical cancer screening: The effectiveness of a computer strategy. *Preventive Medicine, 26*, 801–807.

Campbell, M. K., DeVellis, B. M., Strecher, V. J., Ammerman, A. S., DeVellis, R. F., & Sandler, R. S. (1994). Improving dietary behavior: The effectiveness of tailored messages in  primary care settings. *American Journal of Public Health, 84*, 783–787.

Campbell, M. K., Tessaro, I., DeVellis, B., Benedict, S., Kelsey, K., Belton, L., et al. (2002). Effects of a tailored health promotion program for female blue-collar workers: Health works for women. *Preventive Medicine, 34*, 313–323.

Cappella, J. N. (2006). Integrating message effects and behavior change theories: Organizing comments and unanswered questions. *Journal of Communication, 56*, S265–S279.

Cassell, M. M., Jackson, C., & Cheuvront, B. (1998). Health communication on the internet: An effective channel for health behavior change? *Journal of Health Communication, 3*, 71–79.

Champion, V., Skinner, C. S., Hui, S., Monahan, P., Juliar, B., Daggy, J., et al. (2007). The effect of telephone versus print tailoring for mammography adherence. *Patient Education and Counseling, 65*, 416–423.

Curry, S. J., Wagner, E. H., & Grothaus, L. C. (1991). Evaluation of intrinsic and extrinsic motivation interventions with a self-help smoking cessation program. *Journal of Consulting and Clinical Psychology, 59*, 318–324.

de Bourdeaudhuij, I., Stevens, V., Vandelanotee, C., & Brug, J. (2007). Evaluation of an interactive computer-tailored nutrition intervention in a real-life setting. *Annals of Behavioral Medicine, 33*, 39–48.

de Nooijer, J., Lechner, L., Candel, M., & de Vries, H. (2004). Short-and long-term effects of tailored information versus general information on determinants and intentions related to early detection of cancer. *Preventive Medicine, 38,* 694–703.

Dijkstra, A. (2005). Working mechanisms of computer-tailored health education: Evidence from smoking cessation. *Health Education Quarterly, 20,* 527–539.

Dijkstra, A. (2008). The psychology of tailoring-ingredients in computer-tailored persuasion. *Social and Personality Psychology Compass, 2,* 765–784.

Dijkstra, A., Conijn, B., & de Vries, H. (2006). A match-mismatch test of a stage model of behaviour change in tobacco smoking. *Addiction, 101,* 1035–1043.

Dijkstra, A., & DeVries, H. (1999). The development of computer-generated tailored interventions. *Patient Education and Counseling, 36,* 193–203.

Elder, J. P., Ayala, G. X., Campbell, N. R., Slymen, D., Lopez-Madurga, E. T., & Engelberg, M. (2005). Interpersonal and print nutrition communication for a Spanish-dominant Latino population: Secretos de la beuna vida. *Health Psychology, 24,* 49–57.

Etter, J. F. (2005). Comparing the efficacy of two internet-based, computer-tailored smoking cessation programs: A randomized trial. *Journal of Medical Internet Research, 7,* 1–10.

Evers, K. E., Prochaska, J. O., Van Marter, D. F., Johnson, J. L. & Prochaska, J. M. (2007). Transtheoretical-based bullying prevention effectiveness trials in middle schools and high schools. *Educational Research, 49,* 397–414.

Ezendam, N. P., Oenema, A., van de Looij-Jansen, P. M., & Brug, J. (2007). Design and evaluation protocol of "FATaintPHAT," a computer-tailored intervention to prevent excessive weight gain in adolescents. *BMC Public Health, 7,* 324.

Fishbein, M., & Ajzen, I. (1975). *Belief, attitude, intention and behavior: An introduction to theory and research.* Reading, MA: Addison-Wesley.

Fretheim, A., Oxman, A. D., Havelsrud, K., Treweek, S., Kristoffersen, D. T., & Bjorndal, A. (2006). Rational prescribing in primary care (RaPP): A cluster randomized trial of a tailored intervention. *Plos Medicine, 3,* 783–791.

Friedman, R. H., Kazis, L. E., Jette, A., Smith, M. B., Stollerman, J., Torgerson, J., et al. (1996). A telecommunications system for monitoring and counseling patients with hypertension impact on medication adherence and blood pressure control. *American Journal of Hypertension, 9,* 285–292.

Geller, A. C., Emmons, K. M., Brooks, D. R., Powers, C., Zhang, Z., Koh, H. K., et al. (2006). A randomized trial to improve early detection and prevention practices among siblings of melanoma patients. *Cancer, 107,* 806–814.

Gielen, A. C., McKenzie, L. B., McDonald, E. M., Shields, W. C., Wang, M. C., Cheng, Y. J., et al. (2007). Using a computer kiosk to promote child safety: Results of a randomized, controlled trial in an urban pediatric emergency department. *Pediatrics, 120,* 330–339.

Glasgow, R. E., Nutting, P. A., Toobert, D. J., King, D. K., Strycker, L. A., Jex, M., et al. (2006). Effects of a brief computer-assisted diabetes self-management intervention on dietary, biological and quality-of-life outcomes. *Chronic Illness, 2,* 27–38.

Goldberg, M. E., Fishbein, M., & Middlestadt, S. E. (Eds.). (1997). *Social marketing: Theoretical and practical perspectives.* Mahwah, NJ: Erlbaum.

Grunig, J. (1989). Publics, audiences, and market segments: Segmentation principles for campaigns. In C. Salmon (Ed.), *Information campaigns: Balancing social values and social change* (pp. 199–228). Newbury Park, CA: Sage.

Haerens, L., Deforche, B., Maes, L., Brug, J., Vandelanotte, C., & de Bourdeaudhuij, I. (2007). A computer-tailored dietary fat intake intervention for adolescents: results of a randomized controlled trial. *Annals of Behavioral Medicine, 34,* 253–262.

Haerens, L., Deforche, B., Vandelanotte, C., Maes, L., & DeBourdeaudhuij, I. (2007). Acceptability, feasibility and effectiveness of a computer-tailored physical activity intervention in adolescents. *Patient Education and Counseling, 66,* 303–310.

Halder, A. K., Tiro, J. A., Glassman, B., Rakowski, W., Fernandez, M. E., Perez, C. A., et al. (2008). Lessons learned from developing a tailored print intervention: A guide for practitioners and researchers new to tailoring. *Health Promotion Practice, 9,* 218–288.

Harrington, N. G., Lane, D. R., Donohew, L., & Zimmerman, R. S. (2006). An extension of the activation model of information exposure: The addition of a cognitive variable to a model of attention. *Media Psychology, 8,* 139–164.

Harrington, N. G., Lane, D. R., Donohew, L., Zimmerman, R. S., Norling, G. R., An, J., et al. (2003). Persuasive strategies for effective anti-drug messages. *Communication Monographs, 70,* 16–38.

Hawkins, R. P., Kreuter, M., Resnicow, K., Fishbein, M., & Dijkstra, A. (2008). Understanding tailoring in communicating about health. *Health Education Research, 23,* 454–466.

Heimendinger, J., O'Neill, C., Marcus, A. C., Wolfe, P., Julesberg, K., Morra, M., et al. (2005). Multiple tailored messages are effective in increasing fruit and vegetable consumption among callers to the Cancer Information Service. *Journal of Health Communication, 10,* 65–82.

Hoffman, A. M., Redding, C., Goldberg, D., Anel, D., Prochaska, J. O., Meyer, P. M., et al. (2006). Computer expert systems for African-American smokers in physicians' offices: A feasibility study. *Preventive Medicine, 43,* 204–211.

Hoffmann, T., McKenna, K., Worrall, L., & Read, S. J. (2007). Randomised trial of a computer-generated tailored written education package for patients following stroke. *Age and Ageing, 36,* 280–286.

Hornik, R. C., & Ramirez, A. S. (2006). Racial/ethnic disparities and segmentation in communication campaigns. *American Behavioral Scientist, 49,* 868–884.

Hornikx, J., & O'Keefe, D. J. (this volume). Adapting consumer advertising appeals to cultural values: A meta-analysis review of effects on persuasiveness and ad liking. In C. S. Beck (Ed.), *Communication Yearbook 33* (pp. 39–71). New York: Routledge.

Hyman, H. H., & Sheatsley, P. B. (1947). Some reasons why information campaigns fail. *Public Opinion Quarterly, 11,* 412–423.

Irvine, A. B., Ary, D. V., Grove, D. A., & Gilfillan-Morton, L. (2004). The effectiveness of an interactive multimedia program to influence eating habits. *Health Education Research, 19,* 290–305.

Janz, N. K., & Becker, M. H. (1984). The health belief model: A decade later. *Health Education Quarterly, 11,* 1–47.

Jerant, A., Kravitz, R. L., Rooney, M., Amerson, S., Kreuter, M. & Franks, P. (2007). Effects of a tailored interactive multimedia computer program on determinants of colorectal cancer screening: A randomized controlled pilot study in physician offices. *Patient Education and Counseling, 66,* 67–74.

Joseph, C. L., Peterson, E., Havstad, S., Johnson, C. C., Hoerauf, S., Stringer, S., et al. (2007). A web-based, tailored asthma management program for urban African-

American high school students. *American Journal of Respiratory and Critical Care Medicine, 175,* 888–895.

Kearney, N., Kidd, L., Miller, M., Sage, M., Khorrami, J., McGee, M., et al. (2006). Utilising handheld computers to monitor and support patients receiving chemotherapy: Results of a UK-based feasibility study. *Supportive Care in Cancer, 14,* 742–752.

Kerr, J., & McKenna, J. (2000). A randomized controlled trial of a new tailored walking campaign in an employee sample. *Journal of Health Communication, 5,* 265–279.

Kiene, S. M., & Barta, W. D. (2006). A brief individualized computer-delivered sexual risk reduction intervention increases HIV/AIDS preventive behavior. *Journal of Adolescent Health, 39,* 404–410.

Kreuter, M. W. (2008, March). *Promising new variables for message tailoring in diverse populations.* Paper presented at the 29th annual meeting and scientific sessions of the Society of Behavioral Medicine, San Diego, CA.

Kreuter, M. W., Bull, F. C., Clark, E. M., & Oswald, D. L. (1999). Understanding how people process health information: A comparison of tailored and untailored weight loss materials. *Health Psychology, 18,* 487–494.

Kreuter, M. W., Caburnay, C. A., Chen, J. J., & Donlin, M. J. (2004). Effectiveness of individually tailored calendars in promoting childhood immunization in urban public health centers. *American Journal of Public Health, 94,* 122–127.

Kreuter, M. W., Farrell, D., Olevitch, L., & Brennan, L. (2000). *Tailoring health messages: Customizing communication with computer technology.* Mahwah, NJ: Erlbaum.

Kreuter, M. W., & Holt, C. L. (2001). How do people process health information? Applications in an age of individualized communication. *Current Directions in Psychological Science, 10,* 206–209.

Kreuter, M. W., & Skinner, C. S. (2000). Tailoring: What's in a name? *Health Education Research, 15,* 1–4.

Kreuter, M. W., Skinner, C., S., Holt, C. L., Clark, E. M., Haire-Joshu, D., Fu, Q., et al. (2005). Cultural tailoring for mammography and fruit and vegetable intake among low-income African American women in urban public health centers. *Preventive Medicine, 41,* 53–62.

Kreuter, M. W., Strecher, V. J., & Glassman, B. (1999). One size does not fit all: The case for tailoring print materials. *Annals of Behavioral Medicine, 21,* 276–283.

Kreuter, M. W., & Wray, R. J. (2003). Tailored and targeted health communication: Strategies for enhancing information relevance. *American Journal of Health Behavior, 27,* S227–S232.

Kristal, A. R., Curry, S. J., Shattuck, A. L., Feng, Z., & Li, S. (2000). A randomized trial of a tailored, self-help dietary intervention: The Puget Sound Eating Patterns Study. *Preventive Medicine, 31,* 380–389.

Kroeze, W., Oenema, A., Dagnelie, P. C., & Brug, J. (2008). Examining the minimal required elements of a computer-tailored intervention aimed at dietary fat reduction: Results of a randomized controlled dismantling study. *Health Education Research, 23,* 880–891.

Kroeze, W., Werkman, A., & Brug, J. (2006). A systematic review of randomized trials on the effectiveness of computer-tailored education on physical activity and dietary behaviors. *Annals of Behavioral Medicine, 31,* 205–223.

Latimer, A. E., Salovey, P., & Rothman, A. J. (2007). The effectiveness of gain-framed messages for encouraging disease prevention behavior: Is all hope lost? *Journal of Health Communication, 12,* 645–649.

Latimer, A. E., Williams-Piehota, P., Katulak, N. A., Cox, A., Mowad, L., Higgins, E. T., et al. (2008). Promoting fruit and vegetable intake through messages tailored to individual differences in regulatory focus. *Annals of Behavioral Medicine, 35,* 363–369.

Lewis, E., Mayer, J. A., Belch, G., Engelberg, M., Walker, K., Kwon, H., et al. (2005). Disseminating a sun safety program to zoological parks: The effects of tailoring. *Health Psychology, 24,* 456–462.

Lipkus, I. M., Rimer, B. K., Halabi, S., & Strigo, T. S. (2000). Can tailored interventions increase mammography use in HMO women? *American Journal of Preventive Medicine, 18,* 1–10.

Lorch, E. P., Palmgreen, P., Donohew, L., Helm, D., Baer, S. A., & Dsilva, M. U. (1994). Program context, sensation seeking, and attention to televised anti-drug public service announcements. *Human Communication Research, 20,* 390–412.

Lusk, S. L., Ronis, D. L., Kazanis, A. S., Eakin, B. L., Hong, O., & Raymond, D. M. (2003). Effectiveness of a tailored intervention to increase factory workers' use of hearing protection. *Nursing Research, 52,* 289–295.

Lustria, M. L. A., Cortese, J., Noar, S. M., & Glueckauf, R. (2009). Computer-tailored health interventions delivered over the web: Review and analysis of key components. *Patient Education & Counseling, 74,* 154–173.

Marcus, A. C., Mason, M., Wolfe, P., Rimer, B. K., Lipkus, I., & Stretcher, V., et al. (2005). The efficacy of tailored print materials in promoting colorectal cancer screening: Results form a randomized trial involving callers to the National Cancer Institute's Cancer Information Service. *Journal of Health Communication, 10,* 83–104.

Marcus, B. H., Lewis, B. A., Williams, D. M., Whiteley, J. A., Albrecht, A. E., Jakicic, J. M., et al. (2007). Step into motion: A randomized trial examining the relative efficacy of Internet vs. print-based physical activity interventions. *Contemporary Clinical Trials, 28,* 737–747.

Marcus, B. H., Napolitano, M. A., King, A. C., Lewis, B. A., Whiteley, J. A., Albrecht., A., et al. (2007). Telephone versus print delivery of an individualized motivationally tailored physical activity intervention: Project STRIDE. *Health Psychology, 26,* 401–409.

McBride, C. M., Bastian, L. A., Halabi, S., Fish, L., Lipkus, I. M., Bosworth, H. B., et al. (2002). A tailored intervention to aid decision making about hormone replacement therapy. *American Journal of Public Health, 92,* 1112–1114.

McGuire, W. J. (1989). Theoretical foundations of campaigns. In R. Rice & C. Atkin (Eds.), *Public Communication Campaigns* (pp. 43–65). Newbury Park, CA: Sage.

Mendelsohn, H. (1973). Some reasons why information campaigns can succeed. *Public Opinion Quarterly, 37,* 50–61.

Meyer, C., Ulbricht, S., Baumeister, S. E., Schumann, A., Ruge, J., Bischof, G., et al. (2007). Proactive interventions for smoking cessation in general medical practice: A quasi-randomized controlled trial to examine the efficacy of computer-tailored letters and physician-delivered brief advice. *Addiction, 103,* 294–304.

Myers, R. E., Chodak, G. W., Wolf, T. A., Burgh, D. Y., McGrory, G. T., Marcus, S. M., et al. (1999). Adherence by African American men to prostate cancer education and early detection. *Cancer, 86,* 88–104.

Nansel, T. R., Weaver, N., Donlin, M., Jacobsen, H., Kreuter, M. W., & Simons-Morton,

B. (2002). Baby, be safe: The effect of tailored communications for pediatric injury prevention provided in a primary care setting. *Patient Education and Counseling, 46,* 175–190.

Neuhauser, L., & Kreps, G. L. (2003). Rethinking communication in the e-health area. *Journal of Health Psychology, 8,* 7–22.

Neumann, T., Neuner, B., Weiss-Gerlach, E., Psych, D., Tonnesen, H., Gentilello, L. M., et al. (2005). The effect of computerized tailored brief advice on at-risk drinking in subcritically injured trauma patients. *The Journal of Trauma Injury, Infection, and Critical Care, 61,* 805–814.

Noar, S. M. (2005–2006). A health educator's guide to theories of health behavior. *International Quarterly of Community Health Education, 24,* 75–92.

Noar, S. M. (2006a). A 10-year retrospective of research in health mass media campaigns: Where do we go from here? *Journal of Health Communication, 11,* 21–42.

Noar, S. M. (2006b). In pursuit of cumulative knowledge in health communication: The role of meta-analysis. *Health Communication, 20,* 169–175.

Noar, S. M., Benac, C., & Harris, M. (2007). Does tailoring matter? Meta-analytic review of tailored print health behavior change interventions. *Psychological Bulletin, 133,* 673–693.

Noar, S. M., Clark, A., Cole, C., & Lustria, M. (2006). Review of interactive safer sex websites: Practice and potential. *Health Communication, 20,* 233–241.

Noar, S. M., & Zimmerman, R. S. (2005). Health behavior theory and cumulative knowledge regarding health behaviors: Are we moving in the right direction? *Health Education Research: Theory & Practice, 20,* 275–290.

O'Keefe, D. J., & Jensen, J. D. (2006). The advantages of compliance or the disadvantages of non-compliance? A meta-analytic review of the relative persuasive effectiveness of gain-framed and loss-framed messages. In C. S. Beck (Ed.), *Communication yearbook 30* (pp. 1–43). Mahwah, NJ: Erlbaum.

Palmgreen, P., & Donohew, L. (2003). Effective mass media strategies for drug abuse prevention campaigns. In Z. Slobada & W. J. Bukoski (Eds.), *Handbook of drug abuse prevention: Theory, science, and practice* (pp. 27–43). New York: Kluwer Academic/Plenum.

Palmgreen, P., Donohew, L., Lorch, E. P., Rogus, M., Helm, D., & Grant, N. E. (1991). Sensation seeking, message sensation value, and drug use as mediators of PSA effectiveness. *Health Communication, 3,* 217–227.

Palmgreen, P., Lorch, E. P., Donohew, L., Harrington, N. G., Dsilva, M., & Helm, D. (1995). Reaching at-risk populations in a mass media drug abuse prevention campaign: Sensation seeking as a targeting variable. *Drugs and Society, 8,* 29–45

Petty, R. E., & Cacioppo, J. T. (1981). *Attitudes and persuasion: Classic and contemporary approaches.* Dubuque, IA: Brown.

Portnoy, D. B., Scott-Sheldon, L. A. J., Johnson, B. T., & Carey, M. P. (2008). Computer-delivered interventions for health promotion and behavioral risk reduction: A meta-analysis of 75 randomized controlled trials, 1988–2007. *Preventive Medicine, 47,* 3–16.

Prochaska, J. O., Butterworth, S., Redding, C. A., Burden, V., Perrin, N., Leo, M., et al. (2008). Initial efficacy of MI, TTM tailoring and HRI's with multiple behaviors for employee health promotion. *Preventive Medicine, 46,* 226–231.

Prochaska, J. O., & DiClemente, C. C. (1983). Stages and processes of self-change of smoking: Toward an integrative model of change. *Journal of Consulting and Clinical Psychology, 51,* 390–395.

Prochaska, J. O., DiClemente, C. C., & Norcross, J. C. (1992). In search of how people change: Applications to addictive behaviors. *American Psychologist, 47,* 1102–1114.

Prochaska, J. O., DiClemente, C. C., Velicer, W. F., & Rossi, J. S. (1993). Standardized, individualized, interactive and personalized self-help programs for smoking cessation. *Health Psychology, 12,* 399–405.

Prochaska, J. O., Velicer, W. F., Fava, J. L., Ruggiero, L., Laforge, R. G., Rossi, J. S., et al. (2001). Counselor and stimulus control enhancements of a stage-matched expert system intervention for smokers in a managed care setting. *Preventive Medicine, 32,* 23–32.

Prochaska, J. O., Velicer, W. F., Redding, C., Rossi, J. S., Goldstein, M., DePue, J., et al. (2005). Stage-based expert systems to guide a population of primary care patients to quit smoking, eat healthier, prevent skin cancer, and receive regular mammograms. *Preventive Medicine, 41,* 406–416.

Rakowski, W. (1999). The potential variances of tailoring in health behavior interventions. *Annals of Behavioral Medicine, 21,* 284–289.

Resnicow, K., Davis, R. E., Zhang, G., Konkel, J., Strecher, V. J., Shaikh, A. R., et al. (2008). Tailoring a fruit and vegetable intervention on novel motivational constructs: Results of a randomized study. *Annals of Behavioral Medicine, 35,* 159–169.

Revere, D., & Dunbar, P. J. (2001). Review of computer-generated outpatient health behavior interventions: Clinical encounters "in absentia." *Journal of the American Medical Informatics Association, 8,* 62–79.

Richards, K. C., Enderlin, C. A., Beck, C., McSweeney, J. C., Jones, T. C., & Roberson, P. K. (2007). Tailored biobehavioral interventions: A literature review and synthesis.*Research and Theory for Nursing Practice, 21,* 271–285.

Rimal, R. N., & Adkins, A. D. (2003). Using computers to narrowcast health messages: The role of audience segmentation, targeting, and tailoring in health promotion. In T. L. Thompson, A. M. Dorsey, K. I. Miller, & R. Parrott (Eds.), *Handbook of health communication* (pp. 497–513). Mahwah, NJ: Erlbaum.

Rimal, R. N., & Real, K. (2003). Perceived risk and efficacy beliefs as motivators of change: Use of the risk perception attitude (RPA) framework to understand health behaviors. *Human Communication Research, 29,* 370–399.

Rimer, B. K., Conaway, M., Lyna, P., Classman, B., Yarnall, K. S. H., Lipkus, I., et al. (1999). The impact of tailored interventions on a community health center population. *Patient Education and Counseling, 37,* 125–140.

Rimer, B. K., & Glassman, B. (1998). Tailoring communications for primary care settings. *Methods of Information in Medicine, 37,* 171–180.

Rimer, B. K., & Glassman, B. (1999). Is there a use for tailored print communications in cancer risk communication? *Journal of the National Cancer Institute Monographs, 25,* 140–148.

Rimer, B. K., & Kreuter, M. W. (2006). Advancing tailored health communication: A persuasion and message effects perspective. *Journal of Communication, 56,* S184–S201.

Roberto, A. J., Raup-Krieger, J. L., & Beam, M. A. (2008, May). *The effects of targeting and tailoring on the effectiveness of prevention messages for Hispanics.* Paper presented at the annual meeting of the International Communication Association, Montreal, Canada.

Roberto, A. J., Zimmerman, R. S., Carlyle, K. E., Abner, E. L., Cupp, P. K., & Hansen,

G. L. (2007). The effects of a computer-based pregnancy, STD, and HIV prevention intervention: A nine-school trial. *Health Communication, 21,* 115–124.

Rogers, E. M., & Storey, J. D. (1987). Communication campaigns. In C. R. Berger & S. H. Chafee (Eds.), *Handbook of communication science* (pp. 817–846). London: Sage.

Rose, D. K., Cohen, M. M., & Yee, D. A. (1997). Changing the practice of pain management. *Regional Anesthesia and Pain Management, 84,* 764–72.

Ruiter, R. A. C., Kessels, L. T. E., Jansma, B. M., & Brug, J. (2006). Increased attention for computer-tailored health communications: An event-related potential study. *Health Psychology, 25,* 300–306.

Salmon, C. T., & Atkin, C. (2003). Using media campaigns for health promotion. In T. L. Thompson, A. M. Dorsey, K. I. Miller, & R. Parrott (Eds.), *Handbook of health communication* (pp. 285–313). Mahwah, NJ: Erlbaum.

Scholes, D., McBride, C. M., Grothaus, L., Civic, D., Ichikawa, L. E., Fish, L. J., et al. (2003). A tailored minimal self-help intervention to promote condom use in young women: Results from a randomized trial. *AIDS, 17,* 1547–1556.

Shirazi, K. K., Wallace, L. M., Niknami, S., Hidarnia, A., Torkaman, G., Gilchrist, M., et al. (2007). A home-based, transtheoretical change model designed strength training intervention to increase exercise to prevent osteoporosis in Iranian women aged 40–65 years: A randomized controlled trial. *Health Education Research, 22,* 305–317.

Simon-Arndt, C. M., Hurtado, S. L., & Patriarca-Troyk, L. A. (2006). Acceptance of web-based personalized feedback: User ratings of an alcohol misuse prevention program targeting U.S. Marines. *Health Communication, 20,* 13–22.

Skinner, C. S., Campbell, M. K., Rimer, B. K., Curry, S., & Prochaska, J. O. (1999). How effective is tailored print communication? *Annals of Behavioral Medicine, 21,* 290–298.

Skinner, C. S., Schildkraut, J. M., Berry, D., Calingaert, B., Marcom, P. K., Sugarman, J., et al. (2002). Pre-counseling education materials for BRCA testing: Does tailoring make a difference? *Genetic Testing, 6,* 93–105.

Skinner, C. S., Strecher, V. J., & Hospers, H. (1994). Physicians' recommendations for mammography: Do tailored messages make a difference? *American Journal of Public Health, 84,* 43–49.

Skubisz, C., Reimer, T., & Hoffrage, U. (this volume). Communicating quatitative risk information. In C. S. Beck (Ed.), *Communication Yearbook 33* (pp. 177–211). New York: Routledge.

Slater, M. D. (1995). Choosing audience segmentation strategies and methods for health communication. In E. Maibach & R. L. Parrot (Eds.), *Designing health messages: Approaches from communication theory and public health practice* (pp. 186–198). Thousand Oaks, CA: Sage.

Slater, M. D. (1996). Theory and method in health audience segmentation. *Journal of Health Communication, 1,* 267–283.

Slater, M. D. (2006). Specification and misspecification of theoretical foundations and logic models for health communication campaigns. *Health Communication, 20,* 149–157.

Snyder, L. B., Li, S., Huedo-Medina, T. B., Noar, S. M., Kotz, J., D'Alessandro, N., et al. (2008, August). *Tailored interventions are more effective than traditional interventions over time: A meta-analysis.* Paper presented at the annual National Conference on Health Communication, Marketing, and Media, Atlanta, GA.

Sohl, S. J., & Moyer, A. (2007). Tailored interventions to promote mammography screening: A meta-analytic review. *Preventive Medicine, 45*, 252–261.

Spittaels, H., De Bourdeaudhuij, I., Brug, J., & Vandelanotte, C. (2007). Effectiveness of an online computer-tailored physical activity intervention in a real-life setting. *Health Education Research, 22*, 385–396.

Spitzberg, B. H., & Cupach, W. R. (1984). *Interpersonal communication competence.* Beverly Hills, CA: Sage.

Strecher, V. J. (1999). Computer-tailored smoking cessation materials: A review and discussion. *Patient Education and Counseling, 36*, 107–117.

Strecher, V. J., Kreuter, M., Den Boer, D. J., Kobrin, S., Hospers, H. J., & Skinner, C. S. (1994). The effects of computer-tailored smoking cessation messages in family practice settings. *The Journal of Family Practice, 39*, 262–268.

Strecher, V. J., McClure, J. B., Alexander, G. L., Chakraborty, B., Nair, V. N., Konkel, J. M., et al. (2008). Web-based smoking-cessation programs: results of a randomized trial. *American Journal of Preventive Medicine, 34*, 373–381.

Suggs, L. S. (2006). A 10-year retrospective of research in new technologies for health communication. *Journal of Health Communication, 11*, 61–74.

Sutton, S., & Gilbert, H. (2007). Effectiveness of individually tailored smoking cessation advice letters as an adjunct to telephone counseling and generic self-help materials: Randomized controlled trial. *Addiction, 102*, 994–1000.

Tate, D. F., Jackvony, E. H., & Wing, R. R. (2006). A randomized trial comparing human e-mail counseling, computer-automated tailored counseling, and no counseling in an Internet weight loss program. *Archives of Internal Medicine, 166*, 1620–1625.

Velicer, W. F., & Prochaska, J. O. (1999). An expert system intervention for smoking cessation. *Patient Education and Counseling, 36*, 119–129.

Velicer, W. F., Prochaska, J. O., Bellis, J. M., DiClemente, C. C., Rossi, J. S., Fava, J. L., et al. (1993). An expert system intervention for smoking cessation. *Addictive Behaviors, 13*, 269–290.

Velicer, W. F., Prochaska, J. O., & Redding, C. A. (2006). Tailored communications for smoking cessation: Past successes and future directions. *Drug and Alcohol Review, 25*, 49–57.

Vernon, S. W., del Junco, D. J., Tiro, J. A., Coan, S. P., Perz, C. A., Bastian, L. A., et al. (2008). Promoting regular mammography screening II. Results from a randomized controlled trial in US women veterans. *Journal of the National Cancer Institute, 100*, 347–358.

Walters, S. T., Wright, J. A., & Shegog, R. (2006). A review of computer and Internet-based interventions for smoking behavior. *Addictive Behaviors, 31*, 264–277.

Webb, M. S., Hendricks, P. S., & Brandon, T. H. (2007). Expectancy priming of smoking cessation messages enhances the placebo effect of tailored interventions. *Health Psychology, 26*, 598–609.

Webb, M. S., Simmons, V. N., & Brandon, T. H. (2005). Tailoring interventions for motivating smoking cessation: Using placebo tailoring to examine the influence of expectancies and personalization. *Health Psychology, 24*, 179–188.

Weitzel, J. A., Bernhardt, J. M., Usdan, S., Mays, D., Glanz, K. (2007), Using wireless handheld computers and tailored text messaging to reduce negative consequence of drinking alcohol. *Journal of Studies on Alcohol and Drugs, 68*, 534–537.

Werch, C., Jobli, E., Moore, M. J., DiClemente, C. C., Dore, H., & Brown, C. H. (2005).

A brief experimental alcohol beverage-tailored program for adolescents. *Journal of Studies on Alcohol, 66,* 284–290.

Witte, K. (1992). Putting the fear back into fear appeals: The extended parallel process model. *Communication Monographs, 59,* 329–349.

Wolde, G. B. T., Dijkstra, A., van Empelen, P., van den Hout, W., Neven, A. K., & Zitman, F. (2008). Long-term effectiveness of computer-generated tailored patient education on benzodiazepines: A randomized controlled trial. *Addiction, 103,* 662–670.

Woolf, S. H., Krist, A. H., Johnson, R. E., Wilson, D. B., Rothemich, S. F., Norman, G. J., et al. (2006). "A practice-sponsored web site to help patients pursue healthy behaviors: An ACORN study": Corrections. *Annals of Family Medicine, 4,* 148–152.

Yardley, L., & Nyman, S. R. (2007). Internet provision of tailored advice on falls prevention activities for older people: A randomized controlled evaluation. *Health Promotion International, 22,* 122–128.

# CHAPTER CONTENTS

# 4  An Integrated Model of Knowledge Sharing in Contemporary Communication Environments

*Marni Heinz*
Information Systems Project Manager, Google

*Ronald E. Rice*
University of California, Santa Barbara

Why do people share (or withhold) knowledge through online public knowledge management systems (KMS)? What benefits and costs might they experience from doing so? How does one's ability to cognitively integrate the knowledge shared through a KMS affect these costs and benefits? Sharing knowledge, both contributing and collecting, requires active communication and engagement with others; involves complex issues about knowledge, governance structures and public goods, and individual and collective costs and benefits, and is increasingly done through online public knowledge management systems. An interdisciplinary review of these issues leads to an integrated model of individual and collective influences on knowledge sharing behavior through, and use of, knowledge management systems. Primary contributions of the model include the role of cognitive integration in mediating between a knowledge management system's use and resulting costs and benefits, and the notion that such costs and benefits can occur at both the individual and collective level.

K nowledge management, and specifically knowledge sharing, constitutes an important topic of scholarly inquiry and organizational practice. The purpose of knowledge management is to enhance organizational performance by explicitly designing and implementing tools, processes, systems, structures, and cultures to improve the creation, storage, search, retrieval, sharing, re-use, and value of all three types of knowledge (human, social and structured) that are critical for decision making (Alavi & Leidner, 2001; De Long & Fahey, 2000). Knowledge management, in general, comprises both a process and a perspective, one that understands both the cognitive and the social nature of knowledge.

Knowledge management systems (KMS) are social systems, often supported by technology, used for knowledge sharing purposes. They do not have to involve information and communication technologies (ICTs) (consider the

Correspondence: e-mail: rrice@comm.ucsb.edu

office bulletin board or even the familiar water cooler). However, this review presumes that a KMS uses ICTs to support knowledge management processes—most simply, the creation, storage, transfer, and application of knowledge (Alavi & Leidner, 2001, p. 107). Specific types of ICT-enabled KMS include content management tools, knowledge sharing tools, and knowledge search and retrieval systems (see Benbya, Passiante, & Belbaly, 2004, who provided case studies of eight major corporate ICT-enabled KMS and how those support knowledge generation, storage, distribution, and use). An ICT-enabled KMS may emphasize documents, terms, and fields associated with those documents, an internally generated representation of the content or concepts, directories of projects and people, diagrams of relationships within and among experts and information, or social networking features to foster user-generated relationships and interpretations such as collaborative filtering and recommending. Further, with intranets, the Internet, and new multi-media systems, analysis and application of knowledge sharing now extends well beyond the traditional organization with generally clear boundaries and membership. Information communication technologies have been proposed, designed, and implemented to foster intra-, inter-, and extra-organizational knowledge sharing (Maier, 2007; Tapscott & Williams, 2006). So this review also presumes the KMS is online and public.

With the continuing developing of Internet-based information and communication technologies, analysis and application of knowledge sharing now extends well beyond present discussions of the traditional organization with generally clear boundaries and membership. Yet, while ICTs have been proposed to enable knowledge sharing, many studies have identified challenges and disadvantages to their successful use for this purpose (see "Knowledge Sharing through Information and Communication Technologies" below). The primary focus of this review, then, is to integrate prior theory and research to develop a model of the influences on and outcomes of knowledge sharing through knowledge management systems in contemporary communication environments, primarily organizational and professional members that participate in *networks of practice*. Thus, in this review, we ask: Why do people share (or withhold) knowledge through online public knowledge management systems? What benefits and costs might they experience from doing so? How does one's ability to cognitively integrate the knowledge shared through a KMS affect these costs and benefits?

Research in this area would seem to provide relevant opportunities for and challenges to, as well as requiring participation from, a wide range of expertise from the communication discipline (see also "Proposed Theoretical Model and Future Research" below). The most obvious areas include organizational communication, and ICTs/new media. The traditional bureaucratic organizational structure, designed to control the flow of information and centralize knowledge, is inappropriate and ineffective in rapidly changing environments, where members must share perceptions and knowledge within and across organizational boundaries (Taylor & van Every, 1993). Rather than being embodied in formal structures and buildings, organizations are constituted through this communication, knowledge sharing, and sense-making (Taylor & van Every, 2000; Weick, 1995). Information communication technologies both facilitate as well as embody collaboration and knowledge sharing across time, space, social groups, media and knowledge domains, giving rise to virtual teams, social media, ad hoc and mediated networks, and new organizational forms (Benkler, 2006; Gibbs, Nekrassova, Grushina, & Adbul Wahab, 2008; Rice & Gattiker, 2001; Shirky, 2008; Tapscott & Williams, 2006).

## Knowledge and Knowledge Processes

Knowledge is a key driver to sustaining a competitive advantage in today's global economy (Earl & Scott, 1999; Reagans & McEvily, 2003). Knowledge is a primary component of both the inputs (labor) and outputs (goods and services) of production (Grant, 1996).

### Aspects of Knowledge

Familiar concepts such as *knowledge-intensive firm* (Starbuck, 1992), *knowledge society* (Drucker, 1969), *knowledge-based economy* (Adler, 2001), and *knowledge worker* (Due, 1995) reflect the central role of knowledge in the United States and other societies (Jussawalla, Lamberton, & Karunaratne, 1988). Creating, accessing, and sharing knowledge are central to the growth of knowledge based economies and increased employment, health, and well-being of populations in developing countries (Dolfsma, 2006; Rodrigues, 2003; UNESCO, 2005; see also Harris, 2001, for the intellectual origins of the knowledge-based economy as well as the internationalization of knowledge). Theories of production and economies since Adam Smith (1776/1904) have noted the crucial role of knowledge as industrial and societal inputs, processes, and outputs, particularly in affecting market equilibrium in the form of prices, including through information asymmetries, the costs of obtaining information, and imperfect or incomplete information. Endogenous/new growth theory in economics, and, later, resource-based organizational theory, recognized society's ability to use knowledge to generate continuing technological improvements and ongoing returns of knowledge products at low marginal cost, and organizations' ability to develop first-mover advantages, non-substitutable internal competencies, innovativeness and competitive advantages through creating, sharing, and re-using knowledge (Martin, 2008).

Of course, knowledge sharing is much easier recommended than achieved. A survey of knowledge management (KM) projects in 431 U.S. and European organizations found that slightly over half (54%) reported that one of the most notable difficulties in running a successful KM initiative is motivating individuals to change their current behavior (Ruggles, 1998). According to Martin (2008, p. 391), "Extensive knowledge sharing within organizations still appears to be the exception rather than the rule." Even sharing information about, and even more so the implementation of, best practices—what might be expected to seem highly valued by potential adopters—face considerable barriers. Such obstacles can encompass the organizational context (institutional and organizational environment, absorptive capacity, competency traps, identity, culture, and size), the diffusion process (stages of diffusion, attributes of the innovation, the recipient, and the knowledge to be transferred, and the state of relationship between the source of knowledge and the receiving unit), and management-related barriers (the level of managerial commitment and the appropriateness of training and reward systems) (Simard & Rice, 2007). A wide variety of disjunctures between contextual elements and a KMS may inhibit knowledge sharing, such as where incentives to share are limited, where collaboration challenges traditional power structures, where mediated interactions are insufficient to develop trust, or where content, technology, or access are problematic (Barrett, Cappleman, Shoib, & Waltham, 2004). Thus, understanding the range and level of potential influences on how information and communication technologies might be used to foster knowledge sharing, which may lead to both positive and negative outcomes at both the individual and collective level, is a crucial challenge to organizational researchers and practitioners alike.

One of the critical goals of managing knowledge in organizations as well as in other communities and groups involves enabling and motivating members to provide, gain access to, and share each other's knowledge. To be useful, this knowledge must be provided in a form and context useful to others. On the one hand, communicators could simply strive to make very explicit information available, perhaps accompanied by explanations and procedures. More significantly, other cases entail revealing one's personal understanding and knowledge to others in that explicit form; that is, sharing tacit knowledge as explicit knowledge.

*Explicit* knowledge (or "know what") is knowledge that can be codified (Nonaka, 1994; Nonaka & Takeuchi, 1995), easy to imitate (Alavi & Leidner, 2001; Argote & Ingram, 2000), and transferred at low or zero marginal cost (Roberts, 2000). It is embodied in symbols (documents, drawings, manuals, reports), artifacts (machines, tools), or routines (Rice, 2008; Roberts, 2000). *Tacit* knowledge (or "know how") encompasses knowledge that is deeply embedded in human activity and experience (Nonaka, 1994), and difficult to replicate and transfer (Alavi & Leidner, 2001). We can further conceptualize tacit knowledge as including *cognitive knowledge*, consisting of mental models and beliefs, and *technical knowledge*, or skills and crafts (Nonaka, 1994; Nonaka & Takeuchi, 1995).

A significant debate has emerged on the tacit-explicit distinction, centering on whether or not tacit knowledge can be transformed into explicit knowledge (Flanagin, 2002). Additionally, some question whether the two comprise truly dichotomous states of knowledge (Roberts, 2000). Rather, tacit and explicit knowledge may be mutually reinforcing and constitutive dimensions of knowledge (Hislop, 2002; Polanyi, 1966; Schultze, 2000). Indeed, people need tacit knowledge in order to apply explicit knowledge in a meaningful way (Alavi & Leidner, 2001; Wenger, McDermott, & Snyder, 2002). Experience, reflection, and the interpretation of context interact with information to create knowledge (Davenport, De Long, & Beers, 1998). Both organizations and individuals are constrained by their *absorptive capacity*, or the ability to process new knowledge as a function of an existing knowledge base (W. M. Cohen & Levinthal, 1990). Conversely, data and information can add value to knowledge and open up new possibilities for innovation (Grover & Davenport, 2001). Starbuck (1992) observed that even experts in knowledge intensive firms enhance their tacit knowledge through the application of explicit knowledge. Experts in many fields learn not only by doing, but also through courses and books (Davenport & Prusak, 1998).

Many scholars suggest that knowledge resides at the individual level of cognition (Grover & Davenport, 2001; Simon, 1991). However, Nonaka and Takeuchi's (1995) socialization, externalization, combination, and internalization model of organizational knowledge creation proposes that knowledge initially resides in the minds of individuals while spiraling outward through social interactions to form the bases of knowledge at the organizational level. Social participation with others gives meaning to our experiences, and it functions as the foundation from which interactants create and share new knowledge (Alavi & Leidner, 2001; Brown & Duguid, 2000; Nonaka, 1994; Nonaka & Takeuchi, 1995; Roberts, 2000; Vera & Crossan, 2003; Wenger, 1998; Wenger et al., 2002). Others favor a conceptualization of knowledge as residing in organizations (Levitt & March, 1988), a community of practice (CoP), a network of practice (NoP), or, more generally, social networks (Brown & Duguid, 2000; Contractor & Monge, 2002; Iverson & McPhee, 2002; McDermott, 1999; Rice, 1982; Rice, Collins-Jarvis, & Zydney-Walker, 1999; Wenger, 1998; Wenger et al., 2002). Some have argued for a framework that takes both perspectives into account, while drawing attention to the social character of collective knowledge (Alavi & Leidner, 2001). Others have asserted that the location or sources of knowledge extend even to physical structures, technologies, processes, and routines (Argote & Ingram, 2000; Grover & Davenport, 2001; Rice & Gattiker, 2000).

### Managing Knowledge through Knowledge Processes

The processes of creating, transferring, and applying knowledge underlie many discussions of organizational knowledge and subsequent value creation.

Knowledge *creation* or generation encapsulates the development of new organizational capabilities or innovations. Knowledge *transfer* entails the exchange of knowledge from one location/person/organization to another where it is needed and applied. It usually indicates providing knowledge to, or obtaining knowledge from, one or more others, often mediated by technology.

If scholars describe knowledge as an economic transaction that occurs through knowledge markets, they tend to use knowledge *exchange* as the dominant term (Davenport & Prusak, 1998; Nahapiet & Ghoshal, 1998). Knowledge *sharing* emphasizes the socially embedded nature of knowledge and the existence of reciprocity, trust, and an underlying relationship in the exchange (Van den Hooff, Elving, Meeuwsen, & Dumoulini, 2003). Indeed, when expertise is widely distributed in an organization, knowledge sharing becomes a necessary prerequisite for the creation of firm-wide intellectual capital (Huysman & de Wit, 2003; Nonaka, Noboru, & Toyama, 2001) and subsequent value creation (Kogut & Zander, 1992; Moran & Ghoshal, 1996; Nahapiet & Ghoshal, 1998; Tsai & Ghoshal, 1998). This perspective stems from the knowledge-based view of the firm, which treats knowledge as a strategic resource (Grant, 1996). Knowledge *reuse* underscores the possible multiple uses of the same knowledge when shared among multiple people across time (Markus, 2001). Finally, knowledge *application* focuses on the productive use of knowledge for decision-making and problem-solving purposes (Alavi & Leidner, 2001; Alavi & Tiwana, 2003; also utilization, Easterby-Smith & Lyles, 2003). Benbya et al. (2004) provided a nice summary of how various researchers label each phase of the overall knowledge process.

Sharing knowledge entails both *contributing* and *collecting*. Indeed, a willingness, eagerness, or ability to both collect and contribute knowledge underlies the act of knowledge sharing (Jarvenpaa & Staples, 2000; Kalman, Monge, Fulk, & Heino, 2002; Van den Hooff, De Ridder, & Aukema, 2004). Both contributing and collecting knowledge may be highly active processes (Van den Hooff & De Leeuw van Weenen, 2004). For example, many computer bulletin boards or discussion lists are commonly used to post a question or ask for help or advice—an active role oriented toward collecting (Ridings, Gefen, & Arinze, 2002). Thus, knowledge retrieval entails more than just a one-way interaction between contributor and retriever, and it opens up the possibility of a collector-contributor-collector interaction cycle. Knowledge contributing and collecting behaviors can occur as a person-to-person, generalized other-to-person, or person-to-generalized other interaction (see "Collective and Individual Level Influences, Knowledge Sharing Processes, and their Outcomes," which returns to this theme).

Especially in online and public contexts, knowledge sharing comprises essentially a voluntary activity, even under conditions of cooperative mechanisms that might be instituted by an organization (Davenport, 1997; Wenger et al., 2002). Enforcing rules or formalized processes as part of a KM strategy can actually hinder knowledge sharing (Hinds & Pfeffer, 2003). Indeed, when comparing the behavior of voluntary and required online groups, Finholt and Sproull (1990) found that individuals in discretionary groups displayed a greater rate of participation than individuals whose membership in a particular online group was enforced by their employer. Paradoxically, introducing incentives or rewards to encourage cooperative behavior can have the adverse effect of producing a high volume of low quality knowledge contributions (Cabrera

& Cabrera, 2002; Fulk, Flanagin, Kalman, Monge, & Ryan, 1996). For example, while economic incentives did predict increased provision of answers by researchers on Google's Answer Web site, social incentives (comments and ratings) generated greater ongoing (persistent) provision and even higher average gains (Raban, 2008). So mixed incentives seem to generate greater social capital and more information exchanges, in at least this kind of KM site. However, metaknowledge about the importance of one's knowledge for other group members can enhance the quality of contributions to a discretionary database, particularly in combination with a reward system that encourages high quality contributions (Cress, Kimmerle, & Hesse, 2006).

Central to knowledge sharing is a dilemma inherent in theories of public goods (Dawes, 1980). Typically, individuals' incentive structures favor withholding private resources (in this case, knowledge) over contributing these resources for the creation of a public good, which may involve immediate costs but is unlikely to generate a direct, immediate reward to the individual provider. Individuals not only tend to withhold contributions, they also tend to *free ride* off the contributions of others by consuming a collective good to which they did not contribute. Yet, if everyone behaves in this same manner, then they never produce, and everyone is worse off than they would have been otherwise. Dawes referred to this problem as a *social dilemma*, or any situation in which the interests of the collective are pitted against the interests of the individual (see also Liebrand, Messick, & Wilke, 1992). More general concepts of over-consumption of a public good include *social loafing* in group contexts (Latane, Williams, & Harkins, 1979), and *the tragedy of the commons* (Hardin, 1982), such as traffic jams and global warming.

These issues arise from two unique characteristics of public goods: nonexcludability and jointness of supply. Individuals cannot be excluded from consuming a public good, and an individual's consumption of the good does not diminish the amount available to others (in the above examples, this is true only up to a certain level) (Hardin, 1982; Marwell & Oliver, 1993). These characteristics are especially salient for information goods as the material costs of access and distribution approach zero and as social members may easily use (and redistribute) without contributing. In the case of knowledge sharing, a collective knowledge base is the public good (Nahapiet & Ghoshal, 1998; Van den Hooff & De Leeuw van Weenen, 2004; Van den Hooff et al., 2004; Wasko & Faraj, 2000). An undersupply of knowledge sharing among individuals is the public goods problem that must be resolved (Cabrera & Cabrera, 2002; Connolly & Thorn, 1990).

Collective action provides the means by which members produce a public good. Collective action theories assert that individual motivations to contribute or not depend to some extent on the extent to which the good has already been produced at any given point in time (Fulk et al., 1996; Hardin, 1982). Collective action becomes sustainable once a sufficient number of participants, or *critical mass*, contributes (Markus, 1990; Rogers, 2003). However, situations do arise in which a small number of resource-rich individuals can contribute a sufficient number of resources to secure the good for others (Oliver, Marwell, & Teixeira, 1985). Indeed, according to Markus, the first adopters must have quite different resources and interests than later users, or they would have no reason or ability to be an early adopter, and the system would never be used. The *production function* of collective action can be either decelerating or accelerating. In situations of knowledge sharing, the production function is typically accelerating, such that later contributions produce progressively greater rewards for both individuals and the collective—than do initial contributions (Markus, 1990; Monge et al., 1998). It may also be a *reciprocal production function*, where contributions of both early and later users benefit each other.

These functions relate to *network externalities*. The core premise behind network externalities is that interactions among actors, or systems that promote such interactions, can positively or negatively affect others in the social or technical system (Shapiro & Varian, 1999). For example, in one organization, the use of a new desktop video system led to an increase in interrupted meetings—a negative externality—as well as the ability to generate greater awareness through the research group of others' interests and expertise—a positive externality (Kraut, Rice, Cool, & Fish, 1998).

Thus, both short-term and long-term benefits and costs may accrue at both the individual and collective level. Economic problems underlying valuing, generating, and sharing information, for both individual and public benefit, have been well described by information economists (e.g., Arrow, 1984; Lamberton, 1971; Marschak, 1964; Stigler, 1961). Other theoretical approaches to understanding motivations for and rewards of knowledge sharing include economic exchange theory, social exchange theory, and social cognitive theory (Bandura, 1986; Bock & Kim, 2002; Cook, 1987; Homans, 1958).

### Organizations and Networks as Knowledge Governance Structures

Both the process of sharing knowledge and the technological components that accompany most KM initiatives are deeply embedded in their social contexts (groups, organizations, networks, culture, nation). These contexts involve social interactions that foster or constrain learning among their members (Granovetter, 1985). Kogut and Zander (1992) described formal organizations as superior to markets for knowledge transactions because they function as social communities that are upheld by cooperative organizing principles.

However, other forms, neither formal organizations nor markets, may better foster knowledge sharing, especially in contemporary communication environments. The efficiency of the vertically integrated firm, in terms of asset specialization of repeat transactions, no longer offers an optimal governance structure in the marketplace when viewing efficiency from a knowledge perspective (Adler, 2001; Hedlund, 1994; Shirky, 2008). A logic of network forms is a more appropriate conceptualization of transactions that depends highly on idiosyncratic, complex, and dynamic exchanges in mediated environments that significantly reduce transaction costs (Powell, 1990).

Two conceptual subsets of the network perspective—*communities of practice* (CoPs) and *networks of practice* (NoPs)—have been proposed as ideal social contexts for learning and knowledge sharing, offering advantages above and beyond those afforded by an organizational perspective. Huysman and deWit (2003) asserted that networks in general are ideal for knowledge sharing in cases where members struggle to determine available and necessary knowledge. Networks facilitate or constrain access to collective action, trust, and tacit knowledge (Martin, 2008). Communities and networks of practice comprise social processes designed to increase this access for and by its members (though they do not always achieve this in practice).

CoPs and NoPs represent unique types of networks in which a shared practice or common set of concerns binds members together (Brown & Duguid, 2000). Wenger et al. conceptualized practice as "a set of frameworks, ideas, tools, information, styles, language, stories, and documents that community [or network] members share" (2002, p. 29). Practice rests upon a baseline of tacit knowledge shared by all members of a CoP/NoP, but it is embodied in, and arises from, a mutually reinforcing relationship between tacit and explicit forms of participation (Wenger, 1998). Yet, it is also defined by the relations, unspoken norms, implicit rules, underlying assumptions, and shared understandings that may never be formalized, but nonetheless defining characteristics of membership in a CoP/NoP. The combination of a community/network and a shared practice lends credence to the argument that CoPs/NoPs are more effective for knowledge transactions than networks alone, especially for more voluntary forms of knowledge sharing.

A number of attributes blur the boundaries between CoPs and NoPs, while other attributes differentiate them. Membership in both CoPs and NoPs is voluntary, producing emergent organizing structures, although certain measures can be taken to foster their development (Brown & Duguid, 2000; Nonaka et al., 2001; Wenger et al., 2002).

CoPs generally interact face-to-face, continually renegotiating meaning through shared experiences and perspectives, creating a network of strong ties (Brown & Duguid, 2000; Wenger, 1998). They tend to produce a localized sense of belonging through shared codes and narratives, with direct reciprocity and coordination. While knowledge flows easily within a CoP, the physical space between communities can constrain the flow of knowledge across them (Walsham, 2001). Indeed, Heaton and Taylor (2002) demonstrated how two CoPs in the same area of computer supported collaborative workgroups performed work practices quite differently due to the cultural norms and practices embedded in their national identities.

NoPs, however, typically link individuals with others whom they may never meet, constituting a network of weak ties. Thus, NoPs hold a clear advantage over CoPs in terms of their ability to innovate. In addition, NoPs commonly comprise geographically dispersed strangers who communicate through indirect means, such as professional associations, publications, conferences newsletters, Web sites, bulletin boards, and listserves (Brown & Duguid, 2000; Gibbs et al., 2008; Wasko & Faraj, 2005). Since members do not personally know one another, direct reciprocity and coordination are difficult to achieve in NoPs. For this reason, *generalized reciprocity* replaces *direct reciprocity* in loosely coupled systems, such as NoPs (Cohen & Prusak, 2001; Rice, 1982; Wasko & Faraj, 2005). Data from an exploratory study on why individuals participate in an electronic NoP suggested that a primary motivating factor for contributing content stemmed from a desire to give back to the community in return for previously received advice from individuals in the community (Wasko & Faraj, 2000).

Related to these network forms, social capital theory offers a broad framework for identifying some of the collective level influences on knowledge sharing (Nahapiet & Ghoshal, 1998; Tsai & Ghoshal, 1998; Wasko & Faraj, 2005). However, the rich literature on this concept extends beyond the page limitations of this chapter, if not the conceptual scope. Thus, we note only a few particularly salient points.

From a social capital perspective, the resources in which one invests are social relations, which can be "accessed or mobilized for purposive action" (Lin, 2001, p. 29), including collective action (Adler & Kwon, 2002). The three primary dimensions of social capital include *structural* (networks of social interaction that provide advantages to the members), *cognitive* (shared language and vocabulary), and *relational* (trust, norms, identification, and obligations and expectations) (Nahapiet & Ghoshal, 1998).

Social capital may be both a public (available to the community) and private good (available only to members of a network) (Putnam, 2000). By investing in social capital, an individual may reap personal rewards while simultaneously contributing to the production of social relations as a positive network externality (Adler & Kwon, 2002; Coleman, 1988). Social capital can produce additional network externalities aside from social relations, such as *connectivity* and *communality* (Coleman, 1988; Nahapiet & Ghoshal, 1998). Social capital facilitates the flow of knowledge and acts as an agent of social influence (Cohen & Prusak, 2001; Coleman, 1988; Lin, 2001). Inkpen and Tsang (2005) applied a social capital perspective to knowledge transfer by identifying facilitating conditions for each of the three dimensions of social capital.

## Knowledge Sharing via Information/Communication Technologies

Knowledge management initiatives generally emphasize how ICTs can support knowledge sharing (Easterby-Smith & Lyles, 2003; Huysman & de Wit, 2003). However, some theorists, researchers, and practitioners critique this assumption. Nonetheless, concepts described in the prior section provide good foundations for analyzing how KMS might support knowledge sharing.

## The Potential of Information and Communication Technologies to Foster Knowledge Sharing

Information and communication technologies transcend the barriers of time and space, thereby facilitating knowledge-sharing activities among geographically distributed individuals (Constant, Sproull, & Kiesler, 1996; Wasko & Faraj, 2000). Furthermore, ICTs can drastically reduce the perceived costs of contributing knowledge (Bimber, Flanagin, & Stohl, 2005; Cabrera & Cabrera, 2002; Hansen, Nohria, & Tierney, 1999). Human network *weak ties* are characterized by low levels of closeness and infrequent interaction between two parties (Granovetter, 1973). Members primarily use the Internet to support such weak ties, which are especially beneficial for accessing new and useful information and reducing information search costs (Constant et al., 1996; Granovetter, 1973; Hansen, 1999; Katz & Rice, 2002; Kraut et al., 1998; Levin & Cross, 2004; Lin, 2001). For example, collaborative participation in the creation of open-source software has proliferated through online weak ties (Kollock, 1999; Tapscott & Williams, 2006). Individuals are willing to offer helpful advice in online networks despite the lack of a strong personal connection with the requestor (Constant et al., 1996; Finholt & Sproull, 1990).

About three-quarters of companies in a 2007 McKinsey global survey were applying collaborative tools, and "about 20 percent of these companies are trying to use collaborative tools to go beyond classical knowledge management within their companies" (Bollier, 2007, p. 17, referring to Bugbin & Manyiska, 2007). Multinational organizations implement KMS to foster CoPs across divisions, companies, and nations (Pan & Leidner, 2003). KMS may be also be categorized as supporting content management systems, transfer/retrieval/collaboration systems, or collaborative/distributive systems (Martin, 2008, p. 395). Corporate portals may serve as KMS by synchronizing and supporting knowledge processes (Benbya et al., 2004). Intranets, electronic bulletin boards, expert databases, groupware, data warehouses, lessons learned databases, repositories, yellow page catalogs, decision support systems, and e-mail have all been proposed as tools to enable knowledge processes (Alavi & Leidner, 2001; Ruggles, 1998). ICTs that support the voluntary sharing of explicit/codified knowledge are commonly known as *discretionary databases* or "a shared pool of data to which several participants (individuals, departments) may, if they choose, separately contribute information" (Connolly & Thorn, 1990, p. 221). Certain types of ICTs seem highly capable of supporting tacit knowledge sharing and innovation including rich media (simulation tools, videoconferencing), person-to-person computer-mediated communication systems (e-mail), expert locating/mapping tools (electronic yellow page catalogs), and social network media (blogs, wikis, recommender systems) (Alavi & Leidner, 2001; Bolisani & Scarso, 1999; Flanagin, 2002; Rice, 1987; Shirky, 2008).

The term *Web 2.0* represents the new generation of social networking, collaboration, user-produced content, and mediated interaction through software and services such as wikis, blogs, RSS (really simple syndication) feeds, tagging and social bookmarking, video and photography sharing, and filesharing and peer-to-peer tools such as Bittorrent and the descendents of Napster (Bruns, 2008). KM projects implement organizational blogs and reputation systems (Oravec, 2004). These new media represent the phenomena of collective intelligence, decentralized co-creation of value, and crowdsourcing (Bollier, 2007; Howe, 2008; Shirky, 2008; Tapscott & Williams, 2006), with Wikipedia as perhaps the most famous example. Social networking sites can be viewed as KMS for social knowledge sharing—creating, obtaining, and displaying relationships among members of various social networks, supported by a variety of individual, group and automated tools (boyd & Ellison, 2007). Given the shifting and permeable boundaries of organizations and constant interaction and knowledge sharing among organizations and stakeholders made possible by Web 2.0 technologies, the timelines of and formal organizational constraints on innovation are becoming shorter and looser, leading to the *permanently beta* organization (Neff & Stark, 2004, p. 173).

Knowledge management systems provide a means to generate collective benefits through the public good of shared knowledge. Notably, members can choose whether or not to contribute to or collect from the database, leading to both benefits and costs. The primary public good produced through the use of discretionary databases has been described as a special class of public goods known as *communality*, or a commonly available repository of knowledge (Monge et al., 1998). Once a *critical mass* of users and useful knowledge exists, the potential benefit of using the system exceeds the potential cost for the community of users, because of the wide and deep communality (Markus, 1990; Rafaeli & LaRose, 1993).

Another public good generated through successful KMS is *connectivity*, the ability to connect with other people (Fulk et al., 1996; Markus, 1990; Rice, 1982). Attaining universal access throughout the entire potential population of users, however, is not necessarily required. One or more subsets, or coalitions, of the intended collective may be sufficient to constitute a successful use of an interactive, networked medium (Fulk et al., 1996; Rice, 1990; Rice, Grant, Schmitz, & Torobin, 1990). However, a small group of adopting individuals may perceive a lack of sufficient connectivity since those whom they desire to contact have chosen not to adopt the system. Competing, alternative media can impede full connectivity, reducing communality and connectivity, and possibly causing one or more of the alternatives to fail (Fulk et al., 1996; Kraut, Rice, et al., 1998).

## Critiques of the Use of ICTs for Knowledge Management and Sharing

Whether ICTs facilitate or hinder knowledge processes is the topic of many scholarly debates (Alavi & Leidner, 2001; Alavi & Tiwana, 2003; Davenport & Prusak, 1998; Roberts, 2000; Ruggles, 1998; Walsham, 2002). Some scholars contend that ICTs are better suited for the sharing of explicit knowledge than for tacit knowledge (Hinds & Pfeffer, 2003; Roberts, 2000). As discussed above, scholars often assume that the transfer of tacit knowledge depends highly on direct interpersonal interaction, and thus physical proximity, in order to be effective (Nonaka, 1994; Nonaka & Takeuchi, 1995; Roberts, 2000). Hislop (2002), among others, argued that the fundamental nature of knowledge requires very specific conditions for ICTs to support knowledge sharing, because knowledge is grounded in practice, rather than an objective entity that can be easily exchanged. Johannessen, Olaisen, and Olsen (2001) are more critical, arguing that using ICTs to share knowledge will over-emphasize explicit knowledge, relegating important, strategic tacit knowledge to the background, ultimately resulting in knowledge mismanagement. Alternatively, according to Roberts, even if KMS are limited to the domain of explicit knowledge, the sharing of codified knowledge has the potential to produce new knowledge through its integration with existing tacit knowledge, as discussed above.

## Collective and Individual Level Influences, Knowledge Sharing Processes, and Their Outcomes

This section reviews more detailed implications of the prior conceptual foundations, to develop an integrated model of collective and individual influences on knowledge sharing processes, the cognitive integration of that sharing, and related sets of outcomes, both positive and negative, both collective and individual.

### *Collective Level Influences on Knowledge Sharing through a KMS*

The collective level influences noted here draw upon both the NoP and social capital literature. In particular, the three dimensions of social capital—cognitive (shared language), relational (trust, norms of openness and knowledge sharing, social identification/commitment to a NoP), and structural (frequency and networks of interaction)—influence the knowledge sharing behavior of NoP members.

### *Shared Language*

Although innovation generally occurs through the combination of diverse knowledge and experience, sharing knowledge requires at least some degree of shared context and language (Nahapiet & Ghoshal, 1998; Rogers, 2003). Individuals who share a common social, cultural, and linguistic background, and understanding of the acronyms, slang and jargon that are unique to a shared practice (such as a professional domain) will be more likely to benefit from a KMS (De Long & Fahey, 2000; McDermott, 1999; Roberts, 2000). Shared language facilitates individual and group action, thereby producing collective benefits (Tsai & Ghoshal, 1998). It also fosters the use of collaborative technology for various types of work tasks (Majchrzak, Rice, Malhotra, King, &

Ba, 2000). Participation in a NoP commonly requires generally competent use and understanding of the shared codes and jargon of the NoP (Gherardi & Nicolini, 2002). Furthermore, competence in a discursive practice is critical to the process of social learning, which entails both actively contributing to, and passively absorbing, the shared repertoire of a community for the generation and negotiation of meaning (Jacobs & Coghlan, 2005; Wenger, 1998). Lave and Wenger's (1991) idea of *legitimate peripheral participation* proposes that some CoP members exist on the periphery of the community while others reside at the core. Thus, membership within a CoP or NoP entails varying degrees of participation, which may be constrained or facilitated by the extent to which one has mastered the language of the community or network.

### Competence-Based Trust

Trust is a multidimensional concept that includes a belief in the competence, openness, good intentions, and reliability of others (McAllister, 1995; Mishira, 1996). It enables cooperation and knowledge creation within organizations, particularly in terms of knowledge sharing and contributing to a discretionary database (Adler, 2001; Dawes, 1980; Nahapiet & Ghoshal, 1998; Nonaka et al., 2001). Trust in the good intentions of others with whom one conducts knowledge transactions is positively associated with resource exchange in an organizational setting (Tsai & Ghoshal, 1998). Trusting relationships also influence the type of outcome from knowledge seeking efforts (Cross, Rice, & Parker, 2001).

Within the context of a NoP, interpersonal reciprocal trust is replaced by generalized trust such that individuals derive trust from the similarities resident in a collective identity (D. Cohen & Prusak, 2001; Kramer, Brewer, & Hanna, 1996). Under conditions of generalized or intransitive trust, resources are shared with, and expected to be shared with, others in the community, if not reciprocally to the initial provider, and community resources will be available to the initial provider, even if indirectly.

Competence-based trust is of particular importance for many KMS initiatives (Hollingshead, Fulk, & Monge, 2001; Tsai & Ghoshal, 1998; Van den Hooff, Elving, et al., 2003). Trust in the competence of others positively influences individuals' willingness to both contribute to and retrieve information from a virtual community (Ridings et al., 2002) and the extent to which one contributes to a communal public good (Monge et al., 1998).

### Norms of Knowledge Sharing and Openness

Norms constitute an important influence on motivating members to share knowledge (Nahapiet & Ghoshal, 1998), particularly for NoPs of a professional orientation (DiMaggio & Powell, 1991). Moreover, norms influence individuals to contribute to a public good despite a payoff structure that favors free riding (Dawes, 1980). Thus, norms of cooperation (Nahapiet & Ghoshal, 1998), collectivism (Van den Hooff et al., 2004), reciprocity (Hinds & Pfeffer, 2003; Wasko & Faraj, 2005), knowledge sharing (Constant, Kiesler, & Sproull, 1994; Yuan et al., 2005), and openness (Jarvenpaa & Staples, 2000; Nahapiet & Ghoshal, 1998; Van den Hooff, Vijvers, & De Ridder, 2003) have all been proposed as positive influences on knowledge sharing behavior. Norms of openness harbor a tolerance for mistakes or errors, an acceptance of failure, and a willingness to be criticized by others. An organizational or NoP culture with a norm of openness fosters knowledge sharing activities, both interpersonal and technologically mediated (Davenport, 1997; Jarvenpaa & Staples, 2000; Nahapiet & Ghoshal, 1998; Van den Hooff, Elving, et al., 2003; Van den Hooff, Vijvers, et al., 2003).

Sharing and openness in online systems can be represented by something as simple as receiving a reply to one's first contribution. In Joyce and Kraut's (2006) analysis of six public newsgroups, an initial reply to a contribution increased the likelihood of a subsequent contribution by 12%, regardless of the quality (accuracy or emotional tone) of the response. Joyce and Kraut argued that these initial responses constitute a sign of community commitment, which thus fosters repeat contributions.

## Network of Practice Commitment

A strong sense of social identity and belonging to a social collective (Brown & Duguid, 2000; Hinds & Pfeffer, 2003; Kalman et al., 2002; Nahapiet & Ghoshal, 1998; Van den Hooff, Elving, et al., 2003; Wasko & Faraj, 2005), or to an organization in particular (Kalman et al., 2002; Nahapiet & Ghoshal, 1998; Nonaka et al., 2001; Van den Hooff & De Leeuw van Weenen, 2004; Van den Hooff, Vijvers, et al., 2003), is critical for inducing cooperative knowledge sharing behavior. Brewer and Kramer (1986) also concluded that salient group identity increases the likelihood of cooperation in social dilemmas.

Other scholars prefer to leverage the theoretical construct of *organizational commitment* to study the relationship between a strong sense of belonging to a collective and knowledge processes (Kramer et al., 1996; Van den Hooff & De Leeuw van Weenen, 2004; Van den Hooff, Vijvers, et al., 2003; Wasko & Faraj, 2005). Some scholars assert that attitudinal commitment is a conceptually and empirically sound replacement for identity when investigating information or knowledge sharing phenomena in organizations or other collectives (Kalman et al., 2002; Wasko & Faraj, 2005).

Empirical evidence suggests that the degree of organizational commitment to a collective significantly predicts knowledge sharing behavior, both in a technologically mediated environment and in a more traditional social context (Cabrera & Cabrera, 2002; Kalman et al., 2002; Van den Hooff & De Leeuw van Weenen, 2004). Contrary to these findings, Wasko and Faraj (2005) reported a lack of empirical support for the connection between commitment to an electronic NoP and the volume of contributions made to the NoP. Similarly, Van den Hooff and De Leeuw van Weenen determined that organizational commitment only elicited knowledge collecting behavior while commitment to a smaller, more intimate group (a department), elicited both collecting and contributing behaviors.

### Frequency and Networks of Interaction

Frequent interaction among members of a collective strengthens the ties, relational bonds, and trust among actors, creating a dense network structure that facilitates the flow of knowledge and influence (Markus & Benjamin, 1997; Nahapiet & Ghoshal, 1998; Rice & Aydin, 1991; Roberts, 2000; Tsai & Ghoshal, 1998). Most scholars adopt the theoretical framework of social capital in making such claims since such an approach grants favor to interpersonal social relations, and the use of network methods to study the relationship between various aspects of social structure and knowledge processes (Nahapiet & Ghoshal, 1998; Wasko & Faraj, 2005). The strength of social ties and actor centrality have been investigated as facilitators of knowledge sharing behavior, particularly in terms of contributing behavior, such as to an online message board (Hansen, 1999; Wasko & Faraj, 2005). For example, employees from one business unit were more likely to share information with employees of another business unit when they frequently engaged in social interaction with those employees (Tsai & Ghoshal, 1998). Weak or infrequent ties can increase the speed of sharing for highly codified, non-redundant, stand-alone knowledge but may impede the sharing of knowledge that is both non-codified and dependent (Hansen, 1999; Levin & Cross, 2004). In the case of NoPs with geographically dispersed members, face-to-face interaction is highly unlikely. Instead, interpersonal relationships between NoP members more likely develop through a diverse array of less direct communication channels such as professional associations, publications, conferences, newsletters, Web sites, virtual teams, bulletin boards, social networking sites, and listserves (Brown & Duguid, 2000; Gibbs et al., 2008; Wasko & Faraj, 2005).

Beyond mere frequency or strength of interaction, however, the patterns of interaction, for both individuals and organizations, also influence the extent and kinds of knowledge sharing. For example, greater social cohesion (relations among one's contacts) and range of contacts (across different knowledge areas) fostered greater knowledge transfer within a R&D firm, after controlling for the strength/frequency of dyadic communication relationships (Reagans & McEvily, 2003). Further, beyond even this network orientation, the patterns of relationships among members and with artifacts themselves may constitute the nature of knowledge associated with a given practice (Østerlund & Carlile, 2005). Thus, not just the *extent of interactions* among members within a practice, but also *patterns of the relations* will influence the extent and nature of knowledge sharing. Thus, a KMS integrated into one's existing social networks and peer groups is more likely to succeed (Brown & Duguid, 2000; Rice, 1990).

*Propositions about Collective-Level Influences on Knowledge Sharing*

People tend to use a KMS, in general, and specifically for both knowledge contributing and knowledge collecting activities, when they perceive that the members of a NoP: have mastered the language (jargon and codes) of a NoP; adhere to norms of knowledge contributing, knowledge collecting, and openness; exhibit a high level of competence-based trust; perceive a high degree of NoP commitment, and engage in frequent and patterned network interaction.

### Individual Level Influences on Knowledge-Sharing through a KMS

An important characteristic of activities (such as work tasks, or collaborative projects) involves the degree of interdependence required to complete them.

#### Activity Interdependence

The underlying premise of task interdependence is that activities can only be completed as a team effort, whether sequentially, in parallel, or reciprocally, and thus requiring knowledge by more than one team member of at least relevant aspects of each other's task components. Consistent with this perspective, task interdependence is positively associated with knowledge sharing through a KMS (Jarvenpaa & Staples, 2003; Van den Hooff, Elving, et al., 2003). Yet, a KMS holds the potential to benefit more than just those who work in an organizational team-oriented environment. For example, computer programmers' involvement in the opensource software phenomenon highlights the collective nature of their work that would otherwise go unnoticed if we relied solely on a basic description of their daily work routine (Kollock, 1999; Markus, Manville, & Agres, 2000).

#### Tacitness of Knowledge Required for the Activity

From a KM perspective, the extent of tacit knowledge required to successfully complete an activity is an important attribute to consider. Highly equivocal tasks require the use of an interactive and rich communication medium (Daft & Lengel, 1984). Nonaka et al. (2001) argued that face-to-face contact serves as the primary mechanism for converting tacit knowledge into tacit knowledge. Hansen (2002) suggested that weak ties are beneficial for effectively transferring explicit knowledge, while strong ties are necessary for tacit knowledge exchange. In sum, individuals engaged in activities involving tacit knowledge should be less likely to collect knowledge from a KMS because they require a richer form of communication to complete their work.

*Activity Load*

Activity load is manifested by the time pressure experienced when performing a work task that often prevents an individual from doing other activities. Time pressure can create a barrier to participation in knowledge processes (Van den Hooff, Vijvers, et al. 2003). Sharing one's experiences with others, especially through a discretionary database, or learning how to use a KMS can be a burden when time is a valuable resource (Cabrera & Cabrera, 2002). In an industry study, managers reported that KM initiatives experience limited success, at least in part, because employees did not have enough time to participate in knowledge sharing through their KMS (KPMG, 2000). Siemsen, Roth, and Balasubramanian (2007) developed and tested a model involving different roles of the influences of motivation to share knowledge, ability to share knowledge (such as time), and opportunity to share knowledge (as well as control variables). In particular, they tested four different ways in which these central factors relate to affect knowledge sharing. Their *constraining factor* model fit the data best. Low levels of either motivation or ability, and somewhat more complexly for opportunity, stymied knowledge sharing. Especially when time was insufficient, motivation and ability levels had no effect; that is, the person was not able to engage in knowledge sharing regardless of their motivation or ability to share.

*Knowledge Domain Expertise*

One's expertise in the knowledge domain of a NoP can have important ramifications for the likelihood of *contributing* knowledge with other NoP members. For example, Wasko and Faraj (2000) found that some people opted not to contribute to an electronic CoP because they felt uncomfortable about their level of expertise. However, in a later study, they determined no significant link between self-rated expertise and volume of contribution (Wasko & Faraj, 2005). In studies of a non-mediated environment, and a collaborative media environment, people were more willing to share information with others when it was a product of their own knowledge or understanding rather than an information product owned by an employer (Constant et al., 1994; Jarvenpaa & Staples, 2000). However, related to the knowledge sharing social dilemma, assuming that people behave in a rationally self-interested way, they may be motivated to *protect* those resources that are most valuable to them in a competitive environment (Lin, 2001)—that is, undersupply expertise to the collective. In a highly competitive knowledge economy, contributing one's personal expertise to a collective is tantamount to foregoing one's strategic advantage in the labor market (Cabrera & Cabrera, 2002; Constant et al., 1994; Fulk et al., 1996; Fulk, Heino, Flanagin, Monge, & Bar, 2004; Hinds & Pfeffer, 2003). Thus, research is not consistent on whether having greater knowledge domain expertise will foster greater contributing behavior.

A positive relationship between expertise and knowledge collecting behavior is rooted in principles of rational economic behavior. Individuals who have *less* expertise in the knowledge domain of their profession (or other NoP) are more likely to attempt to increase their existing knowledge base through knowledge collecting as a means of securing a better position in the labor market (Lin, 2001).

### ICT Competency

Technological competence may facilitate knowledge sharing through ICTs. One study found that the general use of computer-mediated communication tools, typically assumed to imply greater competency, positively related to knowledge collecting while not significantly corresponding to knowledge contributing (Van den Hooff & De Leeuw van Weenen, 2004). Having sufficient computer skills fostered the use of collaborative media for both contributing and collecting information in a study by Jarvenpaa and Staples (2000). Van den Hooff (2004) reported that prior experience with a collaborative technology positively influenced the use of that technology for knowledge sharing purposes. In a more general assessment of technological competence, Yuan et al. (2005) found that user skill level was positively associated with both contributing and collecting behavior in the use of a discretionary database. However, Majchrzak et al. (2000) discovered that the use of a collaborative technology did not increase over time as users gained more experience with it.

### Other Influences, Context, and Controls

Other potential individual influences include the extent to which one feels their contributions are unique, identifiable, and beneficial for the collectivity (Ling et al., 2005, applying collective effort theory to explaining under-contribution to an online movie recommender system). More generally, each context will have relevant other factors that would need to be controlled or measured in order to avoid confounds and reflect meaningful influences. These issues may range from demographic and professional or organizational characteristics (such as the percentage of problems, information, or relationships involved in one's activities that pertain to the knowledge being shared). Close analysis of the individual's context is necessary to identify and develop valid measures for these controls.

### Propositions about Individual-Level Influences on Knowledge Sharing

People more likely use a KMS in general, and specifically for both knowledge contributing and knowledge collecting activities, when they experience greater activity interdependence, more tacit knowledge in their activities, lower activity load, and greater Internet competence. People who perceive that they are more expert in the knowledge domain of a NoP tend to use a KMS, in general, and possibly more for knowledge collecting than contributing (which in some cases may be negative). Various demographic, activity, and membership factors, operating as control variables in an integrated model, would also influence KMS use, contributing, and collecting.

### Knowledge Contributing and Collecting, and KM System Use

KMS use constitutes a behavioral construct that comprises three mutually reinforcing behaviors: knowledge contributing, knowledge collecting, and general KMS use.

#### Knowledge Contributing

Scholars commonly assume that knowledge collecting precedes knowledge contributing behavior (Fulk et al., 2004; Yuan et al., 2005). Collecting knowledge from a KMS can shed light on the extent to which the content is useful and the likelihood that others will make this same assessment. Lending credence to this assumption, at least two studies found knowledge collecting to be a highly significant predictor of knowledge contributing behavior (Fulk et al., 2004; Van den Hoof & De Leeuw van Weenen, 2004). Alternatively, some individuals might initially contribute to a KMS without collecting much from it in return. Indeed, critical mass theory requires early adoption/contribution by users with greater resources and motivation (Markus, 1990). Applying the concepts of positive and reciprocal productive functions, knowing that one can collect in the future would serve to (1) justify the time and effort expended in making initial contributions and (2) satisfy a desire for generalized or transitive reciprocation.

#### Knowledge Collecting

What about those free-riders or lurkers who primarily collect, without contributing? As discussed above, in the extreme, this practice constitutes an information-based version of the tragedy of the commons, and the community may collapse. However, individuals may feel generally both motivated, as well as compelled, to reciprocate the contributions made by others, perhaps through representing the collective and its norms, after collecting from a KMS. A network-evolution analysis of over-time participation in a computer conferencing system found that users who received (collected), but did not continue to send (contribution), messages quickly became isolates in the computer-mediated communication network (Rice, 1982). Thus, users must navigate between over-contributing (exceeding the carrying capacity of the system and their own processing abilities) and under-contributing (and, thus, perceived as not supporting generalized reciprocity and the collective benefit). Intriguingly, asymmetry of participation may, in fact, have collective benefits. For example, members of some online communities do perceive value from having *lurkers*, those who read but do not post (Nonnecke, Andrews, & Preece, 2006). In general, in spite of the potential for asymmetric free riding, successful KMS do occur, as people come to both collect and contribute.

*General KMS Use*

It would seem likely that a KMS supports other general uses and applications, both to the extent that a KMS is integrated with other ICTs and to the extent that it offers support applications. Further, as with all innovations in general, and ICTs in particular, the various uses of a KMS and their social consequences are particularly difficult to discern during the initial stages of system adoption because the features and uses may be changed by the adopters (Rogers, 2003). That is, an innovation may be adapted after initial adoption, through reinvention, adaptive structuration, technology structuring, or technology adaptation (DeSanctis & Poole, 1994; Johnson & Rice, 1987; Kraut, Rice, et al., 1998; Majchrzak et al., 2000; Orlikowski, 1992). Thus, any model of KMS use would be more realistic by including general system use as well as knowledge sharing.

*Propositions for KMS Use (Contributing, Collecting, General)*

Knowledge collecting relates positively to knowledge contributing through a KMS. Knowledge contributing and knowledge collecting through the system correspond positively to general use, although other uses of the system may exist than contributing and collecting.

### Knowledge Sharing and Cognitive Integration

Individual reflection is important for the creation of both individual and organizational knowledge (Alavi & Tiwana, 2003; McDermott, 1999; Nonaka, 1994; Vera & Crossan, 2003). Knowledge, in and of itself, holds little value if it is not integrated with existing knowledge and applied in a meaningful way (Alavi & Leidner, 2001; Grant, 1996).

*Cognitive Integration*

Knowledge is rooted in prior experiences that we have thought about and made sense of (McDermott, 1999; Walsham, 2001). A core tenet of cognitive theories of learning is that people come to make sense of the world around them by incorporating external stimuli into their existing mental models, either reconfirming or changing them (Nonaka et al., 2001; Polanyi, 1966). Moreover, the cognitive dimension of tacit knowledge suggests that new knowledge arises not simply from prior experiences, but from prior experiences that people have reflected on and made sense of, and through developing shared mental models within an organization (Kim, 1993; Martin, 2008; McDermott, 1999; Nonaka, 1994; Walsham, 2001).

Vandenbosch and Higgins (1996) proposed that new knowledge can be integrated into existing cognitive structures through one of two ways. *Mental model building* occurs when individuals alter existing mental models to accommodate the receipt of new knowledge and perceive them as the primary source of innovation and creativity. *Mental model maintenance* occurs when individuals adapt incoming stimuli to their existing mental models, thereby validating pre-conceptions. Conceptually, this cognitive integration can arise from both contributing and collecting behavior. Collected knowledge may be new or simply a reiteration of previously acquired knowledge, reinforcing and maintaining knowledge. New knowledge more likely leads to a change in, and development of, new mental models. The process of contributing knowledge may help to refine an individual's thinking on an issue, challenge preconceptions, and develop new insight (Wasko & Faraj, 2000), although it primarily codifies and represents current mental models. Cognitive integration, especially mental model building, may enable double-loop learning, or change in the process or criteria for change, rather than single-loop learning, or improvement applying the process or reach the criteria (Martin, 2008).

### Propositions for KMS Use and Cognitive Integration

KMS use, contributing, and collecting relate positively to cognitive integration (mental model maintenance and mental model building). However, such use may foster more model maintenance and collecting than more model building.

### Potential Individual and Collective Costs and Benefits of Knowledge Sharing and Cognitive Integration through a KMS

Outcomes from knowledge sharing—both contributing and collecting—include both costs and benefits, at the individual and collective level. Indeed, Constant et al. (1996) found that both intangible personal benefits, such as earning the respect of others, and collective benefits, such as improved organizational citizenship, motivated contributions to a KMS. Monge et al. (1998) determined that police officers' use of a cross-jurisdictional discretionary database depended largely on the extent to which the database satisfied individual (rewards for individual performance) and collective (officer safety) interests. When examining why people contribute to KM systems, many studies tend to treat costs explicitly in terms of the time and effort that it takes an individual to use a particular system (Yuan et al., 2005). The notion of negative individual and network externalities at the collective level (Shapiro & Varian, 1999) is largely absent from empirical investigations of information or knowledge sharing (Fulk et al., 2004).

*Individual and Collective Costs*

Costs of contributing to a discretionary database can take the form of initial start-up costs as well as recurring costs (Monge et al., 1998).

INDIVIDUAL COSTS: CONTRIBUTING

System usability comprises an important component of time and effort (Davis, Bagozzi, & Warshaw, 1992; Van den Hooff, 2004). Additional expenses implicit to making a useful contribution may include formatting, compiling, or acquiring knowledge prior to using the system (Cabrera & Cabrera, 2002; Fulk et al., 2004; Monge et al., 1998), or physical, cognitive, and social costs in accessing the system (Rice, McCreadie, & Chang, 2001; Rice & Shook, 1988). Further, an individual may face the cost of losing some of his and her competitive advantage by making privately held knowledge publicly available to others (Cabrera & Cabrera, 2002; Constant et al., 1994; Fulk et al., 1996; Fulk et al., 2004).

INDIVIDUAL COSTS: COLLECTING

A number of knowledge collecting costs also result from using a KMS to share knowledge. First, the time and effort expended to collect knowledge from a KMS can vary significantly from one system to the next (Monge et al., 1998). Indeed, a high volume of posts or messages that lack sufficient filtering, evaluation, or recommendation mechanisms will likely deter people from collecting knowledge from a system (Wasko & Faraj, 2000). Even individuals who opt to free ride will likely incur at least some costs through simply accessing and using a system to collect knowledge. Second, an inability to verify the credentials of contributors or a lack of visibility as to who contributed content to a discretionary database can serve to erode trust in the credibility of the content (Cabrera & Cabrera, 2002). Third, to the extent that a sufficient range of perspectives and interpretation is lacking in the content posted to a KMS, the knowledge collected will be deemed less useful, and the system will be perceived as more costly compared to other sources of knowledge (Fulk et al., 2004). Fourth, as Fulk et al. noted, an individual's perceived value of a knowledge good is based on the perceived level of production of that good at a given point in time. When a KMS is initially deployed, the perceived level of provision often represents a cost rather than a benefit (Cabrera & Cabrera, 2002). Such cost can be attributed to a lack of critical mass at the early stages of system adoption relative to later stages; that is, the production function has not yet reached positive or reciprocal levels (Markus, 1990).

COLLECTIVE COSTS

Even when some individuals accrue personal benefits from contributing to a public good, negative collective externalities can result (Adler & Kwon, 2002).

In many knowledge-intensive professions (such as consulting, law, financial services), reputation is a primary source of value. A collective good that holds the potential to threaten a NoP's reputation in some way represents a collective cost to both participating and non-participating members. Finally, people are limited in their ability to process information (March & Simon, 1958). A KMS in which individuals contribute a wide array of competing interpretations or perspectives can lead to confusion rather than clarification for the collective (Kraut et al., 1998).

### Individual and Collective Benefits

Experiencing a positive benefit for the time and effort expended in making a contribution can lead to future contributions by the initial user, and thus prime subsequent contributions by others.

#### INDIVIDUAL BENEFITS: CONTRIBUTING

Tangible benefits, such as monetary rewards or a promotion, may not be applicable for knowledge sharing communities that develop outside of formal organizational boundaries, such as NoPs. Instead, participating in knowledge sharing activities in a self-organizing KMS likely arises from a desire for psychological or intangible rewards (Constant et al., 1996; Osterloh & Frey, 2000; Shirky, 2008; Wasko & Faraj, 2000, 2005). Jian and Jeffres's (2006) test of their multi-dimensional model showed that utilitarian, normative, and collaborative motivations all influenced employees' willingness to contribute to shared electronic databases.

One intangible benefit from knowledge sharing behavior includes an increase in status or reputation in a collective and gaining a positive feeling from helping others (Constant et al., 1996; Huysman & de Wit, 2003; Wasko & Faraj, 2000, 2005). Some mechanism in the KMS must exist for indicating participants' identities, such as listing contributor names or persistent online usernames, affiliations, profession or even NoP affiliation in order for an increase in reputation to extend from an online environment to a NoP environment (Cabrera & Cabrera, 2002). This recognition constitutes one of the primary rationales in social networking sites where users rate and link other users' contributions (boyd & Ellison, 2007). Benefits of economic and professional payoffs can accrue indirectly from this enhanced status in professional or other work-related online groups (Butler, Sproull, Kiesler, & Kraut, 2002).

For example, an individual might receive client referrals from others in a particular geographic area based on a positive reputation that has developed through valuable contributions to a KMS. Lampel and Bhalla (2007) found that status (including prestige and reputation) increased voluntary contributions to online rating communities evaluating information goods (such as books, travel trips, music, services, etc.). In this context, status may be obtained either by contributions that show focused expertise, or a wide range of areas outside of the review topic. Another intangible benefit of contributing arises from the positive feeling that people get from helping others, as in traditional volunteer work, and the open source community (Butler et al., 2002; Kollock, 1999; Wasko & Faraj, 2000).

INDIVIDUAL BENEFITS: COLLECTING

An implicit assumption in theories of collective action is that individuals elect to free ride because they perceive some intrinsic value associated with consuming a public good, low costs to obtaining that good, and few or no sanctions for non-contributing. Online public KMS where users are anonymous provide such contexts. However, the extent to which individuals benefit from the consumption of a public good is rarely raised as an empirical question. If an individual does not receive at least some benefits from the knowledge collected through a KMS, then he or she has no future incentive to collect from, or likely contribute to, the system. Individuals often seek knowledge from a KMS because of an obstacle or challenge in their daily work routine that requires problem resolution through new knowledge in a short time frame without much awareness of specific sources (Brown & Duguid, 2000; Fulk et al., 2004; Vandenbosch & Higgins, 1996).

COLLECTIVE BENEFITS

As discussed earlier, the primary public goods arising from contributing to and collecting from a KMS includes communality and connectivity. Empirical studies of using an ICT for knowledge sharing support both propositions (Katz & Rice, 2002; Van den Hooff et al., 2004; Van den Hooff, Elving, et al., 2003).

## KMS Evaluation

A newly introduced KMS may have to compete in users' evaluations with existing systems or communication channels, especially if those already have established widespread connectivity (Fulk et al., 1996; Kraut, 1998). This perspective reflects the centrality of *relative advantage* in the adoption decision (Johnson & Rice, 1987; Rogers, 2003). However, a KMS that provides communality and connectivity, possibly opportunities for reinvention and additional uses, and is easy to use and compatible with current practices should receive positive evaluations.

## Cognitive Integration, Costs and Benefits, and KMS Evaluation

Cognitive integration likely plays a mediating role between KMS use (contributing, collecting, general use) and outcomes (individual and collective, costs and benefits). As explained earlier in this chapter, the potential for value from sharing knowledge through a KMS depends, at least in part, on the extent to which individuals have cognitively integrated that knowledge. Building or maintaining one's mental models contributes to confidence, improved competency, learning, and a better understanding of how the knowledge relates to individual and collective outcomes. Conversely, without reinforcing current or developing new knowledge, the material and social costs and possible misapplications of the knowledge of a KMS likely increases, also fostering a negative evaluation of the system.

### Propositions for KMS Use, Cognitive Integration, and Costs and Benefits

The use of a KMS, in general, and specifically for both knowledge contributing and knowledge collecting activities, relates positively to perceived individual and collective benefits of contributing knowledge and collecting knowledge through the system and to a positive evaluation of the system.

Cognitive integration (mental model maintenance and mental model building) relates negatively to perceived costs (collective and individual) of contributing through the system. Cognitive integration corresponds positively to perceived benefits (collective and individual) of contributing and collecting as well as to the overall evaluation of the system. Exactly which aspects of cognitive integration (model building or model maintenance) might be associated with which benefits and costs (collective, individual, contributing, collecting) is an important topic for future theory and research. Cognitive integration is likely to be a partial or total intervening process between KMS use and outcomes.

## Proposed Theoretical Model and Future Research

The preceding review provides the basis for the integrative theoretical model in Figure 4.1, which reflects the summary propositions at the end of each portion of the previous section. The main components, each represented by multiple concepts, include (1) collective (network of practice) influences, (2) individual influences, (3) knowledge management system use, (4) cognitive integration, and (5) outcomes.

Other models of knowledge sharing through knowledge management systems exist, of course. Alavi and Leidner (2001) derived rationales for KMS through a conceptual analysis of the main phases of knowledge management. A somewhat similar model emphasizing KMS information output quality, tested using responses from eight public-sector organizations in Singapore, found that major influences on knowledge collection included the perceived output quality and resource availability, especially when activities were more explicit (Kankanhalli, Tan, & Wei, 2005). Wasko and Faraj's (2005) model highlighted the influence of individual and collective factors on knowledge contributing behavior. Benbya et al.'s (2004) model emphasized more of the technical and managerial aspects of knowledge sharing. Chai, Gregory, and Shi's (2003)

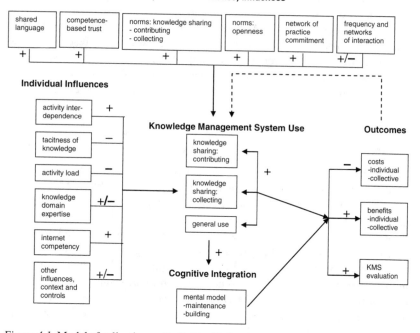

*Figure 4.1* Model of collective and individual influences on knowledge sharing through a knowledge management system, cognitive integration of that knowledge, and costs and benefits at both the collective and individual level.

model, based on case studies in 11 multinational companies, included multiple sharing mechanisms. Kulkarni, Ravindran, and Freeze's (2006–2007) model was oriented toward organizational support factors (leadership commitment, supervisor and coworker support, and incentives) and information systems use research (information and system quality, user satisfaction).

### Future Research

This topic and proposed model generate many possibilities and needs for future research.

### Time

The sources and outcomes of influences on knowledge sharing processes are dynamic and complex. When sharing knowledge through a KMS, the costs, benefits, and overall evaluation of the system are highly relevant outcomes that, in turn, should influence future KMS use and knowledge sharing. The outcomes may also affect collective level influences (such as shared language, trust, openness and knowledge sharing norms, and frequency of interaction) as well as individual level influences (tacitness of knowledge required for an activity, activity load, expertise, and Internet competency). Not only does a feedback loop exist between outcomes and behavior, it also exists among the intermediary components of knowledge contributing, knowledge collecting, general KMS use, and cognitive integration. Therefore, future research should study the over-time reciprocal relationships between outcomes (costs, benefits, and system evaluation), behavior (general KMS use, contributing knowledge, and collecting knowledge), and more indirect influences (collective and individual).

### Culture

Only briefly mentioned, in the context of collective shared language and norms, are differences in cultural norms involving and influencing knowledge sharing either directly or as a moderator. A cultural perspective—whether organizational or social/national—likely emphasizes, among other things, the set of values, practices and relationships that constitute and reconstitute knowledge in use (see Hornikx & O'Keefe, this volume). Organizational culture may, among many other ways, be characterized as clan, ad-hocracy, hierarchical, market, control, collaboration, competence and cultivation (Martin, 2008). Each of these perspectives will have possibly very different assumptions and practices about sharing knowledge, leading to variations in the influences on, use and outcomes of, a KMS. De Long and Fahey (2000) proposed four ways in which culture (specifically, organizational) affects knowledge management processes, and, by implication, use of knowledge management systems. They asserted that (1) culture shapes assumptions about which knowledge is important and relevant, and different subcultures apply different criteria; (2) culture mediates the relationships between levels of knowledge (such as the boundaries between and valuation of individual and organizational knowledge, and the salience of trust and status); (3) culture creates a context for social interaction (both between hierarchical levels, and among peers within levels, such as through network patterns, collaborations, willingness to reuse knowledge, and handling mistakes), and (4) culture shapes the creation and adoption of new knowledge (such as seeking external knowledge, managing internal debates, levels of participation). For example, De Long and Fahey identified differences in the content, quality, and length of contributions to the same topic on four different language versions of Wikipedia. They attributed these differences to Hofstede's cultural dimensions and other cultural markers (e.g., the greater the individualism index, the less likelihood of adding or clarifying information; see Pfeil, Zaphiris, & Ang, 2006). Future research should expand upon the role of culture in knowledge systems and processes.

### Web 2.0

As noted earlier, the concept and forms of Web 2.0 have pushed the venues, participants, and ICTs involved in knowledge sharing well beyond the boundaries of organizations and even nations, and beyond experts and profession-als. One of the most significant phenomena emerging from the Web is the *gift economy* and the *open source movement*, where millions of users volun-tarily spend considerable time, energy, and financial resources developing and sharing knowledge (ranging from replies to questions on discussion boards and comprehensive entries on Wikipedia, to complex modifications of online multiplayer games, to highly sophisticated videos and software) (Kollock, 1999; Shirky, 2008; Söderberg (2007). While this review and proposed model presumes a specific knowledge management system (such as a public online database for professionals to share their expertise), the scope and pervasively interlinked components of the Web clearly represent both a massive-scale knowledge management system, as well as opportunities for studies of a wide variety of specific Web 2.0 forms and sites.

*Related Areas of Communication Research*

Research on knowledge sharing holds strong potential implications for a broad array of areas in the communication discipline. As just a few examples from topics in this volume of *Communication Yearbook*, KMS facilitates the shar-ing and disseminating of important research on genetics (see related review by Galvin & Grill, this volume) or statistical risk (see Noar, Harrington, & Aldrich, this volume). Indeed, participation in a KMS can even be considered a form of volunteerism (see related review by Ganesh & McAllum, this vol-ume). Further, KMS are becoming crucial for sustaining large NoPs, such as media advocacy and activism groups, given that sustained collective action requires both communality and connectivity (see related review by Napoli, this volume). Table 4.1 underscores the potential relevance of knowledge shar-ing and ICTs across the field of communication by highlighting possible areas for collaborative research among International Communication Association divisions and interest groups.

## Conclusion

Three questions motivated this review: Why do people share (or withhold) knowledge through online knowledge management systems? What benefits and costs might they experience from doing so? How does one's ability to cognitively integrate the knowledge shared through a KMS affect these costs and benefits? Fundamental concepts about knowledge processes, the social dilemma of knowledge sharing, networks of practice, social capital, and the potential of ICTs to support knowledge management and sharing generated a variety of collective and individual influences on KMS use. *Cognitive integra-tion* is proposed as a primary component of the knowledge sharing process, acting as a mediator between behavior (knowledge contributing, knowledge collecting, and general knowledge management system use) and its outcomes.

*Table 4.1* Summary Possibilities for Different Communication Research Areas with Studies of Knowledge Sharing and Knowledge Management Systems

- Communication and Technology: How users interact with a KMS in social and organizational contexts, and communication-related features of KMS
- Communication Law and Policy: Issues of intellectual property, economic value of networked knowledge, open source KMS
- Ethnicity and Race in Communication: Varying cultural values on what kinds of knowledge should or can be shared publicly, and the communication medium through which credible knowledge is best shared, and how to provide equitable access to knowledge across social and economic strata
- Feminist Scholarship: How gender influences the availability and value of kinds of knowledge and KMS
- Game Studies: How system design and social processes associated with online games fostering high involvement and large-scale collaboration could be applied to KMS
- Gay, Lesbian, Bisexual and Transgender Studies: How KMS may be used to foster support and knowledge sharing within and among specific communities
- Global Communication and Social Change: Globalization may be considered a massive knowledge-sharing system, involving regional, international, transcultural, transnational and global communication
- Health Communication: Certainly access to and sharing and discussing of health information and is being dramatically transformed through online media; especially relevant is how knowledge can be made more salient, accurate, and useful through personally-tailored web-based KMS
- Information Systems: Studies of information flows, human-computer interfaces, cognitive processing of information are central to KMS research and concepts
- Instructional/Developmental Communication: Learning depends on sharing knowledge, and online instructional media can be conceived as KMS
- Intercultural Communication: Meaningful and effective sharing across physical, social and culture contexts requires deep understanding of the differences and interactions among members of different cultures – including professions, and communities or networks of practice
- Intergroup Communication: What are the factors that would encourage or suppress sharing across boundaries of group social identity
- Interpersonal Communication: Developing shared meaning of information available through a KMS requires interpersonal communication processes that often are not well understood, especially across boundaries
- Journalism Studies: How can traditional journalistic practices, norms and media manage the challenge of new ways of sharing news and opinion, such as blogs, user-contributed stories, and newsgroups
- Language and Social Interaction: Core concepts in the study of human discourse and interaction raise a central critique of the concept of knowledge management, and especially KMS: the assumption that words mediated through a KMS could easily generate shared knowledge, much less transform tacit into explicit knowledge
- Mass Communication: The broad reach of online communication, even just among divisions of multinational corporations or members of NGOs in different countries; has blurred or erased the boundary between interpersonal and mass media; agenda-setting through community-based knowledge sources
- Philosophy of Communication: The very concept of knowledge, the nature of tacit and explicit knowledge, and even what it means to share or interpret knowledge are open to philosophical debate
- Political Communication: Analysis and implementation of KMS would seem to be relevant to the rise of the concept and implementation of e-government and concerns about online political communities

*Table 4.1* Continued

- Popular Communication: Popular communication and cultural studies research is increasingly focused on social media that can be thought of as non-professional KMS
- Public Relations: Relationships between organizations, whether for-profit or non-profit, and their stakeholders, are increasingly being developed and maintained through knowledge-sharing media, with varying effectiveness
- Visual Communication Studies: There has been little research on the visual (or audio!) representations of knowledge in KMS, such as how visual aspects of the interface or content influence use and effectiveness; whether credibility and trust change with different visual representations of participating individuals, groups, and communities on KMS sites

Those outcomes are potentially both positive and negative, and occur at both individual and collective levels.

## Acknowledgments

We would like to acknowledge the very helpful guidance of editor Christina Beck and three anonymous reviewers, and Dr. Bart Van den Hooff, Dr. Ann Majchrzak, and Dr. Samer Faraj for their early suggestions and knowledge sharing.

## References

Adler, P. (2001). Market, hierarchy, and trust: The knowledge economy and the future of capitalism. *Organization Science, 12,* 215–234.

Adler, P., & Kwon, S. (2002). Social capital: Prospects for a new concept. *Academy of Management Review, 27*(1), 17–40.

Alavi, M., & Leidner, D. E. (2001). Review: Knowledge management and knowledge management systems: Conceptual foundations and research issues. *MIS Quarterly, 25,* 107–136.

Alavi, M., & Tiwana, A. (2003). Knowledge management: The information technology dimension. In M. Easterby-Smith & M. A. Lyles (Eds.), *The Blackwell handbook of organizational learning and knowledge management* (pp. 104–121). Malden, MA: Blackwell.

Argote, L., & Ingram, P. (2000). Knowledge transfer: A basis for competitive advantage in firms. *Organizational Behavior and Human Decision Processes, 82,* 150–169.

Arrow, K. J. (1984). *The economics of information. Collected papers of Kenneth J. Arrow* (Vol. 4). Cambridge, MA: Belknap Press/Harvard University Press.

Bandura, A. (1986). *Social foundations of thought and action: A social cognitive theory.* Englewood Cliffs, NJ: Prentice-Hall.

Barrett, M., Cappleman, S., Shoib, G., & Walsham, G. (2004). Learning in knowledge communities: Managing technology and context. *European Management Journal, 22*(1), 1–11.

Benbya, H., Passiante, G., & Belbaly, N. A. (2004). Corporate portal: A tool for knowledge management synchronization. *International Journal of Information Management, 24,* 201–220.

Benkler, Y. (2006). *Wealth of networks: How social production transforms markets and freedom.* New Haven, CT: Yale University Press.

Bimber, B., Flanagin, A. J., & Stohl, C. (2005). Reconceptualizing collective action in the contemporary media environment. *Communication Theory, 15,* 365–368.

Bock, G. W., & Kim, Y.-G. (2002). Breaking the myths of rewards: An exploratory study of attitudes about knowledge sharing. *Information Resources Management Journal, 15*(2), 14–21.

Bolisani, E., & Scarso, E. (1999). Information technology management: A knowledge-based perspective. *Technovation, 19,* 209–217.

Bollier, D. (2007). *The rise of collective intelligence: Decentralized co-creation of value as a new paradigm of commerce and culture.* Washington, DC: The Aspen Institute, Communications and Society Program.

boyd, d. m., & Ellison, N. B. (2007). Social network sites: Definition, history, and scholarship. *Journal of Computer-Mediated Communication, 13*(1), article 11. Retrieved July 15, 2008, from http://jcmc.indiana.edu/vol13/issue1/boyd.ellison.html

Brewer, M. B., & Kramer, R. M. (1986). Choice behavior in social dilemmas: Effects of social identity, group size, and decision framing. *Journal of Personality and Social Psychology, 50,* 543–549.

Brown, J. S., & Duguid, P. (2000). *The social life of information.* Boston: Harvard Business School Press.

Bruns, A. (2008). *Blogs, Wikipedia, Second Life, and beyond: From production to produsage.* New York: Peter Lang.

Bugbin, J., & Manyiska, J. (2007, March). *How businesses are using Web 2.0: A McKinsey global survey.* Retrieved July 15, 2008, from http://mckinseyquarterly.com/article_page.aspx?L2=13&L3=11&ar=1913&gp=1&pagenum=1

Butler, B., Sproull, L., Kiesler, S., & Kraut, R. (2002). Community effort in online groups: Who does the work and why? In S. Weisband & L. Atwater (Eds.), *Leadership at a distance* (pp. 346–362). Mahwah, NJ: Erlbaum.

Byrne, S. & Hart, P. S. (this volume). The boomerang effect: A synthesis of findings and a preliminary theoretical framework. In C. S. Beck (Ed.), *Communication yearbook 33* (pp. 3–37). New York: Routledge.

Cabrera, A., & Cabrera, E. G. (2002). Knowledge-sharing dilemmas. *Organization Studies, 23,* 687–710.

Chai, K-H., Gregory, M., & Shi, Y. (2003). Bridging islands of knowledge: A framework of knowledge sharing mechanisms. *International Journal of Technology Management, 25,* 703–727.

Cohen, D., & Prusak, L. (2001). *In good company: How social capital makes organizations work.* Boston: Harvard Business School Press.

Cohen, W. M., & Levinthal, D. A. (1990). Absorptive capacity: A new perspective on learning and innovation. *Administrative Science Quarterly, 35,* 128–152.

Coleman, J. S. (1988). Social capital in the creation of human capital. *The American Journal of Sociology, 94,* S95–S120.

Connolly, T., & Thorn, B. K. (1990). Discretionary databases: Theory, data, and implications. In J. Fulk & C. W. Steinfeld (Eds.), *Organizations and communication technology* (pp. 219–233). Newbury Park, CA: Sage.

Constant, D., Kiesler, S., & Sproull, L. (1994). What's mine is ours, or is it? A study of attitudes about information sharing. *Information Systems Research, 5,* 400–421.

Constant, D., Sproull, L., & Kiesler, S. (1996). The kindness of strangers: The usefulness of weak ties for technical advice. *Organization Science, 7,* 119–135.

Contractor, N., & Monge, P. (2002). Managing knowledge networks. *Management Communication Quarterly, 16,* 249–258.

Cook, K. (Ed.). (1987). *Social exchange theory.* Newbury Park, CA: Sage.

Cress, U., Kimmerle, J., & Hesse, F. (2006). Information exchange with shared databases as a social dilemma: The effect of metaknowledge, bonus systems, and costs. *Communication Research, 33,* 370–390.

Cross, R., Rice, R. E., & Parker, A. (2001). Information seeking in social context: Structural influences and receipt of information benefits. *IEEE Transactions on Systems, Man, and Cybernetics—Part C: Applications and Reviews, 31,* 438–448.

Daft, R. L., & Lengel, R. (1984). Information richness: A new approach to managerial behavior and organizational design. In L. L. Cummings & B. M. Staw (Eds.), *Research in organizational behavior* (Vol. 6, pp. 191–233). Newbury Park, CA: Sage.

Davenport T. H. (1997). *Information ecology: Mastering the information and knowledge environment.* New York: Oxford University Press.

Davenport, T. H., De Long, D. W., & Beers, M. C. (1998). Successful management projects. *Sloan Management Review, 39*(2), 43–57.

Davenport, T. H., & Prusak, L. (1998). *Working knowledge: How organizations manage what they know.* Boston: Harvard Business School Press.

Davis, F. D., Bagozzi, R., & Warshaw, P. (1992). Extrinsic and intrinsic motivation to use computers in the workplace. *Journal of Applied Social Psychology, 22,* 1111–1132.

Dawes, R. M. (1980). Social dilemmas. *Annual Review of Psychology, 31,* 169–193.

De Long, D. W., & Fahey, L. (2000). Diagnosing cultural barriers to knowledge management. *The Academy of Management Executive, 14,* 113–127.

DeSanctis, G., & Poole, M. S. (1994). Capturing the complexity in advanced technology use: Adaptive structuration theory. *Organization Science, 5,* 121–147.

DiMaggio, P., & Powell, W. (1991). The iron cage revisited: Institutional isomorphism and collective rationality in organizational fields. In W. Powell & P. DiMaggio (Eds.), *The new institutionalism in organizational analysis* (pp. 63–82). Chicago: University of Chicago Press.

Dolfsma, W. (2006). Knowledge, the knowledge economy and welfare theory. In W. Dolfsma & L. Soete (Eds.), *Understanding the dynamics of a knowledge economy* (pp. 201–221). Cheltenham, England: Edward Elgar.

Drucker, P. (1969). *The age of discontinuity: Guidelines to our changing society.* New York: Harper & Row.

Due, R. T. (1995). The knowledge economy. *Information Systems Management, 12*(3), 76–79.

Earl, M. J., & Scott, I. A. (1999). Opinion: What is a Chief Knowledge Officer? *Sloan Management Review, 40*(2), 29–38.

Easterby-Smith, M., & Lyles, M. A. (2003). Introduction: Watersheds of organizational learning and knowledge management. In M. Easterby-Smith & M. A. Lyles (Eds.), *The Blackwell handbook of organizational learning and knowledge management* (pp. 1–15). Malden, MA: Blackwell.

Finholt, T., & Sproull, T. (1990). Electronic groups at work. *Organization Science, 1*(1), 41–64.

Flanagin, A. J. (2002). The elusive benefits of the technological support of knowledge management. *Management Communication Quarterly, 16,* 242–248.

Fulk, J., Flanagin, A. J., Kalman, M., Monge, P. R., & Ryan, T. (1996). Connective and communal public goods in interactive communication systems. *Communication Theory, 6*, 60–87.

Fulk, J., Heino, R., Flanagin, A. J., Monge, P. R., & Bar, F. (2004). A test of the individual action model for organizational information commons. *Organization Science, 15*, 569–585.

Galvin, K. & Grill, L. (this volume). Opening up the conversation on genetics and genomics in families: The space for communication scholars. In C. S. Beck (Ed.), *Communication yearbook 33* (pp. 213–257). New York: Routledge.

Ganesh, S., & McAllum, K. (this volume). Discourses of volunteerism. In C. S. Beck (Ed.), *Communication yearbook 33* (pp. 343–383). New York: Routledge.

Gherardi, S., & Nicolini, D. (2002). Learning the trade: A culture of safety in practice. *Organization Articles, 9*, 191–223.

Gibbs, J., Nekrassova, D., Grushina, Y., & Abdul Wahab, S. (2008). Reconceptualizing virtual teaming from a constitutive perspective: Review, redirection, and research agenda. In C. S. Beck (Ed.), *Communication yearbook 32* (pp. 187–229). New York: Routledge.

Granovetter, M. (1973). The strength of weak ties. *American Journal of Sociology, 78*, 1360–1380.

Granovetter, M. (1985). Economic action and social structure: The problem of embeddedness. *The American Journal of Sociology, 91*, 481–510.

Grant, R. M. (1996). Toward a knowledge-based theory of the firm. *Strategic Management Journal, 17*, 109–122.

Grover, V., & Davenport, T. H. (2001). General perspectives on knowledge management: Fostering a research agenda. *Journal of Management Information Systems, 18*(1), 5–21.

Hansen, M. T. (1999). The search-transfer problem: The role of weak ties in sharing knowledge across organizational subunits. *Administrative Science Quarterly, 44*(1), 82–111.

Hansen, M. T. (2002). Knowledge networks: Explaining effective knowledge sharing in multiunit companies. *Organization Science, 13*, 232–248.

Hansen, M. T., Nohria, N., & Tierney, T. (1999). What's your strategy for managing knowledge? *Harvard Business Review, 77*, 106–116.

Hardin, G. (1968). The tragedy of the commons. *Science, 162*, 1243–1248.

Hardin, G. (1982). *Collective action.* Baltimore: Johns Hopkins University Press.

Harris, R. G. (2001). The knowledge-based economy: Intellectual origins and new economic perspectives. *International Journal of Management Reviews, 3*(1), 21–40.

Heaton, L., & Taylor, J. R. (2002). Knowledge management and professional work. *Management Communication Quarterly, 16*, 210–236.

Hedlund, G. (1994). A model of knowledge management and the N-form corporation. *Strategic Management Journal, 15*, 73–90.

Hinds, P., & Pfeffer, J. (2003). Why organizations don't "know what they know": Cognitive and motivational factors affecting the transfer of expertise. In M. Ackerman, V. Pipek, & V. Wulf (Eds.), *Beyond knowledge management: Sharing expertise* (pp. 3–26). Cambridge, MA: MIT Press.

Hislop, D. (2002). Mission impossible? Communicating and sharing knowledge via information technology. *Journal of Information Technology, 17*, 165–177.

Hollingshead, A., Fulk, J., & Monge, P. (2001). Fostering intranet knowledge sharing: An integration of transactive memory and public goods approaches. In P. Hinds

& S. Kiesler (Eds.), *Distributed work: New research on working across distance using technology* (pp. 335–355). Cambridge, MA: MIT Press.

Homans, G. C. (1958). Social behavior as exchange. *American Journal of Sociology, 63*, 597–606.

Hornikx, J., & O'Keefe, D. (this volume). Adapting consumer advertising appeals to cultural values: A meta-analytic review of the effects on persuasiveness and ad liking In C. S. Beck (Ed.), *Communication yearbook 33* (pp. 39–71). New York: Routledge.

Howe, J. (2008). *Crowdsourcing: Why the power of the crowd is driving the future of business.* New York: Crown/Random House.

Huysman, M., & de Wit, D. (2003). A critical evaluation of knowledge management practices. In M. Ackerman, V. Pipek, & V. Wulf (Eds.), *Beyond knowledge management: Sharing expertise* (pp. 3–26). Cambridge, MA: MIT Press.

Inkpen, A. C., & Tsang, E. W. K. (2005). Social capital, networks, and knowledge transfer. *Academy of Management Review, 30*, 146–165.

Iverson, J. O., & McPhee, R. D. (2002). Knowledge management in communities of practice. *Management Communication Quarterly, 16*, 259–265.

Jacobs, C., & Coghlan, D. (2005). Sound from silence: On listening in organizational learning. *Human Relations, 58*(1), 115–138.

Jarvenpaa, S. L., & Staples, D. S. (2000). The use of collaborative electronic media for information sharing: An exploratory study of determinants. *Journal of Strategic Information Systems, 9*, 129–154.

Jian, G., & Jeffres, L. (2006). Understanding employees' willingness to contribute to shared electronic databases: A three-dimensional framework. *Communication Research, 33*, 242–261.

Johannessen, J.-A., Olaisen, J., & Olsen, B. (2001). Mismanagement of tacit knowledge: The importance of tacit knowledge, the danger of information technology, and what to do about it. *International Journal of Information Management, 21*, 3–20.

Johnson, B. McD., & Rice, R. E. (1987). *Managing organizational innovation.* New York: Columbia University Press.

Joyce, E., & Kraut, R. E. (2006). Predicting continued participation in newsgroups. *Journal of Computer-Mediated Communication, 11*(3), article 3. Retrieved July 15, 2008, from http://jcmc.indiana.edu/vol11/issue3/joyce.html

Jussawalla, M., Lamberton, D. M., & Karunaratne, N. D. (Eds.). (1988). *The cost of thinking: Information economies in ten Pacific countries.* Norwood, NJ: Ablex.

Kalman, M. E., Monge, P., Fulk, J., & Heino, R. (2002). Motivations to resolve communication dilemmas in database-mediated collaboration. *Communication Research, 29*, 125–154.

Kankanhalli, A., Tan, B., & Wei, T. (2005). Understanding seeking from electronic knowledge repositories: An empirical study. *Journal of the American Society for Information Science and Technology, 56*, 1156–1166.

Katz, J. E., & Rice, R. E. (2002). *Social consequences of Internet use: Access, involvement and interaction.* Cambridge, MA: The MIT Press.

Kim, D. H. (1993). The link between individual and organizational learning. *Sloan Management Review, 35*(1), 37–50.

Kisselburgh, L. G., Berkelaar, B. L. & Buzzanell, P. M. (this volume). Discourse, gender, and the meaning of work: Rearticulating science, technology, and engineering careers through communicative lenses. In C. S. Beck (Ed.), *Communication yearbook 33* (pp. 259–299). London: Routledge.

Kogut, B., & Zander, U. (1992). Knowledge of the firm, combinative capabilities, and the replication of technology. *Organization Science, 3*, 383–397.

Kollock, P. (1999). The economies of online cooperation: Gifts and public goods in cyberspace. In M. A. Smith & P. Kollock (Eds.), *Communities in cyberspace* (pp. 220–239). London: Routledge.

KPMG. (2000). *Knowledge management research report 2000*. London: KPMG Consulting Reports. Retrieved July 15, 2008, from http://www.providersedge.com/docs/km_articles/KPMG_KM_Research_Report_2000.pdf

Kramer, R. M., Brewer, M. B., & Hanna, B. A. (1996). Collective trust and collective action: The decision to trust as a social decision. In R. M. Kramer & T. R. Tyler (Eds.), *Trust in organizations: Frontiers of theory and research* (pp. 357–389). Thousand Oaks, CA: Sage.

Kraut, R. E., Patterson, M., Lundmark, V., Kiesler, S., Mukophadyay, T., & Scherlis, W. (1998). Internet paradox: A social technology that reduces social involvement and psychological well-being? *American Psychologist, 53*, 1017–1031.

Kraut, R. E., Rice, R., Cool, C., & Fish, R. (1998). Varieties of social influence: The role of utility and norms in the success of a communication medium. *Organizational Science, 9*, 437–453.

Kulkarni, U., Ravindran, S., & Freeze, R. (2006–2007). A knowledge management success model: Theoretical development and empirical validation. *Journal of Management Information Systems, 23*, 309–347.

Lamberton, D. M. (Ed.). (1971). *Economics of information and knowledge: Selected readings*. Harmondsworth, England: Penguin Books.

Lampel, J., & Bhalla, A. (2007). The role of status seeking in online communities: Giving the gift of experience. *Journal of Computer-Mediated Communication, 12*(2), article 5. Retrieved July 15, 2008, from http://jcmc.indiana.edu/vol12/issue2/lampel.html

Latane, B., Williams, K., & Harkins, S. (1979). Many hands make light the work: The causes and consequences of social loafing. *Journal of Personality and Social Psychology, 37*, 822–832.

Lave, J., & Wenger, E. (1991). *Situated learning: Legitimate peripheral participation*. Cambridge, England: Cambridge University Press.

Levin, D. Z., & Cross, R. (2004). The strength of weak ties you can trust: The mediating role of trust in effective knowledge transfer. *Management Science, 50*, 1477–1490.

Levitt, B., & March, J. G. (1988). Organizational learning. *Annual Review of Society, 14*, 319–340.

Liebrand, W., Messick, D., & Wilke, H. (Eds.). (1992). *Social dilemma*. Oxford, England: Pergamon Press.

Lin, N. (2001). *Social capital: A theory of social structure and action*. Cambridge, England: Cambridge University Press.

Ling, K., Beenen, G., Ludford, P., Wang, X., Chang, K., Li, X., et al. (2005). Using social psychology to motivate contributions to online communities. *Journal of Computer-Mediated Communication, 10*(4), article 10. Retrieved July 15, 2008, from http://jcmc.indiana.edu/vol10/issue4/ling.html

Maier, R. (2007). *Knowledge management systems: Information and communication technologies for knowledge management* (3rd ed.). Berlin, Germany: Springer.

Majchrzak, A., Rice, R. E., Malhotra, A., King, N., & Ba, S. (2000). Technology adaptation: The case of a computer-supported inter-organizational virtual team. *MIS Quarterly, 24*, 569–600.

March, J. G., & Simon, H. A. (1958). Cognitive limits on rationality. In J. G. March & H. A. Simon (Eds.), *Organizations* (pp. 136–171). New York: Wiley.

Markus, M. L. (1990). Toward a critical mass theory of interactive media. In J. Fulk & C. W. Steinfield (Eds.), *Organizations and communication technology* (pp. 194–218). Newbury Park, CA: Sage.

Markus, M. L. (2001). Toward a theory of knowledge reuse: Types of knowledge reuse situations and factors in reuse success. *Journal of Management Information Systems, 18*(1), 57–93.

Markus, M. L., & Benjamin, R. I. (1997). The magic bullet theory in IT-enabled transformation. *Sloan Management Review, 38*(2), 55–68.

Markus, M. L., Manville, B., & Agres, C. E. (2000). What makes a virtual organization work? *Sloan Management Review, 42*(1), 13–26.

Marschak, J. (1964). Problems in information economics. In C. P. Bonini, R. K. Jaedicke, & H. M. Wagner (Eds.), *Management controls: New directions in basic research* (pp. 38–74). New York: McGraw-Hill.

Martin, B. (2008). Knowledge management. In B. Cronin (Ed.), *Annual review of information science and technology* (Vol. 42, pp. 371–424). Medford, NJ: Information Today.

Marwell, G., & Oliver, P. (1993). *The critical mass in collective action: A micro-social theory.* New York: Cambridge University Press.

McAllister, D. J. (1995). Affect- and cognition-based trust as foundations for interpersonal cooperation in organizations. *The Academy of Management Journal, 38*(1), 24–59.

McDermott, R. (1999). Why information technology inspired but cannot deliver knowledge management. *California Management Review, 41*(4), 103–117.

Mishira, A. K. (1996). Organizational responses to crisis: The centrality of trust. In R. M. Kramer & T. R. Tyler (Eds.), *Trust in organizations: Frontiers of theory and research* (pp. 261–287). Thousand Oaks, CA: Sage.

Monge, P. R., Fulk, J., Kalman, M., Flanagin, A. J., Parnassa, C., & Rumsey, S. (1998). Production of collective action in alliance-based interorganizational communication and information systems. *Organization Science, 9,* 411–433.

Moran, P., & Ghoshal, S. (1996). Value creation by firms. *Academy of Management Best Paper Proceedings 1996,* 41–45.

Nahapiet, J., & Ghoshal, S. (1998). Social capital, intellectual capital, and the organizational advantage. *Academy of Management Review, 23,* 242–266.

Napoli, P. M. (this volume). Public interest media advocacy and activism as a social movement. In C. S. Beck (Ed.), *Communication yearbook 33* (pp. 385–429). New York: Routledge.

Neff, G., & Stark, D. (2004). Permanently beta: Responsive organization in the Internet era. In P. Howard & S. Jones (Eds.), *Society online: The Internet in context* (pp. 173–188). Thousand Oaks, CA: Sage.

Noar, S. M., Harrington, N. G., & Aldrich, R. S. (this volume). The role of computer tailoring in the development of persuasive health communication messages. In C. S. Beck (Ed.), *Communication yearbook 33* (pp. 73–133). New York: Routledge.

Nonaka, I. (1994). A dynamic theory of organizational knowledge creation. *Organization Science, 5*(1), 14–37.

Nonaka, I., Noboru, K., & Toyama, R. (2001). Emergence of "Ba." In I. Nonaka & T. Nishiguchi (Eds.), *Knowledge emergence* (pp. 3–9). New York: Oxford University Press.

Nonaka, I., & Takeuchi, H. (1995). *The knowledge-creating company: How Japanese companies create the dynamics of innovation.* New York: Oxford University Press.

Nonnecke, B., Andrews, D., & Preece, J. (2006). Non-public and public online community participation: Needs, attitudes and behavior. *Electronic Commerce Research, 6*(1), 7–20.

Oliver, P., Marwell, G., & Teixeira, R. (1985). A theory of critical mass: I. Interdependence, group heterogeneity, and the production of collective action. *The American Journal of Sociology, 91*, 522–556.

Oravec, J. A. (2004). The transparent knowledge worker: Weblogs and reputation mechanisms in KM systems. *International Journal of Technology Management, 28*, 767–775.

Orlikowski, W. (1992). The duality of technology: Rethinking the concept of technology in organizations. *Organization Science, 3*, 398–427.

Osterloh, M., & Frey, B. S. (2000). Motivation, knowledge transfer, and organizational forms. *Organization Science, 11*, 538–550.

Østerlund, C., & Carlile, P. (2005). Relations in practice: Sorting through practice theories on knowledge sharing in complex organizations. *The Information Society, 21*(2), 91–107.

Pan, S. L., & Leidner, D. E. (2003). Bridging communities of practice with information technology in pursuit of global knowledge sharing. *Journal of Strategic Information Systems, 12*(1), 71–88.

Pfeil, U., Zaphiris, P., & Ang, C. S. (2006). Cultural differences in collaborative authoring of Wikipedia. *Journal of Computer-Mediated Communication, 12*(1), article 5. Retrieved July 15, 2008, from http://jcmc.indiana.edu/vol12/issue1/pfeil.html

Polanyi, M. (1966). *The tacit dimension.* London: Routledge & Kegan Paul.

Powell, W. W. (1990). Neither market nor hierarchy: Network forms of organization. *Research in organizational behavior, 12*, 295–336.

Powell, W. W. (1996). Trust-based forms of governance. In R. M. Kramer & T. R. Tyler (Eds.), *Trust in organizations: Frontiers of theory and research* (pp. 51–67). Thousand Oaks, CA: Sage.

Putnam, R. (2000). *Bowling alone: The collapse and revival of American community.* New York: Free Press.

Raban, D. R. (2008). The incentive structure in an online information market. *Journal of the American Society for Information Science and Technology, 59*(12), 1–12.

Rafaeli, S., & LaRose, R. J. (1993). Electronic bulletin boards and "public goods" explanations of collaborative mass media. *Communication Research, 22*, 277–297.

Reagans, R., & McEvily, B. (2003). Network structure and knowledge transfer: The effects of cohesion and range. *Administrative Science Quarterly, 48*, 240–267.

Rice, R. E. (1982). Communication networking in computer-conferencing systems: A longitudinal study of group roles and system structure. In M. Burgoon (Ed.), *Communication yearbook 6* (pp. 925–944). Beverly Hills, CA: Sage.

Rice, R. E. (1987). Computer-mediated communication and organizational innovation. *Journal of Communication, 37*(4), 65–94.

Rice, R. E. (1990). Computer-mediated communication system network data: Theoretical concerns and empirical examples. *International Journal of Man-Machine Studies, 32*, 627–647.

Rice, R. E. (2008). Unusual routines: Organizational (non)sensemaking. *Journal of Communication, 58*(1), 1–19.

Rice, R. E., & Aydin, C. (1991). Attitudes towards new organizational technology: Network proximity as a mechanism for social information processing. *Administrative Science Quarterly, 36*, 219–244.

Rice, R. E., Collins-Jarvis, L. & Zydney-Walker, S. (1999). Individual and structural influences on information technology helping relationships. *Journal of Applied Communication Research, 27*(4), 285–303.

Rice, R. E., & Gattiker, U. (2001). New media and organizational structuring. In F. Jablin & L. Putnam (Eds.), *New handbook of organizational communication* (pp. 544–581). Newbury Park, CA: Sage.

Rice, R. E., Grant, A., Schmitz, J., & Torobin, J. (1990). Individual and network influences on the adoption and perceived outcomes of electronic messaging. *Social Networks, 12*(1), 27–55.

Rice, R. E., McCreadie, M., & Chang, S-J. (2001). *Accessing and browsing information and communication.* Cambridge, MA: MIT Press.

Rice, R. E., & Shook, D. (1988). Access to, usage of, and outcomes from an electronic message system. *ACM Transactions on Office Information Systems, 6*, 255–276.

Ridings, C. M., Gefen, D., & Arinze, B. (2002). Some antecedents and effects of trust in virtual communities. *Journal of Strategic Information Systems, 11*, 271–295.

Roberts, J. (2000). From know-how to show-how? Questioning the role of information and communication technologies in knowledge transfer. *Technology Analysis Strategic Management, 12*, 429–442.

Rodrigues, M. J. (2003). *European policies for a knowledge economy.* Cheltenham, England: Edward Elgar.

Rogers, E. M. (2003). *Diffusion of innovations* (5th ed.). New York: Free Press.

Ruggles, R. (1998). The state of the notion: Knowledge management in practice. *California Management Review, 40*(3), 80–89.

Schultze, U. (2000). A confessional account of an ethnography about knowledge work. *MIS Quarterly, 24*(1), 3–42.

Shapiro, C., & Varian, H. (1999). *Information rules: A strategic guide to the network economy.* Boston: Harvard Business School Press.

Shirky, C. (2008). *Here comes everybody: The power of organizing without organizations.* New York: Penguin.

Siemsen, E., Roth, A. V., & Balasubramanian, S. (2007). How motivation, opportunity, and ability drive knowledge sharing: The constraining factor model. *Journal of Operations Management, 26*, 426–445.

Simard, C., & Rice, R. E. (2007). The practice gap: Barriers to the diffusion of best practices. In C. R. McInerney & R. E. Day (Eds.), *Re-thinking knowledge management: From knowledge objects to knowledge processes* (pp. 87–124). Dordrecht, The Netherlands: Springer-Verlag.

Simon, H. A. (1991). Bounded rationality and organizational learning. *Organization Science, 2*(1), 125–134.

Smith, A. (1904). *An inquiry into the nature and causes of the wealth of nations* (5th ed.). London: Methuen. (Original work published in 1775)

Söderberg, J. (2007). *Hacking capitalism: The free and open source software (FOSS) movement.* London: Routledge.

Sproull, L., & Kiesler, S. (1991). *Connections: New ways of working in the networked organization.* Cambridge, MA: The MIT Press.

Starbuck, W. H. (1992). Learning by knowledge-intensive firms. *Journal of Management Studies, 29*, 713–739.

Stigler, G. J. (1961). The economics of information. *Journal of Political Economy, 69*, 213–225.

Tapscott, D., & Williams, A. D. (2006). *Wikinomics: How mass collaboration changes everything*. New York: Portfolio/Penguin.

Taylor, J. R., & van Every, E. (1993). *The vulnerable fortress: Bureaucratic organization and management in the information age*. Toronto, Canada: University of Toronto Press.

Taylor, J. R., & Van Every, E. (2000). *Emergent organization: Communication as its site and surface*. Mahwah, NJ: Erlbaum.

Tsai, W., & Ghoshal, S. (1998). Social capital and value creation: The role of intrafirm networks. *The Academy of Management Journal, 41*, 464–476.

UNESCO. (2005). *From the information society to knowledge societies*. Paris: UNESCO.

Vandenbosch, B., & Higgins, D. (1996). Information acquisition and mental models: An investigation into the relationship between behavior and learning. *Information Systems Research, 7*, 198–214.

Van den Hooff, B. (2004). Electronic coordination and collective action: Use and effects of electronic calendaring and scheduling. *Information & Management, 42*, 103–114.

Van den Hooff, B., & De Leeuw van Weenen, F. (2004). Committed to share: Commitment and CMC use as antecedents of knowledge sharing. *Knowledge and Process Management, 11*(1), 13–24.

Van den Hooff, B., De Ridder, J. A., & Aukema, E. J. (2004) Exploring the eagerness to share knowledge: The role of ICT and social capital in knowledge sharing. In M. H. Huysman & V. Wulf (Eds.), *Social capital and information technology* (pp. 163–186). Cambridge, MA: MIT Press.

Van den Hooff, B., Elving, W., Meeuwsen, J., & Dumoulini, C. (2003). Knowledge sharing in knowledge communities. In M. Huysman, E. Wenger, & V. Wulf (Eds.), *Communities and technologies* (pp. 119–141). Dordrecht, The Netherlands: Kluwer Academic.

Van den Hooff, B., Vijvers, J., & De Ridder, J. (2003). Foundations of a knowledge management scan. *European Management Journal, 21*, 237–246.

Vera, D., & Crossan, M. (2003). Organizational learning and knowledge management: Toward an integrative framework. In M. Easterby-Smith & M. A. Lyles (Eds.), *The Blackwell handbook of organizational learning and knowledge management* (pp. 104–121). Malden, MA: Blackwell.

Walsham, G. (2001). Knowledge management: The benefits and limitations of computer systems. *European Management Journal, 19*, 599–608.

Walsham, G. (2002). What can knowledge management systems deliver? *Management Communication Quarterly, 16*, 267–273.

Wasko, M. M., & Faraj, S. (2000). "It is what one does": Why people participate and help others in electronic communities of practice. *Journal of Strategic Information Systems, 9*, 155–173.

Wasko, M. M., & Faraj, S. (2005). Why should I share? Examining social capital and knowledge contribution in electronic networks of practice. *MIS Quarterly, 29*(1), 35–37.

Weick, K. (1995). *Sensemaking in organizations*. Thousand Oaks, CA: Sage.

Wenger, E. (1998). *Communities of practice*. Cambridge, UK: Cambridge University Press.

Wenger, E., McDermott, R., & Snyder, W. M. (2002). *Cultivating communities of practice: A guide to managing knowledge.* Boston: Harvard Business School Press.

Wernerfelt, B. (1984). A resource-based view of the firm. *Strategic Management Journal, 5,* 171–180.

Yuan, Y., Fulk, J., Shumate, M., Monge, P. R., Bryant, J. A., & Matsaganis, M. (2005). Individual participation in organizational information commons: The impact of team level social influence and technology-specific competence. *Human Communication Research, 31*(2), 1–29.

Zander, U., & Kogut, B. (1995). Knowledge and the speed of the transfer and imitation of organizational capabilities: An empirical test. *Organization Science, 6*(1), 76–92.

# CHAPTER CONTENTS

# 5 Communicating Quantitative Risk Information

*Christine Skubisz*
*Torsten Reimer*
University of Maryland

*Ulrich Hoffrage*
University of Lausanne

People often seek quantitative risk information, but, at the same time, many have problems understanding risk messages that contain statistics and numbers. Common hurdles with comprehending such messages can be related to the risk message itself, the message sender, and the message receiver. In this chapter, we review literature indicating that some representations and formats of quantitative risk information are easier to understand than others. These representations provide an important tool for risk communicators. Second, we detail the ways in which the message sender, a risk communicator, may hinder effective communication. Third, we discuss receiver characteristics, including literacy and numeracy skills, which can affect how the message is comprehended. For each of these three classes, we give practical recommendations that may help risk communicators to effectively communicate quantitative risk information. We conclude with a discussion of quantitative risk information in relation to risk perception and provide future research directions.

As Benjamin Franklin eloquently stated, "In this world nothing is certain except death and taxes" (Smyth, 1907). Uncertainty is part of our daily lives. Ironically, to the extent that we, as a society, have gained control over more and more diseases and hazards, our awareness of risk has increased. At the same time, our willingness to accept risk has declined (Wiedemann, 1993). In other words, as our lives become safer (as affirmed by the increase of life expectancy over time), we become more aware of the threats to our lives. Technological developments drive and amplify such concerns, making it possible to detect even the slightest abnormalities. As a result, people want to be provided with information about risks and uncertainties (Frewer et al., 2002), and risk communication plays an important role in modern life—up to the point that relatively trivial news, such as weather reports, now include probabilities (Gigerenzer, Swijtink, et al., 1989; Gigerenzer, Hertwig, van den Broek, Fasolo, & Katsikopoulos, 2005).

In popular terms, risk often refers to an uncertain negative outcome or event, but it may also indicate the probability that such an event happens, or this prob-

Correspondence: e-mail: skubisz@umd.edu

ability multiplied by the perceived negative consequences of the event. Leiss (1996) defined risk communication as "the flow of information and risk evaluations back and forth between academic experts, regulatory practitioners, interest groups, and the general public" (p. 86). Risk communication can serve several functions. Most broadly, it can inform or persuade. A risk message can elicit outrage and action, or it can provide reassurance and peace of mind. Some risk communication focuses on the prevention of a risk, such as a medical screening, while other risk communication comprises a response, like after a natural disaster. Risk messages can cover a variety of topics, including natural hazards, accidents, risks associated with industrial technologies, insurance rates, and political events. These messages are communicated by corporations, federal institutions, the military, health practitioners and other experts in various domains, or journalists, to name only a few. Risk information can be exchanged interpersonally, in a family conversation (see Galvin & Grill, this volume) or in a doctor's office, or it can be expressed to many, on television, through public speeches, on the Internet, or in a mass mailing to the general public.

Traditionally, persuasion research has emphasized what type of evidence should be presented to make a message more persuasive, memorable, or vivid. The research has focused on the differences between narrative, qualitative evidence and statistical, quantitative evidence (Allen & Preiss, 1997; Baesler & Burgoon, 1994; Kazoleas, 1993; R. Kopfman, Smith, Ah Yun, & Hodges, 1998; Reinard, 1988; A. Reynolds & J. L. Reynolds, 2002). Quantitative evidence has been broadly defined as empirically quantifiable information about objects, persons, concepts, or phenomena (Church & Wilbanks, 1986; Kazoleas, 1993). Research on receiver understanding of quantitative risk information holds importance for communication scholars as well as anyone who communicates risks professionally and who faces the challenging task of presenting complicated risk information in a clear, understandable way.

Goals of risk communication include building trust, influencing policy, fulfilling legal obligations, denying responsibility, justifying past actions, or simply helping people to understand risks that they face (Weinstein, 1999). In this chapter, we concentrate on common obstacles to message comprehension when communicating quantitative risk information. These obstacles can be related to (1) the risk message, (2) the sender of the message, or (3) its receiver.

## The Quantitative Risk Message

Quantitative risk messages, if used correctly, can provide precise and accurate descriptions of risks, explaining why some message receivers prefer numerical risk information (e.g., Hallowell, Statham, Murton, Green, & Richards, 1997; Mazur, Hickam, & Mazur, 1999). Quantitative information can assist message receivers to make informed decisions under uncertainty regarding their financial investments, insurance policies, or health and medical treatments, to name just a few domains in which people commonly form decisions under uncertainty. However, even though people often seek quantitative risk information, at the same time, many people have problems understanding risk messages that involve numbers (Gigerenzer, 2002; Gigerenzer, Gaissmaier, Kurz-Milcke, Schwartz, & Woloshin, 2008; Hoffrage, Lindsey, Hertwig, & Gigerenzer, 2000; Lloyd, Hayes, London, Bell, & Naylor, 1999). Thus, communicating risks to the public and the public's understanding of these risk messages are not necessarily the same thing. Simply providing accurate quantitative risk information does not necessarily ensure that receivers understand the risk message. The following examples illustrate several hurdles that can obstruct the goal of communicating risks effectively.

Consider a 25-year-old man who receives the results of an HIV test from his doctor. The doctor tells him that the test is positive. He asks the doctor, "What does a positive test result mean? Does it mean that I have HIV?" The doctor is faced with the difficult task of explaining this test result to the patient so that the patient can make an informed decision about how to proceed. What does the doctor tell this patient? The doctor will likely say "yes;" this man has HIV (Casscells, Schoenberger, & Grayboys, 1978; Eddy, 1982; Gigerenzer, 2002). Yet, as we describe in detail later, the probability that this man has HIV could actually be quite low (Gigerenzer, Hoffrage, & Ebert, 1998).

Communicators commonly use quantitative risk information to alter attitudes and behavior concerning public hazards. For instance, quantitative risk information can be provided as evidence that performing a particular behavior is risky, which leads us to our second example. To deter people from talking on their cell phones while driving, a message might state that "You are 400% more likely to get into a car accident while talking on a cell phone." People are left with the question, "more likely than what?" As we will explain further, such statements are usually based on a comparison of events, or more precisely, a comparison of two ratios of events. In this example, the statistic compares the number of accidents caused by drivers who were using a cell phone while driving with the number of accidents caused by drivers who were not using a cell phone while driving. Of course, these numbers need to be controlled for driving time—thus, we have to deal with ratios and not only with numbers of accidents. These ratios pertain to a particular reference class, the who or the what to which a risk applies. In fact, according to the frequentist school (e.g., von Mises, 1939), a probability, and let us add a risk, cannot be defined unless a reference class is specified. In other words, the meaning of a probability or a risk depends upon the definition of the reference class, and often, misunderstandings about the meaning of a particular risk message can be attributed to confusion about the identity of the reference class (Gigerenzer & Edwards, 2003; Hoffrage & Hertwig, 2006).

### Basic Concepts

Risk communicators—government officials, politicians, managers, bankers, brokers, doctors, epidemiologists, engineers, journalists, and many others— face several choices to make when communicating quantitative risks. The uncertainty of a patient's HIV status, the risk of driving while talking on a cell phone, and the uncertainty of a bio-terrorism threat can all be expressed in terms of probabilities, percentages, or frequencies. When determining the probability of a negative event or outcome, as a first step, a risk communicator must begin by choosing a reference class. The reference class determines which numbers will be presented. For example, will the frequencies of plane crashes be computed per month, year, decade, air company, category of distance traveled, or plane size? When it comes to comparing accidents in air transportation and rail transportation, what should the denominator be—accidents per a certain number of passengers, total miles traveled, passenger-miles traveled, or a certain number of trips? These decisions may lead to different conclusions about which mode of transport seems more risky. Thus, by choosing what to count and within which class to count, the communicator greatly influences what numbers will result, how receivers will perceive the risk, and, ultimately, even what decisions people will make.

In a second, equally important step, risk communicators specify how the acquired numbers should be represented. Quantitative risks can be expressed in terms of probabilities or frequencies. Probability values range from 0 (an event will definitely not happen) to 1 (an event will definitely happen). In contrast, frequencies result from counting specific cases (e.g., fatal accidents, bankruptcies) within a specific reference class (e.g., a group of people, a sample of events, often coupled with restrictions concerning the time interval during which the counting has been done), leading to relative frequencies of observations in a class of events. Percentages can be found either when messages include probabilities (e.g., a firm's probability of becoming bankrupt within the next 5 years is 20%) or estimated (relative) frequencies (e.g., experts expect 20% of firms in this industry and country to become bankrupt within the next 5 years).

Moreover, these numbers can be communicated in words, orally or in written form, or they can be represented graphically, in a chart or in a diagram. Like the choice of a reference class, the choice of a representation format can influence the understanding and choices of the receiver (Edwards, Elwyn, & Gwyn, 1999; Gigerenzer & Edwards, 2003; Hoffrage et al., 2000; Paling, 2003; Sackett, 1996).

### Types of Numerical Representations

In this section, we elaborate upon the basic notion of a probability and base rate, and we demonstrate that it is much simpler to understand a risk message when it presents numbers as frequencies rather than probabilities. Fortunately, research indicates that common quantitative information is neither difficult nor time consuming to master, if messages present it in the right way (Hoffrage et al., 2000; Sedlmeier & Gigerenzer, 2001).

#### Probabilities

A probability is a numerical expression of the likelihood that a particular event will happen. Probability values can range from 0 (x will definitely not happen) to 1 (x will definitely happen) (Kolmogorov, 1956). Probabilities can be distinguished into prior probabilities and posterior probabilities. Prior probability (the base rate or prevalence) is the probability of an event before any new evidence. For example, the probability that a man will have side effects from a medication may be .03. HIV prevalence can also be expressed as prior probability; for example, the probability that a heterosexual man has HIV is .0001 (see Table 5.1). Posterior probability is the updated prior probability—a conditional probability that includes additional information. In the HIV example, the additional information involved a positive test result, and the prior probability of .0001 has to be updated accordingly. The posterior probability that a man who receives a positive result in a HIV test actually has HIV if he tests positive is about 50% (Gigerenzer et al., 1998). The doctor in the earlier example could have explained the patient's HIV test result in terms of this percentage. As illustrated in Figure 5.1, the prevalence of HIV infections (p(HIV)) in heterosexual males in Germany in 1988, aged 20 to 30 who did not belong to a high-risk group, was about 0.01% or 0.0001.[1] The HIV test has a high sensitivity: Among those who are infected, the test detects the infection in 99.9% (p(POS | HIV) = .999). Likewise, an HIV test rarely produces false alarms: If someone is not infected, the test yields a positive result in only 0.01% of such cases (p(POS | NO HIV) = .0001). The doctor could use these

*Table 5.1* Representations of Quantitative Risk Information

| *Representation* | *HIV* | *Mammography* |
| --- | --- | --- |
| Base rate in terms of probabilities: $p$(DISEASE) | The probability that a man is infected with HIV is 0.0001. | For a 40-year-old woman, the probability of having breast cancer is 0.01. |
| Base rate in terms of percentages | 0.01% of men are infected with HIV. | 1% of 40-year-old women have breast cancer. |
| Base rate in terms of absolute frequencies | 1 out of 10,000 men is infected with HIV. | 10 out of 1,000 40-year-old women have breast cancer. |
| Sensitivity: $p$(POS I DISEASE) | The probability that a HIV test result is positive if a man is infected with HIV is 0.9980. | The probability that a 40-year-old woman, who has breast cancer, receives a positive mammogram is 0.80. |
| False positive rate: $p$(POS I NO DISEASE) | The probability that a HIV test result is positive if a man is not infected with HIV is 0.0001. | The probability that a 40-year-old woman, without breast cancer, receives a positive mammogram is 0.10. |
| Posterior probability or Positive predictive value PPV: $p$(DISEASE I POS) | The probability that a man is infected with HIV if his HIV test result is positive is 0.5. | The probability that a 40-year-old woman, who has a positive mammogram, has breast cancer is 0.075. |

*Note:* These values are taken from Gigerenzer et al. (1998) and Gigerenzer (2002).

numbers to compute the critical probability, namely the probability that the man is infected given that he tested positively, by using the Bayes theorem (Gigerenzer & Hoffrage, 1995):

$$PPV = \frac{p(HIV)\,p(POS \mid HIV)}{p(HIV)\,p(POS \mid HIV) + p(NO\ HIV)\,p(POS \mid HIV)}$$

The positive predictive value (PPV) of the test and, thus, the critical probability is about .5 or 50%. Note that the relevant probability is not almost 1, but equals the probability that you get "heads" when you toss an unbiased coin.

### Frequencies

Research indicates that recipients understand a positive test result (and other conditional probabilities) much more easily when the message presents numbers in the form of frequencies instead of probabilities. Over their evolutionary history, humans learned from direct experience rather than from books with statistics—and, for animals, this kind of learning (compared to others, such as imitation or instruction) plays an even larger role in knowledge acquisition (Gigerenzer & Hoffrage, 1995). Consider a physician who observes, case by case, whether or not her patients have a new disease and whether the outcome of a test is positive or negative. Scholars refer to this process as natural sampling (Gigerenzer & Hoffrage, 1995, p. 686; Kleiter, 1994). In contrast, a researcher using systematic sampling in scientific research may conduct a study and select 100 people with disease and 100 without the disease. The difference is that, in natural sampling, the proportions of people who have and who do not have the disease are naturally observed; whereas, in systematic sampling, they are artificially fixed a priori (see also Hoffrage, Gigerenzer, Krauss, & Martignon, 2002). Aggregating the individual observations obtained by natural sampling results in natural frequencies (Gigerenzer & Hoffrage, 1995; Kleiter, 1994). Specifically, in a naturally sampled population, natural frequencies result from counting individuals according to their features (e.g., disease vs. no disease, positive test result vs. negative test result; see Brase, Cosmides, & Tooby, 1998). Note that an isolated number, such as 18 infected people who test positive, is not, by itself, a natural frequency; it only becomes one because of its relationship to other numbers that result from counting different cases within the same sample.

Going back to the man receiving his HIV test result, his doctor could use natural frequencies for a fictitious sample of, say, 10,000 men to explain what a positive result actually means (see Figure 5.1). The doctor could say, consider 10,000 men in the United States with the same HIV risk as you. Of these 10,000 men, 1 will be infected with HIV and test positive. Out of the 9,999 men who are not HIV positive, one will test positive also. Therefore, the chance that you have HIV, if you test positive, is 1 in 2. When presented in the form

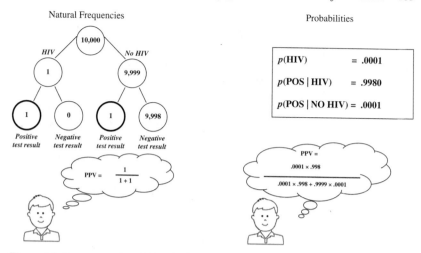

*Figure 5.1* Representation of identical information in terms of natural frequencies and in terms of probabilities. *Note:* In both representations, the positive predictive value (PPV) is .5. However, the computational demands are quite different. While the frequency format requires only two operations (one addition, one division) computing the PPV using probabilities involves three additional operations (three multiplications in addition to one addition and one division). Moreover, the attention demands are much lower when the numbers are presented in frequencies. Here, one only has to consider two pieces of information: true positives and false positives (see bold circles). Base rates need not to be attended to in the natural frequency format (see Gigerenzer, 2002; Gigerenzer & Hoffrage, 1995; Kurzenhäuser & Hoffrage, in press). In contrast, the standard probability format requires paying attention to three pieces of information (see the rectangle above).

of frequencies, risk professionals as well as laypeople, are better able to realize the relative degree of certainty regarding conclusions that can be drawn from a possible test result (Casscells, Schoenberger, & Grayboys, 1978; Eddy, 1982; Gigerenzer, 2002; Gigerenzer et al., 1998).

Notably, it does not make a mathematical difference if message senders write statistics as probabilities, percentages, or frequencies as in Figure 5.1, but it does make a psychological difference (Hoffrage et al., 2000; Slovic, Monahan, & MacGregor, 2000). When message senders express statistics as natural frequencies, they improve statistical thinking. The computations with natural frequencies make it simpler to understand what a positive result actually means.

*Risk Reduction*

Information about relative risk concentrates on how two or more risks relate to each other or how a particular risk in one group compares to the same risk in another group (see Gigerenzer, 2002; Sackett, Haynes, Guyatt, & Tugwell, 1991). Risk communicators commonly use this type of information to highlight the risks of certain activities or life-styles (e.g., does living next to a nuclear power plant increase the risk of getting leukemia?), the effectiveness of diagnostic instruments (e.g., does participating in screening program reduce mortality?), or therapies (e.g., how useful is homeopathy?). In all these cases, researchers compare two or more groups of people to each other with respect to how often a defined outcome occurs. For example, when seeking information about the benefits of mammography screening with respect to the risk of dying from breast cancer, women can read in brochures that, for women over 40 years old, undergoing routine mammography screening may reduce their risk of dying from breast cancer within the next 10 years by 25% (see Kurzenhäuser, 2003; Kurzenhäuser & Hoffrage, in press). This number is a relative risk reduction (RRR), derived from a ratio. The proportion of breast cancer deaths among women who receive mammography screening can be divided by (i.e., expressed relative to) the proportion of deaths among women who do not receive mammograms.

$$\text{Relative Risk Reduction} = 1 - \frac{O_T / N_T}{O_C / N_C}$$

$O_T$ and $O_C$ refer to the number of critical outcomes within a defined time period in the treatment (participation in screening) and control group (no participation), respectively; in this example, the number of breast cancer deaths in the next 10 years. $N_T$ and $N_C$ represent the number of people in the treatment and in the control group, respectively. As we can observe from this formula, if the proportion of women dying of breast cancer in the treatment group is identical to that in the control group (and, hence, the two complements, namely the two survival rates, are also identical), then the relative risk reduction of the treatment is zero. Conversely, if the proportion of women dying of breast cancer in the treatment group is reduced to zero, then the relative risk reduction is 100%.

The relative risk reduction is based on a comparison of two different groups of women, but receivers could likely understand it better if interpreted hypothetically, that is, for the same group of people. In the case of 1,000 women, if none of the women receive mammography screening, four will die of breast cancer in the next 10 years. If all 1,000 undergo screening, three of those four who would die without the screening would still die. That is, for three of the four women, the screening would not prevent this outcome (see Figure 5.2). However, for one of those four women (25%), the screening would make the difference between life and death. Note that this proportion does not reveal how many women would have to have mammograms to prolong the life of one woman, even though it is based on and was derived from numbers that allow us to answer this question.

Alternatively, the benefits of mammography can be framed in terms of *absolute risk reduction* (ARR)—the proportion of women who die from breast cancer without undergoing mammography screening minus the proportion of those who die despite being screened:

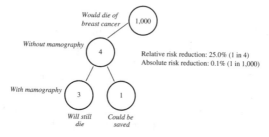

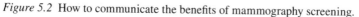

*Figure 5.2* How to communicate the benefits of mammography screening.

$$\text{Absolute Risk Reduction} = \frac{O_C}{N_C} - \frac{O_T}{N_T}$$

When presented in the form of absolute risk reduction, the numbers differ. Screening reduces the proportion of women who die from breast cancer from 4 in 1,000 to 3 in 1,000, that is, it prevents the bad outcome for 1 in 1,000. The inverse of the absolute risk reduction is the *number needed to treat* (NNT) or, in this case, the number needed to screen, in order to save one life (within a specified time interval). In the present example, the expected number of women who would have to be screened so that one woman could benefit (i.e., only survive because she was screened) is 1,000.

The relative risk reduction (in the present example, 25%) looks more impressive than the absolute risk reduction (0.1%). Unfortunately, health organizations inform patients about the benefits of mammography screening almost exclusively in terms of the relative risk reduction (Kurzenhäuser, 2003; Kurzenhäuser & Lücking, 2004). Perhaps not surprisingly, people more likely prefer an intervention if it is advertised in terms of relative risk reduction than in absolute risk reduction (Bucher, Weinbacher, & Gyr, 1994; Gigerenzer, 2002; Heller, Sandars, Patterson, & McElduff, 2004; Sarfati, Howden-Chapman, Woodward, & Salmond, 1998; for a recent review, see A. K. Ghosh & K. Ghosh, 2005), and grant agencies are more likely to fund research on the effectiveness of interventions if the benefits of those interventions have been communicated in terms of relative rather than absolute risk reduction (Fahey, Griffiths, & Peters, 1995). Conversely, people make more rational decisions about whether or not to accept a particular medical treatment when message senders communicate risk reduction in absolute rather than relative terms (Hembroff, Holmes-Rovner, & Wills, 2004; however, see Sheridan, Pignone, & Lewis, 2003).

Importantly, both absolute and relative representations of the frequencies are mathematically correct. Yet, each representation suggests different amounts of benefit or harm, potentially elicits different expectations, and ultimately leads to different decisions (Hanoch, 2004). Some representations, like relative risk, typically do not specify the reference class or do not specify any base rate information regarding the reference class.

### Reference Class

With any representation of risk information, the primary source of confusion for the message receiver is the reference class (Gigerenzer & Edwards, 2003). A reference class comprises the class of events to which a probability applies (von Mises, 1939). Therefore, a reference class needs to be chosen carefully. Even more importantly, messages should clearly state which reference class has been chosen. Each reference class gives the probability of a negative outcome a different meaning. For example, consider the claim that "smoking accounts for 30% of all cancer deaths." Person A may understand this message as, "of all people who will die of cancer, 30% will die of lung cancer." Person B may think, "of all people who will die of cancer, 30% are smokers." Person C may interpret it as, "of all people who die of cancer, 30% only die because they are smokers." Person D may understand the message as "30% of smokers will die of cancer." Finally, Person E may think that "30% of all people who have lung cancer will die from it." Persons A, B, and C's reference class encompasses all people who die of cancer; person D's reference class refers to people who smoke, and person E only considers people with lung cancer.

Gigerenzer et al. (2005) investigated how the public understands the quantitative probability of rain and demonstrated that different understandings correspond to different assumptions about which reference class is underlying meteorologists' probability statements. Pedestrians in five countries—the Netherlands, Greece, Germany, Italy, and the United States—were surveyed in public places. Participants were told, "there is a 30% chance of rain tomorrow." The people in these countries have different degrees of exposure to probabilistic weather forecasts. Results indicated that two-thirds of Americans understood the probability of rain as the meteorologists intended, "When the weather conditions are like today, in 3 out of 10 cases there will be rain the next day." However, only one-third to one-fifth of respondents in the Netherlands, Germany, Italy, and Greece interpreted the probability as it was intended. The most common interpretations in these countries were "It will rain tomorrow 30% of the time" and "It will rain tomorrow in 30% of the area." The authors suggested that confusion about the meaning of probabilities might stem from three common practices in the media. First, in some countries, like Greece, weather forecasts do not typically include probabilities. Second, when the media provides probabilities, they do not typically include the class of events to which they refer. Third, in the few cases when a message mentions a reference class, it is often the wrong reference class. Gigerenzer et al. advocated that a reference class should always be given when message senders provide probabilities. An important lesson can be learned from the smoking example and the weather probability study—the meaning of a probability hinges on the choice of the reference class.

### Message Framing

In addition to the format of the numerical presentation and the specification of a reference class, other message characteristics can also influence risk perception. One type of framing effect suggests that people organize information in terms of potential gains or potential losses (Kahneman & Tversky, 1979, 1982; Tversky & Kahneman, 1981). Therefore, information can be presented in a way that encourages people to process it in terms of potential benefits or potential costs. A gain-frame message presents the benefits of adopting a particular behavior. For example, "if you take an HIV test, the disease can be detected early, and early detection, in turn, increases the number of treatment options that you have." A loss frame message presents the costs of not adopting a particular behavior. For example, "if you do not have an HIV test, the disease cannot be detected early, and the lack of information decreases the number of treatment options you have if you are infected."

Research indicates that people respond differently to information presented as a gain or presented as a loss. According to Salovey, Schneider, and Apanovitch (2002), loss frame messages encourage people to consider the negative consequences of the decision. Therefore, people are motivated to engage in a risky behavior if the behavior helps them to avoid a loss. Alternatively, gain-frame messages have the potential to make people feel less endangered. Therefore, they less likely perform a behavior with uncertain outcomes. These predictions contribute to prospect theory's four-fold pattern, which states that for medium and for high probabilities, people are risk-seeking for losses and risk-averse for gains (Kahneman & Tversky, 1979). Thus, gain-frame messages more likely cause individuals to become adverse to risk; they do not want to do anything to jeopardize the gains presented in the message. As a consequence, if a message sender frames a health message in terms of a gain, and the risk is medium to high, people will not want to lose the benefit of treatment options and will be more likely to be tested. Based on this research, Paling (2003) recommended framing statistical information in both positive and negative terms.

O'Keefe and Jensen (2007) argued that, for some risk messages, the influence of framing may be quite small. O'Keefe and Jensen conducted a meta-analysis using 93 studies (N = 21,656), and they found that, for disease prevention messages, gain-framed appeals were statistically significantly more persuasive than loss-framed appeals. However, this difference was small (r = .03), and O'Keefe and Jensen asserted that this effect may be due to a large and statistically significant effect for messages advocating dental hygiene behaviors. They did not find statistically significant differences in persuasiveness between gain and loss-framed messages for other preventive behaviors, including safer-sex behaviors, skin cancer prevention behaviors, or diet and nutrition behaviors (also see O'Keefe & Jensen, 2008).

*Message Format*

In addition to selecting numbers and text, message senders also select a format for the message. Quantitative evidence can be presented in many different formats—spoken verbally, presented as written text, or presented visually with a graph or picture. The format of the message can affect comprehension and influence the quality of the risk communication (Civan, Doctor, & Wolf, 2005). Usually, doctors only give medical information verbally to patients. Quantities can be expressed verbally using labels like *rarely, occasionally,* and *frequently.* Fischer and Jungermann (1996) concluded that people interpret verbal labels differently depending on the context. If people interpret verbal expressions as representing frequencies that are higher or lower than reality, their interpretations could cause serious implications for health decisions and behavior. Fischer and Jungermann (1996) maintained that "numbers are better than words" (p. 170). In addition to the labels, people should be told what each verbal label means in numerical terms.

Thomson, Cunningham, and Hunt (2001) contended that giving information verbally is not always the best method to facilitate patient understanding and comprehension. Additionally, Kessels (2003) described the obstacles of written information for individuals with low education, low literacy, or individuals who speak a different native language than their doctor. Therefore, visual representations may be better than verbal or written information at times.

Various types of visual formats can present quantitative risk information, including pictures, bar graphs, histograms, pie charts, and pictographs. Each visual format has unique advantages. For example, bar graphs can show ungrouped frequency distributions, while histograms can illustrate continuous, grouped frequency data. Pie charts are good for showing part to whole relationships. In addition to these traditional formats, advances in technology allow for innovative formats with distinct advantages. Interactive multimedia, such as that found on Web pages or on CD-ROMS, requires active involvement of the user and can be adapted to the ability and characteristics of the message receiver (Strecher, Greenwood, Wang, & Dumont, 1999). In this volume, Noar, Harrington, and Aldrich discuss a new approach of tailoring persuasive messages at the individual level. Computer algorithms can create personalized messages based on an individual's characteristics.

Overall, the research exploring the effects of graphical representations is inconclusive, and it suggests that one representations format is not always superior. Specifically, visual representations are not always effective (Lipkus, 2007; Parrott, Silk, Dorgan, Condit, & Harris, 2005). Lipkus discussed the advantages and disadvantages of visual, graphical displays and suggested that graphical displays are able to summarize a lot of information and show patterns in the data (e.g., interaction effects, regression lines). Some numerical data may be overwhelming, and graphical displays can be used to change a numerical, computational task into a perceptual task for the message receiver. On the other hand, graphical displays may discourage people from considering details, like numbers. Also, individuals may lack the skills to interpret a graph, and graphs can be misleading by amplifying the effects of certain elements and diminishing the effects of others (Huff, 1954). Moreover, while visual formats may enhance the risk communication process, we know little about how these formats affect risk-related behaviors (Civan et al., 2005).

*How Can Obstacles Related to the Risk Message Be Avoided?*

We propose that risks should be communicated in terms of natural frequencies, rather than in terms of probabilities, to give people a better chance to realistically assess their magnitudes. At a minimum, both types of information should be provided (Edwards, Elwyn, & Gwyn, 1999; Gigerenzer & Edwards, 2003; Paling, 2003; Sackett, 1996). As Figure 5.1 illustrates, when message senders express statistics as frequencies, they facilitate understanding the meaning of new information; for instance, a result of a diagnostic test. In a study involving 48 physicians, Hoffrage and Gigerenzer (1998) provided base rate information and the statistics of the corresponding diagnostic tests. The physicians had, on average, 14 years of professional experience, with a range from one month to 30 years. They worked on four diagnostic problems in which they had to infer the presence of breast cancer from a positive mammography test, colorectal cancer from a positive hemoccult test, phenylketonuria from a positive Guthrie test, and Bekhterev's disease from a positive HL-Antigen-B27 test. When researchers presented the information in probabilities, the physicians correctly inferred the posterior probability that a patient with a positive test actually has the disease in only 10% of cases. In contrast, when the researchers shared the same information in natural frequencies, that percentage increased to 46%.

For relative risk representations, Heller et al. (2003) pointed out that relative risk measures do not consider the prevalence of a risk in a given population. These authors also asserted that communicating numbers that show the impact of a risk in a specific population make the information easier to calculate and understand. By providing the full information, both the absolute and the relative risks can be easily extracted. For instance, the risk of anthrax exposure can be communicated by explaining, according to the CDC, the chance that any one individual in the United States will contract anthrax in a given year is about one in 300 million people (Centers for Disease Control and Prevention, 2008). In 2001, with the intentional release of anthrax spores in some environments, the nationwide risk was about 23 in 300 million people. Communicated this way, people can realize that the risk has increased by a factor of 23, but they can also understand that the risk is still quite small, compared to fatal car accidents for instance.

With regard to visual format selection, the choice should depend upon the purpose of the risk communication. Some messages intend to enhance quantitative understanding or promote good judgments, while others strive to promote behavior change (Ancker, Senathirajah, Kukafka, & Starren, 2006). Parrott et al. (2005) maintained that graphical displays should be used with caution. A graph can have a considerable amount of face validity. Therefore, a graph may look like it makes sense, so a person may not look closely at the information within the visual. Parrott et al. determined that visual representations of data did not significantly enhance understanding of health risk, and the general public was less proficient in understanding data in this way. Given that health frameworks often consist of several components (e.g., genetics, personal behavior, and environment), it is difficult to include all relevant details in a single graph. Therefore, as Parrott et al. argued, individuals may have difficulty translating a visual form of quantitative evidence associated with one scientific study into something meaningful.

In addition, the choice of graphical representation may make a difference. For example, bar charts constitute one of the most widely used forms of conveying statistical information (Parrott et al., 2005). Receivers presumably have experience processing information presented in this way, and they probably also possess the skills needed to interpret such information. Graphically representing health risk information in other forms (e.g., stick figures, smiley faces) may take longer for people to understand because they must first educate themselves about how to interpret the information, before they are able to make it meaningful to themselves. Unfortunately, no best way exists to present risk information in all situations. The same format may not work with different audiences. Most importantly, the format needs to be appropriate for both the message content and the message receiver. Lipkus et al. (2001) called for more research on developing and testing useful formats for communicating risk.

## The Message Communicator

We do not lack studies showing that the general population has problems processing quantitative information (e.g., Doyal, 2001; Lemaire, 2006; Lloyd, 2001; Schwartz, Woloshin, Black, & Welsh, 1997; Weinstein, 1989). Astonishingly, research shows that experts, including doctors and judges, often experience difficulties with understanding and calculating risks as well. Thus, one obstacle of successful risk communication is that even communicators have trouble grasping quantitative information at times (Barke, Jenkins-Smith, & Slovic, 1997).

### Difficulties in Processing and Calculating Risk

In a classic study, Eddy (1982) asked physicians to estimate the probability that a woman has breast cancer, given that she has a positive mammogram. Eddy provided the following information: (1) the probability that a patient has breast cancer is 1%; (2) if the patient has breast cancer, the probability that the radiologist will classify the mammogram as positive is 79%; and (3) if the patient has a benign lesion (no breast cancer), the probability that the radiologist will still provide a positive test result is 9.6%. In this study, 95 of 100 physicians estimated the probability of breast cancer after a positive mammogram to be about 75%. The correct answer is 7.7%, considerably lower than most physicians concluded.

In a related study, faculty, staff, and students at Harvard Medical School were asked to estimate an individual's probability of having a disease (Casscells et al., 1978). The researchers told participants that "if a test to detect a disease whose prevalence is 1/1000 has a false positive rate of 5%, what is the chance that a person found to have a positive result actually has the disease, assuming you know nothing about the person's symptoms or signs?" Only 11 out of the 60 participants gave the correct answer of 2%. Most of the participants estimated that the individual would have a 95% chance of having the disease.

Experts in other fields have problems drawing the correct inferences from conditional probabilities as well. In a study conducted in Germany, legal professionals who would soon qualify as judges and advanced law students were asked to evaluate two court cases involving rape (Hoffrage et al., 2000; Lindsey, Hertwig, & Gigerenzer, 2003). Researchers informed participants that investigators found a match between the defendant's DNA and some DNA that could be recovered at the crime scene. In addition, they provided participants with the necessary statistical information to quantify the uncertainty associated with the inference from data (positive match) to hypothesis (the defendant was the perpetrator). When researchers disclosed this information in probabilities, only 13% of the legal professionals and less than 1% of the law students correctly inferred the probability that the defendant was the source of the recovered DNA profile.

Many people, including experts, often believe that diagnostic tests are more accurate and more predictive than they actually are (Kurzenhäuser & Hoffrage, in press). Diagnostic test results remain central to decision making in a number of domains, and they can influence medical decisions, court rulings, and policy decisions. Thus, the experts who interpret and provide this information should realize the fallibility of these tests. Tests make correct as well as incorrect identifications. With medical screenings, a positive test result does not necessarily indicate that a person has the corresponding disease. Typically, the probability of infection or disease given a positive test result is still rather low. For example, based on their review of published studies, Gigerenzer et al. (1998) concluded that, among low-risk, heterosexual men who test positive in a HIV test, only about 50% actually are infected with the HIV. With mammography, the likelihood of breast cancer given a positive test is even much lower, about 8% (Gigerenzer, 2002).

Considering the HIV test example once again, most people, including health professionals, are astonished when they hear or read that the probability of infection is 50%. Most expect that a person with a positive test result has a 99.9% chance of being infected. Gigerenzer et al. (1998) conducted a study in which a low-risk client went to 20 German public health centers and obtained an HIV test at each of these centers. Before taking the tests, the client interviewed the counselors, focusing on numerical information in the context of HIV testing. Most counselors used percentages or probabilities to explain the risks. In the majority of the counseling sessions, the information that the counselors provided was either inconsistent or incorrect. For instance, one counselor estimated the base rate and the false-positive rate to be around 0.1%, and the sensitivity to be 99.9%. He then stated that the client's probability of infection, given a positive test, was also 99.9%. In fact, 15 out of the 20 counselors told this low-risk client that it is 99.9% or 100% certain that he has HIV if he tests positive. As we have detailed in the section regarding risk formats (see Figure 5.1), an effective method exists to make this information more transparent. The key is to present the information in a frequency format.

Even if risk communicators understand the quantitative risk information that they need to communicate, several reasons impact why they may not discuss risk or give statistical information to the public. American physicians most frequently mentioned lack of time as the reason for not discussing risks and benefits of cancer screening tests with their patients (Dunn, Shridharani, Lou, Bernstein, & Horowitz, 2001). In addition, many risk communicators are not trained in the communication skills required for discussing risks and benefits with their patients (Gigerenzer, 2002; Towle, Godolphin, Grams, & Lamarre, 2006). As Dunn et al. (2001) concluded, between a quarter and a third of the American physicians, who participated in the study, acknowledged that the complexity of the topic and a language barrier between themselves and their patients would keep them from discussing the benefits and risks of mammography screening.

### How Can Obstacles Related to the Message Communicator Be Avoided?

Some of these obstacles can be avoided with proper training about interpreting numerical values, the appropriate use of statistical information, and effective communication skills. Communicators can be explicitly trained to translate conditional probabilities into a more understandable format for themselves and for their message receivers. For example, when researchers provided statistics regarding DNA profiles in terms of natural frequencies, 68% of legal professionals and 44% of law students made the correct inference (Hoffrage et al., 2000; Lindsey et al., 2003). Sedlmeier and Gigerenzer (2001) demonstrated that training people to encode information in terms of natural frequencies improves the accuracy of their probability judgments, compared to a control group in which students received traditional training (i.e., they learned how to apply mathematical formulas such as Bayes' theorem). When Kurzenhäuser and Hoffrage (2002) implemented representation training in a traditional classroom setting, they replicated Sedlmeier and Gigerenzer's finding that such training is much more effective in improving diagnostic inferences than training people how to insert probabilities into mathematical formulas. In both studies, researchers evaluated the success of the representation training by testing students with problems in which statistical information was given in terms of probabilities—the format that health professionals frequently encounter in medical textbooks (Kurzenhäuser & Hoffrage, in press).

In addition to proper skills training, risk communicators should adapt their quantitative messages to their audience and monitor if message receivers understand the statistical information. Freimuth, Linnan, and Potter (2000) suggested that effective communication must identify receiver characteristics, deliver accurate, scientifically based messages from credible sources, and reach audiences through familiar channels. If the message arouses fear, the communicator should provide ways to alleviate the fear. We now turn our focus to such characteristics of the message receiver that may hinder effective communication.

## The Message Receiver

Risk communicators cannot assume that everyone possesses the same ability to understand risk information. Research indicates that a receiver's literacy and numeracy skills affect risk comprehension (Freimuth, Chervin, Hovick, Johnson-Turbes, 2007; Lipkus, Samsa, & Rimer, 2001; Schwartz et al., 1997). Likewise, studies show that the perception and processing of quantitative risk information may also depend on demographic factors and the emotional state of a receiver (e.g., Peters, Lipkus, & Diefenbach, 2006; Reyna & Brainerd, 2007).

### *Literacy*

To understand quantitative risk information, people first must understand basic issues, like the term "risk" and the concept of a reference class. In an earlier example, a doctor tells a man that his test result is positive. An individual with low health literacy may hear "positive result" and form the conclusion that he is not infected because, in most other contexts, the word *positive* signals good news. Although an extreme example, studies confirm that some receivers of risk messages experience difficulty with understanding basic terminology (Lipkus et al., 2001). In addition to familiarity with basic general terms, receivers must also grasp more specific concepts to which a statistic refers (e.g., mean, median, mode). The literacy and numeracy levels of the message receiver should be considered when sharing quantitative risk information.

Public health scholars have long been aware of the relationship between literacy and health education (Horner, Surratt, & Juliusson, 2000; Tappe & Galer-Unti, 2001). The U.S. Department of Health and Human Services (2000) defined health literacy as the degree to which individuals possess the capacity to obtain, process, understand, and act upon the spoken, written, and visual health information and services needed to make appropriate health decisions (also see Zarcadoolas, Pleasant, & Greer, 2006). Health literacy consists of a broad range of skills that allow people to make health decisions, including functional literacy (reading ability, writing ability, and speaking skills) as well as numeracy skills (the ability to manipulate numbers). A person's health literacy may be better or worse than his or her functional literacy, and functional literacy can be context specific. For example, people across high and low literacy levels may struggle to understand cancer screening recommendations (Davis, Williams, Marin, Parker, & Glass, 2002). On the other hand, a patient with low functional literacy, who is chronically ill and has been managing a disease for many years, may have more health knowledge that is specific to her illness than a person with high functional literacy who was diagnosed only recently or is not ill. Thus, one can expect that health knowledge varies considerably—both within a person across different domains and within a domain across different people.

In addition to the knowledge level of the receiver, a common problem in risk communication entails the use of complex technical terminology and jargon (Davis et al., 2001). Due to the use of complex terminology, the format of the information, and the literacy skills of the patient, researchers estimate that patients immediately forget 40% to 80% of the information that they obtain from medical practitioners (Anderson, Dodman, Kopelman, & Fleming, 1979; Kessels, 2003; Ley, 1979; McGuire, 1996). When unfamiliar information is combined with numerical data, this information is even more difficult to understand.

### Numeracy

Numeracy refers to the ability to understand and manipulate numbers (Schapira et al., 2008; Zarcadoolas et al., 2006). According to Rothman, Montori, Cherrington, and Pignone (2008), it "is a multidimensional skill that involves assessing when to use numerical skills, deciding which skills to use, using the skills effectively to solve the problem, and then interpreting the results appropriately" (p. 592).

Numeracy skills become particularly important when decisions have to be made concerning medical treatment or lifestyle changes to lower a risk. Such decisions often benefit from taking evidence presented with numbers into account. However, as with health literacy, individuals possess different levels of proficiency in numeracy depending on their background and experiences (e.g., Adelsward & Sachs, 1996; Fagerlin et al., 2007; Grimes & Snively, 1999; Lipkus et al., 2001; Peters, Västfjäll, et al., 2006). In the United States, researchers estimate that half of the general population struggles to perform simple numeric tasks, like using a calculator or finding the difference between the regular price and the sale price while shopping (White & Dillow, 2005). Reyna and Brainerd (2007) established that low numeracy skills predict poorer health outcomes, less accurate perceptions of health risks, and compromised ability to make medical decisions. Reyna and Brainerd concluded that numeracy is essential to making health and social decisions in everyday life.

Individuals who are unable to perform simple tasks with numbers may experience even more difficulties when it comes to complicated manipulations and risk assessments. Lobb, Butow, Kenny, and Tattersall (1999) investigated the ability of women to understand breast cancer risk information. In this research, 53% of the women could not calculate how therapy would reduce their risk, and 73% did not understand the statistical term *median* when researchers used it to describe how long it takes for cancer to return. Black, Nease, and Tosteson (1995) concluded that numerate women were less likely to overestimate their chances of dying from breast cancer as well as the absolute risk reduction obtained by mammography.

Like individuals with low literacy, individuals with low numeracy skills are not always uneducated. Paulos (1988) was one of the first to shed light on the fact that even well educated people understand very little about mathematics and that intuitions about numbers often do not conform to simple mathematical rules. For instance, many people fall prey to the so-called ratio bias, according to which the ratio nx/ny appears to be larger than the ratio x/y. Yamagishi (1997) illustrated this point. For 11 well-known risks, college student participants were given estimations of the number of deaths in the population (i.e., 2,414 out of 10,000 or 24.14 out of 100) and asked to assess the riskiness of each. Yamagishi predicted that, for two mathematically identical ratios, the one with the larger numbers (in the numerator and the denominator) would lead people to assess a cause as riskier. Results supported this prediction; participants rated cancer as riskier when they were told that it "kills 2,414 out of 10,000 people" and rated cancer as less risky when they were told "cancer kills 24.14 out of 100 people." The same results were found across all 11 causes of death. As an explanation for the ratio-bias, Slovic, Finucane, Peters, and MacGregor (2004) posited that people usually find it easier to visualize the numerator of a ratio than its denominator.

Lipkus et al. (2001) measured the performance of educated participants on a numeracy scale. Most of the participants had more than a high school education, yet 16% were unable to correctly determine risk magnitude (i.e., what represents a larger risk: 1%, 5%, or 10%). Sheridan and Pignone (2002) investigated the numeracy skills of medical students. In their study, almost 25% of first year medical students could not manage basic numerical calculations. The students who had difficulty with the numeracy questions also experienced challenges with interpreting the treatment benefit of a hypothetical disease.

While it is a problem that educated individuals may have low literacy and numeracy skills when it comes to risk comprehension, individuals with low socio-economic status and minorities, who are often at the greatest risk, more likely have low literacy and numeracy skills, which may add to their health risk (Fagerlin et al., 2007; Zarcadoolas et al., 2006). Although communicating health risks to these groups is especially important, only a few studies have examined how different cultural groups respond to risk information or the most effective approaches in communicating risk to diverse populations (Keller & Stevens 1997; Paling, 2003; Vaughn, 1995). This research has found that cultures view illness and health outcomes differently. For example, Hispanic women were more likely than non-Hispanic women to believe that illness constitutes a matter of chance and recovery can be attributed to good luck (Tortolero-Luna, Glober, Villarreal, Palos, & Linares, 1995).

### Affect and Emotion

Risks are inherently threatening, and, at times, we cannot avoid arousing the emotions of a message receiver (Dillard & Nabi, 2006; Rudd, Comings, & Hyde, 2003). For instance, at the doctor's office or during a crisis like a natural disaster, people feel stressed, and this reaction influences the way that they process messages. Affective responses (e.g., mild positive or negative mood states), as well as emotional reactions (e.g., fear, sadness, anger, and anxiety), hold the potential to influence the processing of quantitative risk information. When risk decisions need to be made, people should be in a psychological and emotional position to comprehend the information that they receive, including the potential benefits and risks. However, when asked to make decisions or form judgments, people often rely on their internal affective responses and cues from the situation and may overlook important information (Peters, Lipkus, & Diefenbach, 2006; Slovic, Finucane, Peters, & MacGregor, 2002). When receivers experience affect at the moment that they attempt to process risk information, their emotions can influence cognitions, information processing, judgments, and decisions (Peters, Lipkus, et al., 2006; Slovic et al., 2004). For example, research indicates that people who rely on affect may pay less attention or give less weight to the numerical information in a message (Rottenstreich & Hsee, 2001; Watson et al., 1999). In addition, mood congruency can occur. Under negative mood states, perceptions and judgments skew toward greater negativity. As a consequence, if perception and judgments are negatively impacted, a person may make a different decision than he or she would in a positive mood state.

Raghunathan and Pham (1999) investigated the differential effects of sadness and anxiety on risk decision making. When asked to evaluate and make choices between two wagers, participants induced into a sad emotional state preferred the high risk and high reward option. The participants induced into an anxious emotional state preferred the low risk, low reward option. Doctors often ask patients to make medical treatment decisions very soon after receiving a diagnosis. Emotion can lead the patient to make a different decision than he or she would make under normal circumstances.

Considering that emotion and mood can affect decision making, we should recognize that some risk information, like a medical diagnosis or a bio-terrorism threat, can cause emotional distress and may affect the processing of risk information. Considerable research reveals how stress affects message processing (e.g., Baron, Inman, Kao, & Logan, 1992; Lazarus & Folkman, 1984). During a crisis, people must deal with processing information as well as hearing, understanding, and remembering what they have been told. Anxiety caused by a stressful situation can prompt people to assume the worst (Covello, 1998), greatly influencing the interpretation of a diagnosis or risk information (for related review, see Galvin & Grill, this volume).

### How Can Obstacles Related to the Message Receiver Be Avoided?

Rowan (1999) identified a number of frequent sources of confusion when explaining science to the public. First, familiar concepts to experts (e.g., exposure, toxic, and emission) are not well understood by the public. In addition to making sure that the receiver has a basic understanding of the concept of risk, communicators should avoid unnecessary jargon that the message receiver may not understand. Rowan suggested that we cannot simply define unfamiliar terms. She asserted that communicators should explain what a word, like *exposure*, means and also explicitly describe what it does *not* mean. In addition, a range of examples is more useful than providing just one instance. For example, a message could explain, "You can be exposed to a poison by eating it, touching it, or breathing it in." Finally, some risks are difficult to imagine— for example, we cannot see or smell carbon monoxide, but it is poisonous. This distinction needs to be made clear to the public.

In addition to clarifying any confusion, to be most effective, risk messages need to be culturally meaningful and provided in the native language of the receiver (Huerta & Macario, 1999; Keller & Stevens, 1997). Moreover, we should recognize that people with low socioeconomic status face barriers that influence their ability to address health risks including limited financial resources, a lack of knowledge about ways to address health problems, and inadequate health care or insurance coverage. A health message should consider these barriers and include ways to address these issues (Freimuth et al., 2007).

If health information is involved, risk communicators must explore and consider the general and domain specific health literacy of the message receiver. If necessary, message senders can utilize assessment tools, including the Rapid Estimate of Adult Literacy in Medicine (REALM; Davis et al., 1993) and the Test of Functional Health Literacy in Adults (TOFHLA; Parker, Baker, Williams, & Nurss, 1995) to evaluate the health literacy skills of potential receivers. Accordingly, health messages should be adapted to the knowledge level and skills of likely receivers.

When message senders communicate risk information to the public, they must make important considerations. Rudd et al. (2003) analyzed the content of two recent U.S. federal government mailings (the 1998 *Understanding AIDS* brochure, and the 2001 postcard in the aftermath of September 11) regarding the safety of the U.S. mail during the anthrax attacks. Researchers used the SMOG readability assessment tool to determine the reading level of both documents (McLaughlin, 1969). Government officials crafted the AIDS brochure at an eighth grade reading level, and the anthrax postcard was written at a 10th grade reading level, which means that both documents were written above the average reading level for half of American adults. Further, these materials were inappropriate for the 11 million American adults who are not literate in English (Kutner, Greenberg, Lin, Paulsen, & White, 2006). Simple changes could make materials like these easier to read and understand. For example, Rudd et al. pointed out that "notify local law enforcement authorities" can be more simply stated as "call the police." Notably, the text that is used in conjunction with the quantitative risk information matters just as much as the numbers themselves. Unnecessary jargon, which includes acronyms and multiple terms for the same condition, should be avoided.

Finally, risk communicators should consider the range of possible emotional reactions to their message. Peters et al. (2006) suggested that messages should explicitly mention common emotions. For example, if a mammography result is being given, the doctor could say that "it is normal to be worried about an abnormal mammogram. However, you should know that, in order to avoid missing any cancers, we react if there is even the slightest reason to be suspicious. As a necessary consequence, there will be many women for whom we want to take a second look, and for whom we will later find out that there was nothing. In fact, most women your age, without a family history, who have an abnormal mammogram, do not have cancer."

## The Communication and Perception of Risk

It is beyond the scope of this chapter to review the literature on risk perception due to the vast amount of research on that topic. Rather, we present a few core findings that are useful for considering risk perception in the context of communicating quantitative risk information.

### *Expert versus Public Perceptions of Risk*

In a classic study on risk perception that included summaries of eight earlier research projects, Slovic (1987) argued that perceived risk is quantifiable, predictable, and that the concept of risk means different things to different groups of people. Slovic asserted that experts typically judge risk based on their estimates of annual fatalities. In fact, for experts, the term *risk* was synonymous with expected annual mortality.

Conversely, laypeople evaluate risks based upon other characteristics of the hazard, like catastrophic potential and the threat to future generations. According to Sandman (1993), laypeople concentrate on two components of risk. Sandman labeled the first component as the hazard, the technical side of the risk, the magnitude and probability of an undesirable outcome. In addition, people focus on the non-technical side of the risk, including the negative aspects of the situation itself. Variables including voluntariness, controllability, fairness, memorability, and familiarity of the risk determine public outrage, explaining why many laypeople think that flying in an airplane is more dangerous than driving a car. Airplane crashes are more memorable, less familiar, and regarded as being less fair than car accidents. In addition, laypeople consider an airplane crash to be uncontrollable and dreaded.

Some evidence indicates that the public tends to believe that the knowledge of scientific experts is limited. For instance, Sjöberg (2001) reported that experts on nuclear waste believed that there is little unknown information in their field; however, politicians and the public held that many unknown effects exist. The unknown effects factor served as a better predictor of risk perception than trust for politicians and the public. This finding is consistent with Slovic (1987) who, by means of a factor-analytic model, identified the perceived level of knowledge about a particular risk as one of the two main dimensions of risk perception (the other factor was dread). These results suggest that an expert may have difficulty communicating a reassuring message because of the public's view that the expert may not have all of the relevant information. Science can only offer a reasonable assessment and can never provide proof.

Expert judgments are not always more accurate than lay judgments (Fiorino, 1989, 1990). The public can sometimes see problems and solutions that the experts may miss. From a communication perspective, we must acknowledge that experts and laypeople may construe risk in different ways (Slovic, 1987). Whenever possible, the public should be part of the message development process. Communication is enhanced when members of the intended audience participate in crafting the communication (Institute of Medicine, 2002). When target audience members assist with developing materials, the reading level of messages matches the ability of proposed readers more appropriately (Roter, Rudd, Keoge, & Robinson, 1986–1987; Rudd & Comings, 1994). Rudd et al. (2003) suggested that key reviewers should consult with members of the lay public, including people with less than a high school education before they distribute messages. In general, systematic differences between experts and a target group could affect risk communication.

## *Cultural Differences*

While some differences in lay versus expert risk perception seem to be similar and stable across cultures, research offers evidence for cultural differences in perceptions of personal risks. Two of Hofstede's (1980) dimensions of culture can be used to understand cultural differences in risk perception. According to Hofstede, some cultures have a higher tolerance for uncertainty and ambiguity. Members of uncertainty avoiding cultures try to minimize the possibility of uncertain situations by embracing strict laws, rules, safety, and security measures. On a philosophical and religious level, these cultures believe in absolute Truth. On the opposite end of the spectrum are uncertainty-accepting cultures. These cultures express more tolerance for competing opinions and try to have as few rules as possible. In addition, these cultures accept competing religious and philosophical viewpoints simultaneously. Hofstede reported that uncertainty avoidance scores were higher in Latin countries, Japan, and German speaking countries and lower in Anglo, Nordic, and Chinese speaking countries.

Power distance also accounts for cultural differences in risk perception (Hofstede, 1980). This concept reflects the extent to which less powerful members of society accept and expect that power is distributed unequally. According to Hofstede's research, power distance scores were higher for Latin, Asian, and African countries and smaller for Germanic countries. Xie, Wang, and Xu (2003) suggested that citizens in eastern countries, like China, with a higher power distance and a hierarchical Confucian cultural heritage, worry more about war and social deviance that threaten the established forms of social relations, and worry less about technology risks. Research confirmed this prediction. Xie et al. conducted two surveys in China, one in Beijing and the other in the northeastern province of Shandong, in which they asked participants about the perceived risks of various threats. Results indicate that the Chinese participants were concerned most about risks that threaten national stability and economic development and less concerned with high-technology risk, such as threat from a nuclear power plant.

Bontempo, Bottom, and Weber (1997) investigated cross-cultural differences in the perception of financial risk. Participants from the U.S., the Netherlands, Hong Kong, and Taiwan rated the risk of several lottery gambles, decided if they would be willing to play, and indicated how much risk they would be taking if they did play. Participants from the United States and the Netherlands were less sensitive to the magnitude of potential losses than participants from Taiwan and Hong Kong. Also, positive outcomes had a smaller reducing effect on perceived risk for the Taiwan and Hong Kong participants than participants from the two western cultures.

Differences in risk perception also emerged with regard to gender and age. Females across cultures and age groups tend to perceive risks as being higher than males perceive them to be (Flynn, Slovic, & Mertz, 1994; Jelalian et al., 1997; Slovic, 1999; Xie et al., 2003). In addition, younger people tend to perceive less personal risk than older people. Compared to adults, teenagers minimize the perceived risk of health-threatening activities (Cohn, Macfarlane, Yanez, & Imai, 1995). Gender and age differences in the perceptions of risks can already be observed during childhood. In their study comparing 6, 8, and 10-year-old children, Hillier and Morrongiello (1998) found that boys rated risk as lower than girls and that 6-year-olds identified fewer risk factors (and identified risk factors more slowly) than 10-year-olds.

## Qualitative Risk Information

Most research comparing qualitative and quantitative information does not suggest that one form of evidence is superior to others (Cacioppo, Petty, & Morris, 1983; Reinard, 1988). This chapter provides an overview of common obstacles in the communication of quantitative risk and describes how quantitative information should be presented. Yet, quantitative information may not always be available, and, at times, it is more appropriate to give qualitative risk information. Qualitative evidence includes narratives, personal anecdotes, case histories, personal stories, and testimonies (Baesler & Burgoon, 1994; Beck, 2001; Harter, Japp, & Beck, 2005; Kahneman & Tversky, 1982; Kazoleas, 1993; Kopfman et al., 1998).

Like numbers, narratives can serve as evidence for a particular conclusion. Beck (2001) suggested that personal stories provide a way of understanding risk that cannot be provided by giving "just the facts." By being able to merge fact, values, reason, and emotional content, such stories may be used in combination with quantitative information to inform or persuade. Kreuter et al. (2007) argued that narrative constitutes an appealing form of evidence due to its familiarity. People communicate and learn about the world through stories (Fisher, 1987).

According to Kreuter et al. (2007), narrative communication (including entertainment education, journalism, literature, testimonials, and storytelling) offers four distinctive capabilities. First, narrative communication can address the bases for resistance to change. A narrative can model a behavior by telling

a story about a person who performed it successfully. Next, narratives facilitate information processing. The authors suggest that humans are hardwired to process stories and narrative communication. Third, narratives provide surrogate social connections. People can develop relationships with characters in stories. Thus narratives serve a social support function. Finally, narratives can address emotional and existential issues where other forms of evidence cannot.

## Discussion

Research on the communication of quantitative risk information is relevant to scholars across the communication discipline. Communicators exchange risk information in both interpersonal and mass communication settings. Further, risk communication occurs in a variety of domains, including health, environmental, public policy, and technology. Risk communication takes place at the organizational level where policies are being made, but also in the family. An organization must assess the risk of an intentional attack in the United States, but a family then must understand this risk and decide if they need to create a disaster preparedness kit and make an evacuation plan. Finally, on the individual level, communication scholars must look at the differences in message receivers. We could benefit from more research regarding cultural differences, including religion, and the processing of quantitative risk information. An important topic for future research involves the communication of risks to people with a low functional literacy. Likewise, we should conduct more research to better understand how different racial and cultural groups process risk messages and how risks can be communicated most effectively to diverse populations (Keller & Stevens, 1997; Paling, 2003; Vaughn, 1995).

Qualitative and quantitative evidence have been studied extensively in the field of communication (Reinard, 1988; R. A. Reynolds & J. L Reynolds, 2002). Most of the research has focused on determining what types of messages are most vivid, memorable, or persuasive. A meta-analysis of 15 studies, conducted by Allen and Preiss (1997), indicates that statistical evidence is generally slightly more persuasive than qualitative messages that use examples or narratives. However, although people may learn quantitative information and be persuaded, they may be unable to apply it accurately in the future. Both qualitative and quantitative evidence can be effective in changing attitudes (Kazoleas, 1993).

Despite this large body of work, many questions remain unanswered. Research should continue to systematically explore the different dimensions of quantitative and qualitative evidence. Hample (2006) suggested that a theory of evidence would help to organize the research in this area. He asserted that a theory could be generated by descriptive study of evidence in use. Future research endeavors should investigate how people distinguish pieces of evidence and systematic investigations of the effects of evidence should be conducted.

Finally, more research that considers the role of emotion in risk communication is needed. Separate actions are involved in experiencing an emotion or a mood state, and in then relying on those feelings to make a risk related decision. People differ in terms of their emotions and affect when processing risk information, and further research can elucidate when such differences may occur.

## Conclusion

Unfortunately, we recognize some truth to Mark Twain's (1907) statement, "there are three kinds of lies: lies, damn lies, and statistics." Numbers can be deceiving, misleading, and misinterpreted. What is most objectionable is when experts will sometimes make intentional use of false numbers. Although we hope that this deception does not happen very often, a false number that is understood correctly, and a correct number that is misunderstood, may ultimately have the same effect. While no universal or magic way of communicating quantitative risk exists, this chapter reviewed a number of steps that can be taken to make risk information more understandable.

Effective risk communication begins with the message sender. Health practitioners have an obligation to inform the public in an appropriate way, particularly in situations when a patient is not ill, such as preventative health campaigns (Kurzenhäuser & Hoffrage, in press). In preventive screening, the number of participants who benefit from the test (those who have an early stage of the disease and would profit from early treatment) is rather small; whereas, the side effects of the test (e.g., exposure to x-rays during mammography) affect all participants.

The characteristics of the message receiver also should be taken into consideration. Doak, Doak, Friedell, and Meade (1998) offered several strategies to improve the comprehension of patients with low literacy skills. First, for verbal communication, Doak et al. asserted that the communicators provide an agenda for the conversation and limit new information to key points that are needed immediately. Second, the communicator should focus on behaviors and actions, and partition long lists of recommendations into smaller parts. Third, the communicator should present the context first, then the new information. Examples (such as pictures, sketches, models, or visuals) should be used, if appropriate. Finally, the message sender must obtain feedback from the message receiver to verify comprehension of quantitative risk information. Most importantly, a risk message has to be clear and understandable. Representations of quantitative information constitute communication tools. A communicator should select the best tools available to communicate his or her message. The selected statistical representation affects how receivers will understand the numbers. Thus, this choice can influence a number of receiver decisions. For example, a patient may choose a treatment option, select a medication, or make lifestyle changes based on the risk information presented.

Research indicates that some numbers, like natural frequencies, are easier to understand than others. Several studies have shown that frequencies improve Bayesian reasoning compared to probabilities and percentages (Brase, 2002; Hoffrage et al., 2000; Kurzenhäuser & Lücking, 2004; Lindsey et al., 2003; Mellers & McGraw, 1999). Statements with absolute frequencies also have another major advantage—they resolve the ambiguity of which reference class is chosen. The reference class, to which a single-event probability pertains, should always be given.

Communication scholars and practitioners who confront the difficult task of communicating quantitative risk information to the public and to consumers of their messages especially benefit from research regarding representation formats. Our review provides a spotlight rather than an exhaustive overview of the rich literature on risk communication. We focused on quantitative risk communication, which has notoriously been interpreted as being complex and difficult to understand. Research on risk formats comprises one area in which communication theories can help us improve the effectiveness of our messages. However, we need more research to better understand and overcome the hurdles inherent in risk communication. We believe the reviewed literature provides some promising avenues for future research, and we hope it inspires communicators who face the challenging task of communicating quantitative information.

## Notes

1. The prevalence rates of HIV and, therefore, also the positive predictive value of the HIV test refer to heterosexual men in Germany who are 20 to 30 years old and do not engage in risky behavior. This rate "is in the range of the prevalence of HIV in blood donors in the U.S. (a group with low prevalence within the U.S.), which has been estimated at one in 10,000 (Busch, 1994, p. 229) or two in 10,000 (George & Schochetman, 1994, p. 90)" (Gigerenzer et al., 1998, p. 199). A recent study on prevalence of HIV among young adults (18–28 years) in the United States (Morris et al., 2006) found similar prevalence rates for women (8.7 in 10,000) and for men (10.6 in 10,000). Note that these rates are about 10 times higher than the rates in the 1994 American samples. Moreover, in the Morris et al. study, the prevalence rate for non-Hispanic Blacks (49 in 10,000) differed remarkably from the prevalence rate found for members of other ethnic groups (22 in 10,000). The sample refers to 14,322 individuals out of 18,924 targeted individuals of a representative sample who agreed to participate (a participation rate of 75.7%).

2. Similar to HIV tests, the results of mammography screenings are not always correct. In fact, HIV tests are more accurate than mammography screenings (see Table 5.1). As a consequence, analyses similar to those displayed in Figure 5.1 revealed that the chance that a low-risk woman between the age of 40 and 50 suffers from breast cancer given that she has a positive result in a mammography is about 8% (Gigerenzer, 2002). In empirical studies, women typically overestimate this probability (Kurzenhäuser & Hoffrage, in press).

# References

Adelsward, V., & Sachs, L. (1996). The meaning of 6.8: Numeracy and normality in health information talks. *Social Science Medicine, 43*, 1179–1197.

Allen, M., & Preiss, R. W. (1997). Comparing the persuasiveness of narrative and statistical evidence using meta-analysis. *Communication Research Reports, 14*, 125–131.

Ancker, J. S., Senathirajah, Y., Kukafka, R., & Starren, J. B. (2006). Design features of graphs in health risk communication: A systematic review. *Journal of the American Medical Informatics Association, 13*, 608–618.

Anderson, J. L., Dodman, S., Kopelman, M., & Fleming, A. (1979). Patient information recall in a rheumatology clinic. *Rheumatology and Rehabilitation, 18*, 245–255.

Baesler, E. J., & Burgoon, J. K. (1994). The temporal effects of story and statistical evidence on belief change. *Communication Research, 21*, 582–602.

Barke, R. P., Jenkins-Smith, H., & Slovic, P. (1997). Risk perceptions of men and women scientists. *Social Science Quarterly, 78*, 167–176.

Baron, R. S., Inman, M. L., Kao, C. F., & Logan, H. (1992). Negative emotion and superficial social processing. *Motivation and Emotion, 16*, 323–346.

Beck, C. S. (2001). *Communicating for better health: A guide through the medical mazes.* Boston: Allyn & Bacon.

Black, W. C., Nease, R. F., & Tosteson, N. A. (1995). Perceptions of breast cancer risk and screening effectiveness in women younger than 50 years of age. *Journal of the National Cancer Institute, 87*, 720–731.

Bontempo, R. N., Bottom, W. P., & Weber, E. U. (1997). Cross-cultural differences in risk perception: A model based approach. *Risk Analysis, 17*, 479–488.

Brase, G. (2002). Which statistical formats facilitate what decisions? The perception and influence of different statistical information formats. *Journal of Behavioral Decision Making, 15*, 381–401.

Brase, G., Cosmides, L., & Tooby, J. (1998). Individuation, counting, and statistical inference: The role of frequency and whole object representations in judgment under uncertainty. *Journal of Experimental Psychology, 127*, 3–21.

Bucher, H. C., Weinbacher, M., & Gyr, K. (1994). Influence of method of reporting study results on decision of physicians to prescribe drugs to lower cholesterol concentration. *British Medical Journal, 309*, 761–764.

Busch, M. P. (1994). HIV testing in blood banks. In G. Schochetman & J. R. George (Eds.), *AIDS testing: A comprehensive guide to technical, medical, social, legal, and management issues* (pp. 224–236). New York: Springer.

Cacioppo, J. T., Petty, R. E., & Morris, K. J. (1983). Effects of need for cognition on message evaluation, recall, and persuasion. *Journal of Personality and Social Psychology, 45*, 805–818.

Casscells, W., Schoenberger, A., & Grayboys, T. (1978). Interpretation by physicians of clinical laboratory results. *New England Journal of Medicine, 299*, 999–1001.

Centers for Disease Control. (2008). *Anthrax Q & A: Risk.* Retrieved April 17, 2008, from http://emergency.cdc.gov/agent/anthrax/faq/risk.asp

Church, R. T., & Wilbanks, C. (1986). *Values and policies in controversy: An introduction to argumentation and debate.* Scottsdale, AZ: Gorsuch Scarisbrick.

Civan, A., Doctor, J. N., & Wolf, F. M. (2005). What makes a good format: Frameworks for evaluating the effect of graphic risk formats on consumers' risk-related behavior. *AMIA Symposium Proceedings* (p. 927).

Cohn, L. D., Macfarlane, S., Yanez, C., & Imai, W. (1995). Risk-perception: Differences between adolescents and adults. *Health Psychology, 14*, 217–222.

Covello, V. (1998). Communicating risk information: A guide to environmental communication in crisis and non-crisis situations, with principles of effective risk communication in crisis and non-crisis situations. In R.V. Kolluru (Ed.), *Environmental strategies handbook: A guide to effective policies and practices* (pp. 497–538). New York: McGraw Hill.

Davis, T. C., Dolan, N., Ferreira, M. R., Tomori, C., Green, K. W., Sipler, A. M. et al. (2001). The role of inadequate health literacy skills in colorectal cancer screening. *Cancer Investment, 19*, 193–200.

Davis, T. C., Long, S. W., Jackson, R. H., Mayeaux, E. J., George, R. B., Murphy, P. W., et al. (1993). Rapid estimate of adult literacy in medicine: A shortened screening instrument. *Journal of Family Medicine, 25*, 391–395.

Davis, T. C., Williams, M. V., Marin, E., Parker, R. M., & Glass, J. (2002). Health literacy and cancer communication, *CA: A Cancer Journal for Clinicians, 52*, 134–149.

Dillard, J. P., & Nabi, R. L. (2006). The persuasive influence of emotion in cancer prevention and detection messages. *Journal of Communication, 56*, 123–139.

Doak, C. C., Doak, L. G., Friedell, G. H., & Meade, C. D. (1998). Improving comprehension for cancer patients with low literacy skills: Strategies for clinicians. *CA: A Cancer Journal for Clinicians, 48*, 151–162.

Doyal, L. (2001). Informed consent: Moral necessity or illusion? *Quality in Health Care, 10*(Suppl. 1), 29–33.

Dunn, A. S., Shridharani, K. V., Lou, W., Bernstein, J., & Horowitz, C. R. (2001). Physician–patient discussion of controversial cancer screening tests. *American Journal of Preventive Medicine, 20*, 130–134.

Eddy, D. M. (1982). Probabilistic reasoning in clinical medicine: Problems and opportunities. In D. Kahneman, P. Slovic, & A. Tversky (Eds.). *Judgment under uncertainty: Heuristics and biases* (pp. 249–267). Cambridge, England: Cambridge University Press.

Edwards, A., Elwyn, G., & Gwyn, R. (1999). General practice registrar responses to the use of different risk communication tools in simulated consultations: A focus group study. *British Medical Journal, 319*, 749–752.

Fagerlin, A., Zikmund-Fisher, B., Ubel, P. A., Jankovic, A., Derry, H. A., & Smith, D. M. (2007). Measuring numeracy without a math test: Development of the subjective numeracy scale. *Medical Decision Making, 27*, 672–680.

Fahey, T., Griffiths, S., & Peters, T. J. (1995). Evidence based purchasing: Understanding results of clinical trials and systematic reviews. *British Medical Journal, 311*, 1056–1060.

Fiorino, D. J. (1989). Technical and democratic values in risk analysis. *Risk Analysis, 9*, 293–299.

Fiorino, D. J. (1990). Citizen participation and environmental risk: A survey of institutional mechanisms. *Science, Technology, & Human Values, 15*, 226–244.

Fischer, K., & Jungermann, H. (1996). Rarely occurring headaches and rarely occurring blindness: Is rarely = rarely? *Journal of Behavioral Decision Making, 9*, 153–172.

Fisher, W. (1987). *Human communication as narration: Toward a philosophy of reason, value, and action.* Columbia: University of South Carolina Press.

Flynn, J., Slovic, P., & Mertz, C. K. (1994). Gender, race, and perception of environmental health risks. *Risk Analysis, 14*, 1101–1108.

Freimuth, V. S., Chervin, D., Hovick, S., & Johnson-Turbes, C. A. (2007, November). *Patterns of response to health risks among the southern poor.* Paper presented at the annual meeting of the American Public Health Association, Washington, DC.

Freimuth, V. S, Linnan, H. W., & Potter, P. (2000). Communicating the threat of emerging infections to the public. *Journal of Emerging Infectious Diseases, 6,* 337–347.

Frewer, L., Miles, S., Brennan, M., Kuznesof, S., Ness, M., & Ritson, C. (2002). Public preferences for informed choice under conditions of risk uncertainty. *Public Understanding of Science, 11,* 363–372.

Galvin, K., & Grill, L. H. (this volume). Opening up the conversation on genetics in families: The space for communication scholars. In C. S. Beck (Ed.), *Communication yearbook 33* (pp. 213–257). New York: Routledge.

George, J. R., & Schochetman, G. (1994). Detection of HIV infection using serologic techniques. In G. Schochetman & J. R. George (Eds.), *AIDS testing: A comprehensive guide to technical, medical, social, legal, and management issues* (pp. 62–102). New York: Springer.

Ghosh, A. K., & Ghosh, K. (2005). Translating evidence-based information into effective risk communication: Current challenges and opportunities. *Journal of Laboratory and Clinical Medicine, 145,* 171–180.

Gigerenzer, G. (2002). *Calculated risks: How to know when numbers deceive you.* New York: Simon & Schuster.

Gigerenzer, G., & Edwards, A. (2003). Simple tools for understanding risk: From innumeracy to insight. *British Medical Journal, 327,* 741–744.

Gigerenzer, G., Gaissmaier, W., Kurz-Milcke, E., Schwartz, L. M., & Woloshin, S. (2008). Helping doctors and patients make sense of health statistics. *Psychological Science in the Public Interest, 8*(2), 53–96.

Gigerenzer, G., Hertwig, R., van den Broek, E., Fasolo, B., & Katsikopoulos, K. V. (2005). "A 30% chance of rain tomorrow": How does the public understand probabilistic weather forecasts? *Risk Analysis, 25,* 623–629.

Gigerenzer, G., & Hoffrage, U. (1995). How to improve Bayesian reasoning without instruction: Frequency formats. *Psychological Review, 102,* 684–704.

Gigerenzer, G., Hoffrage, U., & Ebert, A. (1998). AIDS counseling for low-risk clients. *AIDS Care, 10,* 197–211.

Gigerenzer, G., Swijtink, Z., Porter, T., Daston, L., Beatty, J., & Kruger, L. (1989). *The empire of chance, how probability changed science and everyday life.* Cambridge, England: Cambridge University Press.

Grimes, D. A., & Snively, G. R. (1999). Patients' understanding of medical risks: Implications for genetic counseling. *Obstetrics and Gynecology, 93,* 910–914.

Hallowell, N., Statham, H., Murton, F., Green, J., & Richards, M. (1997). "Talking about chance": The presentation of risk information during genetic counseling for breast and ovarian cancer. *Journal of Genetic Counseling, 6,* 269–286.

Hample, D. (2006). Toward a theory of evidence: Perceptual dimensions and their relationships to persuasiveness. In P. Riley (Ed.), *Engaging argument* (pp. 453–460). Washington DC: National Communication Association.

Hanoch, Y. (2004). Improving doctor–patient understanding of probability in communicating cancer-screening test findings. *Journal of Health Communication, 9,* 327–335.

Harter, L., Japp, P., & Beck, C. S. (Eds.). (2005). *Narratives, health, and healing.* Mahwah, NJ: Erlbaum.

Heller, R. F., Buchan, I., Edwards, R., Lyratzopoulos, G., McElduff, P., & St. Leger,

S. (2003). Communicating risks at the population level: Application of population impact numbers. *British Medical Journal, 327,* 1162–1165.

Heller, R. F., Sandars, J. E., Patterson, L., & McElduff, P. (2004). GP's and physicians' interpretation of risks, benefits, and diagnostic test results. *Family Practice, 21,* 155–159.

Hembroff, L. A., Holmes-Rovner, M., & Wills, C. E. (2004). Treatment decision-making and the form of risk communication: Results from a factorial survey. *BMC Medical Informatics and Decision Making, 4,* 1184–1120.

Hibbard, J. H., & Peters, E. (2003). Supporting informed consumer health care decisions: Data presentation approaches that facilitate the use of information in choice. *Annual Review of Public Health, 24,* 413–433.

Hillier, L. M., & Morrongiello, B. A. (1998). Age and gender differences in school-age children's appraisals of injury risk. *Journal of Pediatric Psychology, 23,* 229–238.

Hoffrage, U., & Gigerenzer, G. (1998). Using natural frequencies to improve diagnostic inferences. *Academic Medicine, 73,* 538–540.

Hoffrage, U., Gigerenzer, G., Krauss, S., & Martignon, L. (2002). Representation facilitates reasoning: What natural frequencies are and what they are not. *Cognition, 84,* 343–352.

Hoffrage, U., & Hertwig, R. (2006). Which world should be represented in representative design? In K. Fiedler & P. Juslin (Eds.), *Information sampling and adaptive cognition* (pp. 381–408). New York: Cambridge University Press.

Hoffrage, U., Lindsey, S., Hertwig, R., & Gigerenzer, G. (2000). Communicating statistical information. *Science, 22,* 2261–2262.

Hofstede, G. (1980). *Culture's consequences: International differences in work related values.* Thousand Oaks, CA: Sage.

Horner, S. D., Surratt, D., & Juliusson, S. (2000). Improving readability of patient materials. *Journal of Community Health Nursing, 17,* 15–23.

Huerta, E. E., & Macario, E. (1999). Communicating health risk to ethnic groups: Reaching hispanics as a case study. *Journal of the National Cancer Institute Monographs, 25,* 23–26.

Huff, D. (1954). *How to lie with statistics.* London: Gollancz.

Institute of Medicine. (2002). *Speaking of health: Assessing health communication strategies for diverse populations.* Washington, DC: National Academy Press.

Jelalian, E., Spirito, A., Rasile, D., Vinnick, L., Rohrbeck, C., & Arrigan, M. (1997). Risk taking, reported injury, and perception of future injury among adolescents. *Journal of Pediatric Psychology, 22,* 513–531.

Kahneman, D., & Tversky, A. (1979). Prospect theory: An analysis of decision under risk. *Econometrica, 47,* 263–291.

Kahneman, D., & Tversky, A. (1982). The psychology of preferences. *Scientific American, 247,* 160–173.

Kazoleas, D. C. (1993). A comparison of the persuasive effectiveness of qualitative versus quantitative evidence: A test of the explanatory hypotheses. *Communication Quarterly, 41,* 40–50.

Keller, C. S., & Stevens, K. R. (1997). Cultural considerations in promoting wellness. *Journal of Cardiovascular Nursing, 11,* 15–25.

Kessels, R. P. C. (2003). Patient's memory for medical information. *Journal of the Royal Society of Medicine, 96,* 219–222.

Kleiter, G. (1994). Natural sampling: Rationality without base rates. In G. H. Fischer &

D. Laming (Eds.), *Contributions to mathematical psychology, psychometrics, and methodology* (pp. 375–388). New York: Springer.

Kolmogorov, A. N. (1956). *Foundations of the theory of probability* (2nd English ed.). New York: Chelsea.

Kopfman, J. E., Smith, S. W., Ah Yun, J. K., & Hodges, A. (1998). Affective and cognitive reactions to narrative versus statistical evidence in organ donation messages. *Journal of Applied Communication Research, 26,* 279–300.

Kreuter, M. W., Green, M. C., Cappella, J. N., Slater, M. D., & Clark, E. M. (2007). Narrative communication in cancer prevention and control: A framework to guide research and applications. *Annals of Behavioral Medicine, 33,* 221–235.

Kurzenhäuser, S. (2003). Welche Informationen vermitteln deutsche Gesundheitsbroschüren über die Screening-Mammographie? [What information is provided in German health information pamphlets on mammography screening?] *Zeitschrift für ärztliche Fortbildung und Qualitätssicherung, 97,* 53–57.

Kurzenhäuser, S., & Hoffrage, U. (2002). Teaching Bayesian reasoning: An evaluation of a classroom tutorial for medical students. *Medical Teacher, 24,* 531–536.

Kurzenhäuser, S., & Hoffrage, U. (in press). Designing risk communication in health. In P. M. Todd, G. Gigerenzer, & the ABC Research Group, *Ecological rationality: Intelligence in the world.* New York: Oxford University Press.

Kurzenhäuser, S., & Lücking, A. (2004). Statistical formats in Bayesian inference. In R. Pohl (Ed.), *Cognitive illusions: A handbook on fallacies and biases in thinking, judgment, and memory* (pp. 61–77). Hove, England: Psychological Press.

Kutner, M., Greenberg, E., Lin, Y., Paulsen, C., & White, S. (2006). *The health literacy of America's adults: Results from the 2003 national assessment of health literacy* (NCES 2006–483). Washington, DC: U.S. Department of Education.

Lazarus, R. S., & Folkman, S. (1984). *Stress, appraisal and coping.* New York: Guilford.

Leiss, W. (1996). Three phases in the evolution of risk communication practice. *The Annals of the American Academy, 545,* 85–94.

Lemaire, R. (2006). Informed consent—A contemporary myth? *Journal of Bone and Joint Surgery, 88,* 2–7.

Ley, P. (1979). Memory for medical information. *British Journal of Social Clinical Psychology, 18,* 245–255.

Lindsey, S., Hertwig, R., & Gigerenzer, G. (2003). Communicating statistical DNA evidence. *Jurimetrics: The Journal of Law, Science, and Technology, 43,* 147–163.

Lipkus, I. M. (2007). Numeric, verbal, and visual formats of conveying health risks: Suggested best practices and future recommendations. *Medical Decision Making, 27,* 696–713.

Lipkus, I. M., Samsa, G., & Rimer, B. K. (2001). General performance on a numeracy scale among highly educated samples. *Medical Decision Making, 21,* 37–44.

Lloyd, A. J. (2001). The extent of patients' understanding of the risk of treatments. *Quality in Health Care, 10*(Suppl. 1), i14–i18.

Lloyd, A. J., Hayes, P. D., London, N. J. M., Bell, P. R. F., & Naylor, A. R. (1999). Patients' ability to recall risk associated with treatment options. *Lancet, 353,* 645.

Lobb, E. A., Butow, P. N., Kenny, D. T., & Tattersall, H. N. (1999). Communicating prognosis in early breast cancer: Do women understand the language used? *Medical Journal of Australia, 171,* 290–294.

Mazur, D., Hickam, D., & Mazur, M. (1999). How patients' preferences for risk information influence treatment choice in a case of high risk and high therapeutic uncertainty: Asymptomatic localized prostate cancer. *Medical Decision Making, 19*, 394–398.

McGuire, L. C. (1996). Remembering what the doctor said: Organization and older adults' memory for medical information. *Experimental Aging Research, 22*, 403–428.

McLaughlin, G. H. (1969). SMOG grading: A new readability formula. *Journal of Reading, 12*, 639–646.

Mellers, B., & McGraw, P. (1999). How to improve Bayesian reasoning without instruction: Comment on Gigerenzer and Hoffrage. *Psychological Review, 106*, 417–424.

Morris, M., Hancock, M. S., Miller, W. C., Ford, C. A., Schmitz, J. L., Hobbs, M. M., et al. (2006). Prevalence of HIV infection among young adults in the United States: Results from the Add Health Study. *American Journal of Public Health, 96*, 1091–1097.

Noar, S. M., Harrington, N. G., & Aldrich, R. S. (this volume). The role of message tailoring in the development of persuasive health communication messages. In C. S. Beck (Ed.), *Communication Yearbook 33* (pp. 73–133). New York: Routledge.

O'Keefe, D. J., & Jensen, J. D. (2007). The relative persuasiveness of gain-framed and loss-framed messages for encouraging disease prevention behaviors: A meta-analytic review. *Journal of Health Communication, 12*, 623–644.

O'Keefe, D. J., & Jensen, J. D. (2008). Do loss-framed persuasive messages engender greater message processing than do gain-framed messages? A meta-analytic review. *Communication Studies, 59*, 51–67.

Paling, J. (2003). Strategies to help patients understand risks. *British Medical Journal, 327*, 745–747.

Parker, R. M., Baker, D. W., Williams, M. V., & Nurss, J. R. (1995). The test of functional health literacy in adults: a new instrument for measuring patients' literacy skills. *Journal of General Internal Medicine, 10*, 537–541.

Parrott, R., Silk, K., Dorgan, K., Condit, C., & Harris, T. (2005). Risk comprehension and judgments of statistical evidentiary appeals: When a picture is not worth a thousand words. *Human Communication Research, 31*, 423–452.

Paulos, J. A. (1988). *Innumeracy: Mathematical illiteracy and its consequences.* New York: Hill & Wang.

Peters, E., Lipkus, I. M., & Diefenbach, M. A. (2006). The functions of affect in health communications and the construction of health preferences. *Journal of Communication, 56*, 140–162.

Peters, E., Västfjäll, D., Slovic, P., Mertz, C. K., Mazzocco, K. & Dickert, S. (2006). Numeracy and decision making. *Psychological Science, 17*, 407–413.

Raghunathan, R., & Pham, M. T. (1999). All negative moods are not equal: Motivational influences of anxiety and sadness on decision making. *Organizational Behavior and Human Decision processes, 79*, 56–77.

Reinard, J. C. (1988). The empirical study of the persuasive effects of evidence: The status after fifty years of research. *Human Communication Research, 15*, 3–59.

Reyna, V. F., & Brainerd, C. J. (2007). The importance of mathematics in health and human judgment: Numeracy, risk communication, and medical decision making. *Learning and Individual Differences, 17*, 147–159.

Reynolds, R. A., & Reynolds, J. L. (2002). Evidence. In J. P. Dillard & M. Pfau (Eds.), *The persuasion handbook: Developments in theory and practice* (pp. 213–232). Thousand Oaks, CA: Sage.

Roter, D. L., Rudd, R. E., Keoge, J., & Robinson, B. (1986–1987). Worker produced health education material for the construction trades. *International Quarterly of Community Health Education, 7*(2), 109–121.

Rothman, R. L., Montori, V. M., Cherrington, A., & Pignone, M. P. (2008). Perspective: The role of numeracy in health care. *Journal of Health Communication, 13*, 583–595.

Rottenstreich, Y., & Hsee, C. K. (2001). Money, kisses, and electric shocks: On the affective psychology of risk. *Psychological Science, 12*, 185–190.

Rowan, K. E. (1999). Effective explanation of uncertain and complex science. In S. Friedman, S. Dunwoody, & C. L. Rogers (Eds.), *Communicating uncertainty: Media coverage of new and controversial science* (pp. 201–224). Mahwah, NJ: Erlbaum.

Rudd, R. E., & Comings, J. P. (1994). Learner developed materials: An empowering product. *Health Education Quarterly, 21*(3), 33–47.

Rudd, R. E., Comings, J. P., & Hyde, J. N. (2003). Leave no one behind: Improving health and risk communication through attention to literacy. *Journal of Health Communication, 8*, 104–115.

Sackett, D. L. (1996). On some clinically useful measures of the effects of treatment. *Evidence-Based Medicine, 1*, 37–38.

Sackett, D. L., Haynes, R. B., Guyatt, G. H., & Tugwell, P. (1991). *Clinical epidemiology: A basic science for clinical medicine.* Boston: Little Brown.

Salovey, P., Schneider, T. R., & Apanovitch, A. M. (2002). Message framing in the prevention and early detection of illness. In J. P. Dillard & M. Pfau (Eds.), *The persuasion handbook: Developments in theory and practice* (pp. 391–406). Thousand Oaks, CA: Sage.

Sandman, P. M. (1993). *Responding to community outrage: Strategies for effective risk communication.* Fairfax, VA: American Industrial Hygiene Association.

Sarfati, D., Howden-Chapman, P., Woodward, A., & Salmond, C. (1998). Does the frame affect the picture? A study into how attitudes to screening for cancer are affected by the way benefits are expressed. *Journal of Medical Screening, 5*, 137–140.

Schapira, M. M., Fletcher, K. E., Gilligan, M. A., King, T. K., Laud, P. W., Matthews, B. A., et al. (2008). A framework for health numeracy: How patients use quantitative skills in health care. *Journal of Health Communication, 13*, 501–517.

Schwartz, L. M., Woloshin, S., Black, W., C., & Welsh, H. G. (1997). The role of numeracy in understanding the benefit of screening mammography. *Annals of Internal Medicine, 127*, 966–972.

Sedlmeier, P., & Gigerenzer, G. (2001). Teaching Bayesian reasoning in less than two hours. *Journal of Experimental Psychology: General, 130*, 380–400.

Sheridan, S. L., & Pignone, M. (2002). Numeracy and the medical student's ability to interpret data. *Effective Clinical Practice, 5*, 35–40.

Sheridan, S. L., Pignone, M. P., & Lewis, C. L. (2003). A randomized comparison of patients' understanding of number needed to treat and other common risk reduction formats. *Journal of General Internal Medicine, 18*, 884–892.

Sjöberg, L. (2001). Limits of knowledge and the limited importance of trust. *Risk Analysis, 21*, 189–198.

Slovic, P. (1987). Perception of risk. *Science, 236*, 280–285.

Slovic, P. (1999). Trust, emotion, sex, politics, and science: Surveying the risk-assessment battlefield. *Risk Analysis, 19*, 689–701.

Slovic, P., Finucane, M., Peters, E., & MacGregor, D. G. (2002). Rational actors of rational fools: Implications of the affect heuristic for behavioral economics. *Journal of Socio-Economics, 31*, 329–342.

Slovic, P., Finucane, M. L., Peters, E., & MacGregor, D. G. (2004). Risk as analysis and risk as feelings: Some thoughts about affect, reason, risk, and rationality. *Risk Analysis, 24*, 311–322.

Slovic, P., Monahan, J., & MacGregor, D.G. (2000). Violence risk assessment and risk communication: The effects of using actual cases, providing instruction, and employing probability versus frequency formats. *Law and Human Behavior, 24,* 271–296.

Smyth, A. H. (Ed.). (1907). *The writings of Benjamin Franklin* (Vol. 10). New York: Macmillan.

Strecher, V. J., Greenwood, T., Wang, C., & Dumont, D. (1999). Interactive multimedia and risk communication. *Journal of the National Cancer Institute Monographs, 25,* 134–139.

Tappe, M. K., & Galer-Unti, R. A. (2001). Health educators' role in promoting health literacy and advocacy for the 21st century. *Journal of School Health, 71,* 477–481.

Thomson, A. M., Cunningham, S. J., & Hunt, N. P. (2001). A comparison of information retention at an initial orthodontic consultation. *European Journal of Orthodontics, 23,* 169–178.

Towle, A., Godolphin, W., Grams, G., & Lamarre, A. (2006). Putting informed and shared decision making into practice. *Health Expectations, 9,* 321–332.

Tortolero-Luna, G., Glober, G. A., Villarreal, R., Palos, G., & Linares, A. (1995). Cancer research in Hispanic populations in the United States. *Journal of the National Cancer Institute Monographs, 18,* 49–56.

Tversky, A., & Kahneman, D. (1981). The framing of decisions and the psychology of choice. *Science, 211,* 453–458.

Twain, M. (1907). Chapters from my autobiography. *North American Review, DXCVIII.*

U.S. Department of Health and Human Services. (2000). *Healthy people 2010: understanding and improving health.* (2nd ed.). Washington, DC: U.S. Government Printing Office.

Vaughn, E. (1995). The significance of socioeconomic and ethnic diversity for the risk communication process. *Risk Analysis, 15,* 169–180.

von Mises, R. (1939). *Probability, statistics, and truth.* (J. Neyman, D. Scholl, & E. Rabinowitsch, Trans.). New York: Macmillan.

Watson, M., Lloyd, S., Davidson, J., Meyer, L., Eeles, R., & Ebbs, S. (1999). The impact of genetic counseling on risk perception and mental health in women with a family history of breast cancer. *British Journal of Cancer, 79,* 868–874.

Weinstein, N. D. (1989). Optimistic biases about personal risk. *Science, 246,* 1232–1233.

Weinstein, N. D. (1999). What does it mean to understand a risk? Evaluating risk comprehension. *Journal of the National Cancer Institute Monographs, 25,* 15–20.

White, S., & Dillow, S. (2005). *Key concepts and features of the 2003 National Assessment of Adult Literacy* (NCES 2006-471). Washington, DC: National Center for Education Statistics.

Wiedemann, P. M. (1993). Taboo, sin, risk: Changes in the social perception of hazards. In B. Rück (Ed.), *Risk is a construct: Perceptions of risk perception* (pp. 41–63). Munich, Germany: Knesebeck.

Xie, X., Wang, M., & Xu, L. (2003). What risks are Chinese people concerned about? *Risk Analysis, 23,* 685–695.

Yamagishi, K. (1997). When a 12.86% mortality rate is more dangerous than a 24.14%: Implications for risk communication. *Applied Cognitive Psychology, 11,* 295–506.

Zarcadoolas, C., Pleasant, A. F., & Greer, D. S. (2006). *Advancing health literacy: A framework for understanding and action.* San Francisco: Jossey-Bass.

# CHAPTER CONTENTS

# 6 Opening Up the Conversation on Genetics and Genomics in Families

## The Space for Communication Scholars

*Kathleen M. Galvin*
*Lauren H. Grill*
Northwestern University

Advances in genetics and genomics research allow increasing numbers of family members to learn of their susceptibilities for inheriting genetic diseases. A family member diagnosed with a genetic disease is expected to notify other family members who may be at risk; these individuals confront the ongoing dilemmas of how to discuss familial genetic health. The complexities of family communication dynamics surrounding genetic health-related issues raise key challenges for many family members. Although communication-related research literature exists in genetic counseling, communication studies, and other social sciences, little scholarship integrates these findings. This chapter provides an interdisciplinary review of the available literature pertaining to the ways in which family members disclose and discuss genetic test results among family members; it discusses implications of genetic knowledge within the family and identifies areas of future related research. The authors call for increasing contributions from interpersonal, family, and health communication scholars to address the needs of families that are managing genetic health issues.

## Introduction

Advances in genetics and genomics research have changed, and will continue to change, the ways in which families talk about health. Until recently, researchers recognized the hereditary nature of certain diseases but, in many cases, knew little about which family members might be affected, remain unaffected, or be carriers. Thus, due to ignorance and ambiguity, many families manage their unpredictable genetic circumstances through silence and highly rule bound interactions. Today, primarily as a result of the Human Genome Project, a 13-year endeavor completed in 2003, new genetic findings are being revealed as researchers investigate the impact and interactions of an estimated 30,000 human genes (Human Genome Project, n.d.).

Correspondence: e-mail: k-galvin@northwestern.edu

According to Francis Collins, Director of the Human Genome Project, "If this is the Book of Life, we should not settle for a rough draft over the long term, but should remain committed to producing a final, highly accurate version" (1999, p. 29). As the Human Genome Project identifies generic variations which may be associated with clinical or health conditions, it creates a need for powerful biopsychosocial and cultural resources to address the interpersonal impact on individuals and family members as they learn of their genetic susceptibilities.

In the Human Genome Project's early stages, some scholars viewed these findings as highly predictive, asserting that families of the future "will more and more be confronted with deterministic predictions of their fate" (Rolland, 1999, p. 123). Today, scholars emphasize genomics, which incorporates the interaction of genetic findings and behavioral choices (Miller, McDaniel, Rolland, & Feetham, 2006) in determining risk for hereditary conditions. Nonetheless, ongoing discoveries from the Human Genome Project challenge families to confront implications of relatives' genetic heritage and health and to engage in disclosure and discussion of familial genetic diseases. Furthermore, conversations regarding issues such as adopting or modifying particular health-related behaviors and future family planning will likely become more commonplace.

Current conversations in this area relate to developments in genetics and genomics. *Genetics* refers to the study of individual genes and their impact on relatively rare single-gene disorders (Feetham & Thomson, 2006). Today, according to Feetham and Thomson, the lexicon also includes *genomics*, a term first used in 1987 "to reflect the study of all the genes in the human genome together, including their interactions with each other, the environment, and other psychological and cultural factors" (p. 5). Advances in genomic science opened the door to understanding the "genetic contribution to some common chronic illnesses such as heart disease, diabetes, Alzheimer disease, and familial breast cancer" (McDaniel, 2005, p. 26).

Although much of the available literature within genetic research focuses on the medical implications of genetic testing, this chapter attempts to open up a space for interpersonal, family, and health communication scholars to join the recent research efforts of genetic counselors and social scientists and to examine changes in family interactions sparked by advances in genetic and genomic research. By addressing communication oriented genetics and genomics research questions, scholars will advance theoretical and applied knowledge in interpersonal, family, and health communication and in other communication areas.

This chapter addresses developments in genetic research that impact family interaction, including research on family disclosure and discussion of genetic disease, the potential contributions of family and interpersonal theories to dialogues about genetics, and scholarship regarding the media's role in creating awareness and encouraging conversations. We conclude by outlining future directions for family and health communication related to this important topic.

## Developments in Genetic Research Related to Family Interactions

Genetic diseases tend to be familial diseases. Genetic research and testing impacts the individual who is undergoing testing and it presents serious implications for that individual's relatives. Specifically, knowledge of hereditary disease within a family has been demonstrated to affect the ways in which family members communicate with each other; likewise, a family's ability to openly discuss a genetic disease may also determine how well members can manage and treat the disease or even prevent transmission to future generations. This section, therefore, presents a brief background of genetic research developments and explains how such advancements impact family interactions.

### *Genetic Diseases in Families*

Family members may be diagnosed with a genetic disease, serve as carriers of a genetic disease, or share a "susceptibility" to a genetic condition (Featherstone, Atkinson, Bharadwaj, & Clarke, 2006). When partners become parents to a biological child, the adult pairing may pass on a genetic abnormality due to their mutual carrier status. Different models of genetic inheritance display various patterns of impact. For example, siblings of unaffected parents tend to show concordance for recessive diseases. Conversely, mild, sex-linked recessive diseases usually occur in grandfather-grandson pairs (Crews & Balcazar, 1999). According to Crews and Balcazar, determining genetic influences in chronic diseases is difficult because "degenerative or chronic diseases have extended and variable periods of onset and risk of onset increases with age" (p. 616). Thus, genetic testing may not only reveal information about an individual but also about potential risks to the affected individual's relatives (Claes et al., 2003).

In the United States, family-oriented genetics emerged between the mid-1930s and the mid-1950s, an era that reflected a negative reaction to the concepts of eugenic thought and was guided by the overarching metaphor of genes controlling human beings (Condit, 1999a). The field changed dramatically through the discovery of the structure of DNA in 1953 and the Human Genome Project, initiated in 1990 and completed in 2003. By the end of the 20th century, according to Condit, "the blueprint provided the dominant metaphor for genetics" (Condit, 1999b, p. 20). By 1999, over 4,000 diseases had been identified as containing genetic predispositions (Wood-Harper & Harris, 1999). Currently, genetic testing is available for more than 1,000 conditions (Van Riper, 2005). The five common types of genetic testing include: (1) prenatal testing, often due to a history of genetic anomalies; (2) newborn screening; (3) carrier testing, intended to identify recessive mutations; (4) diagnostic testing, for diseases such as Down syndrome or Huntington's disease (HD), and (5) predictive testing (McDaniel, 2005).

To date, genetic counseling literature contains much of the research on family interaction and genetic disease. Genetic counseling involves communicating the risk of genetic disease or disorders, the impact of the risk of the disease or disorder, and the treatment options available for the patient and his or her family members (Broadfoot, 2008; Clark, 1997). Resta et al. (2006) described genetic counseling as:

> ...the process of helping people understand and adapt to the medical, psychological and familial implications of genetic contributions to disease. This process integrates the following: Interpretation of family and medical histories to assess the chance of disease occurrence or recurrence; Education about inheritance, testing, management, prevention, resources and research; Counseling to promote informed choices and adaptation to the risk or condition. (p. 77)

Such research provides insights into family communication patterns regarding genetic disease.

### Family Communication about Genetics

Historically, family members managed genetic concerns informally through intergenerational communication networks and, more specifically, shared familial health histories. These family communication patterns dramatically impact members' risk awareness, genetic testing decisions, and outcomes (Croyle & Lerman, 1999). We have witnessed an increase in studies addressing family communication regarding hereditary genetic diseases such as cystic fibrosis (CF), Huntington's disease (HD), hereditary breast and ovarian cancer (HBOC), and hereditary nonpolyposis colorectal cancer (HNPCC) (Forrest et al., 2003; Gaff et al., 2007). The genetic mutation for hereditary hemochromatosis (HH) was only discovered in 1996, and research that explores family disclosure patterns related to the disease continues (Reyes, Dunet, Isenberg, Trisolini & Wagener, 2007). Such studies represent the type of knowledge available to assist individuals in coping with, disclosing, and discussing their genetic histories with family members (Gaff, Collins, Symes, & Halliday, 2005; Holt, 2006).

Increasingly, individuals, subgroups, and entire families will be confronted with communication concerns, ranging from how to manage the transmission of information regarding relatives' genetic health to discussion and decision making. Critical family communication tasks involve accurately exchanging health risk and disease information among family members and integrating communication about genetic risk into the family culture. Thus, understanding family communication patterns plays an increasingly important role in the professional lives of medical practitioners and genetic counselors (Biesecker, 2003; Biesecker et al., 1993).

Currently, much of the research addressing family communication regarding genetic disease involves empirical clinical studies focusing on specific genetic diseases (Forrest et al., 2003; Gaff et al., 2007). According to Gaff et al., a limited number of theory-based studies examine family interaction regarding genetic heritage. Scholars, such as those at the Centre for Economic and Social Aspects of Genomics, take an interdisciplinary approach to address social, economic, and policy aspects of development in genomics, and they include family communication in their research agendas (Centre for Genetics and Society, n.d.). Social scientists and genetic counselors in the British Isles, Australia, New Zealand, and the Netherlands incorporate family communication issues in their research; as Gaff et al. observed, some even advocate that "greater attention needs to be paid to the process of communication with family members" (p. 12).

### Contributions of Communication Scholars

To date, a number of scholars in the communication discipline have published in the areas of genetics, although few focus on family communication about genetic health. Celeste Condit (1999b, 2004, 2008) has pioneered communication-related research, opening up a significant place for rhetorical scholarship while contributing uniquely to public understanding of genetics. Michael Hyde (2008) raised the issues of perfection and postmodern culture when addressing ethical issues including biotechnology and genetics. A growing number of communication scholars are contributing to an understanding of genetic issues in health communication scholarship (Bates, 2005; Bates, Poirot, Harris, Condit, & Achter, 2004; Bates, Templeton, Achter, Harris, & Condit, 2003; Condit, Parrott, & O'Grady, 2000; Duncan, Parrott, & Silk, 2002; Parrott & Condit, 1996; Parrott et al., 2004; Thompson & Parrott, 2002). Morgan and Hacker (2007) extended this conversation by exploring the implications of the Human Genome Project and the HapMap Project, expanding upon an initial understanding of how people who self-identify themselves into different racial and ethnic groups differ significantly in their attitudes toward genomics.

The current communication-oriented genetic and genomics research displays strong connection to and reliance on research in intercultural communication (Awwad, Veach, Bartels, & LeRoy, 2008; MacDonald et al., 2008), rhetoric (Condit, 1999b, Hyde, 2008), and media (Warner, Curnow, Polglase, & Debinski, 2005), and the interfaces among these areas (Condit et al., 2001; Parrott et al., 2004).

In addressing family communication, Weiner, Silk, and Parrott (2005) examined African Americans and European Americans' knowledge, attitudes, and behaviors that are associated with genetics and family communication. A set of studies focused specifically on the management, negotiation, and reduction of uncertainty among health providers and family members related to the diagnosis of childhood CF (Dillard & Carson, 2005; Dillard, Carson, Bernard, Laxova, & Farrell, 2004; Dillard, Shen, Laxova, & Farrell, 2008). In her extensive ethnographic and discursive study of living with genetics within a clinical context, Broadfoot (2008) explored the communication practices of family participants and professionals in genetic clinics. Recent research addresses sibling interactions after one is diagnosed with HH (Galvin, Bylund, Reyes, & Dunet, 2006). Finally, an ongoing project attempts to merge theories related to family communication with the practice of genetic counseling (Gaff & Bylund, in press).

Once some family members become aware of the potential for genetic diseases in their family, they have to decide whether or not to share this information with other family members. The method and timing of this disclosure may impact the health and well-being of other family members. Researchers must understand families' communicative dynamics during disclosure and discussion of genetic disease, given that such conversations may have consequences for their relatives. In the following sections, we explore contemporary understandings of disclosure and discussion of genetic disease within families and suggest critical areas for future research.

## Review of Family Disclosure and Discussion Research

Communication about genetic information within families is a topic of growing research and interest (Sorenson & Botkin, 2003). Diseases—such as CF, HD, oculocutaneous albinism (OCA), and hemophilia (HA)—have been understood practically as hereditary; historically, family members have shared knowledge of the diseases that appear to pass through generations and engaged in surveillance activities as members surreptitiously looked for signs of a disease in other relatives (Featherstone et al., 2006). In their study of how family members talk about genetic health, Weiner et al. (2005) asked a diverse group of subjects to respond to items such as "My family has talked about whether to get genetic testing." Weiner et al. concluded that "families are not yet talking about this issue as revealed by 607 (84.7%) of the participants who answered that they had 'never' discussed genetic diseases in their families" (p. 320). Furthermore, 8.4% indicated that they had seldom discussed this matter; another 5.2% revealed that they sometimes had such discussions. Only 1.9% mentioned discussing genetic testing often in their families. Essentially, many families seldom, if ever, talk about this topic without a specific reason to do so. The families that addressed the disease tended to have a history of an illness moving across generations.

Today, a growing need exists for such conversations, given the numerous genetic revelations derived from the ongoing work of the Human Genome Project (Gaff et al., 2007); future research based on gene identification will likely uncover even further evidence of genetic changes. As a result, an increasing number of families will be faced with an exceptionally delicate task—communicating within families about their genetic heritage when one person becomes symptomatic or when indicators of genetic risk could be identified or have already been identified in certain members. As recently as 30 years ago, these types of family discussions were rare and highly situational (Forrest et al., 2003); however, the pace of scientific advances in the identification of risk indicators and in the management of infertility render such discussions much more pertinent for families today.

A physician may reveal news that an individual has a genetic mutation, or may eventually develop symptoms of one in the future, but many other family members learn about their genetic risk from an already affected family member who sounds the warning. In some cases these alarm messages are vague or medically inexact; often, other family members ignore or reject such messages (Forrest et al., 2003). In other situations, the affected member does not share information for varying reasons. Family members need to confront the sometimes thorny issues of what, when, how, and to whom to reveal the possible genetic risks and, in some instances, to discuss the complex implications of a relative's test results. If a partner has a genetic disease or may be a carrier for a disease, the couple may hold discussions before childbearing, including issues such as whether to test the partner for a recessive gene, undergo pre-implantation genetic diagnosis of embryos, or plan for gene therapy. Such topics will become increasingly commonplace as more discoveries are revealed. Essentially, "[t]he new genetics not only positions individuals as responsible for their own health, but also for the health of others" (Hallowell, 1999, p. 599). Peterson (2005) captured the importance of communication processes to family genetic testing, arguing that "[t]he most important communication function from a clinical standpoint may be to accurately exchange health risk and disease information among family members" (p. 629).

Existing research on family disclosure and discussion is limited. Studies which have addressed family communication about genetic risk focus primarily on the medical concerns of late-onset diseases such as HD and HBOC (Forrest et al., 2003). Most studies examine the process of disclosure of information by one or more affected individuals to their immediate or extended family members, some of whom may share the risk for that genetic disease. For instance, Wilson and her colleagues (2004) identified 30 studies completed through 2003 in their review of research on family communication about genetic risk. They made a case for the importance of family communication in clinical genetics, asserting that "[i]t may influence the accuracy of information brought to a consultation; the issues raised by communication or non-communication may lead to emotional distress; and non-disclosure of relevant information undermines the decision-making autonomy of at-risk relatives" (p. 15).

Additionally, Peterson (2005) summarized studies on family communication and concluded that "[i]ntegrating communication about genetic risk into the family culture also may be instrumental in families' desires to address both physical and emotional problems related to inherited disease, and to buffer present and future against its negative effects" (p. 629). Finally, Gaff et al. (2007) reviewed 29 papers that addressed communication in families about genetic risk and identified three themes: deliberation before communication, communication strategies, and outcomes of communication. Most of these studies involved families confronting HBOC or HD and focused on disclosure of risk to family members.

The most highly developed area of communication research relating genetics and genomics is the disclosure process—specifically, disclosure by the proband, the first person in the family to be medically diagnosed with a disease. Although advances in genomics will broaden the nature of discussion and disclosure, research to date has concentrated almost exclusively on the disclosure of single-gene genetic diseases. Yet, these initial and ongoing family communication patterns related to single-gene diseases may provide groundwork for responding to more general issues of genetic health in broader terms (Weiner et al., 2005). Thus, the following sections review research on proband communication and general family members' disclosure of such information.

## Disclosure of Genetic Disease

This section emphasizes single-gene genetic disclosure because the current literature does not yet reflect attention to disclosure of genomic information. Furthermore, this research focuses heavily on HD and HBOC. The following five factors significantly influence the disclosure interactions in countless families: (1) identifying who may be at risk for a variety of inherited conditions; (2) deciding whether to reveal this genetic history to other family members; (3) deciding how to inform other members that they or their offspring may be at risk; (4) interacting with family members after some members have chosen testing while others have not, and (5) supporting members painfully affected by their genetic knowledge and discussing how to bring future offspring into the family (McDaniel, 2005). Decisions about the disclosure of genetic information cannot be considered as, or reduced to a matter of individual choice because, "in decisions about whether, when, or how genetic information should be shared, one must always be aware of both the interests of the individual and the interests of those who they are linked to genetically" (Van Riper & Gallo, 2006, p. 196).

### Proband

The *proband,* as the first person in the family to be medically diagnosed with a disease, is often the one who initiates family disclosure and further discussions about genetic concerns (Julian-Reynier et al., 2000). Issues of privacy and confidentiality restrict disclosure by medical professionals to a proband's relatives in most cases; therefore, the task of telling falls to the proband. Proband decisions regarding disclosure critically affect the impact of the message on other members. Frequently, the proband determines what information to disclose and how; however, this process is often confounded by a lack of preparation for such a role (Daly et al., 2001). When preparing for such disclosure, many probands are still coping with the emotional effects of learning their test results (Gaff et al., 2005), which makes it more difficult for them to initiate discussions with other members of the family. The proband's response upon receiving the news influences if, when, and how other members learn about their potential risk. Most probands share their news with one or more family members but when and how they do so affects the entire family system (Forrest et al., 2003).

Although the proband serves as the gatekeeper of genetic risk information, in some families, only the parents are expected to convey the news to any children at risk (Forrest et al., 2003), effectively limiting the number of relatives with whom a proband may speak. According to Forrest et al., when disclosing their condition to family members, most probands indicate that they do not share the message equally among all relatives. Thus, not all relatives may be thoroughly debriefed and educated about the benefits of testing because probands' messages may be more persuasive regarding testing than disclosure by other family members. In fact, as Peterson et al. (2003) determined, "family members who were persuaded to seek those services by the proband were more likely to have counseling and testing and were more likely to seek those services sooner" (p. 78).

A proband's decision as to whether or not to tell other family members and the effectiveness of the resulting messages depends, in part, on the extent to which the proband understands genetic inheritance, such as the recessive nature of certain genes. Additionally, factors such as proband gender may influence disclosure patterns (Gaff et al., 2005). Individuals faced with stigmatization are less likely to disclose their health status, given that they perceive their own risk as ambiguous or uncertain (Featherstone et al., 2006; J. Green, Richards, Murton, Statham, & Hallowell, 1997; see also related discussion by Petronio, 2002). As we detail later in this chapter, an additional concern for probands may also relate to balancing the choice to tell relatives about their potential risk with the desire to avoid causing alarm (Forrest et al., 2003).

Without actual transcripts of such discussions, we cannot be certain about the specific messages imparted to family members. However, genetic risk information should not be envisioned as discrete packages of knowledge that all probands receive and understand equally because concepts such as a "risk value" may be interpreted in multiple ways, resulting in varying levels of comprehension among other family members (Featherstone et al., 2006). However, we should note that the continuing revelations of the Human Genome Project, coupled with increased understanding of genomics, may result in more frequent discussions of genetic inheritance within more families; such a change could diminish the proband's role in initiating the discussion process.

### Family Members

Scholars consider informing family members of their potential genetic risks to be the responsibility of all members and generations of a family, but many factors influence the enactment of such disclosure messages (Forrest et al., 2003; Gaff et al., 2007).

RELATIONAL HISTORIES

Relational conflicts, lack of contact, or superficial contact among members can inhibit or block the transmission of critical genetic information. Hughes et al. (2002) determined that not being close to a sister comprised an important reason for not communicating breast cancer test results to 45% of sisters. Distant relatives may be informed in a more haphazard and less timely manner because sporadic contact reduces opportunities for individuals to share genetic news (Claes et al., 2003). Lack of contact also limits the extent to which individuals share test results with second-degree relatives; first-degree relatives are most often the only family members informed (J. Green et al., 1997). Likewise, some individuals decline to tell other relatives about HD or HBOC due to pre-existing conflicts or rifts within the family (Forrest et al., 2003).

FAMILY STRUCTURE

Although disclosing genetic risk generally involves a family responsibility, the family structure influences its transmission (Forrest et al., 2003). Information tends to be passed to first-degree relatives (FDRs), including parents, children and siblings, as well as to emotionally connected relatives; however, families that experience structural variations (such as divorce, step-relationships, or adoption) tend to engage less in genetically linked disclosures. Obligations to relatives also tend to be stronger along lineal links (parents/children) than along lateral links (siblings/cousins) (Foster, Eeles, Ardern-Jones, Moynihan, & Watson, 2004).

POSITIONS AND ROLES

Relational titles generally determine positions, such as "mother" or "aunt." Typically, parents hold the primary responsibility for passing information to their children; for example, relatives such as aunts and uncles have reported frustrations when their siblings forbid them to pass genetic information on to nieces or nephews (Forrest et al., 2003). Discussion of HNPCC tends to occur within nuclear families, and aunts and uncles refrain from discussing such risk information (Koehly et al., 2003); rather, adult siblings talk to each other and then pass the information along to their own respective children. Members of family networks may establish informal roles, such as the "hub" of the network or the person who functions as the knowledge manager for a group of family members. In the case of serious diseases, such as HD or HBOC, Forrest et al. also identified a category of family members who did not "need" to be told, due to factors such as gender or adoption.

GENDER

Gender frequently impacts disclosure because women tend to be considered gatekeepers of genetic knowledge and a link to relatives in older generations

(Foster et al., 2004; Koehly et al., 2003). In their study of proband disclosure in cases of HNPCC, Gaff et al. (2005) found such gender differences in disclosure. Whereas women reported that talking about health felt normal, men did not. Most men expressed a desire for guidance or support in telling relatives; women did not feel the need for such assistance. Featherstone et al. (2006) identified familial beliefs that men "can't talk about things like that" (p. 106) and that, when men in the family were informed, they would not act upon the information appropriately. Some women used this belief to justify not telling the men in the family about genetic conditions. In cases of HNPCC, Koehly and her colleagues determined that mothers tended to be the most influential person in the family network and called for further study of the role of mothers in the familial culture in the context of talking about genetic counseling and testing.

Not surprisingly, similar research on disclosure in families affected by HBOC revealed that "[t]here was much more communication with female relatives than with male, reinforcing the idea that women are the 'kin-keepers'" (J. Green et al., 1997, p. 57). Participants perceived mothers as vital players due to their links to relatives in other generations. Men, although possible carriers for the disease, did not participate actively in the communication networks (Forrest et al., 2003) and frequently were excluded from relevant conversations (McAllister, Evans, Ormiston, & Daly, 1998). Rates of communication among sisters were high in cases of breast and ovarian cancer (*BRCA1/2*). One study of *BRCA1/2* mutations reported that probands usually communicate their results quickly to sisters (Hughes et al., 2002). In part, we know more about female disclosure because much of the research focuses on HBOC which is perceived as a female genetic disease. Male relatives are less frequently informed than female relatives about the genetic test for HBOC and the subsequent results (Claes et al., 2003).

Age factors into some gendered disclosures of *BRCA1/2*. One study of women's attitudes toward family disclosure of positive breast cancer genetic testing results concluded that "the older a woman is, the more likely she is to inform her children and the less likely she is to inform her mother" (Julian-Reynier et al., 2000, p. 17). Moreover, a focus group study of female dyads (formed by a breast/ovarian cancer patient and close female relative) revealed diversity in the ways in which family members communicated and made decisions about their health, persistently worried for their families, lacked knowledge about inherited cancer, and perceived barriers present in communicating about genetic risk (Mellon, Berry-Bobovski, Gold, Levin, & Tainsky, 2006).

Family members may pay a high price for the gendered inequity of access to family genetic health information, especially in the cases of a gendered disease such as HBOC. Foster et al. (2004) found that "both before and after the *BRCA1/2* test result these women experienced tensions in their multiple roles as kin-keepers, health promoters and support-seekers in the realm of genetic testing" (p. 444). Furthermore, according to Foster et al., "[m]en felt a strong sense of privacy and respect for their relatives in the context of disease, a need to hold on to control and to preserve relationships through silence in the context of talk about cancer and genetic cancer in particular" (p. 452). A related study of men's decision making about predictive *BRCA1/2* testing determined that female partners perceived themselves as having a role in their male partner's decision to be tested, a position supported by the male subjects (Hallowell et al., 2005).

The processes of surveillance and searching for inheritance patterns may lead family members to believe that a genetic condition is transmitted through males or through females (Featherstone et al., 2006), resulting in predictions regarding who might be affected or included in conversations on the topic. Because of these assumptions, family members may ignore the importance of opposite gender relatives who may be carriers, such as in the case of HBOC.

### FAMILY COMMUNICATION PRIVACY RULES

As we detail later in this chapter, privacy boundaries within families dictate who talks to whom about certain topics and which networks are used to relay critical family information (Petronio, 2002). Such rules also establish secrets. For example, privacy rules surface when parents forbid their adult siblings from providing genetic information to their nieces and nephews (Forrest et al., 2003). Until recently, members treated certain diseases (e.g., cancer) as family secrets; even today, older family members may hold the view that disease and illness should not be discussed (Kenan, Ardern-Jones, & Eeles, 2004). According to McAllister (2002), participants identified family talk about cancer as a causal condition that influenced engagement (cognitive or emotional involvement with cancer risk). In a study of family members' discovery of their family history of HD, Etchegary (2006) concluded that in families where "awareness of the illness was usually gradual and the family history of HD was not deliberately hidden from family members...there was greater willingness to decide about genetic testing" (p. 113). In African American families, the cultural emphasis on the wisdom of elders may privilege the rules established by their older generations with regard to the provision of health guidance or information (Crews & Balcazar, 1999). When family members consider genetic conditions to be secrets, communication rules prevent revelation even to family members who might benefit from the information.

### NATURE OF THE DISEASE

Family members more often share news about a preventable, manageable, or reversible disease than information about a disease perceived as highly devastating or deadly (J. Green et al., 1997). For example, in their study of families with genetic risks for HD and HBOC, Forrest et al. (2003) found three reasons for withholding the news: the wish to protect relatives from painful knowledge, difficulty in overcoming a conflictual relational history, and the lack of "need" for certain relatives to be told. A telephone survey of 200 Jewish women revealed that nearly all the respondents believed a patient should inform at-risk relatives if the disease was deemed preventable; whereas, only 85% believed that a duty exists to inform others about a non-preventable disease (Lehmann, Weeks, Klar, Biener, & Garber, 2000). Essentially, the decision reflects a dilemma. Gaff et al. (2007) explained that "the desire to protect relatives from potential harm is weighed against the wish to provide them with information that may have important health consequences" (p. 3).

Non-disclosure may be a function of caring for and protecting family members or hesitancy to cause others concern or alarm (Koehly et al., 2003). According to Featherstone et al. (2006), disclosures reflect practical psychology or assumptions about family members' abilities to cope with certain information. Featherstone et al. noted that participants perceive genetic knowledge as a burden because it could have severe consequences for other family members. Affected members struggled to reconcile their feelings about another relative's right to know and their duty to protect them from such painful information. Essentially, Featherstone et al. argued that members of families with a known genetic condition engaged in everyday bioethical decision making, experiencing "high levels of anxiety in dealing with the moral, ethical and practical dilemmas they faced in disclosing such information" (p. 95). They asserted that "[b]ased on their own experience and by observing others' reactions, many thought that it was often better not to know about a condition in advance than to have their actual risk assessed" (p. 110). Those holding such a belief may engage in active surveillance, waiting for a sign that might indicate a relative is affected, before disclosing.

CULTURE

Certain genetic diseases present extensively within cultural (racial or ethnic) groups (Miller, McDaniel, et al., 2006; Morgan & Hacker, 2007; Weiner et al., 2005). For instance, a significantly higher incidence rate of sickle cell anemia (SCA) occurs within the African American community compared to the European American community (Wethers, 2000). Weiner et al. found racial (African American and European American) differences in familial discussions of medical history and encouragement to behave in healthy ways, but they determined no racial differences in family conversations about genetic testing. These authors additionally suggested that a greater predisposition to a disease or condition linked to genetics in a particular racial or ethnic group may lead to a pattern of concealment.

Cultural influences may also impact how and why families disclose genetic health information. In the first multicultural study to include Latinas' beliefs (39% of subjects), MacDonald et al. (2008) reported great similarities among all women; Latinas were more likely to believe a health care provider was responsible for relaying information about genetic cancer risk; slightly more than half of all the women studied believed that information about such a risk should be done in person. In an instance of decision making (related to the desire to inform other relatives who might be at risk), Warner et al. (2005) found members of the Australian Ashkenazi Jewish community reported a very high level (94% or 300 respondents) of family-related motivation to be tested for colorectal cancer risk for altruistic reasons. Additionally, 93% of the participants indicated their reason for disclosure as the benefit to other family members and to know if their own children were at risk (85%).

### TIMING OF DISCLOSURE

When to tell another family member about his or her potential genetic risk varies according to factors such as age, perceived nature of the disease, and life circumstances. Age significantly affects what children learn of their risk for a genetic disease. In their study of families facing issues of HD and *BRCA*, Forrest et al. (2003) found that parents identified the "right time" to tell their children as when "the first key life decision affected by the disease needed to be made" (p. 322), such as the point when their children developed serious romantic relationships, planned to be married, or considered conceiving biological children.

The nature of the disease also affects timing. Affected individuals may wish to have complete assurance of the diagnosis before mentioning the concern to other relatives. For instance, parents of children tested for hearing loss (*GJB2/GJB6*) indicated a need for complete test results before informing multiple relatives (Blase, Martinez, Grody, Schimmenti, & Palmer, 2007). Finally, adverse family dynamics, such as a cutoff or family rift, may influence the timing of disclosure (Forrest et al., 2003). A relative's impending divorce or personal illness may deter disclosure.

Affected family members differ in their styles of disclosure in the timing of the message. Forrest et al. (2003) found two styles of revealing genetic information: (1) *pragmatism*, or telling in direct, practical terms, and (2) *prevarication* or attempting to find the right moment, such as a family gathering. For instance, J. Green et al. (1997) concluded that family members more often share information regarding HBOC when the news could be conveyed in face-to-face meetings or when the news could be integrated into communication that was taking place for other reasons, such as including information in a Christmas letter. This prevarication strategy runs the risk of putting off the revelation for months or years, but it avoids potentially awkward and "out of the blue" disclosures between family members. Because of differing styles of telling, and the fact that sometimes disclosure can take a long time to occur, J. Green et al. suggested that members should perceive telling as a "process" rather than an event.

### SCIENTIFIC MISUNDERSTANDINGS REGARDING GENETIC TRANSMISSION

Disclosure processes may be confounded by the target's ability to process the message accurately. Individual mental models of health, disease causation, and inheritance may match or differ from scientific positions. Some individuals do not understand the transmission process of a particular disease. For example, Claes et al. (2003) concluded that knowledge of HBOC by the "messengers" revealed shortcomings. Featherstone et al. (2006) asserted that family members' "beliefs about the origin of the condition and the mechanisms of transmission exert a powerful influence over who is informed" (p. 88). Such beliefs frequently result in family members' mistaken conclusions about who needs to be informed. Thus, depending on the level of scientific understanding, the proband's message may bear only limited resemblance to the information received in the counseling or medical office.

Individuals may worry about the health of the wrong family members and avoid communicating with a member at risk; in the case of HH, affected members may not understand that their siblings are at significantly great risk (Galvin et al., 2006). In cases of CF, the hereditary nature of the disease or knowledge of who else in the family needs to get tested may be misunderstood. In their study of women talking to relatives about HBOC, Foster et al. (2004) found that some women experienced difficulty with the concept of genetic transmission and were not sure if male relatives should be told about genetic testing. Interpretation of specific events, such as the death of a relative, may differ with one family member attributing it to old age and another to HH: Thus, "the development of a personal sense of vulnerability is not a linear process" (Walter, Emery, Braithwaite, & Marteau, 2004, p. 591).

Finally, in addition to the aforementioned factors, we should note that message effectiveness depends on listener receptiveness, creating circumstances in which repeated disclosure becomes necessary. News about a relative's genetic condition generally meets a range of responses from various family members. According to Walter et al. (2004), "A single affected relative is perceived by some as sufficient, whereas others need several affected relatives before the family history is perceived as important" (p. 588). Essentially, messages must reach persons willing to hear. When individuals direct messages to those who do not listen (Kenen et al., 2004), the effect of the conversation is negligible.

Overall, the 10 issues addressed above represent significant developments in research over the last two decades. Despite the significance of these findings, they do not address disclosure related to predispositions for diseases that reflect complex multifactorial etiology or diseases arising from the interaction of several genes and possibly non-genetic factors. Although individuals may be familiar with concepts of single-gene testing and predictive familial transmission, this practice represents only one approach to identifying health vulnerability. Current genomic research reveals diseases of complex origin involving the interactions of genetics, environment, and behavior. For example, although most cases of Type-1 diabetes involve inheriting risk factors from both parents, this family history does not sufficiently predict children's future health because most individuals at risk do not present with the disease; environmental factors contributing to the onset of this disease include climate, diet, viruses, and autoantibodies (American Diabetes Association, 2008). Thus, as the potential for communication about genomics becomes more commonplace, the issues of effective disclosure will likely be compounded.

Many factors influence disclosure of genetic information within families, and most key relatives eventually hear the news. According to Julian-Reynier et al. (2000), only 8.6% of women attending genetic cancer clinics said that they would inform none of their living first-degree relatives if the gene test were positive. Likewise, Koehly et al. (2003) found that, even in cases when they would not feel comfortable discussing other matters with relatives, people were likely to share the presence of a HNPCC predisposition mutation with relatives. Furthermore, in their study of HNPCC, Peterson et al. (2003) reported that, in four out of five families, the proband shared information about the HNPCC mutation with at least one first-degree relative within the first two weeks of receiving their results.

Family members report a desire to control the information shared about them. In a study of almost 600 participants with strictly genetic conditions and participants at risk for other serious medical conditions, respondents maintained that family members should not be able to get information about them without their knowledge, and they felt they should disclose information about hereditary conditions with other family members (Plantinga et al., 2003).

Disclosure issues are complex. Some researchers stress the importance of thinking and sharing "…in terms of fragmentary disclosure, partial disclosure, or even 'family secrets.' The entirely 'open' family may be an ideal, but it is rarely reflected in our own research experience" (Featherstone et al., 2006, p. 52). This extant research, although valuable, reflects extensive attention to specific diseases, usually HD and HBOC. As further research on genetic risk unfolds, issues will predictably become more varied and complex.

### *Review of Family Discussions of Genetic Health*

Much of the research pertaining to genetic diseases and health risk focuses on the process of how individuals disclose their diagnosis and/or test results to other family members. A growing number of studies address the ongoing familial disclosure and discussion of genetic risks across family networks. While families participate in discussion of genetic health issues outside of the context of disclosing test results or revealing a diagnosis, we know less about the communicative management of this information over time.

Scholars often integrate findings of family discussions about genetic health into disclosure research, making it difficult to distinguish between these types of family interactions (e.g., Claes et al., 2003; Daly et al., 2001; Dillard et al., 2008). However, when the distinction can be made, it becomes evident that, in certain cases, family discussions serve to help family members to make important life decisions regarding their own health (and their relatives' health), decide about future parenting, provide social support for relatives undergoing genetic testing, and disseminate vital health-related information throughout the family network (Dillard et al., 2004; Foster et al., 2004; Kenen et al., 2004).

Many of the same factors that influence disclosure also affect ongoing family discussions of health-related issues. A review of related literature reveals that family ongoing "discussion" about genetic health appears to focus on the following topics: (1) patterns of health communication in families; (2) gender differences in discussions of family health; (3) couples' decisions about pregnancy when a partner realizes the risk for passing on a genetic disease, and the implications of those decisions, and (4) the impact of disease disclosure on future family communication patterns.

*Communication Patterns*

Family discussions of genetic health issues are somewhat predictable. In their investigation of how the family context and genetic clinical context affect family communication in families with a history of HBOC, Kenen et al. (2004) used a family script approach to identify five communication patterns: open and supportive, directly blocked, indirectly blocked, self-censored, and use of third parties. The *open* pattern involved supportive interactions. Family members spoke freely, unless concern about worrying a particular family member limited interaction with that relative. This pattern tended to be gendered (i.e. women talked more freely than men), perhaps an outcome of the nature of HBOC. Some subjects also conversed with close friends in addition to family members. The *directly blocked* pattern occurred when the family directly rejected the topic or when they firmly established a pattern of topic avoidance.

According to Kenen et al. (2004), *indirect blocking* encompasses indirect messages—usually nonverbal—indicating the relatives' desire to avoid talking about the cancer. Males evidenced this style more frequently in response to cancer talk initiated by their female family members. Secrets also limit such conversations. The *self-censored* pattern played out in two ways—self-censoring and proactive censoring. The former occurred when an individual perceived another member's desire to avoid the topic and thus refrained from talking about it; the latter unfolded when the individual did not wish to discuss the cancer with specific family members for fear of invoking a high-anxiety response. Finally, *the use of third parties* patterns involved gaining the cooperation of an intermediary in contacting another family member family, or seeking the advice of third parties to discuss how to approach the topic.

A second communication patterns approach, developed by Suzanne Miller (1995) in her work with cancer patients and later applied to family genetics, entails monitoring and blunting styles (McDaniel, Rolland, Feetham, & Miller, 2006). Monitoring describes scanning for and amplifying threatening cues and searching for related information; whereas, blunting refers to attempts to distract from or avoid threatening cues. Such verbal and nonverbal strategies communicate the actor's anxiety.

*Gender Differences*

Discussion of health-related information occurs much more prevalently among female relatives than male. (Again, it should be noted that one of the two most-studied diseases is HBOC which most directly impacts female relatives.) Numerous studies have observed that the role of "kin-keepers" or "gatekeepers" in their families is almost always filled by women (e.g., Forrest et al., 2003; Foster et al., 2004; Gaff et al., 2005). Likewise, according to Forrest et al., women are more likely to assume responsibility for "keeping" health-related information and creating "implicit rules about who gets told, or not, and who gets to take precedence in being 'allowed' to tell" (p. 324). These trends can be seen in the context of disease discussion as well as disease disclosure. According to Foster et al., when asked, women reported feeling more responsible for the well-being of others and felt more obligated to provide care for others. Thus, these studies suggest that women practice health-related communication that complements their sense of responsibility for the health of other family members.

Additionally, women tend to use health-related communication within their family for different reasons than men. Women are more likely than men try to control others' health, as well as to encourage partners, friends, and relatives of the opposite sex to seek health care (Foster et al., 2004). Foster et al. revealed that women reported a greater reliance on communication with other family members as a source of social support when coping with sadness or anxiety; those who were comfortable talking about these topics generally provided support rather than advice. In their study of *BRCA1/2* patients, McGivern et al. (2004) found that, when faced with an abnormal test result, women often went beyond disclosure with close female relatives as a strategy to cope with their test results, a finding which reinforces the notion that women use family health communication for social support purposes (Albrecht & Goldsmith, 2003).

Alternatively, men frequently utilize distracting behaviors to avoid thoughts of sadness and report feeling the need to protect others' privacy through maintaining silence about health issues in the family. As Foster et al. (2004) explained, "men's 'silence' was not so much about the stereotypical ideal of men's reticence but rather a need to maintain 'strength in silence'" (p. 452).

*Couple Communication about Pregnancy: Possibilities, Risks, and Implications*

Increasingly, couples are confronted with genetic-related issues and decisions regarding pregnancy. Klitzman, Thorne, Williamson, Chung, and Marder (2007) examined family communication surrounding couples' decisions to have children when one or both parents were carriers for HD. They determined that couples usually discuss reproductive decisions at length, often with input from close family members. Usually these discussions became more prevalent after the birth of the couple's first child. According to Klitzman et al., "over time with each pregnancy, some individuals here were uncertain and/ or changed their perspectives and decisions (e.g., 'taking the gamble' with a first pregnancy, but subsequently being more cautious, using pre-implantation genetic diagnosis, or avoiding other pregnancies altogether)" (p. 358). Klitzman et al. asserted that, although couples sometimes sought external family input, many couples also reported that family members would voice their preferences without solicitation, sometimes making the couple feel pressured into making certain reproductive choices. In this case, and perhaps in many others, family discussions of genetic health played a large role in reproductive decision making.

An earlier study indicates, by implication, the nature of discussions that confront couples facing the risk of transmitting a genetic disease. Schover, Thomas, Falcone, Attaran, and Goldberg (1998) found that 14% of couples with this risk would consider using a donated gamete (a sperm or egg cell) to avoid transmitting the disease, but we lack specific insights into the decision-making processes that they used to reach such decisions. The choice of gamete donation has long-ranging communication implications. Secrecy dominated early decisions to use donated sperm, but a move toward greater openness (Burns, 2006) now prompts individuals or couples to confront the issues of disclosure to, and ongoing discussion with a child regarding his or her biological heritage. Culture also impacts the role of family members in dealing with pre-natal testing and discussing genetic information with immediate or extended family members (Awwad et al., 2008). Further research should explore these issues.

## *The Impact of Disease Disclosure*

Given the range of family openness towards discussions of genetic health, several studies have explored the impact that a family member's disclosure has on future family discussions about health. Forrest et al. (2003) reported that an individual's experience while finding out about a genetic condition in the family could hold implications for subsequent family discussion patterns. Likewise, Kenen et al. (2004) found that family support for each person's ability to cope with genetic information "reduces family friction" in the future and "helps foster an atmosphere of normalcy" (p. 342). Some studies concluded that positive and negative impact on future family communication was mixed, depending upon the family and the disease. For example, in their study of families with HD, Sobel and Cowan (2000) revealed that, for some families, a positive test result constricted future family communication; for others, "the impact of the testing has allowed them not only to discuss HD, but other subjects that were previously off limits" (p. 54). In both cases, however, the effects of the disclosure on family communication extended beyond the scope of genetic issues.

Foster et al. (2004) reported a slightly different impact of disclosure on family discussions. In their study of women and cancer, these researchers determined that future communication was often hindered depending upon the test results of other family members, asserting that "some women who tested negative could not talk to those who tested positive, or relatives with cancer, due to feelings of guilt. Some women who tested positive felt isolated and felt they could not talk to relatives with a negative result or those with cancer" (p. 453). In such instances, differing test results among female relatives influenced family discussions, not a lack of interest in discussing health issues.

These studies demonstrate the profound impact genetic testing can have on family dynamics and communication. Future research should delve into other ways that family discussions help (or hinder) the prevalence of genetic testing in families, how these discussions occur (and with whom), and the dynamics of the discussions themselves and their impact on families.

*Phases of Family Discussion*

In their study of genetic risk communication processes, Dillard et al. (2004), a team of communication scholars and medical professionals, placed disclosure into a larger frame of a process of risk communication while examining newborn screening for CF, the "most common, life-threatening, autosomal recessive genetic disease in Caucasians" (p. 196). Risk communication involves "the exchange of information among interested parties about the nature, magnitude, significance, or control of a risk" (Covello, 1992, p. 359). The researchers videotaped clinic visits of 17 families identified through newborn screening whose infants tested positive on the CF test. Phase 1 occurred from birth until results of a second round of blood tests for identified infants were completed. Phase 2 involved the initial contact with the CF health care system, between 1 and 4 weeks after the birth of the child. Phase 3 involved the sweat test when the child was between 1 and 6 weeks of age.

Although their study concluded after the third phase, Dillard et al. (2004) called for an extension of the phase analysis maintaining that the risk communication process does not end in the early months of a child's life. They argued that family members would likely talk to others about the diagnosis and seek social support from friends and family, some of whom may eventually request testing. Most importantly, they predicted other moments of risk communication, such as when the child reaches sexual maturity, and parents may discuss his or her reproductive risks.

Many other moments of risk communication were also likely to occur as parents reminded children about the importance of taking their medication, the necessity of airway clearance to loosen mucus in the lungs, and the need to develop and strengthen their muscles. The authors concluded, "Understanding the later phases of this communication process is surely as important as understanding those that go before" (Dillard et al., 2004, p. 203). Although many other genetic diseases necessitate predictable conversations regarding the necessity of health- related practices, other developmental-stage issues also impact these ongoing conversations as children become teenagers and gain independence from constant parental supervision. As children develop, many of them have to explain their conditions to key adults as well as to friends.

Although specific written or media materials may exist to help individuals with a certain condition manage life transitions, health professionals will benefit from additional communication-oriented research to prepare family members for these developmental changes.

*The Determinism/Medicalization Issue*

Currently, genetic information can indicate, with high probability, one's chances of presenting with a particular genetic disease. For instance, someone who carries the genetic mutation for HD will eventually present with the disease unless death intervenes; a woman with the genetic mutation for HBOC also has a high probability of experiencing breast or ovarian cancer before dying. Some geneticists express concern that the availability of such personal genetic information will result in the medicalization of family life across life stages. Finkler (2001) contended that the "medicalization" of family and kinship could convert people into perpetual patients, with lives incessantly punctuated with future health concerns. Finkler further asserted that the medicalization of family and kinship alters people's perceptions from "if I get breast or colon cancer" to "when I get breast or colon cancer" (p. 250). For example, journalist Masha Gessen (2008) described herself as a "previvor" or a woman who carries the genetic mutation for breast and ovarian cancer and whose life is dominated by continuous medical screening and the decision of whether to undergo radical preventive surgery. Other studies also reveal similar communicative struggles faced in families when presymptomatic members are identified (Etchegary, 2006; Holt, 2006).

The issues discussed in this section reflect key current concerns, but, given the rapid advances in genetic and genomic research, new issues will continue to confront families in the next few years. For example, major advances in the developing area of neuropsychiatric genetics, studies of the heritable nature of psychiatric and other nervous system disorders, characterized at the molecular, cellular, or behavioral levels, will challenge family members to address the potential role genes play in the development of schizophrenia, bipolar, or affective disorders (Genomics Network, n.d.).

## Potential Contributions of Family Communication Theories

Theory-driven research creates a framework to guide the accumulation of related knowledge. Although genetic research has relied on a range of theoretical approaches, some scholars have asserted that "greater attention needs to be paid to the use of theoretical models of communication to complement empirical studies" (Gaff et al., 2007, p. 11).

Currently, systems theory research undergirds a limited number of genetically focused family interaction studies evidenced by a review of specific studies and reflected in a general application of the Family Systems Genetic Illness (FSGI) Model (Rolland & Williams, 2006). This model calls for application of a family lens, in addition to an individual lens, in the treatment of individuals affected by genetic disease (Feetham & Thomson, 2006). This theory also informs research in family communication (Galvin, Dickson, & Marrow, 2006).

Communication scholars have developed specific interpersonal communication and family communication theories with potential to contribute to ongoing research involving family communication about genetic health. This section briefly describes four theories developed by these scholars to demonstrate their applicability. These four theories represent ones that scholars have occasionally used in studies on genetic disclosure or that hold the greatest potential for applicability to research on talking about genetics in families. Other communication theorists and their theories will be noted but not developed quite as fully.

### Communication Privacy Management Theory (CPM)

CPM developed from earlier self-disclosure studies (Petronio, 2002; Petronio & Caughlin, 2006). Instead of focusing exclusively on self-disclosure, CPM broadens the focus to incorporate private information about others as well as about oneself. This theory explores the "ownership" of private information, relying on metaphoric boundaries to indicate personal or collective rights to such details. According to Petronio, although a person "owns" his or her private information, it may become shared by design or by accident. Individuals manage their personal or collective boundaries through communication rules.

Petronio (2002) asserted that, through disclosure, an individual draws one or more others into the boundary around his or her private information, turning these others into information shareholders. She also suggested that such communication relies on explicit or implied rules; criteria for establishing these rules include culture, self-esteem, gender, motivations, and the perceived risk/reward ratio. These criteria affect decisions such as whether to tell, who to tell, and the depth and timing of the discussion. The theory's focus on boundary coordination and turbulence in families directly applies to genetics. For example, once a proband discloses his or her genetic disease or predisposition to such, this information becomes owned jointly by the proband and the other person(s). If such sharing is accompanied by a request to keep the information confidential, and all parties comply, boundary rule coordination occurs; if a listener reveals the proband's private information, boundary turbulence results.

Boundary turbulence occurs when an individual discloses another's private information, accidentally learns (e.g., overhears) private information, reveals another's information when faced with a choice as to what is best for self or the other, or spies on another to find out private information (Petronio, 2002). Specific genetic health-related examples of such turbulence include: (1) a husband breaks the couple privacy rule by revealing to his parents that his wife has a mutation for HBOC; (2) a college student overhears a phone conversation between her mother and aunt indicating that her cousin is a mutation carrier for familial adenomatous polyposis (FAP); (3) an older male diagnosed with HH ignores his sister's mandate not to tell his college-aged nieces and informs nieces that they should be tested, or (4) an adult daughter snoops in the medicine cabinet for evidence that her father is being treated for Type 2 diabetes. Family members not only negotiate privacy rules with each other, but they may need to teach established rules to maturing children or new members (e.g., in-laws). This theory's emphasis on private information renders it highly useful when examining disclosure of genetic disease within family systems.

### Family Communication Patterns Theory

Family communication patterns theory emerged from mass media research (McLeod & Chaffee, 1972, 1973) that explored how parents socialize their children to process information, specifically in the media, relying on the concepts of socio-orientation and concept-orientation. Scholars interested in general family communication patterns then adapted this early work (Fitzpatrick & Ritchie, 1994; Koerner & Fitzpatrick, 2006; Ritchie, 1991). Family researchers developed the Revised Family Communication Patterns (RFCP) instrument that establishes two dimensions of family communication—(1) *conversation orientation* and (2) *conformity orientation*. According to Koerner and Fitzpatrick, the interaction of these two dimensions creates "four family types that are qualitatively different: *consensual, pluralistic, protective* and *laissez-faire*" (p. 56). Each orientation ranges from high to low.

Conversation orientation describes "the degree to which families create a climate in which all family members are encouraged to participate in unrestrained interaction about a wide array of topics" (Koerner & Fitzpatrick, 2006, p. 55). High conversation orientation suggests that family members speak freely, frequently, and spontaneously without many limitations in regard to time spent in interaction and topics discussed. Low conversation orientation reflects less frequent interaction around a limited set of topics that all family members openly discuss.

Conformity orientation details "the degree to which family communication stresses a climate of homogeneity of attitudes, values and beliefs" (Koerner & Fitzpatrick, 2006, p. 55). High conformity orientation families typically engage in interactions that emphasize a uniformity of beliefs and attitudes, harmony and conflict avoidance. Low conformity orientation families interact in ways that display heterogeneous attitudes and beliefs. Such families strongly value member independence and the individuality of family members, even children.

This theory has been incorporated in some writings on genetic disease. For example, Kenen et al. (2004) cited Ritchie's (1991) call for viewing communication patterns in terms of "members' *perceptions* of family norms rather than adherence to one agreed upon family norm" (p. 336) and Fitzpatrick and Ritchie's (1994) work on measuring family communication patterns.

*Four Family Types*

As noted above, Koerner and Fitzpatrick (1997) expanded the concepts of communication orientation and conformity orientation into four characterizations of family types—consensual, pluralistic, protective, and laissez-faire. Koerner and Fitzpatrick (2006) explained each of these types in detail.

*Consensual* families rate high in conversation and conformity. They demonstrate pressure to agree as well as commitment to open communication and exploration of new ideas. Parents listen to children and then explain their decisions. Members avoid volatile conflict. The family openly discusses serious health issues, such as genetic diseases, with adaptation for children's levels of understanding. Medical decisions rest with the parent or parental unit although members express their respective positions.

*Pluralistic* families are high in conversation and low in conformity. They engage in open and unrestrained discussions involving members on a wide range of topics. Parents are not invested in control; children wield power in decisions. Their discussions consist of free exchanges. They prize independence. Although open conflict occurs, members tend to use positive conflict resolution strategies. These families address health issues openly and consider ideas or concerns of all members when making decisions. A 19-year-old male will be supported in his decision to be tested for HD, even though his result will essentially reveal his mother's status and affect his siblings.

*Protective* families rate low on conversation and high on conformity. Parents expect children to respond to their authority without discussion. They do not tend to communicate openly; parents make decisions and perceive little value in discussion. Children may be unaware or unclear about health issues facing the family. Parents may refuse to discuss family genetic disease patterns with their children and forbid other relatives from disclosing that information, such as a cousin's diagnosis of HH to their children.

*Laissez-faire* families are low in conversation and conformity. Members raise few topics and actively discuss even fewer. Children make many decisions. These patterns serve to limit conflict. Emotional separation characterizes many of these families. Adults are responsible for their own medical decisions. In cases of genetic testing, each member likely receives encouragement to make his or her own decision and discouragement from discussing the topic with the family.

### Relational Dialectics Theory

This theory, reflecting Russian social theorist Mikhail Bakhtin's (1981, 1986) writings in dialogism, focuses on the development of meaning-making through the interplay of competing perspectives, or discourses. Multiple perspectives can be in play with and against each other. Communicative life in families can be envisioned as a dialectic in which different, often opposing, voices interpenetrate, some more dominant and others more marginalized (Baxter & Montgomery, 1996). Contradictions undergird family interactions, and "[i]t is their interplay that constructs meaning for family members" (Baxter, 2006, p. 132). Related studies focus on internal contradiction management (within the family) and external contradiction management (between the family and the larger system in which it is embedded). Although numerous possibilities exist, extensively studied contradictions include autonomy–connection, openness–closedness, and novelty–predictability. Individuals manage contradictions through communicative strategies such as selection, cyclic alternation, segmentation, neutralizing, and reframing. Although applicable to multiple types of relationships, Baxter recommended that communication scholars apply this theory to couples and families in an attempt to identify their systems of meaning—the discourses, the ideologies, the codes—that are unified yet competing.

Recent dialectics research addresses health-related concerns. In their study of premature birth, Golish and Powell (2003) articulated the dialectical tensions surrounding the ambiguous loss of premature birth because parents experience life and loss simultaneously. The authors represented these couples as struggling with premature birth and facing tensions of control–helplessness, openness–closedness, and joy–grief. The birth of a child with CF may activate similar tensions. In her study of stroke survivors, Pawlowski (2006) found dialectical tensions such as thankfulness–frustration/anger, isolation/loneliness–support, determination–wanting to give up, and dependence–independence. Recently scholars and journalists demonstrate the struggles of certain tensions in families with HD such as hope–futility, openness–closedness, and dependence–independence, among others (Harmon, 2007b; Holt, 2006) as well as different tensions within families with *BRCA* including openness–closedness, hope–futility, and surrender–options (Foster et al., 2004; Harmon, 2007a). This theory provides a unique way to frame and explore communication involving disclosure and discussion of familial genetic predispositions or disease.

### Narrative Theory/Narrative Performance Theory

Narrative theory and narrative performance theory interrelate, as both focus on the role of stories in human life. According to narrative theory (Fisher, 1987), humans experience life in narrative form; personal meanings for their stories emerge through interpretation, not rational observation. Narration involves verbal and nonverbal symbolic actions, words or deeds, set within a sequence of events that have meaning for those who interpret them. Researchers explore questions such as "what interpretations do people construct for their lived experiences? What significance do they assign to the events and moments of their lives?" (Babrow, Kline, & Rawlins, 2005, p. 34). Fisher argued that narrative theory relies upon two criteria to determine its rational quality—cohesion (the extent to which the story is realistic, meaningful and free of inconsistencies) and fidelity (the extent to which the story has direct ties to social reality and resonates with listeners' personal experiences and beliefs). According to Fisher, narratives fall into two overarching types—recounting, or providing a history, and accounting, or offering an explanation. Although much family research focuses on experiences such as birth, death, how-we-met, family histories, and memorable events, health-related stories (such as diagnosis, struggles, hopes, and fears) constitute the family repertoire.

Given the nature of genetic disease, multigenerational stories could reveal much about how members learn to view and cope with CF or HBOC. Stories reflect experiences such as the discovery of a problem or the latest joys or sorrows related to disease progression. In her collection of stories about marriages after the death of a child, communication scholar Judy Pearson (1994) recounted the experience of a couple who lost two daughters to metachromatic leukodystrophy (MLD). Her analysis demonstrates the communication patterns enacted by the grieving parents during the illness and after the deaths of their children. A more recent study of parental narratives about genetic testing for hearing loss details how parents acted on their initially stated attitudes toward genetic testing for hearing loss (Kaimal et al., 2007). Kaimal et al. recommended that genetic counselors use the family's own narrative as a frame of reference for presenting results to the family in a way that is personally meaningful, even while addressing inconsistencies between personal beliefs and medical interpretations.

Petersen (2006) collected narratives through interviews with genetic support group members clustered around the overarching themes of triumphing over tragedy, becoming an expert, and inheritance and risk with regard to negotiating relations with family. The final theme revealed participants who tried to assign responsibility for passing on the gene, struggled with the issues of who to tell and their responsibilities to others, weighed risks about starting a family, and experienced painful times when learning of the illness and death of other family members.

Narrative performance theory focuses on the actual telling of the family narrative because "family storytelling forms a system of shifting relationships among audiences and storytellers, narrators and characters" (Langellier & Peterson, 2006, p. 102). As Langellier and Peterson asserted, these complex performances involve multiple and changing participants dispersed across time and space "that are partial, fragmentary, contradictory, conflicted and sometimes incoherent" (p. 100). Such performances reveal members in operation as a family.

Family storytelling involves constraints that both facilitate and restrict possibilities. Constraints include who can tell or hear which story? What kinds of stories can we tell and how can we tell them? How and when can they be told? Which meanings and identities matter? Most families have explicit or implicit rules about who can tell about or hear about the genetic disease of a particular member and how is the disease characterized, the extent to which stories may change as a member declines or discovers through testing that he or she is unaffected, and the conditions under which members can tell these stories. Answers to such questions provide an understanding of how members construct meanings and identities through joint storytelling. Typically, the interactional work of family storytelling is ordered according to gender and generation. Research on patterns of familial genetic narratives indicates women more often serve as the narrators, particularly in disclosing or discussing test results indicating a *BRCA1* mutation (e.g., Forrest et al., 2003; Foster et al., 2004; Gaff et al., 2005).

### Other Useful Theories and Implications

Several communication theories (individually centered, discourse-centered, and relationship-centered) can provide strong theoretical groundwork for future studies of communicating about genetics in families (e.g., Baxter & Braithwaite, 2008; Braithwaite & Baxter, 2006). These theories include (but are not limited to) uncertainty reduction theory, turning point theory and communication accommodation theory.

Uncertainty reduction theory (Berger & Calabrese, 1975) addresses communication initial interactions and changes in developed relationships assuming that people desire to predict others' behaviors. When they feel uncertain about their ability to do so, they feel anxious. They become highly motivated to reduce their aversive cognitive or behavioral uncertainty by obtaining knowledge that will better predict the other's behavior before enacting communication strategies to reduce the uncertainty (Knobloch, 2008). Uncertainty in developed relationships can lead to a lack of certainty about the status and future of the relationship. Therefore, if one relative is diagnosed with a genetic mutation, uncertainty about other family members' health status, genetic test results, or levels of risk may lead other relatives to engage in a range of active (talking to a third party), passive (observing the proband), or interactive strategies (questioning the proband) to reduce their uncertainty (Berger, 1995). Use of this theory provides a means of response to the assessment by Sarangi and Clarke (2002) that "uncertainty is a major, but neglected, topic in genetic counseling" (p. 144).

Turning point theory poses an alternative framework for stage-based theories of relationship development, in which the impetus for relational change is based upon significant events occurring within the relationship. These significant "transformative events" (Baxter & Erbert, 1999, p. 551) mark numerous moments in relationships (or in an individual's own life) when the ways in which people interact with each other change—either positively or negatively—and create new interaction patterns. Genetic-related turning points include when a proband discloses his or her genetic diagnosis condition to relatives, when other family members receive genetic test results, or when a member dies of a genetic disease. In each of these instances, family members' levels of closeness or distance with each other, and the concomitant communication patterns, may change as a result of these transformative events in family members' lives (Golish, 2000).

Communication accommodation theory, an offshoot of social identity theory, focuses on intergroup relations, with specific attention on how and why people shift their communication styles in relation to those with whom they interact. Depending upon speech patterns, people may demonstrate *convergence orientation* in which they seek social approval and affiliation compliance or *divergence orientation* in which they seek distinctiveness or display social disapproval (Giles, J. Coupland, & N. Coupland, 1991; Giles & Smith, 1979). Based upon these orientations, subgroups may form within families. Some subgroups may be determined by health—for example, members affected by a genetic disease and those who remain unaffected—and membership in one group or another can affect how family members construct their social identities (Harwood, Soliz, & Lin, 2006).

## The Educational Role of the Media

Mainstream media increasingly draws attention to genetics and genetic risk. In 2006, the *New York Times* ran extensive narratives in an article entitled "Cancer Free at 33, but Weighing a Mastectomy" (Harmon, 2007a) and "Facing Life with a Lethal Gene" (Harmon, 2007b). In both cases, the individuals coping with a disease engaged other family members in their decision making regarding potential treatments. Actress Christina Applegate publicly disclosed her decision to undergo a double mastectomy after a biopsy revealed a hereditary cancer in one breast (Bloom, 2008). The documentary *In the Family*, (Rudnick, 2008) and the PBS program *POV* promote awareness of the issue faced by young women with HBOC. NPR's *All Things Considered* presented the struggles of a couple choosing pre-implantation genetic diagnosis after losing an infant to spinal muscular atrophy (SMA). Additionally, television shows, such as *House* and *Grey's Anatomy*, have incorporated storylines featuring patients diagnosed with diseases such as HH, bringing it, and other little-known genetic diseases, into the vocabulary of millions of viewers (Hess & Glatter, 2007; Rhimes, Stanton, & Stanzler, 2005).

Some scholars cite the media as the primary source from which the public gains genetic information (e.g., Bubela & Caulfield, 2004; Weiner et al., 2005), yet little empirical research links media messages to family communication about genetics. Nonetheless, some research indicates that further investigation into this area is worthwhile, as media appear to influence how families talk about genetics. Weiner et al. determined that talk shows, newspaper readership, movies, and television shows were related to families' discussions about human genetics research. We now highlight some other research on the media's influence on the public understanding of genetics and explore how these findings might translate to avenues for future family communication research.

### Internet Influences

Web sites explaining genetic risk and health information provide exceptionally useful tools for helping family members to assess their risk for certain diseases as well as to improve their understanding of diseases already diagnosed within the family. Bernhardt and Hubley (2001) discerned over 20,000 web sites pertaining to health-related information; today, that number has increased dramatically. As a simple series of online searches by the second author revealed, the search word *genetics* on MSNBC.com returned 3,890 articles; the phrase *human genome project* returned 190 articles; even searching for a specific genetic mutation such as *BRCA1* returned 61 articles. She also found similar results on Web sites such as ABCnews.com and CNN.com. As such evidence demonstrates, the Internet provides a wealth of health resources to families because it offers unique informational Web sites and also pools television and newspaper reporting into one, easily accessible location. According to Bernhardt and Hubley, the availability of such resources holds the potential to benefit family members who may experience more difficulty talking about genetic issues with one another without sufficient information regarding the nature or threat of the disease.

An increasing number of individuals report using the Internet to learn about a familial genetic disease; additionally, probands report using e-mails and family Web sites to disclose genetic conditions to other family members (Bernhardt, Lariscy, Parrott, Silk, & Felter, 2002). A study of sibling perception of risk for HH based on proband disclosure of an HH diagnosis and recommendations that siblings seek testing (Galvin et al., 2006) also found that a few probands reported their diagnosis on family Web sites or in family newsletters. Some probands used Internet resources to support their persuasive messages to siblings, and some target siblings sought Internet information on a disease to more fully understand the proband's diagnosis and their personal potential risk.

In their study of the potential of using the Internet for delivering information on human genetics communication, Bernhardt, McClain, and Parrott (2004) concluded that women were much more likely to research health information online and felt more comfortable researching online than men. Echoing our earlier discussion, this gender difference coincides with other research regarding family communication about genetics indicating that female family members comprise the gatekeepers of genetic information, who, possessing such knowledge, may also be more inclined to research information about the implications of health conditions which impact their relatives. Likewise, male relatives' preference for "strength in silence" (Foster et al., 2004, p. 452) also emerged in these findings; even though women claimed greater experience with online health information seeking and higher comfort with online genetics communication, the male participants in the study reported higher preference for online communication.

Much remains to be learned about the Internet's role in providing information that might motivate individuals to get tested, or the effect of receiving personal genetic risk information via e-mail or Web sites and the role of family communication in these processes. Family and health communication scholars need to conduct further research to assess how stakeholders use the media to facilitate family functioning and communicative dynamics at the point of disclosure and the subsequent family discussions that may follow such disclosure.

## Newspapers

Unlike research with other media forms, research pertaining to newspaper coverage of genetic issues has been somewhat more concerned with inaccuracy and exaggeration in the reporting of findings. Such exaggerations—coined "genohype" in the literature—include "the "hyped" portrayal of both the benefits and the risks associated with genetic research and the application of genetic technologies" (Bubela & Caulfield, 2004, p. 1399). Communication scholars have expanded upon the concern for "hype" in newspapers, specifically the way in which headlines contribute to genetic determinism (e.g., Condit et al., 2001). As Condit et al. asserted, hype, defined as an "attribution of genetic causality in a totalistic and absolute fashion, especially where such a casual account does not accurately represent the probabilistic and multifactorial inputs into a particular characteristic of biological entity" (p. 380), genetic determinism often ignores the complexity of factors (e.g., environmental influences, multi-gene interaction) that contribute to a gene's expressivity.

According to Condit and colleagues (2001), the brevity and attention-grabbing nature of newspaper headlines make them particularly susceptible to communicating genetic determinism—an inclination which could have serious implications for how family members learn about gene functioning and genetic risk for particular diseases. Condit et al. distinguished between high and low deterministic accounts, explaining that highly deterministic statements in the media can be characterized by inaccurate suggestions "that single genes generally produce direct and discrete effects that the level of human traits identifiable to the lay observer, such as a 'gene for' intelligence" (p. 381). Alternatively, less deterministic explanations more accurately describe ways in which multiple genes and environmental factors can contribute to the observable expression of genetic traits. Condit et al. suggested that the overabundance of genetic determinism in news headlines generally contributes to public impressions attributing a false and excessive amount of "causal power" to genes (p. 381). However, further research needs to investigate such claims and their potential impact on family discussions of genes and heredity.

Depending upon media preferences, family members might bring varying levels of understanding to the table regarding genetic complexity and pervasiveness within the family. Family discussions about genetics may, therefore, be highly influenced by the type and quality of the media sources favored by family members.

## Television

Limited research assesses the impact that television has on family communication about genetics. Weiner et al. (2005) examined how television programs related to genetic health impact family communication. They demonstrated that TV shows containing information about how the environment harms human genes exhibited the most influence upon family conversations about health, but only for individuals who have participated in genetic testing. Since the publication of this article, medical shows that increase the medical literacy of some viewers by highlighting genetic conditions, their environmental influences and their potential heredity (e.g., *Private Practice*) have become increasingly popular, but the effect, if any, that this trend might have on family communication remains unclear. Since media can impact family discussions of health and genetics, communication researchers, genetic counselors, and medical professionals should further investigate how different media sources may trigger or inhibit productive family discussions or beliefs about genetic health and genetic testing.

## Future Implications and Communication Research Directions

Given ever-expanding research on genetics and genomics, scholars interested in family interaction will be challenged to stay abreast of the implications for family disclosure and discussion of genetic health. We believe that the following issues will emerge as key concerns:

### *Family Definitional Issues*

Although families across the globe are experiencing changing kinship patterns, Western families, particularly those in the United States, represent the forefront of familial redefinition (Galvin, 2006). Currently, kinship relies less on biological/genetic or traditional legal ties and reflects more non-traditional legal ties, complicated fertility options, and practical or fictive kinship. Family communication scholars increasingly stress the constitutive perspective, in which "our families and our images of families are constituted through social interaction" (Vangelisti, 2004, p. xiii). Contemporary families may be envisioned on a continuum, ranging from traditional (biologically/legally linked) to constitutive (linked through communication or self-definition as family). Family scholars interested in genetic disclosure and discussion need to directly confront implications of the constitutive approach and the scientific advances that impact the socio-legal approaches to family.

As family structures become increasingly complicated, their definitional processes expand exponentially, rendering their identity highly discourse-dependent (Galvin, 2006). Although families have always relied on discursive patterns to create or reinforce their identities, a growing number of families rely on discursive processes extensively or fully to create their identity. Therefore, at a time when many family communication scholars argue for an appreciation of practical or voluntary kinship (Braithwaite et al., 2008; Fitzpatrick, 1998; Galvin, 2006; Whitchurch & Dickson, 1999), findings of the Human

Genome Project have reinvigorated the role of biological ties in establishing familial membership. New emphasis on genetics tends "to *strengthen* the conventional categories of reproduction and biological relatedness" (Featherstone et al., 2006, p. 6) at the same time that Western concepts of family are becoming more fluid.

Yet, in discussing the *family tree*, which serves as the basis of much genetic interpretation, Featherstone and her colleagues (2006) asserted that "this is an artifact that straddles the two domains of medical practice and everyday family life. It is grounded simultaneously in the socially constructed facts of biological relations and the equally constructed facts of family relations" (p. x). They called for attention to "practical kinship" or "who in practice is recognized as a relation, who is regarded as 'family' and where the boundaries of 'family' are placed" (p. 12).

Increasingly, the construction of family identity will reflect the efforts of family members to "continuously reconfigure themselves across members' life spans as members' choices create new family configurations through legal, biological, technological, and discursive means" (Galvin, 2006, p. 5). According to Galvin, the majority of these configurations will be transparent to both members and outsiders; some will be transparent to members only; whereas, others will not be transparent to outsiders and one or more family members. For example, families formed through visible adoption, such as interracial adoption, cannot conceal the nature of their ties; whereas, families formed through sperm donation may be transparent only to one or both parents. Since numerous parents indicate they will not reveal the use of gamete donation, (Lasker, 1998) many families will attempt to continuously live a fiction.

In an extension of this position, Feetham and Thomson (2006) described the growth of multiple complex family forms and the advances in reproductive technology, suggesting that any definition of family in genetics and genomics needs to include both issues. As Feetham and Thomson inquired, "Is the 'real' family the individuals who carry out the functions of family life?... In the context of genetic risk assessment and testing, biological factors are paramount. Yet the lived experience of coping and adaptation to genetic knowledge and risk exists in the functional family unit" (p. 24).

Certain ongoing deceptions are ripe for exposure in the age of new genetics; for example, the son born outside of the current marriage, the daughter added through a secret adoption, or the twins born through the use of an anonymous sperm donor and egg donor may undergo a genetic test that reveals their non-biological ties. Just as more families are formed through visible or invisible differences, rendering their ties ambiguous to outsiders as well as to insiders, the ongoing revelations of the Human Genome Project heighten the importance of knowing one's biological ties. In addition, even when non-biological family formations are known to all members, such as in cases of adoption, the communication rules pertaining to maintaining the current family identity may limit discussion of genetic information in order to minimize member differences. In these areas and many more to come, genetic health specialists and communication scholars, working together, have much to contribute to the issues of family identity.

### The Genetic Divide(s) and Communication

The ability of scientists to "map" disease through several generations (Collins, 1999) raises practical and ethical issues of access to resulting opportunities and creates family communication challenges. Currently, prenatal testing for chromosomal diseases has become increasingly common (Moyer et al., 1999). Options such as pre-implantation genetic diagnosis (PGD) can identify over 1,250 disease-related mutations creating an opportunity for parents to select unaffected embryos for implantation in the womb (R. M. Green, 2008). Test results provide potential parents with information that may lead to decisions involving intervention in the genetic makeup of future children. Although some families welcome such options, others may be unable or unwilling to consider such procedures, due to financial concerns or moral/ethical/religious beliefs.

The option of in vitro fertilization (IVF) improves the chances for many individuals to become parents. Recent advances in in vitro fertilization now make it possible for eggs or sperm to be donated and implanted in the mother's uterus so that parents may experience pregnancy and birth of children who are not necessarily biologically related to either of them. These "test tube" babies (Golombok, MacCallum, & Goodman, 2001, p. 599) offer parents struggling with the potential for passing on severe genetic diseases an alternative to adoption or surrogacy. For example, if a woman carrying the gene mutation for HD wants to be pregnant, but also wishes to avoid the risk of passing the HD mutation to her children, IVF provides the solution. However, parents who choose this option will also be faced with deciding whether to disclose their fertility choices and discussing their chosen conception processes with their children. Although far from common, this use of IVF may become more desirable as genetic testing permits parents to calculate the risks for their children's health and potentially prevent such risks using this method. As a result, future communication-oriented scholars will need to collaborate with genetic counselors to address the challenges that such families face when making decisions and discussing choices with their children.

Researchers studying factors that contribute toward a couple's choice to undergo prenatal testing have determined that partners base their decision upon several factors, including, but not limited to: parental beliefs about abortion, attitudes regarding disability and their "perceptions of the usefulness of having the information revealed by genetic tests" (Moyer et al., 1999, p. 522). Abortion beliefs constitute a key issue in the decision-making process. Even though a majority of parents receiving abnormal prenatal test results terminate their pregnancies (Redlinger-Grosse, Bernhardt, Berg, Muenke, & Biesecker, 2002), Moyer et al. noted that, when asked, more families reported that they would make use of prenatal testing than would be willing to terminate a pregnancy. The decision to continue or terminate a pregnancy after prenatal testing comprises a joint decision between both parents (e.g., Awwad et al., 2008; Beeson & Golbus, 1985); however, the nature of the conversations leading to the decision and the involvement of extended family members in the decision-making process remains highly understudied.

Fertility-related genetic advances raise a key communication issue: disclosure of non-biological ties. In addition to changing the ways families think about and discuss options for children, biological or otherwise, these scientific advances raise critical privacy family issues. Just as adoption served as a key issue of family secrecy for much for the last century (Carp, 1998), surrogacy is becoming a critical site of family secrecy in the 21st century. As donor insemination became more common, a high percentage of heterosexual couples indicated a desire to keep it secret (Lasker, 1998). More recently, a percentage of couples plan to reveal this information (Paul & Berger, 2007). Such a choice leads to concern about *resemblance talk*, threat to parents that remarks "about physical appearance could stigmatize their children or cast doubt on the legitimacy of their family structure" (Becker, Butler, & Nachtigall, 2005, p. 1300). In contrast, single women who become pregnant through this intervention are more likely to discuss the known or unknown donor with their children but, in either case, tend to protect the family boundaries between social and genetic kinship as the child ages (Hertz, 2006). In discussing the practice of gamete donation and the growing openness surrounding the practice, Burns (2006) asserted that "questions about disclosure, especially telling the child, are important for potential parents. Their unwillingness or inability to consider these issues may be an indication that they are not prepared for this form of parenthood" (p. 386).

Ethnic and cultural backgrounds may also play a role in the decisions that families make regarding prenatal testing. Moyer et al. (1999) concluded that Caucasian women more often undergo prenatal diagnoses than African American or Asian women, or Latinas. Furthermore, Awwad et al. (2008) found American couples less inclined to involve extended relatives in the prenatal decision-making process than Native Palestinian couples. Both of these examples clearly indicate that cultural differences can impact the ways in which families negotiate prenatal decisions. Further research needs to investigate how different families engage in such discussions and decision-making processes, especially as prenatal testing becomes more common and better able to predict or prevent a wider range of genetic conditions.

Tightly closed ethnic groups remain at high risk of serving as carriers for genetic mutations, but the management of this possibility varies greatly. For example, some Ashkenazi Jewish groups use screening for mutations for Tay-Sachs disease (TSD) as the basis for rabbinical marriage advice; whereas, children born to Amish families in Pennsylvania more often present with glutaric aciduria type 1 (GA1) but, given their beliefs, parents tend not to accept prenatal testing because of the implication of abortion (McKusick, 2000).

The future of genetics and families continues to be addressed by scientists, ethicists, and social scientists, many of whom disagree in their beliefs about what options, such as germline engineering, are realistic and about the desirability of potential scientific advances. R. M. Green (2008) argued that "discussions of human gene enhancement and gene modification tend to divide people into two camps: those bitterly opposed and those overwhelmingly favorable" (p. 11). Much discussion centers on human germline manipulations or changes (inheritable genetic modifications) made to the germinal or reproductive cells, the egg and the sperm. Such a process would result in genetic changes that will be copied into every cell of the future adult, including reproductive cells (Stock & Campbell, 2000), opening the door to irreversibly alter the human species. Inevitably, significant self-disclosure and discussion challenges await families who choose to alter multiple generations of future families (Centre for Genetics and Society, n.d.) because, according to Stock and Campbell, "germline engineering touches the very core of what it means to be human" (p. 3). Scholars strongly disagree regarding the ethics of potential genetic enhancements. As Sandel (2007) explained, "Defenders of enhancement argue that there is no difference, in principle, between improving children through education and improving them through bioengineering. Critics of enhancement insist there is all the difference in the world" (p. 51). Proponents of such genetic alternations believe that it will just make people potentially smarter and healthier; alternatively, others express concern about the "siren call to perfect ourselves" (Condit, 1999b, p. 239).

If some potential parents possess the option to engage in prenatal genetic alterations, and others do not, then Masci (2001) asserted that "genetically endowing children with selected traits will create a social divide between those who can and cannot afford the procedure" (p. 425). It is difficult to imagine how parents would discuss the choice of genetically altering an embryo resulting in changes that will affect all future offspring, yet future scholars in communication and genetic counseling may need to address this area in the future.

## Conclusion

Addressing the critical family communication issues raised by the rapidly changing science of genetics and genomics requires sustained professional collaboration among genetic health professionals, medical professionals, and social scientists, particularly communication scholars. Parrott (2008) advocated translational research programs involving collaboration between those with communication expertise and those with health/medical expertise to plan, implement, and evaluate family communication research focused on genetics and genomics. The interaction among interdisciplinary groups has been limited thus far; however, such complex communication and medical issues require active long-term collaboration. Feetham and Thomson (2006) argued that the lack of attention to family systems and family relationships in the collection and dissemination of genetic information increases the risk for affected family members. The potential value of such collaboration is self-evident; the joint research directions are multiple, yet the challenges are enormous. Within the next decade, research efforts should include attention to the impact of genomics research. Communication scholars focused on family and health issues need to take their place at the table with colleagues in the sciences, social sciences, and counseling to confront the implications of the new genetics and genomics.

As scientists move beyond the gene to explore the rest of the genome, their findings will impact communication scholars across the spectrum. Genetic and genomic research stands to contribute to scholarly conversation in areas as diverse as the rhetoric of science, relational development, social networks, and new technologies. The Book of Life will continue to reveal itself over many decades, and communication scholars offer a great deal as people wrestle with those revelations.

## Acknowledgments

The authors wish to thank a set of five remarkable reviewers who provided detailed and extremely valuable suggestions for strengthening drafts of this chapter. We also would like to thank Christina Beck for her guidance throughout this process.

## References

Albrecht, T. L., & Goldsmith, D. J. (2003). Social support, social networks, and health. In T. L. Thompson, A. M. Dorsey, K. I. Miller, & R. Parrott (Eds.), *Handbook of health communication* (pp. 263–284). Mahwah, NJ: Erlbaum.

American Diabetes Association. (2008). *The genetics of diabetes*. Retrieved March 26, 2008, from http//:www.diabetes.org/genetics.jsp

Awwad, R., Veach, P. M., Bartels, D. M., & LeRoy, B. S. (2008). Culture and acculturation influences on Palestinian perceptions of prenatal genetic counseling. *Journal of Genetic Counseling, 17,* 101–116.

Babrow, A. S., Kline, K. N., & Rawlins, W. K. (2005). Narrating problems and problematizing narratives: Linking problematic integration and narrative theory in telling stories about our health. In L. M. Harter, P. M. Japp, & C. S. Beck (Eds.), *Narratives, health, and healing* (pp. 31–52). Mahwah, NJ: Erlbaum.

Bakhtin, M. M. (1981). *The dialogic imagination: Four essays by M. M. Bakhtin* (C. H. Emerson, Trans.). Austin: University of Texas Press.

Bakhtin, M. M. (1986). *Speech genres and other late essays* (V. McGee, Trans.). Austin: University of Texas Press.

Bates, B. R. (2005). Care of the self and patient participation in genetic discourse: A Foucauldian reading of the Surgeon General's "My Family Health Portrait" program. *Journal of Genetic Counseling, 14,* 423–434.

Bates, B. R., Poirot, K., Harris, T. M., Condit, C. M., & Achter, P. (2004). Evaluating direct-to-consumer marketing of race-based pharmacogenomics: A focus group study of public health understandings of applied genomic medication. *Journal of Health Communication, 9,* 541–559.

Bates, B. R., Templeton, A., Achter, P. J., Harris, T. M., & Condit, C. M. (2003). What does "a gene for heart disease" mean? A focus group study of public understandings of genetic risk factors. *American Journal of Medical Genetics, 119A,* 156–161.

Baxter, L. A. (2006). Relational dialectics theory: An interactional family theory. In D. O. Braithwaite & L. A Baxter (Eds.), *Engaging theories in family communication: Multiple perspectives* (pp. 130–145). Thousand Oaks, CA: Sage.

Baxter, L. A., & Braithwaite, D. O. (Eds.). (2008). *Engaging theories in interpersonal communication: Multiple perspectives.* Thousand Oaks, CA: Sage.

Baxter, L. A., & Erbert, L. A. (1999). Perceptions of dialectical contradictions in turning points of development in heterosexual romantic relationships. *Journal of Personal and Social Relationships, 16,* 547–569.

Baxter, L. A., & Montgomery, B. M. (1996). *Relating: Dialogs and dialectics.* London: Guilford Press.

Becker, G., Butler, A., & Nachtigall, R. D. (2005). Resemblance talk: A challenge for parents whose children were conceived with donor gametes in the US. *Social Science & Medicine, 61,* 1300–1309.

Beeson, D. G., & Golbus, M. S. (1985). Decision making: Whether or not to have prenatal diagnosis and abortion for X-linked conditions. *American Journal of Medical Genetics, 20,* 107–114.

Berger, C. R. (1995). Inscrutable goals, uncertain plans, and the production of communicative action. In C. R. Berger & M. Burgoon (Eds.), *Communication and social processes* (pp. 1–28). East Lansing: Michigan State University Press.

Berger, C. R., & Calabrese, R. J. (1975). Some explorations in initial interaction and beyond: Toward a developmental theory of interpersonal communication. *Human Communication Research, 1*(2), 99–112.

Bernhardt, J. M., & Hubley, J. (2001). Health education and the Internet: The beginning of a revolution. *Health Education Research, 16,* 643–645.

Bernhardt, J. M., Lariscy, R. A., Parrott, R. L., Silk, K. J., & Felter, E. M. (2002). Perceived barriers to internet-based health communication on human genetics. *Journal of Health Communication, 7,* 325–340.

Bernhardt, J. M., McClain, J., & Parrott, R. (2004). Online health communication about human genetics: perceptions and preferences of internet users. *Cyberpsychology & Behavior, 7,* 728–733.

Biesecker, B. B. (2003). Back to the future of genetic counseling: Commentary on "psychosocial genetic counseling in the post-nondirective era." *Journal of Genetic Counseling, 12,* 213–217.

Biesecker, B. B., Boehnke, M., Calzone, K., Markel, D. S., Garber, J. E., Collins, F. S., et al. (1993). Genetic counseling for families with inherited susceptibility to breast and ovarian cancer. *Journal of American Medical Association, 269,* 1970–1974.

Blase, T., Martinez, A., Grody, W. W. Schimmenti, L., & Palmer, C. G. S. (2007). Sharing GJB2/GJB6 genetic test information with family members. *Journal of Genetic Counseling, 16,* 313–324.

Bloom, J. (2008, August 19). *Christina Applegate has double mastectomy.* Retrieved October 22, 2008, from http://www.nytimes.com/2008/08/20/arts/20arts-CHRISTINAAPP_BRF.html

Braithwaite, D. O., Bach, B. W., Baxter, L. A., DiVerniero, R., Hammonds, J., Nunziata, A. M., et al. (2008, November). *Constructing family: A typology of voluntary kin.* Paper presented at the annual meeting of the National Communication Association. San Diego, CA.

Braithwaite, D. O., & Baxter, L. A. (Eds.). (2006). *Engaging theories in family communication: Multiple perspectives.* Thousand Oaks, CA: Sage.

Broadfoot, K. J. (2008). *Living with genetics: Recombining self and health in modern medicine.* Cresskill, NJ: Hampton Press.

Bubela T. M., & Caulfield, T. A. (2004). Do the print media "hype" genetic research? A comparison of newspaper stories and peer-reviewed research papers. *Canadian Medical Association Journal, 170,* 1399–1407.

Burns, L. H. (2006). Genetics and reproductive issues: Psychosocial issues and prenatal testing. In S. M. Miller, S. H. McDaniel, J. S. Rolland, & S. L. Feetham (Eds.), *Individuals, families, and the new era of genetics* (pp. 371–403). New York: Norton.

Carp, E. W. (1998). *Family matters: Secrecy and disclosure in the history of adoption.* Cambridge, MA: Harvard University Press.

Centre for Genetics and Society. (n.d.) *Inheritable genetic modification.* Retrieved April 4, 2008, from http://geneticsandsociety.org/article.php?list=type&type=108

Claes, E., Evers-Kiebooms, G., Boogaerts, A., Decruyenaere, M., Denayer, L., & Legius, E. (2003). Communication with close and distant relatives in the context of genetic testing for hereditary breast and ovarian cancer in cancer patients. *American Journal of Medical Genetics, 116C,* 11–19.

Clark, W. R. (1997). *The new healers: The promise and problems of molecular medicine in the twenty-first century.* New York: Oxford University Press.

Collins, F. S. (1999). Shattuck lecture—Medical and social consequences of the human genome project. *The New England Journal of Medicine, 341*(1), 28–37.

Collins, F. S. (2006). Foreword. In S. M. Miller, S. H. McDaniel, J. S. Rolland, & S. L. Feetham (Eds.), *Individuals, families, and the new era of genetics: Biopsychosocial perspectives* (pp. xv–xvii). New York: Norton.

Condit, C. M. (1999a). How the public understands genetics: Non-deterministic and nondiscriminatory interpretations of the "blueprint" metaphor. *Public Understanding of Science, 8,* 169–180.

Condit, C. M. (1999b). *The meanings of the gene.* Madison: University of Wisconsin Press.

Condit, C. M. (2004). The meaning and effects of discourse about genetics: Methodological variations in studies of discourse and social change. *Discourse and Society, 15,* 391–407.

Condit, C. M. (2008). Race and genetics from a modal materialistic perspective. *Quarterly Journal of Speech, 94,* 383–406.

Condit, C. M., Ferguson, A., Kassel, R., Thadhani, C., Gooding, H. C., & Parrott, R. (2001). An exploratory study of the impact of news headlines on genetic determinism. *Science Communication, 22,* 379–395.

Condit, C. M., Parrott, R. H., & O'Grady, B. (2000). Principles and practice of communication strategies for genetics in public health. In M. J. Khoury, W. Burke, & E. Thomson (Eds.), *Genetics and public health: Translating advances in human genetics into disease prevention and health promotion* (pp. 549–567). New York: Oxford University Press.

Covello, V. T. (1992). Risk communication: An emerging area of health communication research. In S. A. Deetz (Ed.), *Communication yearbook 15* (pp. 359–373). Newbury Park, CA: Sage.

Crews, D. E., & Balcazar, H. (1999). Exploring family and health relationships: The role of genetics, environment, and culture. In M. Sussman, S. K. Steinmetz, & G.

W. Peterson (Eds.), *Handbook of marriage and the family* (pp. 613–631). New York: Plenum Press.

Croyle, R. T., & Lerman, C. (1999). Risk communication in genetic testing for cancer susceptibility. *Journal of the National Cancer Institute Monographs, 25*, 59–66.

Daly, M. B., Barsevick, A., Miller, S. M., Buckman, R., Costalas, J., Montgomery, S., et al. (2001). Communicating genetic test results to the family: A six-step, skills-building strategy. *Family Community Health, 24*(3), 13–26.

Dillard, J. P., & Carson, C. (2005). Uncertainty management following a positive newborn screening for cystic fibrosis. *Journal of Health Communication, 10*, 57–76.

Dillard, J. P., Carson, C. L., Bernard, C. J., Laxova, A., & Farrell, P. M. (2004). An analysis of communication following newborn screening for cystic fibrosis. *Journal of Health Communication, 16*, 195–206.

Dillard, J. P., Shen, L., Laxova, A., & Farrell, P. (2008). Potential threats to the effective communication of genetic risk information: The case of cystic fibrosis. *Health Communication, 23*, 234–244.

Duncan, C. M., Parrott, R. L., & Silk, K. (2002). African American women's perceptions of the role of genetics in breast cancer research. *American Journal of Health Studies, 17*(2), 50–58.

Etchegary, H. (2006). Discovering the family history of Huntington disease (HD). *Journal of Genetic Counseling, 15*, 105–116.

Featherstone, K., Atkinson, P., Bharadwaj, A., & Clarke, A. (2006). *Risky relations: Family, kinship and the new genetics.* New York: Berg.

Feetham, S. L., & Thomson, E. J. (2006). Keeping the individual and family in focus. In S. M. Miller, S. H. McDaniel, J. S. Rolland, & S. L. Feetham (Eds.), *Individuals, families, and the new era of genetics: Biopsychosocial perspectives* (pp. 5–35). New York: Norton.

Finkler, K. (2001). The kin in the gene: The medicalization of family and kinship. *Current Anthropology, 42*, 235–263.

Fisher, W. R. (1987). *Human communication as narration: Toward a philosophy of reason, value and action.* Columbia: University of South Carolina Press.

Fitzpatrick, M. A. (1998). Interpersonal communication on the Starship Enterprise: Resilience, stability, and change in relationships for the twenty-first century. In J. Trent (Ed.), *Communication: Views from the helm for the 21st century* (pp. 41–46). Boston: Allyn & Bacon.

Fitzpatrick, M. A., & Ritchie, L. D. (1994). Family communication patterns: Measuring interpersonal perceptions of interpersonal relationships. *Communication Research, 17*, 523–544.

Forrest, K., Simpson, S. A., Wilson, B. J., van Teijlingen, E. R., McKee, L., Haites, N., et al. (2003). To tell or not to tell: Barriers and facilitators in family communication about genetic risk. *Clinical Genetics, 64*, 317–326.

Foster, C., Eeles, R., Ardern-Jones, A., Moynihan, C., & Watson, M. (2004). Juggling roles and expectations: Dilemmas faced by women talking to relatives about cancer and genetic testing. *Psychology and Health, 19*, 439–455.

Gaff, C. L., & Bylund, C. L. (Eds.). (in press). *Talking about genetics: A family affair.* New York: Oxford University Press.

Gaff, C. L., Clark, A. J., Atkinson, P., Sivell, S., Elwyn, G., Iredale, R., et al. (2007). Process and outcome in communication of genetic information within families: A systematic review. *European Journal of Human Genetics, 15*(10), 1–13.

Gaff, C. L., Collins, V., Symes, T., & Halliday, J. (2005). Facilitating family communication about predictive genetic testing: Probands' perceptions. *Journal of Genetic Counseling, 14*, 133–140.

Galvin, K. M. (2006). Diversity's impact on defining the family. In L. H. Turner & R. West (Eds.), *The family communication sourcebook* (pp. 3–19). Thousand Oaks, CA: Sage.

Galvin, K. M., Bylund, C. L., Reyes, M., & Dunet, D. O. (2006, November). *Sibling communication about genetic risk of hereditary hemochromatosis: Using the health belief model to understand sibling decision making about testing.* Paper presented at the annual meeting of the National Communication Association, San Antonio, TX.

Galvin, K. M., Dickson, F. C., & Marrow, S. R. (2006). Systems theory: Patterns and (w)holes in family communication. In D. O. Braithwaite & L. A Baxter (Eds.), *Engaging theories in family communication: Multiple perspectives* (pp. 309–324). Thousand Oaks, CA: Sage.

Genomics Network. (n.d.). Dr. Katie Featherstone profile page. Retrieved October 19, 2008, from http://www.genomicsnetwork.ac.uk/people/academicstaff/forename,173,en.html

Gessen, M. (2008). *Blood matters.* Orlando, FL: Harcourt.

Giles, H., Coupland, J., & Coupland, N. (1991). Accommodation theory: Communication, context and consequence. In H. Giles, J. Coupland, & N. Coupland (Eds.), *Contexts of accommodation: Developments in applied sociolinguistics* (pp. 1–68). Cambridge, England: Cambridge University Press.

Giles, H., & Smith, P. M. (1979). Accommodation theory: Optimal levels of convergence. In H. Giles & R. St. Clair (Eds.), *Language and social psychology* (pp. 45–65). Oxford, England: Blackwell.

Golish, T. D. (2000). Changes in closeness between adult children and their parents: A turning point analysis. *Communication Reports, 13*(2), 79–97.

Golish, T. D., & Powell, K. A. (2003). "Ambiguous loss": Managing the dialectics of grief associated with premature birth. *Journal of Social and Personal Relationships, 20*, 309–334.

Golombok, S., MacCallum, F., & Goodman, E. (2001). The "test-tube" generation: Parent–child relationships and the psychological well-being of in vitro fertilization children at adolescence. *Child Development, 72*(2), 599–608.

Green, J., Richards, M., Murton, F., Statham, H., & Hallowell, N. (1997). Family communication and genetic counseling: The case of hereditary breast and ovarian cancer. *Journal of Genetic Counseling, 69*, 45–60.

Green, R. M. (2008). *Babies by design: The ethics of genetic choice.* New Haven, CT: Yale University Press.

Hallowell, N. (1999). Doing the right thing: Genetic risk and responsibility. *Sociology of Health and Illness, 21*, 597–621.

Hallowell, N., Ardern-Jones, A., Eeles, R., Foster, C., Lucassen, A., Moynihan, C., et al. (2005). Men's decision-making about predictive *BRCA1/2* testing: The role of family. *Journal of Genetic Counseling, 14*, 207–217.

Harmon, A. (2007a, September 16). Cancer free at 33, but weighing a mastectomy. *New York Times,* pp. A14 –15.

Harmon, A. (2007b, March 18). Facing life with a lethal gene. *New York Times,* pp. A20–21.

Harwood, J., Soliz, J., & Lin, M. C. (2006). Communication accommodation theory: An intergroup approach to family relationships. In D. O. Braithwaite & L. A. Baxter (Eds.), *Engaging theories in family communication: Multiple perspectives* (pp. 19–34). Thousand Oaks, CA: Sage.

Hertz, R. (2006). *Single by chance; mothers by choice.* New York: Oxford University Press.

Hess, S. (Writer), & Glatter, L. (Director). (2007). You don't want to know [Television series episode]. In P. Attanasio (Producer), *House.* New York: Fox Broadcasting.

Holt, K. (2006). What do we tell the children? Contrasting the disclosure choices of two HD families regarding risk status and predictive genetic testing. *Journal of Genetic Counseling, 15,* 253–265.

Hughes, C., Lerman, C., Schwartz, M., Peshkin, B. N., Wenzel, L., Narod, S., et al. (2002). All in the family: Evaluation of the process and content of sisters' communication about BRCA1 and BRCA2 genetic test results. *American Journal of Medical Genetics, 107,* 143–150.

Human Genome Project. (n.d.). *About the Human Genome Project.* Retrieved September 26, 2007, from http://www.ornl.gov/sci/techresources/Human_Genome/project/about.shtml

Hyde, M. J. (2008). *Perfection, postmodern culture, and the biotechnology debate.* Carroll C. Arnold Distinguished Lecture. Washington DC: National Communication Association.

Julian-Reynier, C., Eisinger, F., Chabal, F., Lasset, C., Nogues, C., Stoppa-Lyonnet, D., et al. (2000). Disclosure to the family of breast/ovarian cancer genetic test results: Patient's willingness and associated factors. *American Journal of Medical Genetics, 94,* 13–18.

Kaimal, G., Steinberg, A. G., Ennis, S., Harasink, S. M., Ewing, R., & Li, Y. (2007). Parental narratives about genetic testing for hearing loss: A one year follow-up study. *Journal of Genetic Counseling, 16,* 775–787.

Kenen, R., Ardern-Jones, A., & Eeles, R. (2004). We are talking, but are they listening? Communication patterns in families with a history of breast/ovarian cancer. *Psycho-Oncology, 13,* 335–345.

Klitzman, R., Thorne, D., Williamson, J., Chung, W., & Marder, K. (2007). Decision-making about reproductive choices among individuals at-risk for Huntington's disease. *Journal of Genetic Counseling, 16,* 347–362.

Knobloch, L. K. (2008). Uncertainty reduction theory: Communicating under conditions of ambiguity. In L. A. Baxter & D. O. Braithwaite (Eds.), *Engaging theories in interpersonal communication* (pp. 133–144). Thousand Oaks, CA: Sage.

Koehly, L. M., Peterson, S. K., Watts, B. G., Kempf, K. G., Vernon, S. W., & Gritz, E. R. (2003). A social network analysis of communication about hereditary nonpolyposis colorectal cancer genetic testing and family functioning. *Cancer Epidemiology, Biomarkers & Prevention, 12,* 304–313.

Koerner, A. F., & Fitzpatrick, M. A. (1997). Family type and conflict: The impact of conversation orientation and conformity orientation on conflict in the family. *Communication Studies, 48,* 59–75.

Koerner, A. F., & Fitzpatrick, M. A. (2006). Family communication patterns theory: A social cognitive approach. In D. O. Braithwaite & L. A Baxter (Eds.), *Engaging theories in family communication: Multiple perspectives* (pp. 50–65). Thousand Oaks, CA: Sage.

Langellier, K. M., & Peterson, E. E. (2006). Narrative performance theory: Telling stories, doing family. In D. O. Braithwaite & L. A Baxter (Eds.), *Engaging theories in family communication: Multiple perspectives* (pp. 99–114). Thousand Oaks, CA: Sage.

Lasker, L. N. (1998). In search of parenthood: Coping with infertility and high tech conception. In K. Daniels & E. Haimes (Eds.), *Donor insemination: International social science perspectives* (pp. 7–22). New York: Cambridge University Press

Lehmann, L. S., Weeks, J. C., Klar, N., Biener, L., & Garber, J. E. (2000). Disclosure of familial genetic information: Perceptions of the duty to inform. *The American Journal of Medicine, 109*, 705–711.

MacDonald, D. J., Sarna, L., Giger, J. N., Van Servellen, G., Bastani, R., & Weitzel, J. N. (2008). Comparison of Latina and non-Latina white women's beliefs about communicating genetic cancer risk to relatives. *Journal of Health Communication, 13*, 465–479.

Masci, D, (2001, May 19). Designer humans. *CQ Researcher, 11*(19), p. 425–440. Retrieved September 15, 2007, from http://library.cqpress.com/cqresearcher/document.php?id=cqresrre2001051800

McAllister, M. (2002). Predictive genetic testing and beyond: A theory of engagement. *Journal of Health Psychology, 7*, 491–508.

McAllister, M. F., Evans, D. G., Ormiston, W., & Daly, P. (1998). Men in breast cancer families: A preliminary qualitative study of awareness and experience. *Journal of Medical Genetics, 35*, 739–744.

McDaniel, S. H. (2005). The psychotherapy of genetics. *Family Process, 44*(1), 25–44.

McDaniel, S. H., Rolland, J., Feetham, S. L., & Miller, S. M. (2006). It runs in the family: Family systems concepts and genetically linked disorders. In S. M. Miller, S. H. McDaniel, J. S. Rolland, & S. L. Feetham (Eds.), *Individuals, families, and the new era of genetics* (pp. 118–136). New York: Norton.

McGivern, B., Everett, J., Yager, G. G., Baumiller, R. C., Hafertepen, A., & Saal, H. M. (2004). Family communication about positive BRCA1 and BRCA2 genetic test results. *Genetics in Medicine, 6*, 503–509.

McKusick, V. A. (2000). Ellis-van Crevald syndrome and the Amish. *Nature Genetics, 24*, 203–204.

McLeod, J. M., & Chaffee, S. H. (1972). The construction of social reality. In J. Tedeschi (Ed.), *The social influence process* (pp. 50–59). Chicago: Aldine-Atherton.

McLeod, J. M., & Chaffee, S. H. (1973). Interpersonal approaches to communication research. *American Behavioral Scientist, 16*, 469–499.

Mellon, S., Berry-Bobovski, L., Gold, R., Levin, N., & Tainsky, M. A. (2006). Communication and decision-making about seeking inherited cancer risk information: Findings from female survivor-relative focus groups. *Psycho-Oncology, 15*, 193–208.

Miller, S. M. (1995). Monitoring versus blunting styles of coping with cancer influence the information patients want and need about their disease. *Cancer, 76*, 167–177.

Miller, S. M., Daly, M. B., Sherman, K. A., Fleisher, L., Buzaglo, J. S., Stanton, L., et al. (2006). Psychosocial processes in genetic risk assessment for breast cancer. In S. M. Miller, S. H. McDaniel, J. S. Rolland, & S. L. Feetham (Eds.), *Individuals, families, and the new era of genetics: Biopsychosocial perspectives* (pp. 274–319). New York: Norton.

Miller, S. M., McDaniel, S. H., Rolland, J. S., & Feetham, S. L. (2006). *Individuals, families, and the new era of genetics: Biopsychosocial perspectives*. New York: Norton.

Morgan, E., & Hacker, K. (2007). Boundaries in genetic discourse: Racial and ethnic self-identification. *Communication Research Reports, 24*(1), 1–7.

Moyer, A., Brown, B., Gates, E., Daniels, M., Brown, H. D., & Kuppermann, M. (1999). Decisions about prenatal testing for chromosomal disorders: Perceptions of a diverse group of pregnant women. *Journal of Women's Health and Gender-based Medicine, 8*, 521–531.

Parrott, R. (2008). A multiple discourse approach to health communication: Translational research and ethical practice. *Journal of Applied Communication Research, 36*, 1–7.

Parrott, R. H., & Condit, C. (Eds.). (1996). *Evaluating women's health messages: A resource book*. Thousand Oaks, CA: Sage.

Parrott, R., Silk, K., Weiner, J., Condit, C., Harris, T., & Bernhardt, J. (2004). Deriving lay models of uncertainty about genes' role in illness causation to guide communication about human genetics. *Journal of Communication, 54*, 105–122.

Paul, M. S., & Berger, R. (2007). Topic avoidance and family functioning in families conceived with donor insemination. *Human Reproduction, 22*, 1–6.

Pawlowski, D. R. (2006). Dialectical tensions in families experiencing acute health issues: Stroke survivors' perceptions. In L. H. Turner & R. West (Eds.), *The family communication sourcebook* (pp. 469–489). Thousand Oaks, CA: Sage.

Pearson, J. C. (1994). *Marriage after mourning: The secrets of surviving couples*. Dubuque, IA: Kendall-Hunt.

Petersen, A. (2006). The best experts: The narratives of those who have a genetic condition. *Social Science & Medicine, 63*, 32–42.

Peterson, S. K. (2005). The role of the family in genetic testing: Theoretical perspectives, current knowledge, and future directions. *Health Education & Behavior, 32*, 627–639.

Peterson, S. K., Watts, B. G., Koehly, L. M., Vernon, S. W., Baile, W. F., Kohlmann, W. K., et al. (2003). How families communicate about HNPCC genetic testing: Findings from a qualitative study. *American Journal of Medical Genetics, 119C*, 78–86.

Petronio, S. (2002). *Boundaries of privacy: Dialectics of disclosure*. Albany: State University of New York Press.

Petronio, S., & Caughlin, J. (2006). Communication privacy management theory: Understanding families. In D. O. Braithwaite & L. A Baxter (Eds.), *Engaging theories in family communication: Multiple perspectives* (pp. 35–49). Thousand Oaks, CA: Sage.

Plantinga, L., Natowicz, M. R., Kass, N. E., Chandros Hull, S., Gostin, L. O., & Faden, R. R. (2003). Disclosure, confidentiality, and families: Experiences and attitudes of those with genetic versus nongenetic medical conditions. *American Journal of Medical Genetics, 199C*, 51–59.

Redlinger-Grosse, K., Bernhardt, B. A., Berg, K., Muenke, M., & Biesecker, B. (2002). The decision to continue: The experiences and needs of parents who receive a prenatal diagnosis of holoprosencephaly. *American Journal of Medical Genetics, 112*, 369–378.

Resta, R., Biesecker, B. B., Bennett, R. L., Blum, S., Hahn, S. E., Strecker, M. N., et al. (2006). A new definition of genetic counseling: National society of genetic counselors' task force report. *Journal of Genetic Counseling, 15*, 77–83.

Reyes, M., Dunet, D. O., Isenberg, K. B., Trisolini, M., & Wagener, D. K. (2007).

Family-based detection for hereditary hemochromatosis. *Journal of Genetic Counseling, 16*, 92–100.

Rhimes, S., & Stanton, G. G. (Writers), & Stanzler, W. (Director). (2005). Who's zoomin' who? [Television series episode]. In B. Beers (Producer), *Grey's anatomy*. New York: American Broadcasting Company.

Ritchie, L. D. (1991). Family communication patterns. *Communication Research, 18*, 548–566.

Rolland, J. S. (1999). Families and genetic fate: A millennial challenge. *Families, Systems & Health, 17*, 123–132.

Rolland, J. S., & Williams, J. K. (2006). Toward a psychosocial model for the new era of genetics. In S. M. Miller, S. H. McDaniel, J. S. Rolland, & S. L. Feetham (Eds.), *Individuals, families, and the new era of genetics* (pp. 36–75). New York: Norton.

Rudnick, J. (Director & Producer). (2008). *In the family* [Motion picture]. United States: Kartemquin Films.

Sandel, M. J. (2007). *The case for perfection: Ethics in the age of genetic engineering*. Cambridge, MA: Belknap Press/Harvard University Press.

Sarangi, S., & Clarke, A. (2002). Zones of expertise and the management of uncertainty in genetics risk communication. *Research on Language and Social Interaction, 35*, 139–171.

Schover, L. R., Thomas, A. J., Falcone, T., Attaran, M., & Goldberg, J. (1998). Attitudes about genetic risk of couples undergoing in-vitro fertilization. *Human Reproduction, 13*, 862–866.

Sobel, S. K., & Cowan, D. B. (2000). Impact of genetic testing for Huntington disease on the family system. *American Journal of Medical Genetics, 90*, 49–59.

Sorenson, J. R., & Botkin, J. R. (2003). Genetic testing and the family. *American Journal of Medical Genetics, 119C*, 1–2.

Stock, G., & Campbell, J. (2000). Introduction: An evolutionary perspective. In G. Stock & J. Campbell (Eds.), *The human germline: An exploration of the science and ethics of altering the genes we pass on to our children* (pp. 3–6). New York: Oxford University Press.

Thompson, T. L., & Parrott, R. H. (2002). Interpersonal communication and health care. In M. L. Knapp & J. A. Daly (Eds.), *Handbook of interpersonal communication* (3rd ed., pp. 680–725). Thousand Oaks, CA: Sage.

Vangelisti, A. L. (2004). Introduction. In A. L. Vangelisti (Ed.), *Handbook of family communication* (pp. xiii–xx). Mahwah, NJ: Erlbaum.

Van Riper, M. (2005). Genetic testing and the family. *Journal of Midwifery and Women's Health, 50*, 221–233.

Van Riper, M., & Gallo, A. (2006). Family, health, and genomics. In D. R. Crane & E. S. Marshall (Eds.), *Handbook of families and health: Interdisciplinary perspectives* (pp. 195–217). Thousand Oaks, CA: Sage.

Walter, F. M., Emery, J., Braithwaite, D., & Marteau, T. M. (2004). Lay understanding of familial risk of common chronic diseases: A systematic review and synthesis of qualitative research. *Annals of Family Medicine, 2*, 583–594.

Warner, B. J., Curnow, L. J., Polglase, A. L., & Debinski, H. S. (2005). Factors influencing uptake of genetic testing for colorectal cancer risk in an Australian Jewish population. *Journal of Genetic Counseling, 14*, 387–394.

Weiner, J. L., Silk, K. J., & Parrott, R. L. (2005). Family communication and genetic health: A research note. *The Journal of Family Communication, 5*(1), 313–324.

Wethers, D. L. (2000). Sickle cell disease in childhood: Part I. Laboratory diagnosis, pathophysiology and health maintenance. *American Family Physician, 62*, 1013–1020.

Whitchurch, G. G., & Dickson, F. C. (1999). Family communication. In M. Sussman, S. K. Steinmetz, & G. W. Peterson (Eds.), *Handbook of marriage and the family* (2nd ed., pp. 687–704). New York: Plenum.

Wilson, B. J., Forrest, K., van Teijlingen, E. R., McKee, L., Haites, N., Matthews, E., et al. (2004). Family communication about genetic risk: The little that is known. *Community Genetics, 7*(1), 15–24.

Wood-Harper, J., & Harris, J. (1999). Ethics of human genome analysis: Some virtues and vices. In T. Marteau & M. Richards (Eds.), *The troubled helix: Social and psychological implications of the new genetics* (pp. 274–284). Cambridge, England: Cambridge University Press.

CHAPTER CONTENTS

# 7 Discourse, Gender, and the Meaning of Work

## Rearticulating Science, Technology, and Engineering Careers Through Communicative Lenses

*Lorraine G. Kisselburgh*
*Brenda L. Berkelaar*
*Patrice M. Buzzanell*
Purdue University

In this chapter, we offer communicative perspectives and challenges related to gender representation and the gendered organizing and career processes in science, technology, engineering, and math (STEM) areas. We focus on the meaning of work in STEM and how these meanings are (re)created and communicated through d/Discourses. Using a discursive approach, new perspectives on the issue of the underrepresentation of women in STEM careers derive from the constructed nature of STEM work itself and its meaningfulness to different groups, particularly women. Engagement in STEM careers also provides a context to evaluate and expand theory, research, and practice in communication. We use multi-disciplinary lenses to examine developmental, educational, media, technological, socio-cultural, and organizational perspectives on STEM work and careers. In summary, this chapter examines the discursive roots of contemporary constructions and images of STEM work, careers, education, and organizations, offering an opportunity to address a socially relevant issue and context for further examination and explication of communication research, theories, and practices across specialties.

## Introduction

In 2006, the President of the International Communication Association (ICA), Jon Nussbaum, called for communication scholars to address socially relevant quality of life concerns placing communication at the "very heart of these discussions" (Nussbaum, 2007, p. 5; see also Craig, 2005). For adults, work and careers, and occupational opportunities perceived as accessible and meaningful to particular individuals and groups, comprise a central aspect of quality of life. At the simplest level, careers give form and meaning to paid labor and relevant unpaid work experiences (Buzzanell & Lucas, 2006). The

Correspondence: e-mail: lorraine@purdue.edu

nature, accessibility, and meaningfulness of work and careers, broadly conceptualized[1] (see Arthur, Inkson, & Pringle, 1999; Cheney, Zorn, Planalp, & Lair,
2008; Medved, this volume), have material considerations embedded in their
very conduct and context. The ways in which stakeholders socially construct
these issues are communicative in nature. These constructions center on the *discourses*, or everyday talk, interactions, media depictions, and linguistic choices
surrounding work and careers, as well as on the *Discourses*, or "standardized
ways of referring to/constituting a certain type of phenomenon" (Alvesson &
Kärreman, 2000, p. 1134), such as gender, economics, globalization, and managerialism that people invoke to determine whether or how they might participate in work and careers (Alvesson & Kärreman, 2000; Fairhurst, 2007; Kuhn
et al., 2008). As Kuhn and colleagues noted, *D/discourses* can act as resources
or *tools*, serving as linguistic devices that explain past actions, affect future
practices, and guide our interpretations and constructions of experience, persons, and institutions (see also Fairclough, 1992; Kuhn & Nelson, 2002).

The work of science, technology, engineering, and math (STEM) and associated careers offer a site in which the d/Discourses of work and careers are
complexly manifested and contested. National and international calls for innovative theory, research, assessment, and practices seek to draw in a new generation of participants, especially women, and rearticulate what work in these
areas contributes to society within the context of a contemporary and global-
ized information economy (Congressional Commission on the Advancement
of Women and Minorities in Science, Engineering and Technology Development [CAWMSET], 2000; Domestic Policy Council, 2006; National Academy
of Sciences [NAS], 2007; National Science Foundation [NSF], 2004, 2005).[2]
Because communication constitutes the heart of needed scholarship and practice within STEM, our goals in this chapter are twofold: We strive, first, to set
research agendas with communication at the center of STEM work and career
initiatives, and second, to propose STEM as a site in which innovative communication theory, research, and practice can be undertaken. We believe communication perspectives and research can bring new insights to the continuing
underrepresentation of women in STEM while simultaneously providing a rich
and influential site in which to test and evaluate communication theories from
organizational, family, instructional/educational, cultural, media, technology,
and other communication perspectives.

We focus on STEM because these disciplines do and will continue to play
important roles in 21st century society, particularly given the ubiquity of technology in everyday lives and work. STEM work offers technical solutions to
the world's most urgent problems—from health issues and global warming
to drought-resistant foods and advance warning systems for tsunamis—and
to the world's seemingly more mundane activities—productivity, domestic
work, and education. Solutions require multidisciplinary and diverse insights,
including those from communication, women, and multicultural populations,
to define, evaluate, and identify solutions that hold social as well as techni-

cal influences and implications. Moreover, because of the tremendous workforce demand and monetary rewards of this work, STEM careers can provide opportunities for countries, groups, and individuals to benefit economically and socially.

Given global demands for recruitment and retention of individuals in STEM careers and the underrepresentation of women in these careers, many initiatives are directed toward women and girls (CAWMSET, 2000; Etzkowitz, Kemelgor, & Uzzi, 2000; NAE, 2002, 2008; NSF, 2004, 2005, 2006; Phipps, 2008; Rosser, 2004). Yet, despite decades of effort, women remain underrepresented in most STEM fields even as the demand for a highly skilled and educated workforce grows (U.S. Department of Labor, Bureau of Labor Statistics, 2006–2007; International Labour Organization, 2003; Judy, D'Amico, & Geipel, 1997). Although enrollment rates have risen in certain STEM disciplines, such as the life sciences and biomedical engineering (NSF, 2006), the underrepresentation of women continues (Snyder, Tan, & Hoffman, 2006), particularly in engineering and computer science (Rosser, 2004; Spertus, 1993). In computer science academic programs in the United States, according to Snyder et al., the number of females enrolled has actually declined, and graduation rates have fallen below 25%, the lowest since 1977 (Snyder et al., 2006). For this reason, although we situate our review and discussion within the broad framework of STEM, we focus specifically on engineering and computer science, given the intransigence of growth in those two areas. Underrepresented in the global STEM labor force, both individual women as well as their nations do not receive the economic and social benefits that arise from more equal participation in the research, design, and engineering of systems, technologies, and processes that are ubiquitous in everyday life.

We frame our review around the *meaning of work*,[3] seeking to understand the messages that influence how members of society, particularly girls and women, perceive and construct these meanings—how people *talk* about work matters. Thus, examining work as a discursive construction helps uncover "the very nature and goals of work" within different historical contexts and how these meanings are shaped by Discourses and demographics of race, nationality, gender, and class (Cheney et al., 2008, p. 140). Because doing the work—both the craft and intellectual aspects—is of utmost importance, the language that accompanies STEM work also deserves examination. Employing a discursive approach helps to make sense of, consider the linguistic choices and occupational frames employed by, and locate the ways in which STEM members discursively position themselves and others within macrodiscourses surrounding STEM. In other words, we explore the intersections of d/Discourse, gender, technology, and meaningful work, with the intent of bringing new perspectives to the issue of women's underrepresentation in STEM careers while simultaneously seeing the context of STEM careers as a setting that presents challenges that can lead to new understandings of communication theories and processes.

## Rearticulation of STEM Careers from Cross-Disciplinary Perspectives

We begin with the development/lifespan perspectives and then consider educational, media, technological, socio-cultural, and organizational lenses on the discursive constructions of meaningful work in science, engineering, and technology. In so doing, we provide new and multiple lenses in which to examine both the communicative perspectives of the representation of women in STEM careers, as well as the multiple factors that influence and contribute to the meaningfulness of science and engineering work.

### *Developmental (Lifespan) Perspectives*

From a *lifespan* perspective (Nussbaum, 2007; Pecchioni, Wright, & Nussbaum, 2005), STEM provides a context in which memorable messages (Stohl, 1986/2006) attributed to multiple socialization agents can be considered more or less salient depending on the developmental phase of individuals within particular contexts. Stohl defined messages as memorable if an individual "remembers the message for a long period of time and perceives the message had a major influence on the course of his or her life" (p. 146). With known influences of early parental aspirations and socialization processes, STEM provides an opening for enhancing research in family communication that explores how families talk (or do not talk) about work with their children— both boys and girls (Golden, 2000; see also Lucas, 2006). Children are not simply socialized in the *how* of a particular career but *whether* a particular career or type of work is acceptable through indirect, direct, absent, and ambient messages. For example, a study of Chinese immigrant parents in Canada illustrated that participants considered different types of careers or work to be appropriate for girls and boys (Liu, 2006), and most of the parents in the study associated engineering, science, and computers with boys. As Liu detailed, one mother stated that:

> In terms of occupation for a girl, it ought to be something steady and peaceful, decent and clean, and not very challenging and risky. I hope my son will go out as far as he likes to explore the wide world as much as he likes. But with a girl, I would not have held such high expectations. The most important thing for a girl is to be steady and safe. (p. 496)

Evidence suggests that boys and girls are differently socialized in career views. As early as age 2, girls receive differential reinforcement to engage in play, academic subjects, and occupations that are gender appropriate, subsequently resulting in different educational exposure and perceived expectations (Etzkowitz et al., 2000; Fels, 2004; Lytton & Romney, 1991). As Etzkowitz et al. explained, in the United States, many teachers and parents encourage STEM-valued behavioral traits (such as risk-taking, innovation, and independence) in boys and urge boys to pursue math and science for fiscally rewarding careers, while persuading girls to consider careers that allow family commitments to be prioritized over or balanced with work. These socialization processes circumscribe occupational choice considerations (Gottfredson, 1981, 2002) and can intersect with socio-political and cultural factors. In China, for example, many parents indicate that the "sciences, engineering, construction, computer, politics, military affairs, [and] management" are the most suitable occupations for boys (Liu, 2006, p. 496). However, in response to national agendas, such as the one-child policy, parents now also encourage girls into traditionally masculine careers because such careers can bring prestige, economic value, and honor to families and the country (Liu, 2006; Lucas, Liu, & Buzzanell, 2006). Thus, national Discourses and messages intersect and sometimes contradict traditional economic, culture, and gender Discourses, and reframe and reshape messages and socialization patterns.

Although they may not be able to articulate, from the earliest ages children conceptualize adult labor as separation from family life and recognize adults' attitudes toward work and non-work (e.g., Jablin, 1985, 2001; Van Maanen & Schein, 1979). As children age, they consider and role-play familiar occupations and receive reinforcement for their performances. Boys become firefighters, doctors, and policemen; girls play the parts of teachers, cooperative game players, and nurses (Thorne, 1993). Furthermore, children develop skills and talents by participating in sports, taking lessons, and excelling in subjects that might prove appropriate for desirable careers. Intergenerational research indicates that children may learn the details of particular work through regular interaction with and observations of occupational members (Gibson & Papa, 2000; Lucas, 2006). Through this occupational *osmosis* process, families, friends, and neighbors function as important socialization agents, and the home and local community serve as sites for learning and refining meanings of work (Jablin, 2001).

Parental conversations about work and career continue through adolescence and often eclipse other socializing agents, until youth begin to learn about work, jobs, and careers through part-time employment (Levine & Hoffner, 2006). When parental work and careers and the messages associated with them do not align with the work that their children choose (e.g., in the move from an industrialized to an information economy), children must contend with mixed or contradictory messages that complicate success and perceptions of the meaningfulness of their work or career (Lucas, 2006). Lucas noted that contradictory messages may occur when parents alternate between wanting their children to make use of talents, get an education, find a fulfilling career, remain in their communities, and do work that is not dangerous or marked by instabilities caused by strikes and layoffs. Complicating these messages are conditions of deindustrialization (Lucas, 2006), changes in cultural norms through outsourced work in developing nations (Pal & Buzzanell, 2008), or shifting national social policies (Liu, 2006; Zachmann, 2000).

With regard to socializing agents in Western nations, vocational and career counseling centers in educational institutions frequently impart advice and messages about following one's passions, abilities, and interests, emphasizing the "know thyself" approach (e.g., Butler & Waldroop, 1999; Buzzanell & Lucas, 2006; Collingwood, 2001). In other nations and cultures, such as China (Liu, 2006) and the Chinese Canadian immigrant culture (Li, 2001), family members explicitly state career aspirations for children. According to Li, families encourage participation in science and engineering, and explicitly discourage participation in law, the arts, or politics. Although the political-economic ideologies in China and the United States are dissimilar in many ways, Lucas et al. (2006) demonstrated how both exert control through systematically distorted career and work discourses that appear benevolent but encourage individuals to extend themselves indefinitely and in particular types of work. From desires for jobs that enable individuals to be self-sustaining in the inner city (Newman, 2000) to "real jobs" (Clair, 1996) with advancement and prestige potential, influential adults affirm the nature, perceived accessibility, and meanings of work to children early in life.

The recognition of gender and cultural differences in influences on meaningful work resonates through these cross-cultural and class-based descriptions. Gender differences in work and career start early and are influenced by Western developmental and lifespan processes that emphasize independence for boys and relational development for girls (Gallos, 1989). For example, Helwig (2004) asked elementary school-aged children to identify *desirable* occupations and found that in the second grade both boys and girls tended to select occupations dominated by members of their own gender. However, these aspirations changed with age. In the sixth grade, boys were more likely to select a "male" occupation (93%, vs. 83% in second grade), but girls were less likely to select a "female" occupation (30%, vs. 56% in second grade) as they matured. The fifth- to sixth-grade period, then, may represent a time in which girls (though not boys) are less likely to hold gender-role stereotypes about occupations. This occupational orientation changes again in adolescence when identity and peer identification begin to exert stronger influences in occupational choice (Faber, Brown, & McLeod, 1979; National Academy of Engineering [NAE], 2008).

While there may not be strict boundaries, girls may find that their ambitions are either encouraged or curtailed through sanctions and memorable messages (see Fels, 2004) as well as memorable absences (Arendt, Buzzanell, Dohrman, & Litera, 2008). Furthermore, even when girls select male-dominated university majors and careers, they may be discouraged by an unsupportive climate, little integration of family and community aspects, and instructional styles that perpetuate notions of STEM occupational members as isolated, obsessed with work, and intolerant of those who do not adapt rapidly to the work and material conditions (e.g., Arendt et al., 2008; Grant, Knight, & Steinbach, 2007; Hewlett, Luce, & Servon, 2008; Margolis & Fisher, 2002). They also may learn that organizations discourage or prohibit leave-taking for familial reasons or discuss the implications of technical or scientific skill decay and its material consequences (Allen, Armstrong, Riemenschneider, & Reid, 2006; Galtry & Callister, 2005; Kirby, 2000; Kirby & Krone, 2002; Remke, 2008).

The developmental perspective, then, illustrates that multiple socialization agents (particularly the family, school, and culture) communicate the meaning of STEM work, generating memorable messages throughout the lifespan of an individual. The discursive construction of STEM work (as masculine and isolated, prestigious and academic, and segregated from and often incompatible with other social roles or commitments such as family) provides early and sometimes lasting Discourses with which individuals determine the appropriateness or desirability of pursuing STEM careers.

### Educational Perspectives

In his book, *A Short History of Nearly Everything*, journalist Bill Bryson (2003) detailed his first exposure to science in school. Excited, he rushes home, opens his textbook, ready with "real wonder" to uncover the answers to important questions. Unfortunately, the textbook "wasn't exciting at all…it didn't answer any of the questions…stirred up in a normal inquiring mind…. So I grew up convinced science was supremely dull, but suspecting that it needn't be, and not really thinking about it at all if I could help it" (p. 5).

In contrast to developmental/lifespan perspectives, an *educational* perspective on STEM from kindergarten through college, at both broad and discipline-specific levels, can help communication researchers to understand the institutionalized messages and discourse that influence the enactment of meaning regarding work and career choice within educational institutions. These influences include curricular materials and programs, occupational counseling, academic role models and advisors as well as institutional discourses and policies that influence the perception of meaningful work. STEM and communication researchers as well as STEM practitioners should examine the ambient and indirect messages and strategic absences provided by educational institutions preparing future engineers, scientists, and technologists— the direct and discrete messages evidenced in textbooks, curriculum, teacher language choices, and marketing through organizational documents and Web sites.

Jablin (2001; see also Levine & Hoffner, 2006) regarded schools and school-related activities as significant sources of work, vocational, and career information for children, noting that "school is typically the first socializing institution in a child's life that institutionalizes status differentiation and hierarchical division of labor" (p. 737). These early influences of school continue through adolescence. According to Phillips's (2005) study of 200 youth, "[t]hrough eighth grade, there is no significant difference between boys' and girls' performance in math and science, but by twelfth grade boys tend to outperform girls in both subjects. Girls are more likely than boys to attribute difficulty in math and science to personal ability" (p. 1). However, recent research has demonstrated that these minor differences in academic achievement generally disappear with curricular changes that encourage girls to take advanced level math courses during high school (Hyde, Lindberg, Linn, Ellis, & Williams, 2008; Lubinksi & Benbow, 2006).

In addition to aptitude tests, training opportunities and curricular content also reflect educational influences on the meaning of STEM work. Blue collar, masculine constructions of engineering in the United States (Oldenziel, 2000) historically contributed to women being denied entry to certain areas of hands-on factory training that was essential to industrial engineering careers, in effect excluding them from graduation or future career promotions. Further, Eriksson-Zetterquist (2007) asserted that science education has been "constructed in ways that are not attractive to women in the same degree as to men.... This construction affects women as students, teachers and researchers, as well as the content of the textbook" (p. 306; see also Faulkner, 2000, 2007; Wajcman, 1991). In critiquing the ostensibly inclusive "science for all" U.S. curriculum initiative, Calabrese Barton and Osbourne (2001) argued that critical, postmodern, and feminist discourses remain marginalized, such that traditional renderings of technology, science, and engineering remain dominant and generally do not appeal to marginalized groups, including minorities and women.

The cultural environment of academic programs also influences the desirability and hospitability of climates for female students. Margolis and Fisher (2003) studied women in the premiere computer science program at Carnegie Mellon University and noted the strong masculine culture. According to Margolis and Fisher, "the male norms of who can do computer science exert their influence at many points throughout a student's college career. Curriculum, culture, peer relations, and faculty expectations reflect the traditional male claims on computing" (p. 17). Margolis and Fisher's findings (2002, 2003; see also Sahr, 2008) suggest that the meaning or broader implications of work may be more influential in career choice for women in computer science than for men. While the enjoyment of computing is a primary factor for both female and male students, women also prioritize the versatility offered by the career, its relationship to their interests, the excitement offered by the rapidly changing nature of the field, and encouragement (or lack thereof) from teachers and parents. Male students, in contrast, envision a computing career as "a natural extension of their lifelong passion for computers" (Margolis & Fisher, 2002, p. 50). Thus, for women, enjoyment and passion for computers and computing constitutes a necessary but not sufficient condition for deciding to enter the computer science profession; broader considerations factor into this decision as well.

Eccles (2006) reached similar conclusions, based upon 35 years of research on gender underrepresentation in the physical sciences and engineering. Her research indicates that the main source of gender differences does not come from aptitude or self-efficacy differentials but, rather, from differences in the *value* that men and women place on certain occupational types. However, inaccurate stereotypes about STEM careers persist that "lead some young women and men to reject these careers for the wrong reasons" (p. 209); the messages and information about such careers result in better informed occupational choices. For example, Metz (2007) analyzed popular Web sites about college majors and found that Web sites for fields such as mechanical engineering continue to emphasize "the least interesting aspect of the field" with limited and stereotypical descriptions that emphasize a "love of math and science," enjoyment of "computer games, mazes and jigsaw puzzles"—thus characterizing the field as hard work and lots of math (pp. 196–197). According to Metz, professionals reviewing these Web sites noticed the absence of particular messages. For example, one reviewer suggested that messages about "[h]ard, math, and makes you a nerd but NOTHING that describes what mechanical engineers do—nothing about serving society or building products," will "drum all women out of the field" (p. 198). Furthermore, while attempting to demonstrate the diversity of engineers in a list of 21 well-known artists, astronauts, musicians, leaders, CEOs, and personalities who had earned engineering degrees, Metz only identified one woman, one African American man, and one Hispanic man. Thus, narrow and inaccurate messages and images of STEM careers do not represent work attributes that women value.

Educational perspectives must also address the cultural context(s) and the educational systems within which the students reside. Unlike in nations such as India and China, where educational assessment determines future education and career paths, in the United States, teenagers face at least two important decision points—deciding whether to pursue a college education and then settling on an academic major. Engineering and science majors present an exception to these educational rhythms, however, because more stringent curricular requirements require an early commitment to the major during the freshman year, as well as substantial prerequisite courses in math and science. Individuals who are discouraged (or not encouraged) from taking prerequisite courses perceive themselves to be at a disadvantage and are dissuaded from considering such programs. Flexible curricular programs can encourage diversity and entry to STEM fields. In addition certain types of educational institutions are able to counter broader social patterns (Giguette, Lopez, & Schulte, 2006; Lopez & Schulte, 2002) and enact influences that affect enrollment and the completion of academic degrees. For instance, women are more equally represented in STEM programs in historically Black U.S. colleges and universities, than other institution types (Giguette et al., 2006; Lopez & Schulte, 2002).

Educational influences can be both institutionally and culturally specific. In contrast to the more individualist choice within U.S. culture, Gupta and Sharma (2002) argued that women in Indian culture experience *patrifocality* (Mukhopadhyay & Seymour, 1994; Subrahmanyan, 1998), a system that gives precedence to men in the family and expects women to subordinate their goals. According to Mukhopadhyay and Seymour, within this system of patrifocality, educational decisions arise from family, not individual choices, and, as Subrahmanyan explained, the mother-in-law (on behalf of the husband's family) exercises substantial influence over the educational decisions of the daughter-in-law, who is considered an economic liability. Subrahmanyan noted that women in India (in most classes) historically had very limited access to higher education because of the economic burdens imposed on the family. However, the trend has shifted in contemporary times to recognize the "earning wives" benefit of women with STEM degrees, making these careers palatable and in demand for Indian women. By appealing to economic Discourses as a basis for career meaningfulness, the construct of *economically viable* wives has been created.

In sum, educational perspectives on the meanings and meaningfulness of STEM work do not rely simply on the everyday discourses of teachers and coaches of extracurricular activities but also upon broader societal and cultural Discourses that reveal how social policies, historical periods, cultural norms, economic pressures, and other factors create contexts in which STEM interests are gendered, privileged, curtailed, and reconfigured. Rather than looking solely at educational reforms and governmental policies that correspond with STEM initiatives and outcomes (e.g., Phipps, 2008), communication researchers can ascertain how the d/Discourses portray shifts in educational thinking and practices that encourage or discourage participation of girls and minorities in STEM and examine whose interests these shifts sustain.

### *Media Perspectives*

STEM work generates a plethora of slogans and portrayals of scientists, engineers, mathematicians, and technologists as mechanistic, nerdy, or geeky. From the infamous Barbie chant "Math is hard" to the more recent suggestions that "engineering is elementary" (Museum of Science, 2007) and "[m]ath is cool for girls," proponents increasingly strive to expand the discourse (NAE, 2002, 2008) and portray engineering as a way to individual and national prosperity (Gupta & Sharma, 2002). At national policy levels in the United States, the NSF (2005) discussed the importance of changing the ways in which media sources represent fields such as engineering and the talk and interactions that surround and shape its Discourse (NAE, 2008). Examining the metaphors, images, and media perceptions of STEM in the context of broader discourses of scientific rationality gives insight into the perceptions of meaningful work. Media portrayals of STEM work include dominant archetypes that are constructed and communicated through multiple media—movies, television, music, the Internet, and others—with the intent of engaging a global media perspective. Rhetorical and popular cultural scholars pursue these portrayals with examinations of the myths and stereotypes that infuse television, movies, and cyberspace (Steinke, 2004, 2005; Van den Bulck & Van den Bergh, 2005).

The myths and stereotypes associated with both STEM work and gender roles permeate cultural portrayals (Steinke, 2004; see also Leonardi, 2003; NAE, 2008). In both engineering and computer science careers, considerable research indicates stereotyped views of STEM work influence subsequent career choices (see Clarke & Teague, 1996; NAE, 2008; Whyte, 1984). Clarke and Teague reported that both male and female high school and college students believed that women were not enrolling in computer science programs because of the "images of computing as technical, male sex-typed, and mathematical" (p. 242). According to Clarke and Teague, when asked about the desirability of careers, high-school girls generally panned the idea of computing careers, characterizing such work as *boring* to be "sitting in front a computer all day" (p. 243), in spite of their enthusiastic use of computers at school and home. The girls failed to see the relevance of such careers to factors that they deemed meaningful in work (NAE, 2008; Whyte, 1984). Similarly, despite a decrease in the media portrayal of scientists as "mad," dangerous, and anti-social, Turkish middle school students tended to characterize scientists as elderly Caucasian males who work alone on chemistry experiments (Türkmen, 2007). However, these stereotypes are not globally consistent. In Mauritius, negative stereotypes for computing careers are absent; "instead, computing is seen as fresh, new, modern, and challenging" (Adams, Bauer, & Baichoo, 2003, p. 62).

As children age, peers and media become more prominent socialization agents. Television viewing begins for many around 2 to 3 years old, and it comprises a prominent socializing medium that increases in importance as children reach adolescence. According to Steinke (2005, p. 28), "during this time, adolescents are more likely to look to the media for information on specific 'life tasks' that have the greatest salience to them: developing a gender-role identity, learning how to interact with members of the opposite sex, and selecting an occupation and other future life roles."

During preadolescence and adolescence, the media offer images of possible selves and ways of thinking about and managing femininity and work-life issues. Hylmö (2006) analyzed the messages presented about gender and vocational roles in films for teenage girls, and she noted that films deliver messages that minimize the importance of careers for women and suggest that men (fathers and boyfriends) will be available for "protection, guidance, and financial support" (p. 167). Consistent with this research, Conaway (2007) analyzed television portrayals of teenage girls in programming noting mixed messages when brainy girls "learned to perform more normatively" (p. 242) by neglecting schoolwork for relational benefits (popularity or romance).[4] Even though female scientists and engineers in film appear as competent professionals with high status, Steinke (2005) found that only 20% of the films analyzed in her study depicted scientists as mothers, and only one (of 23) depicted a dual-career family that shared childcare responsibilities. Steinke concluded that films emphasized the femininity of the scientists and engineers—all were or became attractive and were typically romantically involved during the course of the film.

In short, popular depictions of females on television and other media continue to display women as passive, dependent, emotional, social, and more interested in romance and appearance than in work and careers (Signorelli,

1997; Steinke, 2005). Steinke (2005) detailed the implications of these portrayals for women in science and engineering:

> The focus on female scientists and engineers as single and the lack of images of working mothers...represents an important direction for future research. The impact, if any, of the message conveyed by some of the female scientist and engineer primary characters about the difficulties of balancing work and family and the scarcity of characters presented as successfully balancing work and family needs to be examined given recent research on women's perceptions of SET [science, engineering, and technology] careers. (p. 54)

Narrow portrayals of STEM careers have significant implications for girls and adolescents who are beginning to consider how to integrate and balance work and family in future careers. As Hanson (2000) argued, "A critical element in the culture of science occupations involves ideas about having to be wedded to one's work—making it difficult for women with families (spouses and/or children), but not men with families, to succeed" (p. 170).

Representations do not merely occur in traditional mass media. The Internet, new media, and even virtual worlds, such as *Second Life*, have broadened the avenues through which social actors perform and portray occupations and gender roles (Bortree, 2005; Mazzarella, 2005; Stern, 2004), providing an additional source of potentially influential information and portrayals given the number of teens who use the Internet on a daily basis (Lenhard, Madden, Macgill, & Smith, 2007). Steinke (2004) analyzed Web sites targeted toward girls seeking information about science and engineering careers. While a number provided positive portrayals about careers, Steinke observed the many mixed messages conveyed—countering struggles against discrimination and work-life challenges with positive achievements in work that was meaningful and socially important. Furthermore, some of these Web sites are too narrowly focused, neglecting to emphasize elements and opportunities of the profession that are attractive to women, such as civic and global responsibility (Raphael, Bachen, Lynn, Baldwin-Philippi, & McKee, 2006).

The absence of media portrayals of women in STEM professions also communicate volumes. Signorelli (1997) analyzed the messages to which girls are exposed through film, television, music videos, and teen magazines, and she found that most women were not portrayed in occupational contexts. Furthermore, few media portrayals of engineers and scientists exist that one would consider cool, fun, and *sexy*,[5] despite notable exceptions. The *Nickelodeon* network consistently portrays girls as capable, strong, and empowered individuals, who can save others, boys included (Banet-Weiser, 2004). Additionally, PBS launched a new television series aimed at middle- and high-school students to illustrate engineering work. *Design Squad* (WGBH Educational Foundation, 2007; see also Sahr, 2008) follows a multicultural and gender diverse team of students who accept engineering challenges and use the processes of brainstorming, designing, building, and testing to illustrate that engineering can be fun, challenging, and performed with teams of people who look like "you and me."

In addition, numerous social groups—online and off-line—have formed to offer counternarratives to the stereotypical STEM professional as a male nerd or geek. For example, at Tufts University, the *Nerd Girls* group embraces the *nerd* label, challenging the notion that geek pursuits are incompatible with feminine interests in fashion and reframing such activities (and the members who enjoy them) as *geek chic* (Bennett & Yabroff, 2008). Members perform these counternarratives by modeling themselves after popular media figures such as Tina Fey, writer and star of *30 Rock* whose character loves *Star Wars*; by hosting Girl Geek dinners; or even participating in, and winning, *Sexiest Geek Alive* contests typically geared toward men (Bennett & Yabroff, 2008; Newitz & Anders, 2006).

These stories and performances recognize and subvert the familiar stereotypes of STEM work (Tucker, Pawley, Riley, & Catalano, 2008) and offer counternarratives to the existing cultural portrayals of engineers as nerdy, boring, and non-social. In fact, alternative discourses expand and reframe the discourse of engineering work and its members to one of *coolness*—a bit like the Apple *Get a Mac* television commercials that contrast the nerdy, overweight, institutional PC guy with the cool, independent, healthy Mac guy (see http://www.apple.com/getamac/ads/). These discourses also reframe the meaningfulness of STEM work and its careers, when media sources connect the value of innovation and imagination to serving social needs and importance in our future world. Specifically, alternative discourses reframe the meaning of being smart and choosing STEM careers as an opportunity to empower girls. However, critics have warned that the counterdiscourses can themselves be problematic as evident in debates over the culturally dominant stereotypes of attractiveness employed by the *nerd girls*, which some argue demand women fill traditionally hegemonic ideals of feminine sexuality while simultaneously demonstrating intellectual prowess (Pawley, 2008).

The biases inherent in the news media compound this problem of mixed messages in media portrayals. For example, promoting itself as a progressive company in gender equality (Styhre, Backman, & Börjesson, 2005), Volvo created an all-female engineering and design team to develop a new concept car and illustrate the possibilities and products that result when more women participate in engineering design. Through critical discourse analysis of 272 news articles, Styhre et al. found that the media coverage drew upon gendered stereotypes and produced a form of *double articulation*—emphasizing the unique qualifications of the female team, while refusing to admit differences between female and male engineers.

As engineering groups, most notably the NAE (2008), work toward branding engineering in more attractive and accurate fashions, new media campaigns can draw more youth, particularly girls, into STEM majors and careers (see also NAE, 2002). Based upon interviews and surveys of children, youth, and parents, the NAE identified phrases and messages about engineering that have strong appeal to youth of particular age, gender, and racial/ethnic groups. However, these message campaigns can also have opposite, mixed, and contradictory effects. In particular, messages strategically designed to increase interest and participation in STEM areas by women and members of underrepresented groups may have unintended, and opposite effects (i.e., a *boomerang effect*; see Byrne & Hart, this volume) if the targeted audience is already predisposed toward certain behaviors or values. Factors such as gender, age, prior knowledge or behavioral involvement, and media usage can impact potential boomerang effects. In addition to unintended consequences, media campaign efforts might have little effect if they are not aligned with and adapted to cultural values (see Hornikx & O'Keefe, this volume). Furthermore, health campaign message research can provide useful strategies for the development of persuasive STEM message campaigns using both tailored rather than targeted message strategies (see Noar, Harrington, & Aldrich, this volume).

In short, many media portrayals of gender and STEM perpetuate stereotypes about occupational members' appearance, values, behaviors, and work-life intersections in ways that are unappealing to girls, women, and many males. Current and upcoming campaigns to create more inspiring messages and accurate occupational portrayals about the meanings and meaningfulness of STEM work and careers would benefit greatly from critique and research by communication scholars well versed in message construction, unintended consequences, and long-term campaigns.

### Technological Perspectives

Careers in STEM disciplines hold distinct and direct relationships with the technologies believed to be germane to those occupations. In the case of computer science and engineering, intimate relationships exist between the technologies and the occupational members' interests, self-efficacy, feelings of belonging, and retention that have both discursive and material consequences. The tools of the trade carry particular connotations about the nature of work which, in turn, frames occupational members' expression and experience. Even when not stated explicitly, such machine-occupation correspondences underlie gendered orientations to STEM work and careers (Faulkner, 2000, 2007; Frehill, 2004). For example, "working with computers," "building bridges," "fixing engines," or "using Bunsen burners" constitute iconic symbols reinforcing the mechanistic and manual nature of such work in a way that backgrounds the intellectual, creative, and interactive dimensions of these disciplines. Technologies influence individual perceptions and constructions of the meaning of STEM work as well as the experience and skill that people bring to such careers.

Activities in school and play shape interest in technologies. Clarke and Teague (1996) demonstrated that boys participated more in computing activities such as clubs and camps than girls and spent more time in programming and gaming activities, experiences that build both intellectual and physical fluency with the tools that one uses in computer science and engineering. Consistent with this research, Margolis and Fisher (2002, 2003) found that girls in the Carnegie Mellon computer science program did not have the same degree of programming experience, or even gaming skill, as their male counterparts, despite similar academic preparation. This lack of technical fluency influenced female confidence as participants in the program as well as their comfort with the culture of play that pervaded and typified these academic environments (Margolis & Fisher, 2003). Enhancing the fluency of young girls can lead to greater comfort and self-efficacy (Bertozzi & Lee, 2007) and shift attitudes toward valuing such work (and play) in occupational and organizational cultures.

Changes in the nature of technologies themselves can also change interest and engagement with the tools and related environments as well as their associated careers. For example, the gap between technology use in girls and boys in the United States has narrowed, primarily due to the increasingly social nature of technologies. In 2000, the number of teenaged girls using the Internet approached that of the boys in most activities and exceeded them in others (Fallows, 2005). Furthermore, young women were actually more likely than young men to be online but participate in different activities: Women were more likely to engage in socially interactive activities underscoring human connections, while men engaged more in instrumental and recreational activities (Fallows, 2005; Kennedy, Wellman, & Klement, 2003). Furthermore, teenage girls were more likely than their male peers to be content creators on the Internet (Lenhard et al., 2007). Thus, as Lenhard et al. detailed, the prevalence of social technologies appears to have increased interest and participation in the Internet and Web-based technologies among teenage girls and young women, which could change the landscape of users and creators of such technologies.

Researchers recognize, however, that the digital divide—a gap between those with access to and fluency with technologies—continues to persist in nations outside of the United States, particularly in non-industrialized countries without digital infrastructures (DiMaggio, Hargittai, Neuman, & Robinson, 2001). The presence of digital infrastructures is a necessary but not sufficient condition for technical efficacy. In a survey of 700 people in Singapore, a country with an extremely high penetration rate of communication technologies, Cheong (2007) found that efficacy rates among women remained quite low, demonstrating the interaction of social and cultural factors in influencing access to and use of technology.

A growing area of research involves how play and gaming technologies can be used to broaden occupational choice, development (Klawe, 2006; Shaffer, 2006a, 2007), and learning (Prensky, 2007). For example, a new genre of gaming and virtual environments called *serious games* (Gee, 2003; Prensky, 2007) employs gaming for non-entertainment goals such as learning, skill training, and decision-making simulations. These approaches tap into the notion that the use of creativity, imagination, and innovative technologies engages the interest of new millennial students (also called *digital natives,* Palfrey & Gasser, 2008) and holds the potential to attract a broader audience to the STEM disciplines and prime their interest in addressing global societal needs. For example, Shaffer uses epistemic games in the development of professional skills, values, and identities in children (Shaffer, 2006b; Svarovsky & Shaffer, 2006) as they role-play the work of particular professions. In the course of simulations requiring problem solving, students learn the skills, knowledge, and values required in certain professions, that is, the epistemology of a profession. In the *Alternate Routes to Technology and Science (ARTS)*[6] program, Shaffer (2005, 2006b) created engaging learning environments that are relevant to students' interests. In the *Digital Zoo* project, students utilize practices of biomechanical engineering to design virtual creatures and learn physics and biology; in *Ecology 2020*, students use geographic information systems to create urban plans, learning about sustainability and urban growth. These processes convey the value, identity, and meaning of such work.

The integration of creativity, art, design, and fun with engineering processes and technological design environments for learning and doing STEM shift the meaning of STEM work away from existing perceptions of such professions as hard, boring, and mechanistic. Such alternate articulations of STEM can communicate and reinforce ties to work and careers that coincide with what young girls value and find meaningful. In parallel with this increase in the design and production of new games-based learning environments, colleges and universities are developing new academic programs in game design and game studies to address growing industry needs and attract broader interest to the computer sciences (Jackson, 2007).

Determining whether such new learning environments influence gender participation and interest in STEM careers, improve fluency, and affect the perceived meaningfulness of such work constitutes an important area for communication research. For example, the influence of these new learning environments as an extension of play, and the structures that underlie the design of such technologies, calls for more extensive research. Opportunities also exist to integrate such efforts with emerging knowledge on media portrayals and message campaigns in order to re-frame the portrayal of STEM work, in collaboration with STEM educators, professionals, and branding experts. These tools pose exciting possibilities for learning. However, while gaming can also expand occupational interest, technical fluency, and skill competency, designers should also ensure that the structure of such games, traditionally gendered and biased toward activities that are attractive to boys and men—competition, war, violence, and misogynist treatments and portrayals of women—do not serve as tools to further hinder participation by girls and women. A considerable body of research has examined the content of games (Sherry, 2001; Lucas & Sherry, 2004), particularly their trends toward violence and gender-related play preferences (Bertozzi & Lee, 2007), but few have examined the context and structure of games (with the notable exception of Shaffer (see 2005, 2006a,

2006b) or the ambient and discrete career messages (and absences) inherent in such technology designs.

Taylor (2003) found that gender comprises a significant contributor to understanding how gamers approach play and the creation and use of avatars in online gaming, and Consalvo (2004, 2006) described the continuing gendered assumptions that drive the development of new technologies in the games industry[7] (see also Cassell & Jenkins, 2000). Furthermore, Soukup (2007) noted that many digital games are gendered at the structural level of game design and include their assumptions of what elements of play are attractive. The gendered structures of game design suggest the presence of gendered Discourses and messages as well, and additional examination of the messages present and absent in games is necessary to avoid further disadvantaging women considering STEM careers (Kafai, Heeter, Denner, & Sun, 2008). As Jackson (2007) observed, researchers must "consider and critique not only the content of games (which are often violent and sometimes misogynistic), but also the gendered qualities of those things that might be taken for granted (and therefore invisible) in the deeper structure underlying game play" (p. 151).

Social constructionists of technology remind researchers that technologies stem from the societies and members who create them (see Flanagin & Waldeck, 2004; Jackson, Poole, & Kuhn, 2002; Pinch & Bijker, 1984). Technologies are gendered (Wajcman, 1991), and the creation of technologies has generally been considered to be a masculine job, while the consumption of technologies has been rendered either feminine or masculine (Consalvo, 2006; Wajcman, 1991). One of the most powerful reasons to be concerned with fewer women in the fields of engineering and computer science involves realizing the implications of their absence as designers of the ubiquitous technologies that pervade our everyday lives (Eriksson-Zetterquist, 2007; Latour & Woolgar, 1979; Margolis & Fisher, 2002). When, as Margolis and Fisher asserted, "boys invent things and girls use the things boys invent" (p. 5), the consequences extend not only to the technologies being designed but also to the messages created and implied by those technologies.

The construction of technologies and their associated STEM professions intersects with the resulting artifacts, products, and the knowledge as well as the identities of those creators and producers. Scholars have suggested that decoupling the identities of computer science and engineering professionals from the knowledge that is created and produced in such programs and careers holds promise for changing the value and meaning of such work for young women (Leonardi, Jackson, & Diwan, in press; Putnam et al., 2009). Because some young women hesitate to adopt the identities typically associated with STEM professionals, yet embrace the knowledge and preparation, decoupling one from the other holds promise as another form of rearticulating STEM careers. Putnam et al. suggested alternative educational paths toward STEM careers, such as through industrial and architectural design, in which the artifacts and knowledge are similar, but the identities differ.

Furthermore, technology intersects not only with gender identities but also socio-cultural and economic factors. Kennedy et al. (2003) acknowledged that, as industrialized societies moved from the production of things to the production of knowledge and discourse, gender roles (on the Internet and beyond) were also affected, with both material and discursive consequences. For example, the globalization of technological product manufacturing and the outsourcing of customer service industries have changed the locus of work so that women in developing countries now possess breadwinning status and power that previously resided with men in industrialized countries (Eriksson-Zetterquist, 2007). Coupled with this shift comes a re-valuing of meaningful work in these societies as work that empowers women in material and discursive ways.

In a fascinating account of how technology empowers women in STEM careers in other cultural contexts, M. Anderson and Shrum (2007) interviewed female scientists in India. While women in India have been encouraged to pursue STEM careers (Subrahmanyan, 1998), the social and cultural norms of their country continue to limit their mobility in terms of social interaction with men outside of their family. The introduction of communication technologies (such as cell phones and the Internet) provide a way for women to circumvent cultural restrictions, empowering them with greater access to knowledge and professional networks while still respecting the norms of their culture. Thus, participation in workforce economies and societies changes the socio-political and socio-economic elements in which STEM work is embedded.

Similarly, the factors that allow women to participate through virtual or distance work may provide both challenges and opportunities in STEM work. Organizations tend to privilege physical proximity in terms of influence and promotions (Hylmö, 2004); virtual or distance employees receive fewer promotions and pay increases than comparable physically co-located employees, and may face challenges in organizational assimilation and socialization (Gibbs, Nekrassova, Grushina, & Wahab, 2008; Picherit-Duthler, Long, & Kohut, 2004; Waldeck & Myers, 2007). However, distributed and distance work (Hinds & Kiesler, 2002) can facilitate work-family balance (Hylmö, 2004) as well as foster relations among virtual team members (Gibbs et al., 2008; Leonardi, Jackson, & Marsh, 2004). The strategic use of distance work and virtual organizing may change the value and meaning that such work holds for women and provide opportunities to re-examine assumptions and ideas held about work and organizing in fixed contexts (Marsh, 2006).

Thus, engineering's prominence in shaping the artifacts and technologies of the industrial age, and both engineering and computer science's prominence in shaping the artifacts and technologies of the information age, suggest underlying meanings and messages within the tools and technologies themselves. These meanings hold implications for understanding valued and meaningful STEM work and careers as well as grasping the underlying assumptions of the systems, products, and tools designed (or, pointedly, *not* designed) in our 21st century society.

*Socio-Cultural Perspectives*

The examination of STEM careers from class and cultural perspectives provides insights into how careers are constructed differently by classes and cultures (Lucas, 2006; Weinger, 1998; Willis, 1977). Class[8] may constrain STEM career opportunities through omissions. According to Lucas, the absence of specific message types and content may be as significant as the presence of others. Additionally, ambient messages may influence as much as discrete ones. For example, Lucas explained that intergenerational Discourses and discourses in a blue-collar community undergoing deindustrialization are complicated and ambiguous as the children of working-class mining families are forced to transition to careers in an information economy. According to Lucas, with transition periods and "no footsteps to follow" (p. 6), difficulties occur in legacy careers, but opportunities arise for STEM membership. These multiple and intersecting social and cultural discourses produce discursive and material opportunities and constraints on individuals' and group members' consideration and pursuit of careers in STEM fields.

Research on African American socialization practices indicate that parents and members of extended kin relationships promote autonomy and close familial relationships at early ages (Bell & Nkomo, 2001; Suizzo, Robinson, & Pahlke, 2008), socializing young children into expectations of educational achievement within the context of ancestral struggles. As Suizzo et al. argued, these messages reflect a "broader cultural value among African Americans, regardless of class" (p. 308). Parents in middle-class African American families recall direct messages as children of working-class parents that emphasized the value of educational achievement. Early and continued socialization into hard work, development of human capital, and attainment may be more manifest in certain groups, but it remains part of continuities across time and location of American work ethics (Bernstein, 1997).

Economic Discourses play a prominent role in socio-cultural perspectives of class. As corporations become the dominant organizations in contemporary society, embedded values regarding meaningful work align with money, accountability, return on investment, financial sustainability, efficiency, and cost/benefit analyses. Some may question the economic imperatives which appear to change institutional structures and processes (Herrmann, 2007). Herrmann argues that Economic Discourses pay insufficient attention to the specific contexts in which discourses can assist in (re)defining meaningful actions. In terms of meaningful work, individuals reference Economic Discourses in their everyday negotiations, such as: when parents decide who engages in paid labor and who becomes a stay-at-home parent, or when individuals decide to engage in wage work to give their offspring the benefits of travel, private education, and extracurricular training that can foreshadow their adult work or enable them to move from one occupational category to another in insecure economic times. For example, individuals frequently select STEM careers for the economic benefits provided by such professions and that parents identify as sources of future economic security for their children (NAE, 2008).

Economic Discourses, as well as models of social and human capital, still play into discursive equations that education, hard work, and networking yield "good" jobs and entitlements to the good life. In other words, investment into economic indicators equates with positive career outcomes and meaningful work. Such investment constitutes a motivating force, a hope for the future, a hedge against insecurity, and a powerful Discourse that joins with survival of the fittest and individualistic values. Economic Discourses do not simply communicate that work is meaningful because it pays for life's necessities or the extra things that make life enjoyable (Ciulla, 2000); instead, they pervade everyday conversations in subtle ways, negotiated with an eye toward material realities. Today, the Discourse of career passion can supersede money, status, and even class. Those in elite classes prioritize "following your bliss" more than money, which is simply assumed to follow from passion-driven work (Collingwood, 2001).

In addition to classed constructions of work, the cultural environment exerts a significant influence on the construction of meaningful work and occupational choice. International research indicates significant differences in how families, schools, educational institutions, and national socio-political climates portray work in science and engineering which shapes the meaning and value placed on educational and occupational choices (Galpin, 2002; Lagesen, 2005). For example, in the country of Mauritius, girls are just as likely as boys to select academic majors in computer science careers (Adams et al., 2003); and, compared to those in Norway, girls in Malaysia consider computing to be *cool* and a desirable career choice (Jumnongjit, 2007; Lagesen, 2005).

These cultural influences affect academic aptitude as well. Guiso, Monte, Sapienza, and Zingales (2008) analyzed test[9] scores in mathematics and reading for 15-year-old students across 40 countries. Categorizing the countries according to their gender equality using economic, political, educational, and general well-being indices, they found that the gap in mathematics ability was higher in countries with a low gender equality index and disappeared in those countries considered to be gender-equal, suggesting that the gender gap in math ability is culturally influenced.

Across countries and cultures, research on gendered disparity in science, technology, and engineering careers includes substantial discussion about the impact of culture on perceptions of and involvement in these fields (Crump, Logan, & McIlroy, 2007; Gupta & Sharma, 2002). The assumption that individuals have the ability to choose careers may not be prevalent in non-Western cultures where responsibility to one's family, community, and culture are more dominant factors of influence. For example, like women in India, Jorgenson (Jorgenson & Wang, 2008) asserted that women in China may not have the same presumption of individual agency in occupational choice. At the same time, paradoxically, Pinker (2008) demonstrated that, in cultures where choice is more prevalent, the gender gap among STEM professionals may actually be more pronounced. Assessing the prevalence of women in physics professions, Pinker found that, in countries (such as the United States, Norway, Switzerland, Canada, and the United Kingdom) with better financial stability and legal support for job choice, the gender split is higher than in countries (such as the Philippines, Thailand, and Russia) with less support for occupational choice. For example, roughly 30 to 35% of physicists are women in these less supportive countries, compared to 5% in more supportive countries (Canada, Japan, Germany). This research highlights the complexity of intersections of socio-political, economic, and cultural influences in occupational choice of STEM careers and the continuing opportunities to examine the discourses that influence such choice. In ongoing research, we are analyzing the work and career socialization messages received by children in kindergarten through fourth grade in three countries, comparing the United States, Belgium, and China. In this project, we are examining potential differences in both micro- and macro-level discourses received by very young children in diverse cultures (Kisselburgh, Berkelaar, & Buzzanell, 2008).

These cultural discourses of meaningful work deserve greater research attention. Cultural perspectives also yield important insights as the practice of engineering and other STEM careers becomes increasingly global and multicultural, and internationalization essential to economic success (Kumar, Ochieng, & Oyango, 2004). Evetts and Buchner-Jeziorska (2001) argued that professional knowledge (i.e., transmitted through language) is moving beyond national borders as professional associations discuss standards with growing international professional bodies. The internationalization of all professions, not simply science, technology, and engineering professions, makes discourse about these professions relevant to a broad, interconnected community.

## Organizational Perspectives

In this section, we focus on organizational (and occupational) culture literature and career discourses. First, in offering a communicative view of organizational culture, Eisenberg and Riley (2001) defined it as a process that "consists solely of patterns of human action and its recursive behaviors (including talk and its symbolic residues) and meaning" (p. 292). While they encouraged a focus on organizing rather than organizations, given the boundarylessness of organizations (Arthur & Rousseau, 1996), in this chapter, we focus on the culture of specific organizations as well as organizing processes of STEM organizations and occupations. First, we provide an overview of engineering culture, and then, we share a critique of its premises and findings with regard to the meanings and gendering of STEM work.

Classic work on engineering culture (Kondo, 1990; Kunda, 1993; Kvande, 1999; see also Collins, 2003; Kuhn & Nelson, 2002; Leonardi, 2003), suggests that engineering cultures are often organizational manifestations of the stereotypes and typified professional identities of engineers and engineering, implying underlying and broader values of what it means to be a successful engineer. Margolis and Fisher (2003) assessed the culture of CMU's computer science program where students described peers as someone who is "in love with computers, myopically focused on them to the neglect of all else, living and breathing the world of computing" (p. 17). While many of the females in the program denied fitting this profile, the discrepancy between self-identity and the perceived identity of their (mostly male) peers contributed most to their questioning whether they belonged in the field: "I don't seem to love it as much as the men, and therefore I don't belong" (p. 18). Male-dominated cultures persist into organizations as well, and Hewlett and colleagues (2008) identified the pervasiveness of such cultures as the primary reason that 50% of women leave STEM careers after 10 or 15 years. Belkin (2008) asserted:

> Engineers have their "hard hat culture," while biological and chemical scientists find themselves in the "lab coat culture" and computer experts inhabit a "geek culture." What they all have in common is that they are at best "unsupportive and at worst downright hostile to women." (p. 1; see also Hewlett et al., 2008)

The discourses within an organization help shape the culture in ways that reinforce or (re)construct the gendered notions of careers. Ruiz Ben's (2007) research on employees in the software industry in Germany suggests that women talk differently about technology than men and are less arbitrary in their use of technological terminology. Similarly, Peterson (2007) examined the talk of male versus female workers in a Swedish IT firm and found that "male colleagues 'talk more about how competent they are' while [females] preferred to 'tone [their] competence down'" (p. 344). Further examinations of the discourse—or *talk-in-practice*—could provide insight into how different framing strategies and discursive resources shape career meanings and opportunities for different groups (see related work by Drew & Heritage, 1992).

Peterson (2007) also noted the *"feminization* of IT work" (p. 334), discussing how the meaning of valuable work within the Swedish IT sector has been reconstructed in the past decade to re-value and redefine social competence as a masculine quality of "aggression, instrumental, rationalized, competitive" more typically found in men (p. 345). As a result, the roles of women in the firm were (re)constructed according to new norms of value and prestige. Peterson determined clear gendering in the discursive labeling of work. According to Peterson, "Senior developers, systems analysts and systems architects...are male dominated. It is technology. The rest: design, interface profiling and application architects.... In these softer kinds of work, such as design, the majority are women" (p. 339). Thus, the meaning of valuable work was gendered even within the IT firm, depreciating the "softer" fields of work and contrasting them with "real" technology work. Interestingly, the male-dominated areas, such as systems architecture, involve working closer to the machine, while the female-dominated areas (such as design, user interface, and higher-level applications work) involve working closer to the people. In other words, the greater the interface with people rather than machine, the greater the emphasis on the aesthetic versus the manual, the "softer" (less valuable, and less masculine) or more feminized the work, participants tend to more readily perceive and configure the occupation (even STEM occupations) as sex segregated (see also Blackburn & Jarman, 2006).

These gendered dualisms of different aspects of STEM practice are evident in notions of teamwork and collaboration as well. Although organizations herald teamwork and collaboration as valuable for contemporary STEM practices, particularly in engineering (see Accreditation Board for Engineering and Technology [ABET], 2007), Discourses of individualism and individual achievement or skill persist. When incorporated into everyday discourses, an imbalanced dualistic tension emerges—they contrast teamwork with more valued technical skill as a necessary but less important component of professional practice (Faulkner, 2000).

Thus, an organizational lens presents either a singular organizational culture centered on engineering values, or a culture that is adversarial in nature, where members delineate subcultures by gender or some other point of difference (e.g., creators or users of technologies or particular computer systems, or soft versus real work; see W. Anderson & Buzzanell, 2007). Studies rarely reveal the complex and fragmented nature of organizational and occupational cultures in STEM (Martin, 1992). Without exposing the nuances and contradictions inherent in the discourses about and the tasks and tools of STEM work, predominant images and Discourses of masculinity and exclusion persist.

An organizational perspective also encourages researchers to examine not only how STEM work and careers might better be portrayed, but also how the meaning and organization of STEM (and other fields) might be changed to better accommodate the values of women. For example, Rosser (2004) told the story of a female computer scientist who discovered that her desires for broad life experiences conflicted with the views of her male peers, who perceived computing as both work and a "relaxing hobby" and where "respect is conferred upon those who possess knowledge obtained primarily through countless hours investigating the nuances of hardware and operating systems" (p. xxiii).

At its core, this restructuring of organizations and organizational values fundamentally involves discursive practices and incorporation of alternative values and work accomplishment strategies (Buzzanell, 1995). According to Buzzanell, numerical goals for enhancing equity of representation may be necessary, but they are not sufficient. Broader awareness and appreciation of the different values and patterns of thinking embedded in Discourses and interaction (discourse) that affect the construction, validation, gendered composition, and meaning of certain professions is required. For example, research suggests that in countries where the representation of women within STEM careers is more balanced, members link the value of STEM careers more to cultural values and gender roles and identities (e.g., being a good wife and daughter)

(M. Anderson & Shrum, 2007; Gupta & Sharma, 2002; Subrahmanyan, 1998), and the fulfillment of traditional gender roles (e.g., wife and mother) as well as career roles is enabled by social policies and structures (Oldenziel, Canel, & Zachmann, 2000; Zachmann, 2000). These values, however, can conflict with one another as in the case of Chinese American mothers in IT fields who must adopt assertive interpersonal styles in order to defend their work flexibility, which contrasts with their cultural norms (Jorgenson & Wang, 2008).

Young women are less likely to study and choose such careers, but, perhaps even more striking, a significant number of women leave STEM careers early. Hewlett et al. (2008) completed a large-scale study of women in STEM careers, finding that, although 41% of entry-level STEM professionals are women, nearly 55% of these women leave their careers roughly 10 years after beginning, what the researchers called a "key moment" (p. 23). As reasons for this exodus, the women mentioned (a) hostile work climates amidst heavily macho cultures; (b) feelings of isolation; and (c) a disconnect between preferred work rhythms and those rewarded in high-risk, fast turnaround occupations. These results coincide with other research in information technology (IT) work (Major, Davis, Sanchez-Hucles, Downey, & Germano, 2007), where the perceived incompatibility of occupational cultures (e.g., long hours, continual need to stay current with technologies, late nights, and on-call duty) and women's responsibilities as mothers result in turnover (Allen et al., 2006), regardless of whether official policies of flexible or non-standard work arrangements existed (Armstrong, Riemenschneider, Allen, & Reid, 2007). These findings are not organization or culture specific. Indeed, in countries that experience underrepresentation of women, engineering and technology careers are perceived as entailing long, unrelenting hours, with no time for a personal or family life (Sumner, 2008), countering the values that many women hold or that Discourses assert.

An organizational or occupational cultural lens aligned with fragmentation, ambiguities, and multiple realities (see Martin, 1992) offers opportunities to explore how particular discourses about career, meaningfulness of work, and quality of life intersect. For example, because women place a higher value on having a *multifaceted* life (Eccles, 1994; Mainiero & Sullivan, 2005), they are more concerned about selecting occupations that demand the whole of their life. Thus, the perception of the single-minded absorption of computing careers may be less attractive to women and to people of different racial, ethnic, religious, or national backgrounds who desire participation in community (Bell & Nkomo, 2001; Buzzanell & Lucas, 2006). Ironically, computing and other STEM careers may also be perceived as attractive because some women value flexibility and mobility, where work can be done in multiple sites, through virtual and distributed work (Crider & Ganesh, 2004; Gibbs et al., 2008; Hinds & Kiesler, 2002; Hylmö, 2004; Leonardi et al., 2004; Marsh, 2006; Picherit-Duthler et al., 2004), and at different temporal rhythms (Ballard & Gossett, 2006).

The organizational/occupational approach in an organizational perspective opens up discussions about specific organizational practices, occupational cultures, and work-life issues that other lenses consider but do not see as central to the meaning and meaningfulness of STEM work and careers. Understanding how to discursively reframe STEM careers and their associated environments to accommodate work-family and work-life demands offers a challenge to current organizational and family communication studies (Golden, Kirby, & Jorgenson, 2006). Current research on work-life Discourse suggests that the presence of policies is not sufficient for accomplishment of work-life goals, since discursive constructions discouraging their use tend to maintain the status quo even as the presence of official texts suggest their possibilities for work-life balance (Buzzanell & Liu, 2005; Fogg, 2003; Kirby, 2000; Kirby, Golden, Medved, Jorgenson, & Buzzanell, 2003; Kirby & Krone, 2002). Empowering women to take advantage of these work-life policies requires occupational and cultural change as well as acknowledgment of the varied structures and discursive positionings in which careers take place (Buzzanell & Lucas, 2006; Jorgenson, 2002).

Second, the d/Discourses of career and their association with the meaning and meaningfulness of STEM work deserves note. When status, power, compensation and benefits, and perceived competence are defined by a linear career track with few, if any, interruptions, and when the work requires continual monitoring for technological changes, members establish expectations and Discourses for appropriate forms of occupational membership and work. As such, the rapid change of technological and knowledge skills inherent in STEM careers complicates the issue of work-family balance, where taking a mid-career break makes reentry into the field problematic because of potential skill decay. The most common metaphor used in discussing STEM careers is the *pipeline* (or even the *leaky pipeline*), which suggests and constrains career trajectories as linear and hierarchical, a pattern typical for traditional middle-class White males but not for lower income, minority, or female members (Buzzanell & Goldzwig, 1991). Alternative career movement metaphors include "slow burn/ apprenticeship," "multi-faceted life-stage responsive," "Web," and multi-channel careers in which women and men enter full-fledged career commitments later in life or alternate technical or managerial and family work according to life phases. These metaphors promote non-linear career forms that emphasize personal choice, knowledge, and development (Bailyn, 1989, 2004; Buzzanell & Goldzwig, 1991; Buzzanell & Lucas, 2006; Helgeson, 1990). Reconceptualizing the metaphor of the ideal STEM career to allow for non-linear and other alternative career models could permit potential employees to align careers with more realistic gendered career experiences and facilitate reentry and skill maintenance even with sabbaticals or parental leaves. Looking at issues of work-family or work-life through the lens of STEM careers encourages communication scholars to recognize even greater complexities in proposed problems and solutions.

## Reimagining Science, Technology, and Engineering Work and Careers

A discursive lens on the meaning of work in science, technology, and engineering and associated messages provides insights to the nature, portrayal, and material aspects of college majors, work, and careers in these areas across the globe. Throughout this chapter, we have drawn from communication scholarship including family, lifespan, instructional, media, communication technologies, cultural, feminist, rhetorical, and organizational as well as relevant literature from interdisciplinary scholars to address the underrepresentation of women in STEM careers. We sought to provide a comprehensive review of the multidisciplinary literature on gender and STEM careers and to rearticulate this literature from communicative perspectives on meaningful work. Thus, this chapter establishes a foundation that intersects work, gender, and technology, providing a springboard for further collaborations between scholars in the communication and STEM disciplines, as well as STEM practitioners.

In framing this piece around d/Discourse, gender, and career, we implicitly acknowledge the underlying tensions of power implicit in this orientation and embrace the transformative opportunities for rearticulating both the meaning and dynamics of STEM work in global contexts (Mumby, 2005). Specifically, in uncovering and acknowledging the incongruities and ambiguities in the d/Discourses of STEM careers, we envision power as discursive, relational, institutionalized, and embedded in the very core of institutions and careers.

By acknowledging d/Discourse and power, we affirm opportunities for resistance. In this chapter, we have discussed both meaningful work as well as occupational identities as sites of resistance (Ashcraft, 2005, 2006)—contesting the nature of work and the meaning of STEM work, challenging it and opening it up for alternative discourses and images, practices in collaboration and culture, and values of meaningful work (e.g., work that is meaningful to community, environment, and global enterprises; see Waugh, 2001). In addition to examining women who leave such occupations as forms of resistance (Allen et al., 2006; Hewlett et al., 2008), we can explore the everyday resistance that women perform during the course of STEM work, including the mundane processes and dialectics (Fleming & Spicer, 2008; Mumby 2005), and the covert and overt practices (Gabriel, 2008) that members perform within specific cultural and socio-political contexts and as they negotiate identities (Jorgenson, 2002) within such careers.

Furthermore, by framing this chapter around d/Discourse, we argue that the capacities to understand and acknowledge the power relations and struggles, and transform everyday life and institutions are embedded within communication. Specifically, by focusing on the layers and interdependencies embedded within talk-in-interaction, linguistic choices, and cultural Discourses or formations, we gain understanding not only about how power is used in productive ways, but also how it can be used to transform micropractices and macrostructures through attention to the unfolding of talk—whether in developmental, educational, media, technological, socio-cultural, or organizational perspectives—providing a holistic and communication-centered view of gender in STEM work. As such, this chapter goes beyond reviewing related literature to advance an argument for how literature from multiple disciplines can be rearticulated through communicative lenses in a way that foregrounds the distinctive contributions that the field of Communication can bring to the conversation about STEM careers.

In summary, then, research on STEM careers offers broad potential for future communication research. We challenge theorists and researchers in communication to become more fully engaged in communication scholarship that can advance understandings of work and related issues in the STEM disciplines. Communication scholars can contribute to an issue highlighted both nationally and internationally, demonstrating theoretical and practical benefits of a communicative approach as well as potential for programmatic funding. For example, NSF has granted significant funding in the past five years under the ADVANCE program for multidisciplinary research that serves to increase the participation of women in academic STEM careers. Additional programs, such as the Broadening Participation in the STEM initiative, provide funding and incentives for including a more representative population in academic research. Other funding agencies, including the National Institute of Health (NIH), support research addressing issues of underrepresentation not only in work but in the knowledge and research that is produced about and for underrepresented populations.

### *Implications*

This chapter engages broad societal imperatives including technological, gender, organizational, and globalization imperatives. First, both local and global societies are becoming more technological. Individuals, organizations, and countries without access to technology, engineering, and scientific discoveries experience clear disadvantages in access to information but also fail to benefit from the economic, social, educational and other opportunities afforded to those with access. At national and international levels the resources of the STEM disciplines, including an educated workforce, serve as critical drivers for economic and social development in the new knowledge economy.

Second, although this chapter examines gender specifically, research suggests that insights gleaned from patterns of difference among one group may be transferable to others. For example, Carnegie Mellon University investigators found that addressing issues that undermined the retention and graduation of women improved the retention and graduation of cultural minority groups and international students as well (Margolis & Fisher, 2002). Third, technology organizations entail the largest growing sector of many economies and some of the fastest growing professions. The continuing development of STEM disciplines depends on individuals' abilities to understand collaboration and teamwork, processes for which communication is inherent and critical.

Finally, ongoing development of global and multicultural economies rests in large part on communication and technological innovation intersections. Frankel's (1993) book, *In Pursuit of Technological Excellence: Engineering Leadership, Technological Change, and Economic Development*, provides one foundation for understanding these imperatives. Jorgenson's (2002) examination of gender and identity negotiations in engineering work shares a communication-oriented view into broader discourses, such as gender, that underlie these societal imperatives.

Generating research that helps us to understand and address the underrepresentation of women in STEM careers constitutes a societal imperative that requires knowledge, inspiration, and collaboration from multiple disciplines both within and outside of communication. These research issues will appeal to communication scholars from a number of disciplines, including family, lifespan, instructional/educational, cultural, media, communication technology, and organizational, as well as the communication of science. The interest in STEM career issues has already launched new research in the communication discipline that considers these questions from the multi-disciplinary communicative perspectives underlying this social issue. This research includes examinations of cross-cultural career stories, media representations, the new educational approaches of game studies, collaborative work experiences of nanotechnology scientists, and transnational work-family issues (Jackson, 2008; Jorgenson & Wang, 2008; Kisselburgh et al., 2008; Mastronardi, 2008; Putnam et al., 2009; Stoltzfus, 2008). These works exemplify the new articulations possible when communication scholars examine the issue of women in STEM careers and illustrate new avenues of research and interventions that can make an important difference in girls' interests and choices about education and careers.

## Conclusion

In the 20th century, our society was framed by scientific discourse and the orientation of rational, industrialized work. The discourse of this era continues to influence significant sectors of our 21st century society including our court systems, academic institutions, and particularly technological organizations. The 21st century society, however, while still linked to scientific-rational discourse, is evolving beyond the mechanistic industrial frameworks that characterized work and organizations in the previous century. Innovation, knowledge, connectivity, and global perspectives are the new discourses of this century. Yet, meaningful work continues to be driven by the discursive formations of the past. Specifically, work in STEM careers is still framed by science and technology discourses that are linked to masculine, mechanistic, and rational understandings of what is valued and meaningful to members of our society.

As communication scholars progress in the new millennium, it is essential that researchers examine other rationalities and cultural formations, particularly the d/Discourses of work that are meaningful and valued for members of our global society. In addition to the d/Discourses of efficiency, production, and construction, d/Discourses of design, creativity, and innovation provide new meanings and appeal to broader segments of our populations. These alternative d/Discourses can coexist with existing d/Discourses, create and sustain dialectic tensions that are absent from current d/Discourses, and provide opportunities for transformation. Through this discursive lens, we both *rearticulate* and *reimagine* the work and careers of science, technology, and engineering, and broaden the meaning of such work to appeal to both men and women across multiple cultures.

## Acknowledgments

The authors express thanks to Christie Beck and to the anonymous reviewers for their many helpful suggestions regarding this chapter. We also thank Rebecca Dohrman for her research assistance during this project.

## Notes

1. Although work is traditionally defined in terms of paid employment, Cheney and colleagues (Cheney et al., 2008; see also Clair, 1996; Medved, this volume) argue for a reconceptualization of work beyond economic contracts to incorporate unpaid employment such as housework, volunteer work, and other forms of hidden labor.
2. Some of the richest reports on institutional level policy and discourse have focused on U.S. STEM concerns (e.g., *The Task Force of the Future of American Innovation*, 2005; *Council on Competitiveness: Innovate America*, 2004; *Tapping America's Potential: The Education for Innovation Initiative*, 2005). Furthermore, a plethora of summits and conferences, including the 1999 UNESCO World Conference on Science, and the 2003 World Summit on the Information Society, encouraged the development and refinement of STEM policies or initiatives at many educational institutions.
3. Traditionally situated within sociological and psychological perspectives, the study of meaningful work is emerging as an area of interest for communication scholars because of the centrality of *meaning* to organizational communication specifically and communication more broadly (Cheney et al., 2008; Kuhn et al., 2008; see also the set of essays in *Management Communication Quarterly*, 2008, volume 22).
4. There are a growing number of exceptions to these television and film narratives, including *The Suite Life of Zach and Cody*, *High School Musical*, and the gender neutral portrayals of females in *Hackers* and *The Matrix*, that suggest a potential shift in portraying and heralding female characters for their intelligence, work ethic, and ambition. Additional research from media scholars is needed to assess whether such counter narratives are exceptions or reflect cultural shifts, and the effect these messages have on occupational identification and identity construction of teenage girls.
5. The term *sexy* is used in this context to denote something that is trendy, attractive, and exciting, rather than something with sexual connotations (*Merriam-Webster Online Dictionary*, 2008).

6. Notice the construction of an acronym decidedly different from what one would expect of a science and technology program. This strategic use conveys an image that attracts new learners to an unexpected environment.
7. There are exceptions, and the work of Sheri Graner Ray (2003) and the NSF-funded Project IT Girl (http://wiki.laptop.org/go/Project_IT_Girl) in Austin, Texas, are exemplars.
8. Although there are multiple definitions of class, in this work we define class according to economic delineations, distinct from cultural delineations of class used in India (Subrahmanyan, 1998).
9. Tests were designed to be free of cultural bias, by the Organisation for Economic Co-operation and Development (OECD).

## References

Accreditation Board for Engineering and Technology. (ABET). (2007–2008). *Criteria for accrediting computer programs*. Baltimore, MD: ABET Computing Accreditation Commission.

Adams, J. C., Bauer, V., & Baichoo, S. (2003). An expanding pipeline: Gender in Mauritius. *ACM SIGCSE Bulletin, 35*, 59–63.

Allen, M., Armstrong, D., Riemenschneider, C., & Reid, M. (2006). Barriers facing women in the IT workforce. *The DATA BASE for Advances in Information Systems, 37* (4), 58–78.

Alvesson, M., & Kärreman, D. (2000). Varieties of discourse: On the study of organizations through discourse analysis. *Human Relations, 52*, 1125–1149.

Anderson, M., & Shrum, W. (2007) Circumvention and social change: ICTs and the discourse of empowerment. *Women's Studies in Communication, 32*, 229–253.

Anderson, W. K. Z., & Buzzanell, P. M. (2007). "Outcast among outcasts": Gender and leadership in a Mac users group. *Women & Language, 30*, 32–45.

Arendt, C., Buzzanell, P. M., Dohrman, R., & Litera, N. (2008, February). *Performing career stories of engineering women*. Performance presented to College of Engineering, Purdue University. West Lafayette, IN.

Armstrong, D., Riemenschneider, C., Allen, M., & Reid, M. (2007). Advancement, voluntary turnover and women in IT: A cognitive study of work–family conflict. *Information and Management, 44*, 142–153.

Arthur, M. B., Inkson, K., & Pringle, J. K. (1999). *The new careers: Individual action and economic change*. London: Sage.

Arthur, M. B., & Rousseau, D. M. (1996). *The boundaryless career: A new employment principle for a new organizational era*. New York: Oxford University Press.

Ashcraft, K. L. (2005). Resistance through consent? Occupational identity, organizational form, and the maintenance of masculinity among commercial airline pilots. *Management Communication Quarterly, 19*, 67–90.

Ashcraft, K. L. (2006). Back to work: Sights/sites of difference in gender and organizational communication studies. In B. Dow & J. T. Wood (Eds.), *The handbook of gender and communication* (pp. 97–122). Newbury Park, CA: Sage.

Bailyn, L. (1989). Understanding individual experience at work: Comments on the theory and practice of careers. In M. B. Arthur, D. T. Hall, & B. S. Lawrence (Eds.), *Handbook of career theory* (pp. 477–489). Cambridge, England: Cambridge University Press.

Bailyn, L. (2004). The Hughes Award: Time in careers—Careers in time. *Human Relations, 57*, 1507–1521.

Ballard, D. I., & Gossett, L. M. (2006). Alternative times: The temporal perceptions, processes, and practices defining the non-standard work relationship. In C. S. Beck (Ed.), *Communication yearbook 31* (pp. 269–316). Mahwah, NJ: Erlbaum.

Banet-Weiser, S. (2004). (Nickelodeon portrayals) Girls rule!: Gender, feminism, and nickelodeon. *Critical Studies in Media Communication, 21,* 119–139.

Bell, E. L. J., & Nkomo, S. M. (2001). *Our separate ways: Black and white women and the struggle for professional identity.* Cambridge, MA: Harvard University Press.

Belkin, L. (2008, May 15). Diversity isn't rocket science, is it? *New York Times.* Retrieved August 31, 2008, from http://www.nytimes.com/2008/05/15/fashion/15WORK.ht ml?ex=1368590400&en=1661297781a958a6&ei=5124&partner=permalink&expr od=permalink

Bennett, J., & Yabroff, J. (2008, June 16). Revenge of the nerdettes. *Newsweek,* pp. 44–45. Retrieved November 7, 2008, from http://www.newsweek.com/id/140457

Bernstein, P. (1997). *American work values: Their origin and development.* Albany: State University of New York Press.

Bertozzi, E., & Lee, S. (2007). Not just fun and games—Digital play, gender and attitudes towards technology. *Women's Studies in Communication, 32,* 179–204.

Blackburn, R. M., & Jarman, J. (2006). Gendered occupations: Exploring the relationship between gender segregation and inequality. *International Sociology, 21,* 289–315.

Bortree, D. S. (2005). Presentation of self on the web: An ethnographic study of teenage girls' weblogs. *Education, Communication & Information, 5*(1), 25–39.

Bryson, B. (2003). *A short history of nearly everything.* New York: Broadway Books.

Business Roundtable. (2005). *Tapping America's potential: The education for innovation initiative.* Retrieved November 8, 2008, from http://www.businessroundtable. org/sites/default/files/2005.07.01TAP_Report.FINAL.pdf

Butler, T., & Waldroop, J. (1999). Job sculpting: The art of retaining your best people. *Harvard Business Review, 77,* 144–152.

Buzzanell, P. M. (1995). Reframing the glass ceiling as a socially constructed process: Implications for understanding and change. *Communication Monographs, 62,* 327–354.

Buzzanell, P. M., & Goldzwig, S. R. (1991). Linear and nonlinear career models: Metaphors, paradigms, and ideologies. *Management Communication Quarterly, 4,* 466–505.

Buzzanell, P. M., & Liu, M. (2005). Struggling with maternity leave policies and practices: A poststructuralist feminist analysis of gendered organizing. *Journal of Applied Communication Research, 33,* 1–25.

Buzzanell, P. M., & Lucas, K. (2006). Gendered stories of career: Unfolding discourses of time, space, and identity. In B. J. Dow & J. T. Wood (Eds.), *The Sage handbook on gender and communication* (pp. 161–178). Thousand Oaks, CA: Sage.

Byrne, S., & Hart, P. S. (this volume). The boomerang effect: A synthesis of findings and a preliminary theoretical framework. In C. S. Beck (Ed.), *Communication yearbook 33* (pp. 3–37). New York: Routledge.

Calabrese Barton, A., & Osborne, M. D. (Eds.). (2001). *Teaching science in diverse settings. Marginalized discourses and classroom practice.* New York: Peter Lang.

Cassell, J., & Jenkins, H. (Eds.). (2000). *From Barbie® to Mortal Kombat: Gender and computer games.* Cambridge, MA: MIT Press.

Cheney, G., Zorn, T. E., Planalp, S., & Lair, D. J. (2008). Meaningful work and personal/social well-being: Organizational communication engages the meanings of work. In C. S. Beck (Ed.), *Communication yearbook 32* (pp. 136–185). New York: Routledge.

Cheong, P. H. (2007). Gender and perceived Internet efficacy: Examining secondary digital divide issues in Singapore. *Women's Studies in Communication, 32,* 205–229.

Ciulla, J. B. (2000). *The working life: The promise and betrayal of modern work.* New York: Random House.

Clair, R. P. (1996). The political nature of the colloquialism, "A real job": Implications for organizational socialization. *Communication Monographs, 63,* 249–267.

Clarke, V. A., & Teague, G. J. (1996). Characterizations of computing careers: Students and professionals disagree. *Computers and Education, 26,* 241–246.

Collingwood, H. (2001). Leadership's first commandment: Know thyself. *Harvard Business Review, 79*(11), 8–8.

Collins, S. T. (2003). Using ethnography to identify cultural domains within a systems engineering organization. *Bulletin of Science, Technology and Society, 23,* 246–255.

Conaway, S. B. (2007). *Girls who (don't) wear glasses: The performativity of smart girls on teen television.* Unpublished doctoral dissertation, Bowling Green State University, Bowling Green, OH.

Congressional Commission on the Advancement of Women and Minorities in Science, Engineering and Technology Development (CAWMSET). (2000). *Land of plenty: Diversity as America's competitive edge in science, engineering and technology.* Retrieved November 20, 2008, from www.nsf.gov/pubs/2000/cawmset0409/cawmset_0409.pdf

Consalvo, M. (2004, May). *The digital games industry: The changing role of women in and behind games.* Paper presented at the annual meeting of Console-ing Passions. New Orleans, LA.

Consalvo, M. (2006). Gender and new media. In B. J. Dow & J. T. Wood (Eds.), *The Sage handbook of gender and communication* (pp. 355–369). Thousand Oaks, CA: Sage.

Council on Competitiveness. (2005). *Innovate America.* National Innovation Initiative Summit and Report. Retrieved November 8, 2008, from http://www.compete.org/images/uploads/File/PDF%20Files/NII_Innovate_America.pdf

Craig, R. T. (2005) How we talk about how we talk: Communication theory in the public interest. *Journal of Communication, 55,* 659–667.

Crider, J. A., & Ganesh, S. (2004). Negotiating meaning in virtual teams: Context, roles, and computer-mediated communication in college classrooms. In S. H. Godar & S. P. Ferris (Eds.), *Virtual and collaborative teams: Process, technologies, and practice* (pp. 133–155). Hershey, PA: Idea Group.

Crump, B. J., Logan, K. A., & McIlroy, A. (2007). Does gender still matter? A study of the views of women in the ICT industry in New Zealand. *Gender, Work and Organization, 14,* 349–370.

DiMaggio, P., Hargittai, E., Neuman, W. R., & Robinson, J. P. (2001). Social implications of the Internet. *Annual Review of Sociology, 27,* 307–336.

Domestic Policy Council. (2006, February) *American competitiveness initiative.* Office of Science and Technology Policy. Retrieved April 16, 2007, from http://www.whitehouse.gov/stateoftheunion/2006/aci/aci06-booklet.pdf

Drew, P., & Heritage, J. (Eds.). (1992). *Talk at work: Interaction in institutional settings.* Cambridge, England: Cambridge University Press.

Eccles, J. S. (1994). Understanding women's educational and occupational choices:

Applying the Eccles et al. model of achievement-related choices. *Psychology of Women Quarterly, 18*, 585–609.

Eccles, J. S. (2006). Where are all the women? Gender differences in participation in physical science and engineering. In S. J. Ceci & W. M. Williams (Eds.), *Why aren't more women in science? Top researchers debate the evidence* (pp. 199–210). Washington, DC: American Psychological Association.

Eisenberg, E. M., & Riley, P. (2001). Organizational culture. In L. L. Putnam & F. M. Jablin (Eds.), *The new handbook of organizational communication: Advances in theory, research, and methods* (pp. 291–322). Thousand Oaks, CA: Sage.

Eriksson-Zetterquist, U. (2007). Editorial: Gender and new technologies. *Gender, Work and Organization, 14*, 305–311.

Etzkowitz, H., Kemelgor, C., & Uzzi, B. (2000). *Athena unbound: The advancement of women in science and technology.* Cambridge, England: Cambridge University Press.

Evetts, J., & Buchner-Jeziorska, A. (2001). The professionalization of knowledge in European markets: Engineering in the UK and Poland. *Current Sociology, 49*, 133–147.

Faber, R. J., Brown, J. D., & McLeod, J. M. (1979). Coming of age in the global village: Television and adolescence. In E. Wartella (Ed.), *Children communicating: Media and the development of thought, speech, understanding* (pp. 215–249). Beverly Hills, CA: Sage.

Fairclough, N. (1992). *Discourse and social change.* Cambridge, England: Polity.

Fairhurst, G. (2007). *Discursive leadership: In conversation with leadership psychology.* Thousand Oaks, CA: Sage.

Fallows, D. (2005). *How women and men use the Internet.* Washington, DC: Pew Internet & American Life Project.

Faulkner, W. (2000). Dualisms, hierarchies and gender in engineering. *Social Studies of Science, 30,* 759–792.

Faulkner, W. (2007). "Nuts and bolts and people": Gender-troubled engineering identities. *Social Studies of Science, 37,* 331–356.

Fels, A. (2004). Do women lack ambition? *Harvard Business Review, 82*(4), 50–60.

Flanagin, A. J., & Waldeck, J. H. (2004) Technology use and organizational newcomer socialization. *Journal of Business Communication, 41*, 137–165.

Fleming, P., & Spicer, A. (2008). Beyond power and resistance: New approaches to organizational politics. *Management Communication Quarterly, 21*, 301–309.

Fogg, P. (2003, June 13). Family time: Why some women quit their coveted tenure-track jobs. *The Chronicle of Higher Education, 49*(40), A10.

Frankel, E. G. (1993). *In pursuit of technological excellence: Engineering leadership, technological change, and economic development.* Westport, CT: Praeger.

Frehill, L. M. (2004). The gendered construction of the engineering profession in the United States, 1893–1920. *Men and Masculinities, 6,* 383–403.

Gabriel, Y. (2008). Spectacles of resistance and resistance of spectacles. *Management Communication Quarterly, 21,* 310–326.

Gallos, J. V. (1989). Exploring women's development: Implications for career theory, practice, and research. In M. B. Arthur, D. T. Hall, & B. S. Lawrence (Eds.), *Handbook of career theory* (pp. 110–132). Cambridge, England: Cambridge University Press.

Galpin, V. (2002). Women in computing around the world. *SIGCSE Bulletin, 34*(2), 94–99.

Galtry, J., & Callister, P. (2005). Assessing the optimal length of parental leave for child and parental well-being: How can research inform policy? *Journal of Family Issues, 26*, 219–246.

Gee, J. P. (2003). *What video games have to teach us about learning and literacy.* New York: Palgrave Macmillan.

Gibbs, J. L., Nekrassova, D., Grushina, S. V., & Wahab, S. A. (2008). Reconceptualizing virtual teaming from a constitutive perspective: Review, redirection, and research agenda. In C. S. Beck (Ed.), *Communication yearbook 32* (pp. 187–230). New York: Routledge.

Gibson, M. K., & Papa, M. J. (2000). The mud, the blood, and the beer guys: Organizational osmosis in blue-collar work groups. *Journal of Applied Communication Research, 28*, 68–88.

Giguette, M. S., Lopez, A. M., & Schulte, L. J. (2006). Perceived social support: Ethnic and gender differences in the computing disciplines. *36th Annual Frontiers in Education Conference Proceedings* (pp. 9–12).

Golden, A. (2000). What we talk about when we talk about work and family: A discourse analysis of parental accounts. *Electronic Journal of Communication, 10*. Retrieved August 27, 2008, from http://www.cios.org/www/ejc/v10n3400.htm

Golden, A. G., Kirby, E. L., & Jorgenson, J. (2006). Work–life research from both sides now: An integrative perspective for organizational and family communication. In C. S. Beck (Ed.), *Communication yearbook 30* (pp. 143–195). Mahwah, NJ: Erlbaum.

Gottfredson, L. S. (1981). Circumscription and compromise: A developmental theory of occupational aspirations. *Journal of Counseling Psychology, 28*, 545–579.

Gottfredson, L. S. (2002). Gottfredson's theory of circumscription, compromise, and self-creation. In D. Brown (Ed.), *Career choice and development* (4th ed., pp. 85–148). San Francisco: Jossey-Bass.

Graner Ray, S. (2003). *Gender inclusive game design: Expanding the market.* Hingham, MA: Charles River Media.

Grant, D. M., Knight, L. V., & Steinbach, T. A. (2007, June). *Informing young women about computer careers: Examining the pervasiveness of the geek image.* Paper presented at the annual meeting of the 2007 Informing Science and IT Education Conference. Ljubljana, Slovenia.

Guiso, L., Monte, F., Sapienza, P., & Zingales, L. (2008). Diversity: Culture, gender, and math. *Science, 320*(5880), 1164–1165. doi: 10.1126/science.1154094.

Gupta, N., & Sharma, A. K. (2002). Women academic scientists in India. *Social Studies of Science, 32*, 901–915.

Hanson, S. L. (2000). Gender, families, and science: Influences on early science training and career choices. *Journal of Women and Minorities in Science and Engineering 6*, 169–187.

Helgeson, S. (1990). *The female advantage: Women's ways of leadership.* New York: Doubleday.

Helwig, A. A. (2004). Gender-role stereotyping: Testing theory with a longitudinal study. *Sex Roles, 38*, 1573–2762.

Herrmann, A. (2007, November). *Economic discourses and meaningful work in academia.* Paper presented at the annual meeting of the National Communication Association, Chicago.

Hewlett, S. A., Luce, C. B., & Servon, L. J. (2008). Stopping the exodus of women in science. *Harvard Business Review, 6*, 22–23.

Hewlett, S. A., Luce, C. B., Servon, L. J., Sherbin, L., Spiller, P., Sosnovich, E., et al.

(2008). *The Athena factor: Reversing the brain drain in science, engineering, and technology* (Harvard Business Review Research Reports, No. 10094). Cambridge, MA: Harvard Business.

Hinds, P., & Kiesler, S. (Eds.). (2002). *Distributed work*. Cambridge, MA: MIT Press.

Hornikx, J., & O'Keefe, D. J. (this volume). Adapting consumer advertising appeals to cultural values: A meta-analytic review of effects on persuasiveness and ad liking. In C. S. Beck (Ed.), *Communication yearbook 33* (pp. 39–71). New York: Routledge.

Hyde, J. S., Lindberg, S. M., Linn, M. C., Ellis, A. B., & Williams, C. C. (2008). Gender similarities characterize math performance. *Science, 321,* 494–495.

Hylmö, A, (2004). Women, men, and changing organizations: An organizational culture examination of the gendered experiences of telecommuting. In P. M. Buzzanell, H. Sterk, & L. H. Turner (Eds.), *Gender in applied communication contexts* (pp. 47–68). Thousand Oaks, CA: Sage.

Hylmö, A. (2006). Girls on film: An examination of gendered vocational socialization messages found in motion pictures targeting teenage girls. *Western Journal of Communication, 70,* 167–185.

International Labour Organization. (2003). *Facts on women at work*. Retrieved November 15, 2007, from http://www.ilo.org/global/About_the_ILO/Media_and_public_ information/Factsheets/lang--en/docName--WCMS_067595/index.htm

Jablin, F. M. (1985). An exploratory study of vocational organizational communication socialization. *Southern Speech Communication Journal, 50,* 261–282.

Jablin, F. M. (2001). Organizational entry, assimilation, and disengagement/exit. In F. Jablin & L. L. Putnam (Eds.), *The new handbook of organizational communication: Advances in theory, research, and methods* (pp. 732–819). Thousand Oaks, CA: Sage.

Jackson, M. H. (2007). Exploring gender, feminism and technology from a communication perspective: An introduction and commentary. *Women's Studies in Communication, 32,* 149–156.

Jackson, M. H. (2008, May). *Designing interaction, building communities: Game Studies as a new entry into STEM disciplines*. Paper presented at the annual meeting of the International Communication Association, Montréal, Canada.

Jackson, M. H., Poole, M. S., & Kuhn, T. (2002). The social construction of technology in studies of the workplace. In L. Lievrouw & S. Livingstone (Eds.), *Handbook of new media: Social shaping and consequences of ICTs* (pp. 236–253). London: Sage.

Jorgenson, J. (2002). Engineering selves: Negotiating gender and identity in technical work. *Management Communication Quarterly, 15,* 350–380.

Jorgenson, J., & Wang, J. (2008, May). *Pursuing engineering careers in transnational worlds: Chinese American women's reflections on their professional journeys*. Paper presented at the annual meeting of the International Communication Association, Montréal, Canada.

Judy, R. W., D'Amico, C., & Geipel, G. L. (1997). *Workforce 2020: Work and workers in the 21st century*. Indianapolis, IN: Hudson Institute.

Jumnongjit, R. (2007, May 23). *Malaysia: Where computing is cool for girls*. Retrieved August 31, 2008, from http://www.scandasia.com/viewNews. php?coun_code=my&news_id=3292

Kafai, Y. B., Heeter, C., Denner, J., & Sun, J. Y. (Eds.). (2008). *Beyond Barbie® and Mortal Kombat: New perspectives on gender and gaming*. Cambridge, MA: MIT Press.

Kennedy, T., Wellman, B., & Klement, K. (2003). Gendering the digital divide. *IT & Society, 1*, 72–96.

Kirby, E. L. (2000). Should I do as you say or do as you do? Mixed messages about work and family. *The Electronic Journal of Communication/Le Review de électronique de Communication, 10* [Online]. Retrieved August 26, 2008, from http://www.cios.org/EJCPUBLIC$$821733280967$$/010/3/010313.html

Kirby, E. L., Golden, A. G., Medved, C. E., Jorgenson, J., & Buzzanell, P. M. (2003). An organizational communication challenge to the discourse of work and family research: From problematics to empowerment. In P. Kalbfleisch (Ed.), *Communication yearbook 27* (pp. 1–44). Mahwah, NJ: Erlbaum.

Kirby, E. L., & Krone, K. J. (2002). The policy exists but you can't really use it": Communication and the structuration of work-family policies. *Journal of Applied Communication Research, 30*, 50–77.

Kisselburgh, L. G., Berkelaar, B. L., & Buzzanell, P. M. (2008, May). *What kids say: Stories about jobs, science, and engineering from China, Belgium, and the United States.* Paper presented at the annual meeting of the International Communication Association, Montréal, Canada.

Klawe, M. M. (2006, February). *Gender, lies and video games: The truth about females and computing.* Presentation given to the Technology and Social Behavior Speaker Series at Northwestern University, Evanston, IL.

Kondo, D. K. (1990). *Crafting selves: Power, gender and discourses of identity in a Japanese workplace.* Chicago: University of Chicago Press.

Kuhn, T., Golden, A., Jorgenson, J., Buzzanell, P. M., Berkelaar, B. L., Kisselburgh, L. G. et al. (2008). Cultural discourses and discursive resources for meaningful work: Constructing and disrupting identities in contemporary capitalism. *Management Communication Quarterly, 22*, 162–171.

Kuhn, T., & Nelson, N. (2002). Reengineering identity: A case study of multiplicity and duality in organizational identification. *Management Communication Quarterly, 16*, 5–38.

Kumar, A., Ochieng, A., & Oyango, M. S. (2004). Engineering education in African universities: A case for internationalization. *Journal of Studies in International Education, 8*, 377–389.

Kunda, G. (1993). *Engineering culture: Control and commitment in a high tech corporation.* Philadelphia: Temple University Press.

Kvande, E. (1999). "In the belly of the beast": Constructing femininities in engineering organizations. *The European Journal of Women's Studies, 6*, 305–328.

Lagesen, V. A. (2005). *Extreme make-over? The making of gender and computer science.* Unpublished doctoral dissertation, The Norwegian University of Science and Technology, Trondheim, Norway.

Latour, B., & Woolgar, S. (1979). *Laboratory life: The social construction of scientific facts.* Thousand Oaks, CA: Sage.

Lenhard, A., Madden, M., Macgill, A. R., & Smith, A. (2007). Teens and social media (December 19, 2007). *Pew Internet and American Life Project.* Retrieved August 26, 2008, from http://www.pewinternet.org/PPF/r/230/report_display.asp

Leonardi, P. M. (2003). *The mythos of engineering culture: A study of communicative performance and interaction.* Unpublished master's thesis, University of Colorado, Boulder.

Leonardi, P. M., Jackson, M. H., & Diwan, A. (in press). The enactment-externalization dialectic: Rationalization and the persistence of counter-productive technology design practices in student engineering. *Academy of Management Journal.* Accessed July 30, 2008, from http://www.soc.northwestern.edu/leonardi/enactment.pdf

Leonardi, P. M., Jackson, M., & Marsh, N. (2004). The strategic use of "distance" among virtual team members: A multi-dimensional communication model. In S. H. Godar & S. P. Ferris (Eds.), *Virtual and collaborative teams: Process, technologies, and practice* (pp. 156–173). Hershey, PA: Idea Group.

Levine, K., & Hoffner, C. (2006). Adolescents' conceptions of work: What is learned from different sources during anticipatory socialization? *Journal of Adolescent Research, 21,* 647–669.

Li, J. (2001). Expectations of Chinese immigrant parents for their children's education: The interplay of Chinese tradition and the Canadian context. *Canadian Journal of Education, 26,* 477–494.

Liu, F. (2006). Boys as only-children and girls as only-children—Parental gendered expectations of the only-child in the nuclear Chinese family in present-day China. *Gender and Education, 18,* 491–505.

Lopez, A. M., Jr., & Schulte, L. (2002). African American women in the computing sciences: A group to be studied. *SIGCSE Bulletin, 34*(1), 87–90.

Lubinski, D., & Benbow, C. P. (2006). Study of mathematically precocious youth (SMPY) after 35 years: Uncovering antecedents for the development of math-science expertise. *Perspectives on Psychological Science, 1,* 316–343.

Lucas, K. (2006). *No footsteps to follow: How blue-collar kids navigate postindustrial careers.* Unpublished doctoral dissertation, Purdue University, West Lafayette, IN.

Lucas, K., Liu, M., & Buzzanell, P. M. (2006). No limits careers: A critical examination of career discourse in the U.S. and China. In M. Orbe, B. J. Allen, & L. A. Flores (Eds.), *The same and different: Acknowledging diversity within and between cultural groups. International and intercultural communication annual 28* (pp. 217–242). Thousand Oaks, CA: Sage.

Lucas, K., & Sherry, J. (2004). Sex differences in video game play: A communication-based explanation. *Communication Research, 31,* 499–523.

Lytton, H., & Romney, D. M. (1991). Parents' differential socialization of boys and girls: A meta-analysis. *Psychological Bulletin, 109,* 267–296.

Mainiero, L. A., & Sullivan, S. E. (2005). Kaleidoscope careers: An alternate explanation for the "opt-out" revolution. *Academy of Management Executive, 19*(1), 106–123.

Major, D. A., Davis, D. D., Sanchez-Hucles, J., Downey, H. J., & Germano, L. M. (2007). Myths and realities in the IT workplace: Gender differences and similarities in climate perception. In R. J. Burke & M. C. Mattis (Eds.), *Women and minorities in science, technology, engineering, and mathematics: Upping the numbers* (pp. 71–90). Cheltenham, England: Edward Elgar.

Margolis, J., & Fisher, A. (2002). *Unlocking the clubhouse: Women in computing.* Cambridge, MA: MIT Press.

Margolis, J., & Fisher, A. (2003). Geek mythology. *Bulletin of Science, Technology, and Society, 23*(1), 17–20.

Marsh, N. N. (2006). *Reconsidering the conceptual relationship between organizations and technology: Engineering task force as a virtual organization.* Unpublished doctoral dissertation, University of Colorado, Boulder.

Martin, J. (1992). *Cultures in organizations: Three perspectives.* New York: Oxford University Press.

Mastronardi, M. (2008, May). *Girls, "intrinsic aptitude" and the Harvard president: A tale of science and patriarchy*. Paper presented at the annual meeting of the International Communication Association, Montréal, Canada.

Mazzarella, S. R. (2005). Introduction: It's a girl wide web. In S. R. Mazzarella (Ed.), *Girl Wide Web: Girls, the Internet, and the negotiation of identity* (pp. 1–12). New York: Peter Lang.

Medved, C. (this volume). Crossing and transforming occupational and household gendered divisions of labor: Reviewing literatures and deconstructing differences. In C. S. Beck (Ed.), *Communication yearbook 33* (pp. 301–341). New York: Routledge.

Merriam-Webster Online Dictionary. (2008). Definition of *sexy*. Retrieved August 27, 2008, from http://www.merriam-webster.com/dictionary/sexy

Metz, S. S. (2007). Attracting the engineers of 2020 today. In R. J. Burke & M. C. Mattis (Eds.), *Women and minorities in science, technology, engineering, and mathematics: Upping the numbers* (pp. 184–209). Cheltenham, England: Edward Elgar.

Mukhopadhyay, C. C., & Seymour, S. (Eds.). (1994). *Women, education, and family structure in India*. San Francisco: Westview Press.

Mumby, D. (2005). Theorizing resistance in organization studies: A dialectical approach. *Management Communication Quarterly, 19*, 19–45.

Museum of Science. (2007). *Engineering is elementary*. Retrieved November 15, 2007, from http://www.mos.org/eie/

National Academy of Engineering (NAE). (2002). *Technically speaking: Why all Americans need to know more about technology*. Washington, DC: National Academies Press.

National Academy of Engineering (NAE). (2008). *Changing the conversation: Messages for improving public understanding of engineering*. Washington, DC: National Academies Press.

National Academy of Sciences (NAS). (2007). *Rising above the gathering storm: Energizing and employing America for a brighter economic future*. Washington, DC: National Academies Press.

National Science Foundation. (2004). *Women, minorities, and persons with disabilities in science and engineering: 2004*. Retrieved April 11, 2007, from http://www.nsf.gov/statistics/wmpd/pdf/tabh-6.pdf

National Science Foundation (NSF). (2005). *Extraordinary Women Engineers final report*. Retrieved April 11, 2007, from http://www.eweek.org/site/news/Eweek/EWE_Needs_Asses.pdf

National Science Foundation (NSF). (2006). Survey of graduate students and post-doctorates in science and engineering. Division of Science Resources Statistics. Retrieved September 1, 2008, from http://www.nsf.gov/statistics/nsf08306/

Newitz, A., & Anders, C. (Eds.). (2006). *She's such a geek: Women write about science, technology, and other nerdy stuff*. Emeryville, CA: Seal Press.

Newman, K. (2000). *No shame on my game*. New York: The Russell Sage Foundation

Noar, S. M., Harrington, N. G., & Aldrich, R. S. (this volume), The role of message tailoring in the development of persuasive health communication messages. In C. S. Beck (Ed.), *Communication yearbook 33* (pp. 73–133). New York: Routledge.

Nussbaum, J. F. (2007). Life span communication and quality of life. *Journal of Communication, 57*, 1–7.

Oldenziel, R. (2000). Multiple-entry visas: Gender and engineering in the U.S., 1870–1945. In A. Canel, R. Oldenziel, & K. Zachmann. (Eds.), *Crossing boundaries, building bridges. Comparing the history of women engineers, 1870s–1990s* (pp. 11–50). Amsterdam: Harwood Academic.

Oldenziel, R., Canel, A., & Zachmann, K. (2000). Introduction. In A. Canel, R. Old-enziel, & K. Zachmann (Eds.), *Crossing boundaries, building bridges: Comparing the history of women engineers, 1870s–1900s* (pp. 1–10). Amsterdam: Harwood Academic.

Pal, M., & Buzzanell, P. M. (2008). The Indian call center experience: A case study in changing discourses of identity, identification, and career in a global context. *Journal of Business Communication, 45*, 31–60.

Palfrey, J., & Gasser, U. (2008). *Born digital: Connecting with a global generation of digital natives.* New York: Basic Civitas Books.

Pawley, A. (2008, June 16). June 16 Newsweek musings. Blog posted to *Sciencewomen* blog. Retrieved August 27, 2008, from http://scienceblogs.com/sciencewoman/2008/06/june_16_newsweek_musings.php?utm_source=sbhomepage&utm_medium=link&utm_content=channellink

Pecchioni, L. L., Wright, K. B., & Nussbaum, J. F. (2005). *Life-span communication.* Mahwah, NJ: Erlbaum.

Peterson, H. (2007). Gendered work ideals in Swedish IT firms: Valued and not valued workers. *Gender, Work and Organization, 14*, 333–348.

Phillips, L. (2005). *Despite gains, adolescent girls lag on health, safety, other measures.* New York: National Council for Research on Women. Retrieved March 30, 2008, from http://www.ncrw.org/research/grptpres.htm

Phipps, A. (2008). *Women in science, engineering and technology: Three decades of UK initiatives.* Stoke on Trent, England: Trentham Books.

Picherit-Duthler, G., Long, S. D., & Kohut, G. F. (2004). Newcomer assimilation in virtual team socialization. In S. H. Godar & S. P. Ferris (Eds.), *Virtual and collaborative teams: Process, technologies, and practice* (pp. 133–155). Hershey, PA: Idea Group.

Pinch, T. J., & Bijker, W. E. (1984). The social construction of facts and artifacts: Or how the sociology of science and the sociology of technology might benefit each other. *Social Studies of Science, 14*, 399–441.

Pinker, S. (2008). *The sexual paradox: Extreme men, gifted women, and the real gender gap.* New York: Scribner.

Prensky, M. (2007). *Digital game-based learning.* St. Paul, MN: Paragon House.

Putnam, L. L., Kisselburgh, L. G., Berkelaar, B. L., Buzzanell, P. M., Mastronardi, M., Jackson, M. H., et al. (2009). Conversations about women in STEM careers: The impact of communication research in creating occupational and social change in a global information economy. In L. Harter, M. J. Dutta, & C. Cole (Eds.), *Communication for social impact: Engaging communication theory, research, and practice* (pp. 47–62). Cresskill, NJ: Hampton Press.

Raphael, C., Bachen, C., Lynn, K-M., Baldwin-Philippi, J., & McKee, K. A. (2006). Portrayals of information and communication technology on World Wide Web sites for girls. *Journal of Computer-Mediated Communication, 11*, 771–801.

Remke, R. (2008, July). *Challenging the changing workplace: Rethinking family leave policies for knowledge workers.* Paper presented to the European Group for Organizational Studies, conference held in Amsterdam.

Rosser, S. V. (2004). *The science glass ceiling: Academic women scientists and the struggle to succeed.* New York: Routledge.

Ruiz Ben, E. (2007). Defining expertise in software development while doing gender. *Gender, Work and Organization, 14*, 312–322.

Sahr, T. (2008, February 28). *Design Squad.* Presentation given to the College of

Engineering's 2008 ENC Colloquia Series in Engineering Education, Purdue University, West Lafayette, IN.

Shaffer, D. W. (2005, April). *Islands of expertise and ARTS: Developing alternative routes to scientific understanding through informal and out-of-school learning experiences.* Paper presented at the National Association for Research in Science Teaching, Dallas, TX.

Shaffer, D. W. (2006a). Epistemic frames for epistemic games. *Computers and Education, 46(3)*, 223–234. doi:10.1016/j.compedu.2005.11.003

Shaffer, D. W. (2006b). *How computer games help children learn.* New York: Palgrave Macmillan.

Shaffer, D. W. (2007, October). *Epistemic games to improve professional skills and values.* Paper presented at the meeting of the Organisation for Economic Co-operation and Development (Center for Education and Research Innovation) Expert Meeting on Videogames and Education, Santiago, Chile. Retrieved November 16, 2008, from http://www.oecd.org/dataoecd/0/21/39530780.pdf

Sherry, J. L. (2001). The effects of violent video games on aggression: A meta-analysis. *Human Communication Research, 27*, 409–431.

Signorelli, N. (1997). *A content analysis: Reflections of girls in the media.* Report for the Kaiser Family Foundation and Children Now. Retrieved March 30, 2008, from http://www.kff.org/entmedia/1260-gendr.cfm

Snyder, T. D., Tan, A. G., & Hoffman, C. M. (2006). *Digest of Education Statistics 2005.* Retrieved April 1, 2007, from http://nces.ed.gov/pubsearch/pubsinfo. asp?pubid=2006030

Soukup, C. (2007). Mastering the game: Gender and the entelechial motivational system of video games. *Women's Studies in Communication, 32*, 157–178.

Spertus, E. (1993). *Why are there so few female computer scientists?* (MIT Artificial Intelligence Lab Technical Report, No. 1315). Cambridge, MA: MIT.

Steinke, J. (2004). Science in cyberspace: Science and engineering World Wide Web sites for girls. *Public Understanding of Science, 13*, 7–30.

Steinke, J. (2005). Cultural representations of gender and science: Portrayals of female scientists and engineers in popular films. *Science Communication, 27*, 27–63.

Stern, S. R. (2004). Expressions of identity online: Prominent features and gender differences in adolescents' World Wide Web home pages. *Journal of Broadcasting & Electronic Media, 4(2)*, 218–243.

Stohl, C. (2006). The role of memorable messages in the process of organizational socialization. In L. L. Putnam & K. J. Krone (Eds.), *Major works in organizational communication* (Vol. 3, pp. 146–164). London: Sage. (Original work published 1986)

Stoltzfus, K. (2008, May). *Participation, perceptions, and achievement of women scientists in cutting-edge research: A study of nanotechnology.* Paper presented at the annual meeting of the International Communication Association, Montréal, Canada.

Styhre, A., Backman, M., & Börjesson, S. (2005). The gendered machine. Concept car development at Volvo Car Corporation. *Gender, Work and Organization, 12*, 551–571.

Subrahmanyan, L. (1998). *Women scientists in the third world: The Indian experience.* New Delhi, India: Sage.

Suizzo, M-A., Robinson, C., & Pahlke, E. (2008). African American mothers' socialization beliefs and goals with young children: Themes of history, education, and collective independence. *Journal of Family Issues, 29*, 287–316.

Sumner, M. (2008, April). *An investigation of work family conflict among IT Professionals*. Proceedings of the 2008 ACM SIGMIS Conference, Charlottesville, VA.

Svarovsky, G. N., & Shaffer, D. W. (2006, June). *Engineering girls gone wild: Developing an engineering identity in Digital Zoo*. Paper presented at the annual meeting of the International Conference of the Learning Sciences (ICLS), Bloomington, IN. Retrieved August 11, 2008, from http://epistemicgames.org/cv/papers/svarovsky_shaffer_icls_poster_2006.pdf

Task Force on the Future of American Innovation, The. (2005). *The knowledge economy: Is the United States losing its competitive edge? Benchmarks of our innovation future*. Retrieved November 8, 2008, from http://futureofinnovation.org/PDF/Benchmarks.pdf

Taylor, T. L. (2003). Multiple pleasures: Women and online gaming. *Convergence, 9*(1), 21–46.

Thorne, B. (1993). *Gender play: Girls and boys in school*. New Brunswick, NJ: Rutgers University Press.

Tucker, J., Pawley, A., Riley, D., & Catalano, G. D. (2008, October). *New engineering stories: How feminist thinking can impact engineering ethics and practices*. Paper presented at the annual conference of Frontiers in Education: Racing Toward Innovation in Engineering Education, Saratoga Springs, NY.

Türkmen, H. (2007). Turkish primary students' perceptions about scientists and what factors affecting [sic] the image of the scientists. *Eurasia Journal of Mathematics, Science, & Technology Education, 4,* 55–61.

U.S. Department of Labor, Bureau of Labor Statistics. (2006–2007). *Occupational outlook handbook*. Retrieved April 3, 2007, from http://www.bls.gov/oco/

Van den Bulck, J., & Van den Bergh, B. (2005). The child effect in media and communication research: A call to arms and an agenda for research. In P. J. Kalbfleisch (Ed.), *Communication yearbook 29* (pp. 35–47). Mahwah, NJ: Erlbaum.

Van Maanen, J., & Schein, E. (1979). Toward a theory of organizational socialization. In B.M. Staw (Ed.), *Research in Organizational Behavior* (pp. 209–264). Greenwich, CT: Jai Press.

Wajcman, J. (1991). *Feminism confronts technology*. Cambridge, MA: Polity Press.

Waldeck, J., & Myers, K. (2007). Organizational assimilation theory, research, and implications to multiple areas of the discipline: A state of the art review. In C. S. Beck (Ed.), *Communication yearbook 31* (pp. 322–369). Mahwah, NJ: Erlbaum.

Waugh, B. (2001). *The soul in the computer: The story of a corporate revolutionary*. Maui, HI: Inner Ocean.

Weinger, S. (1998). Children living in poverty: Their perception of career opportunities. *Families in Society: The Journal of Contemporary Human Services, 79,* 320–330.

WGBH Educational Foundation. (2007). *About the program: Design Squad program summary*. Retrieved April 20, 2008, from http://pbskids.org/designsquad/parentseducators/program/program_summary.html

Whyte, J. (1984). Observing sex stereotypes and interactions in the school lab and workshop. *Educational Review, 36,* 75–86.

Willis, P. (1977). *Learning to labor: How working-class kids get working-class jobs*. New York: Columbia University Press.

Zachmann, K. (2000). Mobilizing womanpower: Women, engineers and the East German state in the Cold War. In A. Canel, R. Oldenziel, & K. Zachman (Eds.), *Crossing borders, building bridges: Comparing the history of women engineers 1870s–1990s* (pp. 211–252). Amsterdam: Harwood Academic.

# CHAPTER CONTENTS

# 8 Crossing and Transforming Occupational and Household Gendered Divisions of Labor

## Reviewing Literatures and Deconstructing Divisions

*Caryn E. Medved*

Baruch College—City University of New York

In this chapter, I review and critique social research which explores micro-practices of gender transgressions and macro-level transformations of occupational and household divisions of labor. Today, "crossing over," even blurring of hegemonic gendered occupational and relational boundaries occurs more frequently. Yet, it remains a problematic and complex social phenomenon even in the 21st century, particularly with respect to highly sex-typed forms of paid and unpaid work. This review of literatures examines occupational gender crossing and sex segregation studies as well as parallel research on gender violations and/or sex segregation in the division of household labor and marital breadwinning. Literature findings are organized around three discursive fields: sexuality, skill and competence, and inequality. Finally, a critique is offered of the centrality of micro-practices in reproducing sex-segregation, heteronormative and patriarchical bias embedded in these bodies of research as well as related lessons for social change. An intra-disciplinary agenda is also discussed for scholarship with respect to work, family, and difference.

## Introduction

In this chapter, I review and critique social research which explores micro-practices of gender transgressions and macro-level transformations of occupational and household divisions of labor. Today, "crossing over," even blurring of hegemonic gendered occupational and relational boundaries occurs more frequently. Yet, it remains a problematic and complex social phenomenon even in the 21st century, particularly with respect to highly sex-typed forms of paid and unpaid work. Consider the fractious yet path-breaking nature of Senator Hillary Rodham Clinton's 2008 bid for the Democratic Party presidential nomination or the gendered implication of the advertising slogan "Are you man enough to be a nurse?" used by the Oregon Center for Nursing to attract men into the field. Similarly, reflect on the fact that only .006% of

Correspondence: e-mail: caryn_medved@baruch.cuny.edu

heterosexual married men are at-home fathers (Casper, 2007), while 25% of dual-career women significantly out-earn their husbands (U.S. Census Bureau, 2006). Certainly, tremendous individual, organizational, and social transformations can result when individuals break barriers in the sexual divisions of labor. Yet, gendered language and social interactions significantly contribute to persistence of gender barriers (Ridgeway & Correll, 2000, 2004). While communication can create change, it also reproduces rules, relations, structures, and outcomes of *inequality* ubiquitous across our work and family lives. Getting to the roots of these inequalities necessitates digging underneath these taken-for-granted divisions of labor in both lived experiences and their scholarly representations as well as confronting their ideological nature with respect to issues of class, race, and sexuality.[1]

This review of literatures examines occupational gender crossing and sex segregation literatures and, when appropriate, includes parallel research on gender violations or sex segregation in the division of household labor and marital breadwinning (e.g., Doucet, 2004; Drago, Black, & Wooden, 2005; Medved, 2007; Medved & Rawlins, 2007; Meisenbach, 2007; Pilcher, 1998; Smith, 1998; Stamp, 1985; Tichenor, 2005).[2] I structure this literature review around three discursive fields (Deetz, 1992): sexuality, skill and competence, and inequality. Each section examines key findings. The final section of the chapter then further explores the role of language and social interaction micropractices in reproducing sex segregation, displaying the heteronormative and patriarchal bias embedded in these bodies of research as well as related lessons for social change. Finally, I advance an intra-disciplinary agenda for communication scholarship with respect to work, family, and difference.

## Review of Literatures

A vast number of studies published since the late 1970s detail experiences and effects of occupational and marital gender crossing as well as gendered occupational transformations. As such, writing a meaningful review necessitates a few choices. First, research reviewed in this chapter investigates women performing "men's work" specifically in male-dominated or traditionally masculine occupations and men performing "women's work" in female-dominated occupations (Anker, 1998, Reskin & Roos, 1990; Williams, 1993). While important regional variation exists, Anker observed that worldwide "male-dominated non-agricultural occupations are seven times more numerous than female-dominated ones" (p. 407). According to Anker, worldwide women are underrepresented in administrative and managerial work, overrepresented in service and clerical jobs (excepting the latter in China, India, Pakistan, Nigeria, and Ghana), variously represented in sales occupations by region, and greatly underrepresented in production work. Second, given the present focus on sex-segregated occupational and household contexts, this analysis of literatures only occasionally references the broad literature on women in management (e.g., Butterfield & Grinnell, 1990; Fagenson, 1993; Powell, 1990; Sloan

& Krone, 2002; Wood & Conrad, 1983), including leadership sex differences (Eagly & Johnson, 1990; Eagly & Karau, 1991; Eagly, Makhijani & Klonsky, 1992) and women's ways of leading (e.g., Helgesen, 1990; Rosner, 1990). Such research serves to "expose the masculine bias of managerial and professional communication, to suggest resulting dilemmas and barriers faced by women seeing advancement (e.g., 'double binds' and 'glass ceilings'), and even to bill women's alleged leadership differences as a business opportunity or 'feminine advantage'" (Ashcraft, 2006, p. 98). Yet, this review focuses on a narrower set of studies of gender crossing in highly sex-typed work and occupational transformations, both at the margins of social change.

Correspondingly, in the private sphere this review concentrates on studies of explicit "role reversals": men doing "women's work" full time in the home; that is, a growing number of studies on the experiences of at-home fathers (Doucet, 2004; Medved, 2007; Medved & Rawlins, 2007; Petroski & Edley, 2006; Smith, 1998; Varvus, 2002) and women doing "men's work" as primary or sole family breadwinners (Drago et al., 2005; Meisenbach, 2007; Stamp, 1985). I sought to include empirical work representing non-U.S. or non-Western perspectives; however, the gender assumptions underlying this project are admittedly ground in Western intellectual gender history and traditions (Ferree, 1990).

### Discourses of Sexuality

Routinely unquestioned heterosexual assumptions about gender and gender relations often "emerge when traditional gender boundaries are crossed" (Nielsen, Walden, & Kunkel, 2000, p. 292). Within the discursive field of sexuality, three dominant vocabularies emerge—sexual deviance, sexual objectification, and cross-sex relational taboos. Generally speaking, men employed in care-giving occupations and, at times, stay-at-home fathers (Smith, 1998) report being negatively labeled in social interactions as homosexual or dangerously sexually aggressive (e.g., Evans, 2002; Evans & Frank, 2003; Murray, 1996). Kite (2001) explained that "the association between men's femininity and gay male sexuality is stronger than the association between women's masculinity and lesbianism" (p. 223; see also Faludi, 1999; Wentworth & Chell, 2001). As women transgress traditional subordination, they will most likely experience overt heterosexuality in the workplace (DiTomaso, 1993), including sexual harassment (e.g., Doughtery & Smythe, 2004; Jansma, 2000) and objectification (e.g., S. E. Martin, 1994; Prokos & Padavic, 2002; Schroedel, 1990; Shuler, 2003; Yount, 1991).

### Sexual Deviance

Men working the field of midwifery in the early 1800s were rebuked as homosexual or labeled "filthy nondescript(s)" and "full-time lecher(s)" (Donnison, 1988, p. 60). Even today, when men perform feminized care labor, warning signs may go up. Regardless of an individual man's sexual preference, male nurses, elementary school teachers, secretaries, and daycare providers frequently contend with negative homosexual labeling (Camilleri & Jones, 2001; Evans, 2002; Evans & Frank, 2003; Heikes, 1991; Lupton, 2000; Murray, 1996; Pringle, 1988; Taylor, Dwiggins, Albert, & Dearner, 1983; C. L. Williams, 1993) or others' fears of care-giving men as pedophiles or sexual aggressors (Evans, 2002; Murray, 1996; Sargent, 2000). As a result, gender crossing men "are at a greater risk of being unsupported, devalued, viewed as anomalies and gay" (Tokar & LaRae, 1996 as cited in Evans & Frank, 2002, p. 279).

Many men, like women, report going into the field of nursing (as well as teaching and early childcare) desirous of helping others. Nonetheless, gender trouble may arise (Butler, 1990). A male nurse, for example, was accused of molestation when a new father saw him changing his baby's diaper (Evans, 2002). Adolescent and relatively healthy males most often may object to male nurses performing care. One male childcare employee explained that "[a]lmost immediately, he is suspected of not being a 'real man'; there must be something wrong with him…for him to be interested in this work" (C. L. Williams, 1993, p. 3; see also Cockburn, 1988). Some male nurses, like at home fathers, report negative sexual stereotyping more often in their dealings with the public rather than in personal or immediate co-worker relations (C. L. Williams, 1992).

Homosexual labeling "often elicited open and direct denial" from some men nurses who participated in C. L. Williams' (1993, p. 3) study. Other interaction strategies or gender work employed to contradict sexual prejudice or fear includes preemptive use of masculine humor, learning "safe" ways to care and touch, and making casual references to one's own children (erroneously perceived of as: "I *must* not be a homosexual") (Evans, 2002). As one male nurse clarified, "There are things I don't do—talk in a womanly manner, not too soft unless it's a person in a lot of distress…I conduct myself as a man. I talk to my male patients about manly things they do" (Evans & Frank, 2003, p. 281).

In childcare contexts, sexual taboos of physical touch can result in fears of pedophilia. One male teacher stressed that "you're crazy if you hold the kids and sit them on your lap…you have to be cognizant of the fact that you can't put a lot of physical touch in the situation; and, it's understandable" (Sargent, 2000, p. 416). As Sargent reported, another male elementary school teacher well captured this difficult situation, noting that "women's laps are places of love, but men's laps are places of danger" (p. 416). Men also express feeling as if they work under a cloud of suspicion. Murray (1996) contended that men may get negatively judged for performing the same care-giving behaviors as women.

Self-monitoring of behavior (e.g., asking for the assistance of women colleagues, eliminating physical touch, etc.) entails another often reported strategy for managing others' fears (Murray, 1996; Sargent, 2000; Skelton, 1991). Self-monitoring comprises just one way of accepting hegemonic assumptions of male sexuality. Men in paid care-giving jobs themselves may assert that men, more than women, present a higher probability of "threat." As such, patient, parental or organizational caution is "understandable." In addition to this individual-level gender work, organization-level strategies (i.e., gendering organization) become institutionalized ostensibly to protect children/patients, employees, and organizational liability (Acker, 1990). Hospitals often require male nurses to work in teams with female colleagues when checking on female patients, especially on night shifts. Officials also monitor care-giving behaviors in daycare and childhood education (Evans, 2002; Heikes, 1991; Murray, 1996; Sargent, 2000).

Sexual deviance is also ascribed to men performing secretarial or clerical work, albeit in very different ways than intimate care-giving occupations (Henson & Rogers, 2001; Pringle, 1993). Powerlessness, rather than nurturance, epitomizes the "office wife" or secretary. Powerlessness for men can become conflated with homosexuality (Donaldson, 1993), while powerlessness for women can become sexualized (Yount, 1991). At-home fathers also report experiencing emasculation or powerlessness (Smith, 1998). According to Smith, one Australian househusband recalled a conversation, "I was a househusband and she knew I was a househusband and ahh I said 'yes' and she said 'they're all poofs [gay] [sic] y'know' I said 'really, how do you work that out?' 'well, it's obvious isn't it?'" (p. 148). However, when the participant asked why she didn't categorize him as homosexual, she explained that he coached football and drank beer.

Both at-home fathers and male secretaries report managing gender contradictions by linguistically reframing or renaming their jobs and tasks (Doucet, 2004; Henson & Rogers, 2001; Lupton, 2000; Pringle, 1993; C. L. Williams, 1989). Doucet noted that at-home fathers primarily talk about their care-giving roles as "rough and tumble" play with children and frame their identities around building or repair work. Male nurses emphasize the technical aspects of their job (even transferring into nursing specialties assumed to be more masculine, such as psychiatry; Evans & Frank, 2003). Male secretaries and temporary workers describe their jobs and tasks in gender neutral terms, such as being an administrative assistant or bookkeeper. According to Henson and Rogers, men may also characterize their work in relation to the computer environment or software required to do the job (e.g., "I used WordPerfect a lot.... Basically, it's been a lot of word processing" (p. 231). Altering the term *secretary* is one renaming technique used both by men in clerical work as well as their supervisors who are often also reticent to apply feminized labels (Pringle, 1993; see also Medved & Kirby, 2005, for an example of at-home mothers renaming their work per the language of the "Family CEO").

Men also report maintaining masculine identities in the face of feminized work by telling "cover stories" (Henson & Rogers, 2001). These explanations told to others (and themselves) rationalize their sex atypical tasks. For example, male temporary workers admit to presenting themselves as actors or writers to explain why they do not have a "real job" (Clair, 1996). Finally, outright resistance encompasses also a strategy registered by men doing non-traditional labor. Male clerical workers report not performing subservient tasks which align with their feminized work, even at the risk of losing their jobs. Like some low-earning men who resist doing housework, these men "do gender" by refusing to perform particular types of work (Brines, 1994). However, according to Henson and Rogers, women in similar positions disclose using passive strategies, such as forgetfulness, as a means of resistance.

### Sexual Objectification and Harassment

Studies of women working in highly masculine sex-typed workplaces (not necessarily in the home) list experiences of hypersexualization or objectification (i.e., when a person is judged or evaluated primarily in terms of attractiveness to the opposite sex; Buzzanell, 2001; Nielsen et al., 2000; Norander, 2008; Prokos & Padavic, 2002; Shuler, 2003). Shuler, for instance, demonstrated how visual representations of women executives in *Fortune* magazine's issue on the 50 top American women in business depict these high achieving women as "Cosmo CEOs," images reminiscent of Kanter's (1977) sexual stereotype of the "seductress." Nielsen et al. found that women who violated gender norms were often heterosexualized. A woman participating in Nielsen et al.'s study asked about wood at a local building supply store and was told, "You're one of the prettiest carpenters he'd ever seen."

While women often cite financial reasons for working in male-dominated fields (Reskin & Roos, 1990; see related review by Kisselburgh, Berkelaar, & Buzzanell, this volume), their motives can become sexualized, albeit differently from men's motives to enter "women's work." Male co-workers of women coal miners explained the motives of single or attractive women miners as "man-hunting or promiscuity," not work. As one mine supervisor revealed, "A woman would have to be a certain breed of woman to go down there in the first place, not a lady" (Yount, 1991, p. 402). Some women miners actively engaged their sexualized femininity with respect to the performance of work. Those women who constructed and claimed identities as "flirts" were most likely to be objectified and demeaned by both male and female co-workers. One woman miner, a self-identified "flirt," admitted using her sexuality to co-opt men's help. She shared that "[my boss] says, 'I'll help you shove and then you can sit and talk to me.' Like I said, I knew I was manipulating. But it came as second nature..." (p. 407).

Other women reported using sexuality as a defensive maneuver or a way to appease male co-workers. Whether flirting behavior was a conscious form of gender work or a result of depressed aspirations (Kanter, 1977), flirts had the least success for advancement (Yount, 1991). Prokos and Padavic (2002) also illustrated how the sexual objectification of women comprises part of the police academy "hidden curriculum." Various aspects of recruit life and formal instruction denigrated and objectified women through the trivialization of domestic violence and rape, male interactions calling each other "pussies" to indicate "unmanly" behavior, and sexist reactions of men recruits to training videos.

Finally, Tewksbury (1993) examined men doing "women's work" in the lives of male strippers and the objectification of other men in this particular paid work context. Tewksbury found that male strippers (dancing primarily for gay male audiences) effectively reframe their roles in ways not available to women strippers. This reframing maintains patriarchal privilege. Tewksbury explained that male strippers, different from women strippers, become "'cleansed' and presented in more economically oriented, rather than sexual terms.... In order to both maintain a masculine identity and be constructed as a sexual object, it is necessary to restructure the role of the sexual object" (pp. 179–180).

Sexual objectification is tightly coupled with the issue of sexual harassment or "unwelcome sexual conduct that unreasonably and negatively affects individuals' employment conditions and productivity" (Jansma, 2001, p. 165). As an issue well-studied by communication scholars, a complete review of findings is beyond the scope of this chapter (for reviews see Jansma, 2001; Keyton, 1996; Morrison & Van Glinow, 1990). Yet, as Jansma observed, sexual harassment is argued to be more about power than sex. Legal and societal changes have significantly named and raised consciousness about sexual harassment, but incidents still occur. It remains a part of some women's gender crossing experiences in highly sex-typed occupations, such as policing and mining (Prokos & Pavadic, 2002; Yount, 1990), and underreporting of incidents continues (Davey & Davidson, 2000).

One counter-intuitive example, however, is warranted in the context of this review. Clair (1994) analyzed Michael Gray's experiences of female to male sexual harassment through the insight of resistance and oppression as a self-contained opposite. Clair argued that "oppression becomes resistance when the female nurses oppress Michael through sexual harassment in order to resist being infiltrated by a male" (p. 252). Clair notes that "Resistance becomes oppression when the nurses accept sexual harassment from the patients in order to dominate them" (p. 252). The women nurses used sexual harassment as a means of preventing men's invasion of the traditionally female-dominated occupation and to mark a male nurse as an "outsider."

*Cross-Gender Taboos*

Stereotypes surrounding cross-sex heterosexual workplace relationships, including friendships, co-workers, or mentors, abound (Raggins, Townsend, & Mattis, 1998; Rawlins, 1992). Studies of executive women, for instance, often reveal the double bind of high potential women needing to develop cross-sex mentor-protégé relationships yet these relationships being fraught with problems of cross-sex relational taboos (Noe, 1988; Raggins & Cotton, 1991; Raggins et al., 1998). In the blue-collar workplace, women also report needing men as mentors to gather important work-related information and, at times, experiencing sexual stereotyping from colleagues (Holder, 1996; Lillydahl, 1986; Schroedel, 1990; Wetherby, 1977). In addition to formal mentoring, more casual cross-gender socializing experiences result in both difficulties and opportunities. For instance, men and women pilots often stay in the same hotel with time to socialize between flights. As a major component of airline culture, pilots observe private behaviors of their peers in these "down route" situations and judge their value as professional colleagues with respect to these supposed non-work interactions. Many women reported enjoying informal socializing with men colleagues and often became considered "one of the lads" (Davey & Davidson, 2000, p. 212). Other female pilots avoided socializing with their male pilot colleagues and thereby enacted gender; instead, they interacted mostly with women crew members.

While challenges exist, however, successful male-female mentoring also exists in various work environments. Transcending heterosexual relationship taboos may happen through reframing work relations into the logics of family gender roles. Male mentors in U.S. blue-collar work may become "fathers" or "big brothers" (Schroedel, 1990). One female plumbing apprentice in Schroedel's study commented that "I think it's easy for a White man especially to put a White woman like in the role of their kid. Even if they don't think it's good for you to be doing this, a lot of other kids are doing things they didn't plan or want them to do" (p. 250). Other women mentioned taking on desexualized family roles of "mother" or "little sister" in the context of work relationships. A female trucker told Schroedel that she became the "mother" to isolated men truckers as a way to create social networks. This identity work seems reminiscent of Kanter's (1977) four sexual stereotypes of women in the organization: sex object, mother, child, and iron maiden (see also Jamison, 1995; Wood & Conrad, 1983). Alternatively, some women attempt to construct a moral feminized identity as a "lady" in an attempt to discourage objectification or harassment (Prokos & Padavic, 2002; Yount, 1991). Research on women's information seeking strategies in non-traditional occupations identifies women needing to operate without vital information, along with using more overt strategies, despite social costs, with their cross-sex co-workers and supervisors (Holder, 1996). In addition, Holder's skilled trade workers were not granted a socialization "honeymoon" per traditional socialization models (see related review by Waldeck & Myers, 2007), as well as persistent feelings of isolation in relationships both inside and outside the organization.

Finally, social norms or rules surrounding cross-sex friendships and concerns about men in feminized spaces and places also shape men's experiences as caregivers in the private sphere (Smith, 1998). For example, in Smith's study, at-home fathers shared that they did not receive invitations to women's playgroups, at-home mothers' networks, or daily coffees. At-home mothers may be hesitant to strike up a friendship with a male father given the potential interpretations of a sexual relationship or perceptions of a male presence being a threat. One participant in Smith's study noted that "there's morning teas and coffee mornings going on all round Brisbane [Australia] but men don't go to them, ahh cause women just don't invite strange men to them, which I think is partly sexual—um y'know like they don't want to invite strange men into their houses" (p. 152). Smith surmised that these ways of framing sexual relations are partly to blame for the isolation many of these men report feeling in their roles as primary at-home parents.

In sum, private sphere sexuality (i.e., sexual preference, deviance, or motive) is appropriated as an interpretive frameworks to assess men and women's suitability, or lack thereof, to perform paid work in the public sphere. Questions of deviance and fear often surface with ostensible misalignment between individuals' visible sex characteristics and the gender typicality or the status composition of work being performed (Tomaskovic-Devey, 1993). These findings point to the underlying heteronormative nature of studies of the division of labor. Heteronormativity describes an ideology which marginalizes, ignores, or overtly stigmatizes variations of heterosexual discourses, interactions, practices, and related structures (Foster, 2008; Herek, 2004). As discussed in the final section of this chapter, challenging heteronormativity is key to undermining negative stereotypes about men and care-giving.[3]

### Discourses of Skill and Competence

Vocabularies of gender, skill, and competence are complexly and variously related to self and other perceptions of individuals' competence to perform supposed sex atypical work, along with larger macro-discourses and practices of occupational gender transformations. Three clusters of ideas constitute this discursive field: (1) macro-level occupational gender transformations, (2) interpretations of competence, and (3) competence and reproduction.[4]

### Occupational Gender Transformations

Over time, occupations become gender stereotyped based partly on workforce sex composition. The symbolic and material inertia behind occupational gendering makes such markers difficult to change (Jacobs, 1998). Similarly and intimately connected to public sphere occupational gendering, domestic labor in the home remains marked as feminine, devalued, and ironically, also culturally lauded as the most important job in the world (Crittenden, 2001; Ferree, 1990). Although variation in the storyline exists, on the rare occasion when men take over traditionally women's occupations, pay and status generally increase (Phillips & Taylor, 1980). When previously male-dominated occupations become feminized, pay and status by and large decrease (Bradley, 1993; for a contradictory example, see Wright & Jacobs, 1994). Internal segregation (or demarcation), re-segregation, or re-ghettoization can result from occupational feminization (Reskin & Roos, 1990). While few professions or household and family care-giving tasks are entirely the province of singularly for either males or females, more women have historically fought to enter male-dominated occupations than vice versa (Bradley, 1993; Reskin & Roos, 1990). Much research documents the existence, extent, and nature of worldwide occupational or skill sex segregation (e.g., Anker, 1998; Charles & Grusky, 2004). Yet, a narrower set of studies exploring gender transformations of entire occupations or skill categories.

While historical examples of gendered occupational transformations are revealing—such as the cases of Rosie the Riveter in World War II or historic changes in the gendered nature of the teaching profession—occupational transformation processes remain gendered.[5] For example, shortages of men workers in male-dominated occupations often precede or follow a parallel decrease in occupational status and pay, or the downgrading of required *skills*. This devaluing of skills (i.e., feminization) frequently coincides with technological or organizational change, rising competition, and declining union power, none of which are gender neutral processes (Pringle, 1993; Wright & Jacobs, 1994). In addition, employers may recruit women to fill labor demands due to expansion or gaps in employment left by male flight prompted by deskilling. The sex composition of insurance adjusting and examining work, for instance, altered significantly between 1970 and 1990 partly due to legal, social, and technological changes (Phipps, 1990). The content of this once male-dominated, fairly autonomous, and well-respected middle-class white-collar career came to reflect feminized clerical tasks. Legal regulations and technological innovations standardized and routinized claim processing as well as "led to the occupation's sex label to shift, orienting employers to women workers and driving men out" (Phipps, 1990, p. 235). These newly deskilled jobs earned low financial rewards and became less attractive to men. They also expanded in number and became disproportionately filled by women. Data indicate that the occupational category called "loan interviewers and clerks" employed 82.2% female workers in 2007 (Bureau of Labor Statistics, 2007).

Finally, Cockburn's (1988) research demonstrates how technology does not facilitate gender-neutral organizational change but, rather, the redistribution of work so that men's control over the use of technology is maintained. Moreover, members frequently construct technology and its use as "tools of the trade" as masculine (see also review by Kisselburgh et al., this volume). Cockburn illustrated this effect with the case of technological change in British hospitals. Women entering the profession of medical physics, for example, tend to be hired into jobs in nuclear medicine which have more direct contact with patients. As Cockburn noted, men move into positions "that have more to do with the technology. There is more status attached to the latter than to the former, which is seen as being associated with nursing" (p. 34). Thus, technological change comprises a gendered process of occupational transformation.

Three patterns characterize transformation processes, inclusive of language and social interaction practices, when men enter into customarily female-dominated occupations: takeover, invasion, and infiltration (Bradley, 1993). Like feminization processes above, economic incentives combined with social or technological upheavals often accompany men's entrance into "women's work" in significant numbers. Instances of occupational takeover by men have historically been documented in industries, such as baking and brewing during Britain's Industrial Revolution (Clark, 1982), cotton spinning

(Lazonick, 1979; Walby, 1988), and midwifery (Donnison, 1988; see also Turner, 2004).[6]

Invasion, different from takeover, does not drive out women but segregates men and women into particular subspecialties within the occupation. It is often the case that "although not inevitably, men take the positions at the top of the hierarchy or the higher status specialties" during instances of male invasion (Bradley, 1993, p. 20). Midwifery constitutes one well-documented profession which experienced male invasion in the 17th century. Male midwives significantly closed off women's participation and redefined women's roles as assistants to male obstetricians under the guise of new technologies and the growing medicalization of childbirth (Donnison, 1988). This slow but successful occupational transformation resulted from complex and competing gendered social, economic, medical, technological, and rhetorical forces. Today, while midwifery or alternative birthing practitioners enjoy increased legitimacy in the United States, gendered paradoxes and double binds still exist in relation to traditional gendered forms of medicine (Turner, 2004).

Finally, infiltration of men into women's work occurs when "token" or "pioneer" men enter into highly sex-segregated occupations. Women more often infiltrate male-dominated professions than vice versa, yet more male than female dominated occupations exist worldwide (Anker, 1998). Men in today's nursing field offer a prime example of the dynamics of men's occupational infiltration. Men nurses often engage in what Bradley (1993) called internal demarcation of the field by moving into particular sub-specialties. Nursing work in areas such as psychiatry, anesthesiology, and intensive care or emergency nursing align more closely with masculine characteristics like physical strength or technical competence, and these tasks allow men to distance themselves from feminized and homophobic stereotypes of the nursing profession (Evans, 2002).

One final occupation which has experienced infiltration is secretarial work (Pringle, 1993). Pringle's study of secretarial work in Australia finds that men often perform secretarial work but do so under job titles such as assistants or administrative officers. This shifting language of this work harkens back to pre- and early-industrial male-dominated jobs of clerks and stenographers; these jobs were treated as gateways to management. Yet, with new office technologies, secretarial work in the mid-1900s became feminized and constructed as unskilled or semiskilled (i.e., phone work, typing/word processing). Further, such work also became sexualized as the "office wife" whose job duties became more ambiguous. Men secretaries hardly exist, and, according to Pringle, their invisibility also results from shifts in gendered census practices which reclassified men out of secretarial and receptionist classifications. Data from the Bureau of Labor Statistics (2007) in the United States indicates that secretaries and administrative work remains highly sex segregated; 96.7% of these workers are women.

Before we turn our attention to interpretations of individual competence, note that family skill categories, like many public sphere occupations, also go through gender transformations. In early U.S. history, both children's education and moral development were supposed to be the province of fathers (Griswold, 1993; Hays, 1996). Men were more "suited" to this role; they were assumed to be logical, more intelligent, and disciplined while women "were thought to be susceptible to 'passions' and 'affections,' and given to 'indulgence' and 'excessive fondness'" (Demos, 1970, p. 45).

Men were to oversee children's moral and spiritual development and set them to work in the family business as young as possible. The few childrearing manuals, mostly Puritan, were addressed to fathers, not mothers. As the ideologies of domesticity (Ferree, 1990) and burgeoning industrialization began to redefine women as the "moral sex" and protectors of the home from encroaching commerce and consumption, the gendered meanings assigned to childrearing and even definitions of childhood changed. Women slowly became categorized as morally superior to men and, thus, uniquely suited to care for children as men (usually White, middle class) moved out into the newly industrializing world. While the history of parenting and gender extends beyond the scope of this chapter, the roots of today's ideologies of intensive mothering (Hays, 1996), and deficit models of fathering (Dollahite & Hawkins, 1998) lie in the gendering of this account of the public and private split (Douglas & Michaels, 2004; Lopata, 1993).

### Interpretations of Competence

In addition to the transformation of cultural meanings assigned to entire skill categories or occupations, interpretations of an individual's competence to perform particular skills are also laden with assumptions of masculinity and femininity. Gender, while ever-present, plays varying roles in relation to perceived workplace competence, often lurking in the background or in more highly gendered contexts, playing a more central part in perceptions and interactions (Ridgeway & Correll, 2004).[7]

For the present purpose, studies are germane which explore relationships between assumptions of individual competence and the performance of gendered work and family tasks. For example, at times, men who are at-home fathers report being perceived of as being incompetent caregivers. Discourses of ineptitude or "deficit models" of fathering (Dollahite & Hawkins, 1998; Golden, 2007) have been argued to follow from feminized definitions of caregiving. In essence, men who perform fathering differently from the idealized practices of mothering are perceived as unqualified or unskilled caregivers. At-home fathers, single fathers as well as adult male caregivers—paid or unpaid—may experience feelings of self-doubt but also great pleasure and confidence in skillfully caring for children and performing household labor (Doucet, 2004; Risman, 1986; Russell, 1997). While Smith (1998) argued that most male disaffection resulted from others' negative assessments, some fathers did perceive their gender status as a weakness in their ability to give care, for example, to teenaged daughters.

In nurturing or caring careers, some question men's abilities to provide the necessary physical and emotional labor. Curt, a fourth grade teacher in J. Allen's (1993) study of men in elementary education, noted that "I think sometimes female teachers will look at you, especially at first, and say, 'Okay, let's see if you as a male can handle this'.... It's kind of a challenge to me. I want to show them that I can" (p. 118). Some male nurses report perceiving of themselves as not initially competent caregivers; one man revealed that he felt awkward with the physical touch of care-giving in that it "wasn't part of my existence [as a man] to that point" (Evans, 2002, p. 443). Men and women nurses also acknowledge that their styles of expressing care may differ from each other, yet male and female physicians tend to perceive male nurses as more competent and frequently treat them more as junior physicians than nurses (Evans & Frank, 2003). Like women who are implicitly or explicitly assigned to "relational work" in organizations (Fletcher, 1999), male teachers also disclose assignment to tasks closely aligned with masculinity. For example, according to J. Allen, regardless of an individual male teacher's skills or disposition, students with discipline problems may be placed in his classroom per stereotypes that men do not coddle or enable children, and men also reported being steered into coaching as an assumed masculine job.

Women also share that others initially may perceive them to be incapable of performing "men's work" or disproportionately needing to prove their abilities to men colleagues. Further, "clients, co-workers, and supervisors often demand proof of a woman's abilities, yet establish interaction patterns which make it almost impossible to produce such evidence" (Jurik, 1985, p. 375). For example, co-workers assume that women recruits cannot perform the physical labor or handle the stress of police work, and interactions in training programs often serve to reinforce negative stereotypes rather than build the skill and confidence of women recruits. Some women in blue collar jobs also occasionally felt at a disadvantage due to aspects of their gender socialization; for example, a female machinist explained that she was not socialized to feel competent with the tools of her trade. According to the woman, "There are little things that men take for granted, like when they're growing up their fathers teach them how to fix cars, they know what a feeler gauge is, how to set spark plugs..." (Schroedel, 1990, p. 247). Like at-home fathers' learning curves, however, these women often gain confidence and knowledge through training and on-the-job experiences (Risman, 1986; Schroedel, 1990).

Others also doubt women executives' competence or cast it in a negative light. High achieving women may be interpreted as unfeminine, competitive, and tough in the organization (Kanter, 1997; see also Buzzanell, 2001; Norander, 2008) and similarly, domineering or "wearing the pants" in marital relations. This femininity/competence double bind elucidates the paradoxical tensions women in power often experience (Jamison, 1995). Jamison asserted that, because some associate acting "feminine" per se with incompetence and acting "masculine" with competence, women can only lead by being unfeminine. Yet, at the same time, some cultures still sanction women leaders for behaving in too masculine a fashion. The "iron maiden" or "bitch" labels illustrate how gendered skills and characteristics shape perceptions of individual women's competence (Garlick, Dixon, & P. Allen, 1992; Jamison, 1995). Davey and Davidson (2000) contended that superiors initially assumed women pilots lacked competence, particularly in the early years when women were first admitted to the occupation. For example, one female pilot explained, "It always seems to be a test.... You have to do a sector P2 [as the non-handling pilot] before they let you do a landing. The girl before me had to do 30 sectors to prove her performance was ok" (p. 206). Davey and Davidson also noted, however, that negative gendered assumptions of competence, while remaining, have lessened over time.

In a different vein of research, women's assumed relational *effectiveness* in the workplace also provides evidence of the gendered nature of competence assessments. Colleagues expect women engineers, for example, to perform feminized discourses and related practices at work, yet the women end up devalued and not rewarded for doing so (Fletcher, 1999). In a study of what Fletcher referred to as relational practices (e.g., preserving, mutual empowering, self-achieving, and creating a team) at work, she found that women more often than men perform these essential relational practices. In so doing, these women fundamentally contributed to success in achieving tangible work results. Yet, co-workers considered these women to be simply nice or helpful, not highly skilled as managers or leaders. Relational work disappeared, Fletcher argued, because such skills do not appear on performance appraisals nor can they be "found on many lists of leadership characteristics" (p. 115). Even further, when women used their skills to create collaborative, not conflict-laden environments for problem solving, others framed them not as leaders, but as co-workers with dependency issues or having a need to be liked (see also discussions of women and hidden family work, Devault, 1991).

Returning to the issue of masculinity and workplace technology/tools, Yount (1991) found that men co-workers characterized women as "inept with machinery, physically incapable, lazy" among other negative labels. Women miners sought to prove competence by divesting themselves of qualities and physical markers of femininity (e.g., makeup, well-groomed appearance). In a similar fashion, male co-workers perceived women police officers (Prokos & Padavic, 2002) and corrections officers (Jurik, 1985), to be incompetent or safety threats, regardless of physical strength or abilities. Prokos and Padavic observed obstacle-course training during which equal numbers of men and women had difficulty dragging a dummy at the end of the course. Prokos and Padavic note: "Yet one student complained after the exercise that he would not want a woman to be his partner because she would never be able to drag him in an emergency" (p. 451). Exaggerations of gender differences in conjunction with prevailing myths of police work as action-filled and dangerous create interpretations of incompetence for female recruits. In doing so, male police officers often "cling to the image of police officers as crime fighters and downplay the femininely labeled aspects of the job, such as paper work and social services" (p. 442). This selective defining of the job through occupational language and interaction aims to protect its hegemonic masculinity and maintain women as incompetent and as "outsiders."

### Competence and Reproduction

The vocabulary of reproduction, particularly in the context of executive jobs, also intersects with discourses of skill and competence. Women executive and managerial experiences of pregnancy on the job have been related to gender stereotypes (Cuddy, Fiske, & Glick, 2004) and perceptions of competence and motivation (Ashcraft, 1999; J. Martin, 1990).

Cuddy and colleagues (2004) maintained that the assumed transition from being a "female professional" (read: without children) to a "working mother" shifts others' interpretations of women's work competence. Based on their research of gender stereotyping, Cuddy et al. found that "merely adding a child caused people to view the woman as lower on traits such as capable and skillful and decreased people's interests in training, hiring, and promoting her" (p. 711). When women become mothers, they "trade perceived competence for perceived warmth" (p. 701). However, male professionals moving into fathering roles both maintained perceived competence and gained warmth. Related, Coltrane (2004) asserted that colleagues envisioned men who are husbands and fathers to be "family men" and thus, more serious about their careers and deserving of promotion. According to Coltrane, women who get married or become mothers inevitably experience conflict between obligations which will subtly render them less qualified for promotion.

J. Martin (1990) offered insights about the tensions, ironies, and challenges of gender crossing through her deconstruction of a story told by the CEO of a large multi-national organization. J. Martin contended that, in a male-dominated working environment, a woman executive's pregnancy, and related issues of sexuality, become unavoidably visible and subject to organizational control (see also Buzzanell, 2003). Different from a male token doing "women's work," the physicality of her sex contradicts organizational taboos barring the supposed private sphere from entering into the public sphere. Men executives cannot do women's reproductive work in this bodily sense, so their visibility as nurturers remains hidden except in mentoring relations (as noted above, taboos exist for cross-sex work relations; Noe, 1988).

J. Martin's (1990) work also reminds us of the double standard surrounding interpretations of the voluntary sexual behaviors of women, such as taboos against women who sleep with "beneath them" or a lower ranking man. Additionally, if a woman has a sexual relationship with a higher ranking man and subsequently receives a promotion, "her advance is likely to be credited to her seductive abilities, rather than her competence on the job" (p. 349).

Ashcraft's (1999) analysis of a female founder's pregnancy and employee reaction in a small, entrepreneurial firm connects discourses of reproduction and competence. Employees, who until the announcement of her pregnancy, perceived of their female executive as very involved in every aspect of the business, began to expect and articulate changes in her behavior and leadership competencies. Employees began to assume she would undergo personal and professional changes as well as increased levels of empathy. Employees also panicked, observed Ashcraft, as the date of the founder's maternity leave approached and interpreted her level of work commitment and increased delegating behaviors in a gendered manner. One employee explained that "now, I think her attention is diverted by other more family-related concerns...but, I think when, or should I say if, she returns from her leave she'll be playing even less and less of a role" (p. 257). In brief, shifting interpretations and questions about her leadership competences were revealed in the discourse and related practices of employees, as well as the founder's own sense making of maternity experiences in the masculine role of executive.

All in all, the gendering of organizations and families at least partly occurs through reproducing the symbolic linkages between particular skills or competencies and gender. These micro-appropriations perpetuate gendered understandings about an individual's suitability to perform types of work and also affect macro-organizational, economic, and technological change. While much theorizing exists contending that multiple masculinities and femininities exist (Hearn & Collinson, 1994; Schippers, 2007), this research does not significantly explore variations among or within the categories of women and men. This practice allows the category of women to operate as a deceptive generic and the category of men to be used as the singular mechanism of female oppression (Spelman, 1988; see also Connell, 1995; West & Fenstermaker, 1995). In addition to ignoring broad within-category variations for men and women crossing gendered boundaries, differences in the experiences of masculinities and femininities also considerably vary at the intersections of nationality/region, race, class, age, and ability. Later in the chapter, I will elaborate on the idea of intersectionality as a means of theorizing divisions of labor with respect to multiple social identity categories, not singularly based on gender (Ashcraft, 2007; Glenn, 2000).

### Discourses of Gendered Inequalities

Researchers address discourses of inequality in various ways across studies of gender transgressions and transformations. Fundamentally, gender is about power. The very idea of segregation connotes separation and the troubling rhetoric of "separate but (not really) equal." The above detailed discursive fields related to sexuality and competence also tell us much about gendered inequality and power. These three categories represent and constitute interlocking webs of signification and material relations. This final section further points to power imbalances often sustained by discourse or "the range of symbolic activities by which members of a culture name, legitimize and establish meanings" of gender transgression and transformation (Wood, 1994, p. 122).

Thus, I detail discourses of (in)equalities separately for primarily organizational purposes but also as a means of highlighting two specific and linked vocabularies—marital power relations as well as glass ceilings and glass escalators (please see also related earlier section on discourses of sexuality).

## Marital Power Relations

The effects of severely violating gendered work and family norms in heterosexual marital relations, while not widely explored, has increasingly been studied in relation to power, dependency, and the division of labor. Studies, for example, of marital dynamics in couples in which wives earn significantly more than their husbands, or where men are at-home fathers foregoing participation in the paid labor force, provide important insights (Atkinson & Boles, 1984; Brines, 1994; Doucet, 2004, 2007; Hochschild, 1989; Smith, 1998; Stamp, 1985). Although some change has occurred in men's participation in household labor, Brines investigated and theorized the difficult question of why housework primarily remains "women's work" in the United States. Research provides evidence of a gender difference with respect to marital dependency and household labor. That is, as women depend more economically on men, they tend to perform more housework; an economic exchange explanation seems to fit these data. Yet, when men rely more on their wives for financial support, they typically do less household work, contradicting a straightforward economic exchange explanation for the division of household labor. Brines explained this discrepancy by arguing that men "do" gender by not performing household labor. Without the traditional base of breadwinning on which to accomplish their masculinity, low earning men, especially in lower socio-economic situations, actively avoid performing feminine household labor as a means of maintaining their masculine marital identities and power. Bittman, England, Folbre, Sayer, and Matheson (2003) also found that when women's earnings approach or exceed 51% of household income "gender trumps money." Men at the extremes of the income range slightly *reduce* their participation in household work.

Breadwinning women, at the same time, report downplaying their financial contributions also as a means of helping their husbands "save face" when interacting with their spouse and family outsiders (Atkinson & Boles, 1984; Brines, 1994; Hochschild, 1989; Stamp, 1985). These women also participate in performing masculinity in these non-traditional marriages. In a study of couples labeled "wives as senior partners" (WASP), Atkinson and Boles determined that couples used two strategies as a means of minimizing or neutralizing perceived deviance represented by the fact that the woman's career took precedence over the man's professional advancement: (1) concealing, hiding, covering, and (2) denying the importance of the deviance. Wives who are primary breadwinners actively work to equalize marital power relations. For instance, Stamp found that women expressed aversion at the idea of giving their low- or non-earning husbands an allowance or some sort of spending money, a more acceptable practice in traditionally economic dependent marriages where wives might be given spending money.

One interesting, perhaps counter-intuitive strategy related to inequities in the division of household labor is also important to mention here—gatekeeping. S. M. Allen and Hawkins (1999) defined maternal gatekeeping as mothers' beliefs and behaviors that *inhibit* greater involvement in family work. They classified 21% of the women participating in their study as "maternal gatekeepers" reporting high levels of (1) reluctance to relinquish responsibility over family matters or setting rigid standards, (2) needing external validation of a mothering identity, and (3) conceptualizing differentiated family roles. Similar to the women nurses discussed above who harassed their male colleagues, gatekeeping can be a means of preventing male intrusion into feminized arenas of home labor (Clair, 1994). Finally, women's gender crossing in the workplace can also have severe negative repercussions on personal heterosexual relationships in the form of divorce (Heckert, Nowak, & Snyder, 1998; Schroedel, 1990; see Sayer & Bianchi, 2000 for an opposing argument) and potentially, domestic violence (Atkinson, Greenstein, & Lang, 2005).

### Glass Ceilings and Glass Escalators

Given extensive studies of glass ceiling effects and strategies, a comprehensive review of the literature extends beyond the scope of this chapter (Pollard, 2005; Powell, 1999; Weyer, 2007). Rather, this chapter focuses on select barriers to women's advancement into traditionally male dominated levels of organizational hierarchies (i.e., vertical sex segregation) and men's advancement experiences in female-dominated occupations. Glass ceiling research shifts our focus from women's gender crossing experiences within primarily male-dominated occupations (i.e., law enforcement, mining, and engineering) to women's experiences in male-dominated executive jobs across various occupations (i.e., CEOs, CFOs).

Explanations for glass ceiling effects vary with corresponding theoretical explanations, but in the management and organizational literatures, scholars have identified three categories of factors that persistently contribute to inequalities—corporate practices, stereotyping and preferred leadership styles, and structural and cultural explanations (Buzzanell, 1995; Morrison & Van Glinow, 1990; Oakley, 2000). Oakley summarized extant research and explained that, first, organizational practices—such as training and development, hiring, and promotional considerations—can negatively affect women's upward organizational progression. Second, and as explained above in relation to discourses of competence, researchers have partly attributed glass ceiling effects to gendered double binds in women's leadership behaviors and communication styles, along with socialized gender role stereotypes and gendered preferred leadership styles. Third, research consistently concludes that men's negative reactions to powerful women, gendered token effects, as well as the "old boys'" networks also can damage women's promotion opportunities.

While a great deal of the research that Oakley reviewed is grounded in social constructivist and feminist approaches, Buzzanell (1995) embraced the constructivist project even further by arguing that current theorizing is both insufficient and detrimental to fundamental change. Buzzanell developed three critiques of existing definitions and strategies. First, she observed the perilous and inadequate nature of viewing the glass ceiling as primarily a problem of numbers and, by extension, resulting simply from the lack of women in executive positions. The numbers argument fails to recognize that women who make it into the c-suite most likely had to adopt patriarchal organizational practices to achieve this status. Merely increasing the number of women promoted into this system will have little or no fundamental change on the gendered system itself. Buzzanell also noted overlap among affirmative action stereotyping, numbers remedies to the glass ceiling, and discourses of competence. Pointing to work by J. Martin, Price, Bies, and Powers (1987), she stressed that increased representation of women driven by affirmative action still comes with "the presumption of incompetence" (p. 330).

Second, glass ceiling practices and research perpetuate the equality-difference binary. According to Buzzanell (1995), arguments based on equality or that "men and women have identical interests, beliefs, and practices" (p. 330) ostensibly offer women the choice to shatter the glass ceiling if they emulate the male model of organizational success. Framing women as having distinctly different, unique needs and challenges with respect to organizational advancement, however, often deteriorates into polarized debates about "mommy tracks" (Schwartz, 1989) and "Opting Out" (Belkin, 2003, see also Stone, 2007). Finally, programs and policies focused on women's career development/developmental needs frequently add additional layers of responsibility and pressure to women's work activities, ostensibly under the guise of helping women break though the glass ceiling. Buzzanell argued that, instead, we should reconsider the value of "women's work" in our daily practices and macro-discourses and structures as a means of reshaping organizations and work life.

Glass ceiling processes and effects, however, differ greatly from the glass escalator. As alluded to early on in this analysis, Kanter's (1977) original articulation of token experiences in the workplace was revised to acknowledge the gendered nature of tokenism. Research on men's career experiences in female-dominated occupations illustrates this effect across various ways. Starting with hiring decisions, men entering fields such as nursing, elementary education, librarianship, and social work often experience significant advantage; C. L. Williams (1992) emphasized a preference for hiring men. In other words, men's token status, different from the token status of women, can be constructed as a positive deviation from the norm. According to one male librarian interviewed by C. L. Williams, "Because there are so few [male librarians], and the...I don't know, maybe they feel they're being progressive or something, [but] I have had a real sense that they really appreciate having a male" (p. 255). According to the participants in C. L. Williams' study, men felt tracked into masculine-aligned specialties or managerial work, and even negatively evaluated for not being aggressive enough in pursuing advancement opportunities.

Yet as C. L. Williams (1992) maintained, men performing "women's work" effectively get "kicked upstairs" or ride glass escalators into higher status and better paying positions in feminized occupations, an effect which contradicts women's token experiences (see also Pringle, 1993). Industries (such as hairdressing) exist in which the employee base is predominantly female, but men tend to cluster at the top of the hierarchy. As argued by Attwood and Hatton (1983), industry insiders expressed anxiety about the lack of men hairdressers not out of a desire for gender equality but rather because men are future managers and owners. Greater evidence for escalator effects at lower levels and negative effects on men's advancement has been suggested as perceived outcomes of affirmative action policies (e.g., Henson & Rogers, 2001). In addition to many promotion advantages, men's experiences of collegial relations with supervisors and colleagues in feminized occupations also differs from many of the reports of hostile work relations and environments experienced by token women (for an exception, see Clair, 1994). Men are more likely to supervise other men and, differing from women's experience, members tend to construct their gender status as a positive difference.

In short, discourses of inequality and related male privilege span occupational and marital gender crossing with respect to working conditions, experiences of negative and sexualized workplace interactions, marital power relations, and progression upward through the organizational ranks. As much as patriarchy reveals, it also obscures divisions of labor. Patriarchy itself must be questioned as the professed universal and preeminent mechanism of inequalities in divisions of labor (Collins, 1990; hooks, 2001). Of course, male (especially White, middle class, heterosexual) privilege should be acknowledged, but race and class divisions of labor and related inequalities for women may also significantly affect lack of access and differential experiences of occupational and relational life (B. J. Allen, 2004; Parker, 2002).

## Contributions, Critiques, and Research Directions

This literature review makes three contributions to scholarly knowledge about crossing and transforming occupational and household divisions of labor: foregrounding gendered micro-practices, sexualizing across the public and private, and critiquing divisions of labor intersectionalities.

### Foregrounding Gendered Micro-Practices

First, notwithstanding context, this review foregrounds and assembles the variety of micro-practices which constitute reproduction, resistance, or transformation of interconnected gendered occupational and relational boundaries. For example, the social interaction practices described across the studies in this review include denial, deflecting humor, self-monitoring, verbal context shifting, harassment, renaming, reframing, cover stories, overt resistance behaviors, passive resistance behaviors, and interaction avoidance. They constitute the daily practices of "doing gender" in the context of household and occupational divisions of labor (West & Zimmerman, 1987); "doing gender" is a phrase too often evoked without delineation of the discourses and related practices of "doing." As communication scholars, we are particularly well-suited to further theorize and evaluate communicative accomplishments with respect to gendered forms of work and family life.

Organizational and governmental practices can also be pulled together such as sex-specific workplace policies or informal rules in hospitals, daycare centers, and schools, as well as historical gendered census practices of occupational and family labor. In short, this list of micro-practices and policies, although clearly tentative and partial, begins to empirically illustrate how stakeholders continually accomplish sexual divisions of labor in daily workplace and relational interactions. Dominant notions of masculinity and femininity become visible during 'social relational contexts' [these are]...any situation[s] in which individuals define themselves in relation to others in order to act" (Ridgeway & Correll, 2004, p. 511), particularly those of gender violations (Kite, 2001; see also Risman, 1999), and are pivotal to processes of social change (Reskin, 1988). Yet, rigorous empirical analysis of specific language and social interaction strategies of social change and stability remain scant (Ashcraft, 2007; Mills & Chiarmonte, 1991; Rakow, 1996). This literature review underscores the need to deeply explore communication practices in relation to larger organizational structures and societal discourses of household and occupational sex segregation; that is, intersections at the division of labor of micro-level *d*iscourse and macro-level *D*iscourses (Alvesson & Karreman, 2000).

As Acker (1990) explained, "advantage and disadvantage, exploitation and control, action and emotion, meaning and identity" (p. 146) emerge through micro-processes which, simultaneously, also perpetuate the gendering occupations, workplace hierarchies, and skill categories. Gendered discourses and related practices are part and parcel of ongoing occupational infiltration, take-over, re-segregation, ghettoization, and internal demarcation (Reskin, 1988). Bringing these bodies of research together allows us to see the mechanisms of the "structuration" of our gendered public-private relational and occupational structures and inequities (Giddens, 1984); it foregrounds the constitutive role of communicative practices.

This assemblage also reveals the fact that, through these discourses and related practices, both lay and academic, we produce a particular kind of knowledge about the divisions of labor. We often construct women as "normal" caregivers and men as "deviant" caregivers. We give masculine skills and competencies higher social value and treat feminized care-giving skills and competencies as unskilled and devalued. If closely examined, all of the micro-practices of gender crossing embody both power and resistance (Clair, 1994; Mumby, 2005). They constitute dialectical processes which, at times, reify dominant forms of gender hegemony while simultaneously exhibiting resistance. Male daycare providers perpetuate hegemonic forms of masculinity through fighting homosexual occupational stereotypes. Female nurses protect care-giving as "women's work" by labeling men as incompetent caregivers yet concurrently maintaining its devalued status. Breadwinning mothers' attempts at maintaining their husbands' sense of self also devalue their own economic contributions to their families. Sex-specific rules about care-giving both guard organizations against lawsuits and pacify client/customer/patient fears yet perpetuate assumptions of male caregivers as dangerous or deviant. To be clear, sexual abuse does occur or should be problematized, but the individual and social consequences of this way of speaking about and interacting with men choosing to engage in care-giving work must be carefully analyzed. Encouraging men to take on both paid and unpaid care-giving responsibilities in society, despite their perpetual devaluation, is essential to broader feminist and pro-feminist men's goals for social change. Fathering and male care-giving comprises a feminist issue (Silverstein, 1996) which we must cautiously address without glorifying male care-giving or perpetuating patriarchical assumptions. Clearly, gendered tensions constituting the meanings and divisions of labor thread across the public and private spheres.

With respect to worldwide sex segregation, Anker (1998) argued that "the most important changes required, if occupational segregation is to be greatly reduced, are ideational in nature" (p. 417). Members reproduce ideologies and related occupational and family structures through everyday micro-practices. As such, future study and recommendations for practice stemming from the field of communication studies should focus on further delineating and examining these discursive practices and related behaviors. Further research should focus on understanding how specific forms of language and social interaction variably relate to social inequalities of divisions of labor. For example, teams of communication scholars with expertise in media, gender, and organizational communication can explore how recruitment strategies of non-traditional populations into gendered occupations and hierarchical levels enable and constrain particular gendered identities, relations, and choices. Intra-disciplinary groups of scholars may also further explore how men in non-traditional careers reproduce or resist assumptions of hegemonic masculinity or "glass escalator" career advantages. As Buzzanell (1995) aptly argued, social change related to gender and career advantage will not happen as a result of increasing the numbers of women as CEOs (nor men as daycare providers). We need to fundamentally examine, question, and potentially transform how we do gender across everyday organizational and family practices. Further, all communication scholars must question their own research practices and reflect on how they might unintentionally perpetuate narrow understandings of care-giving and wage earning in their choices of literature to consult, questions to ask, and sampling procedures or participation criteria.

### Sexualizing across the Public and Private

Reinforcing the deeply rooted sexualized, not just gendered, nature of occupational and relational divisions of labor entails another vital lesson to be learned from this review. Sexuality can be defined as a political, historical discursive formation constituting the social expression and relations of physical bodily desires (Burrell & Hearn, 1993; Hearn, Sheppard, Tancred-Sheriff, & Burrell, 1993). As Weeks (1986) asserted, gender and sexuality are closely related yet distinct. According to Weeks, "[We] still cannot think about sexuality without taking into account gender...the elaborate façade of sexuality has in large part been built on the assumption of fundamental differences between men and women, and of male dominance over women" (p. 25). Additionally, discourses and practices of heterosexuality privilege and serve to discipline not only sexual desires and behavior but also remain deeply entrenched in occupational and family divisions of labor.

Much of the research discussed throughout this chapter denaturalizes the binary nature of gendered work and family relations, yet underlying heteronormative assumptions remain unproblematized. Gender crossing studies consistently detail discriminatory and homophobic reactions and interactions as a part of the routine experiences of men engaging in paid or unpaid care-giving work. Regardless of sexual preference and for varying reasons, for example, many male nurses reported constantly "doing" heterosexuality particularly in interactions with non-intimate others. One nurse who explained that "I conduct myself like a man" reified heterosexuality and related notions of hegemonic masculinity in his efforts to avoid being labeled homosexual. Homophobia and the avoidance of the feminine both remain fundamental to the performance of hegemonic masculinity (Kimmel, 2001; McCreary, 1994). By extension, changing heterosexual divisions of labor requires a challenging sexual preference stigma and discrimination (Herek, 2004; Kimmel, 2001).

Research detailed in this review explains how organizational members use private sphere sexual preferences to discipline occupational choice and behavior. To date, scholars have only touched on issues of male sexuality in this body of research when they occasionally include gay men engaged in care-giving work for pay as study participants; researchers erroneously treat sexuality as a sampling characteristic, not a fundamental part of the organizing process. Research also reveals heterosexual power relations for at-home fathers sees them as not fulfilling their traditional duties as breadwinners and, as such, requiring identity management help from their primary earning wives. Studies of men as disrupting heterosexualized relations in secretarial work illustrate the inherent sexualizing of many occupational roles. Sexuality also serves as an ingrained and disciplining force for women performing non-traditional career or family work and identities, but the means of regulation play out in ways that are different from those for men. Others less often label women as homosexual or lesbian; rather they become objectified and (hetero)sexualized when they cross gendered occupational boundaries and are required to manage men's hegemonic identities to preserve traditional sexual power relationships in marriage. The studies discussed in this chapter highlight women police officers, miners, CEOs, and senior executives being positioned by others as sex objects, subject to sexual harassment, and needing to distance themselves from feminine behaviors in the context of male-dominated occupations and hierarchical levels. Co-workers simultaneously call upon women to perform relational work in the organization yet devalue them for doing so (Fletcher, 1999). Members reproduce heteronormative assumptions of women's sexual submission and sanction deviations across a range of occupations. These assumptions persist to such a degree that they are reproduced even during times of significant occupational restrictions (Reskin & Roos, 1990). In the private sphere, breadwinning wives often perform the gendered relational work to maintain hegemonic masculinity even in the face of very contradictory experiences. In short, discourses and practices of heterosexuality remain deeply embedded in organizational and marital relations of power and identity, and not sequestered exclusively in the private sphere.

Future communication research needs to examine and challenge the fundamental heteronormative nature of our scholarship and continue this work in relation to occupational and relational divisions of labor (Foster, 2008). Exploring both similarities and differences in the practices and experiences of gays and lesbians in the workplace and in personal relationships allows for a portrait of doing work outside, at times, of the stranglehold of heteronormative power relations. Researchers should further explore similarities between heterosexual and gay/lesbian micro-practices for managing non-traditional identity at work or in personal relations. Studies of *passing*, for instance, or "how one conceals normal information about oneself to preserve, sustain, and encourage others' predisposed assumptions about one's identities" (Spradlin, 1998, p. 598) have some resemblance to men's use of cover stories to preserve their masculine identities when doing "women's work" (Henson & Rogers, 2001). What could communication scholars learn about identity and narrative at the intersection of organization, sexuality, and identity? Scholars in our field could also extend research on the division of household labor by exploring the language and social interactions of gay and lesbian couples. While limited research has argued that same-sex relationships (men or women couples) are more egalitarian than heterosexual couples (e.g., Giddings, 2003; Solomon, Rothblum, & Balsam, 2005) but considerable work remains to be done. Again, communication scholars must also reflect on how their own research practices might take up heteronormative assumptions and the consequences these assumptions have on the knowledge being produced.

### Critiquing Divisions of Labor Intersectionalities

The trenchant nature of discourses and practices of patriarchal gender relations and sexuality have been explored so far in this final discussion section. While these ideologies are important to contest, male domination or heterosexuality should not be mistaken to provide comprehensive explanations for divisions of home and occupational labor and related inequalities. The ubiquitous use of the adjective *sexual* with respect to divisions of labor effectively absences other social identity categories with significant effects on how labor and its associated resources are distributed. Divisions of labor and related inequalities based on class and race significantly affect lack of access and differential experiences of occupational and relational life for people of color and those economically disadvantaged (Williams, 2000; see also B. J. Allen, 2004; Parker, 2002; Yoder & Berendsen, 2001). Further, as Lorde (2004) explained, problems of patriarchy are not necessarily the same for White women and Black women. Lorde says, "it is easy for Black women to be used by the power structure against Black men, not because they are men, but because they are Black" (p. 67). Sexuality is also raced and classed (e.g., West, 2004). Dominant culture assumptions about sexuality affect how we talk about and study problems of divisions of labor and also serve to obscure raced and class intersectionalities, inequalities, and relations (B. J. Allen, 2004; Anderson & Collins, 2004; Glenn, 2000; Hondagneu-Sotelo, 2004; Johnson, 2001).

As I detailed earlier, skill constitutes a gendered social construction (e.g., Ashcraft, 2006; Phillips & Taylor, 1980). For Black men in the United States, however, skill is not only gendered but significantly raced. Moss and Tilly (2004) found that employers rated Black men poorly in terms of "skills, abilities, and traits that pertain to personality, attitude and behavior rather than technological knowledge" (p. 239). These negative evaluations of African American male job candidates are partly driven by racial stereotypes and cultural differences between employers and young Black men. For example, according to Moss and Tilly, one Latino employer applauded the work ethic of Hispanic employees yet dismissed Black workers' motivation as "putting in the time and playing around" (p. 244). Other employers evoked stereotypes of Black men as scary, hostile, or lazy in their justification for not hiring them for jobs requiring "soft skills." The raced nature of assumptions about "traditional" family gender roles also argues that African American heterosexual couples divide work and family labors in ways which vary from dominant culture stereotypes and research (Broman, 1991; Burgess, 1994).

Workplace segregation does not just occur by sex but also by race and class; this insight may shift the viewpoint of some scholars who read the word *segregation*, which has been used up to this point only in conjunction with *sex* segregation. While members shape workplace divisions of labor by gender, they also divide them by race (U.S. Department of Labor, Bureau of Labor Statistics, 2007). Thus, harassment at work is not only sexual but also targeted at race and sexual preference as well. As Tomaskovic-Devey (1993) argued, "Middle-class blacks work in extraordinarily white environments... [and] often experience direct face-to-face discrimination at work" (p. 17). Gay and lesbian individuals also report persistent discrimination and harassment based on sexual preference (Herek, 2004). Some communication scholars have begun to explore intersections among divisions of paid labor and race;

for example, B. J. Allen's (1996) analysis of Black women's standpoints on organizational socialization reveals much about how divisions of university scholarship, teaching, and advising work is racially divided as well as embedded in historically racialized stereotypes for Black women (see also Parker, 2002). Teams of communication scholars need to collaborate and investigate micro-practices of social interaction across a diverse set of occupational or family experiences. In addition to exploring gender crossing experiences, we also need to further problematize the challenges and opportunities of crossing racial and class work and occupational boundaries. Finally, communication scholars need to draw upon diverse literatures and recognize when their own research practices unintentionally perpetuate raced and classed explanations for divisions of labor and related communication phenomenon. As with all of the critiques levied above, much research remains to be conducted and many essays for popular audience based on rigorous scholarship left unwritten.

## Acknowledgments

I would like to express my appreciation to Christina Beck for her guidance, Jennifer Scott for her editorial insights, as well as the views of the three anonymous reviewers. I would also like to acknowledge the graduate students and faculty at Arizona State University who shared ideas with me during my visit in the winter of 2008 and Karen Ashcraft for her insights on this project. I must also express my gratitude to Joe Medved for his support, patience, and daily encouragement.

## Notes

1.  Across social science literatures, a wealth of research investigates micro-practices of marital and workplace gender transgressions (e.g., Bittman et al., 2003; Coltrane, 1996; Conn, 2004; Corcoran-Nantes & Roberts, 1997; Dennis & Kunkel, 2004; Doucet, 2004; 2007; Drago et al., 2005; Evans, 1997, 2002; Evans & Frank, 2003; Fletcher, 1999; Greenstein, 1996; Henson & Rogers, 2001; Kite, 2001; Medved & Rawlins, 2007; Murray, 1996; Pilcher, 1998; Pringle, 1988, 1993; Russell, 2007; Shuler, 2003; Stamp, 1985; C. L. Williams, 1993). Studies investigate, for example, men performing tasks, behaviors, or identities characterized as "women's work" in either in the workplace (e.g., male nurses, elementary teachers, daycare providers) or in the home (e.g., stay-at-home fathers) as well as women doing traditionally male-identified work in the organization (e.g., female CEOs and welders) or in marital or family relations (e.g., breadwinning mothers).

    A second interconnected area of research explores historical and current macro-discourses and processes of occupational gender transformations (e.g., Anker, 1998; Bradley, 1993; Charles & Grusky, 2004; Cohen & Huffman, 2002; Lueptow, Garovich-Szabo, & Lueptow, 2001; Reskin, 1993; Reskin & Roos, 1990; Tichenor, 2005; Wright & Jacobs, 1994). This body of work delves into, for instance, how previously male-dominated fields—such as real estate sales

(Thomas & Reskin, 1990), insurance adjusting and examining (Phipps, 1990), or teaching (Preston, 1997)—became feminized or, alternatively, how women's central role in child birthing as midwives became medicalized and, as a result, male-dominated (Donnison, 1988). Volumes of social research also document continuing inequities in household divisions of labor (e.g., Bittman et al., 2003; Coontz, 1999; McKeon, 2005; Tichenor, 2005) and changes in the gendered nature of family labor (Griswold, 1993; Hays, 1996).

Occupational sex segregation and the division of household labor, however, remain topics sparingly and often indirectly addressed in communication research (e.g., Alberts & Trethewey, 2007; Ashcraft, 2005, 2006; Bergen, Kirby & McBride, 2007; Buzzanell, 1995; Clair, 1994; Clair & Thompson, 1996; Conn, 2004; Jorgenson, 2002; Kisselburgh, Berkelaar & Buzzanell, this volume; Medved, 2007; Medved & Rawlins, 2007; Snavely & Fairhurst, 1984). Scholars in our field more often pursue other diverse issues of gender and organizing (e.g., Ashcraft & Mumby, 2004; Buzzanell, 1994, 2001; Buzzanell & Goldzwig, 1991; Mumby & Putnam, 1992; Sloan & Krone, 2000; Shuler, 2003; Townsley, 2006; Trethewey, 2001; Trethewey, Scott, & LeGreco, 2006) and, as of late, work-life intersections (e.g., Buzzanell et al., 2005; Cowen & Hoffman, 2008; Golden, 2007; Kirby & Krone, 2002; Krouse & Afifi, 2007; Medved 2004, 2007; Medved & Kirby, 2005).

Notably, much about gendered occupational and family roles, identities, and opportunities has drastically changed over the past half century partly as a result of second wave feminism as well as previous centuries' of women's activism. More workplace integration has occurred since 1970 than took place in the previous hundred years (Wright & Jacobs, 1994) and men are doing more domestic work at home (Coltrane, 1996, 2004). Yet, household labor, childcare, and "[o] ccupational segregation by sex [remains] extensive and pervasive and is one of the most important and enduring aspects of labour markets [as well as social, organizational and relational life] around the world" (Anker, 1998, p. 3). Thus, both public and private sphere divisions of labor remain replete with inequalities. Moreover, these inequalities can neither be fully understood nor radically changed in isolation, although some radical feminist scholars might take issue with this claim. Analyzing studies of crossing and transforming these gendered divisions of labor is the primary focus of this chapter.

2. Two reasons exist for examining research findings situated within and across both the public and private spheres: (a) to develop a more complex picture of how gender is reproduced, indeed co-constructed, across occupational and organizational life, and (b) the process of deconstructing gender as *the* singular and dominant difference that "makes a difference" in how we talk about and apportion forms of work in personal and professional life (B. J. Allen, 2004; Glenn, 2000; West & Fenstermaker, 1995).

First, the "separate spheres" ideology, or ways of positioning work and family as autonomous, gender-specific domains of life resulting from economic forces of Western industrial revolutions, has long since been debunked by feminist scholars (e.g., Ferree, 1990). To best capture the messiness and complexity of how gender shapes divisions of labor, we cannot independently focus on either occupational sex-segregation (public) or gendered forms of family labor (private). Doing so "tends to truncate, cut short, and pervert…important distinctions" about work and personal life (Geuss, 2001, p. xx). As such, this chapter organizes and reviews these literatures not as "separate spheres" of intellectual work or as filtered through traditional scholarly divisions of research labor but rather a series of findings which represent and construct overlapping, nondualistic, and multifaceted ideological tensions (Geuss, 2001; Mumby, 2001). This framework for reviewing these bodies of literature allows us to question dominant public/ private logics and forms of knowledge, the politics of critical definitions, as well as articulations of division of labor inequality "problems" and their potential "solutions."

Second, given that gender has been taken up as the central explanatory mechanism for both public and private divisions of labor, a great deal of interpretive effort in this chapter explores extant research findings related to the production of masculinities and femininities. Undeniably, decades of research, feminist and otherwise, demonstrate that gendered language and social interaction is fundamental to the appropriation of meaning and tasks of paid work and unpaid labor. Yet challenging the ubiquitous public/masculine-private/feminine distinction also allows for a wider array of social identities to be problematized regarding divisions of labor and related social inequalities. Questioning divisions and differences stemming from experiences and categories of race, class, and sexuality is essential and intimately connected with gendered meanings and practices. Recognizing these intersectionalities is not only indispensable to gaining a fuller understanding of how language and social interactions create differences in the divisions of labor but also, as will be argued in the final section of this chapter, to creating fundamental social change (B. J. Allen, 2004; Ferree, Lorber, & Hess, 2000; Glenn, 2000; Rosenblum & Travis, 2003).

3. The above discussion, indeed even the broad framing of this entire chapter, extends from a heteronormative stance. That is, the idea of *transgressing* or *crossing* gender norms means moving away from a "legitimate" or accepted mid-point and/or axis. In this case, the center is heterosexuality, its discourses and practices. Critiquing compulsory heterosexuality or heterosexual gender norms is a nascent but growing practice in social research (e.g., for more recent work in communication studies, see Foster, 2008; Haas & Stafford, 2005; Peplau & Beals, 2004; Spradlin, 1998; Suter, Daas, & Bergen, 2008).

4. According to structural/cultural explanations of gender, men and women are assumed to possess innate or socialized personal qualities or abilities which predispose them to aptly perform particular types of skills (Eagly & Karau, 1991). Men are rational, thus better decision makers; women are more emotional, thus better caregivers, so the logic goes. Further, some argue that "both sexes attribute more value to work performed by men than by women" (Cohen & Huffman, 2002, p. 884). So, society tends to value presumed male qualities and skills more than women's qualities and related skills. Not surprisingly, men who act more stereotypically masculine and women who act more stereotypically feminine enjoy higher evaluations of competence by their subordinates. Acting in ways that contradict gender stereotypes can be risky for both men and women but, keep in mind, this condition still exist in the larger cultural context of Western patriarchy (Fletcher, 1999). Double binds for women in leadership positions create unique constraints, not experienced by the majority of men (Jamison, 1995; Wood & Conrad, 1983).

Workplace and care-giving skills associated with femininity, more often than masculinity, tend to be perceived as *unskilled* (e.g., Fletcher, 1999) and unproductive (Folbre, 1991) or performance that requires little training, talent, and ability and deserves minimal financial reward (Reskin & Roos, 1990). In other words, "jobs can take on a gendered or racialized character that is independent of their incumbents and that influences how such jobs are concretely organized" (Tomaskovic-Devey, 1993, p. 12). To illustrate, some cultures frame intellectual work as masculine and, thus, more skilled than service or care-giving (Folbre, 2001; Wood, 1994; see related study by Kisselburgh et al., this volume). In the manufacturing arena, members perceive heavy machine operating as more skilled and laborious than dexterous manual assembly work often performed by women (Phillips & Taylor, 1980). We can also broadly exemplify the hierarchy embedded in types of work by comparing two stereotypical statements: "'My daughter is a physician,' resonates far more favorably in most people's ears than 'My son, the nurse'" (Williams, 1992, p. 262).

Historical constructions of "women's work" as unproductive or unskilled, some argue, stem from Marxist sentiments devaluing forms of work which do not directly produce profits for capitalist owners (Gerstein, 1973). The emergence of discourses of the "unproductive housewife" arose in relation to androcentric 19th century census practices in the United States and England. At this point, women were "formally relegated the census category of 'dependents'" (Folbre, 1991, p. 464), thus not productive in the market. Phillips and Taylor (1980) contended "that the classification of women's jobs as unskilled and men's jobs as skilled or semi-skilled frequently bears little relation to the actual amount of training or ability required for them" (p. 79). Meanings assigned to any skill or job, while not completely devoid of defensible associations between complexity and gendered status, remain largely ideological and often reproduce assumptions of patriarchy, as well as class and race (Ehrenreich, 2001; Tomaskovic-Devey, 1993).

5. Two historic examples of gendered occupational transformations are instructive. First, is the case of "Rosie the Riveter" (Coontz, 1999; Kossoudiji & Dresser, 1992). Between 1940 and 1945, the U.S. government successfully recruited women into wartime manufacturing jobs which had been held by men since early 1900s industrialization, as well as funding extensive childcare programs to support these urgently needed workers. When men returned from World War II, however, most women were laid off or downgraded into "women's jobs," such as clerical and service positions. According to Coontz, the laying off of these women en masse occurred despite economic arguments to the contrary—such as these women were cheaper to employ and an equally productive source of labor as returning male veterans. Women's movement out of customarily male-dominated jobs after World War II, however, proved to be only temporary and foreshadowed a wave of feminist movement that was not long in coming (Goldin, 1991).

Second, the concurrent feminization and professionalization of teaching offers another example of occupational transformation (Preston, 1997). Teaching or so-called school keeping in the 18th century was primarily a male-dominated field. Yet, when the field became increasingly professionalized and more women entered into these jobs, schools created managerial or supervisory positions to oversee the activities of individual teachers. A disproportionate number of men occupy supervisory positions in comparison to women (88% of elementary school teachers and 60% of school principles are women; Sargent, 2000).

Feminization together with professionalization, in this case, resulted in higher wages and increased status for women and men teachers, but it also came with "male-dominated bureaucratic structures, restricting autonomy, wage restructuring leading to greater gender differences in absolute wages while increasing wages overall, and the creation of a cultural representation of the female teacher" (Preston, 1997, p. 331).

6. Discourses and practices of men's occupational takeovers also implicate domestic heterosexual relations. Birnbaum's historical study of 1920s machining in the clothing trade in Britain detailed how men staunchly fought for, and succeeded in maintaining the distinction of male machinists as being skilled and female machinists as being semi-skilled (n.d., cited in Phillips & Taylor, 1980). Yet this resistance "arose out of the struggle of men workers from Russian, Jewish and Polish communities to retain their social status within the family.... Forced as they were to take on machining work usually done by women as semi-skilled, they fought to preserve their masculinity by re-defining (their) machining as skilled labor" (Phillips & Taylor, 1980, p. 85).

7. Discourses of competence are undergirded by opposing and hotly contested relationships among biological sex, gender, and particular workplace or family tasks. Clearly, pink and blue clothing or sex-specific childhood toys mark only the beginning of a lifetime of gender socialization. Reviewing the extensive literature on gender and childhood socialization (e.g., Chodorow, 1978; Peters, 1994), biological sex differences (Fausto-Sterling, 1985; Hrdy, 1999; Urdy, 1994), and the nature/nurture debate (Gander, 2003) is not the focus of this chapter. Still any discussion of appropriating gendered meanings to interpretations of adults' competence to perform paid or unpaid work must be acknowledged as the continuation of ongoing processes of gender socialization (Csikszentmihalyi & Schneider, 2000; Medved, Brogan, McClanahan, Morris, & Shepherd, 2006; see also related reviews by Ganesh & McAllum, this volume; Kisselburgh et al., this volume).

## References

Acker, J. (1990). Hierarchies, jobs, and bodies: A theory of gendered organizations. *Gender & Society, 4*, 139–158.

Alberts, J., & Trethewey, A. (2007, Summer). Building gratitude: Love, honor, and thanks. *Greater Good, 4*, 20–22.

Allen, B. J. (1996). Feminist standpoint theory: A black woman's (re)view of organizational socialization. *Communication Studies, 47*, 257–271.

Allen, B. J. (2004). *Difference matters: Communicating social identity.* Long Grove, IL: Waveland Press.

Allen, J. (1993). Male elementary teachers: Experiences and perspectives. In C. Williams (Ed.), *Doing "women's work": Men in nontraditional occupations* (pp. 113–127). Newbury Park, CA: Sage.

Allen, S. M., & Hawkins, A. J. (1999). Maternal gatekeeping: Mothers' beliefs and behaviors that inhibit greater father involvement in family work. *Journal of Marriage and the Family, 61*, 199–212.

Alvesson, M., & Karreman, D. (2000). Varieties of discourse: On the study of organizations through discourse analysis. *Human Relations, 53*, 1125–1149.

Anderson, M. L., & Collins, P. H. (2004). *Race, class and gender: An anthology* (5th ed.). Belmont, CA: Thompson-Wadsworth.

Anker, R. (1998). *Gender and jobs: Sex segregation of occupations in the world.* Geneva, Switzerland: International Labour Office.

Ashcraft, K. L. (1999). Managing maternity leave: A qualitative analysis of temporary succession. *Administrative Science Quarterly, 44*, 240–280.

Aschcraft, K. L. (2005). Resistance through consent? Occupational identity, organizational form, and the maintenance of masculinity among commercial airline pilots. *Management Communication Quarterly, 19*, 67–90.

Aschcraft, K. L. (2006). Back to work: Sights/sites of difference in gender and organizational communication studies. In B. J. Wood & J. T. Wood (Eds.), *The Sage handbook of gender and communication* (pp. 97–122). Thousand Oaks, CA: Sage.

Ashcraft, K. L. (2007). Appreciating the "work" of discourse: Occupational identity and difference as organizing mechanisms in the case of commercial pilots. *Discourse & Communication, 1*, 9–36.

Ashcraft, K. L., & Mumby, D. K. (2004). *Reworking gender: A feminist communicology of organization.* Thousand Oaks, CA: Sage.

Atkinson, M. P., & Boles, J. (1984). WASP (Wives as Senior Partners). *Journal of Marriage and the Family, 46*, 681–670.

Atkinson, M. P., Greenstein, T. N., & Lang, M. M. (2005). For women, breadwinning can be dangerous: Gendered resource theory and wife abuse. *Journal of Marriage and Family, 67*, 1137–1148.

Attwood, M. & Hatton, F. (1983). "Getting on": Gender differences in career development: A case study in the hairdressing industry. In E. Gamarnickow, D. Morgan, J. Purvis, & D. Taylorson (Eds.). *Gender, class, and work* (pp. 115–130). London: Heineman.

Belkin, L. (2003, October26). The opt-out revolution. *New York Times Magazine*, 42–47, 58, 85–86.

Bergen, K. M., McBride, M. C., & Kirby, E. L. (2007). "How do you get two houses cleaned?": Accomplishing family caregiving in commuter marriages. *Journal of Family Communication, 7*, 287–308.

Bittman, M., England, P., Folbre, N., Sayer, L., & Matheson, G. (2003). When does gender trump money? Bargaining and time in household work. *American Journal of Sociology, 109*, 186–214.

Bradley, H. (1993). Across the great divide: The entry of men into "women's jobs." In C. L. Williams (Ed.), *Doing "women's work": Men in non-traditional occupations* (pp. 10–27). Newbury Park, CA: Sage.

Brines, J. (1994). Economic dependency, gender and the division of labor at home. *American Journal of Sociology, 100*, 562–688.

Broman, C. L. (1991). Gender, work-family roles, and psychological well-being of blacks. *Journal of Marriage and Family, 53*, 509–521.

Bureau of Labor Statistics. (2007). Current Population Survey 11. Employed persons by detailed occupation, sex, race, and Hispanic or Latino ethnicity. Retrieved June 16, 2008, from http://www.bls/gov/cps/epsaat11.pdf

Burgess, N. J. (1994). Gender roles revisited: The development of the "woman's place" among African American women in the United States. *Journal of Black Studies, 24*, 391–401.

Burrell, G., & Hearn, J. (1993). Gender, sexuality, and organizational theory. In J.

Hearn, D. L. Sheppard, P. Tancred-Sheriff, & G. Burrell (Eds.), *The sexuality of organization* (pp. 29–44). London: Sage.

Butler, J. (1990). *Gender trouble: Feminism and the subversion of identity.* New York: Routledge.

Butterfield, D. A., & Grinnell, J. P. (1990). "Re-viewing" gender, leadership, and managerial behavior: Do three decades of research tell us anything? In G. N. Powell (Ed.), *Handbook of gender and work* (pp. 223–238). Thousand Oaks, CA: Sage.

Buzzanell, P. M. (1994). Gaining a voice: Feminist perspectives in organizational communication. *Management Communication Quarterly, 7,* 339–383.

Buzzanell, P. M. (1995). Reframing the glass ceiling as a socially constructed process: Implications for understanding change. *Communication Monographs, 62,* 327–354.

Buzzanell, P. M. (2001). Gendered practices in the contemporary workplace: A critique of what often constitutes front page news in *The Wall Street Journal. Management Communication Quarterly, 14,* 517–537.

Buzzanell, P. M. (2003). Feminist standpoint analysis of maternity and maternity leave for women with disabilities. *Women & Language, 26,* 53–65.

Buzzanell, P. M., & Goldzwig, S. (1991). Linear and nonlinear career models: Metaphors, paradigms, and ideologies. *Management Communication Quarterly, 4,* 466–505.

Buzzanell, P. M., Meisenbach, R. Remke, R., Liu, M., Bowers, V., & Conn, C. (2005). The good working mother: Managerial woman's sensemaking and feelings about work–family issues. *Communication Studies, 56,* 261–285.

Camilleri, P., & Jones, P. (2001). Doing "women's work"?: Men, masculinity, and caring. In B. Pease & P. Camilleri (Eds.), *Working with men in the human services* (pp. 5–36). Crows Nest, Australia: Allen & Unwin.

Casper, C. M. (2007). Daddy takes care of me! Fathers as care providers. *Current Population Reports.* Retrieved January 10, 2008, from http://www.census.gov/prod/3/97pubs/p70-59.pdf

Charles, M., & Grusky, D. B. (2004). *Occupational ghettos: The worldwide segregation of women and men.* Stanford, CA: Stanford University Press.

Chodorow, N. J. (1989). *The reproduction of mothering: Psychoanalysis and the sociology of gender.* Berkeley: University of California Press.

Clair, R. P. (1994). Resistance and oppression as self-contained opposite: An organizational communication analysis of one man's story of sexual harassment. *Western Journal of Communication, 58,* 235–262.

Clair, R. P. (1996). The political nature of the colloquialism, "A real job": Implications for organizational socialization. *Communication Monographs, 63,* 249–267.

Clair, R. P., & Thompson, K. (1996). Pay discrimination as a discursive and material practice: A case concerning extended housework. *Journal of Applied Communication Research, 24,* 1–20.

Clark, A. (1982). *Working life of women in the seventeenth century.* London: Routledge.

Cockburn, C. (1988). The gendering of jobs. In S. Walby (Ed.), *Gender segregation at work* (pp. 28–42). Philadelphia: Open University Press.

Cohen, P. N., & Huffman, M. L. (2002). Occupational segregation and the devaluation of women's work across U.S. labor markets. *Social Forces, 81,* 881–908.

Collins, P. H. (1990). *Black feminist thought: Knowledge, consciousness, and the politics of empowerment.* New York: Routledge.

Coltrane, S. (1996). *Family man: Fatherhood, housework, and gender equity.* New York: Oxford University Press.

Coltrane, S. (2004). Elite careers and family commitment: It's (still) about gender. *Annals of the American Academy of Political and Social Science, 596,* 214–220.

Conn, C. (2004). *Blue collar women at work: A feminist poststructuralist reading of gendered identities and materiality.* Unpublished doctoral dissertation, Purdue University, West Lafayette, IN.

Connell, R. W. (1995). *Masculinities.* Berkeley: University of California Press.

Coontz, S. (1999). *The way we never were: American families and the nostalgia trap.* New York: Basic Books.

Corcoran-Nantes, Y., & Roberts, K. (1997). "We've got one of those": The peripheral status of women in male-dominated industries. In D. Dunn (Ed.), *Workplace/women's place: An anthology* (pp. 271–287). Los Angeles: Roxbury.

Cowen, R., & Hoffman, M. F. (2008). The flexible organization: How contemporary employees construct the work/life border. *Qualitative Research Reports in Communication, 8,* 37–41.

Crittenden, A. (2001). *The price of motherhood.* New York: Metropolitan Books.

Csikszentmihalyi, M., & Schneider, B. (2001). *Becoming adult: How teenagers prepare for the world of work.* New York: Basic Books.

Cuddy, A. J. C., Fiske, S. T., & Glick, P. (2004). When professionals become mothers, warmth doesn't cut the ice. *Journal of Social Issues, 60,* 710–718.

Davey, C. L., & Davidson, M. J. (2000). The right of passage? The experiences of female pilots in commercial aviation. *Feminism & Psychology, 10,* 195–225

Deetz, S. A. (1992). *Democracy in an age of corporate colonization.* Albany: State University of New York Press.

Demos, J. (1970). *A little commonwealth: Family life in Plymouth Colony.* New York: Oxford University Press.

Dennis, M. R., & Kunkel, A. D. (2004). Perceptions of men, women, and CEOs: The effects of gender identity. *Social Behavior and Personality, 32,* 155–172.

Devault, M. L. (1991). *Feeding the family: The social organization of caring as gendered work.* Chicago: University of Chicago Press.

DiTomaso, N. (1993). Sexuality in the workplace: Discrimination and harassment. In J. Hearn, D. L. Sheppard, P. Tancred-Sheriff, & G. Burrell (1993), *The sexuality of organization* (pp. 71–90). London: Sage.

Dollahite, D. C., & Hawkins, A. J. (1998). A conceptual ethic of generative fathering. *Journal of Men's Studies, 7,* 109–132.

Donaldson, M. (1993). What is hegemonic masculinity? *Theory and Society, 22,* 643–657.

Donnison, J. (1988). *Midwives and medical men: A history of inter-professional rivalries and women's rights.* New York: Schocken Books.

Doucet, A. (2004). "It's almost like I have a job, but I don't get paid": Fathers at home reconfiguring work, care, and masculinity. *Fathering, 2,* 277–303.

Doucet, A. (2007). *Do men mother? Fathering, care, and domestic responsibility.* Toronto, Canada: University of Toronto Press.

Dougherty, D. S., & Smythe, M. J. (2004). Sensemaking, organizational culture, and sexual harassment. *Journal of Applied Communication Research, 32,* 293–317.

Douglas, S. J., & Michaels, M. W. (2004). *The mommy myth: The idealization of motherhood and how it has undermined women.* New York: Free Press.

Drago, R., Black, D., & Wooden, M. (2005). Female breadwinner families: Their existence, persistence and sources. *Journal of Sociology, 41*, 343–362.

Eagly, A. H., & Johnson, B. (1990). Gender and leadership style: A meta-analysis.
*Psychological Bulletin, 108*, 233–256.

Eagly, A. H., & Karau, S. J. (1991). Gender and the emergence of leaders: A meta-
analysis. *Journal of Personality and Social Psychology, 60*, 685–710.

Eagly, A. H., Makhijani, M. G., & Klonsky, B. G. (1992). Gender and the emergence of
leaders: A meta-analysis. *Psychological Bulletin, 111*, 3–22.

Ehrenreich, B. (2001). *Nickel and dimed: On (not) getting by in America*. New York:
Metropolitan Books.

Evans, J. (1997). Men in nursing: Issues of gender segregation and hidden advantage.
*Journal of Advanced Nursing, 26*, 226–231.

Evans, J. (2002). Cautious caregivers: Gender stereotypes and the sexualization of men
nurses' touch. *Journal of Advanced Nursing, 40*, 441–448.

Evans, J., & Frank, F. (2003). Contradictions and tensions: Exploring relations of masculinities in the numerically female-dominated nursing profession. *The Journal of
Men's Studies, 11*, 277–292.

Fagenson, E. A. (1993). *Women in management: Trends, issues, and challenges in
managerial diversity*. Newbury Park, CA: Sage.

Faludi, S. (1999). *Stiffed: The betrayal of the American man*. New York: Harper
Collins.

Fausto-Sterling, A. (1992). *Myths of gender: Biological theories about women and
men* (2nd ed.). New York: Basic Books.

Ferree, M. M. (1990). Beyond separate spheres: Feminism and family research. *Journal of Marriage and the Family, 52*, 866–884.

Ferree, M. M., Lorber, J., & Hess, B. B. (2000). Introduction. In M. M. Ferree, J.
Lorber, & B. B. Hess (Eds.), *Revisioning gender* (pp. xv–xxxvi). Walnut Creek,
CA: Altamira Press.

Fletcher, J. K. (1999). *Disappearing acts: Gender, power, and relational practice at
work*. Cambridge, MA: MIT Press.

Folbre, N. (1991). The unproductive housewife: Her evolution in nineteenth-century
economic thought. *Signs, 16*, 463–484.

Foster, E. (2008). Commitment, communication, and contending with heteronormativity: An invitation to greater reflexivity in interpersonal research. *Southern Communication Journal, 73*, 84–101.

Gander, E. M. (2003). *On our minds: How evolutionary psychology is reshaping the
Nature versus nurture debate*. Baltimore: John Hopkins Press.

Ganesh, S., & McAlllum, K. (this volume), Discourses of volunteerism. In C. S. Beck
(Ed.), *Communication yearbook 33* (pp. 343–383). New York: Routledge.

Garlick, B., Dixon, S., & Allen, P. (Eds.). (1992). *Stereotypes of women in power: Historical perspectives and revisionist views*. Westport, CT: Greenwood.

Gerstein, I. (1973). Domestic work and capitalism. *Radical America, 7*, 101–130.

Geuss, R. (2001). *Public goods, private goods*. Princeton, NJ: Princeton University
Press.

Giddens, A. (1984). *The constitution of society: Outline of the theory of structuration*.
Berkeley: University of California Press.

Giddings, L. (2003). But...Who mows the lawn?: The division of labor in same-sex
households. In K. S. Moe (Ed.), *Women, family and work: Writings on the economics of gender* (pp. 85–102). Oxford, England: Blackwell.

Glenn, E. N. (2000). The social construction and institutionalization of gender and race: An integrative framework. In M. M. Ferree, J. Lorber, & B. B. Hess (Eds.), *Revisioning gender* (pp. 3–43). Walnut Creek, CA: Altamira Press.

Golden, A. (2007). Father's frames for childrearing: Evidence toward a "masculine concept of caregiving." *Journal of Communication, 7*, 265–287.

Goldin, C. D. (1991). The role of World War II in the rise of women's employment. *The American Economic Review, 81*, 741–756.

Greenstein, T. N. (1996). Husbands' participation in domestic work: Interactive effects of husbands' and wives' gender ideology. *Journal of Marriage and the Family, 58*, 585–595.

Griswold, R. L. (1993). *Fatherhood in America: A history*. New York: Basic Books.

Haas, S. M., & Stafford, L. (2005). Maintenance behaviors in same-sex and martial relationships: A matched sample comparison. *Journal of Family Communication, 5*, 43–60.

Hays, S. (1996). *The cultural contradictions of motherhood*. New Haven, CT: Yale University Press.

Hearn, J., & Collinson, D. L. (1994). Theorizing unities and differences between men and masculinities. In M. Brod & M. Kaufman (Eds.), *Theorizing masculinities* (pp. 97–118). Thousand Oaks, CA: Sage.

Hearn, J., Sheppard, D. L., Tancred-Sheriff, P., & Burrell, G. (1993). *The sexuality of organization*. London: Sage.

Heckert, D. A., Nowak, T. C., & Snyder, K. A. (1998). The impact of husbands' and wives' relative earnings on marital disruption. *Journal of Marriage and the Family, 60*, 690–703.

Heikes, J. (1991). When men are the minority: The case of men in nursing. *The Sociological Quarterly, 32*, 389–401.

Helgesen, S. (1990). *The female advantage: Women's ways of leadership*. New York: Doubleday.

Henson, K. D., & Rogers, J. K. (2001). "Why Marcia you've changed!" Male clerical workers doing masculinity in a feminized occupation. *Gender & Society, 15*, 218–238.

Herek, G. M. (2004). Beyond "homophobia": Thinking about sexual prejudice and stigma in the twenty-first century. *Sexuality Research and Social Policy, 1*, 6–24.

Hochschild, A. R. (1989). *The second shift: Working parents and the revolution at home*. New York: Viking.

Holder, T. (1996). Women in nontraditional occupations: Information-seeking during organizational entry. *Journal of Business Communication, 33*, 9–26.

Hondagneu-Sotelo, P. (2004). Doméstica. In M. L. Anderson & P. Hill Collins (Eds.), *Race, class, and gender: An anthology* (5th ed., pp. 257–265). Belmont, CA: Thomson-Wadsworth.

hooks, b. (2001). *Feminism is for everybody: Passionate politics*. Cambridge, MA: South End Press.

Hrdy, S. B. (1999). *Mother nature: Maternal instincts and how they shape the human species*. New Haven, CT: Yale University Press.

Jacobs, J. A. (1998). Men in female-dominated fields: Trends and turnover. In C. Williams (Ed.), *Doing "women's work": Men in non-traditional occupations* (pp. 49–63). Newbury Park, CA: Sage.

Jamison, K. H. (1995). *Beyond the double binds: Women and leadership*. New York: Oxford University Press.

Jansma, L. J. (2000). Sexual harassment research: Integration, reformulation, and implications. In P. Kalbfleish (Ed.), *Communication yearbook 23* (pp. 163–225). Thousand Oaks, CA: Sage.

Johnson, F. (2001). The ideological undercurrents of the semantic notion "working mother." *Women & Language, 25*, 21–27.

Jorgenson, J. (2002). Engineering selves: Negotiating gender and identity in technical work. *Management Communication Quarterly, 15*, 350–380.

Jurik, N. C. (1985). An officer and a lady: Organizational barriers to women working as correctional officers in men's prisons. *Social Problems, 32*, 375–388.

Kanter, R. M. (1977). *Men and women of the corporation.* New York: Basic Books.

Keyton, J. (1996). Sexual harassment: A multidisciplinary synthesis and critique. In B. Burleson (Ed.), *Communication yearbook 19* (pp. 93–155). Thousand Oaks, CA: Sage.

Kimmel, M. S. (2001). Masculinity as homophobia: Fear, shame, and silence in the construction of gender identity. In S. M. Whitehead & F. J. Barrett (Eds.), *The masculinities reader* (pp. 265–285). Cambridge, England: Polity Press.

Kirby, E. L., & Krone, K. (2002). "The policy exists but you can't really use it": Communication and the structuration of work-family policies. *Journal of Applied Communication, 30*, 55–77.

Kisselburgh, L. G., Berkelaar, B. L., & Buzzanell, P. M. (this volume). Discourse, gender, and the meaning of work: Rearticulating science, technology, and engineering careers through communicative lenses. In C. S. Beck (Ed.), *Communication Yearbook 33* (pp. 259–299). New York: Routledge.

Kite, M. E. (2001). Changing times, changing gender roles: Who do we want women and men to be? In R. K. Unger (Ed.), *Handbook of psychology of women and gender* (pp. 215–227). New York: Wiley.

Kossoudji, S. A., & Dresser, L. J. (1992). Working class Rosies: Woman industrial workers during World War II. *Journal of Economic History, 52*, 431–446.

Krouse, S. S., & Afifi, T. D. (2007). Family-to-work spillover stress: Coping communicatively in the workplace. *Journal of Family Communication, 7*, 85–122.

Lazonick, W. (1979). Industrial relations and technological change: The case of the self-acting mule. *Cambridge Journal of Economics, 1*, 231–262.

Lillydahl, J. H. (1986). Women and traditionally male blue-collar jobs. *Work and Occupations, 13*, 307–323.

Linstead, S. (1995). Averting the gaze: Gender and power on the perfumed picket line. *Gender, Work & Organization, 2*, 192–205.

Lopata, H. Z. (1993). The interweave of public and private: A women's challenge to American society. *Journal of Marriage and the Family, 55*, 176–190.

Lorde, A. (2004). Age, race, class, and sex: Women redefining difference. In M. L. Anderson & P. H. Collins (Eds.), *Race, class & gender: An anthology* (5th ed., pp. 64–73). Belmont, CA: Thomson-Wadsworth.

Lueptow, L. B., Garovich-Szabo, L., & Lueptow, M. B. (2001). Social change and the persistence of sex typing: 1974–1997. *Social Forces, 80*, 1–36.

Lupton, B. (2000). Maintaining masculinity: Men who do "women's work." *British Journal of Management, 11*, S33–S48.

Martin, J. (1990). Deconstructing organizational taboos: The suppression of gender conflict in organizations. *Organizational Science, 1*, 339–359.

Martin, J., Price, R. L., Bies, R. J., & Powers, M. E. (1987). Now that I have it, I'm not sure I want it: The effects of opportunity on aspirations and discontent. In B. A.

Gutek & L. Larwood (Eds.), *Women's career development* (pp. 42–65). Newbury Park, CA: Sage.

Martin, S. E. (1994). "Outsider within" the station house: The impact of race and gender on black women police. *Social Problems, 41*, 383–399.

McCreary, D. R. (1994). The male role and avoiding femininity. *Sex Roles, 31*, 517–531.

McKeon, M. (2005). *The secret history of domesticity: Public, private, and the division of knowledge.* Baltimore: John Hopkins University Press.

Medved, C. E. (2004). The everyday accomplishment of work and family: Exploring practical actions in daily routines. *Communication Studies, 55*, 128–145.

Medved, C. E. (2007). Investigating family labor in communication studies: Threading across historical and contemporary discourses. *Journal of Family Communication, 7*, 1–19.

Medved, C. E., Brogan, S., McClanahan, A. M., Morris, J., & Shepherd, G. J. (2006). Work and family socializing communication: Messages, gender, and power. *Journal of Family Communication, 6*, 161–180.

Medved, C. E., & Kirby, E. L. (2005). Family CEOs: A feminist analysis of corporate mothering discourses. *Management Communication Quarterly, 18*, 435–478.

Medved, C. E., & Rawlins, W. K. (2007). *At-home fathers and breadwinning mothers: Variations in couples' approaches to homemaking and moneymaking.* Unpublished manuscript.

Meisenbach, R. (2007, November). *Discursive constructions of the female as breadwinner: Negotiating identities at home and at work.* Paper presented at the annual meeting of the National Communication Association, Chicago.

Mills, A. J., & Chiaramonte, P. (1991). Organization as a gendered communication act. *Canadian Journal of Communication, 16*, 381–398.

Morrison, A. M., & Van Glinow, M. A. (1990). Women and minorities in management. *American Psychologist, 45*, 200–208.

Moss, P., & Tilly, C. (2004). "Soft" skills and race. In M. L. Anderson & P. H. Collins (2004). *Race, class & gender: An anthology* (5th ed., pp. 239–247). Belmont, CA: Thomson-Wadsworth.

Mumby, D. K. (2001). Communication, organization, and the public sphere: A feminist perspective. In P. M. Buzzanell (Ed.), *Rethinking organizational & managerial communication from feminist perspectives* (pp. 3–23). Thousand Oaks, CA: Sage.

Mumby, D. K. (2005). Theorizing resistance in organizational studies: A dialectical approach. *Management Communication Quarterly, 19*, 19–44.

Mumby, D. K., & Putnam, L. L. (1992). The politics of emotion: A feminist reading of bounded rationality. *Academy of Management Review, 17*, 465–486.

Murray, S. B. (1996). "We all love Charles": Men in child care and the social construction of gender. *Gender & Society, 10*, 368–385.

Nielsen, W. G., & Kunkel, C. A. (2000). Gendered heteronormativity: Empirical illustrations in everyday life. *The Sociological Quarterly, 41*, 283–296.

Noe, R. (1988). Women and mentoring: A review and research agenda. *Academy of Management Review, 13*, 65–78.

Norander, S. (2008). Surveillance/discipline/resistance: Carly Fiorina under the gaze of the *Wall Street Journal. Communication Studies, 59*, 99–113.

Oakley, J. G. (2000). Gender-based barriers to senior management positions: Understanding the scarcity of female CEOs. *Journal of Business Ethics, 27*, 321–335.

Parker, P. S. (2002). Negotiating identity in raced and gendered workplace interactions: The use of strategic communication by African American women senior executives within dominant culture organizations. *Communication Quarterly, 50,* 251–268.

Peplau, L. A., & Beals, K. P. (2004). The family lives of lesbians and gay men. In A. Vangelisti (Ed.), *Handbook of family communication* (pp. 233–248). Mahwah, NJ: Erlbaum.

Petroski, D. J., & Edley, P. P. (2006). Stay-at-home fathers: Masculinity, family, work and gender stereotypes. *The Electronic Journal of Communication, 16*(3/4). Retrieved March 15, 2008, from http://www.cios.org.remote.baruch.cuny.edu/getfile/01634_EJC

Peters, J. F. (1994). Gender socialization of adolescents in the home: Research and discussion. *Adolescence, 29,* 914–934.

Phipps, P. A. (1990). Occupational resegregation among insurance adjusters and examiners. In B. F. Reskin & P. A. Roos (Eds.), *Job queues, Gender queues: Explaining women's inroads into male occupations* (pp. 225–240). Philadelphia: Temple University Press.

Phillips, A., & Taylor, B. (1980). Sex and skill: Notes towards a feminist economics. *Feminist Review, 6,* 79–88.

Pilcher, J. (1998). Gender matters? Three cohorts of women talking about role reversal. *Sociological review online, 3.* Retrieved February 27, 2008, from http://www.socresonline.org.uk/3/1/10.html

Pollard, P. L. (2005, April). *A critical analysis of the glass ceiling phenomenon: A Sloan Work and Family encyclopedia entry.* Retrieved April 23, 2008, from ttp://wfnetwork.bc.edu/encyclopedia.php?mode=nav

Powell, G. N. (1990). One more time: Do female and male managers differ? *Academy of Management Executive, 4,* 68–75.

Powell, G. N. (1999). Reflections on the glass ceiling: Recent trends and future prospects. In G. N. Powell (Ed.), *Handbook of gender and work* (pp. 325–345). Thousand Oaks, CA: Sage.

Preston, J. A. (1997). Gender and the formation of a women's profession: The case of public school teaching. In D. Dunn (Ed.), *Workplace/women's place: An anthology* (pp. 315–334). Los Angeles: Roxbury.

Pringle, R. (1988). *Secretary talk: Sexuality, power and work.* New York: Verso.

Pringle, R. (1993). Male secretaries. In C. L. Williams (Ed.), *Doing "women's work":\nMen in nontraditional occupations* (pp. 128–151). Newbury Park, CA: Sage.

Prokos, A., & Padavic, I. (2002). There oughtta be a law against bitches: Masculinity lessons in police academy training. *Gender, Work and Organization, 9,* 439–459.

Raggins, B. R., & Cotton, J. L. (1991). Easier said than done: Gender differences in perceived barriers to gaining a mentor. *Academy of Management Journal, 34,* 939–951.

Raggins, B. R., Townsend, B., & Mattis, M. (1998). Gender gap in the executive suite: CEO and female executives report on breaking the glass ceiling. *Academy of Management Executive, 12,* 28–42.

Rakow, L. F. (1986). Rethinking gender research in communication. *Journal of Communication, 36,* 11–24.

Rawlins, W. K. (1992). Theorizing public and private domains and practices of communication: Introductory concerns. *Communication Theory, 8,* 369–380.

Reskin, B. F. (1988). Bringing the men back in: Sex differentiation and the devaluation of women's work. *Gender & Society, 2,* 58–81.

Reskin, B. F. (1993). Sex segregation in the workplace. *Annual Reviews of Sociology, 19*, 241–270.

Reskin, B. F., & Roos, P. A. (1990). *Job queues, gender queues: Explaining women's inroads into male occupations.* Philadelphia: Temple University Press.

Ridgeway, C. L., & Correll, S. J. (2000). Limiting inequality through interaction: The end(s) of gender. *Contemporary Sociology, 29*, 110–120.

Ridgeway, C. L., & Correll, S. J. (2004). Unpacking the gender system: A theoretical perspective on gender beliefs and social relations. *Gender & Society, 18*, 510–531.

Risman, B. J. (1986). Can men mother? Life as a single father. *Family Relations, 35*, 95–102.

Rosenblum, K. E., & Travis, T. C. (2003). *The meaning of difference: American constructions of race, sex and gender, social class, sexual orientation and disability* (5th ed.). Boston: McGraw Hill.

Rosner, J. B. (1990, November/December). Ways women lead: The command-and-control leadership style associated with men is not the only way to succeed. *Harvard Business Review, 68*, 119–125.

Russell, R. (2007). Men doing "women's work:" Elderly men caregivers and the gendered construction of care work. *Journal of Men's Studies, 15*, 1–18.

Sargent, P. (2000). Real men or real teachers: Contradictions in the lives of men elementary teachers. *Men and Masculinities, 2*, 410–433.

Sayer, L. C., & Bianchi, S. (2000). Women's economic independence and the probability of divorce: A review and reexamination. *Journal of Family Issues, 21*, 906–943.

Schippers, M. (2007). Recovering the feminine other: Masculinity, femininity, and gender hegemony. *Theoretical Sociology, 36*, 85–102.

Schroedel, J. R. (1990). Blue-collar women: Paying the price at home and on the job. In H. Y. Grossman & N. L Chester (Eds.), *The experience and meaning of work in women's lives* (pp. 241–260). Mahwah, NJ: Erlbaum.

Schwartz, F. N. (1989). Management women and the new facts of life. *Harvard Business Review, 67*, 65–76.

Shuler, S. (2003). Breaking through the glass ceiling without breaking a nail: Women executives in Fortune magazine's "power 50" list. *American Communication Journal, 6*. Retrieved November 8, 2007, from http://www.acjournal.org/holdings/vol6/iss2/index.htm

Silverstein, L. B. (1996). Fathering is a feminist issue. *Psychology of Women Quarterly, 20*, 3–37.

Skelton, C. (1991). A study of career perspectives in male teachers of young children. *Gender & Education, 3*, 11–22.

Sloan, D. K., & Krone, K. J. (2000). Women managers and gendered values. *Women's Studies in Communication, 23*, 111–130.

Smith, C. D. (1998). "Men don't do this sort of thing": A case study of the social isolation of househusbands. *Men and Masculinities, 1*, 138–172.

Snavely, B. K., & Fairhurst, G. T. (1984). The male nursing student as a token. *Research in Nursing and Health, 7*, 287–294.

Solomon, S. E., Rothblum, E. D., & Balsam, K. F. (2005). Money, housework, sex, and conflict: Same-sex couples in civil unions, those not in civil unions, and heterosexual married siblings. *Sex Roles, 52*, 561–575.

Spelman, E. V. (1988). *Inessential woman: Problems of exclusion in feminist thought.* Boston: Beacon Press.

Spradlin, A. L. (1998). The price of "passing": A lesbian perspective on authenticity in organizations. *Management Communication Quarterly, 11,* 598–605.

Stamp, P. (1985). Research note: Balance of financial power in marriage: An exploratory study of breadwinning wives. *Sociological Review, 33,* 546–557.

Stone, P. (2007). *Opting out? Why women really quit careers and head home.* Berkeley: University of California Press.

Suter, E. A., Daas, K. L., & Bergen, K. L. (2008). Negotiating lesbian family identity via symbols and rituals. *Journal of Family Issues, 29,* 26–47.

Taylor, E., Dwiggins, R., Albert, M., & Dearner, J. (1983). Male nurses: What they think about themselves—and others. *RN, 46,* 61–62, 64.

Tewskbury, R. (1993). Male strippers: Men objectifying men. In C. L. Williams (Ed.), *Doing "women's work": Men in non-traditional occupations* (pp. 168–181). Newbury Park, CA: Sage.

Thomas, B. J., & Reskin, B. F. (1990). A woman's place is selling homes: Occupational change and the feminization of real estate sales. In B. F. Reskin & P. A. Roos (Eds.), *Job queues, gender queues: Explaining women's inroads into male occupations* (pp. 205–224). Philadelphia: Temple University Press.

Tichenor, V. (2005). Maintaining men's dominance: Negotiating identity and power when she earns more. *Sex Roles, 53,* 191–205.

Tomaskovic-Devey, D. (1993). *Gender and racial inequality at work: The sources and consequences of job segregation.* Ithaca, NY: ILR Press.

Townsley, N. C. (2006). Love, sex, and tech in the global workplace. In B. J. Dow & J. T. Wood (Eds.), *The Sage handbook of gender and communication* (pp. 143–160). Thousand Oaks, CA: Sage.

Trethewey, A. (2001). Reproducing and resisting the master narrative of decline: Midlife professional women's experience of aging. *Management Communication Quarterly, 15,* 183–226.

Trethewey, A., Scott, C., & LeGreco, M. (2006). *Constructing embodied organizational identities: Commodifying, securing, and servicing professional bodies).* In B. J. Dow & J. T. Wood (Eds.), *The Sage handbook of gender and communication* (pp. 123–142). Thousand Oaks, CA: Sage.

Turner, P. K. (2004). Mainstreaming alternative medicine: Doing midwifery at the intersection. *Qualitative Health Research, 14,* 644–662.

Urdy, J. R. (1994). The nature of gender. *Demography, 31,* 561–573.

U.S. Census Bureau (2006). SHP-1. Parents and children in stay-at-home parent family groups: 1994 to present. Retrieved December 1, 2007, from http://www.census.gov/population/socdemo/hh-fam/shp1.pdf

U.S. Department of Labor, Bureau of Labor Statistics. (2007). *Household data annual averages.* Retrieved September 1, 2008, from http://www.bls.gov/cps/cpsaat18.pdf

Varvus, M. D. (2002). Domesticating patriarchy: Hegemonic masculinity and television's "Mr. Mom." *Critical Studies in Media Communication, 19,* 352–375.

Walby, S. (Ed.). (1988). *Gender segregation at work.* Milton Keynes, England: Open University Press.

Waldeck, J., & Myers, K. (2007). Organizational assimilation theory, research, and implications for multiple areas of the discipline. In C. S. Beck (Ed.), *Communication yearbook 31* (pp. 322–369). New York: Erlbaum.

Weeks, J. (1986). *Sexuality.* London: Routledge.

Wentworth, D. K., & Chell, R. M. (2001). The role of househusband and housewife as perceived by a college population. *The Journal of Psychology, 135,* 639–650.

West, C. (2004). Black sexuality: The taboo subject. In M. L. Anderson & P. H. Collins (Eds.), *Race, class & gender: An anthology* (5th ed., pp. 455–460). Belmont, CA: Thomson-Wadsworth.

West, C., & Fenstermaker, S. (1995). Doing difference. *Gender & Society, 9,* 8–37.

West, C., & Zimmerman, D. (1987). Doing gender. *Gender & Society, 1,* 125–151.

Wetherby, T. (1977). *Conversations: Working women talk about doing a "man's job."* Millbrae, CA: Les Femmes.

Weyer, B. (2007). Twenty years later: Explaining the persistence of the glass ceiling for women leaders. *Women in Management Review, 22,* 482–469.

Williams, C. L. (1989). *Gender differences at work.* Berkeley: University of California Press.

Williams, C. L. (1992). The glass escalator: Hidden advantages for men in the "female" professions. *Social Problems, 39,* 253–267.

Williams, C. L. (Ed.). (1993). *Doing "women's work": Men in non-traditional occupations.* Newbury Park, CA: Sage.

Williams, J. (2000). *Unbending gender: Why work and family conflict and what to do about it.* New York: Oxford University Press.

Wood, J. T. (1994). *Who cares? Women, care, and culture.* Carbondale: Southern Illinois University Press.

Wood, J. T., & Conrad, C. (1983). Paradox in the experiences of professional women. *Western Journal of Speech Communication, 47,* 305–322.

Wright, R. & Jacobs, J. A. (1994). Male flight from computer work: A new look at occupational resegregation and ghettoization. *American Sociological Review, 59,* 511–536.

Yoder, J. D., & Berendsen, L. L. (2001). "Outsider within" the firehouse: African American and White women firefighters. *Psychology of Women Quarterly, 25,* 27–36.

Yount, K. R. (1991). Ladies, flirts, and tomboys: Strategies for managing sexual harassment in an underground coal mine. *Journal of Contemporary Ethnography, 19,* 396–422.

# CHAPTER CONTENTS

# 9   Discourses of Volunteerism

*Shiv Ganesh*
*Kirstie McAllum*
University of Waikato

Public discourse often promotes volunteerism as a novel and empowering solution to social problems, and it is a significant international phenomenon. In this chapter, we engage in an interdisciplinary review of the literature on the topic. We begin by clarifying three key terms around which we organize our review: *volunteer*, *volunteering*, and *volunteerism*. We take an explicitly discursive approach in our review, treating academic research on volunteerism as instantiations of discourses of representation, understanding, suspicion, and vulnerability (Mumby, 1997), and we use this framework to identify key areas of research and their possibilities and limitations. We conclude with some suggestions for future study.

Scarcely a day goes by without public attention in a range of societies being drawn to the issue of volunteerism. Volunteering, we are invariably told, benefits us, and volunteers themselves are good people (Winter, 1998). Some scholars have argued that volunteerism is *the* means through which citizens build contemporary democratic communities and that volunteer work creates linkages between diverse interests and classes in the face of declining social capital and widening social, economic, and political disparities among large groups of people (Putnam, 2000). Indeed, scholars have suggested that academic and practitioner discussions of volunteerism are characterized by a "language of decline" (Rathgeb Smith, 1999, p. 169) that describes the quality of collective life in terms of erosion and decay, to which volunteering is presented as a solution. In this context, it becomes important to consider what sorts of political and community participation volunteering might engender. Further, what does it mean to interpret civic engagement, which we understand as our personal and collective involvement with social issues, primarily through the lens of volunteerism?

Our collective enchantment with volunteerism is further indexed by the sheer number of academic essays on the subject since Sills's (1957) influential book, *The Volunteers*. Scholars from a broad range of disciplines (including communication, economics, leisure studies, political science, psychology, public administration, and sociology) have studied the subject vigorously. Perhaps unsurprisingly, a large percentage of studies emanate from the United States,

Correspondence: e-mail: sganesh@waikato.ac.nz and kmcallum@waikato.ac.nz and the vast majority of studies are located in "advanced" liberal democracies (Dekker & Halman, 2003).

In this chapter, we take a communication-centered approach to understanding contemporary issues surrounding volunteerism, and we engage in a detailed interdisciplinary review of the literature in order to identify key theoretical assumptions, empirical issues, and areas that we believe are ripe for more inquiry. The field of communication studies provides a particularly good platform upon which to build an understanding of volunteerism, not only because communication constitutes such a crucial empirical issue, but precisely because, as an academic discipline, communication studies is thoroughly multi-theoretical and multi-perspectival (Corman & Poole, 2000). Thus, it offers an ideal vantage point from which to integrate, compare, review, and critique both micro-studies of individual behavior and macro-studies of social structure, policy, and discourse.

Moreover, establishing a communication-centered perspective for studying volunteerism encourages greater exchange among various branches of communication inquiry, including organizational communication, health communication, and communication and social justice. For example, organizational communication scholars are well placed to understand volunteerism in terms of identification and social capital (Lewis, 2005), and health communication scholars are well positioned to investigate discursive connections between volunteering and well-being. Indeed, the United Nations, which designated 2001 as the International Year of the Volunteer, described volunteering itself in terms of efforts to improve the well-being of other individuals and communities (Anheier & Salamon, 1999). Scholars concerned with issues of social justice and dialogue also stand to benefit from enunciating a clearly defined set of terms and concepts to understand student volunteering as part of social justice-oriented service learning projects (Artz, 2001).

Given this context, we aim in this essay to understand who volunteers, what volunteering involves, what volunteerism means, and why these questions emerge as significant, by examining four key academic discourses on the subject. As we examine each discourse, we unpack conceptions and insights into communication processes that each point of view affords researchers. Before we begin our review of these discourses, literatures and approaches, however, we signal our overall direction by discussing our own perspective on the terms *volunteerism*, *volunteering*, and *volunteer*. Following these definitions, we elaborate a theoretical framework, and, finally, as we move through a range of studies of volunteerism, we tease out issues pertaining to each of the three key terms.

## Volunteerism, Volunteering, and Volunteers

While scholars have made implicit distinctions among the terms *volunteerism*, *volunteering* (Cnaan & Goldberg-Glen, 1991) and *volunteer* (Ellis & Noyes, 1990), none offers explicit conceptual treatments of them. Consequently, making clear-cut distinctions is difficult, rendered more so by the fact that some researchers have used the terms interchangeably. For instance, Snyder (2001), for the most part, conflated volunteerism with volunteering, and understood both in terms of processes and activities. However, he did make one reference to volunteerism as a form, framework, or environment in which helping takes place (p. 16311), and that description serves as an interesting starting point from which to fashion a fuller understanding of volunteerism. Notably, Snyder's emphasis on form allows us to appreciate volunteerism in historical terms. Accordingly, we define volunteerism as an overall framework which engenders particular types of economic and political structures, discourses, practices, and contexts for connecting individuals with society that are identifiable either in terms of activity (volunteering) or personhood (volunteer). At first glance, the notion of volunteerism so positioned is feasibly distinct from other possible terms to describe civic engagement such as *charity, activism,* or *engaged citizenship* (Barnill, Beitsch, & Brooks, 2001; Bussell & Forbes, 2002; Tocqueville, 1835/1969), and, in many ways, it is. We offer two such points of distinction between volunteerism and other similar terms: one distinction is structural and the other discursive.

### Volunteerism as Structure

First, volunteerism can be understood structurally, as a social practice produced by the shrinking of the traditional welfare state.[1] As states have attempted to deregulate and globalize markets over the last few decades, their historic welfare role has been reduced considerably (Kingfisher, 2002; Young, 2000). Whereas the precise nature of such structural adjustment has varied considerably from country to country (Kelsey, 1995), the very proliferation of a global "third sector" or a "non-government organization (NGO) sector" can be read as a consequence of state recession (Ganesh, 2005). Predictably then, studies have demonstrated a relationship between the amount of voluntary activity in a country and the overall size of its welfare sector: the less state welfare, the more the volunteering (Anheier & Salamon, 1999; Anheier & Seibel, 1990). The high percentage of the U.S. population that engages in volunteering, popularly estimated at more than 50% (Independent Sector, 2002), could therefore be considered an index of the relatively small size of its welfare sector. New Zealand, for example, has a much lower incidence of volunteering at about 25%, but a much more evolved system of welfare and public health (Statistics New Zealand, 2004).

Moreover, structural pressures emphasizing market forces are creating shifts in the type and nature of voluntary engagement more significant and problematic than the change in numbers initially suggests, even in societies with long histories of volunteerism such as the United States, the United Kingdom, and Australia (Milligan, 1998). For example, the move toward professionalization (Bloom & Kilgore, 2003) is changing the face of volunteerism, with expectations that the voluntary sector acts in rationalized, business-like ways. So, even as it adopts a shadow state role, the voluntary sector, and organizations that deliver welfare services in particular, have begun competing for funds in ways that are not dissimilar to businesses. If funding contracts are to be retained it is necessary that they measure up to standards, demonstrate accountability, and meet state-driven outcomes efficiently. This drive to marketization (Simpson & Cheney, 2007) has instigated claims that the voluntary sector is bifurcated (Knight, 1993; Milligan, 1998). On the one hand, one can identify grass-roots initiatives that emphasize local engagement and empowerment through decision making, and on the other, voluntary organizations that resemble large corporations (Milligan & Fyfe, 2005).

Further, a palpable tension exists between the statistic that 50% of the U.S. population has volunteered at one time or another (Independent Sector, 2002) and competing popular claims about the marked decline of social capital in that country (Putnam, 2000). In this sense, the statistic itself indicates a logic of accountability and rationalization that stems from viewing volunteers solely as the "little fingers of the state" and business (C. Wilson, Hendricks, & Smithies, 2001, p. 132). This narrow view raises the specter of discursive closure (Deetz, 1992) about what actually constitutes volunteerism not only in a legal but also in a profoundly moral sense. Can civic engagement truly be measured in terms of the percentage of population that volunteers? Can it be achieved only in organizational contexts? Postcolonial perspectives, in particular, carry the potential to challenge the reified organizational focus of much research on volunteerism as excluding indigenous forms of communitarian action that position self and other in more complicated and fluid ways. C. Wilson et al. illustrated this point nicely in the context of the contrast, in Aotearoa/New Zealand, between Pakeha (European) and Maori ways of being:

> When I get up as a Pakeha and mow my lawns, I mow my lawns.... When I go down the road to the disabled children's home and mow their lawns I volunteer to do something for the other.... When my friend Huhana gets up and mows her lawns, she mows her lawns, when she goes down to the Kohanga Reo and mows lawns, she mows her lawns. When she moves across and mows the lawns at the Marae and the Hauora, she mows her lawns—because there is no sense of "other." (p. 129)

Volunteerism as morally and culturally positioned implies that, in addition to being a structural phenomenon, it is also profoundly discursive.

### Volunteerism as Discourse

The term *volunteerism*, as we argue below, appears to encompass more and more forms of civic engagement. For example, some scholarship on the subject interprets acts of interpersonal help—assisting a person to cross a street, for example—as constituting a form of informal volunteering (Spoonley, Pearce, Butcher, & O'Neill, 2004). A vivid, if somewhat extreme, example of the extent to which historically distinct forms of civic engagement have been reinterpreted as exemplars of volunteering can be found in Winter's (1998) reinvention of U.S. patriot Paul Revere's famous midnight ride as an act, not of patriotism or revolution, but of "volunteering."

Additionally, volunteerism as a discourse demonstrably emphasizes order over change, cohesion over discord, and individualism over collectivism. Most commonly, regardless of the consequence of acts of volunteering—which might include radical social change—stakeholders link the actual performance of tasks archetypically associated with volunteering with cohesion and coordination, such as answering phones, assisting patients at hospitals, hospice care-giving, or preparing food. Such emphasis upon cohesion and coordination can be explained with reference to the "language of decline" (Rathgeb Smith, 1999, p. 169) that characterizes discussions of volunteerism. Although social problems may seem chaotic, volunteerism comprises an ordered, structured, and functional solution. It makes sense, then, why academic discourses so often position volunteerism in organizational terms, while they frame activism more often as a social movement (see Napoli, this volume). Notably, some scholars consider the consequences of volunteering in terms of its potential to increase social cohesion and social capital (Janoski, Musick, & Wilson, 1998; Putnam, 2000). Others have argued that volunteerism constitutes a key term in promoting managerial participation systems such as quality circles (Stohl & Jennings, 1988).

Additionally, volunteerism also discursively emphasizes individualism over collectivism. With one or two exceptions, much scholarly literature on volunteerism measures volunteering in terms of individuals' attributes (e.g., Clary & Snyder, 1991; Clary et al., 1998; Mesch, Rooney, & Steinberg, 2006; Smith, 1994), rather than groups' interaction (Iverson & McPhee, 2008; McComb, 1995). Indeed, the very term *volunteer*-ism emphasizes *voluntas*, or individual will (Habermas, 1984), which implies agency—the ability to make free, rational, and unencumbered choices. Such assumptions about order and agency occur with great frequency in studies of volunteerism. For example, Cnaan, Handy, and Wadsworth's (1996) extensive review of literature on key characteristics of volunteers emphasizes both free will and an ability to contribute to the public good. Brown (1999), in framing volunteering in the United States as behavior that occurs "in the national interest" (p. 39), began her essay with the claim that "the idea of public life in America is premised upon individual initiative" (p. 17).

## Volunteering

One can understand the more specific concepts of volunteering and volunteer with reference to volunteerism as a general discursive and structural backdrop. We understand the term *volunteering* in performative and action-oriented terms, as contextual activity and experience that individuals, groups and communities may go through. Yet, researchers must unravel what sorts and contexts of activities "count" as volunteering and what does not. The literature on volunteering, as indicated, acknowledges the importance of organizational context (Ashcraft & Kedrowicz, 2002; Barlow, Bancroft, & Turner, 2005; McComb, 1995; Tschirhart, Mesch, Parry, Miller, & Lee, 2005), and, hence, the term *formal* volunteering denotes volunteering for an organization. The idea that volunteering is predominantly organizational makes additional sense in the context of commentary by prominent social critics about the changing nature of the public sphere, and the increasing prominence of organizations as the primary way in which individuals connect with larger social issues and concerns (Habermas, 1989). However, as we mentioned earlier, more and more types of informal civic activities associated with helping and support also appear to be subsumed under the rubric of volunteering, including informal support to neighbors, or spontaneous care offered to strangers.

Moreover, scholars have described volunteering in many different ways, developing disciplinary lenses through which they define and analyze it. Notably, economists have tended to treat volunteering in terms of work, characterizing it as work performed without monetary reward and attempting to calculate the economic worth of volunteer work hours (Brown, 1999). Other scholars, notably in leisure studies, have framed volunteering as a form of "serious leisure" rather than work (Stebbins, 2002). Still others have considered it to be a "third space," independent from work and leisure (Ashcraft & Kedrowicz, 2002). Finally, understood as a form of care, volunteering refers to altruistic acts performed *outside* the intimate sphere of family and friends (J. Wilson, 2000). In this sense, it can be conceptualized as a contained, rather than a radical notion of care that permeates public and personal boundaries.

### Volunteer

The third key term under consideration in this essay is the term *volunteer* itself. We understand the term to be a form of identity produced under volunteerism. Thus, while we are not so much interested in noting essential characteristics of "the" ideal volunteer, we find the number of studies of volunteer characteristics quite telling. A major concern of research on volunteerism has been to answer the question: "Who volunteers?" (Carson, 1999). We will discuss specific characteristics later in this essay. For now, we acknowledge some irony in the attempt to characterize the ideal volunteer in the United States, where the largest number of such studies has been conducted, in the face of the widely cited statistic that 50% of the adult population of the United States has volunteered (Independent Sector, 2002). Given that the only common trait that this vast, diverse, and conflicted culture likely shares is the good fortune to be alive, we can reasonably suggest that attempts to develop personality profiles of volunteers are motivated not so much by sociological curiosity as they are by rationalized managerial volunteer recruitment and coordination needs. Finally, even the managerial character profile of the volunteer increasingly blurs, as more and more forms of social action become classified as volunteerism. J. Wilson (2000), for instance, argued that no good sociological reasons exist to study activists separately from volunteers.

## Theoretical Framework: Discourses of Volunteerism

In this essay, we adopt a largely discursive position, in that we seek to examine the discursive implications of interdisciplinary academic theorizing on volunteerism as much as to summarize the results of such research. Mumby (1997) offered a useful way of understanding academic discourses. Drawing from Ricoeur (1981), Mumby characterized four paradigmatic positions in academic studies of communication: a discourse of representation, a discourse of understanding, a discourse of suspicion, and a discourse of vulnerability. Mumby's fourfold categorization can be contextualized with reference to several attempts by scholars to situate various paradigms of inquiry in organizational studies, in general, and organizational communication studies, in particular.

Perhaps the best known of these comes from Burrell and Morgan (1979), who laid out four paradigms or ways of classifying organizational analysis: functionalism, interpretivism, radical humanism, and radical structuralism, based on distinctions made along two sets of key dimensions: subjective versus objective approaches and theories of order versus theories of change. Deetz (1996) critiqued and reconfigured these four paradigms, instead advocating four discursive positions that did not rely on subject-object dichotomies or functionalist notions of order and change. He labeled these paradigms normative, interpretive, critical, and dialogic discourses, arguing that they more accurately configured the terrain of inquiry in organizational studies. Mumby's four discourses—representation, interpretation, suspicion and vulnerability— frame much research in communication studies and organizational communication, and they largely echo Deetz's formulation. However, his equation of discourses of representation with positivism is more specific than Deetz's rendition of what counts as a "normative" discourse. We take the term *representation* to incorporate positivist, post-positivist, as well as functional points of view, given that none of these points of view enable a critique of representational practices themselves. Indeed, Mumby (1997) concluded that the other three discourses "articulate increasingly transgressive orientations toward the "notions of 'representation' and 'correspondence' as critical attributes of knowledge" (p. 23).

A key advantage of organizing and analyzing academic studies of volunteerism in terms of these four discourses is that they provide a clear sense of where scholarship has been conducted and what possibilities currently exist. Conversely, however, some important continuities might well be lost were one to treat each discourse as a discrete set. Therefore, as we discuss various academic studies organized with reference to four discourses, we observe continuities, parallels, and potentials. To begin, we provide an introduction to each discourse.

### Discourses of Representation

According to Mumby (1997), a realist discourse of representation reflects positivist and functional perspectives on knowledge. Mumby connected this range of research through a singular view of rationality which suggests communication is an outcome of foundational knowledge about the world. According to Mumby, communication thus reflects the world "as it is" as if in a mirror. Positivist assumptions treat communication as "a conduit...for already formed ideas" (p. 4), and, in so doing, they conceptually separate language from thought and cognition. In sum, this framework presents communication as a product of thought in which the substantive content of what is communicated and the topic of conversation reflect the Cartesian subject-object split, with the former reflecting the latter. Communication is, therefore, ancillary to questions about the creation of meaning and, subsequently, larger questions of power and identity. As a discourse then, such research literally represents, reproduces, and legitimates communication in terms of outcomes in reality rather than understanding its implication in the construction of reality itself.

### Discourses of Understanding

Mumby (1997) positioned an interpretivist discourse of understanding within the Modernist project because it attempts to reinterpret and expand the concept of rationality rather than reject it altogether. Such perspectives expand the concept beyond the instrumental reason enshrined in discourses of representation, to include rationality as a broad, inherently value-laden phenomenon. Further, a second tenet of such interpretivism is to understand subjects and objects in terms of interaction (Husserl, 1962), which is resonant with Kantian idealism rather than empiricist positivism. In this way, communication becomes construed as a process of dialogue between the acting subject and the other(s) and contributes to creating social reality as we know it. In organizational contexts, in particular, interpretive scholars pay attention to ways in which communication molds organizational reality via organizational culture, metaphors, or rituals, and certain communication practices constitute different organizational realities (Boden, 1994; Trujillo, 1992).

### Discourses of Suspicion

It can be argued that interpretivism privileges action in the lifeworld (Habermas, 1984) but neglects structural influences (Deetz, 1996), which operate at a deep cultural and ideological level. Mumby (1997) asserted that both Western Marxist thinkers as well as those from the Frankfurt School have not abandoned all modernist assumptions. Rather, they have criticized the ways in which power relations have undermined the modernist project of emancipation, often by excessive emphasis on scientific-technical and bureaucratic notions of rationality. As Deetz contended, these scholars treat communication itself as constructive, dialogic, and dialectical, with the risk of meaning deformation ever present. Moreover, they envision communication as the means through which members reproduce and maintain systems of domination via the construction of particular forms of identity. Ideology operates at the level of meaning, identity, and culture while hegemony reflects the ways in which ideological colonization is played out and sustained dialectically across a myriad of everyday activities and practices. Such critical theory aims to interrogate the deeper structural power tensions covered over by the superficial unity of organizational life.

### Discourses of Vulnerability

Finally, Mumby (1997) maintained that discourses of vulnerability present selfhood in terms of the "de-centered subject" and question the possibilities for representation altogether. This perspective treats individual subjectivity as constructed of shards of multiple, conflicting, and sedimented discourses (Tracy & Trethewey, 2005). In this way, individuals are *sites* of discursive indeterminacy rather than agentic *subjects*, and discourse, thus, precedes acts of individual choice. As such, seemingly sutured individual identities result from dominant discourses, which paradoxically can themselves never capture the wholeness of experience because, according to Mumby, "meaning is always, by definition, partial, incomplete, and subject to slippage and transformation" (p. 16). A discourse of vulnerability, in this sense, implies and requires openness toward indeterminacy.

Discourses of vulnerability sometimes *tout court* reject the ability of discourse to fully represent reality (Derrida, 1976), instead positioning discourse itself as a shifting, self-representative set of signifying practices (Baudrillard, 1983). Studies focus on discursive struggle and acts of resistance rather than transformation. Indeed, as we will discuss later, such post-structural perspectives more likely treat academic representation practices as discourses rather than making claims about the nature of reality and society.

Having described our own position on the key terms of this essay and outlined the contours of four key academic discourses, we now examine how various discourses construct the relationships among volunteerism, volunteering, and volunteers respectively, positing different relationships among these terms. While our review is interdisciplinary, we focus on communication in that we refer to, and indeed revel in, issues of broad significance to communication scholars, highlighting such key constructs as cultures, frameworks, meanings, symbols, definitions, messages, values, discourses, and dialogue.

## Discourses of Representation: Volunteers, Volunteering, and Volunteerism

Studies which draw on the tenets of the discourse of representation focus predominantly upon understanding individual behavior, whether from psychological, economic, or even sociological standpoints. As we demonstrate in this chapter, researchers situated within this discourse are much more concerned with identifying characteristics of volunteers and describing acts of volunteering than they are with analyzing structural or discursive characteristics of volunteerism. Indeed, such studies often conceptualize communication most explicitly at individual levels, rather than at organizational or societal levels. Accordingly, we begin by presenting how positivist and post-positivist studies tend to characterize volunteers and volunteering, and we then move on to a discussion of how such studies see volunteerism itself.

### Representations of Volunteers

Much work on who volunteers and why can be classified as part of a discourse of representation. Here, we outline some assumptions of research typical of this discourse and detail how rationality underpins such studies' considerations of communication.

First, researchers tend to assume that volunteers can be categorized by structural socio-economic or demographic characteristics, which predict particular skills and attitudes. Several studies use data such as age (Omoto, Snyder, & Martino, 2000; Rotolo, 2000), income (Freeman, 1997), educational level (McPherson & Rotolo, 1996), occupation (Hodgkinson & Weitzman, 1996), gender (J. Wilson & Musick, 2003), and race (Musick, Wilson, & Bynum, 2000; Sundeen, Garcia, & Wang, 2007) to identify volunteers, thereby taking for granted that social stratification significantly predicts engagement in voluntary work (Goss, 1999). Volunteers are, therefore, located by "dominant statuses" that they already possess (Smith, 1994). For example, some quantitative studies (McPherson & Rotolo, 1996) have attempted to correlate greater voluntary participation with higher educational levels. J. Wilson and Musick's (1997a) study found a higher incidence of volunteers among more highly educated and public service workers, although Brown and Smart (2007) cautioned against using education as a proxy for ability for non-dominant racial groups.

Brown (1999) concluded that those in the paid work force tend to volunteer more than those who are not. These findings are corroborated by a study of middle income Australians (Pusey, 2000). Clary and Snyder (1999) linked particular skills that volunteers possess, such as communication ability, with high human capital and personal resources, such as transportation and health. Further, Reinerman (1987) exhibited how higher volunteer engagement by public sector workers relates to a specific value position—a less individualistic, compartmentalized view of life than those who did not volunteer.

Second, studies sometimes assume that volunteers have distinct personality traits that dictate communication patterns, notably altruism. While psychological studies (e.g., Boz & Palaz's 2007 analysis of Turkish volunteers) look beyond socio-economic conditions and demographic characteristics, they still reinforce the assumption that an essential version of the "traditional volunteer" exists. From this perspective, the typical volunteer is no longer determined by age, education, race, gender or income level, but rather an identifiable personality type. Accordingly, scholars list attributes such as extraversion, others-oriented empathy (Penner & Finkelstein, 1998), helpfulness (Finkelstein & Brannick, 2007), and appropriate attachment styles (Gillath et al., 2005) as key characteristics of a volunteer that shape their communication with recipients of services rendered.

In turn, studies focused on personality traits often neglect the impact of social and organizational structures. Also, although psychological insights may be helpful in explaining individual engagement, they do not explain the surprising drop in social capital in the United States over the last four decades (Putnam, 2000). Studies that argue that individuals are repositories of altruism simply cannot explain such deep social fluctuations over time in seemingly stable dispositions (Wuthnow, 1991a).

A third assumption that characterizes literature in this area is that individuals act to maximize their own satisfaction. The emphasis in such research upon individual motivation prompts us to discuss the assumption that cost-benefit considerations significantly influence volunteers' motivation and perseverance. Theory development in the area has focused extensively on initial motivation or goals (Omoto & Snyder, 1995), identifying volunteer goals based on underlying needs, such as altruistic, social, instrumental, self-esteem, and other motivations (Clary, Snyder, & Ridge, 1992). Scholars then classify volunteers on a continuum between pure altruism and clear self-interest (Barnett, 1996).

In sum, such research has argued that volunteers' initial decisions to "bring themselves into contact with needy others…are made in part via a *rational process* during which people estimate the kind of emotional experiences they are likely to have during such encounters and then use these anticipated responses to determine *the degree of satisfaction they expect to experience*" (Davis, Hall, & Meyer, 2003, p. 249, our italics). Researchers, therefore, treat rational choice as a useful tool for predicting how organizational settings influence incentive structures for individuals (Boston, Martin, Pallot, & Walsh, 1996). For instance, Tschirhart et al.'s (2005) longitudinal study of stipended volunteers noted that initial altruistic motivations tended to decrease over time unless coupled with other outcomes such as social, instrumental, and self-esteem goals. However, quantifying value-laden goals (such as credibility, integrity, and self-fulfillment) remains difficult, particularly when respondents report multiple motivations (Clary & Snyder, 1999).

### Representations of Volunteering

Studies oriented toward representation treat volunteering in several ways, but two in particular bear mention. First, academic discourses binarize volunteering as occurring in either formal or informal contexts. Second, such scholarship considers volunteering in terms of its parallels with paid work.

Representational discourses define formal contexts as explicitly organizational. Moreover, these studies often focus on how organizations deal with and manage organizational activity around volunteers themselves. Issues include volunteer recruitment (Clary et al., 1992; Sundeen, 1992), socialization and training (Davis et al., 2003), coordination and role ambiguity (Merrell, 2000), or commitment (Wisner, Stringfellow, Youngdahl, & Parker, 2005).

Informal contexts, on the other hand, involve individual acts of helping that are determined more by dispositional attributes such as helpfulness or empathy (Finkelstein & Brannick, 2007). Researchers have characterized informal volunteering within family or neighborhood groups by sporadic occurrence, private impact, casual organizing, and often obligatory character, stemming from strong relational ties (Amato, 1990).

Second, and relatedly, scholars often explore formal volunteering in relation to paid work (J. Wilson & Musick, 1997b). The subtitle of Pearce's (1993) book, *The Organizational Behavior of Unpaid Workers*, indicates the extent to which volunteering references both formal organization as well as the world of work. Within the context of an agency or institutional framework, some researchers attribute work-like attributes to volunteering in terms of organizational ties, timetabling and the need for skills. For example, Davis et al. (2003) defined volunteering as a long term commitment, not a one-off act of helping, as presented by bystander intervention research (Schroeder, Penner, Dovidio, & Piliavin, 1995). Davis et al. argued that establishing commitment requires initiating formal workplace-like contracts.

Conceptual parallels with paid work also emerge in studies that examine individuals' transitions to the workforce, "using" volunteering (J. Wilson & Musick, 2003) as a means to enhance their success in obtaining a job later on (Wuthnow, 1995) due to acquired skills, community networking, and social capital (Onyx & Leonard, 2000). In fact, Duncan's (1999) investment model of volunteering utilized an image of "well-roundedness" to indicate ability to potential employers. Notably, however, empirical research about utilizing volunteering to enhance job seeking success has yielded mixed results. Prouteau and Wolff's (2005) study of French volunteers did not support human capital investment models.

Despite this empirical lacuna, rhetorical associations between volunteering and work predominate, as evident in the growing research on corporate volunteering (Buckley, 2005). Here, studies have interrogated how organizations should manage relationships between volunteering and organizational citizenship behavior (Farmer & Fedor, 2001). The idea that volunteering represents a training ground for future members of the workforce also becomes apparent in some aspects of the service learning movement in high schools and universities in the United States (Droge & Murphy, 1999).

### Representations of Volunteerism

Studies oriented toward representation tend to present volunteerism as a relatively stable concept, which manifests itself differently across the lifespan and across groups of individuals. Most of these studies orient toward describing and predicting individuals' behavior (Stukas, Snyder, & Clary, 1999; J. Wilson & Musick, 1997b) and, consequently, treat institutional influences as stable, and pre-specified (Dutta-Bergman, 2004). Thus, such studies tend to draw from early institutional theories (Scott, 1995).

Liao-Troth's (2005) study of psychological contracts among volunteers provides one example of how research can focus on the individual and take institutional contexts as pre-given. Liao-Troth framed institutional norms and rules for acceptable behavior in terms of the parameters of the relationship, but these norms were not investigated. Likewise, other research designed to understand volunteer characteristics takes institutional features for granted instead of explaining or deconstructing them. For instance, Katz and Rosenberg's (2005) economic interpretation of institutional volunteering sought to model and predict the relationship between altruism and productivity in developed economies without interrogating what it is about developed economies that might cause individuals to volunteer in the first place. Finally, several studies have examined the impact of religion upon volunteering and giving (e.g., Hodgkinson, Weitzman, & Kirsch, 1990; Perry, Brudney, Coursey, & Littlepage, 2008; Ruiter & De Graaf, 2006; J. Kim, Kang, Lee, & Lee, 2007 for the impact of religiosity on volunteering in Korea which differs markedly from U.S. findings). Studies of religious influences tend to support a strong relationship between religious observance and altruistic behavior (Independent Sector, 2002; Lyons & Nivison-Smith, 2006). For instance, Yeung (2004) indicated volunteering in Finland may be viewed as a public expression of one's faith, while Berger (2006) found that conservative Protestant denominations in Canada seem to both volunteer and give more in monetary terms than do Catholics, Muslims, Hindus, Buddhists, and those with no professed religion. Although Berger identified factors which may mediate reasons for giving, such as access to social networks and the importance attributed to community, such studies do not interrogate how religiosity is constructed in the everyday lives of its observers.

## Discourses of Understanding: Volunteering, Volunteers, and Volunteerism

Unlike the overt behaviorism often evident in studies oriented toward a discourse of representation, studies grounded in discourses of understanding tend to attribute a much more fundamental role to communication in constructing volunteer identities, and expectations of reciprocity and relationality establish particular ways of viewing volunteering. Such studies are also inclined to understand larger structures and vocabularies of volunteerism as constructed at the level of micro-practice through everyday talk. We argue that, in contrast to discourses of representation, according primacy to experience and activity emphasizes *becoming* rather than *being* a volunteer. Thus, we begin with the question of how discourses of understanding position and frame volunteering and follow with a discussion of how volunteers are constituted as an object of inquiry. Finally, we appraise how such discourse constructs volunteerism.

## Understanding Volunteering

Interpretive studies are arguably well placed to examine how individuals and organizations interact to create the "warm glow" factor. The value assigned to altruism itself is created by communicative practices that enshrine caring as the type of social interaction deemed most appropriate for volunteering (Rajulton, Ravanera, & Beaujot, 2007). For example, Roker, Player, and Coleman's (1998) description of the lunch organized by adolescent students with a mild to moderate learning disability for residents of a nearby retirement home highlights the communicative issues of mutuality and reciprocal giving. In this situation, the project manager decided elderly residents with dementia were not suitable for the occasion since they "just ended up confusing each other" (p. 735). Other studies highlight such aspects of giving that representational studies do not capture, such as love, surprise, or authenticity. For instance, Ronel's (2006) study of at-risk youth demonstrated that relationships between youth and volunteers developed because "[t]hey are amazed that people give them something for nothing, without payment. This sort of giving also frees those who receive the service from the obligation to give something in return…and this is what enables a genuine relationship to evolve" (p. 1142).

The relational and dialogic nature of volunteering serves as a particular source of emphasis for interpretive studies. However, relationality does not always imply equality (Schervish & Havens, 2002). Whereas some scholars envision constructed reciprocity as a "community commons where people come together to create layers of social connections and relationships" (Nunn, 2002, p. 14), others contest such positive assumptions of "we-ness," arguing that opportunities for social interaction do not always create volunteer satisfaction (Wisner et al., 2005).

Intercultural communication research could provide rich insights into the management of dialogic encounters, such as Western "disaster mental health" professionals who needed to negotiate significant cultural dissonance when training Sri Lankan volunteers in the wake of the 2004 tsunami (J. Miller, 2006). J. Miller's nuanced account of indigenous responses contrasts with research which emphasizes the potential of intercultural exchange to foster reciprocal empowerment via challenging experiences either at home or abroad. Such exchanges may render both parties' "cultural identity…open to further transformation and growth" (Kim & Ruben, 1988, p. 313) by questioning stereotypes and prejudices. For example, community elders were surprised at the positive impact on local children of a group of Australian volunteers involved in a community service project on New Zealand's East Coast. According to McIntosh and Zahra (2007), "The holiday program with the volunteers… helped the kids identify with their culture. These volunteers were interested in them and in their culture and it made them proud to be Maori. They were

important to strangers, to outsiders. These people engaged with them personally" (p. 553). Thus, intercultural researchers track personal paradigm shifts in
both parties which occur as a result of cultural exchanges.

## Understanding Volunteers

Research that adopts a discourse of understanding concentrates far less on
specific types of volunteers as determined by structural or dispositional categories. However, it holds the potential to adapt some psychological constructs
that account for the mutual interplay between dispositions and situations. For
instance, role identity research (Finkelstein, Penner, & Brannick, 2005; Grube
& Piliavin, 2000) can easily be extended to examine the role of communication in the process of how volunteers construct their roles and adopt volunteer
identities, or how empathy is intersubjectively constructed in situations which
incite helping or empathic responses. Indeed, the emphasis on process emerges
as the chief distinction between extant interpretive studies on volunteers and
more quantitative studies on the subject.

Such interpretive research is less likely to classify and categorize societal contributors as inherently altruistic "joiner junkies," instead discussing
how individuals construct and align altruism with other issues such as social
responsibility, in the process creating and developing a social currency. For
instance, a newly retired physician described his participation in a community
clinic run by volunteer professionals as a need, and he concluded that "[w]e
almost owe this to society" (Reynolds, 2006, p. 371).

Researchers have, therefore, asserted that volunteers should be understood
in terms of the communities that construct them (Iverson, 2003). In so doing,
they focus on the way that societal pressures and expectations of altruistic
responses create volunteers who offer help due to privilege, time availability
or the devastation wreaked by a disaster. After registering as a mental health
volunteer during Hurricane Katrina in the U.S. in 2005, Bartley (2007) noted
that "I did not know when or if I would be called to go. The pain in my gut
went away because I had done what I had to do. Now it was out of my control"
(p. 5). Her personal narrative vividly evoked how torn she was with feelings of
anxiety, personal incapacity, and a sense of duty.

## Understanding Volunteerism

Unlike representational studies, research on volunteerism rooted in discourses
of understanding examines the ways in which communication constitutes key
social and cultural constructs associated with volunteerism, such as compassion, care (Andersson & Ohlen, 2005), giving (Jones, 2006), sacrifice, connection (Leonard & Hayward-Brown, 2002), and charity (Cloke, Johnsen, & May,
2007; Lyons, 2001).

Such research sometimes privileges organizational influence. Boden (1994)
discussed how organizational talk can shape norms to such an extent that they

become normalized as accepted "rules of the game" (McDonald & Warburten, 2003, p. 382). Puffer and Meindl (2006), in a study of 200 managers and other professionals, determined that the managers carried extant understandings of organizational culture along with them as they entered particular contexts for volunteering. In a study of pro bono work by lawyers, Granfield (2007) also noted that the characteristics and incentive structures present in legal working environments impacted upon the "vocabularies of motive" (p. 113) and meaning attributed to volunteering.

Further, interpretive studies sometimes examine how everyday talk itself re-creates modes of organizing. Ronel's (2006) study revealed how experiential encounters by at-risk youth framed organizational perceptions. Not only did youth perceive volunteers as external to the "establishment" (professional therapists/welfare officers), but they partly internalized volunteers' altruistic inspiration and the value of non-material gratification.

Interpretive studies have also examined cultural influences which shape both volunteering and volunteers (Dougherty, 2005; Eckstein, 2001; Hustinx & Lammertyn, 2004). Studies consider how family, ethnicity, and religion provide scripts to establish ways of acting and behaving, which are "encoded, enacted, replicated, revised, externalized and objectified" (McDonald & Warburten, 2003, p. 384) selectively by rational organizational participants (Barley & Tolbert, 1997). For instance, studies which describe inter-generational socialization of volunteers by friends and family members assume mutually constructed understandings of volunteerism. Palmer, Freeman, and Zabriskie's (2007) work on family participation in service expeditions challenged the assumption, often found in representational studies, that volunteerism simply comprises an individual pursuit with significant public good properties. Their study also suggested that views of volunteerism developed by adolescents who volunteer with their family diverge significantly from those engaged in school and community-based service learning (Littlepage, Obergfell, & Zanin, 2003). While the latter aimed to acquire personal leadership and life skills, teens within the family circle emphasized quality time together, enhanced relationships, and the development of common familial values and attitudes toward the community. Most interesting perhaps are studies, such as Palmer et al., that detail how individuals and families construct perspectives of sacrifice as positive, purposive, and pivotal to the experience of volunteering. Other scholars have emphasized the importance of understanding ways in which race, gender, and family, create meanings of "care" and "self-sacrifice" (Mesch et al., 2006).

## Discourses of Suspicion: Volunteerism, Volunteering, and Volunteers

Studies grounded in a discourse of suspicion approach volunteerism both structurally and discursively. In fact, it is often difficult to separate highly structural critical scholarship from recent neo-institutional studies that combine resource dependency points of view with detailed understandings of power, society, and culture (Castells, 2001). Therefore, our take on discourses of suspicion is very broad, and it spans some neo-institutional approaches as well as more discursive perspectives on communication and society. Unlike interpretive studies, which take a ground-up approach to understanding volunteerism, critical studies more likely conceptualize individual agency and acts of volunteering with reference to larger systems of control. Therefore, we first take up the issue of how a discourse of suspicion interrogates volunteerism, and we follow this discussion by considering how it constructs volunteering and volunteers in terms of larger systems.

### Volunteerism and Control

Oliver (1992) suggested, from a neo-institutional point of view, that sociopolitical, economic, and structural shifts may alter what are considered appropriate goals for voluntary agencies. Such changes create uncertainty regarding external environments, including funding and statutory requirements. Structural adjustment, in turn, affects on a global scale everyday communication practices and vocabularies and boundaries in non-profit and voluntary sectors. Blurred organizational and sectoral boundaries have dogged the voluntary sector, particularly in the social services, and critical researchers are prone to point that out. Hence, as state-directed institutions abandon the delivery of social services, the voluntary sector can be left to step in as a "shadow state" (Wuthnow, 1991b). On the other hand, corporate discourses of efficiency and contractual obligation may seem to impinge on involvement in community-based social services. Organizations are expected to be "accountable" at all levels (Kearns, 1994). Contracts now communicate expectations of volunteers in terms of time commitment and tasks, and they ensure organizations take on volunteers with clear track records. This two-pronged encroachment of corporate and state interests in the voluntary sector has significantly influenced the legitimation of voluntary activity in most Western nations.

Critical scholars also draw attention to the fact that volunteerism discursively implies that dominant status is ascribed to paid work, with unpaid labor treated as less valuable, even when the actual activities performed are the same (Hustinx, 2007). Scholars have highlighted the gendered nature of such distinctions, which serve to further undervalue the labor that women perform not only in the home, but also in communities (Daniels, 1988; Hochschild, 1983; Raddon, 2003; Waring, 1999).

The orientation toward paid work as the most materially and symbolically rewarded form of engagement between an individual and society holds profound implications for how Rifkin's (1995) clarion call heralding the "end of work" resonates for particular disenfranchised groups. Regardless of the extent to which unemployed individuals may make "civic money" (Beck, 2000) or "social wages" (see Rifkin) by volunteering, the activity guarantees them lesser material and symbolic rewards than paid work. In this sense, volunteers' struggle to professionalize volunteering in the face of societal views which relegate it to a form of occupational therapy, or pseudo-work (Pearce, 1993) actually contributes to its dwindling legitimacy. Further, if scholars persist in viewing volunteerism in terms of work, it is more likely to emerge as a pale shadow to the world of work (Spoonley, 2004).

### Volunteering, Paternalism, Exploitation, and Dialogue

Discourses of suspicion treat volunteering not in terms of relationality and reciprocity but in terms of its capacity for exploitation. Critical scholars have cautioned against the potential for volunteering to descend into paternalism, thereby reinforcing and constructing power inequities among groups of people. Rubin and Thorelli (1984) noted that beneficiaries of "help" may resent volunteers' efforts, seeing their intrusion as a "humiliating experience" (p. 225) and may present an "ambivalent, resistant" (p. 224) face to volunteers, who in turn become disheartened (Bennett & Barkensjo, 2005; Bussell & Forbes, 2002).

Critics of paternalism (Devereux, 2008) argue that pride in helping a needy other (who is expected to gratefully receive this assistance) can be problematic (Illich, 1968) because volunteers may not treat volunteering as a dialogic encounter but rather as a uni-directional handout, even if the comfortably middle-class volunteers experience personal growth and development, through "irreplaceable and enlightening personal experiences" (Artz, 2001, p. 240). Placing volunteers face-to-face with social problems does not ipso facto lead them to seriously delve into the underlying structural causes or to consider potential solutions to these problems. In their discussion of the impact of emergency feeding programs on volunteer attitudes to the experience of hunger, Edlefsen and Olson (2002) observed that, when volunteers were questioned about the *causes* of hunger, "many answers were hesitant and uncertain, or incoherent and difficult to follow. It often appeared that volunteers had never given this question serious consideration" (p. 96).

Paternalism is rife in charity-based models of volunteering, where attendant "institutional arrangements and discursive practices" (Frey, Pearce, Pollack, Artz, & Murphy, 1996, p. 111) tend to privilege individual notions of care, whence "*societal* injustices are issues of *individual* conscience and responsibility" (Artz, 2001, p. 241). According to Artz, one adopts a "doing for" rather than "doing with" (p. 247) stance which, as Frey et al. noted, encourages a "them" and "us" notion of community rather than a radical, non-exclusive "we." In fact, Artz asserted that "institutionally-organized social services mitigating inequality" (p. 241) may, in fact, reinforce those very institutional structures which underwrite interpersonal experiences of helplessness and dependence (W. H. Papa, M. J. Papa, Kandath, Worrell, & Muthuswamy, 2005).

Within the international development NGO sector, for example, volunteering may be counterproductive and unsustainable if short-term interventions create "dependency instead of empowerment and [leave] communities with the feeling that local political choices are useless, or without impact, because the resources of the local health care system are in most cases lower than those of the intervening NGO" (Benzian & van Palenstein Helderman, 2006, p. 413). Lacey and Ilcan (2006) also challenged the perspective that volunteer activity is "automatically advantageous to developing communities...because of the notion that volunteers have a genuine commitment to a project" (p. 42). In fact, they noted that, due to the power imbalance in international NGO work, it is the donors and volunteers that choose where to best spend their efforts, rather than the communities that are the targets of their work.

However, partnership approaches to volunteering, which focus on dialogue and social justice, aim to turn development on its head by requiring a volte-face in the type of communicative practices characteristic of voluntary organizations. Western perspectives suggest that the construction of a collaboratively negotiated direction, rather than reliance on a hierarchical dictate, and a holistic approach instead of a fragmented, sectoral perspective (Zoller, 2000) will facilitate this dialogic approach. This ideal can go horribly wrong. As in any relationship, mutuality is never assured, and, ironically, apparent openness (St. John & Shepherd, 2004) may disguise embedded rules within "an institutionalized arena of discursive interaction" (Fraser, 1990/1991, p. 57).

A second potential pitfall in partnership models for volunteering might lie in the absence of equally developed dialogic communication skills by each party. Zoller's (2000) analysis of a WHO Healthy Communities initiative, which was almost grounded before it flew, showed that trainers' reluctance to direct or constrain participants' understandings and judgments resulted in confusion and apathy. The desire for absolute neutrality and distantiation of any emotive response stifled dialogue. According to Zoller, apparent "fairness" ignored the fact that "excitement is crucial when asking citizens to take personal risks and to accept organizational styles radically different from the structured hierarchy with which most are comfortable" (p. 198).

Even if volunteers act with the best of intentions, they may still dominate decision making—possibly at the behest of those that they intend to help. In a health communication context, Petronio, Sargent, Andrea, Reganis, and Chichocki (2004) problematized the role of "informal healthcare advocates" in physician visits to patients. As Petronio et al. detailed, although advocates positioned themselves as altruistic supporters, emergent themes showed information-seeking privileged the advocate rather than the patient, and that the patient became a superfluous on-looker in the medical interview. Consequently, patients relied heavily on advocates when making medical decisions. Thus, health, environmental, and development communication researchers need to clearly articulate the conditions under which seemingly asymmetrical relationships might still be fruitful (Crabtree, 1998).

### Volunteers, Inclusion, and Exclusion

Generally speaking, critical research that embodies discourses of suspicion tends to focus upon issues of volunteering and volunteerism, rather than characteristics of volunteers themselves, precisely because this perspective assumes that individual agency is located within (and sometimes against) larger power structures and discourses. For now, it bears mention that such research would, as a starting point, be suspicious of the normative context within which notions of who should be considered volunteers are defined. Key questions involve who gets to volunteer, who is pressured to volunteer, and who is *excluded* from volunteering. For instance, Daniels's (1988) study of middle-class women volunteers demonstrated the extent to which the expectation to volunteer at local charities stemmed from their gendered, middle-class positions. Some literature with critical overtones also cites class and ethnicity as contextual factors that prompt individuals to volunteer. That is, volunteers are much more likely to be White and middle class than working class and Hispanic or Black (Goss, 1999). Such pressures make some groups more "open" to volunteerism. For example, "work for the Dole schemes" for unemployed people (Macintyre, 1999, p. 103) [2] as well as subtle pressures on retired seniors to "contribute" (Warburten & Crosier, 2001), can covertly erode the voluntary aspects of volunteering (Mutchler, Burr, & Caro, 2003). Also, marginalized or vulnerable groups (such as women or senior citizens) may be viewed as being open to exploitation due to their ability to be managed easily.

However, the converse is also true. So-called vulnerable groups can be excluded from volunteering (Gaskin, 1998) because of a communicatively constructed "stigma of worthiness" (Hankinson & Rochester, 2005, p. 94) or the normative shaping of who can volunteer well and who cannot. For instance, people with disabilities, often framed as pitiable, passive recipients of aid (Roker et al., 1998) can be treated as second-class volunteers because the quality of their volunteering can be perceived as inferior to that on offer by more "capable" or "powerful" volunteers (Balandin, Llewellyn, Dew, Ballin, & Schneider, 2006). The stigma of worthiness can also translate into feelings of being disposable, as detailed in Dein and Abbas's (2005) study of English hospice volunteers, which established that a major stressor for volunteers was the fear that more able volunteers would take over their roles. Sundeen, Raskoff, and Garcia (2007) also identified social class as a barrier to formal organizational volunteering. The middle classes tend to have more time and resources to volunteer as opposed to working-class communities.

## Discourses of Vulnerability: Volunteerism, Volunteering, and the Vanishing Volunteer

Poststructural perspectives in organizational communication have suggested that the development of a person's "true self" comprises a construction of organizational talk (Tracy & Trethewey, 2005). It stands to reason then, that poststructural studies do not attempt to identify and catalogue characteristics of volunteers. Instead, such studies, which are few, are likely to understand the "face" of the volunteer as a subject position produced by discourses of volunteerism (Glasrud, 2007). In a sense, the "volunteer" in this discourse is vulnerable to the point of absence.

More so than other standpoints, postmodern points of view tend to treat academic studies of volunteerism themselves in discursive terms, and some clear tensions are visible between representational studies and those grounded in a discourse of vulnerability. Specifically, the latter position representational studies as themselves creating identities and subject positions that emphasize altruism, empathy and social responsibility, rather than isolating identifiable, stable features of actual volunteers. The relationship among studies grounded in a discourse of vulnerability with critical and interpretive work is more complex. Indeed, critical, interpretive and postmodern studies in general are not mutually exclusive and, in many ways, constitute a constellation of studies that have varying degrees of agreement and disagreement about the nature of rationality, subjectivity, and reality. Important continuities exist between critical and postmodern work in organizational studies (Mumby, 2001), and, in many ways, it is almost as difficult as it is useful to discuss them as separate categories. Nonetheless, a key advantage of treating studies that emerge from a discourse of suspicion as a category independent of studies that emerge from discourses of vulnerability is that the former enable us to capture a wide range of studies, including those that are grounded in a post-realist and structural worldview. Discourses of vulnerability enable us to focus upon volunteerism itself as a discourse, within which volunteering as activity and practice can be situated. Accordingly, unlike the first three sections where we take up each of our three key terms in varying orders, in the next section, we consider explicitly how volunteerism as a discourse constitutes and shapes both volunteering and volunteers.

## Volunteerism as a Discourse

Like studies oriented toward suspicion, studies emerging from discourses of vulnerability are much more apt to concentrate explicitly about volunteering and volunteerism than essential characteristics of volunteers. Indeed, discourses of vulnerability have much to say about the shifting discursive spaces between paid and voluntary "work." The latter, they say, is increasingly characterized by a discursive shift toward professionalization. The ironic consequences include the privileging of images of "the professional" (Cheney & Ashcraft, 2007; McDonald & Mutch, 2000) and the normalization of discourses of capitalist work (Featherstone, Lash, & Robertson, 1997), epitomized by the greater acceptability of instrumental motivations for volunteering.

This growing professionalization brings with it a responsibility structure, especially the expectation that those with greater expertise must exhibit more responsibility. In this way, professional/professionalized volunteers resemble discursive articulations of Du Gay's (1996) "enterprising subject" and Miller and Rose's (1990) "entrepreneurial self" in search of "meaning, responsibility, and a sense of personal achievement in life, and hence in work" (Miller & Rose, 1995, p. 454).

Thus, volunteer identities are predominantly driven by managerial discourses which focus on control and efficiency (Deetz, 1992), with consumption as a powerful sign (Collinson, 2003) that one has attained self-"real"-ization. For instance, Hankinson and Rochester's (2005) analysis of "branding" specific forms of volunteering, such as governance and campaigning separately from "generic" volunteering to attract a specific skills base, demonstrated the extent to which professionalization can turn volunteering into a discursive object akin to a consumer product.

Other scholars have also made connections among volunteering, enterprise, and commodification. For instance, Glasrud (2007) argued that volunteering is turning into a consumer activity, and volunteers themselves—like students (McMillan & Cheney, 1996)—treat the experience as "consumers" instead of "producers" who need to "feel good" about their volunteering. Rehberg (2005) proposed a brave new world of volunteerism which disengages from traditional forms of organizational commitment based on political or religious adherence to a new "reflexive" form of volunteerism (Hustinx, 2001) which thirsts after experiential learning or a "quest for the new," and self-discovery or the "quest for oneself" (Rehberg, 2005, p. 109). Martinson (2006/2007) also detailed how discourses of volunteerism have resulted in the promotion of a commodified version of volunteering to aging populations as being beneficial to their health and longevity.

The result reflects less commitment to the collective goals of a specific organizations "inspired by coordinating ideology or meaning systems" (Rehberg, 2005, p. 110) and a sort of *bricolage* involving flux and selectivity in choosing projects to construct a temporary personal biography, as is the case with tourists who volunteer (Mustonen, 2005). Further, a barrage of work from other perspectives describes participation in sporting, heritage, environmental, political, and professional contexts as not resonating with social concern but personal development (Dietz, Stern, & Guagnano, 1998; Miles, Sullivan, & Kuo, 1998; Warburten & Gooch, 2007).

Discourses enable the creation of particular forms of identity-centered performance. While discourses create the limits within which we enact personal identities (Ashcraft & Mumby, 2004; Ashcraft & Pacanowsky, 1996; Knights & Wilmott, 1999), space for action emerges from within discursive gaps (Nadesan, 1996). Thus, it stands to reason that, while discursive boundaries can powerfully constrain how individuals act out roles and interact in voluntary settings, significant discursive flux surrounds how we "perform" or practice volunteering.

Such performance is indeterminate—neither work nor leisure. As Ashcraft and Kedrowicz (2002) asserted, volunteering can occupy a third space, distinct from both work and a "personal" life, which cannot adequately be captured in terms of a continuum between work and leisure. Additionally, poststructural studies problematize the boundaries that we draw between intimate spheres of care and more impersonal "helping" relationships. For instance, Adelman and Frey (1996) interpreted the performance of care in poststructural terms in their book *A Fragile Community: Living Together with AIDS*, where they discuss, in dialectical and dialogic terms, the profound ways in which individuals come to care for and with each other in the process of helping. Poststructural perspectives raise significant questions about whether models of volunteering as dialogic collaboration are at all universal. Moemeka (1998), for example, suggested that "community" is differently understood by members of collective and communal cultures, with attendant variance in expected communication strategies.

## Directions for Future Research

To date, a significant portion of extant research has focused on identifying and managing discrete characteristics of "the volunteer." Future investigation would do well to examine how volunteers are both enticed to participate in voluntary experiences and restrained by systemic influences which frame it in particular ways. Therefore, we present the following five potential avenues for future scholarship on volunteerism and volunteering.

### *Culture, Institutions, and Context*

First, we need to acknowledge differences in cultural understandings of what constitutes volunteering, and how institutional frameworks influence these understandings. Cheney, Zorn, Planalp, and Lair (2008), in their exploration of meaningful work, called for research about the historical and cultural situatedness of the understandings groups and individuals develop about work and well-being. However, sometimes it appears that scholars wilfully ignore issues of culture and even remain cognizant of such omissions. For instance, Parboteeah, Cullen, and Lim (2004) stated that they "ignored the possible interactions among national culture and social institutions variables" (p. 440) in their theoretical treatment of cross-national incidence of formal volunteering.

As the majority of studies have been carried out in Western contexts, whether European, (British) Commonwealth, or American, researchers at the very least ought to avoid attributing definitive status or reifying an operational cross-cultural definition of volunteering: this includes situating volunteering as unpaid work within an organization or the free rendering of services without expectation of reward (Dekker & Halman, 2003). Particular challenges include exploring how cultural and postcolonial contexts without a history of charity-based volunteerism make sense of what volunteers do. For instance, Nakano (2000) related how the Japanese *borantia* (volunteer), a concept unknown two decades ago, has been constructed to enhance organizational affiliation for those without it, and to supplement civic participation in ways that the volunteers felt were more meaningful than their primary tasks. She noted the striking differences among different types of volunteers in terms of the extent to which volunteers felt they had stepped outside mainstream values of material security, personal success, and family devotion.

Qualitative researchers are well poised to analyze connections between volunteerism and the construction of personal and collective identities. For instance, the role of *guanxi*, or relational networking, in Asian contexts constructs Web-like linkages which have very little in common with the individualistic/collectivistic dichotomy manifest in Western conceptions of volunteerism (Liu, 2008). Related to such cultural dissonance is the relationship between mainstream conceptions of volunteering and postcolonial perspectives on the subject. Warburten and McLaughlin's (2007) article identifies a range of First Nations peoples whose attitudes to volunteerism do not fit the mainstream. Maori perspectives on volunteering in New Zealand, for example, stem from notions of kinship, in particular the concept of "mahi aroha," which translates into English as a sense of sympathy and caring for all others (Oliver & Love, 2007). Such concepts hold the potential to change our understandings of the discursive boundaries dividing helping, home and work that mainstream perspectives on volunteerism construct.

Moreover, future research would do well to understand and assess the intercultural and power dynamics involved as key concepts related to volunteerism and volunteering travel across the world. For instance, while the service learning movement has particular relevance to the United States and is often characterized by a strong focus on social justice (Trethewey, 1999), scholars need to unravel service learning's potential for cultural domination and transplantation of economic models, before appropriating service learning programs across the world, from Australia to China (for related arguments, see Berry & Chisholm, 1999; Butcher, Howard, McMeniman, & Thon, 2003).

### The "Dark Side" of Volunteerism

Future research needs to question the overly optimistic connotations conjured up by the terms *volunteer, volunteering*, and *volunteerism*, and it should consider that these terms might rather euphemistically describe Band-Aids for societies deeply wounded by the withdrawal of the welfare state and the retreating institutional influences of home, church, and school (Meisenbach & McMillan, 2006). Studies grounded in discourses of suspicion and vulnerability could provide useful insights on such issues. For instance, the relationships that volunteering has with individual and social well-being merits attention. To date, research on volunteering and well-being has discussed difficulties in establishing appropriate work-life balance (MacDonald, Phipps, & Lethbridge, 2005) or the burnout of volunteers through over-commitment (Glass & Hastings, 1998). Future research could draw from multiple academic discourses to examine how volunteers make sense of their activity when the experience of volunteering is negative (Ashcraft & Kedrowicz, 2002; Bennett & Barkensjo, 2005) and discursive influences upon such sense-making processes.

The impact of volunteering on the intended recipient also needs careful consideration, especially in terms of the ethics of help (Cloke et al., 2007). From a global development point of view, researchers from development communication, intercultural communication, volunteer tourism, and social justice perspectives could fruitfully contribute to understanding how the volunteer-cum-international aid worker, engaged tourist, or service learning participant respectively selects and justifies appropriate experiences from a plethora of available environmental or human service projects, and interprets these as distinct from holiday destinations (Coghlan, 2006). Thus, scholars should attend to whether interpretations and practices serve to construct volunteerism as a form of consumption and self-development, or as a vehicle for establishing shared meanings which can contribute to globally just outcomes (cf., Arai & Pedlar, 2003).

## Volunteerism, Meaning, and Work

Communication studies may be able to unpack the complex relationships among shifts in the way people volunteer and work, and changes in the meaning we give these activities. In particular, research needs to examine the ways in which volunteering is communicatively framed solely as an inferior variant of paid work, which is assumed to be the universal membership contract (Ashcraft & Kedrowicz, 2002). Implicitly, what "works" in paid work settings is applied wholesale to other contexts in terms of establishing and maintaining member-organization contracts, developing empowerment strategies (Chiles & Zorn, 1995), and fostering meaningful engagement. Lip service is paid to problems of role ambiguity, support and training, buy-in to organizational goals and responsibility for outcomes.

When full-time employment is privileged as the norm, there is implicit disregard for the growth in non-traditional, non-standard work, characterized by non-hierarchical institutional arrangements, the proliferation of temporary contracts, the expansion of part-time positions, and "extensification" of working hours (Gossett, 2002; Spoonley, 2004). The divide between those employed according to the "standard working model" of the mid-20th century (stable, full-time employment) and non-standard workers has only increased during economic reform processes. Research into volunteering in communities that are beset by "worklessness" (Baines & Hardill, 2008) or poverty (Messias, DeJong, & McLoughlin, 2005) problematizes the existing conceptual boundaries dividing voluntary action from "work."

Another context for evaluating the shifting meanings among volunteering as work, volunteering as leisure, or volunteering as contribution lies closer to home, in the form of what we often refer to as public scholarship (Brouwer & Squires, 1996), which "[connects] the stories of our discipline with the stories of people's lives" (Krone & Harter, 2007, p. 75). The considerable effort involved and the lack of obvious financial payoffs can lead us to cast such scholarship as a form of volunteering, particularly because civic scholarship (Greenwood & Levin, 2005) often goes unrewarded by academic promotion procedures. In this sense, public scholarship is increasingly a process which interrupts—both in terms of creating public space for debating issues which count and also in terms of the time it takes to do so (Cheney, 2007). Yet, univocally categorizing public scholarship as "volunteering," and therefore non-work, ignores the professional benefits it may confer, even if only ancillary ones in effect for scholars whose main work involves teaching students and conducting research.

### Gendering Volunteerism

Studies of volunteerism would also benefit from moving beyond treating gender as one variable (Ashcraft & Mumby, 2004), which may explain or predict voluntary engagement, to descriptions of volunteerism as inherently gendered. Studies to date have yielded insights into how women manage the paid work-volunteering-family nexus differently from men (Kulik, 2000; Taniguchi, 2006), but usually only in terms of time devoted (Gallagher, 1994; Goss, 1999; Herd & Meyer, 2002). However, conceptualizing work as paid employment and volunteering as unpaid labor ultimately sustains the lack of recognition and invisibility of women's domestic and community engagement (Messias et al., 2005, p. 26). New studies should examine the gendered meanings attributed to different types of ostensibly voluntary participation in political, scientific, touristic, and welfare contexts. Moreover, the ways in which these diverse manifestations of social and political engagement differentially emphasize responsibility versus rights or entitlements also require explication (Milligan & Fyfe, 2005).

In order to do so, the impact of gender on the organization of the range of "activities oriented toward collective action, care, concern, and development of others, as well as societal decision making and resource allocation" (McBride, Sherraden, & Pritzker, 2006, p. 153) warrants investigation. Assuredly, highly developed social networks tend to predict participation, as people are more likely to participate when asked by someone else (Hodgkinson, 1995), and those with more linkages to secondary organizations engage more (Lofland, 1996). More importantly, however, communication research needs to examine how gender underwrites "appropriate" forms of participation, and the relative value assigned to various social networks: family, paid work, non-standard work, and community engagement that includes volunteering.

Feminist scholarship offers much potential insight regarding how communication constructs specific gender roles in private and public settings. Volunteering research could add to our understanding of how social milieus in non-private, non-work domains shape a sense of obligation to both family and kin (Rossi, 2001) as well as to those outside one's intimates in formal care-giving contexts. Currently, "formal volunteering" sustains the bifurcations between family and neighbor as another, more distant community member. This distinction becomes problematic, particularly because one relatively small geographic area may have overlapping, multiple communities. Further, the strong link between formal volunteering and the world of work or "real jobs" (Clair, 1996) reinforces the inherently gendered nature of volunteering (for detailed exploration of the relationship between gender and work, see Medved, this volume).

## Volunteerism and Social Transformation

Finally, whether or not volunteerism actually produces genuinely caring and transformative social attitudes and organizations remains under-researched. In his review of Dekker and Halman's (2003) edited text, J. Wilson (2004) corroborated the fact that "people [can] use the idea [of volunteering] to excuse themselves from political responsibility" (p. 1541), neglecting more expansive expressions of compassion in favor of rendering services to a limited circle of care, presumably within existing social networks. Penner (2004) provided a thoughtful appraisal of a system where "politicians…advocate policies that perpetuate or even exacerbate certain social inequities and then almost simultaneously encourage people to volunteer to help the victims" (p. 664) as a smokescreen.

Another important contribution to the volunteerism research involves the elaboration of the relationship among individual action, community development and human rights (e.g., Nagata, 2003). Stakeholders often present the volunteer as an indispensable building block in the construction of social capital and community spirit. Indeed, participation in voluntary associations has been employed as a proxy for democratic participation (Tocqueville, 1835/1969), and cries advancing the need for "active citizenship" on the part of young people (Brooks, 2007) are well documented. Yet, such communities or the societies they construct could well be fascist, not democratic. Volunteerism viewed as a carrier of citizenship may be easily transformed into a form of social control, reinforcing the status quo through the creation of ideal citizens. Coffey (2004), for instance, suggested alternative conceptualizations of volunteerism that lie closer to activism, centering issues of political change and democratic rights. Here, productive tensions might be set up between understanding volunteerism in contrast with activism (Ganesh, Zoller, & Cheney, 2005). Thus, scholars need to analyze the potential of alternative or emergent articulations of civic engagement, and the limitation of volunteerism itself as a metaphor for social action (Flanagin, Stohl, & Bimber, 2006; Melucci, 1996).

## Summary and Conclusion

We summarize the main postulates of each discourse as regards volunteers, volunteering, and volunteerism in Table 9.1.

The four discourses that we have outlined make rather different contributions to our understanding of volunteers, volunteering, and volunteerism. As scholars examine who and what a volunteer is, they make significant assumptions about individuals and individualism. Studies focused on representation, therefore, describe personality attributes of volunteers and ways in which individuals represent particular social classes, ethnic groupings, or gender. In turn, discourses of understanding potentially explain how and why particular traits are appropriated as typical of volunteers, while a discourse of suspicion is well placed to critique such constructed understandings by exposing implicit power

*Table 9.1* Key Features of Various Discourses on Volunteers, Volunteering, and Volunteerism

| *Discourse* | *Key Term* | | |
| --- | --- | --- | --- |
| | *Volunteer* | *Volunteering* | *Volunteerism* |
| Discourse of representation | Volunteers are identifiable by demographics; Volunteers have innate personal characteristics. | Volunteering largely occurs in formal contexts, and has parallels with paid work. | Institutional contexts are pre-given. |
| Discourse of understanding | Volunteers construct their identities. | Volunteering is constructed through reciprocity and relationality. | Larger structures and vocabularies of volunteerism are mutually constructed in everyday talk. |
| Discourse of suspicion | Normative contexts privilege or marginalize individuals as volunteers. | Volunteering is open to coercion, exploitation and privilege. | State and corporate interests legitimate voluntary activity. |
| Discourse of vulnerability | "The volunteer" is a discursive subject position. | Volunteering can create temporary discursive spaces for action. | Volunteerism is discursively constructed through professionalization, enterprise, and consumerism. |

inequalities. A discourse of vulnerability, on the other hand, enables one to treat the entire figure of "the volunteer" with some irony.

In terms of volunteering, the actual activities volunteers engage in can be painted with functional brushstrokes or may be perceived as an exercise of meaning-making by volunteers trying to legitimate and balance both altruistic and egoistic motivations. Alternatively, the network of relationships established by volunteering may be viewed in terms of paternalism, with different sets of problems associated with charity-based and partnership models for volunteering. Finally, postmodern perspectives oriented toward vulnerability describe micro-practices constructed by shifting discursive struggles, which determine what is and is not appropriate fodder for volunteering.

Throughout this chapter, we defined volunteerism as the institutional and discursive framework which society, institutions, and organizations declare appropriate for voluntary involvement, and which provide a web of constraints and resources. The discourses of representation do not problematize systemic influences, either taking them as a given or reifying them in institutional terms. Conversely, the discourse of understanding more likely analyzes how interested parties construct contexts and structures; whereas, the discourse of suspicion pursues the potential to replicate inequality through supposedly benevolent structures. Discussions of volunteerism sometimes complicate sharp distinctions between discourses of suspicion and vulnerability. These two discourses offer much insight about the construction of appropriate spaces for volunteerism.

We hope that this review of the literature will draw further attention to the subject and prompt future investigation. Given the prevalence of popular discourses on volunteerism, the number of non-profit organizations that depend upon it, the millions of individuals and communities that engage in volunteering on a regular basis, and the surprising contexts in which one can see volunteering, it has perhaps never been as important to understand volunteerism in multiple ways and in multiple contexts. We look forward to such research.

## Notes

1. Twentieth century governments have, to varying degrees, engaged in the direct provision and funding of health, education, and welfare assistance to address issues such as unemployment, sickness, or disability.
2. Welfare schemes include a number of government policy initiatives for unemployed persons, including financial assistance (welfare benefits or the "dole"), training options, and work placement agencies. Consistent with an ethos of economic liberalization, citizenship, and self-responsibility, in some cases publicly funded financial assistance has been dependent upon an exchange of labor: "workfare" or "work for the dole" schemes.

## References

Adelman, M., & Frey, L. (1996). *A fragile community: Living together with AIDS*. New York: Erlbaum.

Amato, P. (1990). Personality and social network involvement as predictors of helping behavior in everyday life. *Social Psychology Quarterly, 53*, 31–43.

Andersson, B., & Ohlen, J. (2005). Being a hospice volunteer. *Palliative Medicine, 19*, 602–609.

Anheier, H. K., & Salamon, L. M. (1999). Volunteering in cross-national perspective. *Law and Contemporary Problems, 62*(3), 43–65.

Anheier, H. K., & Seibel, W. (Eds.). (1990). *The third sector: Comparative studies of nonprofit organizations*. Berlin, Germany: Walter de Gruyter.

Arai, S. M., & Pedlar, A. (2003). Moving beyond individualism in leisure theory: A critical analysis of concepts of community and social engagement. *Leisure Studies, 22*, 185–202.

Artz, L. (2001). Critical ethnography for communication studies: Dialogue and social justice in service-learning. *The Southern Communication Journal, 66*, 239–250.

Ashcraft, K., & Kedrowicz, A. (2002). Self-direction or social support? Nonprofit empowerment and the tacit employment contract of organizational communication studies. *Communication Monographs, 69*, 88–110.

Ashcraft, K. L., & Mumby, D. K. (2004). *Reworking gender: A feminist communicology of organization*. Thousand Oaks, CA: Sage.

Ashcraft, K. L., & Pacanowsky, M. E. (1996). "A woman's worst enemy": Reflections on a narrative of organizational life and female identity. *Journal of Applied Communication Research, 24,* 217–239.

Baines, S., & Hardill, I. (2008). "At least I can do something": The work of volunteering in a community beset by worklessness. *Social Policy and Society, 7,* 307–317.

Balandin, S., Llewellyn, G., Dew, A., Ballin, L., & Schneider, J. (2006). Older disabled workers' perceptions of volunteering. *Disability and Society, 21,* 677–692.

Barley, S. T., & Tolbert, P. S. (1997). Institutionalization and structuration: Studying the links between action and structure. *Organization Studies, 18,* 93–117.

Barlow, J. H., Bancroft, G. V., & Turner, A. P. (2005). Volunteer, lay tutors' experiences of the Chronic Disease Self-Management Course: Being valued and adding value. *Health Education Research [NLM-MEDLINE], 20,* 128–136.

Barnett, T. (1996). *Aroha, poha, tikanga [Love, just outcomes, sharing what is of value or treasured]: Volunteering in Aotearoa/New Zealand.* Christchurch, New Zealand: Community Employment Group, Department of Labour.

Barnill, K., Beitsch, L. M., & Brooks, R. G. (2001). Improving access to care for the underserved: State-supported volunteerism as a successful component. *Archives of Internal Medicine, 161,* 2177-2182.

Bartley, A. G. (2007). Confronting the realities of volunteering for a national disaster. *Journal of Mental Health Counseling, 29,* 4–16.

Baudrillard, J. (1983). *Simulations.* New York: Semiotext(e).

Beck, U. (2000). *Brave new world of work.* Cambridge, England: Polity Press.

Bennett, R., & Barkensjo, A. (2005). Internal marketing, negative experiences, and volunteers' commitment to providing high-quality services in a UK helping and caring charitable organization. *Voluntas, 16,* 251–273.

Benzian, H., & van Palenstein Helderman, W. (2006). Editorial: Dental charity work—Does it really help? *British Dental Journal, 201,* 413.

Berger, I. E. (2006). The influence of religion on philanthropy in Canada. *Voluntas, 17,* 115–132.

Berry, H. A., & Chisholm, L. A. (1999). *Service learning in higher education throughout the world: An initial look.* New York: International Partnership for Service Learning and Leadership.

Bloom, L. R., & Kilgore, D. (2003). The volunteer citizen after welfare reform in the United States: An ethnographic study of volunteerism in action. *Voluntas, 14,* 431–454.

Boden, D. (1994). *The business of talk: Organizations in action.* Cambridge, England: Polity Press.

Boston, J., Martin, J., Pallot, J., & Walsh, P. (1996). *Public management: The New Zealand model.* Auckland, New Zealand: Oxford University Press.

Boz, I., & Palaz, S. (2007). Factors influencing the motivation of Turkey's community volunteers. *Nonprofit and Voluntary Sector Quarterly, 36,* 643–661.

Brooks, R. (2007). Young people's extra-curricular activities: Critical social engagement or 'something for the CV'? *Journal of Social Policy, 36,* 417–434.

Brouwer, D. C., & Squires, C. R. (1996). Public intellectuals, public life, and the university. *Argument and Advocacy, 39,* 201–213.

Brown, E. (1999). The scope of volunteering and public service. *Law and Contemporary Problems, 62,* 17–42.

Brown, E., & Smart, R. (2007). Racial differences in civic participation and charitable giving: The confounding effects of educational attainment and unmeasured ability. *Review of Black Political Economy, 34,* 259–271.

Buckley, R. (2005). Unpaid work or serious leisure: Perspectives on volunteering. *Journal of Sustainable Tourism, 13*, 520–521.

Burrell, G., & Morgan, G. (1979). *Sociological paradigms and organizational analysis.* London: Heinemann.

Bussell, H., & Forbes, D. (2002). Understanding the volunteer market: The what, where, who and why of volunteering. *International Journal of Nonprofit and Voluntary Sector Marketing 7*, 244–258.

Butcher, J., Howard, P., McMeniman, M., & Thon, G. (2003). *Engaging community— Service or learning?* Canberra: Australian Government Department of Education, Science and Training.

Carson, E. D. (1999). On defining and measuring volunteering in the United States and abroad. *Law and Contemporary Problems, 62*, 68–71.

Castells, M. (2001). *The Internet galaxy: Reflections on the Internet, business and society.* Oxford, England: Oxford University Press.

Cheney, G. (2007). Organizational communication comes out. *Management Communication Quarterly, 21*, 80–91.

Cheney, G., & Ashcraft, K. (2007). Considering "the professional" in communication studies: Implications for theory and research within and beyond the boundaries of organizational communication. *Communication Theory, 17*, 146–175.

Cheney, G., Zorn, T. E., Planalp, S., & Lair, D. J. (2008). Meaningful work and personal/social well-being: Organizational communication engages the meanings of work. In C. S. Beck (Ed.), *Communication yearbook 32* (pp. 137–185). New York: Routledge.

Chiles, A. M., & Zorn, T. E. (1995). Empowerment in organizations: Employees' perceptions of the influences on empowerment. *Journal of Applied Communication Research, 23*, 1–25.

Clair, R. (1996). The political nature of the colloquialism, "A real job": Implications for organizational socialization. *Communication Monographs, 63*, 249–267.

Clary, E. G., & Snyder, M. (1991). A functional analysis of altruism and prosocial behavior: The case of volunteerism. *Review of Personality and Social Psychology, 12*, 119–148.

Clary, E. G., & Snyder, M. (1999). The motivations to volunteer: Theoretical and practical considerations. *Current Directions in Psychological Science, 8*, 156–159.

Clary, E. G., Snyder, M., & Ridge, R. D. (1992). Volunteers' motivations: A functional strategy for the recruitment, placement and retention of volunteers. *Nonprofit Management and Leadership, 2*, 333–350.

Clary, E. G., Snyder, M., Ridge, R. D., Copeland, J., Stukas, A. A., & Haugen, J., et al. (1998). Understanding and assessing the motivations of volunteers: A functional approach. *Journal of Personality and Social Psychology, 74*, 1515–1530.

Cloke, P., Johnsen, S., & May, J. (2007). Ethical citizenship? Volunteers and the ethics of providing services for homeless people. *Geoforum, 38*, 1089–1101.

Cnaan, R. A., & Goldberg-Glen, R. S. (1991). Measuring motivation to volunteer in human services. *Journal of Applied Behavioral Science, 27*, 269–284.

Cnaan, R. A., Handy, F., & Wadsworth, M. (1996). Defining who is a volunteer: Conceptual and empirical considerations. *Nonprofit and Voluntary Sector Quarterly, 25*, 364–383.

Coffey, A. (2004). *Reconceptualising social policy: Sociological perspectives on contemporary social policy.* Maidenhead, England: Open University Press.

Coghlan, A. (2006). Volunteer tourism as an emerging trend or an expansion of ecotourism? A look at potential clients' perceptions of volunteer tourism organisations. *International Journal of Nonprofit and Voluntary Sector Marketing, 11,* 225–237.

Collinson, D. L. (2003). Identities and insecurities: Selves at work. *Organization, 10,* 527–547.

Corman, S., & Poole, M. S. (Eds.). (2000). *Perspectives on organizational communication: Finding common ground.* New York: Guilford Press.

Crabtree, R. D. (1998). Mutual empowerment in cross-cultural participatory development and service learning: Lessons in communication and social justice from projects in El Salvador and Nicaragua. *Journal of Applied Communication Research, 26,* 182–209.

Cusick, B. (2007). The conflicted individualism of Japanese college student volunteers. *Japan Forum, 19,* 49–68.

Daniels, A. K. (1988). *Invisible careers: Women civic leaders from the volunteer world.* Chicago: University of Chicago Press.

Davis, M. H., Hall, J., A., & Meyer, M. (2003). The first year: Influences on the satisfaction, involvement, and persistence of new community volunteers. *Personality and Social Psychology Bulletin, 29,* 248–260.

Deetz, S. (1992). *Democracy in an age of corporate colonization: Developments in communication and the politics of everyday life.* Albany: State University of New York Press.

Deetz, S. (1996). Describing differences in approaches to organization science: Rethinking Burrell and Morgan and their legacy. *Organization Science, 7,* 191–207.

Dein, S., & Abbas, S. Q. (2005). The stresses of volunteering in a hospice: A qualitative study. *Palliative Medicine, 19,* 58–64.

Dekker, P., & Halman, L. (Eds.). (2003). *The values of volunteering: Cross-cultural perspectives.* New York: Kluwer Academic/Plenum.

Derrida, J. (1976). *Of grammatology* (G. Spivak, Trans.). Baltimore: John Hopkins University Press.

Devereux, P. (2008). International volunteering for development and sustainability: Outdated paternalism or a radical response to globalisation? *Development in Practice, 18,* 357–370.

Dietz, T., Stern, P., & Guagnano, G. (1998). Social structural and social psychological bases of environmental concern. *Environment and Behavior, 30,* 450–471.

Dougherty, G. (2005, April). *Cultural variations and understandings of public service.* Paper presented at the annual meeting of the Midwest Political Science Association, Chicago.

Droge, D., & Murphy, B. O. (Eds.). (1999). *Voices of strong democracy: Concepts and models for service-learning in communication studies.* Washington, DC: American Association of Higher Education.

Du Gay, P. (1996). *Consumption and identity at work.* London: Sage.

Duncan, B. (1999). Modeling charitable contributions of time and money. *Journal of Public Economics, 72,* 213–242.

Dutta-Bergman, M. (2004). Describing volunteerism: The theory of unified responsibility. *Journal of Public Relations Research, 16,* 353–369.

Eckstein, S. (2001). Community as gift-giving: Collectivistic roots of volunteerism. *American Sociological Review, 66,* 829–851.

Edlefsen, M. S., & Olson, C. M. (2002). Perspectives of volunteers in emergency feeding programmes on hunger, its causes, and solutions. *Journal of Nutrition Education, 34*, 93–99.

Ellis, S. J., & Noyes, K. H. (1990). *By the people: A history of Americans as volunteers* (Rev. ed.). San Francisco: Jossey-Bass.

Farmer, S. M., & Fedor, D. B. (2001). Changing the focus on volunteering: An investigation of volunteers' multiple contributions to a charitable organization. *Journal of Management, 27*, 191–211.

Featherstone, M., Lash, S., & Robertson, R. (Eds.). (1997). *Global modernities*. New Delhi, India: Sage.

Finkelstein, M., & Brannick, M. T. (2007). Applying theories of institutional helping to informal volunteering: Motives, role identity and prosocial personality. *Social Behavior and Personality, 35*, 101–114.

Finkelstein, M., Penner, L. A., & Brannick, M. T. (2005). Motive, role identity and prosocial personality as predictors of volunteer activity. *Social Behavior and Personality, 33*, 403–418.

Flanagin, A., Stohl, C., & Bimber, B. (2006). Modeling the structure of collective action. *Communication Monographs, 73*, 29–54.

Fraser, N. (1990/1991). Rethinking the public sphere: A contribution to the critique of actually existing democracy. *Social Texts, 25/26*, 56–80.

Freeman, R. (1997). Working for nothing: The supply of volunteer labor. *Journal of Labor Economics, 15*, S140–S166.

Frey, L. R., Pearce, W. B., Pollack, M., Artz, L., & Murphy, B. A. O. (1996). Looking for justice in all the wrong places: On a communication approach to social justice. *Communication Studies, 47*, 110–127.

Gallagher, S. (1994). Doing their share: Comparing patterns of help given by older and younger adults. *Journal of Marriage and the Family, 56*, 567–578.

Ganesh, S. (2005). The myth of the non-governmental organization: Governmentality and transnationalism in an Indian NGO. In G. Cheney & G. Barnett (Eds.), *International and intercultural organizational communication* (Vol. 7, pp. 193–219). Creskill, NJ: Hampton Press.

Ganesh, S., Zoller, H. M., & Cheney, G. E. (2005). Transforming resistance, broadening our boundaries: Organizational communication meets globalization from below. *Communication Monographs, 72*, 169–191.

Gaskin, K. (1998). *What young people want from volunteering*. London: Institute for Volunteering Research.

Gillath, O., Shaver, P. R., Mikulincer, M., Nitzberg, R. E., Erez, A., & Van Ijzendoorn, M. H. (2005). Attachment, caregiving and volunteering: Placing volunteerism in an attachment-theoretical framework. *Personal Relationships, 12*, 425–446.

Glasrud, B. (2007). Volunteerism vectors. *Nonprofit World, 25*, 3–4.

Glass, J. C., & Hastings, J. L. (1998). Stress and burnout: Concerns for the hospice volunteer. *Educational Gerontology, 18*, 717–731.

Goss, K. A. (1999). Volunteering and the long civic generation. *Nonprofit and Voluntary Sector Quarterly, 28*, 378–415.

Gossett, L. M. (2002). Kept at arms length: Questioning the organizational desirability of member identification. *Communication Monographs, 69*, 385–404.

Granfield, R. (2007). The meaning of pro bono: Institutional variations in professional obligations among lawyers. *Law and Society Review, 41*, 113–138.

Greenwood, D. J., & Levin, M. (2005). Reform of the social sciences and of universities through action research. In N. Denzin & Y. Lincoln (Eds.), *Handbook of qualitative research* (3rd ed., pp. 43–64). Thousand Oaks, CA: Sage.

Grube, J., & Piliavin, J. A. (2000). Role identity, organizational experiences and volunteer experiences. *Personality and Social Psychology Bulletin, 26,* 1108–1120.

Habermas, J. (1984). *The theory of communicative action: Reason and the rationalization of society* (Vol. 1, T. McCarthy, Trans.). Boston: Beacon Press.

Habermas, J. (1989). *The structural transformation of the public sphere: An Inquiry into a category of bourgeois society* (T. Burger with F. Lawrence, Trans.). Cambridge, MA: MIT Press.

Hankinson, P., & Rochester, C. (2005). The face and voice of volunteering: A suitable case for branding? *International Journal of Nonprofit and Voluntary Sector Marketing, 10,* 93–105.

Herd, P., & Meyer, M. H. (2002). Care work: Invisible civic engagement. *Gender & Society, 16,* 665–688.

Hochschild, A. (1983). *The managed heart: The commercialization of human feeling.* Berkeley: University of California Press.

Hodgkinson, V. A. (1995). Key factors influencing caring, involvement and community. In P. G. Schervish, V. A. Hodgkinson, & M. Gates (Eds.), *Caring and community in modern society* (pp. 21–50). San Francisco: Jossey-Bass.

Hodgkinson, V. A., & Weitzman, M. S. (1996). *Giving and volunteering in the United States: Findings from a national survey.* Washington, DC: Independent Sector.

Hodgkinson, V. A., Weitzman, M. S., & Kirsch, A. D. (1990). From commitment to action: How religious involvement affects giving and volunteering. In R. Wuthnow & V. A. Hodgkinson (Eds.), *Faith and philanthropy in America: Exploring the role of religion in America's voluntary sector* (pp. 93–114). San Francisco: Jossey-Bass.

Husserl, E. (1962). *Ideas: General introduction to pure phenomenology* (W. R. B. Gibson, Trans.). London: Collier-Macmillan.

Hustinx, L. (2001). Individualism and new styles of youth volunteering: An empirical exploration. *Voluntary Action, 3,* 47–55.

Hustinx, L. (2007). Brave new volunteers? The value of paid and unpaid work for Flemish Red Cross volunteers. *Voluntas, 18,* 73–89.

Hustinx, L., & Lammertyn, F. (2004). The cultural bases of volunteering: Understanding and predicting attitudinal differences between Flemish Red Cross volunteers. *Nonprofit and Voluntary Sector Quarterly, 33,* 548–584.

Illich, I. (1968). To hell with good intentions. Paper presented at the Conference on InterAmerican Student Projects, Cuernavaca, Mexico.

Independent Sector. (2002). *Faith and philanthropy: The connection between charitable behavior and giving.* Washington, DC: Independent Sector.

Iverson, J. O. (2003). *Knowing volunteers through communities of practice.* Unpublished doctoral dissertation, Arizona State University, Tempe.

Iverson, J. O., & McPhee, R. D. (2008). Communicating knowing through communities of practice: Exploring internal communicative processes and differences among CoPs. *Journal of Applied Communication Research, 36,* 176–199.

Janoski, T., Musick, M., & Wilson, J. (1998). Being volunteered? The impact of social participation and pro-social activities on volunteering. *Sociological Forum, 13,* 495–519.

Jones, K. S. (2006). Giving and volunteering as distinct forms of civic engagement:

The role of community integration and personal resources in formal helping. *Nonprofit and Voluntary Sector Quarterly, 35*, 249–266.

Katz, E., & Rosenberg, J. (2005). An economic interpretation of institutional volunteering. *European Journal of Political Economy, 21*, 429–443.

Kearns, K. P. (1994). The strategic management of accountability in nonprofit organizations: An analytical framework. *Public Administration Review, 54*, 185–193.

Kelsey, J. (1995). *The New Zealand experiment: A world model for structural adjustment?* Auckland, New Zealand: Auckland University Press.

Kim, J., Kang, J.-H., Lee, M.-A., & Lee, Y. (2007). Volunteering among older people in Korea. *The Journal of Gerontology, 62B*, S69–S73.

Kim, Y. Y., & Ruben, B. D. (1988). Intercultural transformation: A systems view. In R. L. Wiseman (Ed.), *Theories in intercultural communication* (pp. 299–321). Thousand Oaks, CA: Sage.

Kingfisher, C. (Ed.). (2002). *Western welfare in decline: Globalisation and women's poverty*. Philadelphia: University of Pennsylvania Press.

Kingston, R., & Levine, P. (2004). What is "public" about what academics do? An exchange. In D. W. Brown & D. Witte (Eds.), *Higher education exchange* (pp. 17–29). Dayton, OH: Kettering Foundation.

Knight, B. (1993). *Voluntary action* (2nd ed.). London: CENTRIS.

Knights, D., & Wilmott, H. (1999). *Management lives: Power and identity in work organizations*. London: Sage.

Krone, K. J., & Harter, L. M. (2007). Forum introduction: Organizational communication scholars as public intellectuals. *Management Communication Quarterly, 21*, 75–79.

Kulik, L. (2000). The impact of gender and age on reactions to unemployment: The Israeli case. *Sex Roles, 43*, 85–104.

Lacey, A., & Ilcan, S. (2006). Voluntary labor, responsible citizenship, and international NGOs. *International Journal of Comparative Sociology, 47*, 34–53.

Leonard, R., & Hayward-Brown, H. (2002). A qualitative analysis of experiences of women volunteers in human services. *Third Sector Review, 8*, 31–50.

Lewis, L. (2005). The civil society sector: A review of critical issues and a research agenda for organizational communication scholars. *Management Communication Quarterly, 19*, 238–267.

Liao-Troth, M. A. (2005). Are they here for the long haul? The effects of functional motives and personality factors on the psychological contracts of volunteers. *Nonprofit and Voluntary Sector Quarterly, 34*, 510–530.

Littlepage, L., Obergfell, E., & Zanin, G. (2003). *Family volunteering: An exploratory study of the impact on families*. Purdue, IN: Center for Urban Policy and the Environment, School of Public and Environmental Affairs.

Liu, L. (2008). Yang and yin in communication: Towards a typology and logic of persuasion in China. *Diogenes, 55*, 120–132.

Lofland, J. (1996). *Social movement organizations*. New York: Aldine de Gruyter.

Lyons, M. (2001). *Third sector: The contribution of nonprofit and cooperative enterprises in Australia*. Crows Nest, Australia: Allen & Unwin.

Lyons, M., & Nivison-Smith, I. (2006). Religion and giving in Australia. *Australian Journal of Social Issues, 41*, 419–436.

MacDonald, M., Phipps, S., & Lethbridge, L. (2005). Taking its toll: The influence of paid and unpaid work on women's wellbeing. *Feminist Economics, 11*, 63–94.

Macintyre, C. (1999). From entitlement to obligation in the Australian welfare state. *Australian Journal of Social Issues, 34,* 103–118.

Martinson, M. (2006/2007, Winter). Opportunities or obligations? Civic engagement and older adults. *Generations, 30,* 59–65.

McBride, A. M., Sherraden, M. S., & Pritzker, S. (2006). Civic engagement among low-income and low-wealth families: In their words. *Family Relations, 55,* 152–162.

McComb, M. (1995). Becoming a traveler's aid volunteer: Communication in socialization and training. *Communication Studies, 46,* 297–317.

McDonald, C., & Mutch, A. (2000). The future of volunteering as institutionalising practice. In J. Warburten & M. Oppenheimer (Eds.), *Volunteers and volunteering* (pp. 125–139). Sydney, Australia: Federation Press.

McDonald, C., & Warburten, J. (2003). Stability and change in nonprofit organizations: The volunteer contribution. *Voluntas, 14,* 381–399.

McIntosh, A., & Zahra, A. (2007). A cultural encounter through volunteer tourism: Towards the ideals of sustainable tourism. *Journal of Sustainable Tourism, 15,* 541–556.

McMillan, J. J., & Cheney, G. (1996). The student as consumer: The implications and limitations of a metaphor. *Communication Education, 45,* 1–15.

McPherson, J., & Rotolo, T. (1996). Testing a dynamic model of social composition: Diversity and change in voluntary groups. *American Sociological Review, 61,* 179–202.

Medved, C. (this volume). Crossing and transforming occupational and household gendered divisions of labor: Reviewing literatures and deconstructing differences. In C. S. Beck (Ed.), *Communication yearbook 33* (pp. 301–341). New York: Routledge.

Meisenbach, R., & McMillan, J. J. (2006). Blurring the boundaries: Historical developments and future directions in organizational rhetoric. In C. S. Beck (Ed.), *Communication yearbook 30* (pp. 99–141). Mahwah, NJ: Erlbaum.

Melucci, A. (1996). *Challenging codes: Collective action in the information age.* Cambridge, England: University of Cambridge.

Merrell, J. (2000). Ambiguity: Exploring the complexity of roles and boundaries when working with volunteers in well women clinics. *Social Science and Medicine, 51,* 93–102.

Mesch, D. J., Rooney, P. M., & Steinberg, K. S. (2006). The effects of race, gender and marital status on giving and volunteering in Indiana. *Nonprofit and Voluntary Sector Quarterly, 35,* 565–587.

Messias, D. K. H., DeJong, M. K., & McLoughlin, K. (2005). Expanding the concept of women's work: Volunteer work in the context of poverty. *Journal of Poverty, 9,* 25–47.

Miles, I., Sullivan, W. C., & Kuo, F. E. (1998). Ecological restoration volunteers: The benefits of participation. *Urban Ecosystems, 2,* 27–41.

Miller, J. (2006). Waves amidst war: Intercultural challenges while training volunteers to respond to the psychosocial needs of Sri Lankan tsunami survivors. *Brief Treatment and Crisis Intervention, 6,* 349–365.

Miller, P., & Rose, N. (1990). Governing economic life. *Economy and Society, 19,* 1–31.

Miller, P., & Rose, N. (1995). Production, identity and democracy. *Theory and Society, 24,* 427–467.

Milligan, C. (1998). Pathways of dependence: The impact of health and social care restructuring—The voluntary experience. *Social Science and Medicine, 46,* 743–753.

Milligan, C., & Fyfe, N. (2005). Preserving space for volunteers: Exploring the links between voluntary welfare organizations, volunteering and citizenship. *Urban Studies, 42,* 417–433.

Moemeka, A. (1998). Communalism as a fundamental dimension of culture. *Journal of Communication, 47,* 118–141.

Mumby, D. K. (1996). Feminism, postmodernism, and organizational communication studies: A critical reading. *Management Communication Quarterly, 9,* 259–295.

Mumby, D. K. (1997). Modernism, postmodernism and communication studies: A rereading of an ongoing debate. *Communication Theory, 7,* 1–28.

Mumby, D. K. (2001). Power and politics. In F. M. Jablin & L. L. Putnam (Eds.), *The new handbook of organizational communication: Advances in theory, research and methods* (pp. 585–623). Thousand Oaks, CA: Sage.

Musick, M., Wilson, J., & Bynum Jr, W. B. (2000). Race and formal volunteering. *Social Forces, 78,* 1539–1571.

Mustonen, P. (2005). Volunteer tourism: Postmodern pilgrimage? *Journal of Tourism and Cultural Change, 3,* 160–177.

Mutchler, J. E., Burr, J. A., & Caro, F. G. (2003). From paid work to volunteer: Leaving the paid workforce and volunteering in later life. *Social Forces, 81,* 1267–1293.

Nadesan, M. H. (1996). Organizational identity and space of action. *Organizational Studies, 17,* 49–81.

Nagata, J. (2003). Local and transnational initiatives towards improving Chinese-indigenous relations in post-Suharto Indonesia: The role of the voluntary sector. *Asian Ethnicity, 4,* 369–381.

Nakano, L. Y. (2000). Volunteering as a lifestyle choice: Negotiating self-identities in Japan. *Ethnology, 39,* 93–107.

Napoli, P. (this volume). Public interest media activism and advocacy as a social movement: A review of the literature. In C. S. Beck (Ed.), *Communication yearbook 33* (pp. 385–239). New York: Routledge.

Nunn, M. (2002). Volunteering as a tool for building social capital. *The Journal of Volunteer Administration, 20,* 14–20.

Oliver, C. (1992). The antecedents of deinstitutionalization. *Organization Studies, 13,* 563–588.

Oliver, P., & Love, C. (2007). *Mahi aroha* [Work performed out of love, sympathy or caring]*: Maori perspectives on volunteering and cultural obligations.* Wellington, New Zealand: Office for the Community and Voluntary Sector.

Omoto, A. M., & Snyder, M. (1995). Sustained helping without obligation: Motivation, longevity of service and perceived attitude change among AIDS volunteers. *Journal of Personality and Social Psychology, 68,* 671–686.

Omoto, A. M., Snyder, M., & Martino, S. C. (2000). Volunteerism and the life course: Investigating age-related agendas for action. *Basic and Applied Social Psychology, 22,* 181–197.

Onyx, J., & Leonard, R. (2000). Women, volunteering and social capital. In J. Warbuten & M. Oppenheimer (Eds.), *Volunteers and volunteering* (pp. 113–124). Sydney, Australia: Federation Press.

Palmer, A. A., Freeman, P. A., & Zabriskie, R. B. (2007). Family deepening: A qualitative inquiry into the experience of families who participate in service expeditions. *Journal of Leisure Research, 39,* 438–458.

Papa, W. H., Papa, M. J., Kandath, K. P., Worrell, T., & Muthuswamy, N. (2005). Dialectic of unity and fragmentation in feeding the homeless: Promoting social justice through communication. *Atlantic Journal of Communication, 13*, 242–271.

Parboteeah, K. P., Cullen, J. B., & Lim, L. (2004). Formal volunteering: A cross-national test. *Journal of World Business, 39*, 431–441.

Pearce, J. L. (1993). *Volunteers: The organizational behavior of unpaid workers.* London: Routledge.

Penner, L. (2004). Volunteerism and social problems: Making things better or worse? *Journal of Social Issues, 60*, 645–666.

Penner, L. A., & Finkelstein, M. A. (1998). Dispositional and structural determinants of volunteerism. *Journal of Personality and Social Psychology, 74*, 525–537.

Perry, J. L., Brudney, J. L., Coursey, D., & Littlepage, L. (2008). What drives morally committed citizens? A study of the antecedents of public service motivation. *Public Administration Review, 68*, 445–459.

Petronio, S., Sargent, J., Andea, L., Reganis, P., & Cichocki, D. (2004). Family and friends as healthcare advocates: Dilemmas of privacy and confidentiality. *Journal of Social and Personal Relationships, 21*, 33–52.

Prouteau, L., & Wolff, F.-C. (2005). Does volunteer work pay off in the labor market? *The Journal of Socio-Economics, 35*, 992–1013.

Puffer, S. M., & Meindl, J. R. (2006). Volunteers from corporations: Work cultures reflect values similar to the voluntary organization's. *Nonprofit Management and Leadership, 5*, 359–375.

Pusey, M. (2000). Middle Australians in the grip of economic reform...Will they volunteer? In J. Warburten & M. Oppenheimer (Eds.), *Volunteers and volunteering* (pp. 19–31). Sydney, Australia: Federation Press.

Putnam, R. D. (2000). *Bowling alone: The collapse and revival of American community.* New York: Simon & Schuster.

Raddon, M.-B. (2003). *Community and money: Men and women making change.* Toronto, Canada: Black Rose Books.

Rajulton, F., Ravanera, Z. R., & Beaujot, R. (2007). Measuring social cohesion: An experiment using the Canadian national survey of giving, volunteering, and participating. *Social Indicators Research, 80*, 461–492.

Rathgeb Smith, S. (1999). Volunteering and community service. *Law and Contemporary Problems, 62*, 169–176.

Rehberg, W. (2005). Altruistic individualists: Motivation for international volunteering among young adults in Switzerland. *Voluntas, 16*, 109–122.

Reinerman, C. (1987). *American states of mind.* New Haven, CT: Yale University Press.

Reynolds, H. (2006). Medical volunteering: Giving something back. *Lung, 184*, 369–371.

Ricoeur, P. (1981). *Hermeneutics and the human sciences* (J. Thompson, Trans.). New York: Cambridge University Press.

Rifkin, J. (1995). *The end of work: The decline of the global labor force and the dawn of the post-market era.* New York: Tarcher/Putnam.

Roker, D., Player, K., & Coleman, J. (1998). Challenging the image: The involvement of young people with disabilities in volunteering and campaigning. *Disability and Society, 13*, 725–741.

Ronel, N. (2006). When good overcomes bad: The impact of volunteers on those they help. *Human Relations, 59*, 1133–1153.

Rossi, A. S. (2001). Domains and dimensions of social responsibility: A sociodemographic profile. In A. S. Rossi (Ed.), *Caring and doing for others: Social responsibility in the domains of family, work and community* (pp. 97–134). Chicago: University of Chicago Press.

Rotolo, T. (2000). A time to join, a time to quit: The influence of life cycle transitions on voluntary association memberships. *Social Forces, 78*, 1133–1161.

Rubin, A., & Thorelli, I. (1984). Egoistic motives and longevity of participation. *Journal of Applied Behavioral Science, 23*, 223–235.

Ruiter, S., & De Graaf, N. D. (2006). National context, religiosity, and volunteering: Results from 53 countries. *American Sociological Review, 71*, 191–210.

Schervish, P. G., & Havens, J. J. (2002). The Boston Area Diary Study and the moral citizenship of care. *Voluntas, 13*, 47–71.

Schroeder, D. A., Penner, L. A., Dovidio, J. F., & Piliavin, J. A. (1995). *The psychology of helping and altruism*. New York: McGraw-Hill.

Scott, R. W. (1995). *Institutions and organizations*. Thousand Oaks, CA: Sage.

Sills, D. (1957). *The volunteers: Means and ends in a national organization*. Glencoe, IL: The Free Press.

Simpson, M., & Cheney, G. (2007). Marketization, participation, and communication within New Zealand retirement villages: A critical-rhetorical and discursive analysis. *Discourse and Communication, 1*, 191–222.

Smith, D. H. (1994). Determinants of voluntary association participation and volunteering: A literature review. *Nonprofit and Voluntary Sector Quarterly, 23*, 243–263.

Snyder, M. (2001). Psychology of volunteerism. In N. J. Smelser & P. B. Baltes (Eds.), *International encyclopedia of the social and behavioral sciences* (pp. 16308–16311). Amsterdam: Elsevier.

Spoonley, P. (2004). Is nonstandard work becoming standard? Trends and issues. *New Zealand Journal of Employment Relations, 29*, 3–24.

Spoonley, P., Pearce, R., Butcher, A., & O'Neill, D. (2004). Social cohesion: A policy and indicator framework for assessing immigrant and host outcomes. *Social Policy Journal of New Zealand, 17*, 85–110.

St. John, J., & Shepherd, G. J. (2004). Transcending tolerance: Pragmatism, social capital, and community in communication. In P. J. Kalbfleisch (Ed.), *Communication yearbook 28* (pp. 167–187). Mahwah, NJ: Erlbaum.

Statistics New Zealand. (2004). *Nonprofit institutions satellite account*. Wellington, New Zealand: Statistics New Zealand.

Stebbins, R. A. (2002). *The organizational basis of leisure participation: A motivational exploration*. State College, PA: Venture.

Stohl, C., & Jennings, K. (1988). Volunteerism and voice in quality circles. *Western Journal of Speech Communication, 52*, 238–251.

Stukas, A. A., Snyder, M., & Clary, E. G. (1999). The effects of "mandatory volunteerism" on intentions to volunteer. *Psychological Science, 10*, 59–64.

Sundeen, R. A. (1992). Difference in personal goals and attitudes among volunteers. *Nonprofit and Voluntary Sector Quarterly, 21*, 271–291.

Sundeen, R. A., Garcia, C., & Wang, L. (2007). Volunteer behavior among Asian American groups in the United States. *Journal of Asian American Studies, 10*, 243–271.

Sundeen, R. A., Raskoff, S. A., & Garcia, M. C. (2007). Differences in perceived barriers to volunteering in formal organizations: Lack of time versus lack of interest. *Nonprofit Management and Leadership, 17*, 279–300.

Taniguchi, H. (2006). Men's and women's volunteering: Gender differences in the effects of employment and family characteristics. *Nonprofit and Voluntary Sector Quarterly, 35*, 83–101.

Thompson, J. A., & Bunderson, J. S. (2003). Violations of principle: Ideological currency in the psychological contract. *Academy of Management Review, 28*, 571–586.

Tocqueville, A. (1969). *Democracy in America*. Garden City, NY: Doubleday. (Original work published 1835)

Tracy, S. J., & Trethewey, A. (2005). Fracturing the real-self–fake-self dichotomy: Moving toward "crystallized" organizational discourses and identities. *Communication Theory, 15*, 168–195.

Trethewey, A. (1999). Critical organizational communication theory, feminist research methods, and service learning: Politicizing the communication course. In D. Droge & B. O. Murphy (Eds.), *Voices of strong democracy: Concepts and models for service-learning in communication studies* (pp. 177–189). Washington, DC: American Association of Higher Education.

Trujillo, N. (1992). Interpreting (the work and talk of) baseball: Perspectives on ballpark culture. *Western Journal of Communication, 56*, 350–371.

Tschirhart, M., Mesch, D. J., Perry, J., L., Miller, T., K., & Lee, G. (2005). Stipended volunteers: Their goals, experiences, satisfaction, and likelihood of future service. *Nonprofit and Voluntary Sector Quarterly, 30*, 422–444.

Warburten, J., & Crosier, T. (2001). Are we too busy to volunteer? The relationship between time and volunteering using the ABS 1997 time use data. *Australian Journal of Social Issues, 36*, 295–314.

Warburten, J., & Gooch, M. (2007). Stewardship volunteering by older Australians: The generative response. *Local Government, 12*, 43–55.

Warburten, J., & McLaughlin, D. (2007). Passing on our culture: How older Australians from diverse cultural backgrounds contribute to civil society. *Journal of Cross-Cultural Gerontology, 22*, 47–60.

Waring, M. (1999). *Counting for nothing: What men value and what women are worth*. Toronto, Canada: University of Toronto Press.

Wilson, C., Hendricks, A. K., & Smithies, R. (2001). 'Lady Bountiful' and the 'virtual volunteers': The changing face of social service volunteering. *Social Policy Journal of New Zealand, 17*, 124–146.

Wilson, J. (2000). Volunteering. *Annual Review of Sociology, 26*, 215–240.

Wilson, J. (2004). The values of volunteering: Cross-cultural perspectives. *American Journal of Sociology, 109*, 1540–1543.

Wilson, J., & Musick, M. (1997a). Work and volunteering: The long arm of the job. *Social Forces, 76*, 251–273.

Wilson, J., & Musick, M. (1997b). Who cares? Toward an integrated theory of volunteer work. *American Sociological Review, 62*, 694–714.

Wilson, J., & Musick, M. (2003). Doing well by doing good: Volunteering and occupational achievement among American women. *Sociological Quarterly, 44*, 433–450.

Winter, M. (1998). Redefining volunteering. *Human Ecology Forum, 26*, 9.

Wisner, P., S., Stringfellow, A., Youngdahl, W., E., & Parker, L. (2005). The service volunteer-loyalty chain: an exploratory study of charitable not-for-profit service organizations. *Journal of Operations Management, 23*, 143–161.

Wuthnow, R. (1991a). *Acts of compassion*. Princeton, NJ: Princeton University Press.

Wuthnow, R. (1991b). The voluntary sector: Legacy of the past, hope for the future? In R. Wuthnow (Ed.), *Between states and markets: The voluntary sector in comparative perspective* (pp. 3–27). Princeton, NJ: Princeton University Press.

Wuthnow, R. (1995). *Learning to care: Elementary kindness in an age of indifference.* New York: Oxford University Press.

Yeung, A. B. (2004). An intricate triangle—Religiosity, volunteering and social capital: The European perspective, the case of Finland. *Nonprofit and Voluntary Sector Quarterly, 33*, 401–422.

Young, D. R. (2000). Alternative models of government-nonprofit sector relations: Theoretical and international perspectives. *Nonprofit and Voluntary Sector Quarterly, 29*, 149–171.

Zoller, H. M. (2000). "A place you haven't visited before": Creating the conditions for community dialogue. *Southern Communication Journal, 65*, 191–207.

## CHAPTER CONTENTS

# 10 Public Interest Media Advocacy and Activism as a Social Movement

*Philip M. Napoli*
Fordham University

This chapter reviews the literature on public interest media advocacy and activism. In so doing, it organizes the literature according to the three primary theoretical perspectives on social movements—framing processes, political opportunities, and mobilizing structures, to reflect the increased tendency in recent years for scholars to conceptualize public interest media advocacy and activism as a social movement. As this review indicates, public interest media advocacy and activism encompasses a movement that has employed a number of distinct, though overlapping, frames. It comprises a movement with political opportunities that are strongly tied to technological developments and to the conceptualization of policy problems within the policy-making sector. It constitutes a movement that, from a structural standpoint, has both emerged from—and can potentially serve the interests of—a wide range of other social movements, including civil rights and democratization movements, the consumer movement, and the anti-globalization movement. This review considers the implications of these and other characteristics of public interest media advocacy and activism as a social movement in an effort to develop strategic recommendations for the movement as well as recommendations for future research.

## Introduction

In recent years, citizen awareness of, and concern for issues related to the performance, structure, and accessibility of our media system has dramatically increased. Issues that range from media ownership regulation to access to communications technologies to the development of community media now resonate globally. These issues resonate far beyond the policy-making sector as information and communication technologies become increasingly important to political participation, cultural expression, and economic opportunity. Consequently, substantial growth in public interest organization activism has occurred in these areas—growth that has taken place along such lines and has had such influence that scholars increasingly characterize the field as a legitimate social movement (e.g., Atton, 2003; Calabrese, 2004; Hackett & Adam,

Correspondence: e-mail: pnapoli@fordham.edu

1999; Hackett & Carroll, 2006; Howley, 2004; Mueller, Pagé, & Kuerbis, 2004; O Siochrú, 1999a; Schiller, 1999; Thomas, 2006). Others have documented recent tremendous growth in policy-making activity in the communications area (see Mueller, Kuerbis, & Pagé, 2004; Scott, 2005), which may reflect and encourage citizen interest and public interest organization activity. The growing profile of public interest activism and advocacy work in the media and communications area underscores the need for scholarship that examines these activities, that places them into broader historical and theoretical contexts, and that assesses the structure and behavior of the organizations engaged in these activities.

This chapter assesses and synthesizes the literature to date that has addressed these issues. This chapter provides a roadmap of the scholarship that examines public interest advocacy and activism in media and communications in terms of its theoretical perspectives. This chapter also synthesizes the key findings of this literature as they relate to the strategies employed by actors in this area and to our understanding of these activities as representative of a social movement.[1] The topics addressed in this review pertain to policy-oriented scholars, as well as to scholars examining the relationship between communication and social movements, and those concerned with information gaps, social justice, minority representation, media and democracy, community media, and other related issues around which public interest media advocacy and activism have mobilized over the years. Scholarship across a wide range of areas within the communication discipline frequently intersects with the issues facing the public interest media advocacy and activist communities, including research on the effects of media on children, the causes and implications of ongoing *digital divides,* and the institutional dynamics surrounding the production and distribution of media content. Scholars across various sectors of the communication discipline also increasingly engage directly in advocacy work in these areas (e.g., Dutton, 2005; Kogen, 2008; Phiphitkul, 2005), which leads to a blurring of the traditional distinction between scholar and advocate. Thus, a deeper understanding of the public interest advocacy community examined in this chapter should be useful to a wide range of communication scholars because it will provide a deeper understanding of the advocacy contexts in which an array of types of communication scholarship can (or should) be brought to bear on issues related to media performance and media policy.

I begin by considering this body of literature through the lens of social movement theory. Specifically, the next three sections outline the three primary (and inter-related) analytical frameworks that have been employed in the study of social movements and organize the literature on public interest media advocacy and activism according to these three analytical frameworks. The concluding section summarizes the key findings and offers recommendations in terms of strategies to be employed within the movement, and in terms of avenues for future research.

## Social Movement Theory and Public Interest Media Advocacy and Activism

Exploring public interest media advocacy and activism through a social movement lens first requires that we establish definitional parameters for a social movement. Social movements have been defined as "sentiment[s] or activit[ies] shared by two or more people oriented toward changes in social relations or in the social system" (Ash Garner & Zald, 1987, p. 293). Many social movements focus on institutional change, which can be conceptualized as systematic adjustments in the "rules-based processes that channel social interaction" (Mueller, Kuerbis, et al., 2004, p. 14). According to Mueller, Kuerbis, et al., these adjustments generally involve changes in rules and norms that alter the distribution of wealth and power in significant ways and that become legitimate and self-reproducing over time.

Social movement scholars increasingly argue that public interest media advocacy and activism meet these criteria, due in large part to the extent to which the issues at the core of the movement (e.g., concentration of media ownership, inequalities in access to communications technologies, the need for alternative media) are beginning to resonate more widely, and thereby, contribute to more intensive public pressure on policy makers and industry actors than has characterized media issues throughout much of their history (Brinson, 2006; Calabrese, 2004; Hackett & Carroll, 2006). However, assessments of this movement still tend to conclude that it remains largely on the periphery of the national and international issue agendas (Hackett & Carroll, 2006; Mueller, Kuerbis, et al., 2004).

The following sections organize and synthesize the literature on public interest media advocacy and activism through a social movement theory analytical lens. Thus, although a review of the broader (and quite extensive) literature on social movements extends beyond the scope of this chapter, I outline the central theoretical perspectives from this field of research in order to then determine how the literature on public interest media advocacy and activism is situated within it.

In a synthesis of the social movement literature, McAdam, McCarthy, and Zald (1996) identified three broad sets of factors—associated with different theoretical traditions—that have been used to explain the emergence and persistence of social movements. These factors include (1) "the collective processes of interpretation, attribution, and social construction that mediate between opportunity and action" (p. 2); (2) "the structure of political opportunities and constraints confronting the movement" (p. 2), and (3) "the forms of organization (informal as well as formal), available to insurgents" (p. 2). According to McAdam et al., social movement scholars often label these three factors as *framing processes*, *political opportunities*, and *mobilizing structures*.

Framing processes refers to "the shared meanings and definitions that people bring to their situation" (McAdam et al., 1996, p. 3). This perspective emphasizes developing an understanding of the values and beliefs that underlie participation in social movements and how these values and beliefs, as well as the movements' key underlying principles and outcome priorities, are conceptualized and communicated (see Caniglia & Carmin, 2005), under the presumption that ideas genuinely matter in mobilizing individuals to take action. According to McAdam et al., an emphasis on political opportunities entails assessing the role of "the broader political system in structuring the opportunities for collective action" (p. 2). Caniglia and Carmin asserted that the analytical emphasis is thus placed on factors external to the movement that can constrain and shape it, such as shifts in the political or policy-making environment. McAdam et al. characterized mobilizing structures as "those collective vehicles, informal as well as formal, through which people mobilize and engage in collective action" (p. 3). According to Caniglia and Carmin, this perspective places the analytical emphasis on the organizational dynamics and structures within the movement, including factors such as resources, leadership, strategies, and organizational culture.

The following sections map the main observations and insights derived from the literature on public interest media advocacy and activism against these three theoretical perspectives. In recognition of the complex dynamics surrounding any social movement, this chapter highlights findings that suggest important points of intersection between these three analytical frames.

### *Framing Processes*

We must recognize that the success of any social movement depends in large part upon the contributions of individuals who become involved because the movement "resonate[s] with their personal values and beliefs" (Caniglia & Carmin, 2005, p. 205). Thus, a key point of emphasis within any social movement involves the crafting of identities and the framing of values and goals in ways that resonate with potential participants and that also effectively communicate the key institutional changes being sought (Caniglia & Carmin, 2005; Oliver & Johnston, 2000). The issue of the focal intellectual and normative underpinnings of public interest media advocacy and activism has been one of the most deeply examined elements of the movement because the movement has grappled with issues of internal divisions and debates over how best to frame its central priorities and desired outcomes to potential movement participants.

In a study focusing on Canada, the United Kingdom, and the United States, Hackett and Carroll (2006) outlined the primary frames that have characterized media activism over the years. These frames include: (1) a *free press, freedom of expression* frame, which emphasizes free speech values, but also encroachment on such values from both government and corporate sources (e.g., Heinz & Beckles, 2005; Venturelli, 1998); (2) a *media democratization* frame, which stresses an informed citizenry and effective self-governance, and the role and responsibilities of the media in relation to these objectives (see

Hackett & Adam, 1999; McChesney & Nichols, 2005; Raboy, 1990); (3) a *right to communicate* frame, which prioritizes the connection between communication and other human rights (Birdsall, 2006; Brinson, 2006; Costanza-Chock, 2002; CRIS Campaign, 2005; McIver, Birdsall, & Rasmussen, 2004; Raboy, 2004; Thomas, 2005, 2006); (4) a *cultural environment* frame that seeks to make strong parallels between media activism and environmental activism, often via an emphasis on harmful or distasteful media content (e.g., Duncan, 1999; Gerbner, 1998; see also Boyle, 1997), and (5) a *media justice* frame, which is relatively new in its explicit articulation, but draws upon many of the civil rights values and concerns with minority representation and participation in the media, and the marginalization of various sectors of society that characterized early media activism (Cyril, 2005; Davis & the Applied Research Center, n.d.; Rubin, 2002).

The existence of these many frames reflects the wide range of concerns that characterize participants in this movement, as well as the movement's international scope (Hadl & Hintz, 2006; O Siochrú, 2005). O Siochrú has noted that "framing the issue is difficult in transnational contexts since diverse cultural, political, and economic circumstances must be addressed" (p. 297). This diversity of frames also reflects a well-documented lack of consensus within public interest media advocacy and activist organizations in terms of the most appropriate means of framing the movement for the broader public. Some sectors of the movement consider particular framing approaches unacceptable for a variety of reasons. For instance, some sectors of the movement find heavy reliance on "democracy" as a core principle problematic, particularly in international contexts where the term *democracy* has developed negative associations with perceived affiliated processes of commercialization and cultural imperialism (Rubin, 2002). Others perceive the democracy frame as inherently ambiguous and lacking in the necessary specificity to achieve widespread appeal and identification (Belden, Russonello, & Stewart, 2006; Hackett & Carroll, 2006). Hackett (2000) observed that, for market liberals, media democratization means private ownership of media, protection from government censorship, and the removal of government-imposed public interest regulations. Such an interpretation of the term runs directly counter to the principles of virtually all sectors of the movement, which undermines the utility of media democratization as a focal concept in the minds of many movement participants.

The communication rights frame, which places communication within a comprehensive human rights framework (CRIS Campaign, 2005; McIver et al., 2004), has undergone similar criticism. Some within the movement perceive the communication rights frame as too abstract and unable to connect concretely with citizens' day-to-day concerns and needs (O Siochrú, 2005; see also Mueller, Kuerbis, & Pagé, 2007). Others perceive it as too legalistic in its orientation (Hackett & Carroll, 2006).

The media justice frame has arisen in response to a general dissatisfaction by some movement participants with the more established frames (Dichter,

2004; Rubin, 2002). Research on members of the media justice community has noted:

> The terms "media democracy," "media advocacy," and "media reform" also are used by those who struggle for progressive change in media policy. Although some feel that the distinction between these terms is largely semantic, whether one chooses "media democracy" rather than "media justice" to describe their[sic] work actually reveals a significant political divide. This divide occurs in part on the basis of race and age— groups run by younger staff, often of color, have consciously developed their media activism through a justice lens…they see the term "media justice" as deliberately addressing issues of race, class, gender, and sexuality within the broad field of media. (Davis & Applied Research Center, n.d., pp. 17–18)

Thus, it should be fairly clear at this point that members of the public interest media activism and advocacy community often perceive significant differences between themselves and those who are part of what can, at least superficially, be considered allied groups (Internaut Consulting, 2006) when it comes to the key guiding frame for the movement (although, as the discussion above suggests, these differences also can run deeper than mere framing). Hackett and Carroll (2004) suggested that the construction of an agreed-upon collective identity may be more difficult for members of this movement than for members of other social movements because the identity of "media reformer" is not as deeply held or resonant an identity as those associated with other social movements (e.g., environmentalism). This tendency may be compounded by the fact that many members of the public interest media advocacy and activism community have migrated from other social movement organizations (Dunbar-Hester, 2008b).

Nonetheless, recent research reflects the potential importance of reconciling these varied approaches to the movement. The Ford Foundation asked members of different sectors of the movement to offer their perceptions of the connotations of different terminologies. This study revealed that media justice, for instance, reflects the perspectives outlined earlier but also indicates an intentional opposition to the traditional media reform sector, which has been perceived by some members of the advocacy community as less radical in its strategic approach and goals than the media justice sector (Belden et al., 2006). Dichter (2004) went so far as to describe the media justice movement as "in contrast and opposition to the existing field of media reformers" (p. 2).

Hackett and Carroll (2006) contended that "a multiplicity of frames is not necessarily a barrier to movement mobilization; there is even an advantage that different frames can appeal to different constituencies," particularly across different national or cultural contexts (p. 79). Belden et al. (2006) suggested that leaders in the organizations that comprise these various sectors "do not think they need an over-arching term, or way of articulating a common goal to their work…most of them are more likely to want to explain their work in some detail rather than with a more approachable shorthand. These leaders also reveal little sense that their work would benefit from having all their efforts fly under one banner" (p. 5).

Arguing on behalf of the development of a unified frame, O Siochrú (2005) contended that "[a]n overarching, unifying frame is needed in order to build the kind of broad movement that alone can be successful" (p. 304). To effectively capture the complexity of the movement, O Siochrú advocated the use of the Right to Communicate as an overarching, "high-level" frame, under which more concrete "sub-frames" could be developed that would divide media issues into several discrete, though inter-related, elements (p. 305). Possible sub-frames identified by O Siochrú included the public sphere, political and cultural diversity, information commons, and civil rights. These sub-frames then could be used to build "horizontal linkages" with related social movements (p. 305). Dichter (2004), in contrast, argued that efforts to develop a single overarching frame for the movement may not be a precondition to a more widespread and influential movement and, therefore, may not be an appropriate point of focus for the movement's energies.

*Outcome Priorities*

A deeper reflection of this issue of the framing of a social movement involves the related issue of determining and clearly articulating the movement's key outcome priorities. Differences in the key framing principles that have characterized different components of public interest media advocacy and activism have, to some degree, been reflected in different areas of emphasis in terms of outcomes. Hackett and Adam (1999) offered a basic "structure" versus "content" categorization scheme, in which some components of the movement emphasize efforts to influence (i.e., improve) media content (particularly in areas such as minority representation, political coverage, and children's/ educational content) (see Blanchard, 1978; Duncan, 1999; Montgomery, 1989; Noriega, 2000; Swanson, 2000), while others focus primarily on structural issues pertaining to ownership and technological infrastructure (i.e., ownership concentration, minority ownership, access to communications technologies, development of alternative media) (Klinenberg, 2007; Opel, 2004; Scott, 2004). These categories are far from mutually exclusive because members of the public interest/advocacy community and, frequently, policymakers presume structural change affects content (Hackett & Adam, 1999; Napoli, 2001). Some analyses of the movement have called for advocates for structural change and advocates for content change to "link more directly" (Wible, 2004, p. 43).

A broad conceptualization of this movement incorporates efforts to affect the structure and content of traditional mainstream media and communications systems as well as efforts to support and develop alternative media systems (Barsamian, 2001; Beatty, 2000; Dagron, 2001; Garcelon, 2006; Joselit, 2007; Pickard, 2006; Stengrim, 2005; Williams, 2001). Alternative media generally refer to media operated and controlled by self-organized, independent groups or associations that often are non-commercial in their orientation and that are less hierarchical, less bureaucratic, and less commercial than traditional mainstream media (Atton, 2004; Downing, with Ford, Gil & Stein, 2001; Hesmondhalgh, 2000; Hintz, 2007a; Howley, 2005; Klein, 1999; Tomaselli & Louw, 1989). Historically, conceptualizations of alternative media have focused on the public broadcasting sector (e.g., Starr, 2001; Williams, 2001) and public access cable (e.g., Engelman, 1990; Higgins, 1999; Steiner, 2005)—particularly in countries with a privatized, commercial broadcast system. However, due to developments in media technology such as the Internet, WiFi, and LPFM, the realm of alternative media is now much more broadly constituted (Atton, 2004; Hamilton, 2001; Howley, 2005). Thus, within the body of literature on public interest media advocacy and activism, a wide range of alternative media sub-movements exist, such as the low power FM, or community radio, movement (e.g., Brinson, 2006; Coopman, 2000; Dunbar-Hester, 2008a) and the Indymedia movement, which focuses on Web-based, non-profit, alternative news outlets (e.g., Garcelon, 2006; Hanke, 2005).

Some disagreement within the field of public interest media advocacy and activism continues regarding the relative value of emphasizing reforming mainstream media versus developing alternative media (e.g., Hackett & Carroll, 2006). McChesney and Nichols (2002), for instance, advised against focusing exclusively on alternative media, arguing that "there are inherent limitations to what can be done with independent media, even with access to the Internet. The alternative media remain on the margins too often, seemingly confirming that commercial media conglomerates have become so massive because they 'give the people what they want'" (p. 123). Kidd, Barker-Plummer, and Rodriguez (2004) offered a related concern:

> [A]lternative media does not always reach the strategic targets of many social justice movements who want to shift the public discourse. While the local alternative media sometimes reaches a small, but critical mass of activists, local policymakers and allies, counter-publics often find that they do not usually reach state and national policy makers, non-English-speaking audiences, or large numbers of the voting public. (p. 5)

Chester (2006), in contrast, perceived efforts to reform traditional mainstream media as largely unsuccessful, emphasizing instead the importance of "parallel efforts...to give the public more access to the airwaves, so that they might create their *own* public interest programming" (p. 6).

Individual advocacy organizations often simultaneously pursue both activities (e.g., Klinenberg, 2004). A recent study of non-profits working in the media reform sector found that equally high proportions (96% of all organizations surveyed) were working on both mainstream and independent media issues, but with a slightly higher percentage (75% versus 69%) expending "significant effort" on mainstream media issues (Louie & Luckey, 2006, p. 10).

Both activities involve engagement in the policy-making process. Such engagement is apparent in relation to the traditional mainstream media, given that public interest media advocates long have concentrated substantial energy on preserving or imposing policies directed at these media that foster goals such as diversity of ownership of media outlets, the availability of public interest-oriented content, and the development of widely accessible communications infrastructures (Napoli, 2001). In many national contexts, fundamental changes in the relationship between the media and the state allow for the development of a media sector with greater freedom from government control (Barnett, 2000; Becker, Tudor, & Nusser, 2004; Price et al., 2001; Wangvivatana, 2005; Yang, 2002). Efforts to develop alternative media also frequently require engagement with the policy sphere, as the development of such media frequently requires specific policy actions (e.g., Engelman, 1990; Price et al., 2001; Siriyuvasak, 1999). Thus, for instance, the recent growth of low power FM radio in the United States depended upon the adoption of specific policies by the Federal Communications Commission (FCC) that allowed for the licensing of LPFM stations (e.g., Hamilton, 2004; Howley, 2004; Opel, 2004). These policies, initiated in large measure due to the prevalence of unlicensed, "pirate" radio (Dick & McDowell, 2000), allowed for community-based broadcasting without the fear of government prosecution. Similarly, the development of public access television in Canada and the United States depended on the adoption of policies that made the cable communications infrastructure accessible by community voices (Engelman, 1990; Stein, 2001). The development of commercial and community broadcasting in Thailand depended upon a dramatic restructuring of the regulatory apparatus in that country (Siriyuvasak, 1999, 2001, 2002). As O Siochrú (1999b) has argued, "Effective intervention into policy formation is critical to the growth of [alternative media]. National (sometimes regional)-level policy is still the most important, but the global level, via intergovernmental or multilateral organizations, is increasing in influence" (p. 151).

*Communicating Media Reform*

Finally, within the context of communicating the values, principles, and goals of any social movement to potential participants, we must also consider the specific communications platforms that are available. The traditional mass media and, increasingly, newer communications technologies such as the Internet, factor significantly in the creation and mobilization of any social movement (e.g., Cogburn, 2004; Coopman, 2000; Dutton & Lin, 2002; Garrett, 2006; Holman, 2005; Klein, 1995; Meikle, 2002; Ostertag, 2006). Mainstream media coverage is necessary for any social movement to: (1) attract public attention and support; (2) achieve a measure of validation and legitimization within public discourse and by association the general public and policy makers, and (3) broaden the scope of the conflict to sympathetic third parties (Gamson & Wolfsfield, 1993; see also Atton, 2004; Zald, 1996). Carroll and Ratner (1999) noted, for instance, that reliance on alternative, or self-generated media restricts the target population of any social movement. Consequently, such communications approaches are best suited only for those social movements "engaged in the politics of recognition and community development" (p. 28; see also Gamson & Meyer, 1996).

Given that public interest media advocacy and activism aims to reform the media system responsible for conveying information about social movements to the public, the movement's ability to attract the mainstream media coverage necessary to accomplish the functions outlined above may be uniquely compromised (Hackett & Carroll, 2004; Wangvivatana, 2005). As Thomas (2006) stated within the context of the global communication rights campaign, "while there are no guarantees for the positive media coverage of any given social movement, reporting the media reform movement is doubly complicated for the simple reason that the primary targets for reform are media structures and practices" (p. 294). This situation creates a disincentive for news outlets to inform the public about the activities and concerns of the movement. Some have described this situation as a conflict of interest (Broderick, 1984). A number of studies have confirmed these suspicions, documenting low levels of news coverage for media policy issues, as well as coverage patterns that suggest that the policy interests of the media organizations influence such editorial decisions (Gilens & Hertzman, 2000; Layton, 2003/2004; Snider, 2005). This situation poses a Catch-22 for public interest media advocacy and activism because one of the key mechanisms by which the movement can accomplish its goals may be foreclosed to it, given the nature of the movement's goals.

This set of circumstances allows for a somewhat different interpretation of the oft-made observation that issues related to media and communications will not likely resonate strongly with citizens, in the face of more tangible concerns such as health care, taxes, or education. Thomas (2005) noted that, within the context of the Communication Rights for the Information Society campaign, "[t]he public salience of a number of issues currently prioritized by the communication rights movement…is low precisely because these issues do not affect the day to day lives of the vast majority of global citizens" (p. 7). Similarly, Broderick (1984) emphasized that many of the effects of communications technologies simply "are not concrete enough to organize people around" (p. 316; see also Toro, 2000). Other scholars also have stressed the communication difficulties associated with articulating the range of concerns associated with media advocacy and activism in the kind of fairly simple language that remains vital to attracting newcomers to the movement and that is essential for the conduct of an effective campaign (O Siochrú, 2005; Thomas, 2006). While these factors may, in fact, comprise characteristics of the movement's core issues that undermine broad public resonance, these limitations may be *significantly* compounded by the fact that the mainstream media coverage that traditionally has been considered essential to generating the kind of issue salience and citizen awareness necessary to support a free-standing social movement (Gamson & Wolfsfeld, 1993) is uniquely difficult to achieve in the realm of public interest media advocacy and activism.

### Political Opportunities

Social movement scholars have recognized that the success of any social movement depends, in large part, on the extent to which the movement can become integrated into the political process. The integration of any movement into the political process depends upon the availability of specific political opportunities. The broader socio-political environment in which social movements operate, therefore, needs to be understood in terms of identifying and understanding those contexts that represent political opportunities (Caniglia & Carmin, 2005). As McAdam (1996) noted, a focus on political opportunities reflects the notion that "the timing and fate of movements [is] largely dependent upon the opportunities afforded insurgents by the shifting institutional structure and ideological disposition of those in power" (p. 23).

Within the context of public interest media advocacy and activism, this notion of political opportunities has been explored by Robert McChesney (2007). McChesney drew upon the concept of *critical junctures* to argue that the contemporary socio-political environment may represent a rare instance in which the necessary conditions are in alignment to allow for meaningful institutional change. Specifically, McChesney contended that critical junctures in the media realm occur when:

> at least two if not all three of the following conditions hold: There is a revolutionary new communications technology that undermines the existing system; the content of the media system, especially journalism, is increasingly discredited or seen as illegitimate; and there is a major political crisis—severe social disequilibrium—in which the existing order is no longer working and there are major movements for social reform. (p. 10)

McChesney asserted that the contemporary environment—particularly in the U.S.—with the growth (and destabilizing effects) of the Internet, increasing dissatisfaction with journalistic coverage related to U.S. activities in Iraq and Afghanistan, and growing dissatisfaction with a wide range of activities of the Bush Administration, may represent such a critical juncture. Perhaps most importantly, McChesney's framework highlights the extent to which new technologies have historically played an important role in the creation of political opportunities because these new technologies immediately represent new points of contention in ongoing struggles over the structure and performance of our media system.

A political opportunities perspective on social movements, in general, and media, in particular, reflects Calabrese's (2004) point that "social movements are, by their very nature, *episodic* and *issue driven*" (p. 324). Thus, within the context of media, a number of analyses illustrate how individual policy issues have, at various times, percolated to the surface of the broader public agenda and gained traction, in part due to the particular socio-political contexts into which they arose (e.g., McChesney, 1993; Mills, 2004). Public interest media advocacy and activism has progressed episodically and has been linked to particular characteristics of the socio-political environment.

A frequently studied example involves the broadcast license challenges initiated by the Office of Communication of the United Church of Christ (UCC) in the United States in the 1960s and 1970s against television stations engaging in racist programming practices. These activities emerged in large part from the significant upheaval and activism in the United States at that time with regard to civil rights (Mills, 2004). Not only did this period of public interest media activism affect the extent to which the mainstream media were sensitive to the needs and interests of minority viewers (Classen, 2004; Clift, 1976; Mills, 2004), but it also reconfigured the institutional dynamics of policy making and, in so doing, contributed to a political opportunity that allowed for public interest media advocacy and activism to blossom and extend its sphere of influence (Branscomb & Savage, 1978; Rubin, 2002; Schneyer & Lloyd, 1976). In the case *Office of Communication of the United Church of Christ v. Federal Communications Commission* (1966) (which emerged as a result of the UCC's efforts to challenge broadcast license renewals), citizens were granted standing in FCC proceedings, which served as a springboard for the continued growth of the movement.

According to Branscomb and Savage (1978) and Hendershot (1998), organizations such as Action for Children's Television (Clark, 2004), the Gray Panther Media Task Force, the Media Committee of the National Organization for Women, Chinese for Affirmative Action, Black Efforts for Soul in Television, and the National Black Media Coalition directly emerged from the UCC decision. Quantitative assessments of the organizational ecology of the communications and information policy advocacy field confirm this perspective, documenting the fastest growth in advocacy organizations over the past 40 years taking place during the 1960s and 1970s (Mueller, Kuerbis, et al., 2004). A key factor in the organizational growth during this time involved the increased ability to attract funding from foundations that had developed an interest in media policy issues, such as the Ford Foundation and the Markle Foundation (Kopp, 1997; Lenert, 2003). Clearly, changes in the socio-political environment surrounding media policy issues (i.e., their higher salience, their tighter linkage with civil rights) represented a political opportunity that simultaneously attracted greater resources to organizations working in the field.

This growth of public interest media activism in the United States was accompanied globally by the growth of the New World Information and Communication Order movement (Nordenstreng, 1999), which was motivated in large part by the expanding prominence of transnational media flows, concerns over cultural imperialism, growing disparities in communications infrastructures (Mowlana, 1993; Mowlana & Roach, 1992; Pickard, 2007; Traber & Nordenstreng, 1992), as well as concerns over increased concentration of media ownership (Senecal & Dubois, 2005). The associated communication rights movement (which has recently reemerged as the Communication Rights for the Information Society movement) first developed out of this movement, via the articulation by the UNESCO-appointed MacBride (1980) Commission of the right to communicate as a distinct and multi-faceted human right.

A number of scholars have, however, traced earlier roots to these movement highpoints in the 1960s and 1970s. As Horwitz (1997) noted, in many respects, the movement that emerged from the UCC decision "represented a resurrection of the old 1930s broadcast reform coalition. But this time the educators, religious people, and intellectuals were part of a broader tapestry of liberal activist groups in civil society" (p. 313). McChesney (1993) provided the most thorough account of the rise and decline of this earlier manifestation of the media reform movement, which developed primarily around the introduction of radio broadcasting and the associated debate over how best to structure and oversee the new system of radio broadcasting in the United States. This new technology served as a vital catalyst in activities of the movement and in the creation of an opportunity for political influence.

Toro (2000) and Williams (2001) provided detailed historical accounts of media reform activity across a wide range of areas (including educational/public broadcasting, broadcaster public interest obligations, license challenges, and even petitioning for citizens groups' rights to participate in the policy-making process) that extend from the 1930s through the 1950s and early 1960s. Schiller (1999) traced the history back even further, chronicling the largely unsuccessful activities of trade unions, civic reformers, and academics from 1894 through 1919 directed at the development of the telephone infrastructure, particularly in terms of advocating on behalf of universal access and municipal ownership during a time of policy-maker uncertainty over how to best regulate telephony. Pike and Winseck (2004) offered a similar historical account of efforts by a diverse array of reform advocates in Britain, Canada, and the United States to prevent the growth of cartels in international telegraphy. An important dimension of these earlier periods of public interest media advocacy and activism is the extent to which they were less explicitly tied to civil rights issues—a factor that may explain their relative lack of success. In an environment that concentrated on civil rights concerns, the political opportunity for public interest media advocacy and activism to attain meaningful institutional change was likely enhanced.

The 1980s and early 1990s have been characterized by many researchers as a period of decline in public interest media advocacy and activism, as the political opportunity window closed (Chester, 2007; Hendershot, 1998; Kopp, 1997; Nordenstreng, 1999). During this time period, the number of public interest and advocacy organizations working in this field diminished dramatically (Mueller, Kuerbis, et al., 2004). This drop-off has been attributed to a number of causes, including changing funding priorities among the relatively few private foundations that supported organizations in this area, the growth of industry lobbying efforts, and the associated deregulatory mindset that took hold in the policy-making sector and undermined public interest media advocacy and activist organizations' traditional avenues of influence (Broderick, 1984; Chester, 2007; Kopp, 1997).

A number of scholars have identified specific alterations in the policy process that both diminished existing political opportunities and reduced the likelihood of new opportunities becoming available. Thus, for instance, in the wake of substantial advocacy group influence on broadcast license renewals in the United States, the FCC altered the license renewal process in ways that effectively insulated broadcasters from the license renewal challenges that were a defining component of the media reform movement in the 1960s and

1970s (Levi, 1996; Toro, 2000). Content regulation mechanisms, such as the Fairness Doctrine, were eliminated in the 1980s, which undermined another common tool of influence (equal time requests) utilized by the advocacy community (Heinki & Tremain, 2000). More broadly, a wide range of deregulatory initiatives that have characterized much of the past 30 years of media policy making (Horwitz, 1989) effectively transferred decision making from government to private parties, thereby undermining many of the traditional channels of influence utilized by public interest organizations (Chester, 2007; Montgomery, 1989).

Focusing also on the deregulatory process, Mueller, Kuerbis, et al. (2004) argued that the transition in the 1980s and the 1990s toward telecommunications liberalization, and its associated emphasis on the benefits of deregulation and the primacy of economic analysis, meant that "media activists who were focused more on culture and content had a difficult time participating in this dialogue" (p. 57). This trend contributed to the marginalization of these groups during this time period because stakeholders recast the nature of communications policy making as more of a technical and economic endeavor than a political or cultural one.

More recently, within the context of the United Nations-sponsored World Summits on the Information Society, grassroots media/ICT activist groups found themselves marginalized as a result of the "'hard-nosed techno-economic and hi-tech' formulations of the key issues and problems to be addressed by WSIS" (Franklin, 2005, p. 40; see also Hadl & Hintz, 2006; Pickard, 2007). Reflecting such observations, a number of studies have emphasized the need for the advocacy community to develop and maintain the knowledge and skill sets necessary to take part in such technologically oriented policy dialogues (Davidson, Morris, & Courtney, 2002; Tacchi, 2005). Researchers have begun to explore how movement participants consider various communications technologies within the analytical and values frameworks of advocacy organizations (Dunbar-Hester, 2008b, 2008c) and how technological changes may impact the effectiveness of various advocacy strategies and tactics (Pekurny, 2000). Nonetheless, the above examples suggest that the de-politicization by policy makers of an area of policy making can undermine the likelihood of political opportunities developing for the movement.

Scholars have noted an upsurge in activity in the mid-1990s, spurred this time by developments in telecommunications technology and infrastructure usage, accessibility, and affordability (particularly in relation to the emergence of the Internet)—and the wide range of policy issues raised by these developments (e.g., Chester, 2007; Powers, 2005). According to Raboy (1998), in the 1990s, we "witnessed an unprecedented growth of projects, groups, and associations of all sorts working on areas which can be clustered under the general heading of democratic communication" (p. 96). These groups included worldwide organizations such as the World Association of Community Broadcasters (AMARC), Videazimut, and the Association for Progressive Communications. Out of the work of these and other organizations emerged the Communication Rights for the Information Society movement (Powers, 2005; Raboy, 1998).

Hackett and Carroll (2004) highlighted the growth in momentum for public interest media advocacy and activism since 1996. During this time, the Cultural Environment Movement (founded by well-known communications scholar George Gerbner) was launched in an effort to explicitly link the concerns and rhetorical approaches of the media reform movement—particularly those related to content—with those of the environmental movement (Duncan, 1999). Also during this time, the first of two Media and Democracy Congresses were held. While these particular institutions did not endure, a significant number of related institutions arose to take their place (see Mueller, Kuerbis, et al., 2004).

Hackett and Carroll (2004) attributed this upsurge in the movement's activity to a number of factors, including widespread discontent in the United States with the Telecommunications Act of 1996, and, years later, to the apparent disinformation—and the role of the news media in the propagation of this information—associated with U.S. involvement in Iraq (see also McChesney & Nichols, 2005), as well as to the tangible demise of local programming in radio, the industry sector most profoundly and visibly affected by the deregulatory initiatives of the 1996 Act (see also McChesney, 2004a). Mueller, Kuerbis, et al. (2004) also emphasized the transformative nature of the Telecommunications Act of 1996, although they interpreted the Act's key significance as reorienting activist groups away from their traditional focus on mass media content and toward infrastructure regulation issues (Drake, 1997; Lenert, 2003). A similar transition has taken place in the context of the United Nations' history of global communications policy activity. Starting with the report of the MacBride (1980) Commission, and moving on through the more recent World Summits on the Information Society, the focus of these international policy debates "has shifted from mass media and information flows to new media and information technology" (Padovani, 2005, p. 333). Other scholars have emphasized the late-1990s attention generated by the pirate/free radio movement (Brinson, 2006) as a key force in the revitalization of public interest media advocacy and activism (Brinson, 2007; Greve, Pozner, & Rao, 2006; Howley, 2000; Opel, 2004; Stavitsky, Avery, & Vanhala, 2001).

This resurgence in the U.S. also has been linked to the FCC's biennial (now quadrennial) media ownership proceeding—particularly the 2002–2003 proceeding (e.g., Brown & Blevins, 2005; Kidd, 2005; McChesney, 2004a; Scott, 2004). The galvanizing of public attention around this issue is well-illustrated by the fact that over 500,000 comments—many of them by individual citizens—were submitted to the FCC in connection with the ownership proceeding (Holman, 2005). FCC Commissioner Michael Copps described the ownership proceeding as awakening "a sleeping giant" in terms of focusing citizen attention, concern, and, most importantly, influence, on media policy issues to an extent never before seen in the United States (quoted in R. Newman & Scott, 2005, p. 25). The movement's success on this front included not only preventing the FCC's effort to further relax the existing media ownership rules, but also the emergence of new organizations devoted to media issues, fostering of new collaborations between existing groups, and generating an overall heightened interest in media policy issues within the broader public (Chester, 2007; Kidd, 2005; Matani, Spilka, Borgman-Arboleda, & Dichter, 2003) and the funding community (Louie & Luckey, 2006). This surge in activity appears to be less concentrated in the legal sector than during the movement's earlier peak in the 1960s and 1970s. Longitudinal research indicates that public interest law organizations devoted an average of 14% of their time and resources to media reform in 1975, but only 5% in 2004 (Nielsen & Albiston, 2006).

Internationally, the rise of international policy-making forums in the late 1990s, such as the United Nations' World Summits on the Information Society (WSIS) and the Internet Corporation for Assigned Names and Numbers (ICANN), further mobilized the broadly constituted global public interest media advocacy and activist community by providing specific avenues of entry into the political process that had not existed previously (Franklin, 2005; Hadl & Hintz, 2006; Hintz, 2007a; Mueller, 2002a, 2002b; O Siochrú, 2004; Padovani & Tuzzi, 2004; Pickard, 2007; Raboy, 1998; Samarajiva & Gamage, 2007; Selian, 2004). However, a key challenge within this context has involved the ability of the advocacy community to achieve sufficient representation in what are supposed to be multi-stakeholder governance contexts (Dany, 2007; Hintz, 2005).

The United Nations-sponsored Internet Governance Forum has served as a recent focal point around which an international collection of public interest media advocacy and activist organizations have gathered in an effort to influence a broad range of Internet-related policies and practices, including the promotion of linguistic diversity on the Web, enhancing Internet access in poor and underdeveloped nations, and protecting freedom of speech and privacy online (Napoli, 2008a, 2008b). The United Nations created the IGF partly in response to criticisms that the UN's World Summits on the Information Society had not given representatives from the public interest media advocacy and activist community sufficient opportunity to take part in the policy dialogue (e.g., Drake, 2004; McLaughlin & Pickard, 2005; Milan, Hintz, & Cabral, 2007). As Milan et al. (2007) noted, grassroots and community level advocacy organizations, in particular, were largely absent from the WSIS process, due to barriers to participation that included not only limited resources (i.e., travel funds), but also strict accreditation requirements that excluded many small grassroots and community organizations (see also Dany, 2007). Researchers have documented significant regional imbalances in WSIS participation, with relatively low levels of participation from African civil society organizations when compared to the participation levels of North American and Western European civil society organizations (Cammaerts & Carpentier, 2005; see also Hintz, 2007b). According to some accounts, such imbalances have been improved upon within the context of the Internet Governance Forum (e.g., Kalas, 2007), though, as Milan et al. indicated, grassroots and community level advocacy organizations—particularly those who envision their role more in terms of developing communications tools and opportunities than engaging in policy advocacy—remain on the margins of the process.

Primary policy concerns at the center of this most recent political opportunity for public interest media advocacy and activism encompass issues such as the universal accessibility of the developing communications infrastructure, the respect for free speech rights and privacy rights, and the importance of diversity and community (Drake, 1997; Munn, 1999; Powers, 2005). During this time period, according to Munn, the movement has been broadly constituted, with "organizations ranging from traditional media watchdogs, civil liberties advocates and consumer groups, to advocates for schools and libraries, children, the elderly, disabled, minorities and the poor" becoming involved (p. 71). Munn attributed this phenomenon to "the widespread perception of advanced information technologies and services as a solution to pressing social problems and to the excitement of their potential and promise for improving the circumstances of people and communities" (p. 77). The potential social, political, and economic significance of these developments in the media sector attracted the attention of funders, many of whom had exited the media policy advocacy arena in the late 1970s and 1980s (Kopp, 1997; Louie & Luckey, 2006). In this regard, changes in the nature of the political opportunities impact the availability of the resources available to develop the movement's mobilizing structures.

### Mobilizing Structures

To fully understand social movements, we must understand the organizations that serve and cultivate these movements as well as their strategies for pursing change—that is, the mobilizing structures that facilitate a particular movement (McCarthy, 1996). Resource mobilization theory, which emphasizes that "collective action is a rational response that only can occur when adequate resources are available," has been credited with reinforcing the idea that "social movements rely upon and are composed of formal organizations" (Caniglia & Carmin, 2005, p. 202). Research on public interest media advocacy and activism has concentrated on these organizations, their relational dynamics, and their strategies and tactics.

For a social movement that has been characterized as relatively small and even (at times) ineffectual (Mueller, Kuerbis, et al., 2004; Rowland, 1982), public interest media advocacy and activism has a complex and dynamic organizational ecology, sustaining a wide range of sectors of activity. Scholars have characterized South Korea's media reform movement, for instance, as comprised of three distinct sub-movements—an independent film movement, a movement critical of mainstream media (commonly referred to as a "viewer's movement"), and a movement of unionized media industry professionals advocating impartiality in news reporting (M. Kim, 2003). Often the various movement sectors all operate simultaneously, although particular sectors rise and fall over time (Mueller, Pagé, et al., 2004). Certain sectors, such as those revolving around the notion of a New World Information and Communication

Order (Galtung & Vincent, 1992; Pickard, 2007; Roach, 1990; Traber & Nordenstreng, 1992) and the Cultural Environment Movement (Duncan, 1999; Fuller, 1998; Gerbner, 1998) have largely come and gone (Carlsson, 2003; Hackett & Carroll, 2004).

A deeper understanding of the organizational ecology of the movement can be obtained by examining the lines of demarcation across the various organizations in terms of their strategic approaches. In efforts to influence industry behavior directly (in terms of content or employment practices), some sectors of the movement have employed tactics such as direct meetings and negotiations, protests, program monitoring, and boycotts (e.g., Fahey, 1991; Garay, 1978; Hendershot, 1998; Y. Kim, 2001; Montgomery, 1981, 1989; Swanson, 2000). Noriega (2000), for instance, documented the efforts of what stakeholders labeled "the Chicano media reform movement" in the 1960s and 1970s to discourage stereotypical portrayals of Latinos in television programs and advertising. Movement organizers emphasized organized boycotts of advertisers' products and targeted television programs as well as direct engagement with programmers and advertisers (see also del Río, 2006; Montgomery, 1989).

In the realm of influencing the structure of the media system, advocates have concentrated on the policy process, with efforts devoted to participation in administrative proceedings, adjudication, and legislative activity (e.g., Schneyer, 1977). A recent assessment of the advocacy work of the Latina/o community (Wible, 2004) concluded that the institutional and philosophical changes that have occurred in the policy-making sector require advocates to appeal to the economic logic of the industries at issue, rather than pursue institutional change via the policy-making process. Further, efforts to develop and support alternative media also have been a key mechanism by which various sectors of the movement have sought to influence the overall structure of the media system (e.g., Dagron, 2001; Garcelon, 2006; Joselit, 2007; Pickard, 2006).

Hackett and Adam (1999) distinguished between "insider" and "outsider" strategies, with outsider strategies encompassing explicit and aggressive media criticism and protest and insider strategies prioritizing efforts to alter the system from within, via tactics such as advocating for changes in hiring practices or seeking regulatory change through traditional policy advocacy mechanisms. Along related lines, scholars distinguish between components of the movement that strive to impact policy making as opposed to directly influencing the behavior of media organizations (e.g., Fahey, 1991; Hanks & Pickett, 1979; Lewis, 1986; Montgomery, 1981, 1989; Schement, Gutiérrez, Gandy, Haight, & Soriano, 1977; Turow, 1984). These different approaches often are related in terms of outcomes, in that via policy avenues reformers typically seek a reorientation of the media system, which they hope will produce many of the performance changes that those advocating more direct strategies also seek.

Some analyses have, however, been critical of the strategies employed by the movement, in terms of their ability to institute meaningful institutional change (e.g., M. G. Cantor & J. M. Cantor, 1986), though, in some instances, these critiques contend that the advocacy community's potential for influence is circumscribed by conditions "not of their own making," given the relatively narrow terms of debate and tools of influence available to them (Streeter, 2000, p. 83). Taking a particularly critical stance, Rowland (1982) described the U.S. media reform movement's record throughout the 1970s as "mixed and uneven" (p. 34), arguing that the policy-making process constrained the movement's impact during this time, that the movement failed to keep pace with techno- logical and institutional change, and that it did not generate a "clear, broad- based national constituency nor any form of organization consistently capable of helping translate their criticisms into comprehensive political action" (p. 36). At best, according to Rowland, "the reform movement has succeeded to date in nudging the policy-making and regulatory process only a degree or two off course" (p. 36), due in large part to the movement's willingness to press for change within—rather than outside of—established institutional channels. More recent analyses have adopted a similar perspective (e.g., Hamilton, 2004; Jakubowicz, 1993; Mueller, Kuerbis, et al., 2004), including within narrower reform contexts such as the Chicano media reform movement (Maxwell, 1988; Noriega, 2000) and global civil society organization activity related to WSIS (Hintz, 2005, 2007a). These analyses conclude that public interest media advo- cacy and activism seldom has been as radical as it needs to be to successfully initiate significant institutional change. However, in some national contexts (e.g., South Korea), scholars have perceived the strategies and tactics employed by advocacy organizations as *too* radical (Yang, 2002).

Hendershot (1998) described the pros and cons associated with employing radical versus more moderate advocacy tactics in public interest media advo- cacy and activism. Her investigation of Action for Children's Television (and related, more radical, advocacy organizations) in the 1970s and 1980s revealed (not surprisingly) that more moderate tactics work in policy-making environ- ments more open to reform but that such approaches fail in less hospitable policy-making environments. Rossman (2000) similarly explored the use of "hostile" versus "cooperative" advocacy tactics in the realm of entertainment programming, and, like Henershot, offered a somewhat more positive assess- ment of cooperative tactics.

Throughout much of its history, the movement has taken a primarily defen- sive stance, often advocating for the preservation of the status quo in the face of potentially substantial deregulatory initiatives, rather than developing and advocating original policy alternatives (McChesney & Nichols, 2002; Mueller, Kuerbis, et al., 2004; O Siochrú, 2004; Pickard, 2008b; Scott, 2005). Trivedi (2006) characterized the movement as "largely reactive" but concluded that with greater legal support, the movement could "begin thinking strategically about how to proceed proactively" (pp. 32–33). An even more recent assess- ment, drawn from survey research conducted among members of the media reform community, similarly stressed the need for the movement to supple- ment its reactive work with a greater capacity for long-term strategizing and vision building (Kulick, 2007). Pickard suggested that a more proactive turn in public interest media advocacy and activism has begun, in light of recent efforts to establish alternative ownership and business models for media out- lets, intensifying advocacy on behalf of public subsidies for alternative media, and "the growing conviction within media industries that radical structural reform is necessary" (p. 25).

## Organizational Critiques

A social movement analytical lens illustrates how many recurring critiques about public interest media advocacy and activism reflect characteristics common to contemporary social movements. For instance, scholars of social movements have recognized that "social movements are often, if not always, two movements in one" (Eyerman & Jamison, 1991, p. 37), with activists at the local grassroots level speaking different languages to different audiences and employing divergent strategies from those used by national advocacy organizations that represent the public interest within the federal policy-making sector. This dynamic has been identified as a source of tension in social movements, and this bifurcation has been reflected in two distinct academic traditions in the study of social movements (Edwards & Foley, 2002; Eyerman & Jamison, 1991). Mueller, Kuerbis, et al (2004) noted just such a distinction. They underscored the importance of distinguishing between the grassroots level of "*activism* or *social movement activity*" and the more formally organized citizens groups that interact directly with policy makers, which they referred to as "*advocacy...*rooted in *advocacy organizations*" (p. 6).

According to some analyses, the movement lacks sufficient coordination and communication between the federally focused and grassroots activist organizations (e.g., Dichter, 2005; Hackett & Adam, 1999; Listening Project, 2004; McChesney & Nichols, 2002; Schneyer & Lloyd, 1976). Studies—ranging from those examining the 1930s and 1940s-era media reform movement in the United States (McChesney, 1993; Pickard, 2008a), to others exploring the contemporary international Communication Rights for the Information Society movement (Thomas, 2006), to investigations of community-based youth media justice organizations (Klinenberg, 2004)—consistently assert that public interest media advocacy and activism has been hampered by a failure of the organizations that comprise the movement to work in unison. Even at the movement's first high point in the 1960s and 1970s, it "did not constitute a unified, coherent set of organizations," but rather "a very loose confederation of groups that shared a common bond" (Munn, 1999, p. 62). Kovacs' (2001) study of activism surrounding British broadcasting policy similarly found that "[l]oose, ad hoc alliances around issues were favored over formal coalitions" (p. 426).

Brinson (2007) examined this issue of cooperation between the grassroots and the national-level activist organizations within the context of the low power FM radio movement in the United States. He concluded that policy change should not be seen as purely the province of the federally focused advocacy organizations, contending instead that "actions by grassroots activists outside the policy arena can contribute in significant ways towards making those changes" (p. 2). He also noted that the influence of the grassroots and the federal-level advocacy organizations on policies that contributed to the development of low power FM radio took place with very little cooperative or coordinated activity taking place between these two groups. These findings suggest that intensive collaboration may not be a prerequisite for successful advocacy.

One explanation for this apparently persistent lack of collaboration and cooperation within the movement may be the intense competition among many groups for a relatively small pool of available funding (Hackett & Adam, 1999; Klinenberg, 2007; Thomas, 2006). Kopp (1997) illustrated how funding for public interest/advocacy work in the media field historically has been confined to very few large foundations (e.g., Ford and Rockefeller); thus, when funding priorities at these organizations changed, opportunities for the continued growth and development of the movement largely dried up (Mueller, 2002b). According to Thomas, organizational survival in the media advocacy and activism field is difficult "in a context in which funding priorities change constantly. New media funding preferences often result in the marginalization of old media projects" (p. 306). This situation has been described as discouraging openness and information-sharing, particularly given the oft-noted tendency of funders in this area to fund specific projects rather than long-term institution building (Fratkin, 2002; Hackett, 2000; Hackett & Carroll, 2006; Kopp, 1997).

More generally, competition fragments the movement, as organizations emphasize establishing and maintaining their own distinctive identity and mission—and even potentially narrowing their focus—in order to stand out to potential funders. These tendencies reflect a broader identity-related phenomenon which Browne (1990) labeled *issue niche theory*, in which advocacy organizations "cultivate specific recognizable identities...by concentrating on very narrow issues" and refraining from imposing on the similarly narrow issue spaces carved out by other interest groups (p. 472; for a critique of issue niche theory, see Heaney, 2007). As one media justice activist interviewed by Klinenberg (2004) observed, "'The fear of collaborating is that funders can just write one of us off—they have to know how each of us is different'" (p. 187).

A second common critique among assessments of the organizational dynamics of public interest media advocacy and activism involves the tendency for key organizations within the movement to be established and sustained through the leadership of a single individual. This centralization of leadership has led, according to some evaluations, to relatively limited efforts on the parts of these organizations to achieve broad, far-reaching memberships or to seek alliances with other organizations, due to reasons ranging from limited resources to a desire to maintain highly centralized and autonomous decision making (e.g., Branscomb & Savage, 1978; Dichter, 2005). Following in a similar vein, Dichter suggested that the movement has long been characterized by a significant centralization and hierarchy of power, a lack of diversity in the leadership ranks, and a failure to integrate the full range of interested stakeholders into the movement's activities and decision making.

Reflecting such critiques, Sherman (2004) provided the most detailed inquiry to date into the extent to which organizations within the movement represent the needs and interests of the broader public. Sherman noted that "[l]eaders of public interest groups, by not actively engaging citizens as part of their daily activities, can easily find themselves perpetuating their own personal interests" (p. 4). Sherman stressed that such tendencies can under-mine the ability of public interest organizations to develop appropriate pol-icy positions and raise questions about accountability for their decisions. As Sherman noted, the public interest community often perceives (perhaps cor-rectly) that the general public is insufficiently informed in regards to media policy issues. Further, Gandy (2003) asserted that public opinion appears to play an insignificant role in media policy debates. If communications policy comprises an area about which the public generally lacks knowledge, then it may be questionable whether the public interest is best served by the advocacy community taking its cues from the public. Nonetheless, Sherman concluded that the public interest/advocacy community is, for the most part, too detached from the broader constituency that they presumably represent.

Such dynamics have led to questions as to whether such a movement can truly be considered representative of the broader public interest (e.g., Padden, 1972). As Y. Kim (2001) argued within the context of audience-based reform movements in South Korea: "what right do audience representative bodies have to speak on behalf of all audiences?" (p. 105). Given that the movement tends to be dominated by groups of individuals who may not be representative of the population as a whole, questions of the legitimacy of these groups may natu-rally arise (e.g., Dichter, 2004; Y. Kim, 2001). Schneyer and Lloyd (1976) noted that "the legitimacy of national media-reform organizations extends no farther than their service to client consumer groups" (p. 21). Generating strong and broad-based public support constitutes a fundamental component of a legitimate social movement (e.g., Ash Garner & Zald, 1987; Eyerman & Jamison, 1991), or, for that matter, to the establishment of a clear identity in the policy-making environment for any interest group (Heaney, 2007). The extent to which public interest media advocacy and activism remains the province of an insular group of committed activists and advocates may undermine its status as a full-fledged social movement and its ability to achieve large-scale institutional change.

Such concerns reflect a broader shift that many social movement scholars argue has taken place in the composition and orientation of social movements since the 1960s. Specifically, "new social movements" have tended to emerge from, and be sustained by, professional, middle class actors, unlike previous iterations of social movements, which tended to have working class origins (Eyerman & Jamison, 1991). In this regard, discussions of the differences between new and old social movements tend to touch upon the issues of elitism and representation reflected in the above discussion of public interest media advocacy and activism. While the viability of the distinction between new and old social movements has been questioned by some social movement scholars (e.g., Pichardo, 1997), public interest media advocacy and activism seems to adhere to the articulated criteria for new social movements.

## Media Reform Linkages with Other Social Movements

One aspect of the organizational dynamics of public interest media advocacy and activism (and one that intersects in very important ways with efforts to develop an understanding of the political opportunities surrounding the movement) that has received a substantial amount of attention, involves its relationship with other social movements. Certainly, the origins of many sectors of public interest media advocacy and activism can be traced to other social movements. The media reform movement in South Korea has been characterized as emerging in the 1980s directly from the broader social movement opposing the country's dictatorship (M. Kim, 2003). In Canada, media reform similarly emerged from oppositional political movements (Raboy, 1990), including the anti-globalization movement (Senecal & Dubois, 2005). In the United States, Mueller (2002b) characterized media policy issues as "completely subordinate to, and reflective of, the agenda of broader social movements regarding civil rights, environmentalism and consumerism" (p. 8; see also Horwitz, 1997). The Indymedia movement has been characterized as emerging primarily from the anti-globalization movement (Garcelon, 2006). Sectors of the movement that have emerged from the consumer movement, include those dealing with issues such as access to communications services (see, for instance, Rhodes' 2006 study of telecommunications reform in Latin America), the quality of media content (Fratkin, 2002; K. Newman, 2002, 2004; Swanson, 2000), and the conduct of advertisers (Ryans, Samiee, & Wills, 1985; Stole, 2000).

Thus, public interest media advocacy and activism appears to have been birthed from a wide array of social movement contexts—a trait that certainly has factored into reflections on how the movement should proceed. A mid-1980s assessment of what strategies and tactics should be employed to foster a legitimate social movement in the area of media reform in the United States concluded that the movement should build upon its original ties to the civil rights movement (Broderick, 1984). More recent studies of the movement similarly emphasize the need to form stronger alliances with other social movements, particularly those driven by social justice issues (M. Kim, 2003; Kulick, 2007). Hackett and Adam (1999) suggested that participants within the movement do not perceive it as able to stand on its own; rather, "media reform must be linked to other progressive movements" (p. 127). Along these lines, stakeholders have sought to link communication rights with the global human rights movement (see CRIS Campaign, 2005).

If public interest media advocacy and activism functions as an integral subcomponent of, and thus primarily subordinate to, other social movements, then its success depends in large part upon developing successful linkages with these movements. Groups with at least a tangential stake in a transformed communications environment—organized labor, human rights organizations, or groups working on behalf of the poor or underprivileged—could prove valuable allies (e.g., Costanza-Chock, 2002). A number of scholars and activists have consequently sought to articulate the specific ways in which a reformed media environment would facilitate improved communication to potential constituencies for other social movements (Brinson, 2006; Garcelon, 2006). Carroll and Hackett (2006) argued that "If media activist groups are successful in their efforts to open up mainstream media to a diversity of voices and to create effective alternative media...the political beneficiaries will be none other than other progressive movements" (p. 91; see also Brinson, 2007). As a result, Brinson asserted that "media reform can change the playing field on which actors compete for media attention, strengthening the positions of some actors (in this case, social movement actors) relative to others" (p. 564).

Reflecting this perspective, Pozner (2005) argued that substantive media reform is a prerequisite for the development of the feminist movement. Similarly, Kidd (2005) illustrated how many U.S. anti-war activists opposed the relaxation of media ownership rules, under the assumption of a relationship between the two areas of activism. McChesney and Nichols (2002) described the media reform movement as possessing a broad array of "natural allies, organizations that should be sympathetic to media reform...organized labor, teachers, librarians, civil libertarians, artists, religious denominations, and groups involved with a broad range of civil rights advocacy" (p. 127). From this vantage point, public interest media advocacy and activism can be envisioned, as one activist has described it, as a "'meta-movement, a movement of movements,' precisely due to the strategic centrality of mediated communication in contemporary society" (Hackett & Carroll, 2006, p. 188).

Unfortunately, the strong linking of media advocacy and activism with other social movements has not, for the most part, been accomplished effectively (e.g., Mason, 2006; Thomas, 2006). Hackett and Carroll (2006) found, for instance, that none of the non-media activists interviewed in their research named media activist groups as important constituents of a potential coalition. Gangadharan (2007) contended that prominent civil rights organizations— such as the National Association for the Advancement of Colored People (NAACP), the Rainbow Coalition, and the Lawyer's Committee for Civil Rights—have been "conspicuously silent on media policy and law" (p. 1).

Brinson (2006) suggested that foregrounding media reform as a mechanism for facilitating the development of other social movements may lack appeal because it represents a long-term strategy at a time when most organizations involved in such initiatives lack the luxury of adopting a long-term orientation. In interviews with representatives of media reform, alternative media, and other social movement groups, Kidd et al. (2004) contended that "most of the groups we talked to agreed that media reform was a critical issue. Not all of the groups could afford to spend time and resources directly on this issue" (p. 3). Brinson went so far as to argue that "it may be unwise or inefficient for most social movements to choose this strategy to achieve their goals since reform of the media may not be a primary movement objective" (p. 561). Similarly, Stein (in press) noted that "social movements have their own priorities and agendas, centered on their own issues; they have few immediate incentives to commit themselves to the cause of media reform, even though it may benefit them in the long run."

Along these lines, a recent investigation of the interaction between law, the media, and environmental policy, which focused in large part on the importance of mainstream media coverage to successful environmental advocacy, contained a series of recommendations about how environmental advocates could better engage the media, but it did not address at all how media reform efforts could play a role in the movement's efforts to obtain more and better media coverage (Plater, 2006). Instead, according to Plater, stakeholders treated the media system—with its intensified concentration, increasingly commercial orientation, and diminished commitment to hard news reporting (all characteristics articulated in the study)—as a static system that environmental advocates needed to figure out how to navigate effectively.

Labor unions, in particular, have been identified in a number of studies as a constituency that would seem to potentially benefit from successful media reform efforts but that has, for the most part, neglected to interact consistently with the movement (Fones-Wolf, 2006a; Hackett & Carroll, 2006). Some scholars have, however, identified exceptions at various points in time. McChesney (1992) documented how organized labor comprised an active constituency in the 1920s and 1930s-era broadcast reform movement in the United States. Similarly, Fones-Wolf (2006a, 2006b) has detailed how organized labor constituted an integral component of the post-World War II U.S. media reform movement, especially in terms of developing the notion of "listener's rights" that has become an integral element of contemporary media reform (Toro, 2000) and spearheading efforts to bring a greater diversity of sources and viewpoints to the airwaves (see also Tracy, 2007). By the 1950s and 1960s, due in large part to the political climate surrounding the Cold War, labor became marginalized from the policy-making process, and, as a result, "labor was never again a major force in the media reform movement, leaving it to become the province primarily of middle-class intellectuals" (Fones-Wolf, 2006b, p. 515).

Along related lines, constituency groups with a potentially more direct stake in media reform outcomes—such as media industry trade unions, the advertising industry, or the creative community (Batt, Katz, & Keefe, 1999; Dolber, 2007; Mosco, 2007)—also represent natural strategic partners if media reform's relationship with labor were conceptualized a bit more narrowly (i.e., to focus only on those labor sectors *directly* affected by changes in the media system). Hackett and Carroll (2006), in their model of the "social sources" for media democratization, placed groups within and around media industries, such as journalists, media workers, and librarians (e.g., Nappo, 2008), at the core of their concentric spheres of actors contributing to public interest media advocacy and activism. In some manifestations of the movement, such as in Indonesia, the Philippines, Thailand, and South Korea, media professionals have, in fact, played an instrumental role in the movement's development (e.g., Siriyuvasak, 2005; Wangvivatana, 2005; Yang, 2002). Yet, as Hackett & Carroll noted, overall, constituent groups, such as journalists, often maintain their distance from media issues, despite the many ways in which their working conditions and career prospects could be improved if the media environment were to change along the lines advocated by reformists. Notably, many advocacy organizations criticize journalists, undermining the likelihood of any alliance-building. Further, as Hackett and Carroll observed, the journalistic culture of objectivity may impede linkages between journalistic organizations and advocacy organizations (for an opposing perspective on this issue, see Foley, 2005).

Although public interest media advocacy and activism theoretically intertwines with other social movements, such embedding of its agenda into those of other movements has not taken place. Hence, we need to explore possible disconnects between theory and practice. Failures to tightly link public interest media advocacy and activism with broader social issues may reflect what Eyerman and Jamison (1991) identified as a key characteristic of many social movements—that they "have been almost aggressively single-issue oriented" (p. 37). If so, we should question whether a long-term strategy in which public interest media advocacy and activism piggy-backs on other public issues comprises an appropriate path for the movement to follow.

## Conclusion

This chapter has reviewed and synthesized the literature on public interest media advocacy and activism. As this review has illustrated, previous characterizations of this literature as sparse seem less appropriate when the parameters of the movement are defined broadly (both geographically and conceptually) and when we take the very recent surge of research on this topic into consideration. Moreover, this chapter has illuminated a number of perhaps defining characteristics of public interest media advocacy and activism as a social movement as well as identified some points for future strategic directions for the movement.

First, from the standpoint of framing processes, public interest media advocacy and activism remains a movement with a number of distinctive, though overlapping, and somewhat complex, frames. Perhaps more important, we lack any indications of a forthcoming consolidation of frames, despite calls from some quarters for such a consolidation. The persistent debate over the details of the various framing options represents a degree of "insider baseball" that introduces a level of complexity that likely should not even be part of a very general and simple frame geared toward achieving broader public resonance. An inclusive frame would seem to be particularly important for a social movement that is inherently narrow in its focus.

Second, in terms of political opportunities, the advent of new media technologies often provides the impetus for the forming and mobilizing of advocacy and activist organizations, and enhances their ability to become integrated into the political process. Consequently, the extent of advocates' knowledge of new technologies and how these technologies fit into their existing value system, become key determinants of if and how they engage in advocacy work surrounding the new technology, and of how successful they are in doing so (Dunbar-Hester, 2008a; Franklin, 2005; Mueller, Kuerbis, et al., 2004).

Additionally, the changing standing of citizens in the process has been fundamental to the evolution of public interest media advocacy and activism. However, alterations to the policy-making process have insulated various dimensions of policy making from public input. Broader ideological shifts in the realm of policy making have recast many policy debates in terms that can marginalize the public interest and advocacy community.

In terms of mobilizing structures, a defining characteristic of public interest media advocacy and activism involves its complex relationship with other social movements. Public interest media advocacy and activism not only has emerged from a number of other social movements; it also may enhance all social movements' abilities to gain greater traction with citizens and policy makers via creating changes in the media system. A key question for future pragmatic and scholarly endeavors relates to determining the most effective approach to creating institutional change in the media system. Should the movement remain ancillary to other social movements, or should it operate instead under the assumption that a distinctive independent identity can and, in fact, must be achieved for the movement to be successful? Does this latter perspective overstate the prominence that media issues can achieve in the broader socio-political environment, particularly one in which garnering mainstream media coverage may be uniquely difficult?

In light of the evidence to date, which suggests that other social movements are not inclined to consistently devote meaningful resources and attention to media issues (e.g., Mason, 2006; Thomas, 2006), the more appropriate strategy for the movement may be for participants to continue to work to solidify and expand public interest media advocacy and activism as a free-standing social movement, while still being opportunistic in regard to potential linkages with other movements. Reliance upon the ebb and flow of the energies, issues, political opportunities, and resources of other social movements puts public interest media advocacy and activism in a position of dependence and subservience that makes it unlikely to be able to respond effectively to the increasingly independent ebb and flow of issues, political opportunities, and citizen attention in the media and communications arena.

Moreover, the continued development and effectiveness of alternative communication channels such as the Internet undermine the extent to which other social movements likely envision media reform issues as central to their needs. At the same time, these alternative communication channels enhance the extent to which media advocates and activists can cultivate the necessary constituency to function as a free-standing social movement without significant mainstream media coverage (see Cooper, 2005).

Further, media issues are, within the contemporary global political-economic environment, increasingly—and recognizably—central to the economic, political, and cultural life of the citizenry. As Mueller (2002b) concluded, "One key difference between this period and …the period of activism thirty years earlier is the greater ability of information and communication policy issues to attract attention and commitment on their own" (p. 17). Thus, the contemporary information society represents an environment in which public interest media advocacy and activism should be more capable and, as the past five to ten years suggests, is more capable, of standing independently as a social movement worthy of the attention and support of the citizenry—although certainly one with underlying motivations that trace very tangibly back to concerns of other social movements. Of course, public interest media advocacy and activism should not divorce itself from the social movements from which it emerged. Such ties can and should be cultivated, but perhaps they should not represent the centerpiece of any strategic approach to building and strengthening the movement.

This review also illuminates another major dimension of public interest media advocacy and activism—the relationship between grassroots activist groups and federal-level advocacy organizations. Clearly, a tendency toward fragmentation and independent operation has characterized assessments of the movement from its earliest days to the present. Early scholarship examining the media reform movement, in fact, identifies as much division back then (e.g., Schneyer & Lloyd, 1976) as today. Hackett and (2006) observed that the movement possesses an "organizational ecology with distinct niches" (p. 65) across national contexts and over time.

The persistent disjuncture between national organizations and grassroots organizations, as well as the tendency toward organizational fragmentation within the field, suggest that strategic thinking within the movement should perhaps focus on developing approaches to transforming these characteristics into sources of strength. That is, how can the movement best capitalize on the different skill sets and areas of expertise of the diverse participants in the movement and on the opportunities for specialization in knowledge and skill sets that presumably arise from the maintenance of distinct divisions between federal and local level activities? As Brinson (2007) suggested, significant policy change can be achieved even when the grassroots activists and federal-level advocacy organizations operate with only loose coordination of efforts. Hackett and Carroll (2006) emphasized how the movement could benefit from a better-coordinated division of labor, something that presumably could be achieved even if the grassroots and federal levels of the movement remain fairly independent.

Perhaps future work should prioritize the creation of liaison-type organizations focused on coordination and communication across levels and sectors of activity, thereby freeing the grassroots- and federal-level organizations from having to try to engage in such tasks. One possible avenue in this regard might involve academic institutions playing a more influential role. While individual academics have been active in public interest media advocacy and activism (e.g., Kogen, 2008; McChesney, 2007; Phiphitkul, 2005), they often do so with little underlying institutional support or encouragement. Indeed, McChesney argued that universities should play a more active and influential role in the development of this movement.

### Future Research

Despite the depth and scope of the existing research on public interest media advocacy and activism, a number of avenues of inquiry still need to be pursued. The literature to date has focused primarily on activities and organizations within the United States and (to a lesser degree) on global policy advocacy (e.g., surrounding WSIS). Comparatively little attention has been devoted to manifestations of the movement within individual countries (Nusser & Hamilton, 2008), and relatively little comparative work has been conducted (for a recent exception, see Hackett & Carroll, 2006). These imbalances in the literature need to be corrected.

Long-term research should track and assess movement activities and organizations over an extended period of time, with a particular eye on assessing the strategies, tactics, and organizational structures that appear most closely related to effecting institutional change. As far back as 1979, Hanks and Pickett called for longitudinal research that examines long-range effectiveness and seeks to "isolate the factors best predictive of change" (p. 105). Unfortunately, 30 years later, other than a few recent exceptions (e.g., Mueller, Pagé, et al. 2004), we still lack research in this vein, and appeals for work of this type persist (Mueller & Lentz, 2004). To the extent that critical analyses of the movement have emphasized a lack of long-term change (e.g., Hanks & Pickett, 1979; Rowland, 1982), additional studies may produce insights that could contribute to improving the long-term success of the movement.

More investigations should also be directed at developing a sufficiently inclusive inventory of the indicators of success or institutional change for the movement. Assessing the effectiveness of any social movement is complicated by the question of where the analyst is looking when she looks for success or influence. Assessing the effectiveness of pubic interest media advocacy and activism organizations has proven to be a difficult methodological challenge (Kovacs, 2001; Rossman, 2000). It may often be the case, for example, that influence has taken place in areas other than the final decision on a particular policy issue. In a 1970s-era analysis of the media reform movement, Chisman (1977) concluded that citizens' groups can have their greatest potential for influence in the early stages of the policy-making process, when issues remain in their infancy. Similarly, in an analysis of 1990s-era advocacy surrounding the development of the National Information Infrastructure in the United States, Munn (1999) concluded that the movement achieved its greatest success in redefining how the policy issues were framed (in this case, successfully foregrounding issues of access). Bauer, Kim, Mody, and Wildman (2005) found that public interest and advocacy organizations play a critical role in introducing research and ideas generated in the academic sector into the policy-making process. More recently, Greve et al. (2006), within the context of microradio, indicated the importance of looking beyond the narrow realm of policy making and considering also the movement's effects within the broader realm of popular culture. Further inquiry into how these various spheres of potential influence can best be identified and assessed would be helpful in providing a more well-rounded assessment of the movement's impact.

Scholars should also explore other social movements (civil rights, consumer rights, anti-globalization, the environment, etc.) and develop a more detailed assessment of exactly where media issues stand within their hierarchy of their perceived needs in order to effect their desired institutional change. Perceptions within media advocacy organizations, and within many academic analyses, of the centrality of media to other social movements and their prospects may not correspond with the perceptions of activists and advocates within these social movements. We could benefit from more research examining if, when, and to what extent the linking of public interest media advocacy and activism with other social movements is an appropriate long-term strategy for the movement to pursue. In the end, developing a deeper understanding of public interest media advocacy and activism enhances our insights into social movements and the dynamics of media policy making. As such, this body of research benefits not only communication scholars in these areas but also communication researchers across a wide range of areas, whose work has the potential to guide, and become integrated into, the activities of this movement.

## Notes

1. This chapter does not seek to provide a detailed history of this movement because a large number of detailed historical accounts of the movement and its key figures already can be found elsewhere (e.g., Classen, 1991, 2004; Fratkin, 2002; Horwitz, 1997; Johnson, 1967; Korn, 1991; McChesney, 1993; Mills, 2004; Mueller et al., 2007; Schiller, 1999; Toro, 2000). However, I will mention key historical moments and figures in the course of addressing the main areas of emphasis.

    In locating and compiling the academic literature on public interest media advocacy and activism, my search strategy involved casting a deliberately wide net, in terms of defining the field, the academic disciplines/fields of interest, and geographical reach. Because I limit this review to English-language publications, it likely is less comprehensive in its review of scholarship related to international manifestations of public interest media advocacy and activism than English-speaking nations.

    I also sought to be inclusive in terms of technological orientation. Traditional mass media, telecommunications, and the Internet have been incorporated under the umbrella framework employed for this review, although scholarly attention to public interest advocacy and activism activities and organizations has tended to focus on mass media (particularly broadcasting) and (more recently) the Internet, with less attention to telecommunications specific areas such as telephony (for exceptions, see Horwitz, 1998; Rhodes, 2006; Schiller, 1999, 2007). In addition to the published scholarly literature, I included as much of the more elusive "gray literature" (i.e., conference papers, reports issued by non-profits and advocacy organizations, dissertations, and theses) as I could locate.

    Finally, I worked to incorporate the full range of advocacy and activism work incorporated within the parameters of the movement. I consider work addressing policy advocacy efforts, as well as research that focuses on advocacy efforts directed at various sectors of the media industry (advertisers, content providers, etc.), and efforts to cultivate and support alternative media. As will become clear, these spheres of activity have been—and continue to be—tightly inter-related.

    The scope of this chapter does not encompass the related, though distinct, area of activity typically referred to as *media development*, which primarily involves efforts to establish media institutions and practices in developing or transitional nations. Although many of the same principles and objectives as public interest media advocacy and activism guide such efforts (Fox, 1986; Kumar, 2006;

Milton, 2001; Price, Rozumilowicz, & Verhulst, 2001; Siriyuvasak, 2001), it is a sufficiently distinct and extensive undertaking in its own right (with its own substantial body of literature) to be defined as beyond the scope of this review.

According to some recent assessments, research attention to public interest media advocacy and activism has been lacking (e.g., Mueller, Kuerbis, et al., 2004; Thomas, 2006). Contrary to these assessments, I found an extensive body of literature on this topic. This discrepancy between previous assessments and current findings may result from a number of factors. First, previous assessments have tended to focus on literature that examines public interest media advocacy and activism *specifically* through the lens of social movement theory. As this review will indicate, the application of this analytical approach to this area constitutes a relatively recent phenomenon, with earlier analyses more often grounded in theories of regulatory decision making or the policy-making process or comprising primarily historical narratives that lack a particular theoretical grounding. In this regard, it is interesting to note that a 1996 analysis by well-known social movement scholars of the relationship between the media and social movements asserted that "ownership and consumption patterns of media, as well as their relation to the state and political parties, are relatively stable and generally beyond the scope of movement claims" (Gamson & Meyer, 1996, p. 287). This statement suggests that social movement scholars had not, at that point, even recognized public interest media activism and advocacy as a distinct social movement.

Second, this movement has operated under many guises, and with a wide array of labels, particularly when the scope of the analysis is global in nature. Further, while those within the movement (or one of its associated sectors) have undeniably legitimate and compelling reasons for the adherence to one particular terminology over another (i.e., media reform versus media justice, versus media democracy, versus communication rights, etc.), I cast a wide net, with the goal of developing a broad-based account of the accumulated scholarship in this area. This approach mirrors other recent studies, which have incorporated all of the relevant subcomponents of the movement into a single analytical frame (Hackett & Carroll, 2006; Internaut Consulting, 2006; Listening Project, 2004). Consequently, I am only secondarily concerned with parsing out the different contours of the media reform movement versus the media justice movement or the communication rights movement. This set of priorities reflects the notion that even those within these different movement sectors would likely acknowledge that the movement for the improvement of the media system, no matter how it is defined or the specific priorities articulated, can be usefully studied as a somewhat integrated whole. As Opel (2004) noted, "Regardless of the term…all refer to a large umbrella of issues and organizations addressing the role of the media in the modern world" (p. 25; see also Klein, 2001).

A final reason for this chapter's departure from earlier assessments of the state of research in this area involves the *very recent* growth in the literature exploring public interest media advocacy and activism. In the past four years, at least 15 books on this topic have been published (Classen, 2004; Fones-Wolf, 2006b; Gangadharan, De Cleen, & Carpentier, 2007; Hackett & Carroll, 2006; Joselit, 2007; Klinenberg, 2007; McChesney, 2004b, 2007; McChesney, K. Newman, & Scott, 2005; Mills, 2004; R. Newman, & Scott, 2005; Opel, 2004; Rhodes, 2006; Stein, Rodriguez, & Kidd, in press; Stole, 2007), in addition to a host of journal articles and book chapters across a variety of disciplines, including sociology (Brinson, 2006; Klinenberg, 2004), communication (Carroll & Hackett, 2006; Garcelon, 2006; Mueller et al., 2007; Pickard, 2006; Raboy, 2004; Thomas, 2006), cultural studies (Calabrese, 2004; O Siochrú, 2004; Stengrim, 2005; Wible, 2004), and history (Fones-Wolf, 2006a; Mason, 2006; Pike & Winseck, 2004).

# References

Ash Garner, R., & Zald, M. N. (1987). The political economy of social movement sectors. In M. N. Zald & J. D. McCarthy (Eds.), *Social movements in an organizational society* (pp. 293–317). New Brunswick, NJ: Transaction.

Atton, C. (2003). Reshaping social movement media for a new millennium. *Social Movement Studies, 2*, 3–15.

Atton, C. (2004). *An alternative Internet: Radical media, politics and creativity.* Edinburgh, Scotland: Edinburgh University Press.

Barnett, C. (2000). Language equity and the politics of representation in South African media reform. *Social Identities, 6*, 63–90.

Barsamian, D. (2001). *The decline and fall of public broadcasting.* Cambridge, MA: South End Press.

Batt, R., Katz, H. C., & Keefe, J. H. (1999, October). *The strategic initiatives of the CWA: Organizing, politics, and collective bargaining.* Paper presented at the Symposium on Changing Employment Relations and New Institutions of Representation, Cambridge, MA.

Bauer, J. M., Kim, S., Mody, B., & Wildman, S. S. (2005, May). *The role of research in communications policy: Theory and evidence.* Paper presented at the annual meeting of the International Communication Association, New York.

Beatty, J. (2000). From cooperative to court case: Struggles for alternative radio at KOOP-FM in Austin, Texas. *Journal of Radio Studies, 7*, 310–328.

Becker, L. B., Tudor, V., & Nusser, N. (2004, July). *Media freedom: Conceptualizing and operationalizing the outcome of media democratization.* Paper presented at the annual meeting of the International Association for Media and Communication Research, Porto Alegre, Brazil. Retrieved July 20, 2007, from http://www.grady.uga.edu/coxcenter/PDFs/Media%20Freedom.pdf

Belden, Russonello, & Stewart (2006, October). *Communicating about communications: Media leaders discuss their work and values.* Report prepared for the Ford Foundation.

Birdsall, W. F. (2006). A right to communicate as an open work. *Media Development, 1.* Retrieved February 15, 2007, from http://www.wacc.org.uk/wacc/publications/media_development

Blanchard, M. (1978). Press criticism and national reform movements: The Progressive Era and the New Deal. *Journalism History, 5*(2), 33–55.

Boyle, J. (1997). A politics of intellectual property: Environmentalism for the net? *Duke Law Journal, 47*, 87–115.

Branscomb, A. W., & Savage, M. (1978). The broadcast reform movement: At the crossroads. *Journal of Communication, 28*(4), 25–34.

Brinson, P. (2006). Liberation frequency: The free radio movement and alternative strategies of media relations. *The Sociological Quarterly, 47*, 543–568.

Brinson, P. (2007, January). *Lessons from the Free Radio Movement about tactical interaction in the Media Reform Movement.* Paper presented at the Social Science Research Council Pre-Conference on Media Policy Research, Memphis, TN.

Broderick, P. (1984). The new electronic technologies and the public interest: Does the "revolution" need a movement? In V. Mosco (Ed.), *Policy research in telecommunications* (pp. 313–319). Norwood, NJ: Ablex.

Brown, D. H., & Blevins, J. L. (2005, May). *The role of the public in the FCC's broadcast policy-making process: Have we entered a new era?* Paper presented at the annual meeting of the International Communication Association, New York.

Browne, W. P. (1990). Organized interests and their issue niches: A search for pluralism in a policy domain. *Journal of Politics, 52,* 447–509.

Calabrese, A. (2004). The promise of civil society: A global movement for communication rights. *Continuum: Journal of Media & Cultural Studies, 18,* 317–329.

Cammaerts, B., & Carpentier, N. (2005). The unbearable lightness of full participation in a global context: WSIS and civil society participation. In J. Servaes & N. Carpentier (Eds.), *Towards a sustainable information society: Beyond WSIS* (pp. 17–49). Bristol, England: Intellect.

Caniglia, B. S., & Carmin, J. (2005). Scholarship on social movement organizations: Classic views and emerging trends. *Mobilization: An International Journal, 10,* 201–212.

Cantor, M. G., & Cantor, J. M. (1986). Regulation and deregulation: Telecommunications politics in the United States. In M. Ferguson (Ed.), *New communication technologies and the public interest: Comparative perspectives on policy and research* (pp. 84–101). London: Sage.

Carlsson, U. (2003, May). *The rise and fall of NWICO—and then? From a vision of international regulation to a reality of multilevel governance.* Paper presented at the EURICOM Colloquium, Information Society: Visions and Governance, Venice, Italy.

Carroll, W. K., & Hackett, R. A. (2006). Democratic media activism through the lens of social movement theory. *Media, Culture & Society, 28,* 83–104.

Carroll, W. K., & Ratner, R. S. (1999). Media strategies and political projects: A comparative study of social movements. *Canadian Journal of Sociology, 24*(1), 1–34.

Chester, J. (2006, September). *The impact of the media reform communities in the decade following the Telecommunications Act of 1996.* Center for Digital Democracy Working Paper.

Chester, J. (2007). *Digital destiny: New media and the future of democracy.* New York: New Press.

Chisman, F. P. (1977). Public interest and FCC policy making. *Journal of Communication, 27*(1), 77–84.

Clark, N. (2004). The birth of an advocacy group: The first six years of Action for Children's Television. *Journalism History, 30*(2), 66–75.

Classen, S. D. (1991). Standing on unstable grounds: A reexamination of the WLBT-TV case. *Critical Studies in Mass Communication, 11,* 73–91.

Classen, S. D. (2004). *Watching Jim Crow: The struggles over Mississippi TV, 1955–1969.* Durham, NC: Duke University Press.

Clift, C. E., III (1976). *The WLBT-TV case, 1964–1969: An historical analysis.* Unpublished doctoral dissertation, Indiana University, Bloomington.

Cogburn, D. L. (2004). Diversity matters, even at a distance: Evaluating the impact of computer-mediated communication on civil society participation in the World Summit on the Information Society. *Information Technologies and International Development, 1*(3–4), 15–40.

Cooper, M. (2005, May). *The importance of collateral communications and deliberate discourse in building Internet-based media reform movements.* Paper presented at the Online Deliberation: Design, Research, and Practice Conference, Stanford University, Palo Alto, CA. Retrieved July 30, 2007, from http://www.online-deliberation.net/conf2005/viewpaper.php?id=1

Coopman, T. M. (2000). High speed access: Micro radio, action, and activism on the Internet. *American Communication Journal, 3*(3). Retrieved May 18, 2007, from http://www.acjournal.org/holdings/vol3/Iss3/rogue4/highspeed.html

Costanza-Chock, S. (2002). The CRIS campaign: Mobilizations and blind spots. *Media Development, 4.* Retrieved February 15, 2007, from http://www.wacc.org.uk/wacc/publications/media_development

CRIS Campaign. (2005). Assessing communication rights: A handbook. Retrieved April 7, 2008, from http://www.crisinfo.org/pdf/ggpen.pdf

Cyril, M. A. (2005). Media and marginalization. In R. McChesney, R. Newman, & B. Scott (Eds.), *The future of media: Resistance and reform in the 21st century* (pp. 97–104). New York: Seven Stories Press.

Dagron, A. G. (2001). *Making waves: Stories of participatory communication for social change.* New York: Rockefeller Foundation.

Dany, C. (2007, November). *Structural power in Internet governance: Enabling and constraining effects of the institutionalization of NGO participation at the WSIS.* Paper presented at the GigaNet Symposium on Internet Governance, Rio de Janeiro, Brazil.

Davidson, A., Morris, J., & Courtney, R. (2002, September). *Strangers in a strange land: Public interest advocacy and Internet standards.* Paper presented at the Telecommunications Policy Research Conference, Alexandria, VA.

Davis, N., & Applied Research Center (n.d.). *Strategic grantmaking & grassroots organizing for media justice.* Retrieved February 15, 2007, from http://www.fex.org/assets/170_media.pdf

del Río, E. (2006). The Latinoa/o problematic: Categories and questions in media communication research. In C. S. Beck (Ed.), *Communication yearbook 30* (pp. 387–429). Mahwah, NJ: Erlbaum.

Dichter, A. (2004). Where are the people in the "public interest"? U.S. media activism and the search for a constituency. *Media Development, 4*(1). Retrieved February 15, 2007, from http://www.wacc.org.uk/wacc/publications/media_development

Dichter, A. (2005, June). *Together, we know more: Networks and coalitions to advance media democracy, communication rights and the public sphere, 1990–2005.* Paper presented to the Social Science Research Council, New York. Retrieved February 15, 2007, from http://www.ssrc.org/programs/media/publications/Dichter.10.final.doc

Dick, S. J., & McDowell, W. (2000). Pirates, pranksters, and prophets: Understanding America's unlicensed "free" radio movement. *Journal of Radio Studies, 7,* 329–341.

Dolber, B. (2007, January). *Missing the boat? The CWA's approach to media policy, 1984–2006.* Paper presented at the Social Science Research Council Pre-Conference on Media Policy Research, Memphis, TN.

Downing, J. D. H., with Ford, T., Gil, G., & Stein, L. (2001). *Radical media: Rebellious communication and social movements.* Thousand Oaks, CA: Sage.

Drake, W. (1997). Public interest groups and the Telecommunications Act of 1996. In H. Kubicek, W. H. Dutton, & R. Williams (Eds.), *The social shaping of information superhighways: European and American roads to the information society* (pp. 173–198). New York: St. Martin's Press.

Drake, W. (2004). *Reframing Internet governance discourse: Fifteen baseline propositions.* Memo #2 for the Social Science Research Council's Research Network on IT and Governance. Retrieved April 7, 2007, from http://programs.ssrc.org/itic/publications/Drake2.pdf

Dunbar-Hester, C. (2008a). *Propagating technology, propagating community? Low-power radio activism and technological negotiation in the U.S., 1996–2006.* Unpublished doctoral dissertation, Cornell University, Ithaca, NY.

Dunbar-Hester, C. (2008b). Geeks, meta-geeks, and gender trouble: Activism, identity, and low-power FM radio. *Social Studies of Science, 38,* 201–232.

Dunbar-Hester, C. (2008c, May). *"Free the spectrum!" Activist encounters with old and new media technology.* Paper presented at the annual meeting of the International Communication Association, Montreal, Canada.

Duncan, K. (Ed.). (1999). *Liberating alternatives: The founding convention of the Cultural Environment Movement.* Cresskill, NJ: Hampton Press.

Dutton, W. H. (2005, June). *Hired gun or partner in media reform: High noon for the social scientist.* Paper presented to the Social Science Research Council, New York.

Dutton, W. H., & Lin, W. (2002). E-democracy: A case study of Web-orchestrated cyberadvocacy. In J. Armitage & J. Roberts (Eds.), *Living with cyberspace: Technology and society in the 21st century* (pp. 98–108). New York: Continuum.

Edwards, B., & Foley, M. (2002). Social movement organizations beyond the beltway: Understanding the diversity of one social movement industry. *Mobilization: An International Journal, 8,* 87–107.

Engelman, R. (1990). The origins of public access cable television, 1966–1972. *Journalism Monographs, 123.*

Eyerman, R., & Jamison, A. (1991). *Social movements: A cognitive approach.* University Park: Pennsylvania State University Press.

Fahey, P. M. (1991). Advocacy group boycotting of network television advertisers and its effects on programming content. *University of Pennsylvania Law Review, 140,* 647–709.

Foley, L. (2005). Media reform from the inside out: The Newspaper Guild-CWA. In R. McChesney, R. Newman, & B. Scott (Eds.), *The future of media: Resistance and reform in the 21st century* (pp. 41–49). New York: Seven Stories Press.

Fones-Wolf, E. (2006a). Defending listeners' rights: Labor and media reform in postwar America. *Canadian Journal of Communication, 31,* 499–518.

Fones-Wolf, E. (2006b). *Waves of opposition: Labor and the struggle for democratic radio.* Urbana: University of Illinois Press.

Fox, E. (1986). Communication research and media reform in South America. *Critical Studies in Mass Communication, 3,* 236–245.

Franklin, M. (2005). *Gender advocacy at the World Summit on the Information Society.* Report prepared for the Ford Foundation. Retrieved April 7, 2008, from http://www.genderit.org/upload/ad6d215b74e2a8613f0cf5416c9f3865/Consultancy_1_.FF.WSIS.Report.Final.pdf

Fratkin, B. C. (2002). *The national citizens committee for broadcasting: A forgotten chapter of the media reform movement of the 1960s and 1970s.* Unpublished master's thesis, University of Utah, Salt Lake City.

Fuller, L. K. (1998). Saving stories: A goal of the cultural environment movement. *International Communication Gazette, 60*, 139–153.

Galtung, J., & Vincent, R. C. (1992). *Global glasnost: Toward a new world information and communication order?* Cresskill, NJ: Hampton Press.

Gamson, W. A., & Meyer, D. S. (1996). Framing political opportunity. In D. McAdam, J. D. McCarthy, & M. Zald (Eds.), *Comparative perspectives on social movements: Political opportunities, mobilizing structures, and cultural framings* (pp. 275–290). New York: Cambridge University Press.

Gamson, W. A., & Wolfsfeld, G. (1993). Movements and media as interacting systems. *Annals of the American Academy of Political and Social Science, 526*, 114–127.

Gandy, O. H. (2003). *The great frame robbery: Strategic uses of public opinion in the formation of media policy.* Report to the Ford Foundation. Retrieved April 7, 2008, from http://mediaresearchhub.ssrc.org/the-great-frame-robbery-the-strategic-use-of-public-opinion-in-the-formation-of-media-policy/attachment

Gangadharan, S. P. (2007, April 3). Why are civil rights groups neglecting media policy? *AlterNet*. Retrieved April 3, 2007, from http://www.alternet.org/story/12841

Gangadharan, S. P., De Cleen, B., & Carpentier, N. (2007). *Alternatives on media content, journalism and regulation.* Tartu, Estonia: Tartu University Press.

Garay, R. (1978). Access: Evolution of the citizen agreement. *Journal of Broadcasting, 22*, 95–106.

Garcelon, M. (2006). The "Indymedia" experiment: The Internet as movement facilitator against institutional control. *Convergence: The International Journal of Research into New Media Technologies, 12*, 55–82.

Garrett, R. K. (2006). Protest in an information society: A review of literature on social movements and new ICTs. *Information, Communication & Society, 9*, 202–224.

Gerbner, G. (1998). Introduction: Why the cultural environment movement. *International Communication Gazette, 60*, 133–138.

Gilens, M., & Hertzman, C. (2000). Corporate ownership and news bias: Newspaper coverage of the 1996 Telecommunications Act. *Journal of Politics, 62*, 369–386.

Greve, H. R., Pozner, J., & Rao, H. (2006). Vox populi: Resource partitioning, organizational proliferation, and the cultural impact of the insurgent microradio movement. *American Journal of Sociology, 112*, 802–837.

Hackett, R. A. (2000). Taking back the media: Notes on the potential for a communicative democracy movement. *Studies in Political Economy, 63*, 61–86.

Hackett, R. A., & Adam, M. (1999). Is media democratization a social movement? *Peace Review, 11*, 125–131.

Hackett, R. A., & Carroll, W. K. (2004). Critical social movements and media reform. *Media Development, 4*(1), 14–19.

Hackett, R. A. & Carroll, W. K. (2006). *Remaking media: The struggle to democratize public communication.* New York: Routledge.

Hadl, G., & Hintz, A. (2006, July). *Framing Our Media for transnational policy: The World Summit on the Information Society and beyond.* Paper presented at the annual meeting of the International Association of Media and Communication Research, Cairo, Egypt.

Hamilton, J. F. (2001). Theory through history: Exploring scholarly conceptions of U.S. alternative media. *The Communication Review, 4*, 305–326.

Hamilton, J. F. (2004). Rationalizing dissent? Challenging conditions of low-power FM radio. *Critical Studies in Media Communication, 21*, 44–63.

Hanke, B. (2005). Toward a political economy of Indymedia practice. *Canadian Journal of Communication, 30*, 41–64.

Hanks, W. E., & Pickett, T. A. (1979). Influence of community-based groups on television broadcasters in five eastern cities: An exploratory study. In H. S. Dordick (Ed.), *Proceedings of the sixth annual telecommunications policy research conference* (pp. 105–133). Lexington, MA: Lexington Books.

Heaney, M. T. (2007). Identity crisis: How interest groups struggle to define themselves in Washington. In A. Cigler & B. Loomis (Eds.), *Interest group politics* (7th ed., pp. 279–300). Washington, DC: Congressional Quarterly Press.

Heinki, R. S., & Tremain, M. H. (2000). Influencing media content through the legal system: A less than perfect solution for advocacy groups. In M. Suman & G. Rossman (Eds.), *Advocacy groups and the entertainment industry* (pp. 44–52). Westport, CT: Praeger.

Heinz, M., & Beckles, T. (2005). *Will fair use survive? Free expression in the age of copyright control.* Report from the Free Expression Policy Project, Brennan Center for Justice, New York University School of Law. Retrieved February 15, 2007, from http://www.fepproject.org/policyreports/WillFairUseSurvive.pdf

Hendershot, H. (1998). *Saturday morning censors: Television regulation before the V-chip.* Durham, NC: Duke University Press.

Hesmondhalgh, D. (2000). Alternative media, alternative texts? Rethinking democratization in the cultural industries. In J. Curran (Ed.), *Media organizations in society* (pp. 107–125). New York: Oxford University Press.

Higgins, J. W. (1999). Community television and the vision of media literacy, social action, and empowerment. *Journal of Broadcasting & Electronic Media, 43,* 624–644.

Hintz, A. (2005, October). *Activist media in global governance: Inputs and outputs at the World Summit on the Information Society.* Paper presented at the RE:activism conference, Budapest, Hungary.

Hintz, A. (2007a). Civil society media at the WSIS: A new actor in global communication governance? In B. Cammaerts & N. Carpentier (Eds.), *Reclaiming the media: Communication rights and democratic media roles* (pp. 243–264). Chicago: Intellect.

Hintz, A. (2007b, September). *Deconstructing multi-stakholderism: The discourses and realities of global governance at the World Summit on the Information Society.* Paper presented at the Standing Group on International Relations Conference, Turin, Italy.

Holman, J. (2005, August). *Strength in numbers? Public participation in the media ownership proceeding at the Federal Communication Commission.* Paper presented at the Telecommunications Policy Research Conference, Arlington, VA.

Horwitz, R. B. (1989). *The irony of regulatory reform: The deregulation of American telecommunications.* New York: Oxford University Press.

Horwitz, R. B. (1997). Broadcast reform revisited: Reverend Everett C. Parker and the "standing" case (Office of Communication of the United Church of Christ v. Federal Communications Commission). *The Communication Review, 2,* 311–348.

Horwitz, R. B. (1998). Telecommunications policy in the new South Africa: Participatory politics and sectoral reform. *Media, Culture & Society, 19,* 503–533.

Howley, K. (2000). Radiocracy rulz! Microradio as electronic activism. *International Journal of Cultural Studies, 3,* 256–267.

Howley, K. (2004). Remaking public service broadcasting: Lessons from Allston-Brighton free radio. *Social Movement Studies, 3,* 221–240.

Howley, K. (2005). *Community media: People, places, and communication technologies.* New York: Cambridge University Press.

Internaut Consulting. (2006, October). *Surveying the capacity to succeed: A baseline review of administrative and issue-based capacity needs of media reform, justice and democracy groups in the U.S.* Report to the Ford Foundation.

Jakubowicz, K. (1993). Stuck in a groove: Why the 1960s approach to communication will no longer do. In S. Splichal & J. Wasko (Eds.), *Communication and democracy* (pp. 33–54). Norwood, NJ: Ablex.

Johnson, N. (1967). *How to talk back to your television set.* Boston: Little, Brown.

Joselit, D. (2007). *Feedback: Television against democracy.* Cambridge, MA: MIT Press.

Kalas, P. P. (2007). *A study of the UN Working Group on Internet Governance: Multi-stakeholder partnerships in communications technology for development at the global policy level.* Diplo Foundation. Retrieved April 7, 2008, from http://www.diplomacy.edu/poolbin.asp?IDPool=455

Kidd, D. (2005). Angels of the public interest: U.S. media reform. In D. Skinner, J. R. Compton, & M. Gasher (Eds.), *Converging media, diverging politics: A political economy of news media in the United States and Canada* (pp. 201–221). Lanham, MD: Rowman & Littlefield.

Kidd, D., Barker-Plummer, B., & Rodriguez, C. (2004). *Media democracy from the ground up: Mapping communication practices in the counter public sphere.* Paper presented to the Social Science Research Council, New York. Retrieved October 4, 2007, from http://programs.ssrc.org/media/publications/rodrig-plummer-kidd.8.final.doc

Kim, M. (2003). *Civil society's global intervention in the area of mainstream, public and alternative media, and consequent network strengthening—is this possible?* Paper presented at the Our Media Network Conference, Barranquilla, Colombia. Retrieved October 4, 2007, from http://www.ourmedianet.org/papers/om2003/Kim_OM3.pdf

Kim, Y. (2001). The broadcasting audience movement in Korea. *Media, Culture & Society, 23,* 91–107.

Klein, H. (1995). *Grassroots democracy and the Internet: The Telecommunications Roundtable, Northeast USA.* Paper presented at the annual meeting of the Internet Society, Honolulu, HI. Retrieved February 15, 2007, from http://www.isoc.org/HMP/PAPER/164/txt/paper.txt

Klein, H. (1999). Making it happen now. *Peace Review, 11,* 41–52.

Klein, H. (2001). Online social movements and Internet governance. *Peace Review, 13,* 403–410.

Klinenberg, E. (2004). Channeling into the journalistic field: Youth activism and the media justice movement. In R. Benson & E. Neveu (Eds.), *Bourdieu and the journalistic field* (pp. 174–194). Cambridge, England: Polity Press.

Klinenberg, E. (2007). *Fighting for air: The battle to control America's media.* New York: Metropolitan Books.

Kogen, L. (2008, June). *The scholar-activist divide in communications policy research: A neo-institutional perspective.* Paper presented at the National Conference on Media Reform, Minneapolis, MN.

Kopp, K. (1997). *The role of private philanthropic foundations in communications policy making: Defining the "public interest"—The Ford and Markle Foundations' influence on policy making at the Federal Communications Commission.* Unpublished doctoral dissertation, University of Pennsylvania, Philadelphia.

Korn, G. E. (1991). *Everett C. Parker and the citizen media reform movement: A phe-*

*nomenological life history.* Unpublished doctoral dissertation, Southern Illinois University, Carbondale.

Kovacs, R. (2001). Relationship building as integral to British activism: Its impact on accountability in broadcasting. *Public Relations Review, 27,* 421–436.

Kulick, R. (2007). *Building a media justice and communication rights movement: Recommendations, challenges, needs, and resources.* Report of the Center for International Media Action. Retrieved April 7, 2008, from http://www.mediaaction center.org/files/Media-Movement-Building.pdf

Kumar, K. (2006). *Promoting independent media: Strategies for democracy assistance.* Boulder, CO: Lynne Rienner.

Layton, C. (2003–2004). News blackout. *American Journalism Review, 25*(8), 18–31.

Lenert, E. M. (2003). *Mapping social entrepreneurship and the role of charitable foundations in electronic media: 1946–1996.* Report prepared for the Ford Foundation. Retrieved April 8, 2008, from http://qcpages.qc.cuny.edu/mediastudies/ff/ report.pdf

Levi, L. (1996). Not with a bang but a whimper: Broadcast license renewal and the Telecommunications Act of 1996. *Connecticut Law Review, 29,* 243–276.

Lewis, C. S. (1986). *Television license renewal challenges by women's groups.* Unpublished doctoral dissertation, University of Minnesota, Minneapolis.

Listening Project (2004). *The makings of a social movement? Strategic issues and themes in communications policy work.* Philadelphia: OMG Center for Collaborative Learning.

Louie, J., & Luckey, A. (2006). *Democracy, social justice and media reform: A baseline study of the emerging field of media policy.* Report prepared for Grantmakers in Film and Electronic Media. San Francisco: Blueprint Research & Design.

MacBride, S. (1980). *Many voices, one world: Report by the International Commission for the Study of Communication Problems.* Paris and London: UNESCO/ Kogan Page.

Mason, R. (2006). The struggle for free time: Media reform in the United States during the 1990s. *Media History, 12,* 313–328.

Matani, S., Spilka, G., Borgman-Arboleda, C. & Dichter, A. (2003, September). *Strength, challenges and collaboration: Advocacy groups organizing together on media ownership and beyond.* Philadelphia: OMG Center for Collaborative Learning/Center for International Media Action.

Maxwell, R. (1988). The Chicano movement, the broadcast reform movement, and the sociology of "minorities and media": A study of cultural hegemony in the United States. *Confluencia, 3*(2), 89–102.

McAdam, D. (1996). Conceptual opportunities, current problems, future directions. In D. McAdam, J. D. McCarthy, & M. N. Zald (Eds.), *Comparative perspectives on social movements: Political opportunities, mobilizing structures, and cultural framings* (pp. 23–40). New York: Cambridge University Press.

McAdam, D., McCarthy, J. D., & Zald, M. N. (1996). Introduction: Opportunities, mobilizing structures, and framing processes—toward a synthetic, comparative perspective on social movements. In D. McAdam, J. D. McCarthy, & M. N. Zald (Eds.), *Comparative perspectives on social movements: Political opportunities, mobilizing structures, and cultural framings* (pp. 1–22). New York: Cambridge University Press.

McCarthy, J. D. (1996). Constraints and opportunities in adopting, adapting, and inventing. In D. McAdam, J. D. McCarthy, & M. N. Zald (Eds.), *Comparative perspectives on social movements: Political opportunities, mobilizing structures, and cultural framings* (pp. 141–151). New York: Cambridge University Press.

McChesney, R. W. (1992). Labor and the marketplace of ideas: WCFL and the battle for labor radio broadcasting. *Journalism Monographs, 134.*

McChesney, R. W. (1993). *Telecommunications, mass media, & democracy: The battle for the control of U.S. broadcasting, 1928–1935.* New York: Oxford University Press.

McChesney, R. W. (2004a). Media policy goes to main street: The uprising of 2003. *The Communication Review, 7,* 223–258.

McChesney, R. W. (2004b). *The problem of the media: U.S. communication politics in the 21st century.* New York: Monthly Review Press.

McChesney, R. W. (2007). *Communication revolution: Critical junctures and the future of media.* New York: New Press.

McChesney, R. W., Newman, R., & Scott, B. (Eds.). (2005). *The future of media: Resistance and reform in the 21st century* (pp. 97–104). New York: Seven Stories Press.

McChesney, R. W., & Nichols, J. (2002). *Our media, not theirs: The democratic struggle against corporate media.* New York: Seven Stories Press.

McChesney, R. W., & Nichols, J. (2005). Creation of the media democracy movement. In C. Alan (Ed.), *Patriotism, democracy, and common sense: Restoring America's promise at home and abroad* (pp. 367–375). Lanham, MD: Rowman & Littlefield.

McIver, W. J., Jr., Birdsall, W. F., & Rasmussen, M. (2004). The Internet and the right to communicate. *Media Development, 4*(3). Retrieved February 15, 2007, from http://www.wacc.org.uk/wacc/publications/media_development

McLaughlin, L., & Pickard, V. (2005). What is bottom-up about global internet governance? *Global Media and Communication, 1,* 357–373.

Meikle, G. (2002). *Future active: Media activism and the Internet.* New York: Routledge.

Milan, S., Hintz, A., & Cabral, A. (2007, November). *Broadening voices: Grassroots tech groups and policy objectives for Internet governance.* Paper presented at the GigaNet Symposium, Rio de Janeiro, Brazil.

Mills, K. (2004). *Changing channels: The civil rights case that transformed television.* Jackson: University Press of Mississippi.

Milton, A. K. (2001). Bound but not gagged: Media reform in democratic transition. *Comparative Political Studies, 34,* 493–526.

Montgomery, K. C. (1981). Gay activists and the networks. *Journal of Communication, 31*(3), 49–57.

Montgomery, K. C. (1989). *Target: Prime time: Advocacy groups and the struggle over entertainment television.* New York: Oxford University Press.

Mosco, V. (2007). The labouring of the public service principle: Union convergence and worker movements in the North American communication industries. *Info: The Journal of Policy, Regulation, and Strategy for Telecommunications, Information and Media, 9*(2/3), 57–68.

Mowlana, H. (1993). Toward a NWICO for the twenty-first century? *Journal of International Affairs, 47*(1), 59–72.

Mowlana, H., & Roach, C. (1992). New world information and communication order: An overview of recent developments and activities. In M. Traber & K. Nordenstreng (Eds.), *Few voices, many worlds* (pp. 4–17). London: World Association for Christian Communication.

Mueller, M. (2002a). *Ruling the root: Internet governance and the taming of cyberspace.* Cambridge, MA: MIT Press.

Mueller, M. (2002b, September). *Interest groups and the public interest: Civil society action and the globalization of communications policy.* Paper presented at the Telecommunications Policy Research Conference, Arlington, VA.

Mueller, M., Kuerbis, B., & Pagé, C. (2004). *Reinventing media activism: Public interest advocacy in the making of U.S. communication-information policy, 1960–2002.* Report prepared for the Ford Foundation. Retrieved January 6, 2009, from http://dcc.syr.edu/ford/rma/reinventing.pdf

Mueller, M., Kuerbis, B., & Pagé, C. (2007). Democratizing global communication? Global civil society and the campaign for communication rights in the information society. *International Journal of Communication, 1,* 267–296.

Mueller, M., & Lentz, B. (2004). Revitalizing communication and information policy research. *The Information Society, 20,* 155–157.

Mueller, M., Pagé, C., & Kuerbis, B. (2004). Civil society and the shaping of communication-information policy: Four decades of advocacy. *The Information Society, 20,* 169–185.

Munn, W. G. (1999). *Constructing the problem of access to information technology: A discursive analysis of the claims of public interest groups.* Unpublished doctoral dissertation, Claremont Graduate University, Los Angeles.

Napoli, P. M. (2001). *Foundations of communications policy: Principles and process in the regulation of electronic media.* Cresskill, NJ: Hampton Press.

Napoli, P. M. (2008a, July). *Diversity as an emerging principle of Internet governance.* Paper presented at the annual meeting of the International Association for Media and Communications Research, Stockholm.

Napoli, P. M. (2008b, November). *From conference themes to foundation principles of global Internet governance: An assessment of the 2007 Internet Governance Forum.* Paper presented at the annual meeting of the National Communication Association, San Diego, CA.

Nappo, C. (2008, June). *Resisting abridgment: Librarianship as media reform.* Paper presented at the National Conference on Media Reform, Minneapolis, MN.

Newman, K. (2002). Poisons, potions and profits: Radio rebels and the origins of the consumer movement. In M. Hilmes & J. Loviglio (Eds.), *Radio reader: Essays in the cultural history of radio* (pp. 157–181). New York: Routledge.

Newman, K. (2004). *Radio active: Advertising and consumer activism, 1935–1947.* Berkeley: University of California Press.

Newman, R., & Scott, B. (2005). The fight for the future of media. In R. McChesney, R. Newman, & B. Scott (Eds.), *The future of media: Resistance and reform in the 21st century* (pp. 21–40). New York: Seven Stories Press.

Nielsen, L. B., & Albiston, C. R. (2006). The organization of public interest practice: 1975–2004. *North Carolina Law Review, 84,* 1592–1622.

Nordenstreng, K. (1999). The context: Great media debate. In R. C. Vincent, K. Nordenstreng, & M. Traber (Eds.), *Towards equity in global communication: MacBride update* (pp. 235–268). Cresskill, NJ: Hampton Press.

Noriega, C. A. (2000). *Shot in America: Television, the state, and the rise of Chicano cinema.* Minneapolis: University of Minnesota Press.

Nusser, N., & Hamilton, J. (2008, May). *De-westernizing theory and practice of new social movements: The indigenous production of transnational media activism in Oaxaca, Mexico.* Paper presented at the annual meeting of the International Communication Association, Montreal, Canada.

Office of Communication of the United Church of Christ v. Federal Communications Commission, 359 F.2d 994 (D.C. Cir. 1966).

Oliver, P. E., & Johnston, H. (2000). What a good idea! Ideologies and frames in social movement research. *Mobilization: An International Journal, 4,* 37–54.

Opel, A. (2004). *Micro radio and the FCC: Media activism and the struggle over broadcast policy.* Westport, CT: Praeger.

O Siochrú, S. (1999a). Democratising telecommunications: The role of organizations in civil society. *Media Development, 2*(2). Retrieved February 15, 2007, from http://www.wacc.org.uk/wacc/publications/media_development

O Siochrú, S. (1999b). Democratic media: the case for getting organized. In R. C. Vincent, K. Nordenstreng, & M. Traber (Eds.), *Towards equity in global communication: MacBride update* (pp. 139–153). Cresskill, NJ: Hampton Press.

O Siochrú, S. (2004). Civil society participation in the WSIS process: Promises and reality. *Continuum: The Journal of Media & Cultural Studies, 18,* 330–344.

O Siochrú, S. (2005). Finding a frame: Toward a transnational advocacy campaign to democratize communication. In R. A. Hackett & Y. Zhao (Eds.), *Democratizing global media* (pp. 289–311). Lanham, MD: Rowman & Littlefield.

Ostertag, B. (2006). *People's movements, people's press: The journalism of social justice movements.* Boston: Beacon Press.

Padden, P. R. (1972). The emerging role of citizens' groups in broadcast regulation. *Federal Communications Bar Journal, 25,* 82–110.

Padovani, C. (2005). Debating communication imbalances from the MacBride Report to the World Summit on the Information Society: An analysis of a changing discourse. *Global Media and Communication, 1,* 316–338.

Padovani, C., & Tuzzi, A. (2004). The WSIS as a world of words: Building a common vision of the Information Society? *Continuum: Journal of Media & Cultural Studies, 18,* 360–379.

Pekurny, R. (2000). Advocacy groups in the age of audience fragmentation: Thoughts on a new strategy. In M. Suman & G. Rossman (Eds.), *Advocacy groups and the entertainment industry* (pp. 105–113). Westport, CT: Praeger.

Phiphitkul, W. (2005). Where there is a dream, there are today and tomorrow: A movement to realize cabinet resolution on children program on TV. In S. Wangvivatana (Ed.), *Media reform going backward?* (pp. 82–97). Bangkok: Thai Broadcast Journalists Association.

Pichardo, N. A. (1997). New social movements: A critical review. *Annual Review of Sociology, 23,* 411–430.

Pickard, V. W. (2006). Assessing the radical democracy of Indymedia: Discursive, technical, and institutional constructions. *Critical Studies in Media Communication, 23,* 19–38.

Pickard, V. W. (2007). Neoliberal visions and revisions in global communications policy from NWICO to WSIS. *Journal of Communication Inquiry, 31,* 118–139.

Pickard, V. W. (2008a, May). *A postwar settlement for U.S. broadcasting: The FCC's Blue Book and the struggle for progressive radio, 1945–1947.* Paper presented at the annual meeting of the International Communication Association, Montreal, Canada.

Pickard, V. W. (2008b). *"Whether the giants should be slain or persuaded to be good": Revisiting the Hutchins Commission and the role of media in a democratic society.* Unpublished working paper.

Pike, R., & Winseck, D. (2004). The politics of global media reform, 1907–23. *Media, Culture & Society, 26,* 643–675.

Plater, Z. J. B. (2006). Law, media, and environmental policy: A fundamental linkage in sustainable democratic governance. *Boston College Environmental Affairs Law Review, 33,* 511–549.

Powers, M. (2005). *Moral arguments for media reform: A study in the ethical universe of the World Association for Christian Communication.* Unpublished master's thesis, Simon Fraser University, Burnaby, Canada.

Pozner, J. L. (2005). Reclaiming the media for a progressive feminist future. *Media Development, 3.* Retrieved February 15, 2007, from http://www.wacc.org.uk/wacc/publications/media_development

Price, M. E., Rozumilowicz, B., & Verhulst, S. G. (Eds.). (2001). *Media reform: Democratizing the media, democratizing the state.* New York: Routledge.

Raboy, M. (1990). *Missed opportunities: The story of Canada's broadcasting policy.* Montreal, Canada: McGill-Queen's University Press.

Raboy, M. (1998). Global communication policy and the realization of human rights. *Journal of International Communication, 5,* 83–104.

Raboy, M. (2004). The World Summit on the Information Society and its legacy for global governance. *Gazette: The International Journal for Communication Studies, 66,* 225–232.

Rhodes, S. (2006). *Social movements and free-market capitalism in Latin America: Telecommunications privatization and the rise of consumer protest.* Albany: State University of New York Press.

Roach, C. (1990). The movement for a New World Information and Communication Order: A second wave? *Media, Culture & Society, 12,* 283–307.

Rossman, G. (2000). Hostile and cooperative advocacy. In M. Suman & G. Rossman (Eds.), *Advocacy groups and the entertainment industry* (pp. 85–103). Westport, CT: Praeger.

Rowland, Jr., W. D. (1982). The illusion of fulfillment: The broadcast reform movement. *Journalism Monographs, 79.*

Rubin, N. (2002, September). *Highlander media justice gathering final report.* New Market, TN: Highlander Research and Education Center.

Ryans, J. K., Jr., Samiee, S., & Wills, J. (1985). Consumerist movement and advertising regulation in the international environment: Today and in the future. *European Journal of Marketing, 19,* 5–11.

Samarajiva, R., & Gamage, S. (2007). Bridging the divide: Building Asia-Pacific capacity for effective reforms. *The Information Society, 23,* 109–117.

Schement, J. R., Gutiérrez, F. F., Gandy, O., Haight, T., & Soriano, M. E. (1977). The anatomy of a license challenge. *Journal of Communication,* 27(1), 89–94.

Schiller, D. (1999). Social movement in telecommunications: Rethinking the public service history of U.S. telecommunications, 1804–1919. In A. Calabrese & J. C. Burgelman (Eds.), *Communication, citizenship, and social policy* (pp. 137–155). Lanham, MD: Rowman & Littlefield.

Schiller, D. (2007). The hidden history of U.S. public service telecommunications, 1919–1956. *Info: The Journal of Policy, Regulation, and Strategy for Telecommunications, Information and Media,* 9(2/3), 17–28.

Schneyer, T. J. (1977). An overview of public interest law activity in the communications field. *Wisconsin Law Review, 1977,* 619–683.

Schneyer, T. J., & Lloyd, F. (1976). *The public-interest media reform movement: A look at the mandate and a new agenda.* Washington, DC: Aspen Institute for Humanistic Studies.

Scott, B. (2004). The politics and policy of media ownership. *American University Law Review, 53,* 645–677.

Scott, B. (2005). Reforming media: Parries and pirouettes in the U.S. policy process. In D. Skinner, J. R. Compton, & M. Gasher (Eds.), *Converging media, diverging politics: A political economy of news media in the United States and Canada* (pp. 187–200). Lanham, MD: Rowman & Littlefield.

Selian, A. N. (2004). The World Summit on the Information Society and civil society participation. *The Information Society, 20,* 201–215.

Senecal, M., & Dubois, F. (2005). The alternative communication movement in Quebec's mediascape. In D. Skinner, J. R. Compton, & M. Gasher (Eds.), *Converging media, diverging politics: A political economy of news media in the United States and Canada* (pp. 249–266). Lanham, MD: Rowman & Littlefield.

Sherman, T. W. (2004). *Champions of the public or purveyors of elite perspectives? Interest group activity in information and communications policy.* Unpublished doctoral dissertation, University of Maryland, College Park.

Siriyuvasak, U. (1999). The Thai media, cultural politics and the nation-state. *International Journal of Communication Law & Policy, 6*(3), 1–19. Retrieved July 30, 2007, from http://www.ijclp.org/3_1999/pdf/ijclp_webdoc_6_3_1999.pdf

Siriyuvasak, U. (2001). Regulation reform and the question of democratizing the broadcast media in Thailand. *Javnost—The Public, 8,* 89–108.

Siriyuvasak, U. (2002, November). Community radio movement: Towards reforming the broadcast media in Thailand. Paper presented at the WSIS Asian Response Meeting, Bangkok, Thailand. Retrieved July 30, 2007, from http://www.wsisasia.org/materials/uajit.doc

Siriyuvasak, U. (2005). People's media and communication rights in Indonesia and the Philippines. *Inter-Asia Cultural Studies, 6,* 245–263.

Snider, J. H. (2005). *Speak softly and carry a big stick: How local TV broadcasters exert political power.* Lincoln, NE: iUniverse.

Starr, J. M. (2001). *Air wars: The fight to reclaim public broadcasting.* Philadelphia: Temple University Press.

Stavitsky, A. G., Avery, R. K., & Vanhala, H. (2001). From class D to LPFM: The high-powered politics of low-power radio. *Journalism & Mass Communication Quarterly, 78,* 340–354.

Stein, L. (2001). Access television and grassroots political communication in the United States. In J. D. H. Downing, with T. V. Ford, G. Gil, & L. Stein, (Eds.), *Radical media: Rebellious communication and social movements* (pp. 299–324). Thousand Oaks, CA: Sage.

Stein, L. (in press). Introduction. In L. Stein, C. Rodriguez, & D. Kidd. (Eds.), *Making our media: Global initiatives towards a democratic public sphere: Vol. 2: National and global movements for media democratization.* Cresskill, NJ: Hampton Press.

Stein, L., Rodriguez, C., & Kidd, D. (Eds.). (in press). *Making our media: Global initiatives towards a democratic public sphere: Vol. 2. National and global movements for media democratization.* Cresskill, NJ: Hampton Press.

Steiner, L. (2005). The feminist cable collective as public sphere activity. *Journalism, 6,* 313–334.

Stengrim, L. A. (2005). Negotiating postmodern democracy, political activism, and knowledge production: Indymedia's grassroots and e-savvy answer to media oligopoly. *Communication & Critical/Cultural Studies, 2,* 281–304.

Stole, I. L. (2000). Consumer protection in historical perspective: The five-year battle over federal regulation of advertising, 1933–1938. *Mass Communication & Society, 3,* 351–372.

Stole, I. L. (2007). *Advertising on trial: Consumer activism and corporate public relations in the 1930s.* Urbana: University of Illinois Press.

Streeter, T. (2000). What is an advocacy group, anyway? In M. Suman & G. Rossman (Eds.), *Advocacy groups and the entertainment industry* (pp. 77–84). Westport, CT: Praeger.

Swanson, D. C. (2000). *The story of Viewers for Quality Television: From grassroots to prime time.* Syracuse, NY: Syracuse University Press.

Tacchi, J. (2005). Supporting the democratic voice through community media centres in South Asia. *3C Media: Journal of Community, Citizen's and Third Sector Media and Communication, 1,* 25–36.

Thomas, P. (2005, October). *CRIS and global media governance: Communication rights and social change.* Paper presented to the Social Change in the 21st Century Conference, Brisbane, Australia.

Thomas, P. (2006). The communication rights in the information society (CRIS) campaign. *The International Communication Gazette, 68,* 291–312

Tomaselli, K. G., & Louw, P. E. (1989). Alternative press and political practice: The South African struggle. In M. Raboy & P. A. Bruck, (Eds.), *Communication for and against democracy* (pp. 203–220). Montreal, Canada: Black Rose Books.

Toro, A. L. (2000). *Standing up for listeners' rights: A history of public participation at the Federal Communications Commission.* Doctoral dissertation, University of California, Berkeley.

Traber, M., & Nordenstreng, K. (1992). *Few voices, many worlds: Towards a media reform movement.* London: World Association for Christian Communication.

Tracy, J. F. (2007). A historical case study of alternative news media and labor activism: *The Dubuque Leader, 1935–1939. Journalism & Communication Monographs, 8*(4).

Trivedi, N. (2006). *The legal needs of local media reform organizations: Report of a national survey.* New York: Brennan Center for Justice at NYU School of Law. Retrieved April 7, 2007, from http://www.fepproject.org/policyreports/localneeds-survey.pdf

Turow, J. (1984). Pressure groups and television entertainment: A framework for analysis. In W. D. Rowland, Jr. & B. Watkins (Eds.), *Interpreting television: Current research perspectives* (pp. 142–162). Beverly Hills, CA: Sage.

Venturelli, S. (1998). Human rights and democracy in cyberspace. *Journal of International Communication, 5,* 11–24.

Wangvivatana, S. (Ed.). (2005). *Media reform going backward?* Bangkok: Thai Broadcast Journalists Association.

Wible, S. (2004). Media advocates, Latino citizens, and niche cable: The limits of "no limits" TV. *Cultural Studies, 18,* 34–66.

Williams, Jr., R. C. (2001). *"Saving radiance": U.S. broadcast reformers, ETV and the invention of national public television.* Unpublished doctoral dissertation, University of New Mexico, Albuquerque.

Yang, S. (2002). The media tax probe and the media reform movement in South Korea. *Harvard Asia Quarterly, 6*(1), 31–36.

Zald, M. N. (1996). Culture, ideology, and strategic framing. In D. McAdam, J. D. McCarthy, & M. N. Zald (Eds.), *Comparative perspectives on social movements: Political opportunities, mobilizing structures, and cultural framings* (pp. 261–274). New York: Cambridge University Press.

# CHAPTER CONTENTS

# 11 Apologia, Image Repair, and Reconciliation

## The Application, Limitations, and Future Directions of Apologetic Rhetoric

*Emil B. Towner*
Texas Tech University

This chapter focuses on two pressing issues facing scholars of apologetic rhetoric—what we talk about and what we do not talk about. I begin this chapter by providing an overview of apologetic rhetoric research, including two diverging approaches—apologia theory as a means of image repair and apologies as part of reconciliation and healing. In the second part of this chapter, I explore what we do not talk about—that is, the gaps and limitations of our current understanding of apologetic rhetoric. In doing so, I argue that we lack research focused on female non-Western apologists, as well as delivery methods such as new media and business or technical documents. Finally, I offer suggestions for future studies of apologia, image repair strategies, and reconciliatory apologies.

Apologies are so pervasive in human interaction that we experience them almost daily—from seemingly simple apologetic waves when one person accidentally cuts off another during rush-hour traffic to public apologies for corporate wrongdoing. On the surface, it may be tempting to view these apologies as cut-and-dried statements of closure for offensive acts, faux pas, and even brutal atrocities. On deeper rhetorical and sociological levels, however, apologies contain critical elements that hold together the fabric of a society; they presuppose a set of social values and an underlying ideology that an offender is charged with fracturing. In this sense, apologies can be thought of not only as acts of contrition but, more importantly, as value-laden negotiations of shame and guilt, of responsibility and liability, of social standing and hierarchy, and of membership in a group, community, nation, or humankind. By studying these complex rhetorical negotiations, we gain a deeper understanding of a group's values and identity at a specific moment in time (Villadsen, 2008). We also discover lasting means for repairing broken relationships, overcoming contention between cultures and communities, and healing victims, in accordance with those societal values.

Correspondence: e-mail: emil.towner@ttu.edu

# The Rhetorical and Sociological Importance of Apologetic Rhetoric

While a large number of articles and books have been published relating to apologetic rhetoric, I argue that this area of research has reached a point at which we must reflect on the diverging concepts and the representative examples that make up our body of knowledge. Since the early 2000s, the field of apologetic rhetoric has branched out in new and exciting ways. Scholars from a variety of fields within communication studies and other disciplines have focused more attention on apologetic exchanges in health care communication, international relations, cultural studies, and race relations. This growth has helped fuel over-arching discussions not only about the terms used to define and analyze apologetic exchanges, but also about how we view the goals of apologetic exchanges. Despite the growth in the subject matter, I argue that potential gaps have silently developed in our tendencies as researchers to examine certain types of exchanges and rhetors instead of others. These gaps limit not only what we understand, but also how broadly and appropriately we can apply our current theories.

## Chapter Overview

To bring these issues to the forefront, I have structured the chapter to focus on two pressing issues facing scholars of apologetic rhetoric today: *what we talk about* and *what we do not talk about*. First, in discussing *what we talk about*, I provide an overview of the deeper negotiations of value and membership that lie beneath the surface of these studies. From there, I discuss two diverging approaches to studying apologetic discourse—apologia theory as a means of image repair and apologies as part of reconciliation and healing. For each approach, I provide a discussion of the major philosophical assumptions, an overview of the theories of analysis and evaluation, and a brief review of studies that demonstrate those theories in action.

In the second part, I explore *what we do not talk about*—the gaps in our knowledge or potential limitations in our application of that knowledge. Specifically, I discuss my survey of 91 articles that have been published in academic journals over the last 40 years. By analyzing the genders/types of rhetors, geographic regions, and media analyzed in these articles, I demonstrate the lack of research that has focused on female and non-Western apologists, as well as various delivery methods such as new media and business or technical documents. In the conclusion, I discuss the implications of *what we talk about* and *what we do not talk about*, as well as offer suggestions for future studies of apologia, image repair strategies, and reconciliatory apologies.

## Additional Areas of Interest to Readers

Before beginning, however, I should clarify that, due to the space constraints and purpose of this chapter, I have limited the scope to focus specifically on the theories and analyses of public apologies and public responses to accusations of wrongdoing. However, readers who are interested in apologies, in general, can find relevant material under the subject area of interpersonal apologies, including recent articles such as Bachman and Guerrero (2006), Hawk (2007), and Tucker, Turner, Barling, Reid, and Elving (2006). In addition, an excellent source for studies on politeness theory in interpersonal apologies can be found in the 2007 special issue of the *Journal of Politeness Research*, which includes articles by Davies, Merrison, and Goddard (2007), Kampf and Blum-Kulka (2007), and Koutsantoni (2007).

Along with these studies of interpersonal apologies, readers may also want to examine the closely related area of account-giving, in which a person provides an explanation or justification for his or her actions. While account-giving and apologia share a similar focus, researchers often examine them from differing perspectives. Specifically, account theory has developed as more of a sociological area of interest, while apologia has generally been a topic of rhetorical studies (Sullivan & Martin, 2001; for a foundational introduction into account-giving theory, see Goffman, 1971; Scott & Lyman, 1968; Sykes & Matza, 1957).

Finally, I should mention the overlapping work of crisis communication. In broad terms, crisis management and communication involves several aspects of crisis prevention, leadership, information dissemination, organization, risk assessment, and communication strategies (for more on communicating quantitative risk information, see Skubisz, Reimer, & Hoffrage, this volume). Among those many aspects involved is the need to sometimes publicly apologize for or to justify a corporation's actions in the face of allegations of wrongdoing. To demonstrate the influence and usefulness of crisis communication studies on theories of apologetic rhetoric, I include Coombs's (1999) book, *Ongoing Crisis Communication*, and Keith Michael Hearit's (2006) book, *Crisis Management by Apology*, in the discussion below. However, readers may find many more tangential theories and applicable discussions in other crisis communication sources, including Ulmer, Sellnow, and Seeger (2007), *Effective Crisis Communication*, Gerald Lewis (2006), *Organizational Crisis Management*, and Kathleen Fearn-Banks (2007), *Crisis Communications*.

Although the various resources and perspectives above provide unique perspectives from which we can analyze and understand apologetic exchanges, in this chapter, I focus on the social values that a person, corporation, or nation-state is accused of fracturing.

## Negotiations of Guilt, Responsibility, and Social Values

As Lazare (2004) described, each apology encompasses a unique and complex negotiation of responsibility that involves shame and remorse on the part of the offender, articulations of suffering on the part of the offended, appropriate explanations, acceptance of responsibilities, and, ultimately, acceptance of an apology as an indication that the offended party's needs have been met (p. 205). Nicholas Tavuchis (1991) referred to such a negotiation as the "middle term in a moral syllogism" or speech act that consists of an accusation, an apology, and acceptance or rejection (p. 20). That idea echoes Ryan's (1982) argument that an apology should be discussed as a response to a specific accusation. Drawing on terms from classical rhetoric, he called for analysis to focus on the speech act of *kategoria* (or accusation) and *apologia* (or speech in defense). Recently, Kevin Stein (2008) added a third element—*antapologia*—to the speech act. According to Stein's description, an offended party issues an accusation (kategoria), and the offender responds with an account or defensive response (apologia). However, if the offended party has an issue with that account or response, he or she initiates a counter-accusation (an antapologia) specifically addressing the content or delivery of the apologia itself. Thus, according to Stein, the antapologia differs from the kategoria in that "the former is designed to be a response to the apologetic discourse and the latter is designed to be a response to the initial harmful act perpetrated by the accused" (pp. 19–20).

With the addition (or acknowledgment) of this third element, the process is more accurately represented and analyzed as a negotiation in which the offender and the offended function as co-creators of the apology (Yamazaki, 2004). Each participant approaches the exchange with many goals that must be woven together. For example, for apologies to heal, the offended party often seeks one or more of the following—a restored sense of dignity and safety, assurance that the harmful act was not their fault, reparations, a meaningful discussion about the act and the pain that resulted from it, the chance to see the offender suffer, and reassurances that the offender shares the same values as the offended (Lazare, 2004, p. 44). As Lazare explained, offenders, on the other hand, typically seek either to expunge guilt and shame or to avoid punishment and damage to their reputation.

The psychological needs of both the offended and the offender underscore the roles of social values, guilt, and redemption in apologetic discourse. In other words, a central underlying figure in accusations and apologies is the social contract (Lazare, 2004) or hierarchy of values (Burke, 1969) that, at least implicitly, defines acceptable behaviors and obligations for members of the community. The breaking of those values leads to a sense of guilt (Brummett, 1981). According to Lazare, guilt entails "the capacity to apply standards of right and wrong to our behavior toward others and to punish ourselves emotionally when we hurt others" (p. 135). As Brummett clarified, for individuals, this guilt leads to a feeling of being incomplete or imperfect. While corporations may not be able to truly *feel* guilt (Tavuchis, 1991), they do, nonetheless, experience "considerable constraints on their actions" (Hearit, 1997, p. 219). Lazare noted that shame comprises another closely related emotion—a sense of failure and self judgment that people experience when they fail to live up to the standards or image they have set for themselves. The emotions of guilt and shame can be further heightened when a sender directs a kategoria at the offender, calling his or her character or actions into question (Hearit, 2006). To alleviate these negative emotions, the offender must expunge the guilt through a ritualistic process shaped by religious worldviews and principles.

## The Role and Influence of Religion

Religion plays two important roles in our understanding of apologetic rhetoric. First, much of the psychology and terminology of apologetic rhetoric—such as redemption, mortification, atonement, absolution, and forgiveness—comes either directly from religious principles or, at the very least, carries strong religious overtones. In other words, religion provides generic norms and concepts that function as lenses for understanding and analyzing apologetic discourse. For example, Kenneth Burke (1969), ties apologies to the religious aspects of guilt and redemption—which, ultimately, help re-establish social order. For Burke, members construct and maintain social order through a set of values and principles that he labeled as hierarchies. Brummett (1981) explained:

> Hierarchies control the terrors of mystery, which is the perception of difference, strangeness, and alienation. Insofar as everyone is somewhat different from everyone else, mystery is inescapable. And insofar as groups of people have values, commitments, and lifestyles that are markedly different from those of other groups, the mystery is threatening. Hierarchies do not eliminate mystery; rather, they provide an order for controlling it. (p. 255)

In other words, hierarchies provide a sense of social order through similar values and obligations. Acceptance of those values maintains the social order of a given group, and serves as terms and conditions for membership within the group. When someone violates one of these values, she or he upsets the natural order of the society, resulting in mystery for the group, as well as a sense of guilt and a loss of membership for the individual. To mitigate mystery and achieve reinstatement in the group, the offender must expunge the guilt.

According to Burke (1970), two major ways exist to efface guilt and achieve redemption: mortification and scapegoating. Mortification consists of the offender confessing his or her sins and receiving some form of punishment, while scapegoating (or victimage) consists of transferring the guilt to another person who represents the sin (Brummett, 1981). However, Burke (1969, 1970) also described a third non-redemptive way to deal with guilt, which he called transcendence. According to Brummett, unlike mortification and scapegoating which seek redemption, transcendence is not a strategy of redemption because it denies that guilt exists and therefore removes the need for redemption. Hearit (1997) offered a deeper understanding of transcendence by arguing that it involves two major elements—redefinition and an appeal to higher order values. The first aspect, redefinition, consists of what Perelman (1982) termed *dissociation*, or an attempt to separate a single concept or unit into two or more distinct elements (p. 49). According to Hearit, transcendence strategies may involve three forms of dissociation—a separation of opinion and knowledge, a separation of business interests and societal interests, and separation of current or short-term considerations from future or long-term issues. Hearit noted that, in the second element of transcendence—an appeal to higher values—the accused attempts to define his or her act in terms of an abstract value that negates the specific or short-term consequences of the act. In short, the rhetorical force of transcendence is that the higher-order, abstract value links and legitimizes the act. By analyzing the use of transcendence, mortification, and scapegoating in apologetic rhetoric, rhetorical analysts better understand the role of guilt, social order, and redemption in negotiations of group membership.

In addition to Burke's (1969, 1970) discussions of guilt, redemption, purification, and mortification, a number of scholars have also founded their theories of apologetic rhetoric on religious concepts. For example, John B. Hatch (2006b) described how religious rituals influence apologies and how religious traditions offer useful examples of genuine reconciliation. Drawing on Rothenbuhler (1998), Hearit (2006) also argued that apologies comprise a sacred ritual in which the offender voluntarily enters the public confessional, seeking absolution and restoration into the community. Moreover, both Hearit (2006) and Tavuchis (1991) likened this ritual of absolution to that of a confession, as described by Michel Foucault (1980):

> The confession is a ritual of discourse…that unfolds within a power relationship, for one does not confess without the presence (or virtual presence) of a partner who is not simply the interlocutor but the authority who requires the confession, prescribes and appreciates it, and intervenes in order to judge, punish, forgive, console, and reconcile; a ritual in which the truth is corroborated by the obstacles and resistances it has had to surmount in order to be formulated; and finally, a ritual in which the expression alone, independently of its external consequences, produces intrinsic modifications in the person who articulates it: it exonerates, redeems, and purifies him; it unburdens him of his wrongs, liberates him and promises him salvation. (pp. 61–62)

Koesten and Rowland (2004) also based their theory of apologetic rhetoric on religious principles—specifically, on the elements of the Jewish prayer *Unetanneh Tokef.* According to their theory, the rhetoric of atonement functions as a sub-genre of apologia and consists of a person purging guilt and seeking redemption when the strategies of denial, deflection or justification will not work because the person is actually guilty. Similarly, Thomas Burkholder (1990) argued that martyrdom speeches function as a sub-genre of apologia in the sense that the people delivering these speeches symbolically sacrifice themselves and, thus, seek salvation in the same way that Christ did—through death.

Religion also impacts our understanding through the examples of apologetic rhetoric that are delivered by religious leaders. These examples provide scholars with case studies that provide fruitful opportunities for applying our understanding of the norms and analytical lenses. For example, academic studies have analyzed the apologetic rhetoric of Martin Luther (Ryan, 1982),

Pope John Paul II (Lazare, 2004; Marrus, 2008), Jerry Falwell (Brown, 1990), televangelist John Ankerberg (Armstrong, Hallmark, & Williamson, 2005), evangelical thinker Francis Schaeffer (Sullivan, 1998), Father James Tunstead Burthchaell (Blaney, 2001), and Jesus (Blaney & Benoit, 1997). In addition, Miller (2002) devoted an entire book to analyzing the apologia of religious figures, including the Apostle Paul, Jimmy Swaggart, and others. He concluded that apologia theory constitutes a useful lens for analyzing the rhetoric of faith and religion.

In addition to religious aspects of contrition and absolution, many scholars of apologetic rhetoric note that the offender's words, actions, and deeds must acknowledge and reaccept a society's rules and values (Goffman, 1971; Hearit, 2006). According to Hearit, through such a commitment, the offender seeks not only to shed guilt but also to be restored back into the community. Other scholars believe that, while apologies presuppose a set of values, their true power is not a restoration of the offender's image. Instead, they affirm that the virtue of an apology is that it serves as a confession that ultimately leads to a relationship steeped in justice (Hatch, 2006a). In other words, sincere apologies that acknowledge responsibility and express regret offer "a form of moral restitution" that enables a group or community to move forward together (Weyeneth, 2001, p. 35).

## The Expanding Rhetoric of Apologia for Image Repair

The term *apologia* has been traced back to the ancient Greek root word *apologos*, meaning "a story" (Partridge, 1977, p. 347). Tavuchis (1991) explained that it first appears in the *Oxford English Dictionary* as *apoloyia—apo*, meaning "away," and *loyia*, meaning "speaking"—and is defined as a speech in defense or as a vindication of a person (p. 15). In ancient Greece, citizens regarded such a defense as an important genre of rhetoric. Plato, Isocrates, and Aristotle characterized *apologia* as a specific genre in which an orator defends himself or his actions against an accusation (Ryan, 1982).

Drawing on this ancient genre of rhetoric, communication scholars in the late 1960s and 1970s began to analyze the characteristics and meanings of apologia in the mass-mediated climate of the 20th century. In one of the first attempts to identify specific characteristics of apologia, Rosenfield (1968) analyzed what he described as the mass-media apologia. In his analysis of speeches by ex-President Harry Truman and vice presidential candidate Richard Nixon, Rosenfield argued that, where similarities exist between these two examples of nationally broadcast apologetic rhetoric, "we have grounds for attributing those qualities to the situation or the genre" (p. 435). To that end, Rosenfield described four initial characteristics of mass-media apologia: (1) they tend to be concise, decisive clashes; (2) the remarks are not limited to defensive messages; (3) mass-media apologia include a preponderance of data in the middle of the speech, and (4) previously used arguments appear to be reused and combined into one cohesive message. A few years later, Sherry Butler (1972) analyzed Edward Kennedy's apologetic rhetoric using Rosenfield's four characteristics. She concluded that the nature of apologetic rhetoric lends itself to Rosenfield's structure; however, she disagreed that future nationally broadcast apologia would provide decisive conclusions to major controversies.

### Philosophical Assumptions

In 1973, Ware and Linkugel defined the genre of apologia as a "public speech of self-defense" issued in response to an attack on one's character or worth" (p. 274). Similarly, Kruse (1977) explained apologia as a defense of one's character in response to public criticism. Later, Kruse (1981b) also expanded the definition to include a wide variety of mediums or methods of delivery in addition to public speeches—including materials such as novels, press releases, plays, and poems. Ryan (1982) also broadened the definition to encompass defenses of one's policies, as well as one's character. In addition to broadening the definition, scholars have worked to more specifically define what apologia is not. For example, Hearit (1994) specified that apologia is not the same as apology. Although an apologia may ultimately consist of an apology, he argued that an apologia, first and foremost, entails "a defense that seeks to present a compelling counter description...to situate alleged organizational wrongdoing in a more favorable context" (p. 115). Finally, in discussing his theory of image restoration—later termed image repair (Benoit, 2000)— Benoit (1995a) explicitly centered the study of apologetic rhetoric around how people and organizations "reduce, redress, or avoid damage to their reputation (or face or image) from perceived wrong-doing" (p. vii). According to this perspective, when offenders offer apologia, they are not seeking to earn forgiveness (Hearit, 2006), but rather "to avoid punishment and damage to their reputation" (Lazare, 2004, p. 134).

By situating analysis and evaluations around these aspects of *apologia* rather than *apologies*, scholars of apologetic rhetoric focus not merely on instances in which organizations offer an admission of guilt, but, instead, more broadly on all situations in which an individual or organization has been accused of wrong-doing and offers some form of defense or justification in response (Kruse 1981a).

### Theories of Analysis and Evaluation

In one of the earliest and most notable examinations of apologetic strategies, Erving Goffman (1971) detailed the remedial work of accounts, apologies, and requests. According to Goffman, an *account* may include denying that the act occurred or admitting it occurred but arguing that the accused isn't responsible for or couldn't foresee the negative outcome. The second remedial strategy consists of an apology, in which the accused essentially splits himself or herself into two parts: the guilty side and the side that "stands back and sympathizes with the blame giving, and, by implication, is worthy of being brought back into the fold" (p. 113). Finally, the accused can defend his or her actions by noting that the victim granted a request prior to the act and, therefore, is partly, if not, solely responsible for the outcome. Regardless of whether a person uses an account, apology, or request, Goffman argued that two distinct processes occur in remedial work. One is restitutive, in which the victim receives some form of compensation; the other is ritualistic, in which the offender relates his or her actions to the values that appear to have been broken. This ritualistic aspect serves a critical function because it establishes the remedial work as a public ritual in which both parties reaccept the society's values.

A couple of years after Goffman (1971), Ware and Linkugel (1973) set out to identify the characteristics of apologia and to describe the forms that these public defenses take. Drawing on Abelson's (1959) theory of belief-dilemma resolution, they described four factors that apologists use when caught in a wrong: denial, bolstering, differentiation, and transcendence. According to Ware and Linkugel, the first two factors—denial and bolstering—should be treated as *reformative* in the sense that the speaker does not "totally invent the identification" nor attempt to completely "change the audience's meaning" of the issue being discussed, but rather the speaker strives to revise or amend the audience's perceptions of it (pp. 275–277). Conversely, the second two factors—differentiation and transcendence—are *transformative* in the sense that communicators employ them to construct new realities and change meanings for the audience.

According to Ware and Linkugel (1973), a denial of an allegation or fact functions as a useful strategy (as long as the truth is not distorted) because it allows the apologist to respond to charges in a way that does not conflict with the values and beliefs of the audience. In contrast to denial, Ware and Linkugel asserted that bolstering takes place when an apologist "attempts to identify himself with something viewed favorably by the audience" (p. 277). While denial and bolstering are reformative, the third and fourth factors—differentiation and transcendence—are transformative. Differentiation comprises a discussion of the specific, detailed aspects of a broader action or accusation; in doing so, speakers attempt to redefine situations or cast their actions in a new, more detailed, and positive light. In contrast to differentiation, the fourth factor, transcendence, shifts the focus away from the particulars of a situation to the larger, conceptual ideals that the audience views favorably.

Ware and Linkugel (1973) also identified four rhetorical postures or subgenres of apologia that each consist of a transformative and a reformative factor: *absolution* (consisting of denial and differentiation), which seeks acquittal; *vindication* (denial and transcendence), which pursues the preservation of the offender's reputation or worth; *explanation* (bolstering and differentiation), which attempts to mitigate condemnation through clarification of motives; and *justification* (bolstering and transcendence), which targets understanding and approval from the audience.

These rhetorical postures get to the heart of image repair theory; that is, they highlight the end goals of apologists as well as how they achieve those goals. Notably, because Ware and Linkugel (1973) specifically examined apologia or "defensive" strategies, they did not identify postures that aimed at reconciling relationships or healing victims, but instead focused only on the goals of the speaker. This defensive perspective would be further developed in a series of articles and a book by Benoit, in which he examines how discourse can restore reputation and public image.

Based on the work of Goffman, Ware and Linkugel, Burke, and a number of account theory scholars (e.g., Schonbach, 1980; Scott & Lyman, 1968; Sykes & Matza, 1957; Tedeschi & Reiss, 1981), Benoit (1995a) offered perhaps the most comprehensive discussion of apologetic rhetoric and strategies. His image restoration theory encompasses five major strategies used by speakers: denial, evading responsibility, reducing offensiveness, corrective action, and mortification. In addition, Benoit advanced subcategories for each. The first strategy, denial, consists of two forms—(1) simple denial, in which the speaker denies the act or, at least, disavows taking part in it, and (2) shifting the blame, also known as scapegoating. The second strategy, evasion of responsibility, comprises (1) provocation, suggesting that the accused responded after being provoked; (2) defeasibility, suggesting that a lack of either information or control is actually to blame; (3) accidents, suggesting it was an accident; and (4) good intentions, suggesting that the accused performed the act with good intentions, despite the negative outcome. The third strategy details how apologists attempt to reduce the offensiveness of their wrongful acts by using (1) bolstering, such as describing the positive attributes and qualities of a person; (2) minimization, attempting to decrease the audience's negative view of the situation; (3) differentiation, focusing on how a particular situation differs from similar, yet much worse acts; (4) transcendence, discussing the act in terms of abstract values and group loyalties; (5) attacking the accuser to undermine his or her credibility; and (6) offering compensation to the victims. The fourth strategy, corrective action, refers to how apologists offer to repair damages caused by their actions, as well as take steps to prevent the event from happening again. The fifth and final strategy, mortification, extends from Burke's discussion of mortification in which the accused "admits wrongful behavior, asks for forgiveness, and apologizes" (Brinson & Benoit, 1999, p. 488).

Thus, scholars have identified a variety of strategies that people and corporations use when facing allegations of wrongdoing (see also Kelley & Waldron, 2006, for related literature review on forgiveness, and Meisenbach & McMillan (2006), for review of literature on organizational rhetoric). Although these diverse lists of strategies contain some similarities, the different terms and perspectives make understanding and applying those practices challenging. To help alleviate the confusion, Coombs (1999) outlined a concise method for evaluating situations and selecting appropriate responses. In his book, *Ongoing Crisis Communication*, Coombs specified the seven most common crisis communication strategies—attack the accuser, denial, excuse, justification, ingratiation, corrective action, and full apology. More importantly, he arranged these strategies on a continuum that moved from a strong defensive position (i.e., attack the accuser) to the most accommodative approach (i.e., full apology). Finally, Coombs positioned this continuum over another one that listed the level of responsibility that audiences perceive the organization to possess—ranging from weak (rumors) to strong (corporate misdeeds). The result of these overlapped continuums entails a visual representation that aligns the appropriate response with the perceived level of responsibility. For example, on the left side of the continuum, Coombs lists *rumors* above *attack the accuser*—indicating that the level of responsibility is low since rumors constitute unfounded statements or gossip. Based on the continuum, then, the appropriate response would be to attack the accuser, calling his or her information and motives into question.

In addition to the strategies and continuum, two important aspects of Coombs's work deserve to be pointed out more explicitly. First, Coombs's (1999) formula was intended to help crisis managers analyze situations and select appropriate responses. In that sense, Coombs offered a prescriptive approach that differed greatly from the descriptive methods of Ware and Linkugel (1973), Benoit (1995a), and others. In 2004, Koesten and Rowland also posed their theory of atonement as a prescriptive method for determining how to effectively respond to allegations of wrongdoing. Angela Jerome (2008, p. 132) affirmed the usefulness of their method as a "preliminary prescriptive framework." Finally, Smudde and Courtright (2008) made a similar case for a prospective approach to image repair theory and application, as opposed to the retrospective approaches that dominate this area of research.

In a second important aspect of his theory, Coombs (1999) explicitly referred to situations in which the communicators emphasize the victims, rather than the apologist. Whereas Benoit (1995a) described apologies as part of the mortification strategy employed by a "rhetor who desires to restore an image" (p. 79), Coombs situated full apologies as "helping the victims, even if it hurts the organization's reputation or financial status" (p. 122). In Coombs's theory, then, we see a shift that accounts for the needs of the victims in apologetic exchanges. This approach to balancing the needs of victims as well as the apologist would later become the main focus on Hearit's (2006) book, *Crisis Management by Apology*.

In an examination of corporate responses to accusations of wrongdoing, Hearit (2006) laid out a method for ethically judging the apologetic decisions of individuals and organizations alike. This method focuses on two aspects of apologetic discourse—the *manner* and the *content* of the apologia. In terms of the manner, Hearit asserted that, ideally, an ethical apologia is truthful, sincere, timely, and voluntary. Such a message also addresses all stakeholders, and communicators perform it in an appropriate context. In terms of the content, an ethical apologia should acknowledge wrongdoing, accept responsibility, express regret, identify with the victims, ask for forgiveness, seek reconciliation, disclose relevant information, provide an explanation that addresses the victims' questions and concerns, and offer corrective actions and compensation.

According to Hearit (2006), apologia involves complex decisions that impact a variety of stakeholders, including victims, stockholders, and employees. Based on these often competing moral obligations, it may not always be prudent to include each aspect in a public acknowledgment of wrongdoing. Consequently, the characteristics should serve more as a guide for the ideal or paradigm case of an ethical apologia. As such, an apologia that fails to meet one or several criteria, based on Hearit's model, is not necessarily unethical. Rather, it may be less ethical than the ideal but still judged ethically acceptable. Moreover, for Hearit, at least five circumstances "...could justify departures from the paradigm case while still retaining the essential ethical character of an apologia," such as catastrophic financial losses, grave liability issues, a "moral learning curve," questions over full disclosure, and even situations where confidentiality or discretion are expected (p. 74). Overall, this method facilitates our understanding of the ethical decisions involved in corporate apologia and enables us to evaluate how we can address the moral obligations to multiple stakeholders.

Inherent in the apologia and image repair theories above is the idea that apologetic exchanges involve more than a mere accusation of wrongdoing followed by a response or defense. Instead, they constitute ritualistic performances in which an individual or corporation seeks redemption back into a community or the repair of one's image after fracturing the values that bind a society together. According to this view of apologetic rhetoric, such redemption and reparation may be achieved by publicly acknowledging the offense, apologizing for it, and reaccepting the societal values. However, apologia and image repair theories also allow for the possibility that offenders may successfully restore their images without ever acknowledging the offense or apologizing but, instead, by merely aligning themselves or their actions with other important and favorable societal values.

### Studies of Apologia for Image Repair

I have noted the philosophical assumptions and theories of image repair at work in the numerous studies of apologia. Among the earliest and most analyzed area is political rhetoric. Dating back to the resurgence of apologetic exchanges as a genre of rhetoric in the late 1960s and 1970s, communication scholars focused on how public officials and political leaders responded to criticisms of the character and policies. Not surprisingly, many of these early studies focused on President Richard Nixon (Benoit, 1982; Harrell, Ware, & Linkugel, 1975; Katula, 1975; King, 1985; Rosenfield, 1968; Vartabedian, 1985a, 1985b). In our post-Watergate skeptical society, a number of presidents and presidential candidates have also garnered attention, due in large part to the controversies that have surrounded their presidencies or candidacies. For example, President Reagan's responses to Irangate have come under scrutiny (Abadi, 1990; Benoit, Gullifor, & Panici, 1991; Brummett, 1981); President Clinton's apologies for historic wrongs and his responses to the Monica Lewinsky scandal have provided fertile ground for analysis (Blaney & Benoit, 2001; Koesten

& Rowland, 2004; Kramer & Olson, 2002; Liebersohn, Neuman, & Beker-man, 2004; Simons, 2000); and most recently, George W. Bush's speeches and responses regarding Hurricane Katrina, Iraq, and the slowing economy have been analyzed as examples of presidential apologia (Benoit, 2006a, 2006b; Liu 2007). In addition, scholars have analyzed the apologetic discourse of various congressional representatives and senators (Kennedy & Benoit, 1997; Morello, 1979; Mueller, 2004; Short, 1987). Similarly, the remarks by Supreme Court Judge Clarence Thomas to the Senate Judiciary Committee regarding allega-tions of sexual harassment also garnered attention (Benoit & Nill, 1998b). As Abadi reflected, the attention on these individuals may be attributed to their prominence and the availability of artifacts as well as the greater likelihood of insincerity due to the nature and high stakes of the politics.

Throughout the 1990s and into the present decade, communication schol-ars have also focused heavily on the role of apologetic rhetoric in crisis com-munication. In fact, companies such as Union Carbide (Ice, 1991), Toshiba (Hearit, 1994; Hobbs, 1995), General Motors and NBC (Hearit, 1996), Sears (Benoit, 1995b), USAir (Benoit & Czerwinski, 1997), Dow Chemical (Hux-man & Bruce, 1995), AT&T (Benoit & Brinson, 1994); Dow Corning Corpora-tion (Brinson & Benoit, 1996), Johnson Controls (Hearit, 1997), Intel (Hearit, 1999), and Texaco (Brinson & Benoit, 1999; Coombs & Schmidt, 2000) com-prise just some of the companies that have been analyzed from a crisis com-munication perspective.

While these studies examined corporate responses to crisis, the nature of their subject matter also impacted other areas of communication studies. For example, the Texaco crisis examined by Brinson and Benoit (1999) and Coombs and Schmidt (2000) dealt with rampant racism within the company. In addition, other studies of apologia and image repair have examined the ongoing debates about race relations in America. For example, Carcasson and Aune (2003) analyzed Supreme Court Justice Hugo Black's 1937 radio address in which Black answered charges that he was a member of the Ku Klux Klan. Similarly, the analyses of Toshiba (Hearit, 1994; Hobbs, 1995) not only detailed how corporations respond to allegations of wrongdoing but also examined inter-national relations. Essentially, Toshiba became the central figure in the trade relations between the United States and Japan, as well as the military technol-ogy race between the United States and the Soviet Union. Taking the topic of international relations even further, other studies have focused on the role of apologetic rhetoric in the contentious relations between the United States and the former Soviet Union (Stein, 2008) as well as between the United States and Japan after the *USS Greenville* collided with the Japanese ship *Ehime Maru* (Drumheller & Benoit, 2004),

Popular culture has also gained popularity in studies of apologia and image repair. Since Kruse (1981a) first focused on the apologies of sports figures, studies of popular culture figures have branched out to include analyses of Billie Jean King (Nelson, 1984), Tonya Harding (Benoit & Hanczor, 1994), Oliver Stone (Benoit & Nill, 1998a), Hugh Grant (Benoit, 1997a), NASCAR driver Tony Stewart (Jerome, 2008), Queen Elizabeth after Princess Diana's death (Benoit & Brinson, 1999), and even King Edward's apologia after deciding to marry a commoner (Ryan, 1984). Perhaps one of the most unique and entertaining, however, was Benoit and Anderson's (1997) study of the fictional television character named Murphy Brown and her response to accusations made by Vice President Dan Quayle. The article examined not only apologia strategies but also the blurring of fantasy and reality.

Studies of apologia also have a long history within the field of mass communications, not only in terms of public relations and crisis communication but also advertising. For example, researchers have examined ads placed by Chrysler (Foss, 1984), Northwest Airlines (Cowden & Sellnow, 2002), Toshiba and Volvo (Hearit, 1994), and Exxon and Dominos (Hearit, 1995). In addition, Benoit and Brinson (1994) analyzed AT&T's letter to the public that was placed as an advertisement. Similarly, Benoit (1995a) explored the attack and defense statements in advertisements and open letters run by Pepsi and Coke during the "Cola Wars" of the 1980s. Other investigations of advertising include Benoit and Czerwinski's (1997) consideration of USAir's open letter ads and Benoit's (1995b) analysis of Sears's open letter ad. Advertising has been employed so heavily to deliver statements of apologetic rhetoric because it functions as an effective method for bypassing media gatekeepers and taking the message directly to the public (Hearit, 1994). Moreover, Veil (2005) also determined that this powerful method of delivery influences, at least to some extent, media coverage.

The field of technical and scientific communication has also gained new insight through the study of apologia. For example, Michael Moran (2003) focused on a commercial report written in 1586. Ralph Lane wrote the report in response to criticisms upon his return to England after leading a failed colony. Moran's project exemplifies the value of apologia theory as a lens for analyzing technical and business communications. Similarly, Johnson (2006) described how studying an apologia artifact may enable scholars to gain insight into technical processes. Johnson analyzed how Peter Hasenclever described the early American iron industry in a letter that he wrote to justify expenditures in 1773, thus, shedding light on the technical process of building ironworks and "the way knowledge traveled" before the use of printed technical manuals and reference books (p. 175). Timothy Sellnow (1993) examined the use of scientific ethos in Exxon's response to the Valdez oil spill, focusing specifically on the use of skepticism. Finally, Sullivan and Martin (2001) described how apologia and account theory can equip technical communicators to better understand and evaluate justifications for their actions. According to Sullivan and Martin, technical communicators who are faced with an ethical dilemma should ask themselves what accusations could result from their decisions and "what story will I tell about it when called to give an account" (p. 269). This body of research exemplifies how business and technical communication can be examined using apologetic rhetoric as a lens; however, a large gap still exists in our understanding of how reports and documents negotiate blame and responsibility.

As these examples demonstrate, apologetic rhetoric comprises a useful form of analysis in a wide range of fields within and related to communications studies. More importantly, the lines between these fields are not distinct; an analysis of one area may well inform another, as demonstrated by Brinson and Benoit's (1996) analysis of Dow Corning, which dealt as much with crisis management as it did with health care communication and the issue of full disclosure. However, not all scholars of apologetic rhetoric favor the rhetor-centered lens that apologia theories provide. Instead, some scholars question whether the underlying image repair theory is adequate or even accurate in examining complex issues such as health care communication, race relations, and political rhetoric.

## The Emerging Rhetoric of Apology for Reconciliation

A number of scholars have moved away from analyzing apologia and image repair theories in favor of analyzing apologies as part of reconciliation (for more on the definition and rhetorical conception of reconciliation, see Doxtader, 2003). In doing so, they distinguish between apologies that focus on the needs of the victims and apologia that focus on the face-saving desire of the rhetor. This distinction has prompted some scholars to argue for sub-genres of apologia that make room for the reconciliatory goal of apologies. For example, Koesten and Rowland (2004) argued that the rhetoric of atonement should be considered a sub-genre of apologia—one that seeks "both forgiveness for a sinful act and restoration of the relationship once the sin has been expiated" (p. 69). Villadsen (2008) agreed that a need exists for a sub-genre such as rhetoric of atonement; however, she preferred the name *official apology* because it was a more religiously neutral, inclusive term. Edwards (2005) identified what he called community-focused apologia, which begins the healing process between communities.

Finally, although Govier and Verwoerd (2002) did not mention apologia specifically, they did divide apologies into three forms: a defense, an excuse or account, and a moral apology, which contains an admission of wrongdoing without a justification or excuse (p. 67). A few years later, Govier (2006) expanded on that discussion by describing the eight characteristics of a moral apology: (1) acknowledging the wrongful act; (2) saying sorry for committing the act; (3) accepting moral responsibility for committing the act; (4) not justifying or excusing the act; (5) inviting forgiveness from the victim; (6) explicitly or implicitly stating that the victim deserved better treatment; (7) reassuring the victim that the harmful act or a similar act will not happen again; and (8) offering amends.

Other scholars have called for a more explicit, stronger separation of apology and apologia. For example, Hatch (2003) argued that apologies should not be considered through the cynical, self-interested lens of apologia at all. Instead, Hatch (2006b) stated that it should be explored in relation to forgiveness and reparations as "constituents of reconciliation" (p. 264). Nick Smith (2008) offered an even more extreme distinction—drawing a line between the ethically ideal *categorical apology* and other forms, including the *purely instrumental apology* (which he defined in a way that connotes apologia).

### Philosophical Assumptions

A critical element in this reconciliatory perspective involves the belief that the ultimate goal of the apologetic exchange constitutes forgiveness and restoration of social harmony (Tavuchis, 1991). This idea starkly contrasts with the image repair position that treats apologies as "a rhetoric of failure" in terms of their ability to repair social relationships (Hearit, 2006, p. 17). Much of the work that focuses on reconciliatory apologies, however, concentrates on rhetorical situations in which discourse must accomplish more than a reacceptance of values; it must pave the way for peaceful coexistence where hate and trauma once lived. Although the goal is lofty, Barkan and Karn (2006) explained how this healing power works:

> [T]he negotiation of apology works to promote dialogue, tolerance, and cooperation between groups knitted together uncomfortably (or ripped asunder) by some past injustice. A sincere expression of contrition, offered at the right pitch and tenor, can pave the way for atonement and reconciliation by promoting mutual understanding and by highlighting the possibilities for peaceful coexistence. (p. 7)

Lazare (2004) took an even stronger position on the role of apologies in reconciliation, stating that in situations "where there are no apologies, reconciliation is unlikely" (p. 232). He explained that it *is* possible to forgive a person who does not apologize, but such forgiveness only functions to remove hatred over a past injustice, rather than reconcile people or groups.

More recently, Melissa Nobles (2008) described how reconciliatory apologies move beyond the reacceptance of values called for in apologia to a redefinition of values that establishes a new social identity. In describing her membership theory of apologies, she argued that official government apologies actually "help change the terms and meanings of national membership" by supporting "certain views of national membership and history while displacing others" (pp. 2–3). Citing apologetic exchanges in the United States, Australia, and Canada relating to race relations, Nobles concluded that "political actors use apologies (or non-apologies) to express support for and advance the ideas and policies they favor…as platforms for announcing new policy directions and promoting societal reconciliation" (p. 111). Similarly, Michael Marrus (2007) argued that official apologies restore victims (not just the offenders) as members in the community. In addition, sincere apologies possess the potential to help alleviate the fear that a hate-filled ideology still lurks beneath the surface and that the shameful acts of human injustice may be repeated (Brooks, 1999; for related reviews, see Grey, 2007; Lacy, 2008; Pörhölä, Karhunen, & Rainivaara, 2006). The crux of such arguments is that official apologies comprise negotiations of guilt and responsibility as well as renegotiations of the society's collective memory, its interpretation of history, and who counts (and is valued) as members of the society (see related arguments by Armada, 1998; Carlson & Hocking, 1988; Dickinson, Ott, & Aoki, 2006; Hasian, 2005; Hasian & Carlson, 2000; Prosise, 1998; Stormer, 2003). As such, sincere exchanges of acknowledgment, remembrance, and contrition hold the power to move beyond *reaccepting* values to *restructuring* identity. Thus, a new internal social order results for the society in question as well as a new identity and way of relating to groups that were once considered nonmembers or even adversaries (Barkan & Karn, 2006; Edwards, 2005; Hatch 2006b). Apologies, then, can be progressive agents of change (Schwartz & Heinrich, 2006) that lead to a "more viable national identity and sense of moral community" (Nytagodien & Neal, 2004, p. 474).

## Theories of Analysis and Evaluation

Like their counterparts who study apologia and image repair strategies, proponents of reconciliation describe typologies or characteristics of successful apologies. For example, Lazare (2004) argued that the apology process includes acknowledging the offense, offering an explanation, communicating remorse, and offering reparations. Similarly, Edwards (2005) stated that community-focused apologies should consist of remembrance (a reckoning or explanation of the wrongs), reconciliation (identifying the victims and pledging to make amends), mortification (expressing remorse and asking for forgiveness), and atonement or some form of corrective action. Hatch (2006a) stated that reconciliation rhetoric consists of the offender confessing the truth and apologizing, the victims forgiving the offenders, and both the offender and victims engaging in discussions of reparations and restorative justice.

Finally, Marrus (2007) and Negash (2006) focused on official apologies as a way toward reconciliation and justice for historical wrongs. According to Marrus, the apology must include an acknowledgment of wrongdoing, acceptance of responsibility, an expression of regret and remorse, and reparation and a commitment to not commit the wrong again. Similarly, Negash argued that successful apologies encompass acknowledgment, accountability, truth-telling, and public remorse. However, Negash distinguished between two types or levels of apologies—those that are meant to mend relationships and those that are meant to heal relationships. Apologies that seek to mend a relationship prioritize repair so that it can function again. As such, apologies that mend need only meet the first two criteria—acknowledgment and accountability—to be successful. Apologies with the purpose of healing relationships, however, aim at reconciling societies. As such, they require all four criteria to be successful.

### Studies of Apologies for Reconciliation

Over the past 20 years, scholars from a wide range of fields and disciplines have helped shed light on the healing and redemptive nature of apologetic exchanges. For example, Tavuchis (1991) examined the sociology of apologies and reconciliation—focusing on offenses as violations of values or morality that require acknowledgment of responsibility, expressions of sorrow and contrition, and corrective action to ensure the offense is not repeated in the future. In addition, he identified and described four types or configurations that apologies can take: apologies from one person to another (One to One), from one individual to a collective group (One to the Many), from a collective group to one individual (Many to One), and from a collective group to another collective group (Many to Many). In doing so, Tavuchis drew insights from disciplines such as philosophy, linguistics, anthropology, law, and religion to examine the meanings, functions, and cultural aspects of apologies. He concluded with a call for further research on the culture of apologies as well as the influence of parents, the media, and popular etiquette guides, such as *The Amy Vanderbilt Complete Book of Etiquette* (Vanderbilt, 1978), *The New Emily Post's Etiquette* (Post, 1975), and *Miss Manners' Guide to Excruciatingly Correct Behavior* (Martin, 1982).

Lazare (2004) and Smith (2005, 2008) offered insight into apologetic exchanges through the lens of psychology. Lazare approached the subject from the perspective of the shame and guilt inherent in apologetic exchanges. He explained the psychology behind why some people apologize while others are hesitant, as well as how apologies lead to healing. Smith (2005), on the other hand, examined the ethics of apologies and identified what he termed a *categorical apology* as the ideal example.

According to Smith (2005), categorical apologies consist of nine elements that people seek in full apologies: a corroboration of the facts, acceptance of causal responsibility, identification of each moral wrong that underlies the harmful event, commitment to shared moral values, unequivocal regret, an actual expression or performance of the apology (rather than alluding to or symbolizing it), reform and reparations as well as the authority to issue an apology for the specific act, and finally the right intentions for offering the apology. Using the standards of the categorical apology as a benchmark, Smith (2008) analyzed collective apologies and described how they often fail to meet the standards and, as a result, obscure important issues such as blame.

Scholars of other disciplines have also focused on apologetic rhetoric. For example, historian Robert Weyeneth (2001) examined the ways that societies apologize for historical wrongs. As part of his survey, he identified acts such as setting aside a day of remembrance, constructing memorials, renaming streets and parks, and issuing pardons as forms of apology. Law professor Roy Brooks (1999), on the other hand, edited a collection of essays and narratives that examined the legal and political issues surrounding reparations for human injustices that cannot be resolved through apologies alone.

In addition, political apologies have been examined through a reconciliatory lens. In contrast to apologia scholars who view such apologies as instances of face-saving or image repair, apology scholars such as Dodds (2003) argued that political apologies are understudied, especially in their ability to promote healing in such areas as the Middle East, the former Yugoslavia, Rwanda, and Burundi. In an effort to shed light on these important instances of apologetic rhetoric, Harris, Grainger, and Mullany (2006) asserted that political apologies involve more important aspects than protecting the reputation of the apologizer. In addition, they specified four characteristics of political apologies: (1) political apologies are offered in the public domain and receive prominent coverage in the media; (2) they are typically the result of high-profile controversies or demands for apologies; (3) they often must include explicit statements of responsibility in order to be viewed as valid; and (4) responses to political apologies rarely contain explicit statements of absolution. Along with these characteristics, Harris et al. identified three distinct types of political apology: social gaffes, serious past offenses, and current offenses that hold serious political implications. An important summative point of their study is that political apologies must not only focus on the needs and reputation of the apologizer but rather must include explicit statements of responsibility. In this sense, we can easily recognize how political apologies that do not meet these expectations of the victims and the audience may ultimately have a boomerang or reverse effect (see Byrne & Hart, this volume, for a deeper discussion of boomerang effects).

Political scientists Negash (2006) and Nobles (2008) have each examined state apologies for past atrocities. Negash studied apologies offered from one nation to another and listed four necessary criteria for healing and reconciliation to take place: acknowledgment of the act, truth-telling, accountability, and public remorse. Conversely, Nobles analyzed the politics involved when a nation delivers an official apology to oppressed people who live within its borders but who are not or have not been considered citizens or full members of that society (such as Native Americans and African Americans in the United States and Aboriginal people in Australia). Danielle Celermajer (2006) also investigated the issue of political apologies in Australia for past wrongs against the Aboriginal people. As such, she contended that such apologies constitute gestures of responsibility that the collective community can and must bear. Similarly, Rebecca Tsosie (2006) discussed the Bureau of Indian Affairs' (BIA's) apology for the brutal acts against Native Americans. In doing so, she illuminated the role of collective memory in establishing collective responsibility for acts of atrocities (see also Schwartz & Heinrich, 2006, for more on public memory, individual responsibility, and apologies). Christopher Buck (2006) also explored the BIA's apology, focusing on the legal ramifications and the legitimacy of it. According to Buck, the apology was an important isolated moment; however, it remains a semi-official gesture due to the federal government's failure to issue an official apology, followed by substantive actions to repair the harm done.

In addition, Hatch (2003, 2006a, 2006b) examined the ongoing debate regarding the past injustices of slavery and the lack of an official apology that might help ease tensions and lead to reconciliation. Dexter Gordon and Carrie Crenshaw (2004) also examined racial apologies, focusing specifically on the role of such apologies in the antiracism movement. Ultimately, Gordon and Crenshaw (2004) argued that racial apologies hold little to no potential for promoting antiracism so long as they discuss racism only in terms of the past, without also acknowledging and addressing the ongoing existence of White privilege (see also related review by Lacy, 2008).

Finally, an important area of research gaining momentum recently focuses on the role of apologetic rhetoric in health care communication. One of the most important discussions to emerge in this area entails the argument for issuing apologies along with full disclosure in the event of medical errors. For example, Leonard Berlin (2006) cited quantitative research that links partial apologies (that do not admit wrongdoing) to reduced malpractice suits. Lazare (2006), on the other hand, described the healing powers of apologies that convey guilt and asserted that "[a]s with other activities that have the power to heal, it is essential that physicians develop skills and ethical principles to use apologies effectively and honestly...with patients" (p. 1404). Similarly, Taft (2005) maintained that pseudo-apologies that do not acknowledge responsibility actually cause additional harm to patients and disrupt the healing process of apologies that both patients and physicians seek. Harter, Stephens, and Japp (2000) alluded to this tension between acknowledging regret and responsibility versus offering pseudo-apologies that do not admit wrongdoing in their analysis of President Clinton's apology for the Tuskegee Institute's syphilis experiments on African Americans. According to their study, rather than offer a statement of acknowledgment and regret for the medical abuses that took place, Clinton minimized the medical abuses by positioning the experiments as a racial incident that merely darkens our past. Then, in an injurious twist, Clinton did not concentrate on the culpability of the medical industry for its role in the experiments but, instead, used his speech to highlight and praise the medical advancements and benefits of the U.S. health care system.

Another prominent example to emerge from the discussion of medical apologetic rhetoric is the decision by the Veterans Affairs Medical Center (VAMC) in Lexington, Kentucky to admit medical mistakes and issue apologies. In analyzing these practices, Jonathan Cohen (2001) remarked that issuing apologies benefits the VAMC financially as well as entails the ethically responsible course of action after injuring another person. In addition, Heather Carmack (2008) conducted an in-depth analysis of the VAMC's practices, focusing on the narrative expressions as well as the emotional redemptive journeys of physicians and staff. In doing so, she argued that the VAMC's policy actually changes the way that stakeholders interact with patients by providing new narratives that shape the discourse surrounding medical mistakes.

## Potential Gaps and Limitations

Taken as a whole, the theoretical framework and wide variety of studies discussed appear to offer a broad array of strategies and components with which to understand, analyze, and, in some cases, evaluate nearly every artifact of apologetic rhetoric that one might come across. The problem, however, may not be in the number of strategies available, but rather in the types of apologetic exchanges—in the artifacts, in the rhetors, in the delivery methods—that have been incorporated into those theories. In other words, has the majority of work focused on articulating subtle differences between mostly similar components, at the expense of branching out to understand different forms of apologia and reconciliation settings? That is, have we, as apologia scholars, broadened the number of strategies without adequately broadening our knowledge base?

Therefore, I argue that the field of rhetoric dedicated to analyzing apologetic exchanges warrants more critical analysis. Questions that deserve exploration include: What artifacts are our current theories based on (e.g., speeches, press releases, transcripts of group-to-group exchanges, and so on)? What media were predominantly used to originally deliver those artifacts? To what extent do those artifacts represent the apologetic rhetoric of non-Western communities, of women, or of minorities? In other words, how have we come to know what we claim to know, and what areas might we have overlooked thus far? Based on this review of the literature,[1] I uncovered four key gaps and limitations of research on this topic to date: (1) steady, yet disproportionate growth; (2) insufficient female representation; (3) overemphasis on oration and traditional media; and (4) lack of non-Western voices.

### *Steady Yet Disproportionate Growth*

The study of apologetic rhetoric has risen steadily since Rosenfield published his 1968 article on apologia (see Table 11.1). However, this growth does not necessarily mean that the field has expanded proportionately in the number of scholars who study and publish academic articles on apologies. To the contrary, in some breakdowns of the decades, a disproportionate number of studies can be attributed to two or three prolific scholars. For instance, 31 articles appear in the 1990s column (see Table 11.1). Of those articles, Benoit wrote 22, either as a sole or coauthor, and Hearit wrote another five. In other words, of the 31 articles listed under the 1990s column, the majority were partially or completely developed by just two scholars, accounting for some of the patterns or tendencies identified in this survey.

### *Insufficient Female Representation*

With the exception of two articles devoted exclusively to the apologetic rhetoric of women, authors almost exclusively cite male rhetors (see Table 11.2).

*Table 11.1* Articles by Decade

| 1960s | 1970s | 1980s | 1990s | | 2000s | |
|-------|-------|-------|-------|-------|-------|-------|
| Rosenfeld (1968) | Butler (1972) | Brummett (1981) | Abadi (1990) | McLennan (1996) | Coombs & Schmidt (2000) | Liebersohn, Neuman, & Bekerman (2004) |
| | Ware & Linjugel (1973) | Kruse (1981a) | Brown (1990) | Benoit (1997a) | Harter, Stephens, & Japp (2000) | Mueller (2004) |
| | Harrell, Ware, & Linkugel (1975) | Benoit (1982) | Burkholder (1990) | Benoit & Anderson (1997) | Simons (2000) | Suzuki & van Eemeren (2004) |
| | Katula (1975) | Ryan (1982) | Benoit, Guillifor, & Paniol (1991) | Benoit & Czerwinski (1997) | Blaney (2001) | Yamazaki (2004) |
| | Kruse (1977) | Blair (1984) | Ice (1991) | Blaney & Benoit (1997) | Courtright & Hearit (2002) | Zhang & Benoit (2004) |
| | Gold (1978) | Foss (1984) | Schultz & Seeger (1991) | Hearit (1997) | Cowden & Sellnow (2002) | Armstrong, Hallmark, & Williamson (2005) |
| | Morello (1979) | Kahl (1984) | Sellnow (1993) | Kennedy & Benoit (1997) | Govier & Verwoerd (2002) | Edwards (2005) |
| | | Ryan (1984) | Benoit & Brinson (1994) | Benoit (1998) | Kramer & Olson (2002) | Veil (2005) |
| | | Nelson (1984) | Benoit & Hanczor (1994) | Benoit & Nill (1998) | Carcasson & Aune (2003) | Buck (2006) |
| | | King (1985) | Hearit (1994) | Sullivan (1998) | Hearit & Courtright (2003) | Hatch (2006a) |
| | | Vartabedian (1985a) | Benoit (1995b) | Thomsen & Rawson (1998) | Moran (2003) | Benoit (2006a) |
| | | Vartabedian (1985b) | Hearit (1995) | Benoit & McHale (1999) | Vartabedian & Vartabedian (2003) | Benoit (2006b) |
| | | Short (1987) | Hobbs (1995) | Benoit & Brinson (1999) | Coombs (2004) | Johnson (2006) |
| | | Benson (1988) | Huxman & Bruce (1995) | Brinson & Benoit (1999) | Drumheller & Benoit (2004) | Liu (2007) |
| | | Hoover (1989) | Brinson & Benoit (1996) | Hearit (1999) | Hearit & Brown (2004) | Tian (2007) |
| | | Nethercote (1989) | Hearit (1996) | | Koesten & Rowland (2004) | Edwards (2008) |
| | | | | | Len-Rios & Benoit (2004) | Jerome (2008) |
| | | | | | | Stein (2008) |
| | | | | | | Villadsen (2008) |

Perhaps somewhat surprisingly, the first female rhetor to appear chronologically in this survey is Tonya Harding. Benoit and Hanczor (1994) analyzed Harding's image restoration strategies that occurred in her television interview with Connie Chung. They concluded that Harding's strategy was ineffective because it put forth an image that was inconsistent with audience perceptions. The only other article in this study that focused exclusively on the apologetic rhetoric of a female was Benoit and Brinson's (1999) analysis of Queen Elizabeth's use of image restoration strategies. After the death of Princess Diana, the Royal Family's silence resulted in a tarnished image. Benoit and Brinson argued that the Queen's use of denial and bolstering (as major strategies) along with defeasibility and transcendence (as minor strategies) were effective in restoring that image.

In addition to the two articles that focused exclusively on female rhetors, one other article did focus partially on a female rhetor. Nelson (1984) analyzed the apologetic rhetoric of Billie Jean King; however, he also concentrated significantly on additional male peers and even the media (as third-party apologetic rhetors). I classified this article as an analysis of multiple rhetors; however, even if I included it in the female category for the sake of argument, only three articles focused on female rhetors out of a possible 91.

### Overemphasis on Oration and Traditional Media

Third, I examined articles according to the type of medium that they analyzed (see Table 11.3). I divided the mediums into oration (such as speeches and other statements addressed to a present audience); traditional media (including rhetoric delivered through television interviews, statements broadcast only via television, print news services, books, and even letters to the public printed in newspapers); new media (which included electronic as well as alternative mediums of rhetoric, such as e-mail, chat rooms, Web sites, mobile text messages, and even comic books); business and technical documents (such as reports, internal letters and memos, product documentation, and corporate press kits); and multiple media (indicating that two or more methods of delivery were analyzed).

Not surprisingly, the two methods most often used for delivery are public oration and traditional media. In fact, only three articles examined new and alternative media. Hearit (1999) analyzed Intel's apologia that was posted on an electronic newsgroup, while Mueller (2004) explored House Speaker Dennis Hastert's Web posting as a pre-emptive apologia regarding his decision to remove the Armenian Genocide resolution from the House schedule. Finally, Short (1987) examined Representative Hansen's comic book apologia. He concluded that the comic book medium allowed for an overly polarized sense of logic. Similarly, only three articles fell under the category of business or technical documents (Coombs, 2004; Huxman & Bruce, 1995; Moran, 2003).

*Table 11.2* Gender/Type of Rhetor/Apologist

| Male | | | Female | Organiz. | Institution | Muliple |
|------|------|------|--------|----------|-------------|---------|
| Rosenfeld (1968) | Burkholder (1990) | Kramer & Olson (2002) | Benoit & Hanczor (1994) | Foss (1984) | Courtright & Hearit (2002) | Nelson (1984) |
| Butler (1972) | Benoit, Gullifor, & Panici (1991) | Carcasson & Aune (2003) | Benoit & Brinson (1999) | Benson (1988) | Drumheller & Benoit (2004) | |
| Ware & Linkugel (1973) | Schultz & Seeger (1991) | Moran (2003 | | Ice (1991) | | |
| Harrell, Ware, & Linkugel (1975) | Sellnow (1993) | Vartabedian & Vartabedian (2003) | | Benoit & Brinson (1994) | Zhang & Benoit (2004) | |
| Katula (1975) | McLennan (1996) | Koesten & Rowland (2004) | | Hearit (1994) | Tian (2007) | |
| Kruse (1977) | Benoit (1997a) | Mueller (2004) | | Benoit (1995b) | Stein (2008) | |
| Gold (1978) | Blaney & Benoit (1997) | Len-Rios & Benoit (2004) | | Hearit (1995) | | |
| Morello (1979) | Kennedy & Benoit (1997) | Liebersohn, Neuman, & Bekerman (2004) | | Hobbs (1995) | | |
| Brummett (1981) | Benoit (1998) | Suzuki & van Eemeren (2004) | | Huxman & Bruce (1995) | | |
| Kruse (1981a) | Benoit & Nill (1998) | Yamazaki (2004) | | Brinson & Benoit (1996) | | |
| Ryan (1982) | Sullivan (1998) | Armstrong, Hallmark, & Williamson (2005) | | Hearit (1996) | | |
| Benoit (1982) | Benoit & McHale (1999) | Edwards (2005) | | Benoit & Anderson (1997) | | |
| Blair (1984) | Brinson & Benoit (1999) | Veil (2005) | | Benoit & Czerwinski (1997) | | |
| Kahl (1984) | | Benoit (2006a) | | Hearit (1997) | | |
| Ryan (1984) | Coombs & Schmidt (2000) | Benoit (2006b) | | Thomsen & Rawson (1998) | | |
| King (1985) | Harter, Stephens, & Japp (2000) | Buck (2006) | | Hearit (1999) | | |
| Vartabedian (1985a) | Simons (2000) | Hatch (2006a) | | Cowden & Sellnow (2002) | | |
| Vartabedian (1985b) | Blaney (2000) | Johnson (2006) | | Hearit & Courtright (2003) | | |
| Short (1987) | Govier & Verwoerd (2002) | Liu (2007) | | Coombs (2004) | | |
| Hoover (1989) | | Edwards (2008) | | Hearit & Brown (2004) | | |
| Nethercote (1989) | | Jerome (2008) | | | | |
| Abadi (1990) | | Villadsen (2008) | | | | |
| Brown (1990) | | | | | | |

Table 11.3  Medium/Method of Delivery

| Oration | | Traditional Media | | New Media | |
|---|---|---|---|---|---|
| Ware & Linjugel (1973) | Benoit & Brinson (1999) | Rosenfeld (1968) | Benoit & Czerwinski (1997) | Short (1987) | |
| Harrell, Ware, & Linkugel (1975) | Harter, Stephens, & Japp (2000) | Butler (1972) | Blaney & Benoit (1997) | Hearit (1999) | |
| Katula (1975) | Govier & Verwoerd (2002) | Blair (1984) | Benoit & Nill (1998) | Mueller (2004) | |
| Kruse (1977) | Hearit & Brown (2004) | Foss (1984) | Sullivan (1998) | | |
| Gold (1978) | Liebersohn, Neuman, & Bekerman (2004) | Kahl (1984) | Benoit & McHale (1999) | **Business/Tech Docs** | |
| Morello (1979) | Suzuki & van Eemeren (2004) | Nelson (1984) | Simons (2000) | Huxman & Bruce (1995) | Coombs (2004) |
| Benoit (1982) | Yamazaki (2004) | Nethercote (1989) | Blaney (2001) | Moran (2003) | |
| Ryan (1982) | Edwards (2005) | Brown (1990) | Cowden & Sellnow (2002) | | |
| Ryan (1984) | Benoit (2006a) | Schultz & Seeger (1991) | Carcasson & Aune (2003) | **Multiple Media** | |
| Vartabedian (1985a) | Buck (2006) | Benoit & Brinson (1994) | Vartabedian & Vartabedian (2003) | Brummett (1981) | Coombs & Schmidt (2000) |
| Vartabedian (1985b) | Hatch (2006a) | Benoit & Hanczor (1994) | Drumheller & Benoit (2004) | Kruse (1981a) | Courtright & Hearit (2002) |
| Burkholder (1990) | Liu (2007) | Hearit (1994) | Armstrong, Hallmark, & Williamson (2005) | King (1985) | Kramer & Olson (2002) |
| Benoit, Guillifor, & Paniol (1991) | Edwards (2008) | Benoit (1995b) | Veil (2005) | Benson (1988) | Hearit & Courtright (2003) |
| Sellnow (1993) | Villadsen (2008) | Hearit (1995) | Benoit (2006b) | Hoover (1989) | Koesten & Rowland (2004) |
| Hearit (1997) | | Brinson & Benoit (1996) | Johnson (2006) | Abadi (1990) | Len-Rios & Benoit (2004) |
| Benoit (1998) | | McLennan (1996) | | Ice (1991) | Zhang & Benoit (2004) |
| | | Benoit (1997a) | | Hobbs (1995) | Tian (2007) |
| | | Benoit & Anderson (1997) | | Hearit (1996) | Jerome (2008) |
| | | | | Kennedy & Benoit (1997) | Stein (2008) |
| | | | | Thomsen & Rawson (1998) | |
| | | | | Brinson & Benoit (1999) | |

### Lack of Non-Western Voices

Finally, the vast majority of apologetic rhetoric articles feature the discourse of Western rhetors (see Table 11.4). In fact, 75 of the 91 articles analyzed examples of Western apologetic rhetoric, and all but six encompassed examples from North America. Four articles focused exclusively on the apologetic rhetoric in Asia (Edwards, 2005; Hobbs, 1995; Suzuki & van Eemeren, 2004; Yamazaki, 2004), which is just two less than the number that focused specifically on the apologetic rhetoric of Europeans (Benoit & Brinson, 1999; Johnson, 2006; Moran, 2003; Ryan 1982; Sullivan, 1998; Villadsen, 2008). Although two articles focused exclusively on the apologetic rhetoric of the Middle East (Blaney & Benoit, 1997; Zhang & Benoit, 2004), an additional two included Middle East rhetoric along with other geographic regions (Abadi, 1990; Liebersohn, Neuman, & Bekerman, 2004). Finally, only two articles examined African apologetic rhetoric in detail (Edwards, 2008; Govier & Verwoerd, 2002), with no articles describing the apologetic rhetoric of South America.

## Implications for the Study of Apologetic Rhetoric

In this chapter, I have argued that recent academic work on apologetic rhetoric has expanded this area of study to a wide array of important fields, including health care communication, race relations, cultural studies, and intercultural communication. However, this growth has also fostered overarching discussions about terms to define and analyze apologetic exchanges. In addition, I contend that, despite the recent growth, gaps have silently developed, given our tendencies as researchers to examine certain types of exchanges and rhetors instead of others. Based on these conclusions, I offer two calls for future work in the area of apologetic rhetoric.

### Commingling of Terms

Recent studies of apologetic rhetoric inherently include discussions relating to how we define—and, ultimately, distinguish—apologia, image repair strategies, and reconciliatory rhetoric. While these definitions are helpful in more deeply analyzing apologetic stances, they may have the unintended consequence of alienating scholars who might otherwise learn from and support each other's research. Already, ascendancy and descendancy searches of the articles in this review indicate that scholars from one perspective may unintentionally overlook the research of the others.

In an attempt to bridge such divides, I have purposely focused on the wide range of perspectives—drawing insights from apologia, image repair strategies, and reconciliatory apologies. I have also tried to use the broader terms *apologetic rhetoric* and *apologetic exchanges* in instances when the use of a specific term (such as *apologia*) might inaccurately define the perspective or multiple perspectives under discussion. I have selected this term—*apologetic*

*Table 11.4* Geographic Regions

| North America | | | | Europe | |
|---|---|---|---|---|---|
| Rosenfeld (1968) | Brown (1990) | Benoit & Anderson (1997) | Hearit & Courtright (2003) | Ryan (1982) | Moran (2003) |
| Butler (1972) | Burkholder (1990) | Benoit & Czerwinski (1997) | Vartabedian & Vartabedian (2003) | Sullivan (1998) | Johnson (2006) |
| Harrell, Ware, & Linkugel (1975) | Benoit, Gullifor, & Panici (1991) | Benoit (1998) | Coombs (2004) | Benoit & Brinson (1999) | Villadsen (2008) |
| Katula (1975) | Ice (1991) | Benoit & Nill (1998) | Drumheller & Benoit (2004) | | |

| | | | | *Mid East* | *Africa* | *Asia* |
|---|---|---|---|---|---|---|
| Gold (1978) | Schultz & Seeger (1991) | Thomsen & Rawson (1998) | Hearit & Brown (2004) | Blaney & Benoit (1997) | Govier & Verwoerd (2002) | Hobbs (1995) |
| Morello (1979) | Sellnow (1993) | Benoit & McHale (1999) | Koesten & Rowland (2004) | Zhang & Benoit (2004) | Edwards (2008) | Edwards (2005) |
| Brummett (1981) | Benoit & Brinson (1994) | Brinson & Benoit (1999b) | Len-Rios & Benoit (2004) | | | Suzuki & van Eemeren (2004) |
| Kruse (1981a) | Benoit & Hanczor (1994) | Hearit (1999) | Mueller (2004) | | | Yamazaki (2004) |
| Benoit (1982) | Benoit (1995b) | Coombs & Schmidt (2000) | | | | |

| | | | | *S. Amer.* | *Australia* | *Multiple* |
|---|---|---|---|---|---|---|
| Blair (1984) | Hearit (1995) | Harter, Stephens, & Japp (2000) | Armstrong, Hallmark, & Williamson (2005) | | Nethercote (1989) | Ware & Linkugel (1973) |
| Foss (1984) | Huxman & Bruce (1995) | Simons (2000) | Veil (2005) | | | Kruse (1977) |
| Kahl (1984) | Brinson & Benoit (1996) | Blaney (2001) | Benoit (2006a) | | | Abadi (1990) |
| Ryan (1984) | Hearit (1996) | Courtright & Hearit (2002) | Benoit (2006b) | | | Hearit (1994) |
| Nelson (1984) | McLennan (1996) | Cowden & Sellnow (2002) | Buck (2006) | | | Liebersohn, Neuman, & Bekerman (2004) |
| King (1985) | Benoit (1997a) | Kramer & Olson (2002) | Hatch (2006a) | | | Tian (2007) |
| Vartabedian (1985a) | Hearit (1997) | Carcasson & Aune (2003) | Liu (2007 | | | Stein (2008) |
| Vartabedian (1985b) | Kennedy & Benoit (1997) | | Jerome (2008) | | | |
| Short (1987) | | | | | | |
| Benson (1988) | | | | | | |
| Hoover (1989) | | | | | | |

*rhetoric*—because it bears strong connections to the defensive strategies of image repair (as conveyed in the term *apologetics*, or the theological defense of a religious belief) as well as to expressions of remorse and regret (as in, being apologetic). Therefore, I offer this chapter's use of the term *apologetic rhetoric* as an example of how apologies and apologia can be discussed in such a way that they are combined, yet remain distinct. Future studies could benefit from using this terminology or a similar umbrella term that allows for connections to be made and for researchers to influence and shape the work of each other, regardless of which specific term they prefer to analyze. Moreover, rather than referring to Koesten and Rowland's (2004) *rhetoric of atonement*, Edwards's (2005) *community-focused apologia*, or Burkholder's (1990) *symbolic martyrdom* as sub-genres of apologia, we might more accurately label them as sub-genres of apologetic rhetoric or apologetic discourse.

### Minding the Gap

This review indicates that the current theories of apologetic rhetoric are based upon studies that largely analyze similar examples of apologetic rhetoric—specifically, the rhetoric of Western males who deliver their apologies through oration or traditional media. As such, gaps clearly exist in the study of the apologetic rhetoric of women and individuals living in Asia, Africa, the Middle East, and South America. The lack of female representation is particularly disturbing in light of Lazare's (2004) claim that woman apologize more frequently than men and are now emerging as leaders of corporate, government, and professional organizations (p. 16). We still lack information about the ways in which female apologists impact apologetic exchanges—not in terms of stereotypes, but in terms of actual discursive practices (for more on gender, communication and social change, see Medved, this volume). The current literature provides little to no understanding of whether women publicly apologize the same as men and whether our current theories of apologetic rhetoric even apply. We need a concerted effort to seek out and examine the apologetic discourse of women—using our current theories as well as remaining open to discover new attributes of apologetic rhetoric.

Similarly, we should explore non-Western apologetic exchanges. Many of the communities most in need of healing and reconciliation exist in seldom visited areas with less formal documentation and distribution of discourse, such as the Middle East (Friedman, 2007), Rwanda (Onyango-Obbo, 2008), Burundi (Gettleman, 2008), the Congo (Polgreen, 2008), Darfur (Gettleman, 2006), and, most recently, Georgia (Tavernise & Siegel, 2008). However, I argue that our heavily Western-based theories and understandings are not yet inclusive enough to be applied in these areas. The field of apologetic rhetoric has made strides in understanding Eastern apologetic situations and meanings (e.g., Huang, Lin, & Su, 2005; Yamazaki, 2005; Sugimoto, 1999). In addition, some cross-cultural studies of apologies have been undertaken (e.g., Renteln, 2008; Howard-Hassman & Lombardo, 2008). However, as Renteln (2008) concluded, "[t]he dearth of empirical data on cross-cultural status of apologies leaves us in a sorry state" (p. 73). In order for us to truly understand apologetic discourse in diverse communities, we should gain access to and learn from apologetic exchanges in a wide variety of locations and cultures. Otherwise, we fall into the trap of analyzing and even evaluating discourse that we don't understand and applying standards that stakeholders in various parts of the world may never have intended to address.

Finally, we cannot ignore that little work has been done regarding the impact on new media rhetoric and business and technical documents. These fields represent burgeoning areas of communication scholarship with the potential to reshape what we know about public apologetic exchanges, and deserve more focused research by scholars of apologetic rhetoric.

Further research on the apologetic exchanges and strategies of these underrepresented individuals and communities could enable us to answer questions such as: What do we know about apologetic exchanges of women, of non-Western rhetors? When do our current strategies apply, and when do they breakdown? Are our Western-based theories even applicable in non-Western settings, or do we need new, more inclusive models that build from rather than subordinate non-Western apologies? What other strategies and perspectives exist? Only by purposefully exploring these often overlooked aspects can we as scholars of apologetic rhetoric truly develop a broader, more all-encompassing foundation from which to analyze and evaluate the wide variety of apologetic exchanges produced in diverse communication and cultural contexts throughout the world.

## Acknowledgments

I would like to thank Dr. Sean Zdenek and Dr. Ken Baake at Texas Tech University, who read earlier drafts of this chapter, asked challenging questions, and provided encouragement and support. I would also like to thank Dr. Christina Beck, her assistant Jennifer Scott, and the four anonymous reviewers who took the time to read this chapter multiple times and to provide insight, advice, and suggestions along the way. Finally, I'd like to thank my wife, Heidi, who read a number of drafts, listened patiently as I talked through my research, and offered a fresh perspective when I needed it most.

## Notes

1. I collected articles using key-term searches (e.g., *apologia, apology, image restoration, image repair*, and *reconciliation*, as well as *strategies* and *typologies*) of two academic databases—JSTOR and EBSCO Academic Search Premiere— as well as Google Scholar. In addition, I conducted ascendancy and descendancy searches to identify additional articles. These searches resulted in 116 academic articles. After conducting these searches, I reviewed the findings to eliminate articles that did not fit the established characteristics of the study (described below).

To be included in the study, articles (a) must have been published in an academic journal between 1968 and 2008; (b) must focus specifically on apologetic rhetoric as defined broadly; and (c) must offer a detailed analysis or evaluation of one or more case studies. Based on these qualifications, I did not include articles that exclusively discussed theory—but did not specifically focus on analysis or evaluation—in the study. Similarly, I excluded news articles, books, and book chapters. The review of the 116 articles resulted in 25 articles not matching the qualifications. After removing the 25 unqualified articles, I focused on 91 academic articles published between 1968 and 2008 that offered a detailed analysis of one or more apologetic exchanges.

I systematically analyzed the 91 remaining articles using pre-defined units of analysis listed on coding sheets relating to the gender or type (organization or institution), geographic region, and medium or method of delivery. In each of the 91 articles, the *rhetor* was analyzed based on these categories. For example, in Hatch's (2006a) analysis of Representative Hall's speech in Africa to a largely African audience, I categorized the article as a male from North America delivering a speech since those categories represent the rhetor that Hatch analyzed. When an article explored more than one instance of the same category (e.g., two different speeches), I still classified the article under the appropriate category (i.e., oration). However, if two different categories comprised the subject of the article (e.g., one male and one female rhetor), I assigned the article to the category of *multiple* (i.e., multiple mediums). Finally, in the event that an article analyzed rhetoric designated as official communications of an organization or institution (e.g., press releases), I labeled the gender/type of rhetor as an organization or institution. However, if a high-profile person acted as the sole rhetor (despite defending the corporation or being employed by the corporation), I put that rhetor into the appropriate category of either male or female. I took every precaution to best identify and accurately categorize the background of the rhetor and the delivery method of the rhetoric that was analyzed in each of the 91 articles. In the event that an article explored more than one person or method of delivery, I did not make a judgment call as to which category the article belonged in more. Instead, I classified that aspect of the article as multiple to help ensure against misrepresentations in the survey data.

During the survey, I made no changes or additions to the categories. In addition, I included all categories (even those without any articles) in the tables and examination of the findings (see MacNealy, 1999). After I compiled and analyzed the statistical data from these coding sheets, I examined major themes and possible oversights in greater detail to provide deeper insight and answer the research questions above.

# References

Abadi, A. (1990). The speech act of apology in political life. *Journal of Pragmatics, 14*, 467–487.

Abelson, R. P. (1959). Modes of resolution of belief dilemmas. *Journal of Conflict Resolution, 3*, 343–352.

Armada, B. J. (1998). Memorial agon: An interpretive tour of the National Civil Rights Museum. *Southern Communication Journal, 63*, 235–243.

Armstrong, R. N., Hallmark, J. R., & Williamson, L. K. (2005). Televangelism as institutional apologia: The religious talk show as strategized text. *Journal of Media and Religion, 4,* 67–83.

Bachman, G. F., & Guerrero, L. K. (2006). Forgiveness, apology, and communicative responses to hurtful events. *Communication Reports, 19,* 45–56.

Barkan, E., & Karn, A. (Eds.). (2006). *Taking wrongs seriously: Apologies and reconciliation.* Stanford, CA: Stanford University Press.

Benoit, W. L. (1982). Richard M. Nixon's rhetorical strategies in his public statements on Watergate. *Southern Speech Communication Journal, 47,* 192–211.

Benoit, W. L. (1995a). *Accounts, excuses, and apologies: A theory of image restoration strategies.* Albany: State University of New York SUNY Press.

Benoit, W. L. (1995b). Sears' repair of its auto service image: Image restoration discourse in the corporate sector. *Communication Studies, 46,* 89–105.

Benoit, W. L. (1997a). Hugh Grant's image restoration discourse: An actor apologizes. *Communication Quarterly, 45,* 251–267.

Benoit, W. L. (1997b). Image repair discourse and crisis communication. *Public Relations Review, 23,* 177–186.

Benoit, W. L. (2000). Another visit to the theory of image restoration strategies. *Communication Quarterly, 48,* 40–44.

Benoit, W. L. (2006a). Image repair in President Bush's April 2004 news conference. *Public Relations Review, 32,* 137–143.

Benoit, W. L. (2006b). President Bush's image repair effort on *Meet the Press*: The complexities of defeasibility. *Journal of Applied Communication Research, 34,* 285–306.

Benoit, W. L., & Anderson, K. K. (1997). Blending politics and entertainment: Dan Quayle versus Murphy Brown. *Southern Communication Journal, 62,* 73–85.

Benoit, W. L., & Brinson, S. L. (1994). AT&T: Apologies are not enough. *Communication Quarterly, 42,* 75–88.

Benoit, W. L., & Brinson, S. L. (1999). Queen Elizabeth's image repair discourse: Insensitive royal or compassionate queen? *Public Relations Review, 25,* 145–156.

Benoit, W. L., & Czerwinski, A. (1997). A critical analysis of USAir's image repair discourse. *Business Communication Quarterly, 60,* 38–57.

Benoit, W. L., Gullifor, P., & Panici, D. A. (1991). Reagan's discourse on the Iran-Contra affair. *Communication Studies, 42,* 272–294.

Benoit, W. L., & Hanczor, R. S. (1994). The Tonya Harding controversy: An analysis of image restoration strategies. *Communication Quarterly, 42,* 416–433.

Benoit, W. L., & McHale, J. P. (1999). Kenneth Starr's image repair discourse viewed in *20/20. Communication Quarterly, 47,* 265–280.

Benoit, W. L., & Nill, D. M. (1998a). A critical analysis of Judge Clarence Thomas' statement before the Senate Judiciary Committee. *Communication Studies, 39,* 179–195.

Benoit, W. L., & Nill, D. M. (1998b). Oliver Stone's defense of *JFK. Communication Quarterly, 46,* 127–143.

Benson, J. A. (1988). Crisis revisited: An analysis of strategies used by Tylenol in the second tampering episode. *Central States Speech Journal, 39,* 49–66.

Berlin, L. (2006). Will saying "I'm sorry" prevent a malpractice lawsuit? *American Journal of Roentgenology, 187,* 10–15.

Blair, C. (1984). From "All the President's Men" to every man for himself: The strategies of post-Watergate apologia. *Central States Speech Journal, 35,* 250–260.

Blaney, J. R. (2001). Restoring the juridical image: *Apologia* for *Ex Corde Ecclesiae. Journal of Communication and Religion, 24,* 94–109.

Blaney, J. R., & Benoit, W. L. (1997). The persuasive defense of Jesus in the Gospel According to John. *Journal of Communication and Religion, 20,* 25–30.

Blaney, J. R., & Benoit, W. L. (2001). *The Clinton scandals and the politics of image restoration.* Westport, CT: Praeger.

Brinson, S. L., & Benoit, W. L. (1996). Dow Corning's image repair strategies in the breast implant crisis. *Communication Quarterly, 44,* 29–41.

Brinson, S. L., & Benoit, W. L. (1999). The tarnished star: Restoring Texaco's Damaged public image. *Management Communication Quarterly, 12,* 483–510.

Brooks, R. L. (Ed.). (1999). *When sorry isn't enough: The controversy over apologies and reparations for human injustice.* New York: New York University Press.

Brown, G. (1990). Jerry Falwell and the PTL: The rhetoric of apologia. *Journal of Communication and Religion, 14,* 9–18.

Brummett, B. (1981). Burkean scapegoating, mortification, and transcendence in presidential campaign rhetoric. *Central States Speech Journal, 32,* 254–264.

Buck, C. (2006). "Never again": Kevin Gover's apology for the Bureau of Indian Affairs. *Wicazo Sa Review: A Journal of Native American Studies, 21,* 97–126.

Burke, K. (1969). *A rhetoric of motives.* Berkeley: University of California Press.

Burke, K. (1970). *The rhetoric of religion: Studies in logology.* Berkeley: University of California Press.

Burkholder, T. R. (1990). Symbolic martyrdom: The ultimate apology. *Southern Communication Journal, 56,* 289–297.

Burns, J. P., & Bruner, M. S. (2000). Revisiting the theory of image restoration strategies. *Communication Quarterly, 48,* 27–39.

Butler, S. D. (1972). The apologia, 1971 genre. *Southern Speech Communication Journal, 36,* 281–289.

Byrne, S., & Hart, P. S. (this volume). The boomerang effect: A synthesis of findings and a preliminary theoretical framework. In C. S. Beck (Ed.), *Communication Yearbook 33* (pp. 3–37). New York: Routledge.

Carcasson, M., & Aune, J. A. (2003). Klansman of the court: Justice Hugo Black's 1937 radio address to the nation. *Quarterly Journal of Speech, 89,* 154–170.

Carlson, A. C., & Hocking, J. E. (1988). Strategies of redemption at the Vietnam Veterans Memorial. *Western Journal of Speech Communication, 52,* 203–215.

Carmack, H. J. (2008). *How to say I'm sorry: A study of the Veteran's Administration Hospital Association's apology and disclosure program.* Unpublished doctoral dissertation, Ohio University, Athens, OH.

Celermajer, D. (2006). The apology in Australia: Re-covenanting the national imaginary. In E. Barkan & A. Karn (Eds.), *Taking wrongs seriously: Apologies and reconciliation* (pp. 153–184). Stanford, CA: Stanford University Press.

Cohen, J. R. (2001). Apology and organizations: Exploring an example from medical practice. *Fordham Urban Law Journal, 27,* 1447–1482.

Coombs, W. T. (1998). An analytic framework for crisis situations: Better responses from a better understanding of the situation. *Journal of Public Relations Research, 10,* 177–191.

Coombs, W. T. (1999). *Ongoing crisis communication: Planning, managing, and responding.* Thousand Oaks, CA: Sage.

Coombs, W. T. (2004). West Pharmaceutical's explosion: Structuring crisis discourse knowledge. *Public Relations Review, 30,* 467–473.

Coombs, W. T., & Schmidt, L. (2000). An empirical analysis of image restoration: Texaco's racism crisis. *Journal of Public Relations Research, 12,* 163–178.

Courtright, J. L., & Hearit, K. M. (2002). The good organization speaking well: A paradigm case for religious institutional crisis management. *Public Relations Review, 28*, 347–360.

Cowden, K., & Sellnow, T. L. (2002). Issues advertising as crisis communication: Northwest Airline's use of image restoration strategies during the 1998 pilot's strike. *Journal of Business Communication, 39*, 193–219.

Davies, B. L., Merrison, A. J., & Goddard, A. (2007). Institutional apologies in UK higher education: Getting back into the black before going into the red. *Journal of Politeness Research, 3*, 39–63.

Dickinson, G., Ott, B. L., & Aoki, E. (2006). Spaces of remembering and forgetting: The reverent eye/I at the Plains Indian Museum. *Communication and Critical Cultural Studies, 3*, 27–47.

Dodds, G. G. (2003). Racial apologies. In J. Rodin & S. P. Steinberg (Eds.), *Public discourse in America: Conversation and community in the twenty-first century* (pp. 135–160). Philadelphia: University of Pennsylvania Press.

Doxtader, E. (2003). Reconciliation—A rhetorical concept/ion. *Quarterly Journal of Speech, 89*, 267–292.

Drumheller, K., & Benoit, W. L. (2004). USS Greenville collides with Japan's Ehime Maru: Cultural issues in image repair discourse. *Public Relations Review, 30*, 177–185.

Edwards, J. A. (2005). Community-focused apologia in international affairs: Japanese Prime Minister Tomiichi Murayma's apology. *The Howard Journal of Communications, 16*, 317–336.

Edwards, J. A. (2008). The mission of healing: Kofi Annan's failed apology. *Atlantic Journal of Communication, 16*, 88–104.

Fearn-Banks, K. (2007). *Crisis communications: A casebook approach.* Mahwah, NJ: Erlbaum.

Foss, S. K. (1984). Retooling an image: Chrysler Corporation's rhetoric of redemption. *Western Journal of Speech Communication, 48*, 75–91.

Foucault, M. (1980). *The history of sexuality* (R. Hurley, Trans.). New York: Vintage.

Friedman, T. (2007, December 9). Making peace with pieces. *New York Times.* Retrieved November 14, 2008, from http:www/nytimes.com

Gettleman, J. (2006, November 8). In a calm corner of Darfur, villagers rebuild ties. *New York Times.* Retrieved November 14, 2008, from http://www/nytimes.com

Gettleman, J. (2008, June 16). After 15 years, hints of peace in Burundi. *New York Times.* Retrieved November 14, 2008, from http://www/nytimes.com

Goffman, E. (1971). *Relations in public: Microstudies of public order.* New York: Basic Books.

Gold, E. R. (1978). Political apologia: The ritual of self-defense. *Communication Monographs, 45*, 306–316.

Gordon, D. B., & Crenshaw, C. (2004). Racial apologies. In P. A. Sullivan & S. R. Goldzwing (Eds.), *New approaches to rhetoric* (pp. 245–266). Thousand Oaks, CA: Sage.

Govier, T. (2006). *Taking wrongs seriously: Acknowledgment, reconciliation, and the politics of sustainable peace.* Amherst, NY: Humanity Books.

Govier, T., & Verwoerd, W. (2002). The promise and pitfalls of apology. *Journal of Social Philosophy, 33*, 67–82.

Grey, S. H. (2007). Wounds not easily healed: Exploring traumas in communication studies. In C. S. Beck (Ed.), *Communication yearbook 31* (pp. 174–223). Mahwah, NJ: Erlbaum.

Harrell, J., Ware, B. L., & Linkugel, W. A. (1975). Failure of apology in American politics: Nixon on Watergate. *Speech Monographs, 42*, 245–261.

Harris, S., Grainger, K., & Mullany, L. (2006). The pragmatics of political apologies. *Discourse & Society, 17*, 715–737.

Harter, L. M., Stephens, R. J., & Japp, P. M. (2000). President Clinton's apology for the Tuskegee syphilis experiment: A narrative of remembrance, redefinition, and reconciliation. *Howard Journal of Communications, 11*, 19–34.

Hasian, M. J. (2005). Authenticity, public memories, and the problematics of post-Holocaust remembrances: A rhetorical analysis of the Wilkomirski Affair. *Quarterly Journal of Speech, 91*, 231–264.

Hasian, M. J., & Carlson, A. C. (2000). Revisionism and collective memory: The struggle for meaning in the "Amistad" affair. *Communication Monographs, 67*, 42–62.

Hatch, J. B. (2003). Reconciliation: Building a bridge from complicity to coherence in the rhetoric of race relations. *Rhetoric & Public Affairs, 6*, 737–764.

Hatch, J. B. (2006a). Beyond *apologia*: Racial reconciliation and apologies for slavery. *Western Journal of Communication, 70*, 186–211.

Hatch, J. B. (2006b). The hope of reconciliation: Continuing the conversation. *Rhetoric and Public Affairs, 9*, 259–278.

Hawk, G. W. (2007). Mending the broken branch: Forgiveness and reconciliation. In W. W. Wilmot & J. L. Hocker (Eds.), *Interpersonal conflict* (7th ed., pp. 297–325). Boston: McGraw-Hill.

Hearit, K. M. (1994). Apologies and public relations crises at Chrysler, Toshiba, and Volvo. *Public Relations Review, 20*, 113–125.

Hearit, K. M. (1995). "Mistakes were made": Organizations, apologia, and crises of social legitimacy. *Communication Studies, 46*, 1–17.

Hearit, K. M. (1996). The use of counter-attack in apologetic public relations crises: The case of General Motors vs. Dateline NBC. *Public Relations Review, 22*, 233–248.

Hearit, K. M. (1997). On the use of transcendence as an apologia strategy: The case of Johnson Controls and its fetal protection policy. *Public Relations Review, 23*, 217–231.

Hearit, K. M. (1999). Newsgroups, activist publics, and corporate apologia: The case of Intel and its Pentium chip. *Public Relations Review, 25*, 291–308.

Hearit, K. M. (2006). *Crisis management by apology: Corporate response to allegations of wrongdoing*. Mahwah, NJ: Erlbaum.

Hearit, K. M., & Brown, J. (2004). Merrill Lynch: Corporate apologia and business fraud. *Public Relations Review, 30*, 459–466.

Hearit, K. M., & Courtright, J. L. (2003). A social constructionist approach to crisis management: Allegations of sudden acceleration in the Audi 5000. *Communication Studies, 54*, 79–95.

Hobbs, J. D. (1995). Treachery by any other name: A case study of the Toshiba public relations crisis. *Management Communication Quarterly, 8*, 323–346.

Hoover, J. D. (1989). Big boys don't cry: The values constraint in apologia. *Southern Communication Journal, 54*, 235–252.

Howard-Hassmann, R. E., & Lombardo, A. P. (2008). Words require action: African elite opinion about apologies from the "West." In M. Gibney, R. E. Howard-Hassmann, J-M. Coicaud, & N. Steiner (Eds.), *The age of apology: Facing up to the past* (pp. 216–228). Philadelphia: University of Pennsylvania Press.

Huang, Y., Lin, Y., & Su, S. (2005). Crisis communication strategies in Taiwan: Category, continuum, and cultural implication. *Public Relations Review, 31*, 229–238.

Huxman, S. S., & Bruce, D. B. (1995). Toward a dynamic generic framework of apologia: A case study of Dow Chemical, Vietnam, and the Napalm controversy. *Communication Studies, 46*, 57–72.

Ice, R. (1991). Corporate publics and rhetorical strategies: The case of Union Carbide's Bhopal crisis. *Management Communication Quarterly, 4*, 341–362.

Jerome, A. M. (2008). Toward prescription: Testing the rhetoric of atonement's applicability in the athletic arena. *Public Relations Review, 34*, 124–134.

Johnson, C. S. (2006). Prediscursive technical communication in the early American iron industry. *Technical Communication Quarterly, 15*, 171–189.

Kahl, M. (1984). Blind ambition culminates in lost honor: A comparative analysis of John Dean's apologetic strategies. *Central State Speech Journal, 35*, 239–250.

Kampf, Z., & Blum-Kulka, S. (2007). Do children apologize to each other? Apology events in young Israeli peer discourse. *Journal of Politeness Research, 3*, 39–63.

Katula, R. A. (1975). The apology of Richard M. Nixon. *Today's Speech, 23*, 1–6.

Kelley, D. L., & Waldron, V. R. (2006). Forgiveness: Communicative implications for social relationships. In C. S. Beck (Ed.), *Communication yearbook 30* (pp. 303–342). Mahwah, NJ: Erlbaum.

Kennedy, K. A., & Benoit, W. L. (1997). The Newt Gingrich book deal controversy: Self-defense rhetoric. *Southern Communication Journal, 62*, 197–216.

King, R. L. (1985). Transforming scandal into tragedy: A rhetoric of political apology. *Quarterly Journal of Speech, 71*, 289–301.

Koesten, J., & Rowland, R. C. (2004). The rhetoric of atonement. *Communication Studies, 55*, 68–87.

Koutsantoni, D. (2007). "I can now apologize to you twice from the bottom of my heart": Apologies in Greek reality TV. *Journal of Politeness Research, 3*, 93–123.

Kramer, M. R., & Olson, K. M. (2002). The strategic potential of sequencing apologia stases: President Clinton's self-defense in the Monica Lewinsky scandal. *Western Journal of Communication, 66*, 347–368.

Kruse, N. W. (1977). Motivational factors in non-denial apologia. *Central States Speech Journal, 28*, 13–23.

Kruse, N. W. (1981a). Apologia in team sport. *Quarterly Journal of Speech, 67*, 270–283.

Kruse, N. W. (1981b). The scope of apologetic discourse: Establishing generic parameters. *Southern Speech Communication Journal, 46*, 278–291.

Lacy, M. G. (2008). Exposing the spectrum of whiteness: Rhetorical conceptions of white absolutism. In C. S. Beck (Ed.), *Communication yearbook 32* (pp. 277–312). New York: Routledge.

Lazare, A. (2004). *On apology.* New York: Oxford University Press.

Lazare, A. (2006). Apology in medical practice: An emerging clinical skill. *Journal of the American Medical Association, 296*, 1401–1404.

Len-Rios, M. E., & Benoit, W. L. (2004). Gary Condit's image repair strategies: Determined denial and differentiation. *Public Relations Review, 30*, 95–106.

Lewis, G. (2006). *Organizational crisis management: The human factor.* Boca Raton, FL: Auerbach.

Liebersohn, Y. Z., Neuman, Y., & Bekerman, Z. (2004). Oh baby, it's hard for me to say I'm sorry: Public apologetic speech and cultural rhetorical sources. *Journal of Pragmatics, 36*, 921–944.

Liu, B. F. (2007). President Bush's major post-Katrina speeches: Enhancing image repair discourse theory applied to the public sector. *Public Relations Review, 33*, 40–48.

MacNealy, M. S. (1999) *Strategies for empirical research in writing.* Boston: Allyn & Bacon.

Marrus, M. R. (2007). Official apologies and the quest for historical justice. *Journal of Human Rights, 6,* 75–105.

Marrus, M. R. (2008). Papal apologies of Pope John Paul II. In M. Gibney, R.E. Howard-Hassmann, J-M. Coicaud, & N. Steiner (Eds.), *The age of apology: Facing up to the past* (pp. 259–270). Philadelphia: University of Pennsylvania Press.

Martin, J. (1982). *Miss Manners' guide to excruciatingly correct behavior.* New York: Atheneum.

McLennan, D. B. (1996). Rhetoric and the legitimation process: The rebith of Charles Colson. *Journal of Communication and Religion, 19,* 5–12.

Medved, C. E. (this volume). Crossing and transforming occupational and household gendered divisions of labor: Reviewing literatures and deconstructing differences. In C. S. Beck (Ed.), *Communication yearbook 33* (pp. 301–341). New York: Routledge.

Meisenbach, R., & McMillan, J. (2006). Blurring the boundaries: Historical developments and future directions in organizational rhetoric. In C. S. Beck (Ed.), *Communication yearbook 30* (pp. 99–142). Mahwah, NJ: Erlbaum.

Miller, B. A. (2002). *Divine apology: The discourse of religious image restoration.* Westport, CT: Praeger.

Moran, M. G. (2003). Ralph Lane's 1586 *Discourse on the first colony*: The Renaissance commercial report as apologia. *Technical Communication Quarterly, 12,* 125–154.

Morello, J. T. (1979). The public apology of a private matter: Representative Wayne Hays' address to Congress. *Speaker and Gavel, 16,* 19–26.

Mueller, A. G. (2004). Affirming denial through preemptive apologia: The case of the Armenian Genocide Resolution. *Western Journal of Communication, 68,* 24–44.

Negash, G. (2006). *Apologia politica: States and their apologies by proxy.* Lanham, MD: Lexington Books.

Nelson, J. (1984). The defense of Billie Jean King. *Western Journal of Speech Communication, 48,* 92–102.

Nethercote, J. R. (1989). The rhetorical tactics of managerialism: Reflections on Michael Keating's apologia, Quo Vadis? *Australian Journal of Public Administration, 48,* 363–367.

Nobles, M. (2008). *The politics of official apologies.* New York: Cambridge University Press.

Nytagodien, R. L., & Neal, A. G. (2004). Collective trauma, apologies, and the politics of memory. *Journal of Human Rights, 3,* 465–475.

Onyanogo-Obbo, C. (2008, October 29). To love and hate: What Rwanda can teach Kenya. *Daily Nation.* Retrieved November 14, 2008, from http://www.nation.co.ke

Partridge, E. (1977). *Origins: A short etymological dictionary of modern English.* New York: Macmillan.

Patel, A., & Reinsch, L. (2003). Companies *can* apologize: Corporate apologies and legal liability. *Business Communication Quarterly, 66,* 9–25.

Perelman, C. (1982). *The realm of rhetoric.* Notre Dame, IN: University of Notre Dame Press.

Polgreen, L. (2008, January 10). Fighting in Congo rekindles ethnic hatreds. *New York Times.* Retrieved November 14, 2008, from http://www.nytimes.com

Pörholä, M., Karhunen, S., & Rainivaara, S. (2006). Bullying at school and in the workplace: A challenge for communication research. In C. S. Beck (Ed.), *Communication yearbook 30* (pp. 249–302). Mahwah, NJ: Erlbaum.

Post, E. L. (1975). *The new Emily Post's etiquette.* New York: Funk & Wagnalls.

Prosise, T. O. (1998). The collective memory of the atomic bombings misrecognized as objective history: The case of the public opposition to the National Air and Space Museum's atom bomb exhibit. *Western Journal of Communication, 62,* 316–347.

Renteln, A. D. (2008). Apologies: A cross-cultural analysis. In M. Gibney, R. E. Howard-Hassmann, J-M. Coicaud, & N. Steiner (Eds.), *The age of apology: Facing up to the past* (pp. 61–76). Philadelphia: University of Pennsylvania Press.

Rosenfield, L. W. (1968). A case study in speech criticism: The Nixon–Truman analog. *Speech Monographs, 35,* 435–450.

Rothenbuhler, E. W. (1998). *Ritual communication: From everyday conversation to mediated ceremony.* Thousand Oaks, CA: Sage.

Ryan, H. R. (1982). *Kategoria* and *apologia*: On their rhetorical criticism as a speech act. *Quarterly Journal of Speech, 68,* 254–261.

Ryan, H. R. (1984). Baldwin vs. Edward VIII: A case study in *kategoria* and *apologia. Southern Speech Communication Journal, 49,* 125–134.

Schonbach, P. (1980). A categorical system for account phases. *European Journal of Social Psychology, 10,* 195–200.

Schultz, P. D., & Seeger, M. W. (1991). Corporate centered apologia: Iacocca in defense of Chrysler. *Speaker and Gavel, 28,* 50–60.

Schwartz, B., & Heinrich, H-A. (2006). Shadings of regret: America and Germany. In K. R. Phillips (Ed.), *Framing public memory* (pp. 115–144). Tuscaloosa: University of Alabama Press.

Scott, M., & Lyman, S. M. (1968). Accounts. *American Sociological Review, 33,* 46–62.

Sellnow, T. L. (1993). Scientific argument in organizational crisis communication: The case of Exxon. *Argumentation & Advocacy, 30,* 28–43.

Short, B. (1987). Comic book apologia: The "paranoid" rhetoric of Congressman George Hansen. *Western Journal of Speech Communication, 51,* 189–203.

Simons, H. W. (2000). A dilemma-centered analysis of Clinton's August 17th apologia: Implications for rhetorical theory and method. *Quarterly Journal of Speech, 86,* 438–453.

Skubisz, C., Reimer, T., & Hoffrage, U. (this volume). Communicating quantitative risk information. In C. S. Beck (Ed.), *Communication yearbook 33* (pp. 177–211). New York: Routledge.

Smith, N. (2005). The categorical apology. *Journal of Social Philosophy, 36,* 473–496.

Smith, N. (2008). *I was wrong: The meanings of apologies.* New York: Cambridge University Press.

Smudde, P. M., & Courtright, J. L. (2008). Time to get a job: Helping image repair theory begin a career in industry. *Public Relations Journal, 2,* 1–20.

Stein, K. A. (2008). *Apologia, antapologia,* and the 1960 Soviet U-2 incident. *Communication Studies, 59,* 19–34.

Stormer, N. (2003). To remember, to act, to forget: Tracing collective remembrance through "A Jury of Her Peers." *Communication Studies, 54,* 510–529.

Sugimoto, N. (Ed.). (1999). *Japanese apology across disciplines.* Commack, NY: Nova Science.

Sullivan, D. L. (1998). Francis Schaeffer's apparent apology in *Pollution and the death of man. Journal of Communication and Religion, 21,* 200–229.

Sullivan, D. L., & Martin, M. S. (2001). Habit formation and story telling: A theory for guiding ethical action. *Technical Communication Quarterly, 10,* 251–272.

Suzuki, T., & van Eemeren, F. H. (2004). "This painful chapter": An analysis of Emperor Akihito's apologia in the context of Dutch old sores. *Argumentation and Advocacy, 41,* 102–111.

Sykes, G. M., & Matza, M. (1957). Techniques of neutralization: A theory of delinquency. *American Sociological Review, 22,* 664–670.

Taft, L. (2005). Apology and medical mistake: Opportunity or foil? *Annals of Health Law, 14,* 55–94.

Tavuchis, N. (1991). *Mea culpa: A sociology of apology and reconciliation.* Stanford, CA: Stanford University Press.

Tavernise, S., & Siegel, M. (2008, August 14). Signs of ethnic attacks in Georgia conflict. *New York Times.* Retrieved November 14, 2008, from http://www.nytimes.com

Tedeschi, J. T., & Reiss, M. (1981). Verbal strategies in impression management. In C. Antaki (Ed.), *The psychology of ordinary explanations of social behavior* (pp. 271–326). London: Academic Press.

Thomsen, S. R., & Rawson, B. (1998). Purifying a tainted corporate image: Odwalla's response to an E. Coli poisoning. *Public Relations Quarterly, 43,* 35–46.

Tian, D. (2007). U.S. and NATO apologies for the Chinese embassy bombing: A categorical analysis. *International Journal of Communication, 1,* 360–376.

Tsosie, R. (2006). The BIA's apology to Native Americans: An essay on collective memory and collective conscience. In E. Barkan & A. Karn (Eds.), *Taking wrongs seriously: Apologies and reconciliation* (pp. 185–212). Stanford, CA: Stanford University Press.

Tucker, S., Turner, N., Barling, J., Reid, E., & Elving, C. (2006). Apologies and transformational leadership. *Journal of Business Ethics, 63,* 195–207.

Ulmer, R. R., Sellnow, T. L., & Seeger, M. W. (2006). *Effective crisis communication: Moving from crisis to opportunity.* Thousand Oaks, CA: Sage.

Vanderbilt, A. (1978). *The Amy Vanderbilt complete book of etiquette: A guide to contemporary living.* (Rev. ed., L. Baldridge, Ed.). Garden City, NY: Doubleday.

Vartabedian, R. A. (1985a). From Checkers to Watergate: Richard Nixon and the art of contemporary apologia. *Speaker and Gavel, 22,* 52–61.

Vartabedian, R. A. (1985b). Nixon's Vietnam rhetoric: A case study of apologia as generic paradox. *Southern Speech Communication Journal, 50,* 366–381.

Vartabedian, R. A., & Vartabedian, L. (2003). Clinton's address to the nation: A case study of apologetic goals. *Speaker and Gavel, 40,* 28–46.

Veil, S. (2005). To answer, or not to answer—that is the question of the hour: Image restoration strategies and media coverage of past drug use questions in the presidential campaigns of Bill Clinton and George W. Bush. *Speaker and Gavel, 42,* 58–78.

Villadsen, L. S. (2008). Speaking on behalf of others: Rhetorical agency and epideictic functions in official apologies. *Rhetoric Society Quarterly, 38,* 25–45.

Ware, B. L., & Linkugel, W. L. (1973). They spoke in defense of themselves: On the generic criticism of apologia. *Quarterly Journal of Speech, 59,* 273–283.

Weyeneth, R. R. (2001). History, memory, and apology: The power of apology and the process of historical reconciliation. *The Public Historian, 23,* 9–38.

Yamazaki, J. W. (2004). The failure of Japanese apologies for World War II. In G. M. Chen & W. J. Starosta (Eds.), *Dialogue among diversities: International and intercultural communication annual 27* (pp. 169–190). Thousand Oaks, CA: Sage.

Yamazaki, J. W. (2005). *Japanese apologies for World War II: A rhetorical study.* New York: Routledge.

Zhang, J., & Benoit, W. L. (2004). Message strategies of Saudi Arabia's image restoration campaign after 9/11. *Public Relations Review, 20,* 161–167.

# About the Editor

**Christina S. Beck** (PhD, University of Oklahoma, 1992) is Professor in the School of Communication Studies at Ohio University. In addition to editing *Communication Yearbook*, she contributed to *Journal of Health Communication: International Perspectives* as book review editor and currently serves on the editorial boards of four communication journals. She has authored two award-winning books on health communication, *Communicating for Better Health: A Guide Through the Medical Mazes* (2001) and *Partnership for Health: Building Relationships Between Women and Health Caregivers* (1997, with Sandra Ragan and Athena duPre), and numerous journal articles and invited book chapters. She also co-edited *Narratives, Health, and Healing: Communication Theory, Research, and Practice* (2005) and *The Lynching of Language: Gender, Politics, and Power in the Hill-Thomas Hearings* (1996). Her research interests span the areas of health communication, language and social interaction, and mass communication.

# About the Contributors

**Rosalie Shemanski Aldrich** (MA, 2006, Michigan State University) is a doctoral student in the Department of Communication at the University of Kentucky. She teaches undergraduate courses in interpersonal communication and public speaking. Her research focuses on persuasive message design in a health behavior context, particularly as it relates to suicide and suicide prevention.

**Brenda L. Berkelaar** (MA, Seton Hall University) is a doctoral student and Andrews Fellow in the Department of Communication at Purdue University. Her research examines the intersections of careers, organizations, technology, and leadership. Current projects include an international study on how children talk about engineering and work, d/Discourses of academic leadership, and research on impacts of emerging information technologies on society and organizations. Past work experiences include academic technology management, information technology fluency programs, training development and delivery for corporate and not-for-profit organizations, and web usability and training consulting. She was also awarded a 2007–2008 Bilsland Strategic Initiative Fellowship for Locating and Disseminating Effective Messages: Research and Strategies to Enhance Gender Representation in Computing Majors Careers. She has a co-authored publication in *Management Communication Quarterly* and has forthcoming chapters in two edited collections.

**Patrice M. Buzzanell** (PhD, Purdue University, 1987) is professor and the W. Charles and Ann Redding Fellow in the Department of Communication at Purdue University where she specializes in career, leadership, and work–life research, particularly from gendered perspectives. She has edited *Rethinking Organizational and Managerial Communication from Feminist Perspectives, Gender in Applied Communication Contexts* (with H. Sterk and L. Turner), and *Distinctive Qualities in Communication Research* (forthcoming with D. Carbaugh). She has published over 80 articles and chapters in *Communication Monographs, Human Communication Research, Communication Theory, Human Relations, Journal of Applied Communication Research, Management Communication Quarterly, Handbook of Applied*

*Communication Research, The Sage Handbook on Gender and Communication*, and other journals and handbooks. She advises the Anita Borg Institute for Women and Technology (ABIWT) team in Purdue's Engineering Projects in Community Service (EPICS) program and currently serves on the College of Engineering Task Force on Diversity and the EPICS Curriculum Committee. She was awarded an Engineering YES Grant, *Encouraging Science and Engineering Interests in Young Children: Toward a Taxonomy of Effective Career Messages and Stories*, for research in China, Belgium, and the United States.

**Sahara Byrne** (PhD, University of California, Santa Barbara) is an assistant professor of communication at Cornell University. Her research examines message disruption processes. Her specific interests are in understanding when and why messages backfire, especially strategies to prevent negative effects of the media on children.

**Kathleen M. Galvin** (PhD, Northwestern University) is a professor in the Department of Communication Studies and a member of the Program on Communication and Medicine at Northwestern University. She is the senior author of *Family Communication: Cohesion and Change* (7th ed.), the editor of *Making Connections: Readings in Relational Communication* (5th ed.), and she has published numerous pieces on family communication that have appeared in *The Handbook of Family Communication*, *The Family Communication Sourcebook*, and the *Journal of Family Communication*. Her current research involves an NIH oncofertility project examining family decision making when a daughter is confronted with fertility threatening cancer treatments and communication between adult survivors of pediatric cancer and their parents.

**Shiv Ganesh** (PhD, Purdue University, 2000) is a senior lecturer in the Department of Management Communication, University of Waikato. His research focuses on the relationships among organizing, social change, social justice and technology, in the context of economic and political globalization. His work has been published in *Communication Monographs*, *Journal of Applied Communication Research*, and *Management Communication Quarterly*, among other outlets. He is co-author, along with George Cheney, Lars Christensen, and Ted Zorn, of the 2004 book, *Organizational Communication in an Age of Globalization: Issues, Reflections, Practices*.

**Lauren H. Grill** (MA Northwestern University) is a fourth year doctoral student at Northwestern University. Her research interests focus on health communication within families, specifically the health-related communication between parents and children. She served as a member of a research team investigating communication between adult survivors of pediatric cancer and their parents. She has co-authored two articles published in the Journal of Pediatric Hematology and Oncology; she developed the *Instructor's Manual* for the 7th edition of *Family Communication: Cohesion and*

*Change.* Her current dissertation research examines the conditions under which young adults will confront their parents about concerns for their parents' health.

**Nancy Grant Harrington** (PhD, University of Kentucky, 1992) is Professor and Chairperson of the Department of Communication, and Associate Dean for Research in the College of Communications and Information Studies, University of Kentucky. She also holds an academic appointment in the School of Public Health and is a faculty associate of the Multi-disciplinary Center on Drug and Alcohol Research. She has been a principal investigator, coinvestigator, or principal evaluator on several NIH-funded and CDC-funded studies. She teaches undergraduate and graduate courses in interpersonal communication, health communication, communication theory, and research methods. Her research focuses on persuasive message design in a health behavior change context, particularly as it relates to substance abuse prevention and interactive health communication using computer technology.

**Philip Solomon Hart** (MS, University of Oregon) is a doctoral candidate in the Department of Communication at Cornell University. His research focuses on framing effects, decision making, persuasion, and environmental communication. He is the recipient of a NSF dissertation improvement grant and an EPA STAR fellowship.

**Marni Heinz** (MA, University of California, Santa Barbara, 2006) has extensive experience in management and information technology consulting, both as an independent contractor and at Big4 consulting companies. She currently is an information systems project manager at Google. She has advised a wide variety of public and private organizations on the design, deployment, and use of information systems.

**Ulrich Hoffrage** (PhD, University of Salzburg, Austria, 1995) is a Full Professor of Decision Theory and Risk in the Faculty of Business and Economics at the University of Lausanne, Switzerland. His research focuses on judgment and decision making, in particular, bounded rationality (both analytical and empirical approaches), consumer decision making, choice deferral, risk communication and risk-taking behavior, so-called cognitive illusions (such as overconfidence, base-rate neglect, hindsight bias, reiteration effect), group decision making, causal reasoning, and evolutionary psychology. He has published in journals that include, *Science, Psychological Review, Psychological Bulletin, Cognition, Journal of Experimental Psychology: Learning, Memory and Cognition, Journal of Experimental Psychology: Applied, Communication Monographs.*

**Jos Hornikx** (PhD, Radboud University Nijmegen, 2006) is an assistant professor in the Department of Business Communication Studies at Radboud University Nijmegen, the Netherlands. His research focuses on argumentation and evidence, the impact of culture on persuasion, multilingual advertising, and the effects of audience adaptation. His work has been published in journals that include *Argumentation, Communication Monographs*, and *Journal of Multilingual and Multicultural Development*.

**Lorraine G. Kisselburgh** (PhD, Purdue University, 2008) is an assistant professor in the Department of Communication at Purdue University. She began her career as a computer analyst and programmer, and directed the development of emerging technologies, applications, and learning environments in higher education. Her research interests include the intersections of technology, organizations, and difference, including the social implications of emerging technologies; privacy; and social networking. She is conducting research on cross-cultural and gendered constructions of science, technology, and engineering work and careers; competition and collaboration in games-based learning environments; difference in organizational contexts, and the social structure and discursive construction of privacy. She has received funding for her research from the Purdue Research Foundation and the Indiana Department of Homeland Security, and she was a research investigator on a grant from Purdue University's College of Engineering to study young children's talk about science and engineering careers. She has published in *Management Communication Quarterly, Communication Studies, the Journal of Motor Behavior, and Acta Psychologica*.

**Kirstie McAllum** (MA, University of Waikato, 1997) is a doctoral student in the Department of Management Communication, University of Waikato. Her research interests include volunteerism and well-being. She has presented several papers at local and national conferences in New Zealand, and she is the recipient of several academic honors and awards.

**Caryn E. Medved** (PhD, University of Kansas, 1998) is an associate professor in the Department of Communication Studies, Baruch College—City University of New York. Her research focuses on the intersections between organizational and family communication particularly in relation to issues of identity, power, and difference. Her work explores issues of work–family socializing communication, discourses of caring and earning, constructions of family labor, and relational work–family negotiations. She is currently the editor of *Journal of Family Communication*. Professor Medved has published in journals that include *Management Communication Quarterly, Journal of Family Communication, Communication Yearbook, Communication Studies*, and *Journal of Applied Communication*.

**Philip M. Napoli** (PhD, Northwestern University, 1997) is an associate professor in the Graduate School of Business and Director of the Donald McGannon Communication Research Center at Fordham University. His research focuses on media institutions and media policy. He is the author of the books *Audience Economics: Media Institutions and the Audience Marketplace* (Columbia, 2003) and *Foundations of Communications Policy: Principles* *and Process in the Regulation of Electronic Media* (Hampton, 2001). His work has been published in journals such as the *Journal of Communication*, the *Harvard International Journal of Press/Politics,* the *Federal Communications Law Journal,* the *Journal of Broadcasting & Electronic Media,* and *Telecommunications Policy.*

**Seth M. Noar** (PhD, University of Rhode Island, 2001) is an associate professor in the Department of Communication at the University of Kentucky. He also holds a secondary appointment in the College of Public Health and is a Visiting Research Fellow at the Rural Center for AIDS/STD Prevention (at Indiana University). Dr. Noar's work addresses health behavior theories, sexual communication, message design and media campaigns, tailored communication, and methodological topics including meta-analysis. He has published articles and chapters in a wide range of outlets in the social, behavioral, health, and communication sciences. Dr. Noar is principal investigator of an NIMH-funded study to develop a computer-tailored safer sex intervention, and he is a co-investigator on other NIH and CDC funded studies. He recently co-edited *Communication Perspectives on HIV/AIDS for the 21st Century* (Erlbaum, 2008).

**Daniel J. O'Keefe** (PhD, University of Illinois at Urbana-Champaign) is Professor of Communication Studies at Northwestern University. His research focuses on persuasion and argumentation. He has received the National Communication Association's Charles Woolbert Research Award, its Golden Anniversary Monograph Award, its Rhetorical and Communication Theory Division's Distinguished Scholar Award, and its Health Communication Division's Distinguished Article Award, the American Forensic Association's Daniel Rohrer Memorial Research Award, the International Communication Association's Best Article Award and its Division 1 John E. Hunter Meta-Analysis Award, and the International Society for the Study of Argumentation's Distinguished Scholar Award.

**Torsten Reimer** (PhD in Social and Cognitive Psychology, Free University of Berlin, Germany) is an assistant professor in persuasion and social influence at the University of Maryland. His research focuses on the role of communication in decision making and organizational behavior. Research topics include the design and reception of persuasive messages, knowledge management in teams and organizations, and risk communication. His research has been published in various outlets in psychology and communication including *Cognitive Science, Journal of Experimental Psychology, Communication Monographs, Theory and Decision*, and *Marketing Letters.*

**Ronald E. Rice** (PhD, Stanford University, 1982) is the Arthur N. Rupe Chair in the Social Effects of Mass Communication in the Department of Communication, and Co-Director of the Carsey-Wolf Center for Film, Television, and New Media, at University of California, Santa Barbara. He has served as President of the ICA (2006–2007) and Fulbright Professor in Finland (2006). He has co-authored or co-edited *Public Communication Campaigns, The New Media, Managing Organizational Innovation, Research Methods and the New Media, The Internet and Health Communication, Accessing and Browsing Information and Communication, Social Consequences of Internet Use, The Internet and Health Care,* and *Media Ownership.*

**Christine Skubisz** (MA, Michigan State University, 2006) is a doctoral student in the Department of Communication and a research assistant in the *Center for Risk Communication Research* at the University of Maryland. Her research focuses on persuasion and social influence. Research topics include risk perception, persuasive message design, and cognitive processing of risk and health related messages. Her work has appeared in the *Journal of Health Communication* and the *Journal of Cancer Education.*

**Emil B. Towner** is a doctoral student in technical communication and rhetoric at Texas Tech University. His research interests include apologetic rhetoric and reconciliation, rhetorical analysis, visual rhetoric, and ethics in communication. His dissertation examines the apologetic rhetoric in Rwanda's *gacaca* trial documents and how blame and responsibility, shared interpretations of history, and societal values and identity are negotiated in those documents.

# Author Index

# Subject Index

22009188